dedication

Stolen Lives
killed by law enforcement

... IS DEDICATED TO ALL THOSE WHO HAVE
LOST THEIR LIVES AT THE HANDS OF BRUTAL
LAW ENFORCEMENT OFFICERS AND TO THE
FAMILIES OF VICTIMS WHO HAVE INSPIRED A
MOVEMENT TO FIGHT FOR JUSTICE AND
DEMAND THAT POLICE BRUTALITY STOP.

LIB
D0940581

NEW ENGLAND INSTITUTE
OF TECHNOLOGY
LIBRARY

7-02   # 43686900

Table of Contents

(Within each state or region, cases are listed in reverse chronological order)

INTRODUCTION

In the fall of 1996, a friend who was organizing for the first National Day of Protest to Stop Police Brutality asked me to help out. In the course of attending meetings, I met some of the relatives of victims of police killings. When I heard their stories of how their loved ones were killed, I was horrified. Like most people, I had believed the news accounts of these killings which usually describe the victims as criminals posing an immediate threat to the community. After meeting with many relatives and eyewitnesses over the course of the past three years, I now know that this widely promoted notion is very far from the truth.

Continuing to attend meetings, I would hear about police killings occurring weekly and decided to keep track of these deaths. I began my own newspaper research and compiled the results. When I could, I contacted family members for their version of events. I have yet to come across an eyewitness account which corroborates the police version of events.

At the same time, three organizations, the Anthony Baez Foundation, named for a Puerto Rican young man killed by an illegal police chokehold, the National Lawyers Guild, and the October 22 Coalition to Stop Police Brutality, Repression and the Criminalization of a Generation initiated the Stolen Lives Project. In 1997, they published the first edition of Stolen Lives which listed 500 cases of people killed and brutalized by police and border patrol agents since 1990.

I soon joined up with the Stolen Lives Project. With a grant from the San Francisco Foundation and a gift of fiscal administration from the Sonoma County Center for Peace & Justice, I collaborated with Project Censored at Sonoma State University and began a search of Lexis-Nexis and other national newspaper databases for cases of police brutality for the year of 1997. That search produced approximately half of the cases listed in this edition.

Simultaneously, public service announcements filmed by artists and families of victims aired on MTV. Organizations such as Physicians for Social Responsibility contributed funds to air the announcements on Black Entertainment Television (BET). These announcements called on people to send any information they had about someone who'd been killed by police to the Stolen Lives Project. Many individuals and organizations, among them the Center for Constitutional Rights, spread the word about Stolen Lives. Victims' families and friends, lawyers who handle police brutality cases, and local civil rights groups sent in stories. These are some of the many ways we uncovered these cases.

Why This Research Is Needed

The government is not informing the public of the true extent of police killings. The 1994 Crime Bill mandated that the U.S. Department of Justice (DOJ) gather and disseminate statistics on the number of people killed by law enforcement. Stating that funding has never been provided, the DOJ has done nothing. In its annual reports for the past few years, the DOJ has reported a fairly consistent finding of 350 cases of justifiable homicides by police. No names, no places, no description of the "justifiable homicides" are provided. How are we to know what really happened? How do we know anything about the lives and dreams of these anonymous, faceless victims, or of the anguish felt by loved ones left behind?

Epidemic numbers of people are being killed by police and no one is being held accountable. People are shot and killed with little or no provocation. They die from chokeholds, hog-tying, pepper-spray, beatings and high speed car chases. They die on the streets, in their own homes, on the border, in jails and prisons. Under the guise of protecting society from crime (at a time when the official crime rate is the lowest in decades), many people, particularly young men of color, are being harassed, brutalized, and, as this book shows, killed.

The officers involved are almost never indicted, prosecuted, or punished in any way. When the families try to bring lawsuits, it can be difficult for them to find an attorney. These cases are often long, drawn-out and expensive to properly investigate and try. Even some lawyers eager to handle these cases are unable to do so for these reasons. Families filing lawsuits are often intimidated by the same law enforcement agencies that killed their loved one. Many families fortunate enough to find attorneys have their cases thrown out in the early stages. Families who win lawsuits receive only monetary compensation; there is no real justice (accountability on the part of police) for their loved one. We know of only a handful of cases where the officers involved were indicted, convicted and sentenced to prison terms.

The general public remains unaware of the enormity of the problem partly because the media is underplaying its significance. With the exception of high profile cases such as Amadou Diallo and Tyisha Miller, a police killing will typically occupy a two-inch column in the back pages of the newspaper. The headlines in most cases are small. It may be a 60-second story on the local television and radio news. And we never hear about it again. This leaves the public with the mistaken impression that police killings are a few isolated incidents. But when we gather the stories together in a book like this, we can see that police killings are a nationwide epidemic.

When media report on cases of police brutality, they generally rely almost exclusively on police reports. Police generally say they had "no choice but to shoot." Many family members say that their loved ones are killed twice: first by the police and then by the press. Often the media does not seek out eyewitnesses or family members for their side of the story. When the media reports only what the police have to say and fails to do a thorough investigation, this helps prevent the public from learning the true extent of police brutality. When I testified about police brutality before the hearings of the U.S. Human Rights Commission held in Sonoma County, I expressed my belief that the failure of the media to act as a strong watchdog amounts to complicity in covering up police brutality.

Goals of the Stolen Lives Project

Stolen Lives' mission is to assemble a national list of people killed by law enforcement agents from 1990 to the present. Stolen Lives attempts to expose the true circumstances and put a human face on a horrifying epidemic. The victims of police violence were part of our society. But rarely are their lives or names publicized, nor are the real circumstances surrounding their deaths investigated and made known. Stolen Lives aims to restore some dignity to the lives that have been lost. Though their lives have been stolen from us, we will not allow them to be forgotten.

Who Are the Victims?

- The main targets of police brutality are Black and Latino people. Yet, many of the newspaper articles we researched failed to report the race or ethnicity of people killed by police. For the people listed in this book whose nationalities we do know, over 3/4 are people of color. Many victims are young. Most are males. From the border with Mexico to the streets of Houston and other cities and towns, people are being killed by police or the border patrol for the simple fact that they are immigrants.
- While it strikes young men of color most, police brutality is increasingly experienced where we would not expect it: in white communities, by women, by the mentally ill and psychologically distraught, the disabled, and even sometimes the elderly, including people in their 80s.
- Most cases we list concern people who were unarmed and/or either committed no crime or were involved in a situation that should have been settled without the use of deadly force.
- Many police killings result from 911 calls for help. Many families of victims never expected police brutality to touch their lives. A mother or father in a family crisis had no expectation when they dialed 911 that their overwrought or suicidal child would be killed by the very agency they had called for help.
- Many victims had no idea they were being confronted by law enforcement agents when plainclothes or undercover police stormed into their homes or communities.
- There are cases where the deaf or non-English speaking people are killed for failing to obey police commands.

Given current trends in law enforcement, we can expect that these abuses will continue, or worse yet, increase. It is our purpose to sound an alarm that will compel people from all walks of life to speak out and act to put a stop to this epidemic of police brutality.

Other Alarming Trends

- When police arrive on the scene, they often escalate the situation rather than diffuse it. There is an increase in the use of paramilitary units (e.g., SWAT teams, Emergency Response Teams) in responding to domestic violence incidents and other types of disturbances. These sieges by domestic police units often involve over 100 SWAT officers, the use of helicopters and other hi-tech military equipment and the evacuation of entire residential neighborhoods for many hours.
- Police, not social workers or psychologists, are called to deal with the mentally ill and psychologically distraught. These incidents are treated as crimes, not as sensitive situations requiring reasoned intervention. In too many cases, the incident rapidly escalates and the person is killed.
- Many police killings occur within minutes or even seconds of when police arrive on the scene.

Policy on Cases Included in this Edition

The authorities have not released the names and accounts of people killed by police nationwide. It is therefore up to us to gather this information, and a verification process of names and circumstances continues. The majority of cases of victims of police killings that we are listing concern people who were unarmed and/or either committed no crime or were involved in a situation that should have been settled without shooting. In other cases, the facts may be in dispute, where the police claim and the media report, that the person killed posed a serious danger to the public or a police officer, while the victim's relatives, friends, and/or witnesses dispute this claim. Then there are cases in which the police claim justifiable homicide and no one has, to our knowledge, contested this. Even in these cases, this may be because of intimidation of family or witnesses, or because of a lack of media coverage. That small slice of cases in which the facts seem less ambiguous are then used to justify a whole climate of police brutality and by extension, the vast majority of clearly unjustified murders by law enforcement officers.

When they are available, we have included reports from families of victims, eyewitnesses and opponents of police brutality. We thank those families, witnesses and activists who are speaking out and telling the truth about the brutality of police. For we believe that they do so at no small risk to their own lives.

Where possible we have reported conflicting accounts from police and families or witnesses. Most entries indicate the source of the account, whether from a newspaper or otherwise.

Our efforts to verify the information we receive continues. We urge anyone who has additional information about the cases presented here to contact us so that we may correct or change the account to more accurately portray what happened. Please accept our apologies for any mistakes made in the 2nd edition. We welcome your corrections, additions and suggestions.

We also continue to seek information about cases that we do not yet know about. We urge those who know about people killed by law enforcement agents to contact us so that we can add their names to the Stolen Lives Project. Families of victims are among the most powerful voices that can speak out and we urge them to do so. As we go to press, we are grateful to exchange research on cases of police brutality with the National Association for the Advancement of Colored People (NAACP). We encourage individuals and organizations to compile and share information about cases of police brutality so that the full extent of this nationwide epidemic can be brought to light. Scholars, students and researchers with access to libraries, computers and university facilities are encouraged to take this up.

So many people around the country have made this 2nd edition of *Stolen Lives: Killed by Law Enforcement* possible. We thank them all for their invaluable efforts.

Karen Saari
on behalf of the Stolen Lives Project

Definition

Law enforcement is defined as police, sheriffs, border patrol, jail and prison guards, security guards acting in the role of law enforcement agents, undercover agents, and agents of the ever-growing and innumerable police agencies of the federal, state and local governments. Retired, former and off-duty officers and guards are included in our definition of law enforcement agents.

Scope of the Project

Stolen Lives aims to collect the names of people killed by law enforcement agents since 1990. We have, however, included stories of people killed prior to 1990 if they were sent to us.

There are many ways that police kill. The following kinds of deaths are included in this edition:

- Shootings. This is by far the largest category.
- Use of excessive force. This category includes the use of chokeholds, hog-tying and other forms of asphyxia, pepper spray, beatings, taser guns, and attacks by police dogs or a combination of these "restraint" tactics. We also include cases where people have died because police chased them off a building or bridge where they fell to their death or where they were chased into a body of water and drowned. We also list cases where police used various incendiary devices, or non-incendiary devices such as tear gas canisters, and the victims were killed in the resulting fires and/or explosions.
- Incarceration / in custody deaths. Places of custody and incarceration include squad cars, police stations, jails, prisons and group homes to which juvenile offenders have been sentenced. Many inmates, such as those in California state prisons, have been shot down by guards who deliberately provoked what they call "gladiator fights" and then opened fire, supposedly to break up the fight. We include deaths in jails and prisons caused by denial of necessary medical treatment. Jail and prison suicides are not included unless a) someone (the victim's family, a local civil rights group, etc.) contests the official finding of suicide or b) when the official report is so ludicrous as to be discounted, as in the case of the Oklahoma man who supposedly shot himself in the back of the head while handcuffed. People who were reported to have died of natural causes in prison are also not included unless a) someone (family, local civil rights group, etc.) contests this finding and charges foul play or medical neglect by jail or prison authorities or b) when someone dies so soon after being taken into custody that it is unlikely that natural causes totally unrelated to their interaction with the police are to blame.
- Deaths reported by police as "suicide by cop." We have included cases where authorities claim that a suicidal victim deliberately provoked the police into killing him. If this is true, as the police contend, what kind of society are we living in when a distraught person contemplating ending their life can count on the police to carry it out? In some of these cases, the families are adamant that the victim was not suicidal. But they are stonewalled in their attempts to unearth the true circumstances.
- Domestic violence in which law enforcement agents kill their current or former spouses or lovers, and their children. Other off-duty killings are also included. These cases help to disclose the pervasive use of violence by many police. Police officers, off duty or retired, routinely request, and too often receive, leniency when they kill a family member or cause a fatal car accident. This practice furthers a tolerance of police officers taking people's lives with impunity.
- Deaths as a result of high-speed police car chases. Most of these deaths reported here do not involve the police car itself, but rather someone fleeing from police, often from stops for minor car equipment violations. Approximately one-third of the people killed in such cases are innocent bystanders. We included these cases because they show a wanton recklessness and blatant disregard for the safety of the community, both the people in the car being chased as well as other motorists and pedestrians. When cops chase someone at 100 mph through a crowded residential neighborhood, it is not surprising when a bystander is killed as a result. Police involved in chases where bystanders or passengers are killed are not prosecuted for homicide, but the people they are pursuing often face murder or manslaughter charges.

Every year since 1997, the names from Stolen Lives have been read at events taking place on October 22, a National Day of Protest to Stop Police Brutality, Repression and the Criminalization of a Generation. A reading of names by actors Ossie Davis and Melvin Van Peebles, filmmaker Michael Moore, and poet Jerry Quickly aired on the radio program, *Democracy Now*. Also, ceremonies to add victims' names to Stolen Lives have taken place in Riverside, California, Greenville, South Carolina and New York City. It is important that the victims be remembered and honored as we demand that police brutality stop. In the two years since the Stolen Lives Project was initiated, a movement to stop police brutality has gained momentum. We hope that the Stolen Lives Project will serve to broaden and strengthen this movement, and compel people from all walks of life to act to stop police brutality.

People killed by brutal police cannot speak for themselves. But we can and will.

The following pages present the circumstances of over 2,000 cases of killings by law enforcement since 1990. Our research is far from complete. We know that there are many cases of which we are not yet aware. What follows is just the tip of the iceberg.

Stolen Lives is a project of:

Anthony Baez Foundation
6 Cameron Place
Bronx, NY 10453
718-364-2879
718-798-2466
718-653-1681 (fax)

National Lawyers Guild
8124 West 3rd Street
Suite 201
Los Angeles, CA 90048
323-658-8627
323-653-3245 (fax)

Oct. 22 Coalition to Stop Police Brutality, Repression & the Criminalization of a Generation
P.O. Box 2627
New York, NY. 10009
212-477-8062
212-477-8015 (fax)
1-888-NO BRUTALITY
email: Oct22@unstoppable.com **web:** http://www.unstoppable.com/22

The Stolen Lives Project aims to speak for victims of police brutality and murder, their families and loved ones and for all of us who demand justice. Contributions to this project are needed. Checks or money orders (tax deductible) should be made out to "Stolen Lives/IFCO/Oct. 22." and mailed to:
October 22
P.O. Box 2627
New York, NY 10009

October 22, 1999 National Day of Protest to Stop
Police Brutality, Repression and the
Criminalization of a Generation!

Stolen Lives is a project of the October 22nd Coalition
to Stop Police Brutality, the National Lawyers Guild
and the Anthony Baez Foundation.

Stolen Lives Project
October 22nd Coalition
P.O. Box 2627
New York, NY 10009
(212) 477-8062
(212) 477-8015 - fax
www.unstoppable.com/22

The mission of the Stolen Lives Project is to assemble a national list of names of people who have been killed by the police and the U.S.-Mexican border patrol. What do we want? What do the people demand? We demand justice! To contribute to the Stolen Lives list, families of victims and others who know of cases of police brutality and murder, need to fill out this form and send it to the Stolen Lives Project at the address above. (To get involved, contact the organizations listed below or the October 22nd Coalition in your area.)

Name of Victim: _____   **Age:** _____   **Nationality:** _____
(Please Print)

Date/Place of Birth: _____   **Date/Place of Death:** _____
*Do you have a photograph of the victim? If so, please attatch it.

Lawyer(s) Name: _____   **Phone No.:** _____

Address: _____
Street   City   State   Zip

What Happened?: _____
_____
_____

Please continue on back if needed.

Please describe any legal proceedings and their outcome. Please include the names of the agencies involved and where they are located:
_____
_____

Are there some things you could tell us about that victim that would help others to know him/her as a person?
_____

How do you want to be contacted, e.g., through your attorney, clergy, work, school or at home?

Name: _____

Address: _____
Street   City   State   Zip

Telephone Number: _____

Please include as much of the information as possible to help us verify and compile what happened.
Photograph(s)   ***Police Reports**   ***Witness Statements**   ***Other** _____

Anthony Baez Foundation
6 Cameron Place
Bronx, NY 10453
(718) 364-2879, (718) 798-2466
(718) 651-1681 - fax

National Lawyers Guild
8124 West 3rd Street, suite 201
Los Angeles, CA 90048
(323) 658-8627
(323) 653-3245 - fax

Oct. 22nd Coalition, National Office
P.O. Box 2627
New York, NY 10009
(212) 477-8062
(212) 477-8015 - fax

The Faces of Stolen Lives

Merle Africa
Pittsburgh / Western Pennsylvania
3/13/98

Travis O'Neill Allen
Texas
7/15/95

Chila Amaya
San Francisco Bay Area / Northern
California
3/7/98

Edward Anderson
Washington State
1/15/96

Michael "Buzz" Arnold
Los Angeles
3/27/98

Frankie Arzuaga
New York City / Westchester / Long
Island
1/12/96

Anthony Baez
New York City / Westchester / Long
Island
12/22/94

Patrick Bailey
New York City / Westchester / Long
Island
10/31/97

Richard Beaty, Jr.
Los Angeles
2/9/96

Hassan Haamid
Cleveland, Oh
4/11/98

Kenneth Maurice Boyd
Washington State
1/4/99

Rudy Buchanan, Jr.
Arizona
1/29/95

Gidone "Gary" Busch
New York City / Westchester / Long
Island
8/30/99

Charles Campbell
New York City / Westchester / Long
Island
10/4/96

**Michael Demonn
Carpenter**
Ohio (outside Cleveland)
3/19/99

Anibal Carrasquillo
New York City / Westchester / Long
Island
1/22/95

2

The Faces of Stolen Lives

Julio Salvador Castillo
Los Angeles
1/10/99

Angel Castro, Jr.
Chicago
10/23/96

Kevin Cedeno
New York City / Westchester / Long Island
4/6/97

Dustin Harley Clark
San Francisco Bay Area / Northern California
9/6/96

Steve Clemons
Los Angeles
9/2/91

Jason Collins
Chicago
7/10/94

Sherly Colon
New York City / Westchester / Long Island
4/24/97

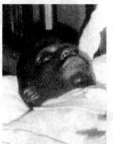

Otis Charles Cooks
Texas
8/8/96

Joseph N. Cooper, Jr.
Washington, D. C.
11/11/95

Stanton L. Crew
New Jersey
6/3/99

Sheila Detoy
San Francisco Bay Area / Northern California
5/13/98

Amadou Diallo
New York City / Westchester / Long Island
2/4/99

Arthur Díaz
San Francisco Bay Area / Northern California
9/10/94

Dario Diodonet
New York City / Westchester / Long Island
11/9/95

Demetrius DuBose
San Diego / Southern California
7/24/99

Harvey Lee Duke, Jr.
South Carolina
5/8/95

3

The Faces of Stolen Lives

Antonio Silo Dunsmore
Washington State
4/22/95

Verlon Dykes
San Francisco Bay Area / Northern
California
6/20/97

Archie "Artie" Elliott III
Maryland
6/18/93

Michael Federici
Arizona
4/16/98

Kenneth Brian Fennell
South Carolina
8/30/93

Johnny Gammage
Pittsburgh / Western Pennsylvania
10/12/95

Mark William García
San Francisco Bay Area / Northern
California
4/6/96

Mike García
San Francisco Bay Area / Northern
California
2/25/98

Yusef Kareem Gause
Connecticut
11/11/97

Anteneh Getachew
Washington, D. C.
10/14/95

Rigoberto González
Los Angeles
12/23/97

Ronald Gordon
Georgia
7/26/93

Joseph C. Gould
Chicago
7/30/95

Lamar Wayne Grable
Michigan
9/21/96

Malice Green
Michigan
November 1992

Preston Green
Los Angeles
10/26/93

The Faces of Stolen Lives

Luke Grinage (Son)
San Francisco Bay Area / Northern
California
7/15/93

Raphael Grinage (Dad)
San Francisco Bay Area / Northern
California
7/15/93

Craig L. Guest
Pittsburgh / Western Pennsylvania
6/26/96

Jorge Guillén
Chicago
10/3/95

Dalon Gunn
Michigan
7/19/97

Robert Wayne Guy, Jr.
Washington State
12/29/97

Tyrone Guyton
San Francisco Bay Area / Northern
California
11/1/73

Adolph Boyd, Jr.
Cleveland, Oh
4/14/97

LaTanya Haggerty
Chicago
6/4/99

Jerrold Hall
San Francisco Bay Area / Northern
California
11/15/92

Danny Harmon
Cleveland, Oh
November 1996

Dwayne Harris
Cleveland, Oh
9/14/91

James Harris
Cleveland, Oh
8/15/98

Kennith "Kenny" Harris
Virginia
8/2/97

Derek Paul Hayward
San Diego / Southern California
11/25/94

Dexter Aubrey Herbert
Los Angeles
3/24/89

The Faces of Stolen Lives

Esequiel Hernandez, Jr.
Texas
5/20/97

Nicholas Heyward, Jr.
New York City / Westchester / Long
Island
9/27/94

Keith Devi Hill
Maryland
1/26/96

Kelsey Lamont Hogan
Chicago
8/14/99

Darryl "Chubby" Hood
Los Angeles
11/15/97

Stephen Horton
Cleveland, Oh
1/1/97

Daryl Howerton
North Carolina
9/8/94

Yong Xin Huang
New York City / Westchester / Long
Island
3/24/95

Dale Allen Hughes
San Francisco Bay Area / Northern
California
11/19/97

Hector Martin Islas
Los Angeles
1/29/97

José Itturalde
Michigan
1993

Antonio Jackson
Washington State
12/14/93

Jaime Jaurequí
Los Angeles
3/9/96

Felix Jorge, Jr.
Upstate New York
7/28/94

Derek Jason Kaeseman
Texas
10/25/98

Kuan Chung Kao
San Francisco Bay Area / Northern
California
4/29/97

The Faces of Stolen Lives

Hong Il Kim
Los Angeles
2/14/96

Brennan King
Chicago
11/28/98

Aaron Kirk
San Francisco Bay Area / Northern
California
11/23/98

Rodney "Banks" Laulusa
Hawaii
1/22/98

Reginald LaVergne
Texas
4/17/99

Leonard Lawton
New York City / Westchester / Long
Island
1/20/96

Paul Anthony Maxwell
New York City / Westchester / Long
Island
7/31/98

Phillip McCall
Philadelphia / Eastern Pennsylvania
5/18/98

Hector Mendez
New York City / Westchester / Long
Island
1988

Anthony Merisier
New York City / Westchester / Long
Island
10/24/94

Dennis Richard Mickel
South Carolina
10/28/96

Tyisha Miller
Los Angeles
12/28/98

Bodegard Mitchell
Washington State
9/30/96

Kevin Morris
Chicago
1/18/98

Terrance Moses
Chicago
5/14/98

Shawn Mottram
Massachusetts
10/11/97

The Faces of Stolen Lives

Kuthurima Mwaria
New York City / Westchester / Long
Island
4/13/95

Jason Nichols
New York City / Westchester / Long
Island
10/17/94

Angry Bear Nieto
Central California
6/2/88

Michael Tebbs Nunn
New York City / Westchester / Long
Island
10/3/87

Frank Olsen
New York City / Westchester / Long
Island
10/16/90

Pedro Oregón
Texas
7/12/98

James Parkinson
San Francisco Bay Area / Northern
California
6/8/96

Tasia Patton
Arizona
4/16/98

Frankie Perkins
Chicago
3/22/97

Leonard "Acorn" Peters
San Francisco Bay Area / Northern
California
4/14/95

Patrick Heslin Phelan
New York City / Westchester / Long
Island
1/21/96

Eric Pitt
New York City / Westchester / Long
Island
12/7/94

Thomas Pizzuto
New York City / Westchester / Long
Island
1/8/99

Marwin Muñoz Prado
San Francisco Bay Area / Northern
California
3/26/98

Sebastián Ramírez
Los Angeles
3/22/96

Douglas Reagan
Washington State
9/30/96

The Faces of Stolen Lives

Leroy Reed
Chicago
1/16/98

James Rhodes
Cleveland, Oh
2/19/97

Jack Brian Richman
Chicago
11/18/97

Freddie Rivera
New York City / Westchester / Long
Island
8/4/98

Dale Hearldeane Robbins
San Francisco Bay Area / Northern
California
1/29/96

Kelvin Robinson
Los Angeles
10/19/97

Oliver Rodriguez, Jr.
Texas
11/29/97

Anthony Rosario
New York City / Westchester / Long
Island
1/12/95

Robert Anthony Russ
Chicago
6/5/99

Michael Russell
Chicago
4/5/98

Tyrone Napolean Salters
South Carolina
4/29/98

Henry Sanchez
Los Angeles
10/19/96

José Manuel Sánchez
Los Angeles
11/30/92

Jose Antonio Sanchez
New York City / Westchester / Long
Island
2/22/97

Ralf C. Sanjurjo
Washington State
11/15/96

Kevin Saunders
San Francisco Bay Area / Northern
California
8/29/96

9

The Faces of Stolen Lives

Gregory Sevier
Kansas
4/21/91

Edward Sheehan
San Francisco Bay Area / Northern
California
11/1/95

Colico Smalls
Ohio (outside Cleveland)
8/4/99

Danny Ray Smith
Los Angeles
8/1/98

Eric Smith
Chicago
4/9/96

Justin H. Smith
Oklahoma
8/14/98

Gustavo Soto-Mesa
San Francisco Bay Area / Northern
California
3/2/96

Frank Valdez
Florida
7/17/99

Miguel A. Valoy-Núñez
New York City / Westchester / Long
Island
1/4/99

Aurea Bonnie Vargas
New York City / Westchester / Long
Island
1/29/93

Bill Earl Vaughn
San Francisco Bay Area / Northern
California
12/21/98

Charles Vaughn, Sr.
San Francisco Bay Area / Northern
California
5/19/98

Hilton Vega
New York City / Westchester / Long
Island
1/12/95

**Aswon "Keshawn"
Watson**
New York City / Westchester / Long
Island
6/13/96

Raynard Anthony White
Chicago
2/12/99

William J. Whitfield
New York City / Westchester / Long
Island
Dec. 25, 1997 (Christmas
Day)

The Faces of Stolen Lives

Aaron Williams
San Francisco Bay Area / Northern
California
6/4/95

Charles Williams
San Francisco Bay Area / Northern
California
3/1/97

40 STOLEN LIVES

Introduction

These are 40 Stolen Lives, the stories of 40 people killed by police since 1990 (though most of the incidents described here have occurred in the past three years). Please read these. Try to find, if you can, the hardened killers of the evening news, the "reality-based" cop shows, or the many prime time dramas on each week. Rest assured that if you do find such characters in these stories, they will not be among the victims.

Who are these victims? Overwhelmingly they were people of color—though the epidemic of police violence has claimed its white victims as well. Overwhelmingly, they were young, though there were some well into middle age too. They were poets, cooks, day laborers, teachers, homeless and well-to-do businessmen. They were people embedded in a human community, with children, parents, lovers, and friends; people with aspirations, dreams, disappointments, loves and hates; people from communities that are themselves under siege, or so it would seem.

It could be said that these are exceptions or aberrations, though our grassroots project has now uncovered over 2,000 law enforcement homicides since 1990. It could be said that the facts are not all in, though the police departments themselves usually refuse to release the information. It could be said that surely the Federal Government will step in, though the Justice Department continues to ignore a 1994 law requiring yearly reports on use of excessive force. Many things could be said, and many things are said, every day, by the police chiefs, the politicians and the other select few who are given a platform. But who will speak for those whose lives have been stolen? Who will give voice to those who can no longer tell their stories? Who will affirm *their* humanity?

ANTHONY BAEZ—KILLED BECAUSE HIS FOOTBALL HIT A POLICE CAR

New York. On December 22, 1994, the four sons of Iris and Ramon Baez were playing football in front of their house, as they waited to leave with their family on a car trip to Florida. When the football hit the car of police officer Francis Livoti, he arrested David, the youngest brother, cuffing him and slamming his head into his brother's jeep and then knocking him to the ground.

Anthony Baez, a 29-year-old Puerto Rican man known as a conciliator in difficult situations, questioned what Livoti was doing. Livoti turned on Anthony, and the other cops on the scene swarmed out of their cars. Livoti wrapped his arm around Anthony's neck in an illegal chokehold. Anthony's father rushed from inside the house and pleaded with Livoti to ease off the chokehold, due to Anthony's asthma. But Livoti only eased off when Anthony was dead. Two of Anthony's brothers were forced to the ground and handcuffed with police guns to their heads.

Widespread community outrage led to a trial. Despite what the judge called evidence of a "nest of perjury" among the officers backing Livoti, he acquitted Livoti. Earlier this year, Livoti was finally found guilty of violating Anthony's civil rights.

Anthony Baez was married and planning to buy a house and start a family in Florida. He loved children and was always surrounded by kids. "Tony was a part of us," his father Ramon has said, "in the prime of life. My family—for us life is not the same …"

CHARLES CAMPBELL—MURDERED BY A COP OVER PARKING SPACE

New York. On October 4, 1996, Charles Campbell pulled into a parking space in front of the delicatessen of Richard DiGuglielmo, Sr. in a Westchester County suburb of New York. DiGuglielmo, his son Richard DiGuglielmo, Jr., and a third man pasted a sticker on Charles' window. When Charles asked them to take it off, they jumped him and began to beat him. When Charles Campbell finally broke free, he picked up a bat to defend himself against the three men. The younger DiGuglielmo—an off-duty New York City police officer—shot Charles three times, twice in the heart, killing him.

Charles Campbell was a 37-year-old Black man, a sanitation worker and youth counselor. After his killing, his fiancée, Vanessa Maldonaldo, spearheaded a battle to win justice for him. One year later, DiGuglielmo was found guilty of second degree murder and sentenced from 20 years to life in prison.

Speaking after the verdict, Vanessa Maldonaldo said, "We must acknowledge and recognize that this definitely was a victory for us as a whole. But the struggle keeps on going and … I'm here for all the other families."

FRANKIE ARZUAGA

New York. Frankie was a 15-year-old Puerto Rican youth, a passenger in a car that was pulled over by police on Jan. 12, 1996 in the Bushwick section of Brooklyn. The police claim that they fired on the car when the driver tried to drive off. Frankie's parents, David and Lillian Flores, later obtained a medical report indicating that Frankie had been shot at close range. No action has ever been taken against the officers involved in the shooting.

On the Mother's Day following Frankie's death, police telephoned to torment his mother, Lillian. The family has a room in their apartment displaying Frankie's favorite things, like a red toy car, and photographs of Frankie, his grave site, and the many protests and police brutality hearings the family has been a part of.

When Abner Louima was beaten and tortured by police in the 70th Precinct, one measure the New York City Police Department took was to replace the 70th's captain. Frankie Arzuaga's parents pointed out to anyone who would listen that the replacement was none other than the captain from the Bushwick precinct where her son had been killed.

ANGEL CASTRO—FAMILY FACES REPRISALS FOR PROTESTING

Chicago. On October 23, 1996, Angel Castro, Jr., a 15-year-old Puerto Rican youth, was on his way to a friend's birthday party. The Chicago teenager crashed into a police cruiser as he rode his bike towards the party. The collision broke Angel's teeth and seriously bruised and scraped his legs and face. When Angel rose from the ground, clearly hurt, the police shouted that he had a gun and opened fire. Angel Castro, Jr. was struck in the side of his head by a cop's bullet, then left to lie handcuffed and shaking in the street until he died. No gun was ever found.

When Angel's mother, Linda Giron, attempted to pursue the case she found herself the victim of slashed tires, broken antennas, a blocked car engine, and frequent hangup calls. Police would cruise by, glare, threaten and even sound their siren at the monthly vigils held for Angel.

"I can't give up," says Linda Giron. "My son had a right to live and they had no right to kill him. I have to fight for my son because he's not here to fight for himself. He's not here to clear his name, so I have to clear his name for him … Before I would be afraid, now I'm not. Because they were the ones that killed my son. And they're out there walking the streets. I surprise myself sometimes, because I snap at them and just look at them dead in their face—like, 'I'm not afraid of you, do whatever you want. I'm not afraid.'"

The Office of Professional Standards, the city agency charged with looking into cases of police abuse, ruled the shooting justified.

JOHN DANIELS JR. and JOHN DANIELS SR.

Los Angeles. On July 1, 1992, John Daniels, Jr., a Black tow-truck driver, was stopped at a gas station by two motorcycle cops. The cops refused to say why they were stopping him and he started to drive away. Officer Douglas Iverson ran beside the truck and shot Daniels once in the neck, killing him. The death of John Daniels, Jr. devastated his family. For in 1985 his father, John Daniels, Sr., was also shot and killed by the LAPD. As a block captain for Neighborhood Watch, he had called police to report a man with a gun. The cops showed up and killed the first Black man they saw.

The killing of John Daniels Jr. was protested by many, including the African-American Tow Truck Drivers Association. Police later admitted that they had organized a task force to harass independent tow truck drivers. A year after the shooting, Officer Iverson was charged with murder. After two trials ending in hung juries, the judge dismissed all charges.

SHEILA DETOY—"SHE WAS JUST A KID"

San Francisco. On May 13, 1998, Sheila Patricia Detoy lost her young life to the San Francisco Police. The police shot into a car of three unarmed youth, striking 17-year-old Sheila Detoy in the head. Police claimed to have been after a suspect who had a bench warrant for failing to appear in court regarding the use and sale of drugs. They used an unmarked green van to block the car in which Sheila was riding and said that they only shot because they feared that the car would hit them.

The police version was inconsistent with the physical evidence and disputed by an eyewitness in a sworn deposition who stated that at no time were the police in the path of the car, nor did they ever shout "police" or in any way identify themselves. Further, the witness maintained that police fired into the rear of the car. Despite attempts to slander Sheila Detoy for "running with the wrong crowd" in the press (a common occurrence in such incidents), it was dragged into the public eye that the officer who fired the fatal shots had been suspended for 20 days in 1992 for unnecessary use of force and lying about his actions, and then faced further disciplinary charges in 1995.

Hundreds of youth protested Sheila's death, and the struggle still goes on. "Why would they shoot Sheila?" her aunt asked. "She was just a kid. Just like everyone else's kid. She was a wonderful, sweet, intelligent girl. We spent all of our summers together… She was a real good student. Socially, she was real popular. She had a job. She worked at a coffee shop. She had plans to go to college. She was extremely close to her sister and mother."

ANDREW "NU-NU" DURHAM—SHOT DEAD FOR RUNNING

Chicago. In the early morning hours of Sunday, August 10, 1997, Andrew "Nu-Nu" Durham lost his life to the Chicago Police Department. He had been hanging out when two police officers ordered him and a friend to come over to their car. Andrew took off running. The cop chasing Andrew first shot him in the thigh. Eyewitnesses say that Durham then stopped running and raised his hands, but the officer grabbed him, shot him in the head, and then shot him again as he fell to the ground. Durham lay in the street for 45 minutes before an ambulance came to pronounce him dead.

Police claimed that Andrew Durham was a suspected car thief who had grabbed for the officer's gun. But at a community-organized inquiry attended by over 400 people a week later, eyewitnesses said that there had been no struggle for the gun, and that the cops had simply pumped bullets into the unarmed and wounded youth. Community residents disputed the charge of "suspected auto theft," asserting instead that Andrew was a kind, soft-spoken young man, and protesting against the "double murder"—first Andrew's life, and then his good name.

MARC FITZSIMMONS—SHOT IN THE BACK, THEN DENIED MEDICAL TREATMENT

Los Angeles. On July 2, 1998, 28-year-old Marc Fitzsimmons left to go to the bank for his mother. That was the last time she would ever see him.

"Five days later the Los Angeles Police Department called the Cleveland Police Department to tell my parents to call me to tell me that my son had been executed," related his mother, Donna Fitzsimmons Dymally. "My son was killed two miles from his home, yet they went all the way to Ohio five days later to notify... Southwest Division. They got a reputation. You know, you never think it could happen to you. My son had no criminal record, no drugs, nothing."

"The police claimed that he had a butcher knife or some kind of meat cleaver and attacked them. And they claimed that they shot him in the chest. And when we got the autopsy report, he was shot in the back. He was taken to UCLA. He was brought in in a police car, handcuffed. The doctor in the autopsy report noted that he felt something was wrong. 'Well, where is this object, this weapon he was supposed to have had?' The police could not show it. It wasn't the police who killed him who brought him in, it was another set of police. The doctors believe he would have lived if he had been given medical treatment. They claim they have witnesses, but of course they won't give us any incident report."

"My child was an honor student. He was a gifted child. He was accepted to UCLA at the age of 15. Never caused me a day's trouble. He was the most spirited, most nice—that's why, when it happened to him, it was just too much for me. To think that it could happen to him, a kid who never gave us a day's trouble. For a long while I didn't want to come out of my house. I'm afraid now when my children leave. It turns your life upside down."

"I felt I had to get mobilized, I felt I had to get involved. It was like 'I cannot stand back,' because I realized it happened to me and it's happening to other people and that maybe I could serve as a source to wake other people up. The only way we're going to make a change is if we stand up and be counted."

JONNY GAMMAGE—DRIVING WHILE BLACK, A CAPITAL CRIME

Pittsburgh. In the early morning of October 12, 1995, Jonny Gammage was stopped by five police officers. Gammage was a 31-year-old Black businessman driving a late-model sports car through an all-white Pittsburgh suburb. Within seven minutes of being stopped Jonny Gammage had been asphyxiated to death by the five police officers.

Police said that they stopped the unarmed Gammage because he had been putting on his brakes "in a suspicious manner" as police followed him. He was suspected of no crime. Police handcuffed and shackled him, then put him face down on the pavement and kneeled on his neck, shoulders and waist. It takes an awful lot of force to suffocate a man like that, but the Brentwood police did it.

Because Gammage's cousin was Ray Seals, a high-profile professional football player, the case attracted national attention. Charges were filed on three of the officers, but an all-white jury acquitted one and the others have since had their cases dismissed.

Jonny Gammage's mother was bitter after the acquittal of Officer John Vojtas, one of the five policemen who killed her son. "We gave the system a chance to work, and it didn't work. I didn't believe the people who told us the system doesn't work for Blacks. I believed it would work. But I don't believe that anymore."

MARK GARCIA—ASKING FOR HELP, PEPPER-SPRAYED TO DEATH

San Francisco. On April 6, 1996, Mark Garcia was robbed. Disoriented, unarmed, and stripped half nude by his robbers, he wandered the streets of San Francisco's Mission District screaming for help. Instead of helping Mark, the police officers who responded pepper-sprayed him and slammed him face-first into the ground. For five minutes an officer ground a foot in Mark's back. No medical attention was provided and no solution was used to wash the pepper spray out of Mark's face. When the police van came, the officers threw Mark into the van face down, and did not monitor his position in the back of the van. When the van reached the hospital, Mark Garcia was dead. To date, no police officer has been penalized for anything relating to the death of Mark Garcia, despite the fact that their behavior involved numerous violations of even departmental rules.

Mark Garcia was a teamster and a recovering drug addict who counselled and helped other people with drug and alcohol problems. He left behind a wife, two children and an extended family that has tirelessly fought for justice.

Daniel Garcia, Mark's brother, speaking at the October 22, 1997 demonstration against police brutality, said, "My brother and the families of all those who died in the hands of the police are here today, right there in the sky. And what they are saying is 'No justice, no peace!' The families, friends, and trade union associates of Mark Garcia nationally and locally are turning their grief into strength and determination. They have joined together for a common cause, to help put an end, once and for all, to the epidemic of police brutality, repression, and the criminalization of a generation. We are coming together this day to honor and pay respect to the people whose lives have been stolen from us. Not just from the families, but from society."

ANTONIO GOLDEN—"WE MUST STOP THIS GENOCIDE"

Lynwood. Antonio Golden's grandmother, Helen Green, gave the following account to the October 22 Coalition:

"My grandson, Antonio Golden, age 18, was murdered February 19, 1997 at 8:40 p.m. by who I believe was the 'Vikings' branch of the Lynwood Sheriffs department. The weekend before he was murdered the sheriff told some teenage children, 'One of you niggers is going to die this weekend.' Witnesses state that my grandson was on his bicycle when he was shot twice in the back, handcuffed, dragged off his bike, given no first-aid by the sheriffs deputies, and died at the scene. His supposed gun was found 20 feet—over two chain link fences—south of his body."

"Whenever one of our children is killed by people in authority it's always reported that the person killed was either a drug dealer or alleged gang member or both. So the listening public will think another menace to society is dead and will not be around to prey on them or their children. My grandson had graduated from Lynwood High and was awaiting assignment, leaving June 9 for boot camp as an E2 with the U.S. Navy. He was not a drug dealer, a drug user, nor was he a member of a gang. He was never arrested or stopped for drug use or gang activities. Innocent men, especially Black and Hispanic children, are being murdered daily by killers with badges. We must stop this genocide."

JOSEPH GOULD—SHOT DEAD FOR TRYING TO WASH A WINDOW

Chicago. Joseph Gould, a homeless vendor of *StreetWise* newspaper, was killed on July 30, 1995. Gould had approached the car of off-duty Chicago police officer Gregory Becker, asking to wash his window for change. Becker shot Gould point blank and then drove away without even calling for help. Joseph Gould died in a pool of blood, still clutching his rag and water bucket.

For nearly two years afterwards a coalition of community, homeless and anti-repression groups organized to demand justice for Joseph Gould. On April 14, 1997, a jury found Becker guilty of armed violence, involuntary manslaughter and official misconduct.

LAMAR GRABLE—"WE CANNOT LET THEM STEAL ONE MORE LIFE"

Detroit. Lamar Grable was a 19-year-old African American active in the Detroit Children's Coalition. He was a photographer and wrote poetry. On September 21, 1996, he left home on his way to his job at K-Mart. Fifteen minutes later he had been shot dead by police.

Witnesses say that after Lamar was shot three times in the back, one of the two cops who shot him turned him over and fired five more rounds point blank into Lamar's chest. This killer cop remains on the force, having received a medal for wearing a bullet-proof vest during the shooting. Lamar had no weapon, and toxicology tests revealed no drugs or alcohol in his bloodstream at the time of death. The police department refused to turn over Lamar's shirt to an independent coroner hired by the family, and now the police harass the family.

Arnetta Grable is Lamar Grable's mother. She has two other children and is an activist in the October

22 Coalition. She has said, "We cannot let them steal one more life."

RAPHAEL and LUKE GRINAGE—FATHER AND SON KILLED OVER A DOG

Oakland. On July 15, 1993, Oakland, California police came to impound Luke Grinage's dog for rabies. Confronted by police in his yard, the 21-year-old Grinage said that the dog had had his shots and he could prove it, and refused to give it up. The police jumped Luke and began to beat him, but he escaped and ran towards his house. Though they shot him as he ran, he made it to the house and returned fire with a shotgun kept inside the door. In the ensuing police barrage both Luke and his father, Raphael—a double amputee in a wheelchair—were killed. And after they finished with father and son, police entered the house and killed the dog as well.

Luke Grinage was a young man who had announced his marriage engagement that day. He had been jailed twice before, only to have the charges dropped, and felt he was being harassed by the police. Raphael Grinage was a musician who at one time played bass for Earl "Fatha" Hines. What does it mean when a dispute over a dog leads police to take two lives? Rashidah Grinage, the wife of Raphael and mother of Luke, has since become an active advocate against police repression.

JORGE GUILLEN—A CALL FOR HELP, FOLLOWED BY MURDER

Chicago. On October 3, 1995, family members called 911 when Jorge Guillen, a 40-year-old immigrant from Honduras, began having schizophrenic hallucinations. When three cops arrived, Guillen was holding a two-by-four used to keep the door shut. The police threw him to the floor, beat his head bloody with a flashlight, and handcuffed him. One cop stepped on the back of Jorge Guillen's neck. Jorge was asphyxiated as he lay face down in a pool of his own blood.

The police department's own Office of Professional Services found the three officers guilty of "excessive and unwarranted" force and recommended short suspensions, but the State's Attorney refused to prosecute the cops.

Ilsa Guillen, Jorge's wife, said, "The case of my husband, Jorge Guillen, has been placed in the dark pages of history. The three corrupt police officers, Chris Anderson, Daniel Parise, Michael A. Ponti—those are the names of those murdering corrupt cops who brutally murdered my husband. None of those three police officers have been fired from their position."

JOSE ANTONIO GUTIERREZ—"WE MUST STAY STRONG"

Los Angeles. On July 29, 1995, 14-year-old Jose Antonio Gutierrez was shot in the back by LAPD officer Michael Falvo, one of 44 police cited as a "problem officer" by the Christopher Commission. Officer Falvo claimed that he saw Tony Gutierrez point a semi-automatic weapon at him. A semi-automatic weapon was found 15 feet away from Gutierrez, but on the other side of a fence. No prints from Tony were on the weapon. Various witnesses have stated that Tony Gutierrez was unarmed when he was shot.

Two days of street-fighting against the police erupted in the Lincoln Heights neighborhood of East LA, where Tony lived. On the second anniversary of her son's death, Ana Maria Gutierrez wrote that "every year around this time as the day of my son's death approaches, I feel this sadness inside of me. Because my son is not here with me. But I also get angry. This anger that gives me the strength to keep on fighting, and continue demanding that justice be served."

"We as victims of police murder and brutality must stay strong and unite our anger and power. I want to give you encouragement to work with the lawyers that will fight for justice. And I want to encourage you to work with the Stolen Lives Project. Because my son Tony was not the only one killed by the police. The police have killed people in cities all across the country. The Stolen Lives Project is important because all of the families that are suffering are connected. And we will continue fighting in the memory of our loved ones."

JERROLD HALL—"ALL OVER THE COUNTRY, THE SAME HORROR STORIES"

San Francisco. On November 15, 1992, Jerrold Hall and a friend were stopped by a Bay Area Rapid Transit officer after arriving at their destination. The officer accused Jerrold of stealing a Walkman from another passenger, though neither Jerrold nor his friend were carrying a Walkman. The cop became verbally abusive and hit Jerrold on the head with his shotgun. The 19-year-old Black youth turned away from the BART cop and began walking towards the Hayward police who had arrived on the scene. The BART cop leveled his shotgun and shot Jerrold in the back of the head, killing him. No charges were ever filed against the officer, who later committed suicide.

Jerrold's father Cornelius, a retired firefighter, became an activist against police brutality and murder. "All over the state, all over the country, I go to different places and I hear these same horror stories. And what happens? DA's don't indict, some people don't even get that far—they don't even get to a grand jury… We can't slack off. We're going to have to continue to push, and make things happen for ourselves… No justice, no peace!"

ESEQUIEL HERNANDEZ—A KILLING ON THE BORDER

Redford, TX. On the afternoon of May 20, 1997, Esequiel Hernandez, Jr. was herding his family's goats in the West Texas border town of Redford. Esequiel, an 18-year-old high school student, carried a .22 caliber rifle to protect the goats from coyotes.

Six U.S. Marines, hidden from sight, stalked Esequiel. Without warning, one of them shot Esequiel dead with a single bullet from his M-16. The Marines waited 22 minutes to radio for medical assistance.

"I don't understand it," said Esequiel's father after the shooting. "I want there to be justice." But the U.S. Marine Corps cleared Esequiel's killers of any wrongdoing.

NICHOLAS HEYWARD, JR.—SENTENCED TO DIE FOR A TOY GUN

New York. On September 27, 1994, Nicholas Heyward, Jr., a 13-year-old African-American boy, was playing cops and robbers in the Gowanus Houses project in Brooklyn, NY. When a police officer saw Nicholas with a toy gun (which had orange day-glo parts on it) he opened fire and killed him. No action of any kind was taken against the cop involved.

Nicholas Heyward, Sr., the youth's father, has fought to expose this case and help others. "I am fighting for my son and I'm gonna fight until the end, until I do get justice. There's no stopping me. I will continue to fight and I will continue to march. I am a member of Parents Against Police Brutality. I support October 22nd and the National Congress of Puerto Rican Rights—I support them all."

DARRYL "CHUBBY" HOOD—KILLED TO 'PREVENT' SUICIDE

Watts. Darryl "Chubby" Hood was 40 years old, a resident of the Jordan Downs housing project in the Watts area of LA. At noon on November 15, 1997, Darryl was attempting to commit suicide with a large kitchen knife. A longtime friend of Chubby's described what happened next:

"I looked behind the building here and I seen Chubby was stabbing himself in the head. So I come from around the fence and asked him—begged him—I said, 'Chubby, Chubby, what you doing to yourself man? You got a wife and kids and everything.' He stopped stabbing himself in the head. I asked him for the knife and he almost gave it to me 'till he looked over my shoulder and saw the police coming. That's when he ran into the field and came back."

"He was shot once in the arm and once in the leg. He fell down and he was on his back and that's when they tried to tase [stun] him and shoot mace in his face. At that time they could have just swarmed him. But they just stood back. And when Chubby got up and ran out in the field I was running after him. I was saying 'Chubby, Chubby, Chubby—please give me the knife, man. If you don't give me the knife they gonna kill you.' Then the police sergeant came up to me and said 'Get your ass out the way!'... Then when I went to turn, that's when all hell broke loose..."

"There was about 20 police around him. They ask me how many times I think he was shot and I said 25 to 30 times. But when he got to the hospital, I guess they saying he was only shot 11 times. They say he lunged at them. He never lunged. He had his arm and his hands pointing backwards. And he couldn't stab them cuz they was 10 or 15 feet away from him. After they shot, after Chubby was dead, they put handcuffs on him."

Several marches involving hundreds of people protested the killing of "Chubby" Hood.

HECTOR ISLAS—FOUR CHILDREN WHO HAVE NO FATHER

Riverside, CA. Frances Islas of Los Angeles has related the following story of her husband, Hector Islas, to the October 22 Coalition:

"On January 29, 1997 Hector Islas ran from the Riverside [California] police. Why the officers chose to pursue Hector on foot and by car, or what crime Hector had committed, remains unknown. Hector was 5'6" tall and weighed 140 pounds. He was alone and exhausted. Although he posed no threat to the officers, he was grabbed, thrown to the ground and brutally beaten to death. Hector Islas was kicked and beaten, stomped on and bashed in the face so severely that both jaws were broken and his teeth were knocked out. By contrast, the Riverside police officers sustained no injuries. The Riverside police department claimed they were simply trying to restrain Hector Martin Islas.

"Can you officers that did this really sleep at night knowing that there are four children that mourn and cry for their father? There are four children who have no father. There is a mother that mourns for her son. Hector, we love you and we will not stop. We will fight until we get justice. I would like to thank everybody for all the support. And I would like to say, 'My God, forgive them for they know not what they do.'"

KUAN CHUNG KAO—"HE REPRESENTED THE ASIAN SUCCESS STORY"

Sonoma County, CA. On April 29, 1997, Kuanchung Kao was shot to death by police in suburban Sonoma County, California.

The 33-year-old Kao was a quality control engineer in Silicon Valley, a husband and father of three young children. At a bar that evening, Kuanchung Kao had been assaulted by a group of white men who had been making anti-Asian slurs. Police refused to arrest the white men, instead calling a cab to take Kao home.

When Kao arrived home at 2 a.m. he was extremely upset. Standing in front of his house, he began shouting for his neighbors to help him, and then assumed a praying position in the middle of the street, clawing at the ground and crying for help. Police arrived at the scene and attempted to scare Kuanchung into dropping a 1-inch diameter stick that he was holding. An officer screeched the squad car to a halt directly in front of Kao who, angry and scared, struck at the car with his stick. When Kuanchung Kao's wife, Ayling Wu, tried to approach Kuanchung for the stick, the police told her to back off.

A second police car came to the scene and within seconds of arrival, Officer Jack Shields emerged from the car, drew his weapon and shot Kuan Chung Kao in the chest. Ayling Wu, a registered nurse, was prevented by the police from administering first aid to her husband. Instead, the police handcuffed Kuanchung and left him face down, unattended for 8 to 9 minutes before any attempt was made to administer medical treatment. When the paramedics finally arrived, Mr. Kao was dead. Claiming that Mr. Kao had assumed a "martial arts pose," Officer Shields was cleared by his own police department of any wrongdoing the day after the murder.

Community outrage came out in numerous memorials, demonstrations and an investigation by the Asian Law Caucus into what turned out to be a police coverup of what happened. Victor Huang, staff attorney for the Asian Law Caucus, said, "A lot of Asians are in denial about race. But Mr. Kao could have been anyone. He represented the Asian American success story. People like to believe that you come to America, you work hard, you succeed. Race isn't a factor. But there is strong recognition now that race was a factor in this killing."

RODNEY "BANKS" LAULUSA—MURDERED IN "PARADISE"

Honolulu. On January 22, 1998, Rodney "Banks" Faatoafe Laulusa, a 30-year-old Samoan man, was murdered by the Honolulu police while visiting with friends. At least 20 shots were fired at him, and 14 bullets were removed from his body.

Rodney was striding through the Palolo Valley Homes with a knife in each hand. Police came on the scene and five cops drew guns and moved towards him. A crowd gathered, yelling "don't shoot." But according to eyewitnesses, the police shot twice, and Rodney fell to his knees, dropping the knives. While he was on his knees, three more shots were fired, and then police continued to pump bullets into him as he lay facedown in the street. The official police log showed an elapsed time of three minutes between the initial reports of a man in the street with knives to the time Rodney was shot.

Police maintained that they tried to reason with Rodney when he began to charge them. But not a single non-police eyewitness agreed with the cops, and the Palolo Tenants Association issued a press release refuting the police story in detail.

As a teenager, Rodney stole a boombox. He received an eight-year sentence for this, his first time. With the exception of this initial charge, his only other "run-ins" with the law were for parole violations. Nonetheless, the police and media portrayed him as a "hardened criminal"—a common theme in these incidents. Neighbors described him as "the nicest kid around" and his killing sparked a series of community protests. It is said that the Hawaii police force is more sensitive to the community than mainland forces. But the killing of Rodney Laulusa was the fifth highly publicized police killing in Hawaii since 1995, and there have been several less publicized cases as well. And the whole scenario from start to finish has a hauntingly familiar ring to it.

THOMAS OCHOA—REVENGE BY POLICE?

Riverside, CA. Thomas Ochoa was 33 years old. On the evening of January 22, 1997 he had fallen asleep in a Riverside, California parking lot. Police said that Ochoa had a knife and came at them. He was shot three or four times and died.

Irma Ochoa, Thomas' mother, has said that "the greater reason he was shot was because his skin was brown. Just one or two weeks prior to his death—and to Hector Islas' death—there were some policemen that were shot by Hispanics. And I know in my heart the police were out to get even. My son did not belong to a gang and he wasn't a drug pusher either. He had been in a rehab program and that day he was on his way home."

PEDRO OREGON—KILLED ON A PHONY TIP

Houston. Acting on a tip at 1:30 a.m. on July 13, 1998, Houston police stormed an apartment complex in the Gulton barrio in search of an alleged drug dealer named "Julio." They busted into the apartment of 23-year-old Pedro Oregón, a Mexican immigrant and landscaper.

The cops had neither arrest warrant nor search warrant. They handcuffed Oregón's brother and beat him in the head and stomach, shouting "Are you Julio?" Pedro insisted they had the wrong man. In the confusion, one cop fired a shot and hit another. Then all hell broke loose as police sprayed the apartment, firing 31 shots in all. Twelve bullets hit Pedro Oregón—nine through his back. And at least one bullet was fired into the back of his head at point-blank range.

Police found no drugs in the apartment, nor did the toxicology report turn up a trace of narcotics or alcohol in Pedro's body. While a gun was found in the apartment, police admit that it was not fired on the night of July 13.

Pedro Oregón left behind a wife and two daughters and a community that respected and loved him. In the week that followed, a protest movement burgeoned in Houston. People in the housing complex and surrounding neighborhood complain that the cops routinely abuse the mainly poor and Latino immigrants, and draw comparisons to the Salvadoran death squads that some in the barrio fled.

ACORN PETERS—AMBUSHED ON THE RESERVATION

Round Valley Reservation, Mendocino County, CA. On the night of April 14, 1995, Bear Lincoln and Leonard "Acorn" Peters were walking up a dirt road in the Round Valley Reservation, located in Mendocino County, California. Deputy sheriffs, who were staked out looking for Acorn's brother, opened fire on the two men without warning. Acorn died immediately and Bear went to ground and returned fire in self-defense. Deputy Bob Davis died as well.

Bear Lincoln, a Native American activist, was put on trial for the killings of both Bob Davis and his friend, Acorn Peters. However, an all-white jury acquitted him of both murder charges and deadlocked 10-2 for acquittal on lesser manslaughter charges.

Lincoln and his supporters credited the massive outcry organized in his support. Bear said, "The public's eyes were opened … A lot of good people came together."

No deputy has ever been charged with the unprovoked shooting of Acorn Peters. Bear Lincoln continues to fight against the remaining charges from that night.

PAUL BRYANT RODRIGUES—THE KILLING FIELDS OF SONOMA COUNTY

Sonoma County, CA. Paul Bryant Rodrigues, a 41-year-old homeless man, was shot and killed by a Petaluma, California police officer on March 10, 1998. Rodrigues thus became the 15th person killed by Sonoma County police in under two years. Paul had no gun, but police justify the shooting by saying that he was holding a metal bicycle part and jogging towards them. Police claim that Paul had been trying to break into a homeless center and that he charged them; they shot him twice when he was 8 to 12 feet away. The entire incident, from when the police exited their car to the shooting of Paul, took less than two minutes. There were no non-police witnesses.

The executive director of the agency that runs the shelter in question said that Paul had never been expelled or suspended from the center for breaking rules and that he did volunteer work to repay the center for services received. "He was a gentle, nice guy," the director told the local newspaper. Other friends remarked on his generosity and his intellectual curiosity.

No action has yet been taken against police involved, in a county where all the previous killings by police (including that of Kuanchung Kao, also listed here) were ruled justifiable homicide.

ANTHONY ROSARIO and HILTON VEGA—SHOT IN THE BACK LYING FACE DOWN

New York. On January 12, 1995, Hilton Vega, Anthony Rosario and Freddie Bonilla went to a friend's house to collect some money for a marriage. Without warning two white men emerged from a dark room with guns drawn, yelling for everyone to get on the floor. One of the men began shooting Hilton Vega. Anthony

Rosario began asking why they were doing that, Hilton hadn't been resisting. According to Freddie Bonilla, who froze at that point, the other white man then came up behind Anthony and began shooting him. An initial police autopsy was later overturned, revealing that Hilton had been shot eight times and Anthony 14 times. The two white men turned out to be plainclothes cops and former bodyguards of Mayor Giuliani. In a close vote a grand jury refused to indict, despite never calling Freddie Bonilla to testify.

Anthony Rosario was 18 years old, described by his mother as "somewhat shy, quiet," a real homebody. Anthony had plans to marry his girlfriend. "When we went into his room we found a magazine," his mother said, "a bridal magazine where him and his girlfriend had been planning what type of dress and outfit he was going to wear for the wedding." Hilton Vega at 21 years had done some time in prison for auto theft and was getting his life together; he and Anthony were thinking about starting a carpet-cleaning business.

After the murder of Hilton and Anthony, Margarita Rosario worked with others to start Parents Against Police Brutality. "My son died as a brave person because my son, from that floor, took a stand and protested against what they were doing. So if my son was able to do that, I am willing to do anything to stand up for his rights. And that's the way people should feel also. They should stand up for what they believe is right, not for what they believe is going to, you know, secure them. If they believe what the cops are doing is wrong, then get up there and fight. Don't be afraid. You cannot be afraid because this is what they want you to do... My son is gone but I still have a younger son here who's 14 years old. So I have to fight for him too, and for other kids that are growing up... It's for the future kids that we're concerned about... So why not get up and do something for our future kids, our future generation so they don't have to go through something like this? We need to change the system. We definitely do."

JAMES RHODES—NO WEAPONS, NO DRUGS, NO PRIOR

Cleveland. With his bookbag full of college books over his shoulder, James Rhodes and his friend were waiting for a bus at 9 p.m. on Cleveland's east side on February 19, 1997. A police cruiser rolled up on them, almost hitting them, and the two men took off running in opposite directions. One of the cops pursued James and five minutes later he lay on the ground—brutally beaten and shot dead.

Police claimed they were busting up a drug deal when James Rhodes had reached for his gun. But neither guns nor drugs were found, and the coroner's reports listed bruises all over James's head and one leg—indicating that he was beaten first, then shot. James was shot in the back.

Protests followed the killing. James' cousin, Anna-Marie Cora, said, "We need to come together. We need to try to fight this issue before too many more situations like this happen ... We need to know why. There was no weapon found, no drugs, no prior record. Now there is a void in our life. This was a 26-year-old man, a young man who had a bright future ahead of him. His mother and family demand answers. And without any justice, there will be no peace."

HENRY SANCHEZ—BEATEN TO DEATH ON THE STREET

Bell Gardens, CA. October 19, 1996: Henry Sanchez, a 35-year-old Chicano man, was riding his bicycle near his home in Bell Gardens, California when he encountered two cops from an anti-gang unit. The police began beating Henry, and other cops on backup came in to prevent bystanders from interceding. Witnesses said that police beat Henry with flashlights and jumped on his head. By the time they were through, Henry Sanchez lay dead on the street. The police did not immediately release any reason for either stopping or beating Henry Sanchez.

Henry Sanchez was a well-liked man in the neighborhood, with a young daughter. Local residents organized a series of marches and protests; at one march following the funeral of Henry Sanchez, police waited until tv crews left the scene and then charged the crowd, clubbing and macing. Carlos de la Cruz, whose nephew Richard Beatty was also killed by police, was at the demonstration: "I was just shocked that there are police like that. It tells you how disrespectful they are towards minorities, waiting there with riot gear all ready. They were the ones who started a riot. We were all peaceful. It shows you how disrespectful they are to the community there… They just treated everybody like animals and they started beating on everybody."

DONALD P. SCOTT—MURDERED FOR WEALTH?

Los Angeles. Donald P. Scott was a 61-year-old white millionaire, living in Ventura County. He was half-blind. Acting on a bogus tip, and despite convincing evidence to the contrary, L.A. County Sheriffs used an illegal and perjured search warrant to search for marijuana plants on his ranch. Scott was awakened by cops crashing into his home. He walked out of his bedroom with a revolver, but raised his hands when he saw it was the police. As his wife begged, "Don't shoot him," the cops ordered him to lower his hands. Then they opened fire, saying that he had pointed a gun at them.

No marijuana plants were found anywhere on the property. The Ventura County District Attorney concluded that the L.A. County Sheriff's Dept. "was motivated, at least in part, by a desire to seize and for-feit the [$5 million] ranch for the government," but declined to prosecute anyone involved.

ERIC SMITH—A DREAM DESTROYED

Chicago. Eric Smith, a 22-year-old African-American man, met his death on April 9, 1996. His mother, Wanda Hogue, had pulled her car off to the side of an expressway to better communicate with Eric, who was deaf. Upset, Eric ran into the traffic and was grazed by a passing car. Two cops from Forest View, a Chicago suburb, pulled up. They trained a gun on Eric's head and brought him to the side of the road. Eric's attempts to communicate by sign language were not understood. The cops beat Eric with metal batons and then shot him six times, with the final bullet going in as Eric lay on his back. The police then handcuffed Eric's mother and grandmother and took them to the station.

At the time of his murder, Eric was a second-year student at Gallaudet University, a well-known school for the deaf and hearing-impaired. He had been an amateur wrestler of some achievement, and was considering a career in either coaching or teaching. He had been previously beaten by Washington, D.C. police in October of 1995 after hailing them to help him with break-ins at his house. The D.C. police issued a written apology; no officer was punished. Eric began suffering from depression, and it was on the way home from a visit to the counsellor that Eric was killed. No officer was ever charged or in any way punished for any of the crimes against Eric Smith.

On October 22, 1997, Wanda Hogue, Eric's mother, said, "I feel that the first step we need to take is to make sure that [the cops] are held accountable or responsible for what they've done. Maybe if they feel flashlights going against their heads…the way they choked [Johnny Gammage] and killed him in cold blood. This is happening too much, and it needs to stop. And I'm going to work with everybody and hope that we can bring about changes."

JULIO TARQUINO—KILLER COP KILLS TWICE

Jersey City. In the early morning hours of May 7, 1995, Julio Tarquino, his fiancée, and a friend stopped at a Jersey City, NJ convenience store to buy food. Witnesses agree that two white men began taunt-ing them, and that Julio and his friends headed to their car to leave.

As they were leaving, Jersey City police officer John Chiusolo drove up. He handcuffed Tarquino and beat him to the ground, repeatedly kicking him in the head. When Julio's fiancée attempted to reason with the off-duty, out-of-uniform officer, she was beaten in turn. Tarquino was a 22-year-old immigrant from Bolivia, working as a housepainter and contractor, and engaged to be married. He was a good-humored and hard-working person, according to his family and friends. On May 11, he died of a fractured skull.

Officer Chiusolo, who in 1991 had killed the unarmed Maximino Cintron, a 23-year-old auto mechanic, was this time indicted for second-degree manslaughter. As of October 1998, he remains out on bail and has not come to trial.

CHARLES VAUGHN

Monterrey County, CA. Charles Vaughn was a 60-year-old Black man, mentally disabled but quite functional, with no history of violence. Yet on May 19, 1998, Monterrey County California mental health authorities called on police to forcibly hospitalize Charles Vaughn, although Vaughn did not meet any of the criteria for involuntary hospitalization.

The cop sent—Sgt. Louis Lumpkin—had a history of harassing Charles Vaughn. And it was Lumpkin, not the mental health social workers, who signed the form for involuntary hospitalization. Along with two other cops, Lumpkin pounded on Vaughn's door. Vaughn told them to leave him alone, and climbed out the back window, a small corkscrew in his hand. Police chased him onto the roof of a one-story apartment building. Rather than defuse the situation, they pursued him onto the roof, where Lumpkin began pepper-spraying him. Lumpkin sprayed an entire can of pepper spray onto Vaughn, who staggered and then ended up sitting on the roof. Lumpkin temporarily left the roof to get more pepper spray. Lumpkin returned and began to spray him again. Then, when Charles Vaughn walked towards Lumpkin one more time, the other officers opened fire, shooting him three times and killing him.

A friend of Charles Vaughn remembered him like this: "We both played sports [in college]. He was a football star… an all-American defensive tackle. In later years he became a political activist. He was also a teacher, [with] three college degrees… He taught from 1969 to 1976…"

"I was in the Black Panther Party in the '60s. Chuck was a strong supporter of the Black Panther Party … He was the leader of an organization of African-American teachers called the Black Educators around Monterey Bay… Chuck was a big influence on me continuing my education and continuing to do the right kind of things—the community activism and the political activism."

"1976 is when he came down with schizophrenia. It pretty much wrecked his life… In the last seven years he started to take care of himself better… I think that the cops were probably shocked when the community rose up the way it did after he was killed—with this outpouring of outrage and people talking about what a great person he was and what a positive and great impact that this man had on their lives. Not that they would have given a damn anyway."

ASWON "KESHAWN" WATSON—18 SHOTS WHILE SITTING IN HIS CAR

Brooklyn, New York. At 3:30 in the afternoon of June 13, 1996, in the Caribbean neighborhood of East Flatbush, Brooklyn, Aswon "Keshawn" Watson came out of a barber shop and got into his car. Suddenly, three plainclothes cops rolled up, blocked his car, and stepped out of theirs. When they drew their weapons, Aswon raised his hands. According to witnesses, one of them said "You're dead, nigger!" and started firing. Aswon "Keshawn" Watson was hit with 18 bullets, dead at the age of 23. Police hurriedly left the scene, but later claimed Watson had "made a motion" of going for a gun. No gun was found.

Community outrage led to days and weeks of protests and demonstrations. Nine months later, a grand jury convened but refused to indict the police.

WILLIAM "SMOKE" WHITFIELD—KILLED ON CHRISTMAS DAY

Brooklyn, New York. On Christmas Day, 1997, William "Smoke" Whitfield was on his way to call his mother. The 22-year-old Black man was going to let her know that he had just proposed to Candy Williams and was going to bring her and her two children to Christmas dinner.

Saying they suspected Whitfield of involvement in reported gunfire in the area, police followed him into a grocery store. The officers then ordered everyone in the store to lie down. One of the officers, Michael

Duggan, claims that Whitfield rose from a crouched position with a "black object" in his hand. Officer Michael Davitt then killed William Whitfield with a single shot to the chest. No gun was found on or near William Whitfield. The only possible object in his possession was a set of keys.

Officer Davitt was involved in more shootings than any other member of the NYPD, including a 1994 shooting in which he opened fire on a "robbery suspect" holding a "dark object" in his hand, which turned out to be a wristwatch.

Hundreds of people rallied and demonstrated in the aftermath of William Whitfield's killing. Willie Mae Whitfield, William's grandmother, said, "I just want justice for my grandson, and not only him, there's plenty more grandsons out here..."

CARL WILLIAMS—POLICE GIVE HIM MEDAL, THEN KILL HIM

Miami. Carl Williams lived in Liberty City, a Miami ghetto, and worked at a warehouse. The 29-year-old Williams received a Silver Medal of Valor from the Miami-Dade police after he subdued an armed man who was struggling with a cop. The Miami-Dade police chief sent him a letter of commendation.

On July 17, 1998, Carl Williams was fatally shot by a Miami cop. According to family members, Williams went outside his house to shoot possums from a tree in the back yard. At the same time, Miami-Dade police detective Mark Bullard was nearby with his gun drawn, reportedly on the trail of a robbery suspect. Pam Mitchell, Williams' fiancée, said, "He had his hands up yelling 'I live here! I live here!'"

Then there was a barrage of gunfire—all from Bullard's 9mm semiautomatic. The medical examiner later counted seven wounds, two on the back of his shoulder.

Police said that Bullard acted in self-defense and the shooting was justified. A spokesperson said that Bullard had ordered Williams to drop his weapon. But eyewitnesses said that there was no order to drop the weapon. Bullard was placed on routine administrative leave.

ALABAMA

Name	Age	Nationality	Photo
Donald Nabors	—	*Black*	

August 3, 1998. Talladega:

Mr. Nabors was shot to death by a white police officer. Authorities refuse to identify the officer or divulge the circumstances surrounding the shooting. On Aug. 17, several hundred Black residents held a protest at city hall to demand justice. **Source:** Yahoo!/States News Service, 8/17/98

Calvin Moore	18	—	

February 21, 1996. Kilby Correctional Facility:

Mr. Moore was serving a two-year sentence for a burglary conviction. He weighed about 160 pounds on Jan. 26, 1996. When he died less than a month later, he weighed 110 pounds. He had lost 56 pounds in less than a month and suffered symptoms of severe mental illness as well as dehydration and starvation after entering the prison. Despite the fact that Calvin was often unable to walk or talk and spent days lying on the concrete floor of his cell in a pool of his own urine, nurses repeatedly failed to provide basic medical care. Not even his vital signs were recorded for the last nine days of his life. An official state autopsy, which concluded that he died of "natural causes," was called a "whitewash" by an internationally renowned expert on forensic medicine. The expert said Calvin's death was "a homicide resulting from criminal negligence." The prison's health-care provider, Correctional Medical Services (CMS), said, "It is clear the health care staff provided appropriate and compassionate care." Calvin Moore's father sued CMS and seven medical professionals, including nurses and doctors, charging malpractice and negligence. A lawyer for the family said, "Calvin was the sickest of the sick and they let him die." A confidential settlement of the civil suit was reached in August, 1998. "I'm angry about it," said Gale Moore, Calvin's mother. "I believe somebody killed him. They can't make me believe he died of natural causes." A lawsuit against Correctional Services Inc., the private health care provider, was confidentially settled with Calvin's father. **Source:** St. Louis Post-Dispatch, 9/27/98

King Casby	37	—	
Bobby Dancy	47	—	
Lorenzo Ingram, Sr.	56	—	
Walter Williams, Jr.	63	—	

December 25, 1995. St. Clair Correctional Facility:

Mr. Ingram, Mr. Dancy, Mr. Williams and Mr. Casby were incarcerated in St. Clair Correctional Facility. They all died after receiving improper dialysis treatment for kidney disease. According to a state health department report, a prison nurse used the wrong chemicals during their treatments, making their blood dangerously acidic. Lawsuits filed by the families of the four men said that they became seriously ill, vomiting and gasping for breath after their treatments on Christmas Eve and Christmas Day, 1995. Mr. Ingram, who was serving a sentence for unlawful distribution of controlled substances, died on Christmas Day. Mr. Williams, who was serving a sentence for a manslaughter conviction, died on Sept. 30, 1996. Mr. Dancy, who suffered from schizophrenia and was serving a sentence for a murder conviction, died on Oct. 30, 1996. Mr. Casby, who was serving a sentence for marijuana possession and distribution of controlled substances, died on Oct. 31, 1996. The Alabama State epidemiologist said that "the people running the system didn't know what they were doing." The prison's health-care provider, Correctional Medical Services (CMS), said, "We believe that Southeast Dialysis (a sub-contractor) employees may have used an incorrect dialysis solution." But in the case of Mr. Casby and Mr. Dancy, CMS claimed that their deaths were "unrelated" to the improper dialysis treatment. The company's contract was terminated. **Source:** St. Louis Post-Dispatch, 9/27/98

ALASKA

Name	Age	Nationality	Photo
Terrance L. Cloyd	20	—	

May 18, 1993. Anchorage:

Mr. Cloyd allegedly "snapped" and shot his mother and sister to death. Police claim they found him covered in blood walking down the middle of the road holding a gun to his 10-year-old brother's head, saying that his brother was an "alien." Police snipers shot him to death. His brother was not hurt. Mr. Cloyd was described as a "celebrated athlete" and a student at Highline Community College. **Source:** Tacoma News-Tribune, 5/20/93

ARIZONA

Name	Age	Nationality	Photo
Antonio Rentería	23	*Mexican*	

September 9, 1998. US-Mexico Border (near San Luis):

An unidentified border patrol agent fired his semi-automatic weapon three times, striking Antonio in the stomach and chest. He died in the Yuma Regional Hospital soon afterwards. The border patrol agent justified the shooting by claiming that Antonio threatened him with a rock and was preparing to assault him. Mexico's consul general in San Diego said, "The migrants just want to make it through. They want to get past the border patrol. They're not looking to fight with border patrol agents." **Source:** SLP Form; The San Diego Union-Tribune, 9/11/98 & 9/29/98

Glenn Alton Haring	42	—	

September 7, 1998. Pima County:

Mr. Haring was shot and killed by Sheriff's Deputies Stephen Carpenter and Eric Maldonado. They shot Mr. Haring twice in the head and five times in the upper body and back from two-and-a-half feet away after an alleged struggle. Cops claim Mr. Haring fired a round at them first. The cops had been chasing Mr. Haring, first in a car, allegedly for suspected drunk driving and later on foot. The victim's fiancee said he may have been trying to avoid arrest because of an outstanding warrant. Friends described Mr. Haring as a hard-working man who was afraid he would never live down his criminal record (He had spent two-and-a-half years in prison for forgery). He leaves behind his mother, a brother, his fiancee and her three daughters for whom he cared. His fiancee said, "He loved me and he loved my kids and it turned his entire life around.... He said he had finally found someone he could love and trust and spend the rest of his life with. I guess he did — I just wanted it to be for a few more years." The deputies were cleared of any wrongdoing by county prosecutors. **Source:** Arizona Daily Star, 9/20/98

Abdiel Burgüeno, Jr.	20	—	

August 2, 1998. Scottsdale:

Mr. Burgüeno was shot in the chest and killed by Scottsdale Police Sgt. Scott Popp outside his apartment complex. Police said Sgt. Popp fired in self-defense. They claimed that Mr. Burgüeno charged at Sgt. Popp with a machete after using it to damage cars and threaten bystanders and that he ignored orders by Sgt. Popp to surrender. Mr. Burgüeno's family feels that Sgt. Popp was too quick to pull the trigger and said they would investigate the matter. Mr. Burgüeno aspired to be a photographer. He leaves behind a two-year-old son. **Source:** Arizona Republic, 8/5/98

Donald Lininger	—	*white*	

July 26, 1998. Phoenix:

Mr. Lininger stopped breathing and died while in police custody. He was arrested by police responding to a 911 call reporting that he was threatening customers with an axe in the parking lot of a bar. A police spokesperson told the press that Mr. Lininger put down the axe when officers arrived, but then resisted being handcuffed. During an alleged struggle, cops took him down on the hot pavement, burning his chest. Officers then put him in the back of the squad car and he supposedly began to fight again when they tried to apply ankle restraints. He then stopped breathing. Cops denied striking or choking him and claimed they didn't know the cause of death. Authorities alleged that Mr. Lininger had a long criminal record and a history of drug abuse and epileptic seizures. **Source:** Arizona Republic, 7/28/98

William Sershon   31   —

July 4, 1998. Glendale:
Mr. Sershon was shot and killed by an FBI fugitive task force, which had William under surveillance at a trailer park in the 8500 block of North 71st Avenue. When he got into his car to drive away, they tried to box him in. According to the FBI account, William tried to escape and crashed into a nearby trailer home. The FBI claims he refused orders to get out of his car and pulled a gun. He was allegedly a murder suspect who had a "long rap sheet." **Source:** The Arizona Republic, 7/5/98

Harold Shover, Jr.   20   —

July 3, 1998. Phoenix:
Mr. Shover was shot and killed by Police Officer Jim Neverman, who fired twice from within two feet. Cops claim that Harold was advancing on them, holding a nearly full Jack Daniel's whiskey bottle over his head in a "threatening manner." A police spokesperson said Harold could have overpowered and injured the cop by hitting him on the head with the bottle and that he grabbed his gun. Eyewitnesses, however, said that the shooting was not justified, that Harold was so drunk that deadly force was not needed. Police had come to the scene after a woman called to report that Harold and a friend were acting "drunk and rowdy" in the Harbor Ridge apartment complex in the 16800 block of North 29th Street. The same woman condemned the shooting, saying, "There was no need for this. The boy was so drunk, I could have stopped him." Harold's sister said, "How can you compare a bottle and a gun?" When cops arrived, Harold, who had just been released from prison, where he had spent six months for violating probation, tried to climb into a man's pickup truck to flee, perhaps realizing that the whiskey would violate his probation. The man ordered him out of the pickup truck, but also condemned the police shooting: "He swung at me twice (with the bottle) and missed both times and I never moved." He reported that whiskey sloshed out of the bottle as Harold swung it and that "That other officer could have knocked the bottle out of his hand." He also reported that Harold told the cops, "You're going to shoot me? Fine. I don't care. Shoot me." Harold's father reported that his son said he was "going to have my little fling (drinking bout)...and then, that's it. It's time for me to get my life together." Harold's father said, "He's gone. We'll never have our son back.... If I had (the officer's) phone number, I'd be his wake-up call every morning. I'd never let him forget what he's done." He also said he was thinking of suing the police department, but, "Probably nothing will ever come of it, because nothing ever does." Harold had had trouble with "violent outbursts" ever since he was struck by a hit-and-run driver at the age of 12 and spent six months in a coma. **Source:** The Arizona Republic, 7/5/98

Janet Zuelzke   85   —

May 19, 1998. Phoenix:
Ms. Zuelzke was killed when a cop car driven by Phoenix Police Officer Jim Jarvis crashed into her car in the 2600 block of North 44th St. Janet was a passenger in the car; the driver was critically injured. Officer Jarvis, who was responding to a call at the time, was not injured. **Source:** The Arizona Republic, 5/20/98

Unidentified Man   —   —

April 28, 1998. Phoenix:
The man was shot and killed by Phoenix police after they stopped the car he and another man were driving for suspicion of bank robbery. Authorities claim that after being ordered to lie on the ground to be handcuffed, he propped himself up, produced a gun and started firing, grazing Officer Steve Rice in the ear. **Source:** Arizona Republic, 4/29/98

Ernie Salas   31   —

April 22, 1998. central Phoenix:
Mr. Salas was arrested and handcuffed after allegedly causing a disturbance at his housing project. During the arrest, he was pepper-sprayed by the cops. He died at Phoenix Memorial Hospital after apparently going into cardiac arrest while in police custody. Police claim Mr. Salas was a known drug user, that marijuana and cocaine were found in his system and that a drug overdose was responsible for the heart attack that caused his death. **Source:** Arizona Republic, 4/23/98

Michael Federici	20	—	👁
Tasia Patton	17	—	👁

April 16, 1998. Mesa:

Michael Federici and Tasia Patton were shot and killed when five officers fired 36 shots at the stolen Toyota in which they were riding. Cops claim the stolen car rammed police vehicles, knocked one officer to the ground and was headed toward another officer when they opened fire. One of the cops involved in the shooting, Detective Andy Fuhrman, had been recommended for dismissal a year before after officials found that he had assaulted a former girlfriend, whom he threw against a wall, pushed, choked and threatened to kill with his police-issued gun. The four other cops were Amanda Keene, Mike Beaton, Jalyn Bellows and Rudy Monarrez. All five were placed on paid administrative leave (paid vacation). Tasia Patton's mother filed a $20 million lawsuit against the city and the five cops, claiming negligence and civil rights violations. **Source:** The Arizona Republic, 5/8/98

J. R. Kvernes	21	—

April 13, 1998. Phoenix:

Mr. Kvernes was allegedly high on drugs and very agitated. His mother's 911 call was answered by firefighters, one of whom was supposedly punched twice in the face by Kvernes. Other firefighters jumped on him to "wrestle him under control." He stopped breathing and died a short time later. The medical examiner ruled that his death was "natural," caused by a medical condition. **Source:** The Arizona Republic, 6/22/98

Michael Johnson	50	*Native American (Apache)*

April 7, 1998. San Carlos Reservation:

San Carlos Tribal Council ordered police to move in against members of Call To Action. Apache member Michael Johnson was beaten to death by police. Arrests of Call To Action members followed. There was a news whiteout.

Unidentified Man	—

March 7, 1998. Phoenix:

The man was shot and killed by police while sitting in the driver's seat of a recreational vehicle in the parking lot of a resort hotel. Police Officers Matthew Shay, Andrew Carlson, Stacey Parks and Erin Murphy arrived in response to a call from a hotel security guard about a suspicious vehicle in the parking lot. Cops claim that when they approached the vehicle, the victim sat up in the driver's seat, started the engine, and pointed an automatic weapon at them. The cops opened fire on the RV. A woman in the RV with the victim was arrested for felony murder on the grounds that she committed an illegal act that caused the man's death. **Source:** Arizona Republic, 3/9/98

Nicholaus Contreraz	16	—

March 2, 1998. Oracle (Arizona Boys Ranch):

Nicholaus, a youth from Sacramento, died at the Arizona Boys Ranch, a detention facility in Oracle, AZ where California youthful offenders were sent. He had been sentenced to that facility by Sacramento authorities. Nicholaus was suffering from a massive chest infection that forced the partial collapse of one lung. Witnesses said that staff members accused Nicholaus of faking illness and forced him to do strenuous exercise as punishment. At least two staff members were fired and four were suspended. The Oracle campus where Contreras died has been shut down. **Source:** The Sacramento Bee, 6/3/98

Richard Snow	57	—

February 12, 1998. north Phoenix:

Mr. Snow was shot twice and killed by Officer Mike Daily. Cops claim he had a knife, refused repeated orders to put it down and lunged at them. Cops were answering a domestic violence call around 10:30 a.m. at an apartment complex in the 11800 block of North 19th Ave. when the incident occurred. The media, citing the cops' version of events, reported that Richard "apparently provoked police into shooting him." Officer Daily was "placed on administrative leave with pay [paid vacation], a routine move pending an internal investigation of the shooting." **Source:** The Arizona Republic, 2/14/948

| **Troy Edward Davis** | 27 | — |

February 12, 1998. Phoenix:
Mr. Davis was shot and killed by a Phoenix police SWAT team. He was the subject of a weeklong manhunt after allegedly shooting at an officer while being chased. Mr. Davis was hiding in a motel when he called for a taxi under an assumed name. When he got into the taxi, police surrounded it and ordered him to surrender. Cops claim he raised his weapon; Officers Vic Roman and Mike Perry fired into the taxi. Mr. Davis was killed. The taxi driver was wounded when chips of glass struck him in the face. **Source:** Arizona Republic, 2/13/98

| **Robert Clermont** | 36 | — |

January 13, 1998. Tucson:
Mr. Clermont went to a store and allegedly told the clerk to call 911 because he wanted a shootout with police. According to police, they attempted to talk him to try to calm him down. But when he put a gun to his head, cops shot him in the chest. Clermont then supposedly shot himself in the head. He died from bullet wounds. **Source:** Associated Press, 4/25/98

| **Unidentified Man** | — | *Latino* |

January 9, 1998. Casa Grande:
The victim was shot and killed by police in the parking lot of a convenience store. Authorities claim he was brandishing a steel prying bar after attempting to break into a car and that he was shot only after approaching an officer in a threatening manner. **Source:** Arizona Republic, 1/10/98

| **Unidentified** | — | — |

1998. Tempe:
A "stolen-car suspect" was shot and killed by a Phoenix cop who had chased him into Tempe. **Source:** The Arizona Republic, 7/21/98

| **José Benito Sáenz** | 18 | — |

November 13, 1997. Glendale:
Mr. Sáenz was shot in the chest and killed by off-duty Police Officer Lee Busch, who fired three shots at the van Mr. Sáenz was in. The police report said that Officer Busch, who was moonlighting as a security guard, ordered the four men in the van to get out, claiming the van looked suspicious. Cops claim that instead of complying, the driver hit the accelerator and tried to plow into Officer Busch, who jumped out of the way and fired at the van. Authorities alleged that two civilians, a husband and wife, backed their account. Prosecutors said they might charge Mr. Sáenz' companions with murder based on a state law that allows people to be so charged when a death occurs during a felony. The victim, known as "Kilo" to his friends, was a former student at North Canyone High School. He is survived by his father and brother, who both felt that Officer Busch was too quick to open fire. **Source:** Arizona Republic, 12/3/97

| **Christopher Foote** | — | — |
| **Spring Wright** | | — |

August 31, 1997. Maricopa County:
Chris Foote and Spring Wright were shot and killed by bounty hunters who raided their house. The bounty hunters had an expired arrest warrant for an alleged fugitive, but they raided the wrong house in any case. Before he and his girlfriend were killed, Chris Foote managed to wound two of the bounty hunters, who broke into the house unannounced, clad in black military uniforms and wielding guns. The bounty hunters later told police that they had botched the raid. All three of the bounty hunters were charged with murder. **Source:** Arizona Republic, 10/1/97

Jason Erin Marsh   26   *white*

February 25, 1997. Glendale:

Mr. Marsh was chased by police on foot for violating his probation. Cops cornered him after 2 1/2 hours and their dog attacked him. Police claim he refused to lie down and reached in his back pocket for a gun. But the cops' statements contain inconsistencies and often contradict each other. Three police officers shot him twelve times and killed him. Nine of the shots were to the victim's back and all but one had a downward trajectory, indicating that the cops were standing over him when they fired. Mr. Marsh had powder burns, indicating that he was shot at close range. He died in handcuffs (it is not clear whether he was handcuffed before or after he was shot). Cops offered him no medical attention and justified this by saying, "He looked like he wasn't going to make it anyways." Police also broke his nose as they were handcuffing him. Mr. Marsh leaves behind a four-year-old son and an infant daughter. The victim's mother said, "He made bad choices in his life, but he was never violent." **Source:** SLP form

Bruno Beltrán   —   *Mexican*

December 20, 1996. Tohono O'odham Indian Reservation:

Bruno Beltrán died after the immigrants' car in which he was traveling was struck from behind numerous times by border authorities, causing it to tumble off the road. Customs agents initiated the high-speed chase of the car with four suspected "illegal" occupants. Border Patrol and Reservation Police were called in to join the pursuit. No drugs were found in the car, but a bag of candy smuggled in to sell in Arizona was confiscated as contraband.

Julio Valerio   16   *Chicano*

November 14, 1996. Phoenix:

Five police officers confronted Julio after his parents called the cops saying he'd left home very upset and had taken a knife. Within one minute of cornering Julio, they shot him 21 times, killing him. His parents are immigrants from southern Mexico. Julio was called a gang member. The police, who claim that Julio raised a kitchen knife and lunged at them, were not charged.

Scott Norberg   —   —

summmer, 1996. Maricopa County Jail:

Scott Norberg suffocated to death due to "positional asphyxia," allegedly during a fight with detention officers. His family filed a $20 million wrongful-death suit against the county, which was still pending as of June, 1998. **Source:** The Arizona Republic, 6/22/98

Houston Dotson   47   —

December 1995. Phoenix:

Mr. Dotson was killed by positional asphyxia when police and firefighters strapped him facedown between two hard plastic boards and bound his hands and legs with handcuffs and gauze. A paranoid schizophrenic, Houston "buzzed" from alcohol and his anti-psychotic medication. He had punched out a window, badly cutting his right hand. Because he was heavily bleeding, a neighbor called 911. When more than half a dozen cops and paramedics crowded into the small living room of the apartment, Houston jumped up from a chair and said, "I've got to get out of here." He allegedly threw several punches at a cop, who knocked him to the ground, at which point several cops or firefighters jumped on him and restrained him. By the time the ambulance arrived, he had stopped struggling and was moaning. He stopped breathing during the two-minute ride to the hospital and died several hours later. Houston's brother, who believes the cops and firefighters came looking for a fight, said, "His biggest crime that night was his contempt of authorities and it turned out to be a capital offense." Houston's death was ruled natural, caused by a medical condition. His family filed a lawsuit, charging the police and fire department with negligence. His brother said it was ludicrous that Houston, whose right hand was badly cut and whose left arm was partially paralyzed, could pose any real threat to fire or police personnel. **Source:** The Arizona Republic, 6/22/98

Rosalia Reyes   38   *Chicano*

July 22, 1995. Cochise County:

Border Patrol Agent Jorge Luis Mancha murdered Mrs. Reyes while off-duty. Agent Mancha was involved in the drug trade in Cochise County.

| **Rudy Buchanan, Jr.** | 22 | *Latino & African American* | 👁 |

January 29, 1995. Phoenix:

Twenty officers surrounded Rudy and shot him 89 times in the back, front, neck and through his heart and lungs. The cops allege that Rudy aimed a shotgun at them and their lives were in danger. Rudy Buchanan Sr. asked, "Whose life was really in danger? They had a helicopter with a beam spot on my kid at about 11:30 or so at night. Twenty officers surrounded him with semi-automatic guns."

| **John Magoch** | 61 | — |

November 1994. Glendale:

Mr. Magoch was shot in the head and killed by former corrections officer and FBI informant Timothy Ring during an armored-car robbery. Mr. Magoch was the driver of the car. Ring was convicted of first-degree murder and received a death sentence in 1997. **Source:** Tucson Citizen, 10/31/97

| **Eduardo José Posada** | 23 | *Chicano* |
| **Sergio Cruz Tapia** | 26 | *Chicano* |

August 4, 1994. Cochise County:

Border Patrol Agent Mark Martinez murdered Sergio Tapia and Eduardo Posada while off duty. Agent Martinez had been accused of using and selling drugs as a border patrolman. Civil suit pending.

| **Edward Mallet** | 25 | *African American* |

August 1994. Phoenix:

Edward was a double amputee with prosthetic legs who died after being pepper sprayed and placed in a choke hold by the police because he was "resisting arrest." In March, 1998, the jury in a civil suit brought by Edward's survivors returned a $45 million verdict against the city of Phoenix. **Source:** The Arizona Republic, 3/28/98; ?

| **Rubén Corona Ortiz** | 18 | *Mexican* |

July 20, 1992. southern Arizona:

Mr. Corona Ortiz was shot to death by Customs Agent Ramos during a confrontation.

| **Darío Miranda Valenzuela** | 23 | *Mexican* |

June 12, 1992. Nogales:

Darío was crossing the border in a remote canyon near Nogales when two border patrol agents (Michael Elmer and Thomas Watson) found him and two friends. The agents claim that they thought they were lookouts for drug smugglers. When Darío and his friends began to run back to the border, the agents chased them and Michael Elmer shot Darío at least a dozen times, hitting him twice in the back. Elmer checked the boy's pulse and told Watson, "I'm going to bury it. Do you have a problem with that?" Elmer then dragged the wounded young man 175 ft. and left him under a tree. His body was found 15 hours later. Noting Darío's clutched hands, the coroner said that he died in agony.

| **Unidentified Man** | 20 | — |

1990. Ajo:

The victim was shot and killed by Sheriff's Deputy Mark Penner, who was initially charged with second-degree murder. A judge threw out the murder charge during a preliminary hearing. The sheriff fired Deputy Penner for refusing to answer questions about the shooting. **Source:** Arizona Daily Star, 9/20/98

| **Unidentified** | teen | — |

June 16, 19??. Oracle (Arizona Boys Ranch):

A Mississippi youth drowned while trying to escape from the ranch employees. The Arizona Boys Ranch has become known for its systemic abuse of inmates and for its paramilitary boot camp style discipline. **Source:** Los Angeles Times, 6/14/98

ARKANSAS

Name	Age	Nationality	Photo
Othel June Striplin	26	—	

October 2, 1997. Fort Smith:

Cops claim Mr. Striplin was suicidal and had barricaded himself in the bathroom, then ran out of the bathroom and lunged at them with a BB pistol. Fort Smith police shot him and he died at the hospital. Four cops were placed on administrative leave during an Arkansas State Police investigation. **Source:** The Commerical Appeal (Memphis, TN), 10/4/97

Name	Age	Nationality	Photo
Marvin Glenn Johnson	28	—	

July 29, 1995. Pulanski County Jail:

Marvin Johnson, who had bussed tables and built cabinets for cash, was jailed for a misdemeanor charge of driving an acquaintance's car without permission. He died three days after entering jail when, despite his repeated pleas to three nurses and six guards that he was an insulin-dependent diabetic, he received no insulin for 30 hours. He coughed up blood, leading guards to alert Correctional Medical Services (CMS) staff that the inmate needed emergency care. CMS did nothing. A nurse said he was "faking" and Mr. Johnson died of diabetic ketoacidosis in their care. CMS claimed that the victim "would not cooperate with health care staff...[who] were unable to confirm immediately whether Mr. Johnson was diabetic." Mr. Johnson's girlfriend had called the jail to warn them of his condition and offered to bring his insulin but she was assured he would be well cared for. When insulin was administered, it was too little too late and Mr. Johnson died of ketoacidosis. The vice president of the St. Louis American Diabetes Association who examined the medical documents stated that, "It's clearly negligence. This is not even the appropriate minimum level of care." The victim's family settled a lawsuit against the county for $20,000 and against CMS for an undisclosed amount. **Source:** Independent, 7/1/98; St. Louis Post-Dispatch, 9/27/98

CENTRAL CALIFORNIA

Name	Age	Nationality	Photo
Unidentified man	—	—	

March 23, 1999. Fresno:

Officers of the Violent Crimes Suppression Unit, who had stopped to talk to two youth, claim that an unidentified man approached, swinging a large broken piece of glass at them. The two unidentified cops, armed with .40-caliber semi-automatic handguns, opened fire. Witnesses said they heard six or seven shots and saw one officer near the hood of the patrol car and the other next to the passenger door. Neighbors reported that the shots came in rapid succession, "It was like pow, pow, pow. There were so many bullets, I couldn't count them all." The man went down, lying on the sidewalk without moving or talking. He died after being taken by ambulance to the hospital. The officers involved were placed on paid administrative leave. **Source:** The Fresno Bee, 3/24/99 & 3/25/99

Name	Age	Nationality	Photo
Kevin Wayne McNeil	32	—	

March 22, 1999. Santa Barbara (near Los Carneros):

Kevin was pulled over on Highway 101 on suspicion of driving under the influence of alcohol. A California Highway Patrol officer fired several rounds, killing Kevin, when Kevin's vehicle allegedly accelerated in reverse. Police claim Kevin knocked down another officer who was not seriously injured. The names of the officers were not disclosed. The officer who killed Kevin was placed on paid administrative leave. **Source:** Associated Press, 3/23/99

Name	Age	Nationality	Photo
Jack Donald Souza	28	—	

March 21, 1999. Sacramento:

Jack was shot in the head and arm and killed after he allegedly fired shots at deputies who were trying to arrest him on a drug-trafficking warrant. **Source:** The Sacramento Bee, 3/22/99

Larry Tobin   53   —

March 12, 1999. Fresno:
According to the authorities, Larry's parents reported that he had an axe and was trying to force his way into their home. Four or five deputies went to Larry's trailer and claim that Larry came out of the trailer with a rifle held across his chest. They fired beanbags, supposedly without effect, then shot and killed Larry when he allegedly pointed a rifle at them. **Source:** The Fresno Bee, 3/13/99

Danny Dunn   37   —

February 19, 1999. Kern County Jail:
Danny was reportedly struggling with manic depression, substance abuse and being HIV positive. His father, Patrick, was the subject of the book, "Mean Justice," which accuses prosecutors of misconduct in Patrick's 1993 murder conviction. Danny suffered a seizure following a bicycle accident. He was later arrested for public intoxication and police claim he struggled with them. Cops pepper sprayed him and bound his hands and legs. Officials said, "Dunn stopped breathing in an instant without even showing labored breathing first." A nurse who examined Danny found a number of scrapes and bruises inflicted before he was arrested. Danny's sister said she wishes her brother had been taken to a hospital instead of jail. **Source:** The Bakersfield Californian, 2/20/99

Jennifer Strobel   teen   —

February 4, 1999. Camp Pendleton:
Jennifer was a teenage participant in the Explorer Ride-Along program for four years. Jennifer's father said while the guidelines call for a couple of ride-alongs per month, Jennifer was going out several times a week, often with the same officer. Mr. Strobel was angry that lax supervision in the program led his daughter to close relationships with two older, married deputies. Jennifer was shot and killed by one of the deputies, César Ramírez. Complaints against both deputies ended with termination of their employment. Deputy Ramírez later shot and killed himself. It is unclear whether Deputy Ramírez killed Jennifer before or after he was fired or whether he killed himself immediately after he killed her. **Source:** The Bakersfield Californian, 2/4/99

Alfredo Ramírez, Jr.   17   —

December 27, 1998. Bakersfield:
Alfredo was shot and killed by police while allegedly burglarizing a sporting goods store. Police claim that Alfredo pointed a shotgun in the direction of the officers and began running. Officers claim that they ordered him to stop and drop the weapon and that when he did not, they shot at him 15 times. The shotgun Alfredo allegedly had was not loaded. Alfredo's family members were shocked to hear what had happened because Alfredo had never been in such trouble before. They questioned the appropriateness of the shooting. **Source:** The Bakersfield Californian, 12/27/98

Michael Franklin   24   —

December 22, 1998. Button Willow:
Four California Highway Patrol officers shot and killed Michael after a three-hour car chase. Investigators allege that Michael rammed a patrol car with his vehicle, fired once at police and ignored orders to drop his gun. Four officers opened fire, hitting Michael eight times. The DA's office stated "the officers acted in accordance of the law and use of deadly force was justified." **Source:** The Bakersfield Californian, 1/4/99

Robert Forrest Murray   51   —

December 7, 1998. Delano:
Robert, a developmentally disabled man, was walking in a cemetery around 1 p.m. with a toy gun. He was well-known to the cemetery staff, who called police out of concern for Robert's safety when he was seen walking slowly in a roadway, scared and confused. When police arrived, they were told Robert was not holding a real gun and that he was mentally disabled. Shortly thereafter, Officer Lewis arrived and got out of his car, pointing his shotgun at Robert. "Without warning Officer Lewis fired one shotgun blast, killing Mr. Murray on the spot. Mr. Murray made no gestures with his hands or arms whatsoever prior to the shotgun blast," states a lawsuit filed on behalf of Robert's family. Witnesses dispute police claims that Robert raised his arm and pointed the gun at police. The cemetery staff said Robert was not presenting a danger to others. **Source:** The Bakersfield Californian, 1/4/99

Michael Van Straaten   32   *Canadian*

December 1998. Corcoran State Prison:

Hoping for better treatment, Michael, with the help of prison rights advocates, parents and friends, had tried for two years to get transferred to a prison medical facility. The Canadian Embassy offered to act as a conduit. After turning down his request for a transfer, guards found Michael hanging in his cell. Instead of cutting him down, they left him there for 18 minutes while they videotaped the scene through metal bars. When a lieutenant and a medical technician arrived, officers spent several more minutes reviewing a prison file that revealed Michael's struggles with epilepsy and HIV. When the officers finally did enter the cell and cut the noose, Michael's body was still warm. Michael was pronounced dead nearly 20 minutes after his body was discovered. No alarms were sounded when Michael was found because the unwritten rule at Corcoran prohibits this on the late-night first watch, due to an officer twisting his ankle responding to such an alarm years ago. **Source:** Los Angeles Times, 12/19/98

Deandre Thomas   —   —

November 11, 1998. Sacramento:

Mr. Thomas was shot and killed by police when he allegedly attacked an officer with a crowbar. **Source:** The Sacramento Bee, 12/19/98

Darryl Howell   45   —

October 7, 1998. Taft:

Darryl, a gun shop owner and father of two, was a law-abiding citizen, who "went by the book" in his gun transactions, according to his family and friends. The U.S. Bureau of Alcohol, Tobacco and Firearms claims Darryl illegally sold two guns without proper paperwork. Taft Police claim that when they tried to arrest Darryl, he shot himself in the head. Then, while Darryl was still standing, Sgt. Ed Whiting, who was known not to get along with Darryl, shot him three times in the side. Police claim Darryl committed suicide, but his family said he would never do that. ""If he [Darryl] did put it (the gun) in his mouth, he had help putting it in there," said his aunt. The family is seeking an independent investigation of Darryl's death. **Source:** The Bakersfield Californian, 10/19/98 & 10/14/98

John Peter Klink   32   —

September 23, 1998. Old Modesto:

John was shot once in the chest and killed by Newman police officers. Cops claim that John was rushing toward them with a shovel in his hand when they shot and killed him. Sheriff's Deputies had been chasing him in his truck. He got out of the truck and continued to run on foot, going to a nearby farmhouse. John got in a fight with the resident of the house, who called 911 for help. As John was leaving the house, shovel in hand, the police saw him and shot him. John was pronounced dead before he could be airlifted to a hospital. The officers involved in this shooting were placed on paid leave, pending further investigation of the shooting. **Source:** Modesto (Calif.) Bee, 9/24/98

Robert Lee Tavalaro   41   —

September 5, 1998. Yolo County Jail:

Robert Tavalaro died in custody at the Yolo County Jail from an enlarged heart, a deputy coroner said. Close friends and relatives were shocked. Several of them, including Robert's pastor have accused officers at the Monroe Detention Center with failing to treat his illness promptly after he requested medical aid. Robert complained of leg pains and multiple hernias two days before he died and had filled out a request to see a physician the following day. Inmates reported that requests by Robert to see a doctor were ignored by jail personnel. Robert, who had been accused by a former friend of trying to kiss her nine-year-old daughter, had been in jail for just over two weeks. **Source:** The Sacramento Bee, 9/8/98 & 9/9/98

Unidentified Man   22   —

July 26, 1998. Ivanhoe (Tulare County):

Sheriff's deputies answered a domestic disturbance call. When they arrived, the man would not come out so the deputies forced their way in. When the man allegedly opened fire on them, they shot and killed him. **Source:** The Fresno Bee, 7/27/98

Israel García   —   *Latino*

July 4, 1998. Fresno:
When authorities received a 911 call that García was threatening his wife, they responded with 12 officers and a helicopter. Claiming that García had his wife on the ground with a gun pointed at her head, they shot and killed him instantly. García, a supervisor at the Lyon's Magnus food processing plant, was the father of three young children. **Source:** The Fresno Bee, 7/5/98

Dwayne Eli Sánchez   26   *Mexican American*

June 13, 1998. Santa Maria:
Mr. Sánchez was shot and killed by two unidentified Santa Maria police officers after his car crashed during a chase. The cops fired up to 18 shots, claiming that the victim put his vehicle into reverse and tried to run them down as they approached. Police had pursued Mr. Sánchez because his car reportedly matched the description of a vehicle whose occupant had "waved a gun in a threatening manner" in an earlier incident. Police supposedly recovered a gun and some methamphetamine from the victim's car. Cops claimed the shooting was self-defense. A lawyer for the victim's family called the shooting "a conscious disregard for human life, community safety and civil rights." A shrine was put up by people in the community at the site where Mr. Sánchez was killed. **Source:** Santa Maria Times, 6/16/98

Tom Neville   36   —

May 9, 1998. Fresno:
Tom Neville, a former 49ers linebacker, escaped from a psychiatric facility and hid in a broom closet in a nearby apartment complex. Cops claim they fired nine beanbag bullets but were unable to subdue him, so they shot him 12 times and killed him. Officials said they had "no choice but to shoot him." Tom lived with his wife and 20-month-old son in Fairbanks, Alaska. His former Fresno State football coach called him a "gentle giant. He was a very quiet, good football player. His chief [assets were] size and intelligence. He was a wonderful kid." Tom went on to play for the Green Bay Packers and S.F. 49ers from 1986-1992. Cops took him to the psychiatric hospital because he allegedly had a hunting rifle and was acting "bizarre" and "out of control." After Tom was killed, his step-sister said, "It's a complete shock to everybody. This is not at all like how he would normally behave. He was a completely rational and calm person. I have no idea what the events were that led up to this." **Source:** The Sacramento Bee, 5/10/98

Octavio Orozco   23   —

May 7, 1998. Fresno (Pleasant Valley State Prison):
Octavio was shot in the head and killed by a prison guard, Officer Brumana, as Octavio and some other inmates were allegedly fighting in the dining hall. Supervisor Patricia Newton defied the prison's code of silence and went straight to the warden with her criticism, stating that the officer had made a grave mistake by using deadly force to break up a routine fight. After voicing her criticism, she was ostracized and harassed, with several commanding officers trying to silence her. A departmental review board later determined that the shooting was unjustified. Supervisor Newton said, "Blood and brain matter were all over the floor, splashed up on the walls. I don't care if he was an inmate. He was still a human being and he didn't deserve to be killed. Not for fighting." **Source:** Los Angeles Times, 12/28/98

Lyle Bradley Federman   43   —

April 21, 1998. Kern County (Sand Canyon):
Lyle was a computer consultant and father of three with no criminal record. Police responded to a complaint that he was igniting bushes and tires around his house. Cops claim Lyle refused to cooperate with them and went into his house carrying a knife in a sheath on his belt, so they called in the sheriff's SWAT team. After a five-hour standoff, the SWAT team went to a window and "doused" Lyle with pepper spray. The victim allegedly responded by firing at the sheriffs. The SWAT officers charged the house, firing wooden bullets. Claiming Lyle lunged at them with a knife, three SWAT members fired 15 9mm bullets and killed him. No one else was in the house and the names of the cops involved were not released. **Source:** The Bakersfield Californian, 4/22/98

Mark Anthony Pérez   —   —

February 22, 1998. Salinas Valley State Prison:
While incarcerated at Salinas Valley State Prison, Mark became involved in a fistfight. He was not armed and did not pose a life-threatening danger to himself or anyone else. After Officer Richardson fired a non-lethal round that did not end the fistfight, prison guard Carlos Jacobo shot Mark in the right thigh. The gunshot penetrated Mark's thigh and caused severe internal injuries. He was taken to the hospital, where he died the following day. Mark's family filed a lawsuit. **Source:** James Chanin, Attorney at Law

Alfonso Hernández   16   *Latino*

January 9, 1998. Visalia:
Alfonso, who at age eight witnessed his father's suicide, was a respectful, polite, smiling, hard-working youth. He felt guilty and frustrated that, due to his young age, he was unable to help support his family since his father's death. A SWAT team stormed Alfonso's apartment to serve an arrest warrant for being part of a gang that shot five people. Alfonso reportedly defended himself. Police admit they knew there were children in Alfonso's apartment, but they fired 65 bullets anyway. Thirty-nine bullets hit Alfonso. Five or six hit a visiting friend, who was reportedly trying to get Alfonso to surrender. The remaining bullets entered neighboring occupied apartments in the building, which was filled with families with young children. Police claim Alfonso shot six bullets at them and killed Officer Rapozo during the raid on his apartment. Magdalena, Alfonso's mother said, "the police knew for at least two hours where my son was that day. If they had come to me and asked for my help, I know I could've talked my son into giving himself up without violence." Believing her son was beaten, Magdalena ordered photographs of her son's face. "He had a big bruise on the bridge of his nose and another on his upper right cheek. His face was disfigured." Peter Kraska, professor of Police Science at Eastern Kentucky University said, "These [SWAT] are police paramilitary units. The no-knock entries are full-out military assaults. This kind of policing is unprecedented in our history." Alfonso's seventh-grade teacher told mourners at his funeral, "I noticed the deep sadness in his eyes that did not seem to match his perennial smile. I was left as a teacher with a child whose profound guilt and anguish were too big for his heart to carry." **Source:** The Fresno Bee, 1/17/98, 1/20/98, & 4/10/98

Jaime García Durán   48   —

January 8, 1998. Tulare County Correctional Center:
Jaime, a prison inmate, had complained of chest pains just after midnight. After being diagnosed and treated at the hospital emergency room for gastroenteritis, he was returned to the correctional center. A few hours later, he was found having a seizure and taken to the hospital in Dinuba, where he died. He was the second inmate to die in the Tulare County prison system in one week. **Source:** The Fresno Bee, 1/10/98; The San Diego Union-Tribune, 1/11/98

Unidentified Man   —   —

January 3, 1998. West Sacramento:
Police from several departments chased an unidentified man who they claim may have been on his way to kill his father. When the man's car crashed, he fled on foot. Police surrounded him both on the ground and in the air. They claim the man raised a gun at officers, at which point police shot and killed him with one round from a shotgun. **Source:** The Sacramento Bee (Metro final), 1/4/98

Juan Cortez   29   —

December 23, 1997. Labor Camp northeast of Visalia:
A deputy sheriff shot and killed Juan at a convenience store in a farm labor camp, claiming Juan approached him carrying two knives. **Source:** The Fresno Bee, 7/27/98

| **Jeffery L. Morgan** | 43 | — |

December 6, 1997. Courtland:

Jeffery grew up in Courtland, where he lived on his boat and walked his Rottweiler, Brutus. He was shot twice in the chest and once in the waist and killed by a Sacramento County sheriff's deputy who was responding to a domestic violence call made by Jeffery's girlfriend from a neighbor's phone. Deputies found Jeffery asleep when they arrived and started to handcuff him. They claim Jeffery attacked them. A cop sprayed him with pepper-spray and used his baton, then was supposedly knocked down a flight of stairs by Jeffrey Morgan. Cops claim the deputy opened fire as Jeffery advanced on him. **Source:** The Sacramento Bee, 12/7/97

| **Ernesto Barajas** | 22 | — |

October 11, 1997. Delano:

In the second fatal shooting in two months by Delano police, Ernesto was shot in the head and killed when he allegedly attempted to hit an officer with his car. Police claim Ernesto rammed at least five vehicles with a stolen pickup before he was confronted by the officer. **Source:** The Sacramento Bee, 10/14/97 & 11/14/97

| **Minerva Gonzales** | 36 | *Latina* |

September 3, 1997. Central Calif. Women's Facility:

Minerva died from medical neglect in prison. She was unable to eat or drink for nine days. After repeated attempts to get medical help, she was told "drink more juice" and that she wasn't sick enough to see a doctor because she wasn't bleeding and didn't have a fever.

| **Manuel García, Jr.** | 30 | *Latino* |

July 31, 1997. Selma (Fresno County):

According to Manuel's family's lawyer, Manuel was in the house, afraid and "threatening to shoot himself. He's not threatening to shoot anyone else." When police arrived, Manuel had barricaded himself in a closet. Cops sent in an attack dog. Manuel reportedly defended himself, stabbing the dog. Three cops fired 30 rounds; 20 of them struck Manuel and killed him. The Fresno County Sheriff's Department and the Selma Police determined that police procedures had been followed appropriately. Manuel's family filed a lawsuit for wrongful death, violation of civil rights and deprivation of liberty without due process of law. **Source:** The Fresno Bee, 5/13/98

| **Francesca Shields** | — | — |

July 21, 1997. Central Calif. Women's Facility:

Francesca was an HIV+ prisoner released too early from an outside hospital and sent back to the prison. She was taken from her cell in horrible pain, left in the infirmary with no pain medication and died.

| **Ramón Gallardo, Sr.** | 64 | — |

July 11, 1997. Dinuba:

Ramón, father of 13 children, was shot 13 to 15 times and killed by a Visalia police officer wielding a submachine gun. The victim was also shot once by another officer when police wearing camouflage uniforms, hoods and masks entered his home at 7 a.m. to serve a search warrant. The search warrant was based on an informant's claim to have sold to one of Ramon's sons a shotgun allegedly used in a murder. No gun was found, and the informant later recanted his statement. Ramón's wife and other relatives at the house were taken to police headquarters after the raid and unlawfully detained until they had given statements. The police said that Ramónhad a knife in his hand during the raid but an attorney for his family called the police liars and pointed out that no fingerprints were found on the knife. The largest award against law enforcement in the nation was given to Ramón's family after a civil trial in which officers were found guilty of numerous civil offenses. Ramón's son said, "My dad is not coming back, but we are going to find justice for somebody else." **Source:** The Fresno Bee, 3/3/99 & 3/13/99

Michael Shane Merriott   30   —

June 14, 1997. Visalia:

Police were seeking Michael for suspicion of petty theft and a parole violation after he was mistakenly released from a detention center. While in a walnut tree in an orchard near his mother's home, Michael was shot 15 times and killed by officers. They claim that Michael refused to surrender and was armed with a small handgun. But Michael's mother filed a lawsuit, naming Police Officer Jeff McIntosh and Sheriff's Deputy Greg Gruich as defendants. The attorney for Michael's mother said that forensic evidence showed that Michael was not attempting to shoot anyone, that he was unarmed and attempting to surrender when he was shot. Michael had no history of violence. **Source:** The Fresno Bee, 1/16/98

Brenda Otto   49   —

May 2, 1997. Central Calif. Women's Facility:

Brenda had a history of strokes and was sent outside the prison to a hospital for treatment. When she returned to prison, she was given three days off work and then told to return to her prison job. She died while walking in the prison yard.

Lisa Pérez   33   *Latina*

January 5, 1997. Central Calif. Women's Facility:

Lisa, a prisoner, was a member of the class action lawsuit Shumate v. Wilson, to challenge the lack of medical care in California women's prisons. She went to sick call for vomiting, pain and dizziness. Lisa was told she had the flu and should not come back throwing up on their floor. She died, apparently from a seizure disorder. **Source:** SLP Form

Sarah Rodarmel   20   —

October 27, 1996. Sacramento:

When police chased a car for suspicion of drunk driving, the car allegedly weaved in and out of traffic at speeds up to 90 mph until it struck the car in which Sarah was a passenger. Sarah was ejected out a rear window, over a bridge railing and onto the ground 65 feet below. She died as result. **Source:** The Sacramento Bee, 10/4/97

Susan Bouchard   44   —

August 30, 1996. Central Calif. Women's Facility:

Susan had a history of heart problems. After complaining of chest pain and trying to see a doctor for three days, she was seen by a prison staff member who gave her an incomplete exam and told her there was nothing to worry about. She died three hours later.

Juan Valdez   16   *Latino*

August 7, 1996. Lamont (Kern County):

Police claim Juan was a car theft suspect. Unarmed, he was shot and killed by Kern County Sheriff Deputy Anthony Chávez. The shooting was subsequently ruled unjustifiable. Juan allegedly crashed into Chávez' patrol car and was running away when he was shot. **Source:** Bakersfield Californian, 5/14/98

Unidentified Man   —   *Mexican*

November 27, 1995. Kerman:

Police report that they shot and killed one man and arrested four others in what cops claimed was a successful attempt to free a kidnapped woman and girl that the men were holding for ransom. **Source:** San Francisco Chronicle, 12/1/95

Suzannah Casas Cody   —   —

July 1995. Taft Highway:

Police claim that after sitting in her minivan for 30 minutes with a pistol, Suzannah got out and aimed it at them. Cops shot and killed her. A federal appeals court sided with the county in a civil rights lawsuit filed by Suzannah's children. The children's lawyer said they are "seriously considering" asking the U.S. Supreme Court to review the case. **Source:** The Bakersfield Californian, 3/1/99

Anna Jackson 27 —

December 2, 1994. Central Calif. Women's Facility:
Anna, a prisoner, went for medical help with extreme pain and bleeding and was told not to worry. She was turned away from the clinic daily when she requested pain medication. Diagnosed months later with cancer, she was admitted to the infirmary and died in great pain after six weeks.

Armando Alegría 17 *Latino*

November 19, 1994. Kern County:
Police claim Mr. Alegría was one of three robbery suspects attempting to flee police in a van. He was shot and killed by Kern County Sheriff's Deputy Lloyd Waters. Deputy Waters shot another person in 1994 (not fatally) and another in 1998, which was ruled unjustifiable. **Source:** The Bakersfield Californian, 5/14/98

Margarite Juárez — *Latina*

September 25, 1994. Central Calif. Women's Facility:
Margarite, a prisoner, went to sick call for chest pains and the staff would not examine her. She was told to take Motrin and passed out the next morning. Two officers administered CPR but were told to stop by a medical staff member even though Margarite had a pulse. She died soon after.

Donald Creasy 31 —

May 1994. Corcoran State Prison:
Mr. Creasy was shot and killed by a prison guard allegedly breaking up a fight. It was rumored that the fight was instigated by the guards. The case was put under investigation. **Source:** The Fresno Bee, 11/24/96

Preston Tate 26 *Black*

April 2, 1994. Corcoran State Prison:
Mr. Tate was shot and killed by a prison guard during a fight staged for the entertainment and betting of prison authorities. **Source:** The Fresno Bee, 11/24/96

Geraldo Jaurequí 34 *white*

December 7, 1993. Madera:
Mr. Jaurequí was killed after being beaten with batons, pepper-sprayed and hog-tied.

Henry Noriega, Jr. 23 —

September 10, 1993. Corcoran State Prison:
Mr. Noriega was shot and killed by a prison guard during a fight staged for the entertainment and betting of prison authorities. **Source:** The Fresno Bee, 11/24/96

Maurice Morrison 43 —

June 7, 1993. Fresno:
Mr. Morrison, who had a history of mental illness, was walking home when he was accosted by three officers. He was pepper-sprayed, beaten, wrestled to the ground and handcuffed. Morrison died. On May 28, 1998, a jury absolved the officers after 35 minutes of deliberations. **Source:** The Fresno Bee, 5/29/98

Michael Mullins 32 —

April 8, 1993. Corcoran State Prison:
Mr. Mullins was shot and killed by a prison guard during a fight staged for the entertainment and betting of prison authorities. **Source:** The Fresno Bee, 11/24/96

Candace Bennett — —

October 27, 1992. Calif. Institution for Women:
After seeking medical help for severe abdominal pain, Ms. Bennett was labeled a "disturbance" by the staff. She received no medical treatment and died the next day.

Fidelino Pascua — 26 —

1992. Marina (Monterey County):
When officers reportedly found Pascua behaving "strangely," they attacked him with pepper spray. Pascua ran into his house and barricaded himself in the bathroom. When he allegedly bolted out with a knife in his hand, he was shot and killed. **Source:** The Herald, 5/24/98

Michael Allen Massengale — *white*

November 27, 1990. Sacramento:
While walking on an overpass of Interstate 80 West, Sacramento police started talking to Michael on their loudspeaker. A police dog to jumped out of the patrol car, perhaps startled by the loudspeaker. The dog attacked Michael, who defended himself and pushed the dog over the side of the bridge. Michael fell to his death after cops either pushed or chased him over the bridge. Legal proceedings on his behalf were settled in his favor. **Source:** James Chanin, Attorney at Law

Andres Cortez Romero — 31 —

February 3, 1990. Corcoran State Prison:
Mr. Romero was shot and killed by a prison guard during a fight staged for the entertainment and betting of prison authorities. **Source:** The Fresno Bee, 11/24/96

William Martinez — 30 —

April 7, 1989. Corcoran State Prison:
Mr. Martinez was shot and killed by a prison guard during a fight staged for the entertainment and betting of prison authorities. **Source:** The Fresno Bee, 11/24/96

Angry Bear Nieto — 27 *Native American (Apache)* ◉

June 2, 1988. New Folsom Prison:
Angry Bear was shot in the back and killed by prison guard Moises Guerrero on the guard's birthday. This occurred a few weeks after Angry Bear had reported Officer Guerrero for repeatedly passing gas to disrupt the Native American prisoners while they were conducting their ceremony of honoring "Grandfather." A lieutenant reprimanded Officer Guerrero in front of everyone, which angered him. Six months after Officer Guerrero killed Angry Bear, he was promoted to sergeant. The guard first claimed that he issued a warning shot before killing Angry Bear, but once that was proven false, he changed his story to say it was a verbal warning. Inmate eyewitnesses say neither happened, but prison officials refused to question them before closing the case and determining that the shooting was justified. **Source:** Tony Nieto, Angry Bear's father

LOS ANGELES

Name	Age	Nationality	Photo
Mario Paz	64	*Latino*	

August 9, 1999. Compton:

Mr. Paz was shot twice in the back and killed in his Compton home by members of the El Monte police SWAT team. The cops, apparently acting out of their jurisdiction, stormed into the victim's home around 11 p.m. by shooting off the locks on the doors. They were reportedly executing a search warrant, looking for drugs and money. But the person named on the search warrant did not live at the house and had moved out of the neighborhood in the 1980's. Cops claim they found four guns in the house but admit that none were in Mr. Paz's reach. Cops justified the use of the SWAT team and the aggressive tactics by saying that recent searches in other neighborhoods that turned up "approximately 400 pounds of marijuana, three high-powered assault rifles, and more than $75,000 in cash." Describing the raid, a lawyer for the victim's family said, "A homicide was committed in this house. Armed gunmen gained entry by shooting shots through windows and doors." A private investigator working for the victim's family said, "Why have they [the police] adopted a policy of shoot first and ask questions later?" Family members reported that they thought they were being robbed when the SWAT team burst into their home. **Source:** The New York Times, 8/28/99; LA Oct. 22 Coalition

Daniel García Zarraga	47	—	

June 25, 1999. Van Nuys:

Mr. Zarraga was shot to death by police, who claim he lunged at them with a shiny object. They supposedly thought the "shiny object" was a knife, but it turned out to be a pen. Mr. Zarraga leaves behind a wife and three children. This was the third in a series of similar fatal shootings by the LAPD in four months. **Source:** Los Angeles Times, 6/26/99

Michael Scott Coolidge	35	—	

June 20, 1999. Westminster:

An unnamed officer with 11 years of service shot and killed Mr. Coolidge after chasing him. Cops claim that they saw the victim reaching into his waistband and that they thought he was reaching for a gun. No weapon was found. **Source:** Los Angeles Times, 6/21/99

Dana Richard de Hertoghe	—	—	

June 19, 1999. Hemet (Riverside County):

Mr. de Hertoghe was killed by Hemet Police Officer Chris Gigandt. Cops arrived on the scene, severely beat Mr. de Hertoghe's companion, whom they supposedly thought was hiding something in his hand, and killed Mr. de Hertoghe. No weapons were found at the scene, nor was anything illegal recovered. Police told two different stories about what happened. The victim's parents described their son as "an outstanding father, husband, son, and electrician, much in demand by electrical companies everywhere." They demanded that Officer Gigandt be put on trial for murder. **Source:** fax from victim's parents

Margaret LaVerne Mitchell	54	*Black*	

May 21, 1999. Los Angeles (LaBrea & 4th):

Margaret Mitchell, a homeless woman well known in the area, was shot to death by police officers who stopped and harassed her for pushing a shopping cart down the street. A motorist saw the police harassing her and jumped out of his car to intervene. Margaret walked away and was shot by the police. A number of witnesses said she was shot in the back. Police claim that she lunged at them with a screwdriver in her hand and that they feared for their lives. Margaret was 54 years old, weighed 102 lbs. and was 5'1" tall. A shopping cart memorial was set up for her at the intersection of La Brea and Fourth Street where she was killed. **Source:** Revolutionary Worker, 6/13/99

Unidentified Woman   30s   *Black*

April 29, 1999. Vernon:
A woman had gotten into a dispute with another woman in her car and had allegedly shot her. The wounded woman ran into a McDonalds and called the police. When cops arrived, the other woman, still in her car, refused to get out but did toss notes out of her window to police. The authorities have refused to reveal the contents of the messages. After about three hours, police approached the vehicle but were still 25 feet away when she allegedly waved a gun and pointed it at the officers. From 100 yards away, a police sharpshooter shot and killed her. **Source:** Los Angeles Times, 6/30/99

Bret Hughes   47   —

April 27, 1999. Los Angeles (Hollywood Hills):
Police arrived at Bret's home and found him sitting in a parked car, very distressed. They were responding to a suspected domestic dispute. According to police, Bret was holding a gun to his head when they arrived. At one point, he got out of the car and they shot at him with bean bags, which startled him. Cops then shot him to death, claiming he pointed a gun at them. **Source:** Los Angeles Times, 4/27/99

Armando Rodriguez   25   *Latino*

April 21, 1999. Whittier Narrows:
Mr. Rodriguez was in a standoff with sheriff's deputies after allegedly robbing a bank and being chased for 20 miles at speeds of up to 60 mph on the freeway. The deputies used a mechanical robot to approach Mr. Rodriguez as he sat in his car. The robot brought him a phone through which he could talk to the cops. The police refused to disclose details of the hour-long discussion. After the discussion, police shot a tear gas canister at Mr. Rodriguez. Cops claim he wiped his eyes from the fumes and raised a gun. A sheriff's marksman then shot him with one round and killed him. Police originally claimed that Mr. Rodriguez shot himself but later had to recant this story and admit that one of their gunman shot him. Questions have been raised about whether officers were ever in serious danger since they were not next to the car at the time they killed him. Also, Mr. Rodriguez had remained in his car throughout the entire standoff, which lasted more than two hours. **Source:** Los Angeles Times, 4/22/99 & 4/23/99

Unidentified Man   —   —

April 2, 1999. Inglewood:
Cops shot and killed a man whom they claimed was the "Westside Rapist." Police and media had been focusing on a man dubbed the "Westside Rapist," who had raped at least seven women over the last couple of months. A few days after cops killed this unidentified man, the "Westside Rapist" attacked another woman. He was apprehended a week later. Police tried to justify the killing of this first man, obviously not the "Westside Rapist," by saying he raped a woman and then approached them with a knife. **Source:** Los Angeles Times, 4/3/99

Unidentified Man   18   —

March 22, 1999. Los Angeles:
A security guard in the parking lot of the Baldwin Hills Shopping Center shot and killed one of two men she claims were trying to rob her with a gun. **Source:** Los Angeles Times, 3/23/99

Lisa Ann Rarick   32   —

March 18, 1999. El Segundo:
Lisa, a political consultant from Rolling Hills Estates, was killed when her car was struck by another vehicle being pursued for a traffic violation by police at speeds of up to 100 mph. Lisa's car smashed into a telephone pole. The force of the crash broke the car in two and ejected her from her car. She died at the scene. **Source:** KCBS TV Los Angeles, Channel 2, 3/18/99

Gus Henry Woods   56   —

March 2, 1999. Los Angeles:
Police shot Mr. Woods once in the chest and killed him as he allegedly held a metal rod in his hand. Cops claim they thought it was a weapon. **Source:** Los Angeles Times, 6/26/99

Ricardo Clos   —   *Latino*

February 23, 1999. East Los Angeles:
Ricardo's wife called 911 to report that her husband had a knife and had cut himself on the neck. Ricardo reportedly ignored police orders to drop the knife and a pair of scissors. After police fired beanbags and pepper-spray at him, he allegedly threw the knife at police. The knife missed. Cops fired 38 rounds and killed Ricardo, who only had a pair of scissors in hand. About 100 people protested and marched to the sheriff's station four days later. Daniel Lopez of the Brown Berets said, "Once again, in our community, the police have appointed themselves judge, jury and executioner." Agustin Cebada, national representative for the Brown Berets said, "They shot him mercilessly, until they ran out of bullets." **Source:** Los Angeles Times, 3/4/99; La Opinion

---

Anthony Gamboa   24   —

February 12, 1999. West Covina:
Anthony was wanted by police for an alleged armed robbery. Cops surrounded his apartment. When Anthony came out, he was grabbed and held by a police dog. Thinking that Anthony might be reaching for a weapon in his bag, police fatally shot him in the chest. Cops claim they found a gun and money in his bag. **Source:** Los Angeles Times, 2/13/99

Stephen Bayer   39   —

January 18, 1999. Simi Valley:
Stephen Bayer was depressed and struggling with financial problems when the police came up to him as he sat in his parked car. Stephen got into an argument with the police and drove off. The police pursued Stephen, chasing him through three counties. Stephen stopped after the police flattened his car tires. Cops claim Stephen shot at them during the chase. Police claim Stephen was holding a gun to his head, threatening to kill himself as he sat in his car after the chase. Officers forced Stephen out of the car by throwing tear gas into his vehicle. They claim he then pointed his gun at them, so they shot him to death. Stephen's family was down the street when the killing happened. They had pleaded with the police to let them talk to Stephen, but the police refused and instead chose to kill Stephen. After the shooting, his family was very angry. Sid Bayer, the victim's father, said "I could have said 'Steve, give me the gun' and he would have done it. But they murdered my son. They took a person's life like it belonged to them and they are going to cover it up... It didn't have to happen. All they had to do was let me talk to him." **Source:** Los Angeles Times, 1/19/99

Unidentified Man   49   —

January 16, 1999. Malibu:
The unidentified man's friends dialed 911 in an attempt to get help for him because he was stabbing himself in the chest with a knife. When police arrived, they "helped" the man by shooting him with stun bags and pepper-spray. The man allegedly dropped the knife and grabbed a pair of scissors. Police claim that the man turned toward them and raised the scissors over his head and that they had no choice but to shoot and kill him. This was one of two killings by police on this day. **Source:** Los Angeles Times, 1/17/99

Dion Goodlow   19   *Black*

January 16, 1999. South Central LA:
Dion was disabled from a car accident and in a wheelchair. Cops answering a report of shots fired claim he matched the description of a person involved in a previous shooting. They further claim that he got out of the wheelchair and ran away, possibly into the house. They supposedly saw him running around the corner pointing a large handgun at them. Police opened fire and killed him. The victim's grandmother accused the cops of lying. Dion had just gotten out of the hospital and had broken bones. She said, "They [the cops] pushed my [grand]son out of the wheelchair and shot him 28 times. They said he was running through an alley, trying to jump a fence. But he had just got out of the hospital, bones cracked, and couldn't have done it. They killed my baby. All I want is justice. I know he wouldn't have done nothing anyway because I had just had a heart attack and that's why he signed himself out of the hospital early to come and be with me." **Source:** Los Angeles Times, 1/17/99; KCBS-TV Channel 2000 News, 1/16/99; statement from victim's grandmother

---

Julio Salvador Castillo   16   *Latino*   👁

January 10, 1999. Lynwood:

Julio's mother called 911, looking for help for her son who had run out of the house with a gun. While she was on hold, her neighbor ran in yelling, "Hang up, they're about to kill your son." When she went outside, she saw a semi-circle of police cars. The cops were standing next to their cars and they were all pointing their guns at her 16-year-old son across the street. She begged them to let her talk to him. Instead, they emptied their guns into him. His 17-year-old friend was with him. Cops tried to claim he was holding her hostage. In reality, he saved her life, blocking her from the bullets with his body. Witnesses say Julio was alive after this barrage of bullets and died hours later when an officer shot him in the head at close range as he was trying to surrender. Witnesses also said cops would not allow the paramedics to give Julio medical attention while he was wounded. Julio's mother described her son as a "little boy, a good person, respectful... He wasn't only my son, he was my companion, in the good times and bad times. Everything we shared is unforgettable... We did a lot of beautiful things together. I was both his mother and father, that's why I hurt a lot for him. With him, the sun shined brighter, now I can't feel the sun's warmth anymore. He was like an angel God lent to me, but his life was taken from me so violently. I know one day we'll see each other again and embrace each other once again." **Source:** SLP Form; Statement from Gloria Santos, victim's mother; Channel 2000 News, 1/11/99; La Opinion, 1/14/99; The Sacramento Bee, 1/11/99

Terry Taylor   —   —

January 1, 1999. Los Angeles:

Mr. Taylor was investigating a noise in his yard at 12:10 a.m. when the LAPD arrived, then shot and killed him. Cops claim he was holding a shotgun. He had committed no crime and was at his home when he was killed. Terry Taylor is survived by his wife and five children.

Unidentified Man   —   —

December 31, 1998. South Central Los Angeles:

Officers assigned to the New Year's Eve Gunfire Reduction Task allege they heard gunshots. They supposedly found a man behind his home and ordered him to put his gun down. Police claim the man refused. They shot and killed him. This was one of four officer-involved shootings, two of them fatal, on the same day. Lt. Anthony Alba said, "The best way to celebrate [the New Year] is to stay inside, keep your hands off your weapons and enjoy life." **Source:** The Sacramento Bee, found on Internet 1/2/99

James Travis McCracken   34   —

December 31, 1998. Studio City / North Hollywood border:

"James hated guns. Many times he didn't want to hunt or fish because he didn't want to kill anything. He didn't like to go fishing — not even catch and release — because he was afraid he would kill a fish," said James' father. So his father was surprised when one of James' friends said James had bought a gun. While wearing a bullet-resistant helmet, James was shot and killed at an apartment complex in an alleged shootout with police. James worked with computers for a telecommunications company. **Source:** Associated Press, 1/3/99

Daniel Rily   —   —

December 28, 1998. El Monte:

Daniel had called 911, apparently distraught. Cops arrived and claim they found Daniel in the front yard holding a large wooden stick that he refused to drop. Daniel allegedly threatened to kill himself and the officers. After police shot Daniel twice with a beanbag gun, he supposedly lunged at officers, who shot him twice more, killing him. **Source:** Los Angeles Times, 12/29/98

Tyisha Miller	19	*Black*	👁

December 28, 1998. Riverside:

Tyisha was killed by four police officers who fired a total of 24 bullets, with 12 hitting her. Friends made a 911 call after finding her after midnight unconscious in the driver's seat of her car with the motor running, doors locked and a flat tire. Friends warned police she had a handgun in her lap. In an effort to awaken Tyisha, police shouted instructions but she remained unconscious. Police then broke the driver's side window to gain entrance; cops claim they heard a loud boom and thought Ms. Miller had fired the gun. Far from threatening the officers, Tyisha was unconscious until she died. Witnesses accuse police of tampering with evidence by cleaning up and repaving the shooting scene, of removing windows from the car and of releasing misleading statements to denigrate the dead woman. The killing of Tyisha Miller unleashed a storm of protest against police brutality. **Source:** Los Angeles Times, 2/11/99, 12/31/98, 1/8/99, & 1/1/99; The Sacramento Bee, 1/23/99 & 1/30/99; The Bakersfield Californian,1/12/99

Unidentified Man	—	—	

November 29, 1998. Culver City:

An unidentified man who cops said was a suspected bank robber was shot and killed by LAPD officers during an alleged shootout. A friend of the victim was also shot four times and it is unclear whether he survived. A cop was also reportedly killed. **Source:** CBS News, Los Angeles, Channel 2 12/1/98

Tracy Joseph Melrose	33	—	

November 25, 1998. Lancaster:

A division of the Lancaster police force were driving by a Walden's Bookstore, when they allegedly spotted a possible multiple-robbery suspect inside the bookstore. They went inside the store, went up to Tracy and a struggle ensued. One of the deputies shot Tracy once in the upper body; he was pronounced dead at the scene. The deputies claim that Tracy had a gun and said he was going to kill them. They later admitted that they could not be exactly sure if the victim was connected to the string robberies that had recently occurred. **Source:** Channel 2000 Web Site,11/26/98

Unidentified Man	—	—	

November 24, 1998. Bellflower:

Police were following a man who had allegedly stolen a Signal Hill Police vehicle. Cops claim that when they ordered him out of the car, the man put the car in reverse and rammed it forward and backward into the patrol cars. Police opened fire, killing him. **Source:** Los Angeles Times, 11/25/98

Unidentified Man	—	—	

November 20, 1998. Los Angeles:

Two deputies reportedly tried to question two men who were wearing purported "gang colors." The deputies allege one of the men opened fire and the cops shot and killed him as he ran. The deputies claim they found two handguns on the dead man. **Source:** Michael Novick, 11/22/98

Unidentified Man	—	—	

November 15, 1998. Marina Del Rey:

An off-duty deputy, who was in a nightclub with three women, alleges two unidentified men began harassing them. An argument and shoving match ensued. One of the men supposedly pulled out a knife, so the cop pulled his gun. The men ran away. According to the deputy, he followed them. While scuffling with one of them, the deputy heard tires squealing and alleges that the second man tried to run over him. The cop opened fire, killing the driver of the vehicle. **Source:** Los Angeles Times, 11/16/98

Unidentified Woman	—	—	

October 13, 1998. Los Angeles (East Vernon Avenue):

Police claim a woman pointed a gun at them. They opened fire, killing her. **Source:** Michael Novick, 10/13/98

Unidentified Woman — —

October 12, 1998. South Los Angeles:
A woman was sitting in her car, allegedly with a gun. Police came up to her car and demanded that she step out and drop the gun. As she got out of the car, two officers fired at her, one with a beanbag shotgun, the other with a regular gun. She died from bullet wounds to the chest. Police whisked off the eyewitnesses before the media could talk to them to verify the police story that the victim pointed the gun at them. A 12-year-old girl who was on her way to school was struck and wounded by a patrol car on its way to the scene. This was the second time in three days that a cop killed someone in South Los Angeles. **Source:** Yahoo News / Channel 2, 10/12/98; Los Angeles Times, 10/13/99

Joe Joshua   76   *African American*

September 30, 1998. Los Angeles (South Central):
Joe Joshua was well liked by the people who knew him. He occasionally rode his bicycle around the neighborhood looking for bottles and cans he could recycle and cash in at the recycling center. Joe was retired and lived on a fixed income, collecting bottles and cans to help supplement his wages. On the afternoon of Oct. 10, his life came to abrupt end. Los Angeles Police officers were investigating a possible robbery. Cops claim that Joe was not complying with their warnings to leave the premises where they were conducting their investigation and brandished a knife instead. Joe Joshua was fatally shot in the chest by a single bullet fired by an LA police officer. Civilian eyewitnesses contradicted the police account, saying that Joe posed no threat to the cops when they shot him down. Witnesses held a protest right on the spot because they were outraged that police would kill this harmless elderly man. As a result, there was widespread news coverage of his death. **Source:** Los Angeles Times, 10/11/98 & 10/12/98; Deadly Crisis Newsletter, 12/98

Yusuf Hasan   47   —

October 2, 1998. Carson:
Mr. Hasan was on his way to get medicine for his desperately ill baby. While he was driving on the freeway, he reportedly crashed through some warning traffic cones and stopped his car. Police shot him in the chest and killed him, claiming he attacked them with a metal pipe. Yusuf's baby also died because he didn't receive his medicine in time. **Source:** Los Angeles Times, 10/2/98; discussion with victim's family members

Ajang Khadivi   35   —

October 1, 1998. Winnetka:
Cops claim Ajang Khadivi walked into a bank and attempted to rob it by threatening to detonate a bomb in his briefcase. A bank guard shot and killed Ajang when he moved and police said they thought he gestured as if he were reaching for a gun or detonator. No bomb or any other weapon was found. Police ruled the killing justified. **Source:** Community News File/Tarzana, 10/3/98

Han Huynh   29   *Vietnamese*

September 22, 1998. Thousand Oaks:
Han suffered from schizophrenia and wandered away from his home. In the past, authorities had picked him up and brought him back home. But this time, Deputies Mark Correia and Michael Rowland pepper-sprayed him, claiming that he brandished a kitchen knife and lunged at Deputy Rowland, who was 10-15 feet away. Han's sister said that her brother always carried a small knife that he used to slice apples and oranges. The deputies shot Han 11 times in the chest and abdomen, killing him. "I have a feeling the police came to the scene and just overreacted. If the police just tried to talk to him, there wouldn't have been a problem," Han's sister said. **Source:** Los Angeles Times (Ventura edition), 3/2/99

Unidentified Man — —

Sept. 17 (?), 1998. Los Angeles:
One man was killed and another was seriously injured when the pickup truck they were driving crashed during a police chase. Cops were chasing them at speeds of up to 90 mph for allegedly driving a stolen vehicle. **Source:** Los Angeles Times, 9/17/98

Dwayne Nelson   41   —

September 13, 1998. Los Angeles (Athens):
Although no injuries or damages were reported, police claim that when they rolled up, Dwayne was walking along the highway with a handgun, shouting incoherently and shooting at passing motorists. According to police, Dwayne was arrested and put in the back seat of a patrol car, where he allegedly began kicking the car window. So, for "safety reasons," police took Dwayne out of the car and restrained him with TARP (total appendage restraint procedure, also known as hog-tying). Dwayne became unresponsive and died less than one and a half hours after his initial contact with the police. All this despite the fact that last year, L.A. city officials agreed to ban hog-tying after the city paid $750,000 to settle a wrongful death lawsuit filed by the family of a Sunland man who died from this practice in 1995. **Source:** Los Angeles Times, 9/14/98

Nick Nelson   43   —

September 9, 1998. Ventura:
Authorities responded to a call at Nick's condo after neighbors heard shots. Nick had apparently shot his television set. After Officers Hewlett and Schindler arrived, Nick supposedly drew a gun and walked toward them. Police fatally shot him. Authorities claimed that the victim was suicidal. His family disputed that, saying he was only depressed. This was the second time Officer Hewlett was involved in a fatal shooting. **Source:** Los Angeles Times, 9/11/98 & 9/12/98

Unidentified Man   —   —

August 30, 1998. San Gabriel:
San Gabriel Police claim an unidentified man pulled a gun from his waistband and fired at officers, who shot and killed him. **Source:** Los Angeles Times (Home Edition), 9/1/98

Thomas Bryant   37   —

August 27, 1998. Los Angeles:
Thomas was arrested on suspicion of being under the influence of drugs and was put in the back seat of a patrol car. While in the car, Thomas stopped breathing. Paramedics were called and Thomas was taken to Antelope Valley Hospital, where he later died. **Source:** Los Angeles Times (Valley Edition), 8/30/98

Unidentified Woman   47   —

August 10, 1998. Temple City:
Family members of the unidentified woman said the previous month she had been the victim of an unreported assault in which she may have suffered a head injury. Police arrested the woman on outstanding warrants for DUI. She died in a hospital shortly after being found unconscious in her jail cell at the sheriff's station, authorities said. **Source:** Los Angeles Times, 8/12/98

Robert Gonzales   —   *Latino*

August 7, 1998. Anaheim:
According to authorities, police were called to Robert's townhouse by his wife, who claimed he had assaulted her. A hundred heavily armed police surrounded the building and a standoff ensued. Police refused to let family members speak to Gonzales during the standoff. Police threw a tear gas canister into the condo. A fire broke out and Gonzales was killed in the fire. Several families lost their homes in the fire. Gonzales was a disabled roofer who had been out of work for four years. He had three children. **Source:** Orange County Register, 8/11/98

Danny Ray Smith   34   *African American*

August 1, 1998. Twin Towers Correctional:

According to other inmates, Danny Smith, an inmate in the mental health wing, balked at being placed in a cell with a Latino inmate. Irritated by his resistance, deputies and a jail worker began beating him while he was still handcuffed. Mr. Smith died from the beating. Speaking at a Stolen Lives induction ceremony in April, 1999, the victim's brother said, "My brother was beat down viciously like a dog! He was beat, choked, etc. How could he struggle and fight when he was in handcuffs? It's a cold thing what they did. Amadou Diallo, Abner Louima, I sympathize with their families. I want justice!" He described his brother as "a loving father, son and supportive and compassionate brother. He instituted principles and values to the youth. Our loving memory of him remains alive in all whose lives he touched.... It is our turn to pick up his baton and carry his message and memory on. Danny, we will meet again when our job here is completed." **Source:** Los Angeles Times, 8/6/98

Unidentified Man   —   —

July 24, 1998. Pomona:

A security guard shot an unidentified man in a bar and the man reportedly returned fire, killing the guard. The wounded man ran from the bar, climbed over a wall and was caught by the police. He was taken to a hospital where he was pronounced dead. **Source:** Los Angeles Times (southland edition), 7/26/98

Lawrence Albert Acosta   27   *Latino*

July 5, 1998. North Hollywood:

According to police, an unidentified off-duty deputy walking at 3:30 a.m. was approached by two men demanding money at gunpoint. The deputy drew his gun and killed Acosta. Acosta's companion, not the deputy, has been charged with the murder. **Source:** Los Angeles Times, 7/6/98 & 7/7/98

Hao Dinh Vu   34   *Vietnamese*

July 2, 1998. Garden Grove:

Officers responded to a 911 call about a man with a knife. According to the police, Vu was shot death after fleeing on foot, refusing to drop the knife and lunging toward the cops. Vu's family said that he had risen, eaten breakfast, showered and gone out for a walk. They described him as a peaceful man who did not carry a knife. He enjoyed cigars and classical music. The family, who immigrated here from Vietnam, is suspicious of the police version of events and wants an investigation. **Source:** Los Angeles Times, 7/3/98

Unidentified Man   60s   —

June 30, 1998. Long Beach:

Police responded to a call about a naked man sitting in a van at a shopping center. He was shot to death when he allegedly grabbed a gun and refused police orders to put it down. **Source:** Los Angeles Times, 7/1/98

Fred Sammons   20   —

June 7, 1998. Van Nuys:

Police on stake-out for the "Lotto Bandit" shot and killed Sammons, claiming he robbed a convenience store. Sammons' mother said he was not the bandit and was a regular known by all the clerks at the store. **Source:** Los Angeles Times, 6/9/98

James Eugene Moore   51   —

June 1998. Compton:

Upon hearing that he had been found guilty of kidnapping, Moore became agitated. When courtroom deputies tried to handcuff him, Moore allegedly attacked them with a homemade plastic knife. When Moore ignored another deputy's order to drop the knife, the deputy shot him once in the head. Moore was killed in front of the jury and 22 witnesses in the courtroom. According to police, Moore left behind a note that said he refused to go to prison for something he didn't do. **Source:** Los Angeles Times, 6/2/98

Francisco Martínez	23	*Latino*

May 25, 1998. Santa Ana:

According to police, two officers noticed Mr. Martínez and a companion "behaving suspiciously" around 4 p.m. The companion fled. An officer opened fire on Mr. Martínez, who died later that day. Police say Mr. Martínez may have had a shotgun. **Source:** Los Angeles Times, 5/27/98

Unidentified Man	20s	—

May 22, 1998. Long Beach:

Passengers on a commuter train told the operator that a passenger had a gun. When the train stopped, police found the man and told him to drop the weapon. When he allegedly pointed it at them, one officer fired several times and killed him. **Source:** Los Angeles Times, 5/24/98

Unidentified Man	—	—

May 12, 1998. Azusa:

Officers tried to stop a car containing two men and a chase ensued. The car crashed. One man ran and allegedly took a hostage who escaped. When he commandeered another car and allegedly backed it up toward police, seven or eight officers opened fire and killed him. **Source:** Los Angeles Times, 5/13/98

Derek B. Myers	26	—

May 7, 1998. Thousand Oaks:

According to police, Myers was shot to death when he threatened Sheriff Scott Streltz with what turned out to be a paint ball gun. Police claim that Myers left behind notes which outlined his plans to "pretend to pull a gun on police." **Source:** Los Angeles Times, 5/9/98

William Edward Meikle	21	—

April 23, 1998. Norwalk:

Police stopped Meikle because he appeared to be intoxicated. When they found a spray can hidden in his jacket, a scuffle ensued. Claiming that Meikle was going for one of their weapons, cops shot and killed him. **Source:** Los Angeles Times, 4/24/98

Jason Todd Hayley	29	—

April 18, 1998. Ventura:

When police attempted to question Jason, he ran. At least 25 officers joined in a chase through a restaurant and onto rooftops during the Artwalk celebration. According to the death certificate, Hayley died from a shotgun wound to the back. **Source:** Los Angeles Times, 4/20/98

Unidentified Man	—	—

April 11, 1998. Los Angeles:

Police responded to a call about a prowler. The man barricaded himself in a crawl space and the SWAT team was called. After a two-hour standoff, they fired tear gas and the man exited. Claiming the man then pointed a gun at them, the SWAT team shot and killed him. **Source:** cbs2.com, 4/12/98

Unidentified Man	—	—

April 8, 1998. Los Angeles:

Off-duty Officer Guzmán was inside a club when he heard gunshots. He rushed out and allegedly saw a man standing over a wounded woman. Claiming to be defending the woman, Officer Guzmán fired six shots at the man. When the man moved, he shot him two more times and killed him. **Source:** Los Angeles Times, 4/9/98

Richard Thorpe   39   —

April 4, 1998. Torrance:

Thorpe was stopped because the registration tags on his car had expired. Claiming Thorpe drew a gun from his waistband when he was asked to exit the car, Torrance police officers shot and killed him. **Source:** Los Angeles Times, 4/7/98

Juan Olvera González   28   *Latino*

April 2, 1998. Costa Mesa:

Mr. González and some family members tried to get readmitted into a bar after they were thrown out for having drunk too much. Claiming Mr. González assaulted him with a pool stick, the security guard shot and killed him. **Source:** Los Angeles Times, 4/4/98

Michael "Buzz" Arnold   39   *white*

March 27, 1998. Los Angeles:

Buzz was disoriented, sitting on the freeway overpass with a BB gun. The officers asked him to exit the freeway, so he got in his car and drove off the exit ramp. The police followed and pulled him over on the street. Cops claim he got out of the car and pointed the BB gun at his head and then at the cops. But a bullet trajectory expert said it was unlikely that he had a gun in his hand when he was killed. Buzz was shot 106 times by multiple police agencies. Nearby homes were hit by police bullets, including one bullet that landed on a pillow, right next to a boy who was sleeping.

Unidentified Male   43   —

March 24, 1998. South Central LA (Athens) (?):

Police responded to call about a strangely behaving man. Cops shot him with a stun gun and then restrained him with a "total appendage restraint procedure." He was having difficulty breathing and died. Paramedics found wadded paper in his throat.

Unidentified male   21   —

March 15, 1998. Long Beach:

A man sped away from a traffic stop and crashed. He then ran from police on foot and supposedly refused to stop. When he allegedly pulled out what looked like a pistol and aimed at three officers, they opened fire and killed him. It was a toy gun. **Source:** Los Angeles Times, 3/17/98

Unidentified Man   43   —

March 11, 1998. Los Angeles (Athens):

The mother of an unidentified man called police for help when her son, allegedly drunk, was "tearing up the house and behaving violently." When police arrived, they claim they found the man nude and "behaving in a bizarre manner." The police shot the man with a dart from an electronic stun gun and then restrained him with a nylon device known as a total appendage restraint procedure. The man had trouble breathing and paramedics were eventually called. Paramedics allegedly pulled three wads of magazine pages from his throat. The man was pronounced dead. **Source:** Los Angeles Times, 3/12/98

Unidentified Man   20   —

March 7, 1998. Long Beach:

Police officers were following a car with three men in it. The men had allegedly been involved in a shooting. According to police, they pulled the car over and the three men got out. Then, one of the men got back into the car and sped off. He was chased by four patrol cars and crashed. The police then claim that he put his car into reverse and drove into one of the patrol cars. Cops shot him multiple times. He died of his wounds the next day. **Source:** Los Angeles Times, 3/9/98

Luis Romero   28   *Latino*

February 20, 1998. Los Angeles:

According to police reports, Romero was stopped for a traffic violation and taken into custody by the LAPD in a case of mistaken identity. As he was being released fifteen hours later, he began having seizures and soon after died in a hospital emergency room. **Source:** Los Angeles Times, 2/25/98

Unidentified	—	—

January 21, 1998. Los Angeles:
According to police, when a driver involved in a traffic stop tried to back into a patrol car, the officer got out of his car. Claiming the car was coming at him, California Highway Patrol Sgt. Ernie García shot and killed the driver.

Juan Gabriel Blanca	28	*Latino*

January 15, 1998. Santa Ana:
Juan Blanca went into a store where he is said to have acted strangely. When police were called, he left the store. When police arrived, an altercation erupted and Blanca was shot and killed. Police allege he tried to rob the store earlier.

Albert Trujillo Flores	46	*Latino*

January 6, 1998. Oxnard:
Oxnard Police Officer Kujawa saw Flores riding his bike erratically. The officer claims that when he approached Flores, the victim threatened him with a screwdriver. He shot Flores in the head and chest several times and killed him. There were no witnesses. **Source:** Los Angeles Times, 1/7/98

Anthony Mosqueda	17	*Latino*

1998. Montebello:
Anthony was running from a fight with some youth who had tried to run him over with a car. Police claim Anthony had a rifle, so they shot and killed him. Anthony's family said he was unarmed and that he was shot in the back while running away.

Mario Machado	17	*Latino*

December 31, 1997. Los Angeles:
According to police, Machado was attending a boisterous New Year's Eve party. He got into an altercation with Officer Steve Gajda and shot him. Moments later, Machado was shot dead by two LAPD officers. Officer Gajda also died. **Source:** Los Angeles Times, 1/2/98

William Hagerman	—	*white*
Tan Van Nguyen	—	*Vietnamese*

December 27, 1997. Huntington Beach:
Both men were killed in a car accident when a car being chased by the California Highway Patrol crashed into their car. The driver of the car being chased was allegedly suspected of DUI. William was a New York Times delivery man; Tan was his supervisor. **Source:** Orange County Register, 12/30/97

Furman Little	27	—

December 27, 1997. Manhattan Beach:
A couple called the police to report an assault. Police arrived to search for the suspects. They located a Jeep Cherokee which they pursued until it crashed. Then, claiming they had been fired upon, police shot the occupants, killing Furman Little. **Source:** Los Angeles Times, 12/30/97

Rigoberto González	18	*Latino*	👁

December 23, 1997. Bell Gardens:
Rigoberto was very depressed and called 911 for help. The police arrived as he was eating dinner. They entered the house, saw Rigo (as his friends called him) with a knife in his hand (from eating dinner) and immediately shot him to death in front of a number of neighborhood kids. A year later the kids were still traumatized and scared of the police. Cops claimed that the victim had attacked them before they opened fire. **Source:** Los Angeles Times, 12/26/97; statement from family

---

Arturo Reyes Torres   41   *Latino*

December 18, 1997. Orange:
Torres, a disgruntled CalTrans worker fired for stealing $106.50 worth of scrap metal, allegedly opened fire and killed his boss and three co-workers. He was stopped by police and then allegedly wounded an officer. Cops shot and killed him. **Source:** Los Angeles Times, 12/19/97

José Luis Mendoza   26   —

December 1, 1997. —:
Cops claim they noticed a pickup truck driving recklessly and began pursuit. They allege that Jose led them on a 15-minute rush-hour chase. Driving against oncoming traffic, police allege he crashed into nine cars, trying to run down some cops and trying to ram his way between stopped cars. He was shot in the head and killed in a freeway underpass by an officer on foot. No cops were injured and civilians whose cars were hit suffered only minor injuries. Cops say that José was not wanted for anything and that the pickup truck belonged to him. **Source:** AP online, 12/2/97

Mark Philyaw   33   *Black*

November 26, 1997. L.A. County Twin Towers jail:
Mark was in jail for some traffic tickets but was expected to be released in time to spend Thanksgiving (the following day) with his family. The Sheriff's Department said he died after a "physical altercation" that occurred when he refused to comply with a strip search. He was beaten to death by at least seven deputies, who beat, kicked and reportedly choked him. He was naked at the time because he was in a strip search area. When ordered to bend over, Mark told the deputies that he could not because of a torn ligament in his leg; according to other prisoners who witnessed the fatal beating, one deputy said "well you want me to help you..." and then started the assault. The coroner finally ruled the cause of death homicide. Mark's windpipe was crushed and asphyxiation was listed as the official cause of death. The sheriffs tried to claim that Mark was in jail for "assault on a officer" when in fact it was for a suspended license. They claimed he refused to comply with a strip search when in fact he could not. They said only three deputies were involved in the beating and later admitted to seven. A deputy supposedly investigating the murder said, "There is nothing to indicate that the deputies did anything other than their jobs." No cops were even suspended for the murder of Mark Philyaw. **Source:** Revolutionary Worker, 4/19/98

Dean Dial   33   —

November 24, 1997. Torrance:
Police responded to a call about a robbery. They chased Dial until he stopped his car. Claiming Dial pointed a handgun at them, officers shot him in the torso. He died a few hours later. **Source:** Los Angeles Times, 11/25/97

Alfredo Joe Arellano   33   *Latino*

November 22, 1997. Garden Grove:
Alleging that Arellano was driving a stolen car, a patrol officer pulled him over. Arellano ran to a nearby parking lot. Claiming that Arellano threatened them with a knife, officers opened fire and shot him several times. He died at the scene. **Source:** The Orange County Register, 11/25/97

Darryl "Chubby" Hood   40   *African American*   👁

November 15, 1997. Watts (Jordan Downs Housing Project):
Chubby was shot and killed by officers responding to a suicide call. He was stabbing himself in the head when police arrived. Refusing orders to drop two knives, police shot him. His killing has outraged the community. Seven hundred people attended his funeral. Community leaders were planning a protest march. Chubby Hood was a loving family man and father who suffered from mental illness. **Source:** Los Angeles Times, 11/25/97

Three Unidentified People — —
___

November 12, 1997. Fontana:

Three people were killed when an officer tried to stop a truck in which they were traveling. Police allege the truck failed to respond and sped away. Police gave chase. The truck crashed into a power pole, killing three of its four occupants. It is not clear why officers originally tried to stop the truck. **Source:** Los Angeles Times (Orange edition), 11/13/97

James Paul Majcherek 25 —
___

November 3, 1997. Seal Beach:

James was found dead in a detoxification cell just seven hours after he was arrested on suspicion of car theft and driving under the influence of drugs. He was being held in a privately operated lockup in the Police Department basement when he stopped breathing, officials said. James' parents have filed a lawsuit claiming that the police, district attorney's office and coroner's office were withholding information about the cause of death. The Majcherek family attorney said, "My clients don't know what the heck happened to their son. How he died. Why he was arrested." **Source:** The Orange County Register, 12/12/97

Walter Chavarría 28 —
___

November 3, 1997. Torrance:

Walter had been in a family argument earlier in the day and police claim he may have been on drugs. Walter died less than an hour after being "restrained" by Torrance police officers. **Source:** Los Angeles Times, 11/4/97

Etone Lewis — —
___

November 1997. Los Angeles:

Etone Lewis was shot and killed by off-duty Police Officer Elpidio Orozco. Officer Orozco claimed that Mr. Lewis was using a gun to rob a man at an automatic teller machine. Orozco said he told him to stop and that instead, Mr. Lewis pointed the gun at him and fired a shot. Officer Orozco, who already had his gun out, then shot Mr. Lewis in the chest, killing him. A confidential report obtained by the Los Angeles Times stated that the gun reportedly used by Etone Lewis could not have fired the bullet that was shot at Officer Orozco. **Source:** Los Angeles Times, 2/3/99

Kelvin Robinson 33 *Black* 👁
___

October 19, 1997. Los Angeles:

Kelvin Robinson was shot three times in the back for no reason by LAPD cops from the Newton St. Division. He was then denied medical attention when the police refused to call the paramedics, so he bled to death. He was a deaf mute and the father of five children. His family filed a lawsuit. **Source:** SLP Form; Deadly Crisis Newsletter, 12/98

Linda Wageman 44 —
___

October 14, 1997. Mission Hills:

Linda, a mother and grandmother, worked as a salesclerk and was the glue that held her family together after the Northridge earthquake forced them from their home. After giving a friend a ride home, her van was broadsided by a car being chased by police for speeding. The car burst into flames, killing Linda and seriously injuring her daughter. The ACLU released a study of 12 law enforcement agencies between 1993-95 that found 47 people killed and more than 1,500 people hurt from police chases. It also said the LAPD accounts for only 37 percent of the region's officers, but was involved in 47 percent of such deaths. Traffic violations are the basis of 70-80 percent of police pursuits. Following Linda's death, the ACLU called on the LAPD to immediately suspend its existing pursuit policy. **Source:** Los Angeles Times, 10/15/97, 10/16/97, & 10/17/97

Unidentified Man 22 —
___

October 13, 1997. Los Angeles:

A sheriff's deputy was hanging up a pay phone near a bar when he was approached by a man who allegedly drew a gun and started shooting. The deputy chased him on foot and claims the two continued to exchange gunfire. The man was hit twice and died two hours later. **Source:** Los Angeles Times, 10/14/97

Unidentified Man   —   —

September 22, 1997. Los Angeles County:
Police responded to a call about a man wielding a knife. When the deputies arrived, the man allegedly attacked them with a machete. Although they were not injured, they shot and killed him anyway. **Source:** Los Angeles Times, 9/23/97

Unidentified Man   —   —

September 16, 1997. Van Nuys:
Two plainclothes security guards — both retired cops — opened fire on four men in a car allegedly putting on ski masks. One of the men supposedly shot back and was killed at the scene. The three others managed to escape. It appears that the guards fired first. There is no evidence that the armed man threatened the two guards. **Source:** Los Angeles Times, 9/17/97

Nicholas Dowey   21   —

September 12, 1997. Ventura County:
Mr. Dowey was attenting a party where he reportedly got into a fight and was hit on the head by another party-goer. Later, Ventura County sheriff's deputies arrived to quiet the party. Deputy Donald Rodarte hit Nick in the head with a can of pepper spray or a flashlight, aggravating his earlier injury. The cops failed to get him medical attention and he died 11 hours later from extensive head trauma. A medical examiner claimed Nick was not killed by the blow from the deputy, but instead from the blow that Nick had received at the party prior to the arrival of the deputies. Although Deputy Rodarte denied hitting Nick, several other cops said Deputy Rodarte told them that he struck Nick a couple of times. A lawsuit filed by Nick's parents said that blows from the deputy led to the death of their son. The lawsuit also stated that Nick yelled at the deputies to leave him alone or to take him to the hospital for treatment of his earlier head wound, which was bleeding profusely. But the deputies stopped Nick from getting a ride with friends to a hospital and instead, "hog-tied and handcuffed [Nick] Dowey who was still bleeding from a head wound." The lawsuit also charged that a deputy maced Nick and inadvertently maced another deputy, who then took out a metal flashlight and struck Nick three times. Deputy Rodarte was exonerated of wrongdoing and the victim's parents lost their federal lawsuit against him and his former partner, Deputy Darin Yanover. But Deputy Rodarte was fired after the incident for lying about hitting Nicholas with a can of pepper spray. Nicholas' father, James Dowey, said, "If this wasn't a case of excessive force, I don't know what is."
Source: Los Angeles Times, 10/3/98, 6/17/99 & 6/24/99

Stephan Ream   47   —

September 4, 1997. Mar Vista:
Police went to investigate reports of a stolen motor home parked in a residential neighborhood. When they opened the door, the occupant allegedly fired on them. The SWAT team was called in to flush out the occupant. The neighborhood was evacuated. Helicopters hovered. Streets were blockaded. A nearby school kept the children inside. SWAT teams went door-to-door with rifles. Officers alleged that when they opened the door of the motor home, a wild gunfight erupted. Then there was a two-hour standoff that ended when officers threw four tear gas canisters into the motor home. They entered the vehicle to find the occupant dead and claimed not to know if he had killed himself or had been shot by them.
Source: Los Angeles Times, 9/9/97

Ebon Leggs   26   —

September 3, 1997. Artesia:
A sheriff's deputy pulled Leggs over for a traffic stop. Leggs allegedly opened fire on the officer and then barricaded himself inside a building. The SWAT team was called and "persuaded" Leggs to come out. Cops claim he emerged holding a gun. When he allegedly pointed it at officers, he was shot and killed. **Source:** Los Angeles Times, 9/4/98

Patricia Kay Gonzales   54   —

August 25, 1997. Pasadena :
Gonzales allegedly fired into the law offices of her former boss. When she reportedly refused police orders to put down her gun, she was shot five times and killed. Police claim that the fatal wound came when she turned her gun on herself. **Source:** Los Angeles Times, 8/30/97

Unidentified Man   60   —

August 23, 1997. Paramount:
A man acting "irrationally" and supposedly carrying a butcher knife down a major thoroughfare was shot killed by a sheriff's deputy when he turned toward the deputy after allegedly slashing at an unarmed community service officer (community police). **Source:** Los Angeles Times, 8/24/97

Alfieri Shinaia   23   —

August 3, 1997. Bell Gardens:
An officer serving a search warrant arrived at Shinaia's home at 5 a.m. and found him in the yard. Shinaia supposedly refused an order to raise his hands. The officer then shot him several times and killed him. **Source:** Los Angeles Times, 8/5/97

Michael Allen Lambert   32   —

July 27, 1997. Temple City:
When sheriffs responded to a domestic disturbance call, Michael's wife was outside while her husband was inside in with his three children. The SWAT team was called and three deputies surrounded the windows of the living room. When Michael, allegedly holding a knife, turned on a deputy, two others shot him several times and killed him in front of his three screaming children. **Source:** Los Angeles Times, 7/29/97

Terry James Parker   —   —

July 23, 1997. Granada Hills:
According to police reports, police tried to pull over Terry for speeding. Terry did not stop. He drove home and ran inside. He opened the door and shot at the cops, hitting one of them (Casillas). He then fled his house and stopped to buy cigarettes and then hid near a tennis court. According to the police, they approached the bushes where he was hiding and heard a shot. The three cops immediately began firing at him. The cops say that Terry shot himself in the mouth and then they shot him right afterward multiple times. One of Officer Casillas' friends said that, "As long as he [Terry] is dead, I don't really care how he got that way." Terry's father had said earlier that his son thought the police had a conspiracy against him.

Unidentified Man   23   —

July 16, 1997. Los Angeles:
Police responded to a call about a man who had reportedly fired a gun inside a house. No one had been hit. When officers arrived, he came out the front gate. Claiming he pointed a gun at them, officers shot and killed him. **Source:** Los Angeles Times, 7/17/97

Unidentified Man   —   —

July 5, 1997. Los Angeles:
Police responded to a domestic disturbance call and allegedly found a man choking a woman. When ordered to move away from her, the man drove away. A pursuit followed. Police fired 20 or 30 shots into the van to stop it. The driver died at the scene. **Source:** Los Angeles Times, 7/5/97

Fernando Hernandez   28   *Mexican American (?)*

July 2, 1997. Azusa:

Mr. Hernandez was fighting with the mother of their children in front of the police station. The cops showed up and claim Mr. Hernandez charged at them with a knife. They shot him 17 times and killed him. His family questions whether he would have charged at the officers. His brother Danny said, "Either way, they could have backed off and brought in the Taser gun. They were in front of the police department." The three cops involved in the incident, Sgt. Andrew Sutcliff, Sgt. Frank Chavez, and Det. Stephen Hunt, were put on paid leave while the police investigated the case. Fernando is survived by three young children and his wife, Rosalinda Martinez. Police handcuffed, dragged and detained his wife for three hours, waiting a long time to tell her that Fernando was killed. Fernando's brother Danny described him as a gentle man who enjoyed playing with his three children. Rose Banuelos, Fernando's sister, said "It's not fair what they did, They should have never done this. This police said he had a weapon, but he never carried a knife." A number of eyewitnesses said that Fernando's hand was in his pocket but they never saw a knife or other weapon. **Source:** San Gabriel Valley Tribune, 7/3/97 & 9/19/97; Los Angeles Times, 7/3/97; Pasadena Star News, 7/3/97; Police Reports supplied by victim's family

---

Unidentified Man   —   —

June 27, 1997. Littlerock:

As a sheriff's deputy on a truck theft investigation spoke to a woman near a camper, a man allegedly approached pointing a shotgun at the deputy. The deputy grabbed the gun barrel, pointed it away from himself and then shot and killed the man. This was the second known killing by sheriff's deputies in this county in two days. The previous day, deputies had shot and killed Robert Paiz. **Source:** Los Angeles Times, 6/28/97

Robert Paiz   39   —

June 26, 1997. Rosemead:

Sheriff's deputies responded to a domestic disturbance call. Paiz had allegedly threatened his wife and child. When the wife and child were inside, deputies claim Paiz tried to grab a gun from the officer's holster. He was shot to death. **Source:** Los Angeles Times, 6/28/97

Unidentified   37   —

June 20, 1997. midtown Los Angeles:

Officers were called to an inpatient mental health facility in midtown LA. When they arrived, they were allegedly confronted by a hostile patient who allegedly tried to grab an officer's gun. Cops shot and killed him. **Source:** Los Angeles Times, 6/21/97

William Anthony Ramos   29   *Latino*

June 14, 1997. Ventura:

Eyewitnesses saw Ramos quietly talking to officers. Cops claim that Ramos suddenly lunged and tried to grab an officer's gun. Another officer arrived and shot him three times. After some time, Ramos was taken to a hospital where he died. Several eyewitnesses were unable to corroborate the police version of events. Many did not understand why the police shot a light-weight, unarmed man. **Source:** Los Angeles Times, 6/18/97

Daniel Collins   39   —

June 11, 1997. Pico Rivera:

Mr. Collins, distraught over an eviction notice, holed up inside his repair garage. The SWAT team was called and a 19-hour standoff ensued. Deputies threw in an exploding device in an attempt to scare him out. A gun battle erupted and Collins was killed. A hundred employees at nearby businesses were evacuated. Gunfire could be heard a block away. An 11-year old was terrified; this was the second such incident he had witnessed. Collins was described as a hard-working man who had his shop for 19 years. **Source:** Los Angeles Times, 6/12/97

Johnny Armendariz	18	*Latino*
James Martínez	21	*Latino*

June 8, 1997. Corona:
Responding to a call of "a large party" at the Five Star Nurseries near Corona, Riverside Sheriff's Deputies said they saw two men firing a shotgun and a handgun. A young woman at the party said that Johnny and James "had a rifle and they shot it up into the air, but they did not fire a shot at the cops." Another person said that the two men did not fire and that the officers fired without warning. Both men were shot and killed by the cops. James was DJ-ing at the party. **Source:** San Francisco Chronicle, 6/9/97

Israel Chapa González	28	—

May 28, 1997. Glendale:
Searching for Mr. González, Glendale police checked a warehouse. Mr. González allegedly shot and killed an officer. In a dramatic rescue attempt captured by some TV crews, the dead officer was carried from the building on the hood of a black-and-white patrol car. The siege lasted another five hours, a night filled with the sounds of a helicopter, gunfire, tear gas bombs and flash bang grenades. It ended when LAPD SWAT officers stormed the building and found Mr. González dead. Police contend he shot himself. **Source:** Los Angeles Times, 5/30/97

Simón Velásquez	22	—

May 16, 1997. Panorama City:
Simon thought that he was being watched by "a lot of people," so he approached them to find out what was going on. The men he thought were watching him turned out to be two cops on a stakeout (for something else). The cops (Dana Adams and Joe Garcia) claim that Simon threatened them and lifted his shirt to show them the gun in his waistband. At this point, the cops identified themselves as being undercover officers. The cops say that he then began to withdraw his gun and they fired on him, killing him. Simon's family said that he was shot many times, including two or three times in the back while he was running away from the police. His cousin said, "They shouldn't have done this. They could have arrested him, but not killed him."

James Gibbs	31	—

April 27, 1997. Hawthorne:
A simmering neighborhood dispute started by a fight between two dogs led to tragedy as a two-year-old boy was wounded, allegedly by a neighborhood gunman. James Gibbs, the toddler's uncle, charged at the men who had wounded his nephew, waving a handgun. Police responding to a call about the fight shot him in the back of the head and killed him. Emanda Norman, James Gibbs' companion of 13 years, said that several family members had been enjoying the sunshine in the front yard when shots rang out from across the street, one hitting the two-year-old boy's arm. Ms. Norman said that James charged after the group of four shooters, waving his handgun. "He wasn't thinking — who was?" she said. But she also said that James did not need to be shot in the back of the head by police. Police say they confronted James and he fled. **Source:** Los Angeles Times (Home edition), 4/29/97

Dwight Stiggons	18	*Black*

April 26, 1997. West Covina:
According to police reports, the cops began to chase Dwight when they saw him jaywalking. When they cornered Dwight, they shot him in the back and killed him. The cops said they thought he was reaching for a gun. But the "gun" was a bible. He was killed at 9:30 a.m. on a Saturday morning. The police did not contact his family until 30 hours later.

Unidentified Youth	13	—

April 25, 1997. South Central:
While the cops were questioning someone they had stopped for a traffic violation, they claim they saw a youth leave a liquor store with a gun sticking out of his pants. Police claim the youth ran for a block and pulled out the pistol after falling on the sidewalk. When Officer Eric Rodgers tried to take the gun away, the youth supposedly put the barrel of the gun to Rodgers' cheek. Officer Rodgers, claiming he feared for his life, shot the youth twice, killing him. **Source:** Los Angeles Times, 4/27/97

Unidentified Man	20+	—

April 8, 1997. Los Angeles:

A motorist being pursued by police lost control of his vehicle and crashed into a light pole. Officers shot him dead, claiming he exited his car and pointed an assault rifle at them. **Source:** Los Angeles Times, 4/10/97

Unidentified Male	—	—

April 5, 1997. Los Angeles:

Officers were investigating serial numbers on camera equipment two men wanted to sell to a shop. Police claim that one of the men drew a large caliber pistol and a struggle ensued. The officer fired one shot and killed one man; the other man fled. **Source:** Los Angeles Times, 4/7/97

Richard Boyd	32	—

April 4, 1997. Los Angeles National Forest:

Deputies stopped to check a car parked on the side of the road. Police claim that when they approached, a man pointed what looked like a large, silver pistol at them. Both deputies opened fire on and killed Boyd. The pistol was a replica. **Source:** Los Angeles Times, 4/6/97

Unidentified Male	—	—

March 28, 1997. Los Angeles:

Officers followed a car that allegedly ran a red light. When it stopped, they attempted to remove the driver. According to police, the driver slammed the door on the officer's arm and drove off dragging him alongside the car. Claiming he feared for his partner's life, the other officer shot and killed the driver. **Source:** Los Angeles Times, 3/29/97

Gregory Brandon	34	—

March 22, 1997. Los Angeles:

Sheriff's deputies spotted Brandon running through a mall with something under his jacket. They told him to raise his hands, which he did. Deputies saw an object in his hand and claim they thought he was pointing a gun, so they began shooting him. They continued to fire until he fell. The object in his hand was a cash box. **Source:** Los Angeles Times, 3/23/97

Todd Tetrick	35	—

March 8, 1997. Lancaster:

Sheriffs responding to a call about a domestic dispute forced their way into a motel room, where they allegedly found Tetrick stabbing a woman. Claiming he did not obey their commands to drop the knife, they shot and killed him. The woman was taken to a hospital. She was treated for her wounds and released. **Source:** Los Angeles Times, 3/9/97

Emil Matasareanu	—	—
Larry Eugene Phillips	—	—

February 28, 1997. North Hollywood:

Emil and Larry were armed and robbing a bank and when LA police surrounded them, a gun battle erupted. More than 1500 rounds were fired. Both men were shot and killed. Emil took 29 shots. An attorney for Emil's family filed a lawsuit that maintained that cops deliberately allowed him to bleed to death on the ground from a leg wound in which no large blood vessels were injured. **Source:** CNN website, 4/12/97

Unidentified Male	—	—

February 27, 1997. Mar Vista:

An LAPD officer pulled a transient riding a bicycle over for a traffic violation. The officer claims the man became belligerent and lunged at him with a small knife, at which point the cop shot and killed him.

Kim Benton	20s	—
Kirk Deffenbaugh	20s	—
Eric Fields	20s	—

February 25, 1997. Northridge:

Officers from LAPD's Special Investigations Section (SIS) opened fire on a car and killed three of four robbery suspects they chased into a Northridge neighborhood. They were suspects in the armed holdup of about 20 patrons in a nearby blues bar. SIS has been the cause of a number of deaths. "Even though department policy generally prohibits shooting from or at a moving vehicle, I find this instance an exception," said Los Angeles Police Chief Parks. In May 1998 the LA police commission and chief of police concluded that the officers had acted "in policy." SIS had been surveilling the four alleged robbers for about a month and had watched them commit the robbery without intervening and then chased them, resulting in the deaths of the three. Critics have accused SIS of carrying out surveillance operations as an excuse to confront — and often kill — people suspected of serial crimes. They also charge that the practice jeopardizes innocent bystanders. In this case, one such bystander was shot and badly wounded by police who mistook him for the fourth suspect who got away. **Source:** Los Angeles Times, 2/27/98 & 5/6/98

Antonio Golden	18	—

February 19, 1997. Lynwood:

Antonio was on his way home in the evening with some friends when sheriff's deputies approached and started questioning the group. Antonio tried to ride away on his bike but the deputies followed him in a patrol car. The deputies struck Antonio with their car and then shot him in the back and thigh, killing him. **Source:** Los Angeles Times, 2/22/97

Juan Hugo Gonzales	—	*Latino*

February 11, 1997. Anaheim:

Corona police were questioning Gonzales in the parking lot of the warehouse where he had been employed for more than six years. Claiming that he pulled a gun on them, the two plainclothes officers shot and killed him. **Source:** Los Angeles Times, 2/13/97

Juan Ramírez	35	*Latino*

February 8, 1997. El Monte:

Police allege that when officers responded to a domestic dispute call, Mr. Ramírez emerged from the house and knocked an officer to the ground with a billy club. Claiming that Mr. Ramírez kept advancing, the second officer shot him numerous times in the upper body and killed him. **Source:** Los Angeles Times, 2/9/97

Hector Martin Islas	—	—	👁

January 29, 1997. Riverside:

Mr. Islas was chased by Riverside police for unknown reasons. Police kicked, stomped, and brutally beat him to death. The victim's face was bashed so severely that both jaws were broken and his teeth were knocked out. Cops claimed they were simply trying to restrain him. **Source:** victim's family

Jack Sexton	26	—

January 26, 1997. Port Hueneme:

Jackie, who had been drinking heavily at a Super Bowl party, drove his car into a ditch. Intoxicated, he wandered around the neighborhood knocking on doors to ask for help. He wandered into one house and was confronted by an off-duty sheriff. The sheriff became abusive and shot him once in the back. Jackie stumbled out of the house and collapsed and died in the driveway.

Eduardo Ramírez	24	*Latino*

January 24, 1997. Buena Park:

Eduardo's mother called police to help her disarm her severely depressed son. When Eduardo allegedly failed to obey commands to drop a kitchen knife, they shot him 10 or 12 times and killed him. Eduardo was on medication for depression and anxiety. **Source:** Orange County Register, 1/30/97

Thomas Ochoa   33   *Latino*

January 22, 1997. Riverside:

An epileptic, Thomas had fallen asleep on the street. A cop came and called for backup. Cops said he had a knife and came at them. Thomas was shot three or four times and killed.

Jarred Joe Arnett   19   —

January 14, 1997. Garden Grove:

Arnett, pursued at high speeds by police, crashed into a light pole. He exited the vehicle and fled to a nearby mobile home. Police followed him and opened up with a barrage of gunfire that killed Arnett and left a dozen bullet holes. **Source:** Los Angeles Times, 1/16/97

Larry Pankey   36   —

January 13, 1997. Oxnard:

The Oxnard SWAT team responded to a call about a domestic dispute. A four-hour standoff ended when a team marksman mistook shots fired by his fellow officers for shots from Pankey. The marksman shot and killed Pankey, who was standing unarmed on his front lawn. In a conversation with a police negotiator just before the shooting, Pankey had said he was unarmed and that his unloaded rifles were in the garage. He wanted the SWAT team to leave because he believed that he had not done anything wrong. In one of his last statements, Pankey said, "My rights are I can defend my property, and nobody can come on my property that I don't want on my property. Now that's the law. I have not pointed a gun at nobody or nothing else." **Source:** Los Angeles Times, 3/15/97

Roger Marito   30   *Latino*

January 13, 1997. West Hollywood:

Officers were called to a vintage car dealership about a "suspicious" person. Police tried to calm him by yelling orders, using pepper-spray and hitting him with a baton. (What do cops do when they want to upset someone?) When Marito pulled a silver pen from his pocket, deputies said they thought it was a gun, so they shot and killed him. **Source:** Los Angeles Times, 1/15/97

William Ramos   29   —

Spring, 1997. Ventura:

Ramos, mentally ill, was shot and killed by a Ventura police officer.

Darryl Hawkins   26   —

1997. Gardena:

Darryl, a security guard, was shot to death after police tried to stop him for allegedly speeding and having an expired registration. Officers Zachary Hutchings and Ronald K. Moy claim that Darryl aimed an AK-47 at them. Attorneys for Darryl's family said he was in possession of the rifle but that it was in the trunk of his car. A court ruled the cops used justifiable force in the shooting death. **Source:** Los Angeles Times, 3/5/99

Marco Marangoni   29   —

December 31, 1996. Ventura County:

Ventura County sheriff's deputies responded to complaints about a man acting and speaking incoherently. Deputies say they used pepper-spray in an effort to restrain Mr. Marangoni, who weighed more than 300 pounds and was allegedly high on marijuana. He died in custody. The coroner ruled that the cause of death was "cardiac arrhythmia due to asphyxia during prone restraint" and did not list pepper-spray as a factor. **Source:** Los Angeles Times, 4/30/98

Abraham Camarena	14	—	
Claudia Quiñonez	16	—	
Lizett Quiñonez	22	—	

December 24, 1996. Anaheim:

Lizett, Claudia, and Abraham were killed when their car was hit by a driver fleeing Cypress police in a high-speed chase. The driver of the car being chased allegedly ran a red light in Anaheim and crashed into the victims' car, killing all the occupants. In June, 1998, the driver was found guilty of murder and faces up to 120 years in prison. **Source:** Los Angeles Times, 6/3/98

Angela Chimienti	19	—	
Serafina Chimienti	25	—	

December 24, 1996. Chatsworth:

On Christmas Eve, former LA County Sheriff's Deputy Edward Vizcarra, 31, went to his estranged girlfriend's parents' house. Neighbors believed that Angela and Vizcarra got in an argument and Serafina interceded. Vizcarra shot and killed the two sisters and then himself. Angela had just graduated from a school where she completed a medical assistant course. The two sisters were daughters of Saverio Chimienti, a high fashion tailor in Beverly Hills.

Henry Sanchez	35	*Chicano*	👁

October 19, 1996. Bell Gardens:

Henry Sanchez, a 35-year-old Chicano man, was riding his bicycle near his home in Bell Gardens, Calif. when he encountered two cops from an anti-gang unit. The police began beating Henry and other cops on backup came in to prevent bystanders from interceding. Witnesses said that police beat Henry with flashlights and jumped on his head. By the time they were through, Henry Sanchez lay dead on the streets. The police did not immediately release any reason for either stopping or beating Henry Sanchez. Henry Sanchez was a well-liked man in the neighborhood who had a young daughter. Local residents organized a series of marches and protests. At one march following his funeral, police waited until TV crews left the scene and then charged the crowd, clubbing and macing. Carlos de la Cruz, whose nephew Richard Beatty was also killed by police, was at the demonstration: "I was just shocked that there are police like that. It tells you how disrespectful they are towards minorities, waiting there with riot gear all ready. They were the ones who started a riot. We were all peaceful. It shows you how disrespectful they are to the community there... They just treated everybody like animals and they started beating on everybody."

Luther Thomas Allen	55	—	

October 1, 1996. Oxnard:

Luther was arrested after a traffic accident on suspicion of driving under the influence. He complained of injuries but police claim he refused medical treatment by paramedics and did not show any external signs of injury. He was taken to the police station and placed in a cell. Two hours after his arrest, he became unconscious and died in custody. The coroner and police state that Luther died of internal injuries suffered during the accident. But if this was true, why would he have refused medical attention? His wife has filed a civil suit against the city for violations of his civil rights and received a $325,000 settlement. Mr. Allen's lawyer, Samuel Paz, believes that he did not need to die. **Source:** Los Angeles Times, 1/27/98

Theodore Franks	77	—	

September 11, 1996. Huntington Beach:

Police investigating a burglary call in an office building stumbled upon the unarmed Mr. Franks and shot him at point blank range in the leg. It took more than two hours to get him to a hospital and he bled to death. Franks often stayed in the office overnight to avoid a long commute. He was wearing his pajamas. Officials called it an "unfortunate incident." Family members were outraged at the findings of a five-month investigation by the DA and Sheriff which found no wrongdoing by police. **Source:** Los Angeles Times, 2/28/97

Fernando Herrera, Jr.   25   *Latino*

July 18, 1996. Oxnard:

Fernando died of asphyxiation because six cops sat on his back while he was handcuffed. His family has filed a civil suit against the city.

Raúl Madera   23   *Latino*

July 9, 1996. Ventura County jail:

Raúl died of septic shock due to tonsillitis while he was held in the Ventura County jail. The jail stated that he was treated by various medical personnel in the weeks before his death. His family filed a civil lawsuit against the city. His lawyer, Samuel Paz, said, "In this day and age, nobody should die of tonsillitis."

Joseph "Gangster" Sánchez   15   —

June 21, 1996. Los Angeles:

"Gangster" was riding in a car with friends in Pico-Union when someone on the street in back of them opened fire on their car. It was only after his friends drove him to the hospital in an unsuccessful attempt to save his life that they found that he had been shot and killed by cops from the CRASH unit.

Hong Byong Chul   40   *Korean*

May 10, 1996. Los Angeles:

"You killed him," shouted an onlooker to the L.A.P.D. cops. Hong Byong Chul had been making a lot of noise at a downtown L.A. corner, banging on signs, yelling, running into the street. When the cops arrived, they swarmed him and one cop put his knee on his neck for four to five minutes. The police later said he died of "natural causes."

Ray Lee Carter   42   —

May 1996. Oxnard:

Police allege that Mr. Carter was high on cocaine when they attempted to restrain him. They hog-tied and pepper-sprayed him and realized he had stopped breathing. Paramedics were not able to revive him. Authorities said Mr. Carter, "brought this on himself." The family says Carter did not use drugs and that police lied about the circumstances of his death. His family filed a wrongful death lawsuit. **Source:** Los Angeles Times, 4/30/98

Sebastián Ramírez   19   *Latino*   👁

March 22, 1996. East L.A.:

Sebastián was crossing the street coming home when plainclothes cops chasing a youth ran into Sebastián. Sebastián had his arms up, but the cops shot him 14 or 15 times without warning, killing him.

Jaime Jaurequí   23   *Latino*   👁

March 9, 1996. Northridge:

After chasing Jaime's car, five police officers shot 36 bullets into the vehicle. Jaime was killed. He was unarmed.

Hong Il Kim   27   *Korean*   👁

February 14, 1996. Orange:

Hong Il Kim lived and attended school in Orange County for several years before returning to his native Korea on business. He was visiting his family when he was pursued by police, ending in the fatal shooting in a parking lot in the City of Orange. His death caused protests from Korean organizations and others. Banners protesting the killing were posted in shopping centers in LA's Koreatown. His mother has kept a large color portrait surrounded by beautiful flowers as a memorial for him in the family living room.

Richard Beaty, Jr.   21   *Mexican American*   👁

February 9, 1996. Montebello:

Richard was shot and killed by police in Montebello, where he was visiting his aunt for her birthday. He was unarmed.

Ivan Ortiz	27	—

February 1, 1996. Los Angeles:

People from the Ramona Gardens projects in East L.A. reacted with rocks and bottles when the L.A.P.D. gunned down Ortiz. Police from a special "anti-gang" unit, one of many squads that occupy the projects, later admitted they stopped him near his house because he was a "known gang member" and they were going to do a "field interrogation." Moments later, Ivan was on the ground, his body riddled with bullets. He was killed.

Keith Dapheney	20	*Black*

1996. Los Angeles:

An off-duty cop saw a gun in Keith's waistband and pulled his gun. Keith ran and the off-duty cop shot Keith once. Some on-duty cops showed up and shot Keith multiple times, killing him. Keith never pulled out his gun.

Tony Gutiérrez	14	*Latino*

July 29, 1995. Los Angeles:

Tony was shot in the back and killed by L.A.P.D. officer Michael Falvo (one of 44 problem officers cited by the Christopher Commission). Officer Falvo claimed he saw Tony point a semiautomatic weapon at him. A semiautomatic weapon was found 15 feet away from Gutiérrez on the other size of a fence. Various witnesses have come forth to state that Tony Gutiérrez was unarmed when he was shot. Criminal investigation pending.

Jesús Vargas Trejo	25	*Mexican*

July 12, 1995. Los Angeles:

Jesús was talking to friends outside his home when LA. County Sheriffs drove up. Jesús started to walk into his house when the cops ran after him. They said later that he "fit the description" of a shooting suspect and they thought he had a gun. Then they said that he went for one of the cops' guns. But his girlfriend and an eyewitness told a different story. The cops shot him twice. The first time was in the doorway of his home. They then forced his girlfriend into the house and dragged Jesús outside, closing the door so she couldn't see anything. It was then that she heard a second shot. He was killed with a bullet to the chest. Her account agrees with the eyewitnesses, who said the police took him out, threw him on the ground and shot him in the chest. No action was taken against the deputies.

Unidentified	—	—

June 26, 1995. Los Angeles:

LA's notorious SIS (Special Investigations Section) shot and killed a suspected robber. The family's attorney, Stephen Yagman, claims the unit acted wrongly and that the city failed to control the unit. This is one of five such cases against the SIS. **Source:** Los Angeles Times, 1/8/98

Unidentifed	17	—

January 5, 1995. Riverside:

A student allegedly led officers on high speed chase to his high school. According to police, in front of dozens of parents and teachers at a PTA meeting, he pretended to draw a weapon. He was shot to death. **Source:** Associated Press, 4/25/98

Santiago López	17	*Latino*

1995. Los Angeles:

Santiago was shot and killed by L.A. county sheriff's deputies. Santiago had been playing basketball. He had a cigarette lighter that resembled a gun. The deputies arrived and shot Mr. López. After Mr. López fell to the ground, a deputy came up to Mr. López and fired two shots to his head. Santiago was unarmed. The district attorney did not file any criminal charges against the deputies.

Jennifer Lyn Clawson	20	—

December 16, 1994. Corona:

Jennifer was killed when her car was hit by a Corona Police Department vehicle. Her aunt said the family believes the officer was speeding recklessly through a residential area. They plan to push for manslaughter charges against the officer. **Source:** San Diego Union-Tribune, 12/19/94

Michael Fierro Arocha	27	—

August 4, 1994. El Sereno:

Police said they got a 911 call about a "man with a gun" and found Arocha walking out of a convenience store near his home in Lincoln Park. They said when they confronted him, he started to draw a gun from his waistband and they shot in self-defense. After they killed him they claimed that he was carrying a plastic toy gun. But witnesses dispute this, saying they couldn't see a gun on him.

John Huffman	29	—

June 16, 1994. Los Angeles:

Drunk, off-duty LA County Sheriff's Deputy Thomas Kirsch shot unarmed John Huffman to death following an argument in a bar. Deputy Kirsch was not charged with a crime or fired from his job. A jury awarded John's family a judgment of $750,000, which was thrown out by an appeals court. John Huffman's father Gerald, said "If we can stop one family from going through what we went through, it would be worth it." **Source:** Los Angeles Times, 12/15/96 & 6/24/98

Charlie Mulford	25	—

June 10, 1994. Anaheim:

Anaheim police officers responded to a call about a burglary at an apartment complex. When they were confronted by Charlie, who was mentally ill and was allegedly threatening them with a metal bar, they shot and killed him. Charlie's mother said her son was not dangerous. **Source:** The Orange County Register, 1/23/97

Juan Penilla	40s	—

May 15, 1994. Huntington Park:

Penilla, a former armed forces medic, was found by neighbors passed out and irregularly breathing. A teenager called 911 and asked for paramedics. Instead, the dispatcher sent two cops, Officers Joseph Settles and Ioane Tua. They dragged Penilla to the house. Then they broke into the front door and left him inside. The cops locked the door behind them. Family members entered the house the next day and found Penilla on the floor, dead of respiratory failure. Doctors said he could have been saved. **Source:** The Sacramento Bee (AP), 6/1/98

John Wighley	—	—

March 1994. (in custody):

John was beaten to death while in custody by L.A. Sheriff's Deputies. This murder was witnessed by a female deputy named Janina who reported the murder to authorities. Janina then herself became a victim of sexual harassment by the male deputies. Janina had also witnessed a previous killing but was too afraid to report it. Although one of the deputies resigned, none of them were charged, dismissed or punished in any way. **Source:** SLP form

Miguel Ruíz	—	Latino

1994. Los Angeles:

Miguel was shot and killed by L.A. County sheriff's deputies. He was shot point blank within one foot of the guns of the deputies, who had responded to a 911 call that a person was brandishing a gun. Mr. Ruíz was in his home, watching television. The door was locked when the deputies kicked in the door. The deputies claimed they saw a gun pointed at them. The deputies fired two rounds at Mr. Ruíz. According to his wife, who was sitting next to Mr. Ruíz, he did not have any weapon in his hands. [Mr. Ruíz did have a weapon in his rear waistband]. The breaking down of the door was in violation of L.A. County Sheriff's regulations. The district attorney did not file any criminal charges, claiming the wife lacked credibility.

José Ricardo Campa-Frías   —   *Latino*

1994. Los Angeles:

Mr. Campa-Frías was shot and killed by City of Torrance police officers, who responded to a 911 call reporting gunfire at the home Mr. Campa-Frías shared with friends. The police entered the home and shot to death Mr. Campa-Frías, who cops claimed was armed, without giving a warning before shooting. Claiming the officer acted in self-defense, the D.A. did not file criminal charges.

Sonji Taylor   27   *African American*

December 16, 1993. Los Angeles:

On the last evening on her life, cops from L.A.P.D. Rampart Division cornered Sonji Taylor on the roof of St. Vincent Medical Center in Pico-Union, where she had parked her car to go Christmas shopping. The cops claimed she was holding her three-year-old son hostage with a kitchen knife while repeating "the blood of Jesus." They claimed they charged her, sprayed her with pepper-spray and took her son. She then "lunged" at them, they claimed and they shot her in self defense. Sonji Taylor had done everything a Black person is supposed to do to "make it" in the U.S. She finished high school where she was a cheerleader and homecoming queen, graduated from college, sang in the church choir and was getting ready to start a new job. Her family pointed out several lies in the police version of her death: She was surrounded for half an hour before she was killed and she never harmed her son, whom she loved. "The blood of Jesus" is a phrase from her Pentecostal upbringing that she repeated when she was in danger. The knife was a Christmas present. An autopsy later found that she had been shot twice in the chest and seven times in the back. Some of the bullets had mushroomed, showing that she had been shot lying on her face. Despite these police lies, a report written by Deputy D.A. Christopher Darden, later one of the prosecutors of O.J. Simpson, said the police should not be prosecuted because Sonji Taylor may have "twisted around" as the police unleashed their fatal gunfire.

Preston Green   25   *African American*   👁

October 26, 1993. Lynwood:

Sheriff's Deputies Todd Kocisco and Thomas Davoran shot Mr. Green in the back and killed him. The officers fired 18 shots, hitting the victim 11 times in the head, torso and legs. Witnesses said the two officers reloaded their weapons and continued firing. Mr. Green was complying with the officers' orders and had his back toward them when he was killed. While the Sheriff's Department was investigating the crime scene, Mr. Green was still lying on the ground in need of medical attention. He died nine hours later at the hospital. As of June, 1999 — more than five years later — the victim's family has not been notified by the Sheriff's Department of his death. **Source:** statement from victim's family

---

Ricky Nickerson   15   —

June 26, 1993. Los Angeles:

Ricky was leaving an outdoor rap concert with friends when their car was surrounded by sheriff's deputies. People in the area said that these cops told the youth "drop your weapons" and then opened fire. Ricky was killed and another youth, identified as 10-years-old, was wounded.

Richard Coleman   35   —

May 1993. Hollywood:

The cops claim they spotted Richard banging his head against the pavement. They hog-tied him and when paramedics arrived, he was strapped face down on a gurney. Richard went into cardiac arrest on the way to the hospital. The LAPD, Fire Department and district attorney found that there was no wrongdoing by the officers or paramedics even though the coroner ruled Richard's death a homicide. Two and a half years later, the LA City Council decided to award his family $500,000.

Justice Hasan Netherly	47	African American

April 25, 1993. Los Angeles:

Mr. Netherly was a single father of five children. He spent the evening at a Muslim mosque and got into an argument with his brother when he got home. He called 911 when his brother wouldn't leave. Police claimed that they fired in fear of their lives when Netherly walked out of the door carrying a large stick that looked like an axe. He was killed. A witness said the cops drove onto the lawn and started firing from 25 feet away. "They got out of the police car and never said anything," said the witness. A three-foot stick was later found on the ground near Mr. Netherly's body.

Darrell Harts	—	—

April 5, 1993. Los Angeles (South Central):

Darrell was shot to death in front of his house in South Central Los Angeles. The cops said Darrell shot his neighbor's dog, which he had threatened to do before. They claim after they were called, he pointed a gun at them and they fired in self-defense. A gun was found under Darrell's body. An eyewitness who spoke to a reporter from the LA. Times said Darrell was unarmed and fleeing from the police who chased him down and shot him. The gun he used as a security guard was later taken from the trunk of his nearby car and placed under his body. The dog owner said that she didn't tell the cops about the threats to her dog until after the shooting and added, "My husband reminded me to say that Darrell shot the dog." Animal Control officers noted on their report that the dog was shot by the L.A.P.D. A high school football player, Darrell Harts was known as the only person within blocks of his South Central home who had finished college. He had a history of working with the police as a security guard and had applied to become a Compton cop. He was a key witness in a police brutality case which was about to come to trial.

Michael Bryant	37	African American

March 9, 1993. Los Angeles:

Michael Bryant was a barber and a political and community activist in Northwest Pasadena. One of his former customers was Rodney King. Cheryl Hubbard, a long time friend, recalled how Michael would help give free haircuts to 200 kids the week before the start of school. He was also a member of the Black Freedom Fighters, who work to teach children about Black and African History. The day after his death, 60 people gathered at his barber shop to remember him. There were no witnesses to his death but the police claimed that Bryant was pursued in his car by police from San Marino, an upper class community near Pasadena. The L.A.P.D. joined the chase. According to police, Michael Bryant left his car and ran into an apartment complex, jumping in the pool to avoid officers. L.A.P.D. officers shot with a Taser gun when he was standing in a swimming pool, then hog-tied him and left him lying on his stomach. He was put in the back of a police car, still on his stomach and died on the way to jail. An autopsy showed that he died of asphyxiation as a direct result of the police practice of hog-tying. The L.A. Times found three other cases in L.A. of deaths from hog-tying in the year after Michael Bryant was killed.

Lorenzo Monzalvo	—	Latino

1993. Los Angeles:

Mr. Monzalvo had been stabbed by an unknown individual. When the police arrived, Mr. Monzalvo was standing by himself and holding his stomach area. The police claim they saw a weapon. The police shot Mr. Monzalvo four times, once in the back, killing him. Mr. Monzalvo was unarmed. There was no criminal prosecution of the police officers.

José Manuel Sánchez	15	Mexican	⊛

November 30, 1992. Los Angeles:

On a Monday evening a group of youth was hanging out in the front yard of an apartment building in Athens, an area of South Central L.A. four miles west of Watts. Some of the teenagers found a .22 pistol and fired it into the air a few times. Two L.A. County sheriff's deputies who were cruising nearby pulled up in front of the apartment house and opened fire on this group of youth. Fifteen-year-old José Sánchez was killed. A 17-year-old was hit by a bullet, tried to run and was shot five more times while he was on the ground. Almost all of their wounds were in the back. José was the son of a Mexican immigrant couple, the youngest in the family of 10 children. The police later prevented his mother from finding out the truth of his killing by destroying the clothing he was wearing when he was killed. The cops said they shot him only once, but someone who handled the body said that there were three bullet holes in his clothes. The deputies who killed him were back on the street and the youth in the neighborhood said the police were harassing them more than ever.

Efraín López   18   *Latino*

November 9, 1992. Los Angeles:

"Nine times for a broom!" was the angry reaction of two young Black women in Pacoima to the killing of this 18-year-old Latino youth. Efraín was distraught, running around the streets at 1 a.m. dressed only in his underwear and swinging a broom. Two cops from the L.A.P.D.'s Foothill Division arrived and shot Efrain nine times in the chest. They claimed the broom was a "deadly weapon." They were there only 30 seconds before they opened fire. Witnesses said Efraín López swung his broom once and the cops killed him.

Butres Samaan   —   —

November 1992. San Bernardino:

A Federal Appeals Court in San Francisco decided that San Bernardino police officers were justified when they shot and killed shopkeeper Butres Samaan and kicked another man, even though they were at the wrong address. Officer Michael Blechinger got a radio call about a burglar alarm at a store. The dispatcher gave the right address but the store had moved and Officer Blechinger went to the old location, thinking he knew better. Butres Samaan, the owner's brother, had been given a gun by his brother to protect him from robberies. While his brother went out the back door with the day's receipts, Butres Samaan went out the front and encountered Officer Blechinger. The cop allegedly ordered Mr. Samaan to drop the gun, then killed him in the ensuing "gun battle." Officer Blechinger claims to have identified himself as a policeman. Later, the court overturned a verdict of $34,000 for damages awarded by a jury to Mohammed Alfaorr, who had been kicked by another officer at the scene. That officer claims he mistook Mr. Alfaorr for an armed robbery suspect when he tried to rise from the floor. **Source:** Los Angeles Times, 3/24/99; Associated Press, 3/23/99

Donald P. Scott   61   *white*

October 2, 1992. Ventura County:

L.A. County Sheriffs used an illegal search warrant for marijuana plants to lead to a raid on the ranch of Donald Scott, a 61-year-old white millionaire. Scott was awakened by cops crashing into his home. He walked out of his bedroom with a revolver, but raised his hands when he saw it was the police. As his wife begged, "Don't shoot him," the cops ordered him to lower his hands. Then they opened fire and killed him, saying he "pointed the gun" at them. No marijuana plants were found.

John Daniels, Jr.   —   *African American*

July 1, 1992. Los Angeles:

A tow truck driver, John Daniels Jr., was stopped at a gas station by two motorcycle cops. The cops refused to say why they were stopping him and he started to drive away. Officer Douglas Iverson ran beside the truck and shot Daniels once in the neck, killing him. The death of John Daniels Jr. was devastating for his family. In 1985, his father, John Daniels Sr., was killed by the L.A.P.D. As a Neighborhood Watch block captain, he had called police to report a man with a gun. The cops showed up and killed the first Black man they saw. The killing of John Daniels Jr. was protested by many, including the African American Tow Truck Drivers Association. Police later admitted that they had organized a task force to harass independent tow-truck drivers. A year after the shooting, officer Douglas Iverson was charged with murder. After two trials ending in hung juries, the judge dismissed all charges.

Kenny Moore   16   *African American*

June 25, 1992. Los Angeles:

The L.A.P.D. said he was stopped driving a stolen car and he pointed a gun at them. Witnesses said the cops rammed Kenny's car and he got out. His shirt was unbuttoned and he was clearly unarmed. One of the cops dropped to his knee and fired several shots. When Kenny went down, the cops shot him twice more in the back. He was killed.

De Andre Harrison   17   —

April 29, 1992. Los Angeles:
Official statistics say that 55 people were killed in the LA. Rebellion. In Nickersons Gardens in Watts, there was a fierce gun battle when residents defended themselves against the L.A.P.D. At least three people were killed in the Nickersons that night, among them 17-year-old De Andre Harrison. There has never been an official explanation of De Andre's death. Some say he was standing with a group of friends when they were ambushed by the police. There were other reports from that night of SWAT-type cops with high-powered rifles who were shooting people in the area. At the time, people heard many stories from others about police "kill squads" — cops dressed "like red necks," as one Black man put it, in civilian clothes and unmarked cars.

Emiliano Camacho   —   *Latino*

1992. Los Angeles:
Mr. Camacho was shot and killed by L.A. County Sheriff's deputies. His daughter called 911 to reporting that her parents were arguing. Deputies responded to a routine family disturbance call. Two deputies arrived at the Camacho residence and positioned themselves in front of the door of the apartment with their guns drawn. As Mr. Camacho, who was unarmed, opened the front door, he was shot in the chest by a deputy. The gun shot residue indicates that the deputy was less than five feet from Mr. Camacho when he shot him. The deputy reportedly had his finger on the trigger even before Camacho came to the door. Mr. Camacho was unarmed. There was no criminal prosecution of the deputy.

Henry Peco III   27   *Black*

November 29, 1991. Watts:
Henry tried to dodge gang members who turned out to be the LAPD. More than 43 shots were fired. Henry was left to bleed to death for five hours. No weapon was found on him.

Joseph Ornelas   25   *Latino*

October 14, 1991. Montebello:
Joseph was said to be acting crazy when he stole a broom from a store, ran past deputies and tried to hijack a truck. He was beaten and choked to death.

Steve Clemons   28   *Black*

September 2, 1991. Willowbrook (LA County):
Steve was at a Labor Day picnic with his wife and four children. He was shot as he ran from a deputy. He was left to bleed to death.

Darryl A. Stephens   27   *Black*

September 2, 1991. West Covina:
A SWAT team burst into Darryl's apartment to search for evidence in a murder case (he was not a suspect). They shot him 28 times in the back, killing him.

Keith Hamilton   33   *Black*

August 13, 1991. Ladera Heights:
Keith was kicked, beaten and tased by deputies, Keith was shot nine times as he lay face down. He was killed after being hog-tied and left to bleed on the ground.

David Ortiz   15   *Latino*

August 28, 1991. Los Angeles:

David was shot by a L.A. County Sheriff's deputy. In the early morning, around 1 a.m., two deputy sheriffs saw youths in a vehicle in a Jack in the Box. The deputies claimed they thought the car was stolen and they stopped the two youths. The deputies exited their vehicles with their guns drawn and fired several shots at the car of the two youths. The youths took off in their car and they were chased for a few miles. The youths drove up to a house belonging to one of them. David then ran out of the vehicle. He was shot in the back of the neck and killed. Another shot hit David, who was unarmed, in the waist. There was no criminal prosecution of the deputy sheriff.

Arturo Jimenez   19   *Latino*

August 3, 1991. Los Angeles:

Arturo was shot and killed by L.A. County Sheriff's deputies. There was a house party attended by young people. A sheriff's police vehicle, out of its jurisdiction, arrived in front of the area of the house and observed several youths. The deputy claimed one youth threw a bottle at the police vehicle. One of the deputies starting hitting one of the youths [not Arturo]. This same deputy claimed Arturo began hitting his partner and he fired three or four shots at Jimenez. One bullet entered Jimenez in the back, another in the front, another in the side. Arturo Jimenez was unarmed. There was no criminal prosecution of the officers.

Italia Tualaulelei   22   *Samoan*
Pouvi Tualaulelei   34   *Samoan*

February 12, 1991. Compton:

Italia was shot eight times and killed by a Compton cop who was responding to a domestic call. Pouvi was shot 12 times and killed by the same cop. They were kneeling and most shots went into their backs, but the cop claimed he shot them in self-defense.

Nicolas Contreras   26   *Latino*

January 1, 1991. South Central:

Nicolas was shot and killed by the LAPD because he was firing a pistol into the air on New Year's. He was tossing the pistol away when the cops started shooting him.

Pedro Castaneda   28   *Mexican*

January 1, 1991. El Monte (LA County):

Pedro was celebrating New Year's by firing a small caliber pistol into the air. He dropped the pistol when a man with a flashlight approached. He was shot five times and killed without warning by a deputy.

Tracy Mayberry   31   *Black*

November 3, 1990. Hollywood:

Tracy was kicked and beaten by LAPD. He was hit more than 60 times with batons and died at the feet of four officers. The coroner called it a drug overdose.

Frankie Taffolla   35   —

August 16, 1990. Santa Ana:

Cops responded to a 911 call of a man (Frankie) yelling and jumping around in people's backyards. Witnesses say Frankie was crying for help and screaming that someone was going to shoot him. The cops say that Frankie did not respond to their requests to calm down, so they unleashed a police dog on him. He died three hours later in police custody. The cops and county coroner said that he died from respiratory failure as a result of a drug overdose. The family took his case to court and introduced a witness who said that the cops beat Frankie with a baton and flashlight, handcuffed him and kicked him before unleashing the dog to attack him. The family believes that Frankie bled to death from his wounds. The Federal jury rejected the family's lawsuit, accusing the cops of excessive force. After the decision, Frankie's mom, Eva Taffolla, said, "I don't think the verdict was fair. I don't have any faith in the justice system. This shows that you can't beat city hall."

Oliver Beasley, Jr.   27   *Black*

January 23, 1990. South Central LA (Athens):
Oliver was a Muslim who was beaten and shot to death by LA deputies after a traffic stop.

Dexter Aubrey Herbert   20   *Black*   👁

March 24, 1989. Gardena:
Dexter Herbert's life was cut short by Gardena Police who shot him in the back of the head during an alleged drug bust. The victim was unarmed when police fired their weapons at him. His family filed a lawsuit against the City of Gardena. Dexter's mother described her son, saying "He wasn't a troublemaker, he didn't like gossip, didn't like violence. He was a very loving person — nothing like they portrayed him to be." **Source:** SLP Form; Deadly Crisis Newsletter, 12/98

Melvin Edward Thompson   32   *Black*

January 16, 1989. Bellflower:
Upset over the Miami shooting, the Don Jackson brutality case on Martin Luther King's birthday, and his wife wanting a divorce, Mel challenged the deputies to shoot him. They did, 25 times. It is unclear whether he died or survived.

James Earl Bailey   27   *Black*

September 22, 1988. Compton:
James was beaten, kicked and shot to death by LA deputies. He died in his father's arms.

Chester Briggs   —   *Black*

February 14, 1988. Lennox (LA County):
Chester was killed after he was kicked, beaten, tased twice and shot five times by LA deputies.

Michael Wayne Johnson   36   *African American*

1988. Gardena:
Gardena police shot Michael in the back multiple times, zapped him all over with stun guns and gouged a huge portion from his neck. Police gave several conflicting accounts of what happened. They removed all his I.D. It is unclear whether he died or survived.

Eddie Ropati   41   *Latino*

August 27, 1987. Whittier:
Eddie grabbed a deputy who was running through his house in pursuit of his stepson. Eddie was beaten, shot by several deputies and killed.

Eliberto Saldana   20   *Latino*

May 19, 1987. East L.A.:
Deputies tried to restrain Eliberto, then zapped him twice with a taser gun. He picked up a pan and was killed when three deputies emptied their guns into him.

Manuel Hernandez   27   *Latino*

May 11, 1987. Whittier:
Manuel was kicked and beaten by deputies, then shot four times and killed when he picked up a discarded push-broom to deflect the baton blows.

Pascual Solis   —   *Latino*

March 9, 1987. East L.A.:
Called to a domestic dispute, a deputy shot Mr. Solis six times, re-loaded his gun, and shot four more times, killing him. Three years later, the same deputy shot and wounded Elzie Coleman.

Manuel Diaz | 16 | *Latino*

February 20, 1987. Los Angeles:
A call was made to LAPD complaining of some kids with a loud radio. The cops came to the scene and got out the police vehicle with their guns drawn. Several of the youths took off running. Manuel Diaz ran through a garage and the carport area. A police officer shot and killed Manuel with one round, claiming he tripped and the gun went off. There was no criminal prosecution of police officer. Manuel Diaz was unarmed.

Cornelius Garland Smith | 35 | *Black*

April 11, 1985. —:
Cornelius was reportedly high on PCP and break-dancing in the street. He died after the LAPD gave him four taser shocks.

Santiago Calderon | 58 | *Cuban*

March 12, 1985. East LA:
A SWAT team burst into Santiago's home on a pre-dawn raid looking for evidence in a murder trial. He was shot multiple times in bed. It is unclear whether he died or survived.

Damian Garcia | — | *Latino*

April 22, 1980. East LA:
Damian was a member of the Revolutionary Communist Party. In April, 1980, Damian, along with two other people, got on top of the Alamo in Texas, took down the U.S. and Texas flags and put up the Red Flag (representing oppressed peoples around the world). People heard about this all around the world and the government was furious. A few weeks later, he was killed in the Pico Aliso housing projects. Damian, along with some other people building for May Day, were attacked by some people no one in the neighborhood recognized who said they were from the government. By the end of the attack, Damian was laying on the ground with this throat cut and stab wounds to his lungs and kidneys. As the attackers left, someone overheard them saying, "Don't worry, the cops won't come." All day, the organizers were being followed by police but during the time of the attack, all the cops were gone. They re-appeared five minutes after Damian was stabbed. Through investigation and a trial, it was discovered that the man standing next to Damian when he was murdered (who Damian thought was his friend) was an undercover cop and that Damian had been under constant police surveillance for weeks before his death and there was a major escalation in this surveillance a week before he was killed.

Steve (last name unknown) | — | —

1976. Lynwood County jail:
Steve was hung by his belt in the Lynwood County jail. When he was first put in jail, however, they took all his clothes away. His friends don't believe he would have killed himself.

Freddy Santana | 26 | *Latino*

May 19, 19??. Exposition Park (LA):
Mr. Santana was shot by LAPD officers who wanted him to lay face down. As he tried to remove a paint can from his belt, he was shot three times. He moaned and was shot more. It is unclear whether he died or survived.

Bruce Klobuchar | 25 | —

Date Unknown. Los Angeles:
Mr. Klobuchar died after being hog-tied by LAPD officers. His family received a $750,000 settlement and forced police to abandon the use of hog-tying. This may be reversed in light of a new study that contends that hog-tying does not affect blood oxygen levels **Source:** Los Angeles Times, 1/17/98

SAN DIEGO / SOUTHERN CALIFORNIA

Name	Age	Nationality	Photo

Demetrius DuBose — 28 — *African American* — 👁

July 24, 1999. San Diego (Mission Beach):
Mr. DuBose, a former football linebacker for the Tampa Bay Buccaneers, was shot 11 times by San Diego police. Witnesses reported that cops then stood over him with their guns pointed at him while he writhed in the street. He bled to death before he reached the hospital. Police were in the predominantly white Mission Beach neighborhood, where Mr. DuBose lived, to investigate a burglary call. Cops claim that after several minutes of questioning Mr. DuBose, he resisted arrest, and fled when they sprayed him with Mace. He supposedly grabbed an officer's nunchakas and threw a cop into a planter box before being shot. But a lawyer for the victim's family talked to five to ten witnesses who said that the first shot was to Mr. DuBose's back and that he had merely picked up the nunchakas. The lawyer said, "You can't kill everybody because you're scared.... Do I think race played a role in the way the cops reacted? Absolutely. But there would be no fewer buckets of tears if he had been white... The main pattern is that the police of San Diego shoot to kill, and it doesn't matter who you are. They shoot first and ask questions later." **Source:** New York Daily News, 8/22/99

Gonzalo Cardena Solorza (?)	25	*Mexican*	
José Angel Leobardo Márquez (?)	39	*Mexican*	
Daniel Toro López	26	*Mexican*	

March 27, 1999. East San Diego County (Dulzura):
Mr. Toro was one of the three men, all Mexican immigrants, suspected of illegally crossing the U.S.-Mexico border who had been arrested by Border Patrol Agent Stephen Sullivan. They were killed, along with the agent, when his overloaded Ford Bronco crashed down a steep embankment east of San Diego. Four other immigrants were taken to area hospitals. Dulzura is a very rugged area that many immigrants have been forced to use for crossing into the U.S. since Operation Gatekeeper has increased border patrol activity in the less rugged areas. Rosemary Johnston, a leader with an inter-faith group that calls for change in the U.S. immigration policy said, "We wonder how many deaths it will take before our government takes a more humane approach to our neighbors to the south." Mr. Toro was from Mexico City. The other two men killed, Mr. Leobardo and Mr. Cardena, respectively were from Puebla and Vera Cruz. **Source:** Los Angeles Times, 3/28/99; San Diego Union Tribune, 3/31/98

José Luis Ramírez — 30 — *Latino*

March 17, 1999. San Diego (Logan Heights):
José was standing outside a convenience store, allegedly holding a gun. When police arrived, he ran away. Cops chased him down an alley and reportedly ordered him to freeze. Police claim he pulled a revolver from his waistband and pointed it at them. No shots were fired at the police, who opened fire, striking José several times in the chest and killing him. A week later, 200 people demonstrated at the construction site of a new police sub-station being built near the scene of the shooting. **Source:** San Diego Union-Tribune, 3/24/99; Michael Novick, 3/17/99

Robert Gomez — 46 — —

March 2, 1999. Placentia (in custody):
Robert had been arrested for a drug violation. While in jail, he had shortness of breath and fainted and was put in an Orange County jail medical isolation unit. As he walked back to a cell after receiving heartburn medication, he stopped to talk to another inmate, then slumped to the ground and died an hour later. **Source:** The Orange County Register, 3/5/99

Unidentified Woman — — — —

February 22, 1999. Mira Loma:
California Highway Patrol officers were chasing a woman at speeds up to 95 mph on the freeway. She made a sharp turn, drove over an embankment and crashed through a fence. She died at the scene. Officer Dennis Welch claims the victim wasn't wearing a seat belt. The cop's motive for engaging in the chase was under investigation. **Source:** Los Angeles Times, 2/23/99

Yachun June Meng   32   —

February 19, 1999. Mira Mesa:

Yachun Meng was killed when a speeding patrol car crashed into her car as she was leaving a shopping mall parking lot. The cop who ran into her was chasing suspected burglars. Police claim that the suspects' car ran a red light and they followed. The lead police car hit the Ms. Meng's vehicle. She died shortly thereafter at the hospital. Police Chief Jerry Sanders said, "The pursuit policy is reviewed constantly and has held up in the courts. I think we have a good pursuit policy, a strong pursuit policy. I think it's the training." **Source:** Michael Novick, 2/24/99; Los Angeles Times, 2/20/99

Ryan O. Cooty   18   —

February 8, 1999. San Diego:

Pvt. 1st Class Cooty had been in the Marines for one month. He was one of 11 marines headed for a few days leave who were stuffed into a van built to carry only seven. The van was struck by another vehicle that was being chased by police. Ryan suffered abdominal injuries and later died. **Source:** Los Angeles Times, 2/9/99

Irvin Landrom, Jr.   19   *Black*

January 17, 1999. Claremont:

Mr. Landrom was shot to death by police after they pulled him over for speeding. Cops claim he had a gun but refused to show it to his wife, Tracy Lee. She said, "I'm sick of hearing stories about him being a criminal. He was an honest working man with a job at IKEA... I cut out the story of Tyisha Miller's killing, but didn't know that 14 days later I'd be in the same spot!... Irvin was a father, a son, a grandson, a friend, and an employee.... If he knew what was gonna happen, maybe he would have kept driving until the helicopter lights, etc. showed up, it would have been another car chase, but he would have lived." **Source:** statement from victim's family

---

Edward Castillo   24   —

January 10, 1999. Newport Beach:

Edward and a friend allegedly stole a car and were involved in a high-speed chase with police. When Edward's car crashed, both occupants were thrown from the car. Edward died at the scene and his friend was charged with murder on the grounds that a participant in a felony that results in a death is liable for murder. **Source:** The Orange County Register, 1/11/99

Unidentified Man   —   —

December 14, 1998. Riverside:

The man was shot numerous times and killed by the Riverside police. Cops claim he threatened them with a vehicle. **Source:** letter to U.S. Senator Dianne Feinstein from Paul Hayward, father of police brutality victim Derek Paul Hayward

---

Christine Turner   9   —

December 9, 1998. San Diego:

Christine died on Dec. 11, 1998, two days after she and her best friend, Adina González were struck by a pickup truck that was fleeing California Highway Patrol (CHP) Officers. The chase began after CHP officers spotted a man speeding on the wrong side of the road. It continued near Lemoncrest Elementary, where the driver lost control, striking the two girls. Officers involved in the chase are not being investigated for any charges in relation to the crash. The driver of the pick up truck was charged with evading arrest and may be charged in connection with Christine Turner's death.

Michael P. Generakos   45   —

November 23, 1998. Costa Mesa:
Michael, a chemist, was described as a devoted father. His 16-year-old son was deaf and possibly going blind. Michael recently had lost custody of his children to his estranged wife. These events led to a dispute between Michael, his ex-wife and the Board of Education over how to teach his son. Instead of having his son learn Braille, Michael held out hope that a new medical treatment would reverse his son's deteriorating eyesight. When his son began Braille lessons, Michael reportedly went to the Board of Education offices with a gun and held two administrators hostage. When Michael came out of the building, allegedly holding a gun on an administrator, a SWAT team member fatally shot Michael in the head. Having lost his hearing and going blind, Michael's son must now deal with the additional loss of his father. **Source:** Los Angeles Times, 11/24/98

Christopher Lloyd   32   *Black*

October 28, 1998. San Diego (Kensington area):
Christopher was shot at least 20 times and killed by three San Diego police officers. When the cops arrived, Christopher was leaving a jewelry store he had apparently decided against robbing after someone called the police. **Source:** San Diego Union-Tribune, 10/29/98

Lonnie Wagner   —   —

October 16, 1998. Fontana:
San Bernardino County sheriff's deputies shot and killed Mr. Wagner as he was surrendering to them for outstanding warrants in front of his house. The victim's roommate was there when it happened and called the killing an assassination. **Source:** Local TV News, 10/16/98

Tuan Thanh Tang   19   *Asian*

October 10, 1998. Westminster:
Tuan's family says the college sophomore was a courteous, loyal brother and son, who "tried to get the best for everybody." When Tuan vomited and had trouble breathing, allegedly from a cocaine overdose, his family called 911. According to a family attorney, the emergency team asked Tuan several questions, consulted with police and then left, never examining Tuan. After repeated requests that their son get medical attention, police told Tuan's family to leave the room. When Tuan's father returned, he found three cops pinning Tuan against the couch, with one on each knee and the third cop pressing Tuan's face against the couch. Tuan was hog-tied and taken to jail. Two hours later Tuan's family was notified that he had stopped breathing. He was placed on a ventilator, virtually brain-dead and died a week later on Oct. 17. "I was shocked that a 911 call turned into this," said Tuan's father, holding back tears. "Had they taken him to the hospital, he would be alive today." Tuan's family filed a $10 million claim against the city of Westminster for wrongful death, excessive force and civil-rights violations. Tuan's father said, "You can help by applying the pressure of public scrutiny and concern on the investigative agencies so that circumstances surrounding Tuan's death will not be swept under the rug. We don't want anything other than justice for my son and hope that other families won't go through what we're going through." **Source:** The Orange County Register, 10/23/98

Leonel Valenzuela   38   *Mexican*

September 27, 1998. Goat Canyon (2 miles west of San Ysidro):
An unidentified border patrol agent who was combing Goat Canyon looking for "illegal border crossers" alleged he was "pelted with rocks." He claimed that Leonel had emerged from the darkness, pelted him with rocks and ignored orders to stop. He shot Lionel in the torso and killed him. This shooting was the second in a 24-hour span that also claimed the life Oscar Velez one day earlier. Leonel was killed while attempting to cross into the U.S. There are no other known witnesses to the shooting. The border patrol agent was put on paid leave. The Justice Department has ruled this and two other shootings during the same period as "justified." Leonel was from Navajoa, Sonora, Mexico. **Source:** SLP Form; Los Angeles Times, 9/29/98; San Diego Union Tribune, 9/29/98 & 1/16/99

Oscar Abel Cordoba Velez   23   *Mexican*

September 26, 1998. San Ysidro Border Crossing:
Oscar was shot and killed by a border patrol agent while crossing the US-Mexico border with two other men. A boxer, Oscar was going to San Diego to buy boxing gloves for a match the following Wednesday. After climbing over the ten-foot border wall, the men saw the border patrol agent approaching and tried to retreat back over the wall. One of Oscar's companions was tackled by a border patrol agent, who tried to pull him down off the wall as he was climbing back over to Mexico. Oscar was almost over but came back down to try to distract the agent and aid the other man. The agent pulled his gun on Oscar and fired into his chest, killing him instantly. The agent later claimed that Oscar had a rock in his hand and raised it over his head as he approached the agent. But six witnesses said Oscar had no rock or weapon. Within a few days, Oscar's family and friends held a demonstration at the Tijuana/San Ysidro Border crossing, chanting "Border Patrol — Murderers" and demanding justice and punishment of the border patrol agent. Mexican consular officials expressed "deep concern" over the shooting. A civil suit against the U.S. government was undertaken on behalf of Oscar's two children, ages two and four. Since the shooting, there have been numerous press conferences denouncing the border patrol for the rash of shootings in September, 1998. People carried pictures of Oscar at the Oct. 22, 1998, March to Stop Police Brutality in San Diego. Oscar was from Guadalajara, Mexico. **Source:** San Diego Union-Tribune, 9/28/98 & 9/29/98; El Heraldo (Tijuana, Mexico), 10/3/98; El Mexicano (Tijuana, Mexico), 10/3/98

José Manuel Campos   28   *Latino*

Sept. 5-7, 1998. Santa Ana:
Officers pulled over José, claiming he was driving a stolen car. Cops claim that José attempted to run them over with his car and that the killing was justified. But at least six eyewitnesses say that police provoked José before Officer James Tavener fired a bullet into his ear at point blank range and killed him. This incident sparked community protests and the filing of a federal civil rights lawsuit against the city. Almost a year later, an Orange County grand jury refused to indict the cops involved, leading to a protest in Santa Ana. Officer Tavener had also killed another man a few years earlier. **Source:** Los Angeles Times, 4/3/99

Raymond W. Quiroz   20   —

September 1998. Camp Pendleton:
Lance Cpl. Raymond Quiroz was a decorated Marine from Kane, Illinois. Cops claim he jumped on the hood of a San Bernardino Police squad car, yelled at the officer and "attacked her." The officer shot him once, killing him. Raymond was unarmed. **Source:** unidentified newspaper article

Raad Wadie Jabro   31   —

August 3, 1998. San Diego:
Police say the behavior of Mr. Jabro was odd in the driveway outside the lobby of the Holiday Inn Hotel. He was allegedly holding a knife in each hand and threatening to stab himself. Harbor Police fired 11 shots and killed him, claiming he lunged at them from ten feet away. **Source:** San Diego Union-Tribune, 8/6/98 & 11/7/98

Geremeskel Gebreselassie   36   *Ethiopian*

July 7, 1998. San Diego:
San Diego Police Officer Gordon Leek shot and killed Mr. Gebreselassie, claiming that the homeless man swung at him with his cane. A leader of the Ethiopian community expressed outrage at what had happened and said the police had killed a peaceful man. Members of the East African community and homeless activists held a demonstration against police brutality, carrying a coffin draped in an Ethiopian flag from city hall to police headquarters. A week before he killed Geremeskel Gebreselassie, Officer Leek had shot and wounded another unarmed homeless man. **Source:** San Diego Union-Tribune, 7/29/98 & 9/4/98

Anthony Reed   22   —

June 23, 1998. Rincon Indian Reservation:
Deputy Chuck Kett went on the Rincon Indian Reservation with his pistol in his lap, allegedly responding to a call of a man standing in the road firing a gun into the air. Deputy Kett claims Anthony Reed tried to conceal the gun and that after the deputy got out of his car, Anthony supposedly "raised his shotgun to eye level" and walked toward him, pointing the gun at him. Deputy Kett shot Anthony in the head, arm and shoulder, killing him. The man who was with Anthony contradicted the police account, saying Anthony never pointed the gun at the deputy. **Source:** The San Diego Union-Tribune, 9/4/98

Unidentified   —   —

June 14, 1998. Fallbrook:
San Diego County sheriff's deputies responded to a call of a domestic disturbance and an unidentified person was shot and killed. No other information was provided. **Source:** San Diego Union Tribune, 6/15/98

Unidentified Man   20s   —

June 4, 1998. Temecula:
A Riverside County sheriff's deputy responded to a call about a suspicious person at an apartment complex. Claiming that the man he approached opened fire on him, the deputy shot and killed him. Police reports say the deputy received minor wounds before he returned fire and killed the victim. **Source:** Los Angeles Times, 6/5/98

Ettore Capitumini   85   —

May 22, 1998. Chula Vista:
According to eyewitnesses and police, an un-uniformed Border Patrol agent in a marked cruiser ran a red light and broadsided the 85-year old Mr. Capitumini's car. Mr. Capitumini was taken to the hospital, where he died. **Source:** San Diego Union Tribune, 5/23/98

Mark Kulok   31   —

April 25, 1998. Acton:
When police attempted to rescue a kidnap victim from him, Kulok fled into the brushy hillside. After an alleged exchange of gunfire, Kulok was found dead. Police claim they do not know if they killed him or he committed suicide. **Source:** Los Angeles Times, 4/27/98

Kenneth Putt   64   —

April 18, 1998. Oceanside:
Officers were called to the Putt home by Kenneth's wife because her husband, a former Marine with a history of mental illness, was holding a rifle. When Kenneth allegedly pointed the rifle at police, they shot and killed him. **Source:** San Diego Union Tribune, 4/20/98

Rubén Joseph Cortez   35   —

April 6, 1998. Escondido:
When he fled a traffic stop for expired tags, police gave chase. Mr. Cortez' car crashed. Badly injured, he exited the car. Claiming he charged at officers with an object in his hand, two officers shot and killed him. The object was an 11-inch lighter. District Attorney Paul Pfingst said "each officer's use of deadly force was justifiable and not unlawful." **Source:** San Diego Union-Tribune, 6/11/98

Kevin L. Silva   37   —

February 24, 1998. San Diego:
Police report that California Highway Patrol officers tried to arrest Mr. Silva when he was found running in the freeway after a traffic collision. A struggle took place and Mr. Silva was subdued with some form of mace. He died while being taken to the county jail. **Source:** San Diego Union-Tribune, 2/26/98

Apolinaria Santiago Hernández   —   *Mexican*

February 12, 1998. near El Centro:
Mr. Hernández was killed when the car in which he was riding crashed while being chased by the border patrol. The agent claimed he turned off his flashing lights and slowed down before the crash took place. Mr. Hernández was from Oaxaca, Mexico. **Source:** San Diego Union Tribune, 2/13/98

Theodore Paul Miodusewski   37   —

January 20, 1998. San Diego:
According to the police, the victim ran from them. When caught from behind, he allegedly fired a gun over his shoulder at the officer but accidentally shot himself in the head. Police claim that initial reports that they had killed the man were incorrect. **Source:** San Diego Union-Tribune, 1/22/98

Martin Santos Castro, Jr.   17   —

January 17, 1998. San Diego:
Martin and another person were allegedly burglarizing a home around 5 a.m. A woman who lived there called the police. Cops came and found the rear door open. As Martin ran from the kitchen, Officer Phillip Bozarth shot him four times, once in the head and killed him. Officer Bozarth claims Martin ran at him with a gun. **Source:** The San Diego Union-Tribune, 4/24/98

Arnold Damon Perez   25   —

January 1, 1998. Placentia:
Arnold spent his last conscious hours with Sharron Serna. Sharron said that just before midnight on New Year's Eve, the two of them had strolled out of Arnold's mother's apartment and heard what they thought were firecrackers or gunfire. Moments later, as they started back to their apartment, police arrived. Three cops confronted Arnold, claiming he was wanted for a parole violation. "One of the cops yelled, 'Damon, is that you? Where are you going?' and ordered him to turn around," said Sharron. As Arnold turned, police shot Arnold in the chest without warning. Cops claim Arnold had a handgun and pointed it at them. Sharron angrily disputed the police story and maintained that Arnold's hands were empty. Sharron said she had seen Arnold get dressed and he was not armed. Arnold died in the early morning hours on New Year's day. Police alleged that they found a gun "in the close proximity." **Source:** The Orange County Register (Morning Edition), 1/2/98

Bernardino Chavarría   21   —

December 13, 1997. San Marcos:
Mr. Chavarría was a passenger in a car pulled over for a traffic stop by Sheriff's Deputy Remy Dang. Deputy Dang, claiming Mr. Chavarría fired a weapon at him, shot and killed him. Evidence showed Mr. Chavarría did not fire a weapon. **Source:** San Diego Union-Tribune, 3/5/98

Chessmur Nicolo Cucchiara   —   —

November 25, 1997. San Diego:
Mr. Cucchiara, a homeless alcoholic with a history of mental problems, was asleep in some bushes being searched by police. He was shot to death after allegedly cursing and throwing bottles at the officers who tried to arouse him. **Source:** San Diego Union-Tribune, 2/8/97

Michael Bangaan   54   —

November 25, 1997. San Diego:
Responding to a domestic call, police found Mr. Bangaan crouching in the back yard. Claiming Bangaan came at them with a knife, police shot him five times and killed him. **Source:** San Diego Union-Tribune, 1/22/98

Jorge Figueroa   —   *Latino*

November 22, 1997. Nestor:

Police were called when Mr. Figueroa (allegedly high on methamphetamines) began firing a shotgun believing that people were chasing him. The SWAT team arrived, evacuated the neighborhood and conducted a four-hour standoff. Negotiators using bullhorns failed. When Figueroa fired once out the front door, the SWAT team shot him four times. Figueroa also was hit by a tear gas missile that penetrated his chest. The DA ruled that since Figueroa had pointed a shotgun at the SWAT team, deadly force was justified. **Source:** San Diego Union-Tribune, 1/29/98

Adán Canseco   20   *Latino*

November 8, 1997. Vista:

Deputy González was struggling with Mr. Canseco, who was down on the ground while his unrestrained companion was a short distance away. Claiming he feared for his life, the deputy shot the unarmed Canseco in the back and killed him. The shooting was ruled justified. **Source:** San Diego Union-Tribune, 1/28/98

Edwin Miller   31   —

October 23, 1997. San Bernadino County (Colton):

Police allege that Edwin robbed a 7-11 store. A Union Pacific Railroad police officer, who said he saw the whole thing, shot and killed Edwin after he claimed Edwin pointed a gun at him. **Source:** The Press Enterprise (Riverside, CA), 10/25/97

Richard R. Webber   46   —

September 13, 1997. San Diego:

According to the medical examiner's report, Richard Webber, who suffered from schizophrenia and was taking medication for it, died from "acute excited delirium" when his heart stopped beating while he was handcuffed in the back seat of a sheriff's car. Authorities claim that Richard threatened several elderly party-goers at a swimming pool and threw two women against a wall. Richard's mother said that she begged deputies and paramedics to put her son in an ambulance but they refused. "They scared him to death," she said. "They didn't have to throw him down on the concrete. He would have sat in the car if they would have let him…He didn't have to be murdered." **Source:** San Diego Union-Tribune, 11/5/97

Miguel Valentín-Lorenzo   34   —

September 10, 1997. San Diego:

Miguel was fatally shot in the chest by an officer who claimed Miguel charged him with a 15-inch wooden stake following a three-hour standoff with a SWAT team. **Source:** San Diego Union-Tribune, 11/15/97

Unidentified man   —   —

Unidentified woman   —   —

May 2, 1997. National City:

Police went to a house to arrest two suspects in the daring Saks Fifth Avenue jewelry heist and a gun battle allegedly broke out. Cops shot tear gas into the house, which ignited, as did a palm tree. When the fire was out, police found two people dead. Their bodies were so severely charred that authorities said they were unable to determine if they had been killed by gunshot, died in the fire or committed suicide. **Source:** Los Angeles Times, 5/3/97

Alfonso Guillén   21   *Mexican*

April 23, 1997. San Diego County:

Mr. Guillén was hit by a car and killed on Interstate 8 during a chase by INS.

Richard Narváez	34	*Chicano*

April 1, 1997. National City:
Richard Narváez suffered from schizophrenia. He was shot five times and killed by two California Highway Patrol (CHP) officers after a moderate-speed chase. The police claimed that Richard grabbed Officer Brean's gun and fired a shot into one of the officers' leg during a struggle. The San Diego County district attorney and sheriff dismissed the accounts of the two eyewitnesses who were 50-100 feet from the shooting and said that Mr. Narváez never had a gun, that he was subdued and face down on the ground when he was shot and that the wounded officer was shot by a fellow cop. The two eyewitnesses later told the press that they feel Richard Narváez was killed without justification and that they came forward because they wanted Richard's parents to know the truth about their son's death. They also said that during an interview by sheriff's department detectives, three hours after the incident, they were discouraged from saying anything negative about the police and when they did so, the detectives repeatedly turned off their tape recorders. Latino activist groups and the Narváez family told the press, "We're not satisfied with the conclusions of the DA. We think they are protecting the cops." **Source:** The San Diego Union-Tribune, 9/6/97 & 10/4/97

Enríquez Santos	26	*Mexican*

January 22, 1997. East San Diego County:
Enríquez Santos died in a crash in which others were injured while being pursued by the INS in a high speed chase.

Adam Williamson	25	—

December 14, 1996. Riverside:
Mr. Williamson was believed to be under the influence of amphetamines (speed) and police claim they thought he was a "peeping Tom." Someone had called 911, but Adam was found someplace other than the reported crime area. He was unarmed. After an alleged altercation, police put him into a carotid neck hold and killed him. This neck hold, in which the officer places an arm around the victim's neck and restricts blood flow to the two main arteries (the carotids), was used to kill Derek Paul Hayward several years earlier. **Source:** letter to U.S. Senator Dianne Feinstein from Paul Hayward, father of police brutality victim Derek Paul Hayward

Rosa María Gutiérrez	53	—

November 1996. Riverside County (Moreno Valley):
Rosa was on her way to a seminar for religious education teachers. She was killed when her car was struck by a van being chased by police. Cops claim the van was stolen. The Gutiérrez family filed a lawsuit against the Moreno Valley police for negligent operation of police cars. City officials rejected their claim and an internal administrative investigation found the police actions within the department's pursuit policy. **Source:** The Press-Enterprise, 10/3/97

2 died, 19 injured	—	*Mexican*

April 26, 1996. San Diego County:
Two persons died and 19 were injured on I-8 Alpine as a result of a high speed chase in which a border patrol van hit the vehicle carrying the immigrants, forcing it off the road.

Felipe Arias Bautista	31	—
Fernando Ocampo Franco	25	—
Benjamin Chávez Múñoz	33	—
Jaime Chávez Múñoz	21	—
Salvador Chávez Múñoz	19	—
Unidentified	—	—
Unidentified	—	—
Leodegario Avilés Varela	42	*Mexican*

April 6, 1996. Riverside County (Temecula checkpoint):
Eight people died and 17 others were injured as a result of a high speed chase by border patrol agents . The truck in which the immigrants were riding allegedly went out of control and crashed.

Eliseo Santos Carmona	24	*Mexican*	

January 23, 1996. San Diego:
Eliseo died of injuries after he fell off a cliff near the border while being chased by Migra (Border Patrol) agents at night. Members of his group of 15 immigrants said they started running after they were fired upon. It was then that Eliseo and five others fell off the cliff.

Antonio Silva Frías	40	*Mexican*	
Richard Horton	—	—	
Roberto López	38	*Mexican*	

May 3, 1995. Route 94, San Diego County:
Three died and 16 were injured as their van slammed into a pickup truck as it was being pursued by border patrol agents in a high speed chase.

Unidentified man	—	—	

1995. San Diego:
A disturbed man stole a five-ton National Guard tank and drove it on a destructive rampage. Police stopped him by shooting him to death. **Source:** San Diego Union-Tribune, 3/23/98

Ricardo Fernando Ziadie	34	—	

1995. Oceanside:
Sgt. John Lamb shot and killed Mr. Ziadie on a downtown street because he thought the man was going to pull a knife on him. Ziadie had been taking medication for schizophrenia. **Source:** San Diego Union-Tribune, 4/20/98

Michael C. Colvette	23	—	

December 30, 1994. Donovan Correctional Facility:
A prison guard shot and killed Michael during a fistfight with another prisoner in the exercise yard. Neither Michael nor the other prisoner had a weapon. Prison policy states that a correctional officer should shoot only to disable, but Michael was shot in the head with a high-power 9mm rifle from an elevated tower. Prison official Lt. Marion Daniels said, "We're satisfied right now with the shooting." **Source:** San Diego Union-Tribune, 12/31/94

Derek Paul Hayward	30	*white*	👁

November 25, 1994. Riverside:
Derek Hayward had shut himself in the bathroom of his sister Toni's apartment. She called 911 for help. When the police arrived, they kicked in the door and placed Derek in a carotid neck hold. This neck hold, in which the officer places an arm around the victim's neck and restricts blood flow from the two main arteries (the carotids), is legal in Riverside even though this is not the first time it has killed someone. After cops put Derek in a carotid hold a second time, his sister overheard the officer say, "this one ought to keep him down". When Derek's fiancee saw that he had stopped breathing, she tried to give him CPR, explaining to the police that she was a licensed vocational nurse. But the cops refused to let her try to save his life and he died. Derek is survived by three daughters, his fiancee, his sister and his parents. A jury deadlocked six to three in favor of convicting the cops of excessive force and a new trial was scheduled for the spring of 1999. In describing Derek, his friend Scott Draddy, said, "If it was between him and one of his good friends getting shot, he would jump in the way of the bullet." **Source:** SLP Form; letter from victim's sister; The Press-Enterprise (Riverside, CA), 11/29/94; letter to U.S. Senator Dianne Feinstein from victim's father, Paul Hayward

Francisco Jiminez	—	*Latino*	

September 9, 1994. San Diego:
Officers Patrick Lenhart and Jeffery Sterling shot Francisco after he allegedly called 911 with a false report. When they arrived at his home, cops claim he came out with two knives and "ignored orders to drop them". They shot and killed him. **Source:** San Diego Union-Tribune, 12/3/94

| **Daniel L. Price** | 35 | — |

June 30, 1994. San Diego County:

Mr. Price got into an altercation with police and was hog-tied, face down on the ground. His heart stopped while he was on the pavement. Although he was revived, he died two days later. Authorities continued to insist that hog-tying does not kill. **Source:** San Diego Union Tribune, 1/14/98

| **Martín García Martínez** | 30 | *Mexican* |

May 28, 1994. San Diego:

Mr. Martinez was shot at close range with an expansive type of bullet by an INS agent who was verbally and physically abusing his brother and sister-in-law. They were all on their way to work in the Coachella Valley. He died on July 3, after being in a coma for more than a month.

| **Juan Carlos Segura Camarena** | 22 | *Mexican* |

May 11, 1994. Imperial County:

INS agents who picked up Juan in Gorman, Ventura County refused to allow him to take his heart medicine when he was being transported to Calexico, CA. Immediately after being deported, he died from secondary pulmonary edema and heat exhaustion while walking into Mexicali, Mexico.

| **Melodee Beleu** | — | — |

1993. Oceanside:

Officers shot and killed Ms. Beleu as she allegedly waved a kitchen knife at them from the bathroom of her home. She had been diagnosed with a longtime mental illness. **Source:** San Diego Union-Tribune, 4/20/98

| **Charles "Chuck" Hill** | — | *Black* |

April 15, 1992. Riverside:

Mr. Hill was beaten to death by Riverside police. **Source:** statement from victim's family

| **Roger Varela** | 22 | — |

February 2, 1991. San Diego:

Roger was killed at the border by the Border Crimes Intervention Unit. He had a plastic gun in his hand. Police said they suspected Roger and a friend were going to rob immigrants.

| **Humberto Robles Valenzuela** | 33 | *Mexican* |

November 2, 1990. San Diego:

Mr. Valenzuela was shot to death with a bullet to the forehead by a patrol agent at the border near Interstate 5.

| **Anthony Tumminia** | 21 | — |

September 13, 1990. San Diego:

Anthony was shot and killed by the same cop who killed Jorge Robles in February. Police claim he used nunchakus against them but witnesses denied it, saying he only pushed police away and attempted to run when they tried to arrest him. Police unsuccessfully tried to pressure his girlfriend to say he was violent and no good.

| **William Slusar** | 39 | — |

September 11, 1990. San Diego:

Mr. Slusar was shot twice through the chest and killed after the police and fire department responded to a call from his parents that he had taken a drug overdose and was contemplating suicide.

Victor Mandujan Navarro	17	*Mexican*

September 8, 1990. San Diego:
Victor was killed at the border trying to cross. A U.S. border patrol agent out of uniform knocked Victor down and then shot him twice in the stomach as he was fleeing back into Mexico with his 23-year-old brother. Three witnesses told Mexican authorities that the agent pulled Victor from the border fence, pinned him to the ground and put the muzzle against his chest before firing. No charges were brought against the border patrol agent. **Source:** Los Angeles Times, 10/90

John Joseph Kelley	30	—

August 6, 1990. San Diego:
Mr. Kelley was shot three times and killed while sitting in the driver's seat of his car because a cop said he reached down between his legs. He had no weapon.

Bruce Todd Riddle	29	—

July 21, 1990. San Diego:
Mr. Riddle was killed by police. He was threatening to kill himself. Police claimed he threatened them with a knife.

Walter Andrew Welch	41	—

June 20, 1990. San Diego:
Mr. Welch was shot and killed by police from 10 feet away as he was breaking car windows with a baseball bat.

Luis Francisco Perez	28	*Mexican*

June 16, 1990. San Diego:
Luis was shot and killed. Police claim he waved a baseball bat at them. Police falsely reported he was on drugs and 4-1/2 inches taller than his actual height.

Jose Eleazar Lopez-Ballardo	24	*Mexican*

May 21, 1990. San Diego:
Jose was a mentally ill man shot and killed while standing on the freeway. Police said they thought he was dangerous because he had a cement trowel in his hand.

Gregory Markley	27	—

April 8, 1990. San Diego:
Gregory, a homeless man, was killed by police. Cops claimed he pulled a knife when they were arresting him.

Jorge Robles	29	*Mexican*

February 9, 1990. San Diego (Ocean Beach):
Jorge was killed by police who claimed he pointed a .22 caliber pistol at an officer.

Maria Juventina Resendiz Soto	17	*Mexican*

January 18, 1990. San Diego County:
Maria was killed in a high speed chase by border patrol agents.

Ana Recia Ponce	22	*Mexican*

August 23, 1989. San Diego-North County:
Ana was killed in a high speed chase with border patrol agents.

Luís Eduardo Hernández	14	Mexican

August 20, 1989. San Diego:
At the border, Luis was struck and killed by a border patrol four-wheel drive vehicle as he was running back toward Mexico after trying to cross the border.

SAN FRANCISCO BAY AREA / NORTHERN CALIFORNIA

Name	Age	Nationality	Photo
Fatt Lai	64	—	

August 25, 1999. Antioch:
Mr. Lai was shot in his home by two Antioch police officers as he allegedly stabbed his daughter-in-law. He died at the hospital of "multiple gunshot wounds to the chest and abdomen." The two cops arrived in response to a 911 call. The newspaper reported, "Once they got to the front door, they saw Fatt Lai stabbing his daughter-in-law.... The two officers fired their guns at Lai in an attempt to stop the attack." There is no mention of any orders to stop or any attempts to use non-lethal force. The two officers were placed on routine administrative leave. **Source:** San Francisco Chronicle, 8/27/99

Richard Rosenberg	36	—	

April 18, 1999. Fremont:
Police responded to the report of a man acting suspiciously and prowling around a car. When cops arrived, they confronted Richard, who allegedly "brandished a knife at them." One officer grazed him with a shot from a bean-bag gun, but Richard reportedly failed to drop the knife. Police killed him with five shots to the torso. **Source:** San Francisco Chronicle, 4/20/99

Jesús Julio Morales	40s	Mexican	

April 13, 1999. San Jose:
Police responding to a 911 call regarding a disturbance and a possible suicide shot and killed Jesús, who they claim threatened them with a knife. Cops allege that they found Jesús holding a blade to his stomach and that when they gave him verbal orders, he raised the knife threateningly. Police shot him twice with "non-lethal" projectiles. Jesus then supposedly raised the knife "in a manner that appears he's going to throw it," said Sgt. Derek Edwards. Officer Brad Rossmiller shot and killed Jesús. This was the eighth homicide of the year in San Jose. Of those, four were killed by police. **Source:** San Jose Mercury News, 4/14/99

Long Phi Tran	26	Vietnamese	

March 1, 1999. San Jose:
Long attended San Jose State University. He was working as a martial arts instructor and hoped to open his own studio. Claiming Long had threatened to kill his ex-girlfriend and her companion the previous night, police entered his home and found him in a bedroom. First, cops said that when they knocked on the bedroom door, Long fired at them and was shot and killed by police as he exited his room. Later, they changed their story and claimed that Long had shot himself. Long's sister-in-law said, "I don't believe them. He's dead; he can't speak for himself. It's an easy way for them to get out, but the family will not take that as an answer. No way. They never identified they were cops. How would you know who it was? It could be a robber." According to the family, police barged into their home at 2:30 a.m., took some members into the kitchen and handcuffed them as they searched for Long. Long's family said they would re-investigate his death and called a press conference to clear his name. **Source:** San Francisco Chronicle, 3/2/99

Naim Ayub	30	—	

February 24, 1999. Hayward:
In a drug sting operation, police surrounded Naim, then shot and killed him, alleging that Naim tried to run over police. The three cops who shot Naim were placed on paid administrative leave. **Source:** San Francisco Chronicle, 3/2/99

Anthony Manuel Montiel   31   —

February 6, 1999. San Jose:

Police saw Anthony and his friend in a car parked by a 7-Eleven store. Claiming they thought perhaps the two were casing the store for a robbery, police approached them. Anthony drove away and following a high speed chase, the car crashed. Cops sent in a police dog and when they found Anthony, Officer John Tepoorten shot and killed him, contending that Anthony had a handgun and refused to drop it. Cops also claimed the car was stolen. No shots were fired by Anthony. **Source:** San Jose Mercury News, 2/7/99

Unidentified man   —   —

February 2, 1999. Mountain View:

Police answered a domestic disturbance call. When they arrived, a woman reportedly came out of an apartment and told them a man inside had a gun. Cops claim the man came out the front door with what appeared to be a semi-automatic pointed downward. Officers claim they ordered him to drop the gun, but the man allegedly pointed it at them instead. One officer fired three shots, killing him. The weapon turned out to be an unloaded pellet gun. **Source:** San Jose Mercury News, 2/3/99

Buford White   45   *African American*

January 15, 1999. San Francisco:

Buford White, a construction worker, was known as a hardworking man. According to people who shared a house with him, "He was as nice as could be, always willing to help out around here. He just treated every single person with respect." Cops claim he tried to rob a bank. After the attempted bank robbery, which left one customer seriously wounded with a gunshot to the head, Buford was shot and killed in a barrage of police gunfire on a busy street during rush hour. At least 30 shots were fired by the cops, two of whom were injured by "friendly fire." After an evening of "debriefing and filling out forms," the officer in charge of the operation died after crashing his car. He was found to have a blood alcohol level four times the legal limit. **Source:** San Francisco Chronicle, 1/16/99 & 1/19/99; Associated Press, 1/15/99

Phuc Nguyen   —   *Vietnamese*

January 1, 1999. San Francisco (North Beach):

Mr. Nguyen allegedly pulled a gun on another man on a crowded North Beach street on New Year's Eve. Police claim Nguyen then pointed the gun at them and police shot and killed him. Deputy District Attorney Paul Cummins said Mr. Nguyen was shot ""almost immediately" after the police arrived. **Source:** San Francisco Chronicle, 1/2/99

Steven A. Reibin   43   —

December 31, 1998. San Francisco:

Police say Steven was stopped by undercover officers who suspected him of drug possession. According to the cops, he tried to flee but was caught and handcuffed. Moments later, they say, he slumped to the ground and died. **Source:** San Francisco Chronicle, 1/2/99

Bill Earl Vaughn   24   —

December 21, 1998. Oakland:

Bill was born and educated in Oakland. He was married and had three daughters. Bill was shot numerous times in the torso and was killed by an undercover narcotics cop who authorities claim he tried to rob. **Source:** family of victim

Aaron Kirk	25	—	👁

November 23, 1998. Pleasant Hill:

Aaron had been laid off for one month from his job as a heating and ventilation repairman. He had no criminal record and had gone to visit a friend and watch the 49ers game. Officer Reef Mowers, who claimed that Aaron tripped a burglar alarm at an adult store, got in a struggle with him near Aaron's pickup, which was parked outside the store. Officer Mowers fatally shot Aaron in the arm and chest. Police refused to say how many times Aaron was shot or to provide details of the alleged struggle because the DA's office "hadn't determined if the shooting was justified." Aaron's parents say that police have never explained to them why their son had to be killed. "I had to read in the newspaper that the officer who killed my son had been cleared and was back on the streets just three weeks after my boy's death," said Aaron's father as tears streamed down his face. "They didn't even have the decency to call us and let us know. We're prepared to believe the truth. But first we have to get it." A lawsuit has been filed, not for money, but as a way to demand details. "We don't know what happened and we're not going to speculate," said the Kirk's lawyer, "But based on statements police have made to witnesses, we have a huge suspicion that it was not a justified shooting." **Source:** San Francisco Chronicle, 12/4/98 & 2/9/99; Contra Costa Times, 11/25/98

Unidentified Man	—	*Latino*	

November 16, 1998. Pittsburg:

According to press reports, the California Highway Patrol began chasing a speeding car. The car careened off the highway, flipped and landed on its roof in a shopping center parking lot. The driver was killed and a passenger was injured. **Source:** San Francisco Chronicle

Unidentified Woman	—	—	

November 7, 1998. Santa Rita Jail:

A woman inmate died the day after being admitted to Santa Rita jail. She was found ill in her cell. She died before jailers allowed her to see a doctor. **Source:** San Francisco Chronicle, 11/10/98

James Robert	31	—	

November 6, 1998. Alameda:

James, a homeless man, was shot and killed by Officer Sean Lynch. Cops claim he "brandished a knife." The officer said he was checking inside vacant buildings along the railroad right-of-way after an earlier fire. Other details of the confrontation were not given, but other homeless persons say that they have increasingly been harassed, beaten and even killed by law enforcement agents and others. **Source:** San Francisco Chronicle, 11/10/98

John M. Smart, Jr.	40	*white*	

October 6, 1998. San Francisco (Tenderloin District):

John Smart, a millionaire advertising executive for Interbrand, headquartered in New York, was reportedly seen arguing with a woman in the Tenderloin district of San Francisco. Cops claim that when they approached, John jumped into his Mercedes and tried to flee. Police fired 14 rounds at John, hitting him five times. Wounded, John lost control of his car and crashed into a building across the street where, according to several witnesses, John was "finished off" by police with two shots to the head. Police denied this, but could not explain why two shell casings were found at that site of the crash, more than 40 feet away from all the others. This was the 12th police shooting in San Francisco this year, the third resulting in a death. **Source:** San Francisco Examiner, 10/11/98 & 10/13/98; San Francisco Chronicle, 10/13/98

Jason Raymond Harritt	25	—	

September 24, 1998. Pittsburg:

Narcotics officers from a multi-agency task force reported that they shot and killed Jason during an attempt to take him into custody. Police claim he tried to run from them and tried to shoot at a cop before being gunned down. **Source:** Contra Costa Times, 10/4/98

Martin Robles Arias　　　　　　32　　　　　　—

September 16, 1998. Antioch:

After responding to a complaint about loud music, an Antioch police officer pepper-sprayed Martin, then shot him five times at close range. Martin died immediately in the yard of his home. Police said he was "acting erratically," but would not say whether he had a weapon. **Source:** San Francisco Chronicle, 9/12/98

Mark Smith　　　　　　—　　　　　　*Black*

September 11, 1998. Oakland:

Mark was reportedly distraught. His family called the police for help. Officer Ron Lighten came and shot him him dead. The National People's Democratic Uhuru Movement called a demonstration at the Oakland Police Department Headquarters on Sept. 22 to protest Mark's killing, as well as the policy of police containment of the Black community. **Source:** Onsale, Inc., Wendy Snyder, writer, 9/20/98; victim's family

Glafira Campos　　　　　　55　　　　　　*Mexican*

September 2, 1998. Hayward:

Glafira was from Jalisco, Mexico. She had been married for 32 years and was known as a kind-hearted woman who enjoyed selling Mexican pottery at swap meets. "She was just an angel on earth," said her son. "She was probably the most caring person ever. She was the glue of the family." Every weekend for 18 years, Glafira traveled from her home in Fremont to work the night shift cleaning an office building in San Francisco's financial district. She was killed when an allegedly stolen vehicle being chased by police slammed into the car in which she was riding. Her two cousins were injured. "It was a price that didn't need to be paid," said her son. The Campos family questioned how the hunt for those who stole a $7000 custom truck led to Glaria's death. "I don't understand how any innocent victim has to die in a police chase," said Glafira's cousin. **Source:** The San Francisco Chronicle (final edition), 9/4/98

Brandon Auger　　　　　　26　　　　　　—

September 1998. San Jose (in custody):

Brandon, arrested for suspected rape, died in custody after seven police officers hog-tied him. Local police claim they are banning the Total Appendage Restraint Procedure and are encouraging the use of Velcro straps and belts to tie up people's legs instead. Last month, the National Institute of Justice advised law enforcement agencies that recent legal decisions have found that the "hog-tie" is not considered deadly force, but medical studies have shown people do suffocate this way. The Institute said departments should consider revising their methods for restraining people. **Source:** Michael Novick, 12/3/98

Phillip Joseph Hourigan　　　　　　50　　　　　　—

August 22, 1998. Placer County (Roseville):

According to deputies, Mr. Hourigan was walking in a "suspicious manner" at 2 a.m and tried to run away when they approached. Claiming Mr. Hourigan attacked them with a large, sharp knife, Deputies Dennis Walsh and John Poutti fired several shots, hitting him. When he allegedly attacked again, they shot and killed him. **Source:** The Sacramento Bee, 8/23/98

Durk Chavis　　　　　　25　　　　　　—

August 18, 1998. Oakland:

According to Oakland police, a patrol officer spotted a stolen 1991 Explorer and initiated a pursuit. The Explorer ran a stop sign and broadsided a car with three people inside. Durk Chavis, the driver of the Explorer, died at the scene. Johnny Benson, a passenger in the car that was hit, died later at the hospital. **Source:** San Francisco Examiner, 8/20/98

Johnny Benson　　　　　　24　　　　　　—

August 18, 1998. Oakland:

Johnny Benson was a passenger in the car that was broadsided by an Explorer being chased by the police. He died at the hospital from his injuries. The driver of the Explorer, Durk Chavis, was also killed. **Source:** San Francisco Examiner, 8/20/98

| **Marvin Noble, Jr.** | 45 | *African American* |

July 16, 1998. Ukiah:
County mental health workers asked the police to detain Mr. Noble, a diagnosed paranoid schizophrenic, because he was not taking his medication. When police approached him at a Foster Freeze, he allegedly "revealed" a hunting knife and left the restaurant and police doused him with pepper-spray. He returned to his nearby apartment building. Police followed him there and then sicced a dog on him. When Mr. Noble allegedly attacked the dog with a knife, police shot and killed him. An ambulance arrived and took the dog for treatment, leaving Marvin Noble to die near the door to his apartment. Protection and Advocacy Inc., a statewide agency empowered to protect the rights of the mentally ill, is investigating. Marvin's family said they doubted local authorities could give them the answers they need. "My family needs to know the truth," said Marvin's mother. "I don't need one police agency clearing another. I need someone from the outside telling me what happened to my son." **Source:** The Press Democrat (Santa Rosa, CA), 7/21/98 & 7/27/98

| **Leslie Baranowski** | 39 | — |

June 6, 1998. Newcastle:
Rocklin Police Officer Marc Baranowski shot his wife, Leslie, to death as she slept and then killed himself. Apparently, he was upset about having to take care of the children (ages 16 and 14) while she was away at her job in Salt Lake City, Utah. Two days later, Officer Baranowski was to have started a new assignment dealing with community-oriented policing and problem solving. **Source:** The Sacramento Bee, 6/9/98

| **Sean Seibel** | 28 | *white* |

May 29, 1998. Manteca:
About 5:30 p.m., a neighbor got a call from Sean's roommate that Sean was despondent. "Please go over there," he said, "Sean has a gun to his head." When she arrived, Sean asked her to give him a hug. "I just want my friends around me right now," he said. He was reported to have fired four shots over a fifteen minute period, which cops claimed were fired at them. But eyewitnesses and people who knew him don't believe they were aimed at anyone. The neighbor went home to call police, but asked them not to send any units. But the Manteca Police Department SWAT team had already arrived. They opened fire and shot Sean three times, killing him. The neighbor said she and a girlfriend had to dive on the floor, covering their three children, and that the SWAT team fired recklessly into neighboring apartments containing children. Her apartment was also shot up. The daughter of the apartment manager said, "They [the cops] shot up the place when there were still people inside. They didn't evacuate people until after they started shooting." "It could have all been avoided," said the neighbor, "If they had let him talk to his roommate, none of this would have happened." **Source:** The Modesto Bee, 5/30/98; Michael Novick

| **Unidentified Male** | — | — |

May 29, 1998. San Francisco:
Police claim that during a drug bust, the victim fired out his passenger window at an undercover cop and a marked patrol car. Another officer shot and killed him. **Source:** SF Examiner, 5/29/98

| **Victor Duran** | 32 | — |

May 28, 1998. Santa Clara County Jail:
Victor had cirrhosis of the liver and was waiting for a transplant. When police spotted him riding his bicycle, they arrested him on outstanding warrants. Police claimed he had a sawed-off shotgun under his coat. Victor phoned his family from jail to say he had been beaten by four officers. The Dept. of Corrections said Victor complained of pain in his side and stomach and told the jail doctor he had been hit with a stick by San Jose police. After 12 hours at the jail, Victor was taken to the infirmary, where he was later found unconscious. Victor died. A county medical examiner said he died of asphyxiation caused by a blow to the left side of his neck. "Something happened and they're not letting us know what happened," said Victor's sister Irene. His family filed a $20 million lawsuit charging that Santa Clara corrections officers strangled Victor while he was in the infirmary. **Source:** San Francisco Chronicle, 5/29/98; San Jose Mercury News, 5/29/98

Charles Vaughn, Sr.	60	*African American*	

May 19, 1998. Seaside:

Charles Vaughn Sr., an accomplished citizen, was afflicted with mental illness late in his life. He had climbed onto the roof of his one-story apartment to avoid mental health workers. He laid down on his stomach and asked the police who arrived to leave him alone. Instead, one of the officers followed him onto the roof and sprayed him with mace. When Mr. Vaughn stood up, he was fatally gunned down by Seaside Police Officers Joseph Bertaina and Ronald Guth, who were on the ground. They claim Charles threatened another officer with a corkscrew. The outraged community and family united to memorialize, protest and demand justice, including holding a national tribunal on police misconduct and brutality. **Source:** family; The Herald, 5/24/98

Sheila Detoy	17	*Filipina*	

May 13, 1998. San Francisco:

Sheila was in a car with her two friends, both young men. All three were unarmed. Plainclothes drug cops Breslin and Moran rushed the car with guns drawn in an attempt to arrest one of the young men for missing a court appearance for a non-violent drug offense. The youth, thinking that they were about to be robbed, started to drive away. Police opened fire into the side and back of the car, shooting Sheila in the head and killing her. The youth drove on and a massive manhunt to arrest Sheila's friends ensued. Police rules allow them to shoot at a car coming at them, but Officer Breslin fired from the side of the car when he was out of harm's way. Officer Breslin had been suspended from the police force in 1992 for beating a man so severely that the jail would not accept him. Police claimed that the car was in reverse and coming at them, but an eyewitness contradicted this, saying, "At no time were the officers in the path of the car and they weren't in any danger from the car." When the driver of the car turned himself in, he was charged with causing Sheila's death, even though it was the cops who killed her. Hundreds of outraged people memorialized Sheila, protested her murder and demanded that the charges against the driver be dropped. **Source:** San Francisco Chronicle (Final Edition), 5/14/98, 7/14/98 & 8/13/98; San Francisco Examiner, 2/26/99 & 2/27/99

Robert Roy Davis	58	—	

May 11, 1998. Alameda:

According to police, Officer Pat Wyeth saw Mr. Davis make a "squealing turn" and decided to stop him for "exhibition of speed." Davis fled and police pursued him. Davis' car crashed into a guardrail. He was thrown from the vehicle and died at the scene. **Source:** San Francisco Chronicle, 5/12/98

Eligio G. Dator	29	—	

May 10, 1998. Sunnyvale:

Officers looking for Mr. Dator found him in a parking lot. Police claim they fired when he pointed a pellet gun at them. Mr. Dator fled into a nightclub crowd and is alleged to have again pointed a gun at officers. Police fired again and killed him. **Source:** San Francisco Chronicle, 5/12/98

Carol Frye	48	*white*	

April 25, 1998. San Francisco City Jail:

Carol had been arrested for being under the influence of narcotics and possession of a hypodermic needle. She had a history of intravenous heroin use. Once jailed, her medical condition rapidly deteriorated and she died in C Tank at the city jail. Her cause of death was listed as a natural one due to drug related cardiomyopathy. **Source:** San Francisco County Medical Examiner Case No. 98-0561; San Francisco Coalition on Homelessness

Thomas Peter Stav   21   —

April 21, 1998. Santa Clara (Highway 17):
Thomas was a U.C. Irvine student and the son of a Department of Defense worker. He was allegedly driving erratically and got into a non-injury hit-and-run accident, hitting a parked car. In what the California Highway Patrol and the media touted as "A Pursuit On Highway 17," officers followed Thomas for 20 minutes at speeds of "up to 45 mph." When a CHP patrol car blocked him in, Thomas allegedly "clipped the front" of the patrol car and then stopped, surrounded by officers. As he got out of his car, CHP cops opened fire and killed him. Police claim he announced he had a gun and "appeared to reach in his waist." The highway was closed for hours while police conducted an extensive search, but no gun was ever found. Witnesses say the victim was pulling out his cellular phone. **Source:** The San Francisco Chronicle, 4/22/98 & 4/23/98

Steve Silver (Akkadet Pathomkrut)   33   *Cambodian*

April 9, 1998. Sacramento County (Roseville):
Akkadet Pathomkrut (a.k.a Steve Silver) was born in Thailand of Cambodian parents. A former supply sergeant who had spent eight years in the US Air Force, he was also a supervisor at the Yuba City Post Office. He had no criminal history. Police allege that Akkadet robbed a bank, out of "boredom," and in the police chase that followed, ran a red light and crashed his car. Cops claim he refused to surrender and opened fire. Police shot and killed him. **Source:** The Sacramento Bee, 5/25/98

Larry Edward Glendowne   49   *white*

March 30, 1998. San Jose:
Los Gatos Police Sgt. Dave Moody and Officer Steve Wahl pulled Mr. Glendowne over in a traffic stop. He gave the cops his driver's license but then reportedly drove away. The officers pursued him to a residence in San Jose, where he banged on the door. Cops claim Mr. Glendowne pulled out a handgun and fired at them. Both officers opened fire and killed him. **Source:** San Francisco Chronicle, 3/31/98; San Francisco Examiner, 3/31/98

Marwin Muñoz Prado   21   *Filipino*   👁

March 26, 1998. Vallejo:
Marwin attended a friend's party and was drunk. Police responded to a call about a man behaving strangely, tearing up the kitchen and garage. A cop found Marwin sitting on a curb, allegedly with a .38 caliber gun in his pocket. Cops claim Marwin refused to obey police orders and a confrontation ensued. The cop shot him three times, once in the shoulder and twice in the back, killing him. It was around 12:41 a.m. Marwin Muñoz Prado was an auto mechanic. He was described as a helpful, friendly person. **Source:** SLP form

Paul B. Rodrigues   41   *Pacific Islander & Latino*

March 10, 1998. Petaluma:
Paul Rodrigues, a mentally ill homeless man, was allegedly attempting to dismantle the alarm at the local homeless center. Claiming Mr. Rodrigues lunged at him with a bicycle fork, Officer Loden shot him twice, killed him. A friend of Paul said, "Those of us who knew Paul would agree, he simply was not the confrontational type. This portrayal and Paul's rap sheet given by police to the newspapers appears to be an explanation to justify the killing by character assassination." **Source:** SLP Form; Petaluma Argus-Courier, 3/13/98; San Francisco Chronicle, 7/7/98

Chila Amaya   35   *Latina*   👁

March 7, 1998. Union City:
Union City police shot Chila four times, killing her as she stood behind her locked security door. They had been called on a non-emergency basis. Police ordered her father and daughter into a rear bedroom. When the door shut, the shooting began. Police claim Chila threatened to kill her father and daughter and was on her way toward them. But Chila was shot by the front door and witnesses say no threat was ever made. Chila's brother witnessed the shooting, yet was never interviewed by the district attorney or the Union City Police. Chila had a son, age six and a daughter, age 16. She was a receptionist, a cosmetologist and a floral designer. Chila's door was always open. She was very kind and loving and a great cook. Her family filed a lawsuit and is organizing the community for a system of police accountability with civilian oversight. Chila is the fourth Latina known to have been killed by the Union City Police in the last ten years. **Source:** victim's family

Michael Scott Carter   34   —

March 7, 1998. Truckee (Placer County):
Police received a report that Michael had assaulted his girlfriend in the Truckee Pines Apartments and had fled in a pick-up truck. He was reported to have a handgun. Placer County sheriff's deputies spotted the truck traveling on Highway 267 south of Truckee in the Sierra Meadows area. Cops claim they tried to stop Carter but he refused to yield and turned back toward Truckee. They claim they pursued him at high speed as he returned to the apartments. There, Carter allegedly jumped out of his vehicle, refused orders to halt and appeared to reach for a weapon. He was shot to death by Deputy Troy Minton-Sander, who was placed on paid administrative leave (paid vacation). No gun was found at the scene. **Source:** Reno Gazette-Journal, 3/8/98; The Sacramento Bee, 3/8/98

Kisha Davis   18   —

March 1, 1998. Sacramento:
Kisha was a passenger in a car involved in a high speed chase with Sacramento police. She was killed when the driver lost control, veered off the road, plowed through a guard rail, flipped over and smashed into a duplex. This was the fifth such death in a year in Sacramento.

Kenneth Michael Duckett   28   —

February 26, 1998. Ceres (Sacramento County):
Cops responded to a call about a break-in and allegedly found Kenneth holding a knife. He tried to run, but fell. Police claim they ordered him to drop the knife and that he reached to his waistband, pulled out a gun and aimed it at them. Kenneth was shot numerous times in the torso and killed. He was the second person killed by Ceres police in two months. **Source:** The Sacramento Bee, 2/28/98 & 3/1/98

Mike García   28   *Puerto Rican*   👁

February 25, 1998. San Francisco:
Someone had said a man was robbing people in the neighborhood. A crowd of guys who were gathered on the corner reportedly pointed Mike out to police, saying he had a gun and that they thought he was going to rob them. Police followed Mike as he walked. Mike kept his back to them and kept walking. Police Officer Andy Castro got out of the car and shot him four times in the back, claiming Mike had quickly turned around. Fifteen minutes later, police called an ambulance. Mike was unarmed and cops found no gun, but they found another man a few blocks away who was carrying a gun. They questioned and released him. Mike's sister went to the San Francisco Office of Citizens Complaints and worked closely with them for awhile, but they suddenly cut off all communications with her after she gave them information on several witnesses. The family has filed a lawsuit against the city. Mike was well loved in the community. A spontaneous outpouring of grief and anger created a memorial alter of flowers, cards, signs and stuffed animals at the site where he was murdered. Mike was working for Goodwill Industries collecting furniture and donations, a job he had held since getting out of jail. Friends said Mike had a good heart. One young woman said that her mother considered him one of her own, that they had long talks about life and what he wanted to do with his. Mike left behind a 12-year-old daughter, who had just started to receive the fatherly attention she had missed while her dad was in jail. **Source:** San Francisco Chronicle, 3/2/98; victim's family

David Torres   29   *Latino*

February 4, 1998. High Desert State Prison:
According to authorities, when ten Asians attacked eight Latinos, guards fired warning shots. The guards claim they shot and killed Mr. Torres to protect other inmates who were down and could not defend themselves. **Source:** The San Diego Union-Tribune, 2/5/98

Michael Moore   23   —

February 4, 1998. Oakland:
Police received a 911 call from a resident near their substation who said a man was pointing a shotgun at her mother. When police arrived, the caller was with two men who had come to help her. One of these good Samaritans was Michael Moore, who police claim held his hand in his waistband, prompting police to try to search Michael, who cops claim ran. Police chased him and shot him to death. Police claimed a gun was found near Michael's body. **Source:** San Francisco Chronicle

Carlos Alberto Topete   26   —

January 27, 1998. Pittsburg:
Even though a man had already confessed, police alleged that Carlos may have been a "second shooter" in a 1997 murder and were seeking him for a parole violation. Carlos was chased through backyard fences and cornered. Police claim he opened fire on a SWAT team and wounded two officers. SWAT officers Carl Webb and Eric Solzman, armed with submachine guns, opened fire on Carlos, striking him in the head and chest, killing him. Bullets ripped through a nearby home and a parked pickup. Police would not release how many shots were fired. **Source:** San Francisco Chronicle, 1/29/98

Paul Edward Sánchez   44   —

January 26, 1998. Jamestown (Tuolomne County):
Paul wore a metal plate in his head after he suffered brain damage from a 1970s diving accident. According to his brother, Paul "walked slow and it took him longer to think. Other than that, he was still Paul. But it was like he was cut in half." Three times in January, Sonora police stopped Paul on minor charges and after the first two incidents, Paul was seen at the hospital. The first time he complained of being "roughed up" by police. The second time, he was treated for fractured ribs and told a doctor he had been tackled and hit with clubs by police. Six days after his third arrest, an ambulance was called to Paul's home when he collapsed and went into a coma, apparently from heart and lung arrest. He was flown to Sacramento and died three days later. **Source:** The Modesto Bee, 1/30/98

Tommy Carl Valdez   29   *Latino*

January 21, 1998. Sacramento:
According to police, Tommy was alone, talking to himself, while standing at the base of a storm drain in a creek on the campus of California State University at Sacramento. CSUS police claim he was switching what they thought was a blue steel semi-automatic revolver from hand to hand and putting it in and out of his pocket. Then, he lit a cigarette. Cops allegedly "feared for their lives" after they had surrounded Tommy, who supposedly pointed the gun at them. They shot him six times and killed him. The gun turned out to be fake. **Source:** The Sacramento Bee, 1/23/98

Unidentified Man   —   —

January 3, 1998. Sacramento County:
Law enforcement initiated a ground and air chase by three police agencies and sheriffs, claiming the man had threatened his father. Finally surrounded by police on the ground and in the air, the man was killed with one round when he allegedly pointed a gun at officers. **Source:** The Sacramento Bee, 1/4/98

Ronnie Caldwell, Jr.   29   —

January 2, 1998. Ceres (Sacramento County):
When police tried to arrest Ronnie, he fled and was shot. When he started to get up, he was shot again in the back and killed. Ronnie was unarmed and the community was outraged. One of the officers involved in the killing, Detective Puryear, was found dead five weeks later. It was rumored that Det. Puryear died of opiate poisoning.

Roland Andrew Sorgatz   49   —

December 27, 1997. Sacramento:
Mr. Sorgatz was an innocent motorist killed when his car was broadsided by a police car involved in a high speed pursuit. His family filed a wrongful death claim against the city charging that the unnamed officer was using excessive speed and was not using emergency lights or a siren. This fatal accident is one of five in the last 18 months involving city police officers. Mr. Sorgatz was a well-liked telecommunications employee. **Source:** The Sacramento Bee, 5/28/97, 12/31/97 & 8/21/98

John Pruitt III   —   *white*

December 26, 1997. High Desert State Prison:
According to his family, John Pruitt III was shot by prison guards in the buttocks during a fight in the exercise yard, then left unattended for more than an hour while he bled to death. He was scheduled to be released in a few months. He is profoundly missed by his family. **Source:** John Pruit II, his father

Raymond E. Stoddard   31   —

December 26, 1997. Napa:

Raymond was gunned down by Napa Special Investigations Bureau agents who allegedly thought he was an armed suspect. Raymond was a passenger in a car leaving an area where undercover drug police were attempting to serve a warrant. He was also known as Ray McClean and had no criminal record. **Source:** Napa Valley Register, 1/11/98

Donald Morell Cook   64   —

December 7, 1997. Sacramento:

Donald Cook was struck and killed by a speeding police car as he was pushing a shopping cart across an intersection. The officer, whose name was still not released months later, was responding to an assault call at about 9:30 p.m. Six of Donald's children filed a wrongful death lawsuit against the City of Sacramento. This is the third claim stemming from five such fatal crashes in a year. The city manager set up a committee to investigate possible changes in the city's policy on how police drive to crime calls and handle chases. Committee head George Caplan, Dean of McGeorge School of Law said, "We now know many of the accidents in the past have been caused by responses to minor crimes or traffic violations." **Source:** The Sacramento Bee, 5/28/98

Clifford Archer   53   *white*

December 7, 1997. San Francisco:

Clifford, a homeless man, had been living in Golden Gate Park until park police and SFPD officers conducted a series of sweeps of the park's residents. His camp was torn down and all his possessions were taken, including his heart medications. A few days later, he was found in the bushes in front of McDonald's across from the park. His cause of death was listed as heart disease. **Source:** San Francisco County Medical Examiner Case No. 97-1523; San Francisco Coalition on Homelessness

Michael Ray Atencio   30   —

December 6, 1997. San Jose:

Michael Atencio, a warehouse worker, was pulled over by Officer Jason Herr for suspicion of car theft. Police then chased Michael on foot and shot him in the chest, killing him. Cops claim Michael had "turned around with a handgun in his right hand" before he was killed. **Source:** San Francisco Chronicle, 12/8/97

Dale Allen Hughes   35   *white*   👁

November 19, 1997. Santa Rosa (Sonoma County):

Dale was shot more than 11 times and killed by Santa Rosa Police Officer Wojcik. Officer Wojcik claims he decided to talk to Dale after hearing a whistle "similar to those that signal a drug transaction" and that Dale fired first. Dale's parents have been contacted by witnesses who gave accounts "180 degrees different" from the official police version. The eyewitnesses say Dale never drew a weapon and that police, mistaking him for a drug dealer, surreptitously surrounded him and gunned him down in cold blood. "I think the policeman thought he [Dale] was a drug dealer and didn't think he deserved to live," said Dale's mother. Dale was the fourth man shot and killed by Santa Rosa police during a two-year span. **Source:** The Press Democrat (Santa Rosa, CA), 4/10/98; victim's family

Erasmo Antonio Bolanos Cortez   22   *Latino*

November 16, 1997. San Rafael:

San Marin County sheriff's deputies tried to stop Erasmo after allegedly seeing him drive erratically. They chased him at speeds of more than 70 mph along Los Ranchitos Road. Erasmo was killed after he allegedly ran a red light and hit a culvert, rolling the vehicle over. **Source:** San Francisco Chronicle, 11/18/97

John Calvin Dine   41   —

November 14, 1997. Santa Cruz:

John was described as a well-known, peace-loving hippie. "Go to the Haight 30 years ago; that's what John was like. He was fixated with the hippie era. When he was down to earth, he was a fun-loving guy to deal with," is how a care provider at a residential facility for the mentally ill described him. "Happy John" became a victim of the Santa Cruz Police campaign to drive the homeless out of this resort and university city. During a police sweep, he was shot and killed by Officer Conner Carey after he allegedly refused to obey a command to show his hands and instead pulled out a toy gun, pointed it at the cops and took what police called a "combat stance." The police produced a gun which they claimed John had pulled. But at least ten witnesses disputed the police version of events, saying that John did not have a weapon, did not point a weapon at the police and was not in a combat stance. **Source:** The Chronicle Publishing Co., Andreas Tzortzis; Becky Johnson, friend of victim; Homeless United for Friendship and Freedom

Solano Sivano   47   *Latino*

November 9, 1997. San Francisco (Bayview District):

Police shot and killed Mr. Sivano, who lived at a homeless encampment. Police claim he had fired a 20-gauge, double-barreled sawed-off shotgun at them from the shadows of a Highway 101 on ramp. A San Francisco police officer allegedly ordered him to drop the shotgun in English, which the Spanish-speaking Mr. Sivano may not have understood. There are reports that the gun was never found. This was the third known time in 1997 that police killed someone. Mr. Sivano had sought mental health treatment at San Francisco General Hospital for paranoia at five programs in one month, just seven months before his death. His cause of death was listed as firearm homicide through legal intervention. **Source:** San Francisco Examiner, 11/10/97; San Francisco County Medical Examiner Case No. 97-01384; San Francisco Coalition on Homelessness

Mong Van Pham   25   —
Tho Van Pham   27   —

November 9, 1997. Menlo Park:

Mong and Tho were killed instantly along Highway 101. The car in which they were riding as passengers was going 90 mph, according to a San Mateo Sheriff's patrol officer. When the deputy gave chase, the driver tried to pull off the freeway but lost control and slammed into a tree. **Source:** San Francisco Chronicle (final edition), 11/11/97

Judith Harris   49   *white*

November 7, 1997. Los Gatos:

Judith's throat was slashed by her husband, San Jose Police Officer Tom Harris. Officer Harris tried to cover up the murder by putting her body in the trunk of her car and saying she was missing. When his story fell apart a few days later, Officer Harris killed himself. **Source:** San Francisco Chronicle, 12/10/97

Jeffrey Tharp   49   —

November 7, 1997. Vallejo:

Officers responded to a call about domestic violence. Cops claim they shot Mr. Tharp when he failed to drop the gun he was supposedly pointing at them.

John Leroy Banks, Sr.   45   —

October 28, 1997. Sonoma County Jail:

Police arrested John, his son and nephew for a family fight. According to John's sister, "It didn't seem like it was serious. Everybody walked away." While in jail, John went into heroin withdrawal. His son said, "They didn't give him any methadone or anything. He was throwing up and was real sick. They just told him, 'Here's some aspirin.'" Four days later, John and his family were released from jail. On the drive home, his son says, John "was real cold." He had lost bowel control, was vomiting and had chills. Within six hours of being released from jail, he was pronounced dead. This was the third death of a drug addict associated with the jail in the past five months. Medical services at the jail are provided by Correctional Medical Services, a St. Louis-based firm which functions in 20 jails and prisons across the country. Dr. John Hibbard, medical director in the jail, called heroin withdrawal "more unpleasant than dangerous." **Source:** The Press Democrat (Santa Rosa, CA), Bob Klose, staff writer

Brian Prosser   39   *white*

October 20, 1997. Novato (Marin County):

Brian, an asthmatic who used an inhaler, was repeatedly pepper-sprayed by police, then handcuffed, hit at least once with a baton, and placed face down in a position which further restricted his breathing. He died an hour later at the hospital. Brian was an accountant who lived in the upscale community of Novato. Police claim they encountered Brian in a carport of an apartment complex in his neighborhood. Brian may have been robbed. A resident of the apartment complex told investigators that a man had knocked on his door asking him to call the police because he had been robbed. Police claim that when they found Brian, he was incoherent, dressed only in his shorts, with his hands in his pockets. The coroner claimed that Brian had a substantial amount of cocaine in his blood and died of "cardio-respiratory arrest due to agitated delirium due to substance abuse." Friends do not believe the official account fits with the man they knew. An attorney who had defended Brian in a previous case (Brian had been beaten by police in 1991 during an arrest for drunk driving) said, "He was not armed. Why was there a need for force?" A friend who had traveled with Brian to Russia had one explanation for the event, "He [Brian] had a problem with sleepwalking. And I know that he would sleep in his shorts." The cops involved in the incident are on paid leave during the investigation. The Novato Police Department has refused to release the names of the cops involved. **Source:** San Francisco Chronicle, 10/22/97

David Hamilton   52   —

October 4, 1997. San Jose:

David was shot several times and killed by Officer Robert Reichert, who claimed David "made contact" with him. Officer Reichert and two other cops pulled David over on the freeway after a couple allegedly told them that David had pulled alongside their vehicle, made an obscene gesture and waved a gun at them. The couple left after telling their story and the police do not know who they are. Cops allege David had a gun in a holster on his belt. They admit that David raised his hands when ordered to do so, but claim he then reached for the gun before they shot him to death. **Source:** San Francisco Chronicle, 10/7/97

Robert McMaster   30   —

September 29, 1997. Napa:

Robert was shot twice in the chest and killed by a sheriff's deputy, who claims Robert threatened to shoot him. Robert was unarmed. He had allegedly broken into a detached garage/living space and confronted the owner, whom he knew. When Robert refused to leave, the owner called the police. Deputies claim that when they arrived, Robert shouted that he was armed and refused to show his hands, which were allegedly concealed behind his back. The deputy opened fire. Robert was declared dead at a local hospital. Mr. McMaster, a PhD pharmacist, had a brain tumor and had been behaving erratically in recent months. His parents, who lived nearby, were not notified that he had been shot and taken to the hospital until many hours after his death. **Source:** The Press Democrat (Santa Rosa, CA), 9/29/97

Albert Glen Thiel   35   *Black*

September 28, 1997. Sacramento (Arden-Arcade Area):

Albert is alleged to have been driving a stolen car that went out of control and crashed after a 17-minute high speed chase by police. As he tried to run away, police set their dog on him and Albert suffered numerous dog bites. The DA's office claims Albert was combative. Police struck Albert with batons on the chest and arm and used a carotid constriction hold on him. Handcuffed, Albert was put in the back seat of a patrol car. Police claim Albert was breathing heavily, but paramedics found no pulse and he was pronounced dead shortly thereafter. A coroner's report stated that Albert died of blunt force trauma to the neck and said, "there appears no doubt that force was utilized to subdue the decedent." Another report said Albert died as a result of a carotid control hold that crushed his windpipe. His death was classified as a homicide. Meanwhile, according to a written statement from DA's office, cops maintained they had no reason to believe that Albert had been seriously injured and none of the officers involved recalled hitting Albert in the neck. They called Albert's death "an unfortunate accident." Albert was unarmed. **Source:** The Sacramento Bee, 10/1/97,12/3/97 & 1/15/98

| **Venus Renee Beaird** | 37 | *Black* |

September 10, 1997. Oakland:

Neighbors called police about a family argument. Renee's family wanted the police to leave. In an ensuing scuffle, Renee was shot in the chest and killed by police in front of her family. Police allege that she attacked them with a butcher knife. Myeshia Hayward, the victim's niece, said, "We have to let people know this is not an isolated incident. The police didn't just kill my aunt. They killed my father. When you shoot someone 14 times you're not trying to stop him, you're trying to kill him. And they were trying to kill my aunt, too." Ms. Hayward's father, Johaun S. Hayward, was shot and killed by police in 1981. **Source:** San Francisco Chronicle, 9/11/97

| **Doron Robert Lifton** | 33 | — |

September 1997. Vacaville:

Claiming Doron struck an officer with a steel pipe and fled an accident scene, three officers shot Doron eight times, killing him. It was reported that Doron had been suffering from psychological problems. **Source:** unidentified newspaper article

| **Hue Truong** | 38 | *Vietnamese* |

August 3, 1997. San Francisco:

Hue Truong was a homeless man. Officer Glenn Ortega of the SFPD responded to a report of a transient trying to start a fire in the doorway of an abandoned building. Officer Ortega claims Hue pulled a pocket knife out of a bag. The cop pepper-sprayed him, but supposedly, "it had no effect." Officer Ortega alleged that Hue then jumped on him and slashed his face in the ensuing struggle, then did not comply with an order to drop the knife. The cop shot Hue in the left side of the chest, killing him. The cause of death was listed as "firearm homicide through legal intervention." Hue had been diagnosed five years earlier as having an impulse control disorder and an intermittent explosive disorder. This was the second person fatally shot by San Francisco police within one month. **Source:** San Francisco Chronicle, 8/5/97; San Francisco County Medical Examiner Case No. 97-0928; Coalition on Homelessness

| **Mildred Porter** | 60 | — |

August 2, 1997. Oakland:

Ms. Porter was killed in a car crash when a motorist being chased by an unmarked police car crashed into her car.

| **Kenneth Wm. Beeby, Jr.** | — | — |

July 21, 1997. Manteca:

Kenneth was shot to death by three Manteca police officers who were cleared of any wrongdoing following a lengthy investigation. No other information was available in this article. **Source:** Modesto Bee, 5/30/98

| **Johnny Williams** | 20 | — |

July 11, 1997. San Francisco:

Johnny was fatally shot in the chest by motorcycle cop Les Adams after Johnny allegedly tried to ram the officer with his car after a high-speed chase. Johnny died three days later. **Source:** San Francisco Chronicle, 7/11/97 & 8/5/97

| **Verlon Dykes** | 26 | *Black* | 👁 |

June 20, 1997. Oakland:

Verlon was shot twice in the back and once in the arm by officer Jude Siapno during a foot chase. Cops claim he had a loaded 10mm and a .38 caliber on him, but admit neither had been fired. Verlon's family said that he was unarmed and that guns were planted on him. Family members also said that Vernon was trying to surrender when he was killed. **Source:** San Francisco Chronicle, 6/27/97

Sammy Marshall — —

June 15, 1997. San Quentin State Prison:

Sammy was given a full reversal of his conviction in February of the year he was killed. There is a pattern at San Quentin of harassment of men with reversals. In June, prison authorities decided to change Sammy's cell. He was asked by guards to come out of his cell to be transferred to another one. He was suspicious and feared for his safety based on what had happened to other prisoners. So Sammy refused to come out of his cell. Rather than try to defuse the situation or just go away and choose another approach, guards sprayed three cans of pepper-spray into the 4 x 11 foot cell, beat him and killed him. The papers said Sammy died at the hospital; he actually died on the spot. **Source:** account of Charla Green, prison activist who knew Sammy; San Francisco Chronicle, 2/11/98

Tartommie Bivens   26   *African American*

June 7, 1997. Oakland:

Tartommie, raised a Jehovah's Witness, was an "easy going, down-to-earth individual, who took pleasure in life," said his sister Darlene. "He had aspired to be a lyrical entertainer. He loved children and had two of his own. An intelligent, outgoing, compassionate and proud young man, Tartommie was never ashamed of who he was. He became a victim of the system, and was soon to be labeled a criminal." Police claim that when they confronted Tartommie after an armed robbery of a taqueria truck, Tartommie ran away, dropping his gun and the money along the way. According to the police story, one cop grabbed Tartommie's legs when he attempted to scale a fence and a struggle allegedly ensued. Cops claim that the struggle caused the officer's drawn handgun to point in the direction of other police officers. Officer Jad Jadallah shot Tartommie in the chest from a distance of one to two feet, the force of the shot reportedly sending Tartommie over the fence. But according to eyewitnesses, Tartommie fell to his knees as he was running away from police and Officer Jadallah walked up and shot him. Autopsy findings show that the bullet entered Tartommie's clavicle (collar bone) area and traveled downward, and that he died within minutes of being shot. The shooting was ruled justified. The victim's sister Darlene said that, despite her requests, she never received a copy of the police report and was told by the Oakland Police Department that if she was given the report, portions of it would be blacked out. **Source:** family; death certificate; autopsy report; San Francisco Chronicle, 6/9/97; Oakland Tribune, 10/14/97

Joannie Marie Holmes   35   *white*

June 4, 1997. Sonoma County Jail:

Joannie had two little children. She was booked into Sonoma County jail on an outstanding prostitution warrant and died less than three days later. According to fellow inmates, Joannie became very ill, "throwing up constantly, gasping for air." A heroin addict well known to police, she and other inmates repeatedly requested medical attention. None was ever provided. Describing Joannie after two days in jail, one inmate said, "I couldn't believe it was the same person. Her skin was gray, almost black; her bottom eyelids were pulled away from her eyeballs. She had deep black circles under her eyes, and her skin was wrinkled, hanging. Her face looked like death." A coroner found she died of a seizure and complications of heroin withdrawal. "That was torture, what they did to her," said an inmate, "I've never seen anything so inhumane. I couldn't do that to my worst enemy." **Source:** Women's Voices, 8/97; Purple Berets

Shiloe Ray Johnson   21   *white*

May 29, 1997. Napa:

Shiloe was artistic, creative, humorous and generous, with a positive outlook on life. He played the harmonica and taught himself the guitar. He always had time to talk to his many friends and to share the money he made from his two jobs. While walking his bicycle over a bridge, he was jumped from behind by a police officer. Shiloe was wearing a Walkman and could not hear police commands to him. Officer Monica, who was later kicked off the Los Angeles police force for brutality, shot Shiloe at point blank range in the head, killing him. Shiloe was unarmed. No gun or weapon was found at the scene. **Source:** SLP form; The Napa Sentinel, 1/16/98

Kuan Chung Kao   33   *Chinese*   ◉

April 29, 1997. Rohnert Park:

While celebrating a new job and a promotion, Kuan was the brunt of a racial slur at a local bar. Later, angry and intoxicated, he stood in the driveway of his home shouting and pleading for help from his neighbors and waving a broomstick. Police arrived. His wife approached to take the stick away from him. The police ordered her to stand back and shot him once through the chest. They would not let his wife, a registered nurse, give medical aid as he lay dying. Cops justified the shooting by saying that Kuan was holding the broomstick in a "martial arts manner." Ayling Wu, Kuan's widow, filed a $50 million wrongful death suit. On Chinese New Year, the U.S. Attorney announced he would not press charges against Officer Jack Shields. Supporters of Kuan's family denounced the decision and took the case to the U.S. Commission on Civil Rights. Mr. Kao was originally from Taiwan. **Source:** The Press Democrat (Santa Rosa, CA), 1/29/98

Michael Stallworth   —   —

April 14, 1997. Stockton:

Police shot Michael 23 times and killed him in front of his family, which was pleading that he not be shot. Michael was unarmed.

Esteven Velez   31   *Latino*

April 11, 1997. Concord:

After a chase, the car Esteven was driving with his girlfriend and their baby skidded into the yard of a residence. When Esteven got out of the car, police pumped him full of bullets, killing him. They said he aimed a gun at them. Two days later, police "found the gun."

Tria Lor (daughter)   13   —
Ge Vue (mother)   31   —

April 7, 1997. Sacramento:

A mother and daughter were killed when their car collided with a police car involved in a high-speed chase. Police were chasing a crime suspect through an intersection. The victims' family received a $1.85 million settlement eight months after the incident. **Source:** The Sacramento Bee, 5/28/98

Charles Williams   23   *Black*   ◉

March 1, 1997. Oakland:

Charles was shot to death by police during a traffic stop.

Corey Glenn Goodwin   36   —

February 23, 1997. Rohnert Park:

Corey Goodwin was described by neighbors as a quiet man who often was seen walking his dog and sometimes seemed troubled. He suffered from stomach cancer and may have been on medication. A Sonoma County Sheriff's SWAT Team was called to Corey's apartment complex following reports of a man, barricaded in his apartment, shooting randomly into the street. Police evacuated the area and a six-hour siege ensued. After allegedly returning Corey's gunfire, the SWAT team threw a tear gas canister into the apartment, knowing that a fire was likely to erupt. Rohnert Park Public Safety Commander Bob Cassel said SWAT also shot a "flash bang" grenade into the house. When a fire broke out, no effort was made to put it out even though the fire department was present. The fire consumed the apartment, where Corey's charred and incinerated body was found hours later with several gunshot wounds as well. **Source:** Comm. Voice, 2/27/97; The Press Democrat (Santa Rosa, CA), 2/24/97

Salomon Arambula Hernandez   28   *Mexican*

February 15, 1997. Santa Rosa:

After pumping gas into his car, Salomon and a friend drove away. They realized that they forgot to pay and Salomon quickly returned and paid the five dollars. The cashier told him he had already called the police, so Salomon returned to his car to wait. Officer Goldschlag, who killed Damon Lansing in Nov., 1989, arrived and approached the car. He shot Salomon three times, killing him. Police claim Salomon attacked them with a screwdriver. It was the third time in 13 months a Santa Rosa cop shot and killed someone. Salomon's wife said, "It was exactly like him to come back. He never would steal. Most people would have just left. But Salomon always kept his word. He was very responsible and a very, very, very good dad." Salomon is sorely missed by his two children. He played video games and baseball with his son and took him for pizza and to the movies. He spent hours in the park everyday with his one year old daughter. He also ran his own furniture and antique refinishing business. **Source:** The Press Democrat (Santa Rosa, CA), 2/19/97; victim's family

Robert Greer   30   *white*

February 3, 1997. San Francisco:

Robert, a homeless man, had sought a place to sleep at the Powell Street BART station at night. He was later awakened by BART police and told he would have to leave. While being escorted outside, police claimed he fell from the escalator to the station floor. His cause of death was listed as an accidental fall. No alcohol was found in his body. **Source:** San Francisco County Medical Examiner Case No. 97-0156; San Francisco Coalition on Homelessness

Isan Richard Frost   33   *white*

January 3, 1997. Santa Rosa:

Sonoma County sheriff's deputies pulled Isan over for a "suspicious car." Deputy Michael Raasch, who had severely beaten Isan in a previous incident, hit him in the chest with a flashlight. Sheriff Mark Ihde defended the actions of the deputies, who, after hitting Isan, chased him into a flooded roadside creek and then canceled a search for him, declaring Isan had escaped on foot. The victim's body was found the next day in the creek; his death was ruled a drowning. Sheriff Ihde said there were no obvious violations of policy in the pursuit or altercation. "His [Officer Raasch's] action, striking with the flashlight, appeared to be consistent with the training we provide." According to Isan's sister, Isan was "quite a charmer and a lot of people cared about him. He was everybody's friend, from young to old." Isan had attended El Verano Elementary school and then private school. He was a carpenter, mechanic and welder. Isan's family filed claims worth $2 million charging misconduct by the officers. **Source:** The Press Democrat (Santa Rosa, CA), 1/4/97

Brad David Fast   36   —

December 1, 1996. Oakley:

Contra Costa sheriff's deputies responded to a domestic disturbance call. The deputies claim Brad came out of the door of his home with a knife raised over his head. They shot and killed him. **Source:** San Francisco Examiner, 12/1/96

Carl Harlow   —   *white*

November 28, 1996. Santa Clara:

Police shot and killed Carl while he was barricaded in his house.

Anthony Gilbert   30   *African American*

October 24, 1996. San Jose:

Anthony got into an altercation with a security guard at a mall. Supposedly, the guard suspected him of shoplifting. When Anthony tried to drive away, he was shot in the head and killed by former Mountain View Police Officer and off-duty San Jose Fire Captain Robert Gremminger. Gremminger claimed Anthony was trying to run him down. He was convicted of involuntary manslaughter and sentenced to prison. Gremminger was one of the leaders in a reverse discrimination lawsuit by a group of white firemen, claiming that they had been denied promotions by San Jose's African-American Fire Chief. (The suit was thrown out of court by a white judge who determined that it had no merit.) **Source:** San Francisco Chronicle, 2/7/98; NAACP (San Jose Branch)

Thomas Palkowski	26	*white*	

October 22, 1996. Benicia:

After a traffic stop, police say Thomas' car lurched at officers. He was shot numerous times and tried to get away. He drove onto the freeway, where he pulled over and died a short distance away. The two cops who shot him are still working for the Benicia police. Thomas left behind a five-year-old son. **Source:** San Francisco Chronicle, 10/23/96

Dustin Harley Clark	23	*Italian*	👁

September 6, 1996. Sonoma County (Santa Rosa):

Dustin was concerned about the feelings of others, willing to give the shirt off his back. For allegedly being under the influence, "my son was brutally beaten by police, pepper-sprayed, attacked by a police dog, hog-tied, and smothered by police," said Dustin's mother. Ambulance personnel revived him and took him to the hospital. His mother was not allowed to see him until five or six hours later. His stepfather was denied visitation under threat of arrest. "I was totally unprepared for what I saw," said Dustin's mother. "My son's face was distorted almost beyond recognition and it was very painful to witness. He was trembling and I was told that he was having seizures. His eyes were open, but unseeing, and his eyelids were fluttering uncontrollably. Dustin was wearing a neck brace and his cheek bone was protruding beyond his nose." Doctors said Dustin died from "massive brain swelling." County Coroner's Office personnel told his mother, "It's just another dead body ... you wouldn't want to see him." Said his mother, "Some nights I am awakened by the thoughts of his fear, pain and suffering; his unheard screams echo through my mind. I miss my only son.... I will live with the image of his suffering body burned into my brain until the day I die... it eats me up inside. And it hurts me so much more than words can even explain." **Source:** SLP form; statement from Kathleen Cooley to the U.S. Civil Rights Commission Hearings 2/20/98 in Santa Rosa

Kevin Saunders	37	*Native American*	👁

August 29, 1996. Santa Rosa:

Distraught and perhaps suicidal, Kevin was shot three times and killed as he "was just standing" in the street. Police said he went for his pocket as if he had a gun. Witnesses say that wasn't true, that his hands were in the air. Kevin was unarmed. DA said "victim wanted to be shot." Official ruling –"Suicide by Police."

George Orozco Intiriano	27	—	

July 7, 1996. San Jose:

Mr. Intiriano was shot and killed by Officer Payne after a call to police from a security guard that a restaurant customer was creating a disturbance. Mr. Intiriano was pointed out to the police as he left the restaurant. Officer Payne called out to him, and when the victim turned, he was shot. Cops claim that Mr. Intiriano had a gun. He was an equipment operator for the nearby city of Palo Alto and had never had contact with law enforcement other than for a traffic ticket. **Source:** San Jose Mercury News, 7/9/96

James Parkinson	25	*white*	👁

June 8, 1996. Fairfield:

James died while in the custody of the Fairfield Police. He had been sprayed with pepper-spray multiple times and shot with a Taser gun. James had schizophrenia and had been doing well on medication. There had been a lapse in his medications, which resulted in the event leading to his death. **Source:** victim's family

| **Mark William García** | 41 | *Latino* | 👁 |

April 6, 1996. San Francisco:

Mark was a husband and loving father of two daughters. He came from a family of Teamsters and was a Teamster himself. Mark had been robbed and partially stripped of his clothing. He was calling for help and in need of medical attention. When cops arrived, they beat and pepper sprayed him and ground a foot into his back for five minutes while he lay face-down in handcuffs. The ambulance called to the scene was diverted to a non-injury accident and Mark was hog-tied, thrown into the back of the police van like a sack of potatoes and left face down to die. The three-minute ride to the nearest hospital took the police ten minutes. Mark died of a massive heart attack. The family and community waged a tenacious struggle for justice in forums, on the streets and in the courts. The Office of Citizen Complaints found the officers involved in the brutality that led to Mark's death guilty of several violations. The García family filed a wrongful-death lawsuit which a Superior Court judge dismissed. An appeal was filed. **Source:** San Francisco Chronicle, 12/5/98; victim's family

| **Gustavo Soto-Mesa** | 33 | *Latino* | 👁 |

March 2, 1996. San Jose:

Gustavo, who had a wife and three young children, ran from a sheriff's deputy after a traffic stop. He was shot in the back of the head at 50 feet and killed. The shooting was ruled accidental. The deputy first claimed that he dropped his gun and it discharged. He later changed his story to one in which as he drew his gun, the hammer cocked as it caught on his badge and then the gun fired when the trigger caught on the pen in his breast pocket. Gustavo's family sued the county, with the case still pending. Gustavo's murder led to several mass marches and a new grassroots organization fighting police abuse in San Jose. **Source:** San Jose Mercury News, 11/15/96

| **Bradley Davis** | 40 | — | |

January 31, 1996. Concord:

Bradley was shot to death as he stood in the doorway of his house allegedly holding a knife.

| **Dale Hearldeane Robbins** | 40 | *white* | 👁 |

January 29, 1996. Santa Rosa:

Police say Dale walked into the lobby of the police station carrying a metal pipe. He was shot and killed when he allegedly attacked cops. Strangely, the lobby surveillance camera, which is on 24 hours a day and which would have recorded what actually happened, was "broken" during the incident.

| **Flores** | — | *African American* | |

1996. New Folsom State Prison:

Flores was killed by prison guards. **Source:** James Chanin, Berkeley attorney

| **Tracy Shaman** | 25 | *Irish American* | |

1996. Alameda County (Santa Rita Jail):

Tracy was picked up on a parole violation. She was high and knew she would have to come down in jail. She said she had a medical problem and begged for medical attention. She was sick with symptoms from withdrawal, but she knew there was something else wrong as well. Jail personnel ignored her and she died in a holding cell within 12 hours of being arrested. Tracy was told she could see a doctor after court, but she never made it. Her mother settled a lawsuit she filed over her daughter's death. **Source:** SLP form

| **David King** | 22 | — | |

December 16, 1995. Fort Bragg (Mendocino County):

Police said that David rammed their patrol car. Police killed him with one shot to the head.

| **Dozell Thomas** | — | *Black* | |

November 19, 1995. Oakland:

Police beat Dozell Thomas to death.

| **Edward Sheehan** | 40 | *white* | 👁 |

November 1, 1995. San Francisco:

Police spotted Edward's vehicle and engaged in a short chase to "check him for a parole violation." After Edward crashed into a parked car and while still sitting in his van, Sgt. John Haggett opened Edward's door and shot him dead. Edward was unarmed. By the end of 1995, Sgt. Haggett had on his record 18 complaints of racism or excessive force, four of which the city paid claims to settle. They included viciously assaulting a motorist who ran a red light, pistol whipping an Asian youth, breaking another teenager's nose with his walkie-talkie and driving his car into the path of a disabled man and saying, "You're my n*gger and I'm taking your Black ass to jail." Still on the force after killing Edward Sheehan, Sgt. Haggett took part in a brutal attack on people attending an AIDS benefit. **Source:** flyer from victim's family

| **Ricky Pierre** | — | *Black* |

September 19, 1995. East Palo Alto:

The car in which Ricky was riding was pulled over by police. According to witnesses, Ricky jumped out and ran, but was hit by a UPS truck. While he was laying face down in the road, badly injured, the officer walked up and shot him in the head, killing him. **Source:** victim's mother

| **William Hankston** | 29 | *Black* |

September 6, 1995. San Francisco:

While a drug bust was going on in a park near William's home, he rode his bicycle by the activity. A plainclothes cop, without identifying himself, yelled at William to stop, then ran up beside him and shot him in the head, killing him.

| **Thomas Trevino** | 38 | — |

July 26, 1995. San Jose:

Thomas was shot 15 times and killed by Officers Sima, López, Dasaq and Jackson, who arrived at his house in response to a neighbor's call of a disturbance. Thomas refused to open the door, but his girlfriend came out to show that she was OK. Officers kicked in the door and fatally shot Thomas, claiming he had a small knife. **Source:** San Jose Mercury News, 6/28/95 & 9/20/95

| **David Boss** | 42 | — |

June 14, 1995. San Francisco:

Police claimed David had a knife. They shot him to death.

| **Robert Olin Jacobson** | — | — |

June 8, 1995. San Jose:

Robert died in custody while being transported in a police van, hog-tied and face down. This violated police policy that hog-tied arrestees are not supposed to be transported face down. Sgt. Unland and Officers Chewy and McMullin, who were transporting Robert when he died, were cleared of wrongdoing. **Source:** San Jose Mercury News, 6/9/95

| **Aaron Williams** | 35 | *Black* | 👁 |

June 4, 1995. San Francisco:

A burglary "suspect," Aaron was at his home when police arrived. They asked him to come out and talk with them. When he did, they swarmed him, ramming his head into a wall. Twelve cops brought him down, hog-tied him, beat and pepper-sprayed him, with one cop kicking him in the head so hard that it left a boot print. They placed a surgical mask over his nose and mouth to keep the pepper spray in. The police did not wash Aaron's face with water, but used the water to clean their own hands and to wash Aaron's blood into the gutter. He was thrown into the back of a police van and taken to the station, passing three hospitals on the way. He was left in the back of the parked van at the station until he was dead. None of the officers involved faced criminal charges and the police commission dismissed brutality charges brought by department officials against Officer Andaya. That prompted a torrent of criticism and protest and three commissioners subsequently resigned. Officer Andaya was later fired for lying about excessive force complaints and lawsuits filed against him while he worked at the Oakland Police Department.

Leonard "Acorn" Peters — *Native American*

April 14, 1995. Mendocino County (Ukiah):

We received the following account of the case from Cora Lee Simmons of Round Valley Indians for Justice: "On April 14, 1995, Leonard 'Acorn' Peters was murdered in cold blood by Mendocino County sheriffs deputies on a lonely road to Little Valley that is within the boundaries of the Round Valley Indian Reservation. Acorn and his lifelong friend Eugene "Bear" Lincoln were ambushed by Mendocino County Deputies Dennis Miller and Bob Davis. Bob Davis was killed, probably by 'friendly fire.' Neither Acorn nor Bear had broken any law that fatal night. This tragedy rocked the Round Valley Indian Reservation as Acorn was one of the most kind, gentle men on the reservation. He always greeted the day with a song of his own and, most importantly, was the the father of six children whom he dearly loved. This precious brother and loving companion cared deeply about nature and loved all people. The lies as told by Mendocino County deputies, including the lie that Leonard was a cop killer and fired on the officers first, were told to a courtroom daily filled with concerned citizens from as far away as Hawaii. Of course, as with all the news about this case, it was proven by forensic testing that Acorn's gun had never fired a single shot. Yet for this lie, Leonard lost his life. According to the coroner's testimony, Leonard lived approximately 45 minutes and could have survived if officers had only felt him worthy of medical attention. He was left to lie in the dirt road for nine hours before his body was hauled away in a pickup truck by Mendocino County sheriff's deputies. This notorious case was shown on America's Most Wanted with a $100,000 reward for the capture of Bear Lincoln offered by California Governor Pete Wilson. Round Valley Indians for Justice and others insisted that Leonard's death would not be in vain and fought to bring to light the corruption and cover-up within the law enforcement brotherhood. The Indians and others said, 'No more. No more.' The U.S. system has never authorized a single officer to enforce his or her own definition of justice whether black, yellow, brown, red, or multi-color." **Source:** Round Valley Indians for Justice

James Hopper — 37 —

April 1, 1995. Santa Rosa:

Police responded to a call of a fight between James and his brother. James left the scene and police pursued him in their car. Police say when they caught him, he knocked one cop to the ground and was coming at another with a pipe. But an eyewitness reported that another witness was beaten because he refused to go along with the police version of what happened. James was killed.

David Arnold — 54 —

February 23, 1995. San Francisco:

Arnold, a vice president of Citicorp, was arrested for being drunk and asleep in the lobby of the Hotel Fairmont. He was taken to jail, where the following morning he was found to be in a coma from a fractured skull and internal injuries. He remained in a coma for 13 months before dying.

Derek Wallace — 29 —

January 18, 1995. Antioch:

Police claim they found Derek banging on doors of homes. They tried to subdue him physically and then used pepper spray. Witnesses reported hearing Derek, an asthmatic, scream that he couldn't breathe. He died soon afterwards. The city of Antioch agreed to pay his family $362,000. The city attorney said that the city did not want to pay, but "the risk of going to a jury trial was too great." Derek's father said, "No amount of money compensates for anything like this." **Source:** San Francisco Chronicle, 2/11/98

Jeremy Emerseon Redd — 24 —

November 3, 1994. San Jose:

Jeremy died in a hail of police gunfire after a 90-minute chase. He reportedly pointed a gun to his own head before being killed by police. **Source:** San Jose Mercury News, 9/21/98

Timothy Pride — —

September 30, 1994. San Quentin Prison:
Timothy was shot two times in the back by a prison guard. Officials contend they had to break up a fight. Eyewitnesses deny this story. Pride had just received a reversal of his conviction and was probably innocent of the charges that landed him in prison.

Moses Pardo, Sr.   68   *Mexican*

September 27, 1994. SAN JOSE:
Moses, born in Mexico, led a hard life. He was abused as a child and orphaned at age nine. He served as a police officer in Mexico before coming to San Jose to work as a laborer and in the canneries. Moses also took medication for schizophrenia. He had a disagreement with a grocery clerk over how much he owed and allegedly chased a security guard with a knife. When police arrived, they maced Moses, then shot him to death when he supposedly lunged at them. Moses' son said, "That doesn't sound like my dad. If he was that violent, I wouldn't have had him here. He'd just sit in front of the house and smoke his pipe. I have to say one thing: My dad was sick most of his life, but he was never violent." Moses was surrounded and cornered by five cops, and witnesses state he was trying to surrender when he was shot. He is survived by three sons, a daughter and 15 grandchildren. **Source:** San Jose Mercury News, 9/29/94 & 9/21/98; Moses Pardo, Jr.

Arthur Díaz   38   *Latino*

September 10, 1994. San Jose:
Arthur accompanied a friend to a dumpster behind Save-on. A Santa Clara sheriff's deputy arrived and ordered Arthur out of the dumpster. He didn't want to be taken in for traffic warrants, so he ran toward his home several blocks away. He was running on the sidewalk with his arms up, according to a witness. He was run down by a sheriff's vehicle from behind. Then the deputy backed up and ran over him again. No crime, no weapons, no threat. The Deputy denied running Arthur down, saying the victim ran into his car. The California Highway Patrol report found that the physical evidence did not support the deputy's statement. Arthur left behind three children. **Source:** www.thediazfamily.com

Charles Mann   43   *white*

July 14, 1994. Placer County:
Charles was killed by police, who beat, hog-tied, and pepper-sprayed him.

George Lockhard, Jr.   34   *Black*

July 11, 1994. San Francisco:
Police were called to the family's home when George locked himself in his sister's room and was acting strangely. When cops arrived, they found him crouching in a downstairs corner. The police struggled with George and handcuffed him. He died at the scene. **Source:** San Francisco Chronicle, 7/13/94

Peter Anthony Knauss   38   *white*

June 30, 1994. San Jose:
Peter was killed by a single shot to the chest after allegedly charging cops with a knife. He had just been released early from a 72-hour hold at a Veterans Medical Center psychiatric ward. **Source:** San Jose Mercury News, 9/21/98

Tony Johnson   28   *white*

April 18, 1994. Sacto County:
Tony was pepper-sprayed to death by police.

David Del Real   21   *Latino*

April 8, 1994. Solano County:
David was pepper-sprayed, hog-tied and killed by police.

Mark Adams   30   —

March 1994. San Quentin State Prison:

Mark Adams was killed by a prison guard during an altercation he was having with another inmate. Timothy S. Reynolds, a prison guard at San Quentin Prison, fired one shot that hit Mark in the back of the head, killing him instantly. A former girlfriend said that Officer Reynolds bragged about the killing afterwards. On Nov. 30, 1998, a federal jury found the guard had used excessive force. The jury also found that the director of the California state prison system and the warden of San Quentin had put into place an unconstitutional policy on lethal force. The jury awarded Mark's mother and widow $2.3 million. The succeeding director of the state prison system announced plans to revise policy to end the use of guns to break up fights between inmates. Leroy Lounibos, a lawyer for the Adams estate said, "I think we've sent the message with this verdict that they're not to break up fist fights with guns." **Source:** Los Angeles Times, 12/1/98 & 1/1/99

Richard Townsend   33   —

February 4, 1994. San Jose:

Richard, a homeless man, reportedly created a disturbance by trying to set fire to a Burger King counter. Employees called 911. Police claim Richard had a gun and refused to drop it. Three officers shot and killed him. He had a long history of psychiatric problems.

Jeffrey Scott   33   *Latino*

December 8, 1993. Napa County:

Jeffrey was pepper-sprayed and killed by police. He had committed no crime.

José Martínez   26   *Latino*

September 15, 1993. Fresno:

José was beaten, hog-tied and pepper-sprayed. He died from this brutal treatment.

Baraka Hull   19   *Black*

August 30, 1993. Oakland:

Baraka Hull was sitting in a car with another man when a cop rolled up. Baraka jumped out of the car and ran. The cop said Baraka pointed a gun at him as he was running, but witnesses say he never pulled a gun or threatened the police. One 15-year-old boy said, "He was running for his life, like a track star." After a chase on foot of less than 100 feet, the cop stood behind a tree and fired twice, shooting Baraka in the back and killing him. The City of Oakland and the cop settled the civil case. The cop, who has been sanctioned for similar incidents since this shooting, continues to patrol the streets. **Source:** victim's family

Nathan Cosby   32   *Black*

August 19, 1993. Oakland:

Nathan was asleep in the early morning hours in a rear bedroom when his house was surrounded by more than 20 officers from the Oakland and Pleasanton Police, the Secret Service and the U.S. Postal Police. They were looking for evidence in a credit card fraud case but they were at the wrong house. While cops were breaking down the front door, cops in the back yard shot Nathan's dog when it barked at them. Nathan woke up, grabbed a gun and stuck his head out the window to see what was going on. Police opened fire and killed him.

Kevin Joice   17   —

August 18, 1993. Oakland (?):

Police chased Kevin into a dark alley, where they shot him 10 times, five times in the back. A gun without identifiable fingerprints that had not been fired was supposedly found next to his body. Kevin's family received a $300,000 settlement from the county, which feared that a jury would return a $1 million verdict. **Source:** Los Angeles Times, 5/14/97

Patrick Adams	—	*white*

August 9, 1993. Fremont:

Police were called to the family home of Patrick Adams, a registered nurse who was apparently threatening suicide. After Patrick shot himself, the cops opened fire, claiming "self-defense." They fired 34 to 50 rounds, hitting Patrick at least 20 times. Patrick's wife and 13 children filed a lawsuit and in 1996 were awarded $4 million by an Alameda County Superior Court, which found the police negligent. A state appellate court overturned the decision, saying Fremont police have no legal duty to act with care to prevent a suicide. Fremont city attorney Harvey Levine stated, "We thought our police did their job and we're glad the court agreed." The appellate ruling became binding on trial courts statewide, strengthening police departments' protection against negligence suits. The Alameda County coroner claimed that Patrick's self-inflicted gunshot wound was the mortal wound. **Source:** San Francisco Chronicle, 12/4/98

Jesse Castillo	20	—

August 6, 1993. Pelican Bay Prison:

Guards stood by in the general population prison yard when two rival gangs — the Bulldogs and Nortenos — began fist fighting. Three guards fired into the melee, killing Jesse Castillo and wounding two others. Mr. Castillo's family won a $600,000 settlement.

Richard García	28	*Latino*

August 5, 1993. Sacramento:

Richard was beaten with batons, pepper-sprayed, hog-tied and killed by police.

William John Blattner	34	—

July 29, 1993. San Jose:

Hoping to find William asleep, the San Jose Police Department Special Tactical Squad used a battering ram to break down the door to his apartment to search for drugs. Police claim William shot at them. Officers Larry Esquivel, Tim Porter, David Yazzolino and David Hober opened fire and hit William four times, killing him. A 12-year-old youth and his mother, who were in the apartment at the time, were taken to police headquarters for questioning. No drugs were found in the apartment. William was the fifth person to die at the hands of San Jose police in 1993. **Source:** San Jose Mercury News, 7/30/93

Raphael Grinage (Dad)	62	*Black*	👁
Luke Grinage (Son)	21	*Black*	👁

July 15, 1993. Oakland:

Luke Grinage had been harassed by the police before. Twice he had been jailed on phony charges that were later dropped. On the day Luke became engaged to be married, Oakland police came to impound his dog for rabies. Luke said he could prove the dog had shots and refused to give up his pet. The police jumped Luke and beat him, but he was able to escape and run to the house. Though they shot him as he ran, he was able to get to the house and was able to return fire with a shotgun kept inside the door. Luke's father, Raphael, a double-amputee in a wheelchair and a bass musician who played with Earl (Fatha) Hines, was also killed in the barrage. After police killed father and son, they went into the house and shot the dog.

Brian Sullivan	22	*white*

July 15, 1993. San Francisco:

Brian was running from police after he was spotted on the street with a shotgun. He dropped the gun and was trying to climb to the roof of his parents' home when he was shot in the buttocks. He bled to death before the police summoned help. The family received $295,000 in an out of court settlement. The shooter, Officer William Wohler, was put back on duty. **Source:** San Francisco Chronicle, 7/23/95

Scott Hodgson	38	*white*

June 13, 1993. San Jose:

Authorities allege Scott became engaged in a struggle with police. After cops pepper-sprayed and handcuffed him, he died.

Douglas James Moore   21   —

June 3, 1993. San Jose:

Douglas was part of a VW car club and had recently lost his job at Home Depot. He was wanted for allegedly killing his girlfriend and her son. Police chased Douglas for several miles in a car. Then, he left his car and began running up a row of trees. Cops surrounded him and claim he turned around and lifted a gun at them. All five officers opened fire, killing him. Douglas did not fire any shots at the police. **Source:** San Jose Mercury News, 6/4/93 & 6/5/93

Lance Rubalcava   32   —

May 30, 1993. San Jose:

Lance suffered severe mood swings due to brain damage since being beaten almost to death seven years earlier. At the Adult Independent Development Center, he won an award for his hard work to overcome his disabilities and was one year away from a degree in computer assisted design. Lance visited his parent's house with a belated mother's day gift . When he was asked to leave, he became despondent and reportedly pulled out a knife, threatening to kill himself. After 911 was called for help, Lance's father met Officer Lloyd outside and told him his son had brain damage. Officer Lloyd drew his gun and when he told Lance to drop the knife, Lance answered "why?" When Lance moved, the cop shot and killed him. Lance's parents said their son had poor coordination and had probably just lost his balance. Lance's former medical case worker said, "We're concerned about how they train police officers to assess mentally disabled behavior as compared to criminal behavior. I wasn't there. All I can say is that people in the mental health field deal with violence a lot. But they don't resort to guns." **Source:** San Jose Mercury News, 6/3/93 & 9/21/98

Carl Sciabarra   22   *white*

May 7, 1993. San Jose:

Carl was shot numerous times in the chest and back and killed by San Jose police, who claim he was acting irrationally and threatening people with a pair of scissors. While Officers Daniel Carley and Glen Baldwin were talking to the complainants, Carl approached the officers. The cops allege that they ordered him to surrender but that he ran instead. Cops chased and pepper-sprayed him and broke his arm with their baton as they allegedly tried to knock the scissor out of his hand. According to press reports, Carl then "wheeled to confront police, who fired their guns in 'self-defense.'" Police later entered his apartment and claimed they found a letter to his girlfriend in an envelope with "crazy" statements written all over it. But witnesses disputed the police version of events, denying that officers first tried pepper spray. An acquaintance pointed out that the police fired at least 15 shots at Carl, some after he was already on the ground. He also noted that Carl was clutching his neck chain and had possibly been robbed. Carl's mother said, "Carl was coming home from a friend's house late at night. He was walking, when suddenly he was mugged. Has was beaten by the muggers. When he approached a policeman for help, the mugger told the cop that Carl was drunk. After 32 seconds he was dead." A civil trial was held in San Jose three and a half years after Carl's death. Judge Aguilar ruled his mother had good and just cause for bringing the two cops to trial to answer for what they did. Carl's mother said of her son, "Carl was very intelligent and sensitive. He had an incredible sense of humor and the most wonderful smile. He loved deeply with all his heart and respected everyone." Carl was an IBM engineer. He was on his way home from the bus stop when he was killed. **Source:** San Jose Mercury News, 5/8/93; victim's mother

Quincy Jackson	20	Black

April 14, 1993. San Jose:

Quincy, his family and even his probation officer had complained that the police had been harassing and threatening him for a few years. He was fatally shot in the back of the head while fleeing police after they had stopped a car in which he was a passenger. Quincy's mother Robina, who learned about her son's death five hours later on the six o'clock news, explained, "Prior to being convicted and incarcerated on bogus charges, Quincy was taken to an isolated warehouse and beaten by the San Jose Police Department." Quincy spent eight months at Elmwoon Correctional Facility, where he earned a high school diploma. On Feb. 8, 1993, he was released and moved to Oakland, believing he had a new lease on life and freedom to attend Grambling University in August to study law. But there were constant reminders from friends informing him that police had been asking, "Where is Quincy?" Quincy wrote the court, "I just want to go to school and be left alone. That's all." The day before Quincy's murder, a friend's house was raided and his cousin said they ordered everyone out except Quincy. Then police entered yelling, "Where have you been?" and left with the warning, "We're gonna get you yet, n★gger." "Quincy had a life, a future ahead, but instead was murdered, the contract carried out by SJPD's special task force unit. Approximately one and a half years before, I wrote to the courts about receiving phone calls from police threatening to kill Quincy. The final living chapter — a conspiracy. Behind closed doors they made plans and with four bullets shot from the back, they committed murder one. Known perpetrators were SJPD Officers Avila and Sandoval," said Quincy's mother. **Source:** San Jose Mercury News, 5/23/93; victim's family

Robert Moore	—	white

1993. Calipatria State Prison:

Robert was shot and killed by prison guards. **Source:** James Chanin, Berkeley attorney

Jerrold Hall	19	Black	👁

November 15, 1992. Hayward:

Jerrold and a friend were stopped by a Bay Area Rapid Transit (BART) officer after arriving at their destination. The officer said that he had a report that they had stolen a Walkman from another passenger. Jerrold denied stealing a Walkman and neither he nor his friend had one on them. The cop got verbally abusive to Jerrold and hit him over the head with the barrel of his shotgun. Jerrold turned away from the BART cop and started walking toward the Hayward police who had arrived on the scene. The BART cop leveled his shotgun and shot Jerrold in the back of the head.

Michael Acosta	21	Filipino

November 1, 1992. San Francisco:

Police Officer Daniel Yawczak supposedly had a report of a purse snatching and a car was pointed out to him. Michael was at the steering wheel of the parked car. His hands were on the wheel and the engine was turned off. The cop came up to the driver's side and shot Michael point blank through the heart, killing him. The cop testified that Michael "had a surprised look on his face when I shot him." The cop then went up to Michael and shot him again. Michael's father said that his son was a good boy who helped in the family's catering business. He had just graduated as a mechanic from Sequoia Institute. **Source:** San Francisco Chronicle, 12/30/96; victim's family

Spencer Mobley	24	Black

September 27, 1992. Oakland:

Spencer, who lived in Lexington Park, Md., was visiting relatives in Oakland. He was stopped and searched by Officer John Jarrett after a burglar alarm went off in a business in the neighborhood. Officer Jarrett claims that he tried to confiscate a concealed .22 caliber handgun and that Spencer was "acting suspiciously." Spencer had reportedly broken free and was running away when Officer Jarrett shot him in the back and killed him. A subsequent investigation determined that the business had not been broken into. Officer Jarrett was given five paid days off and returned to duty. **Source:** San Francisco Chronicle, 9/29/92

| **Rosebud Denovo** | 22 | *white* |

August 1992. Berkeley:

Rosebud was a popular street person and anti-war activist. She was non-violent. Under very suspicious circumstances, the police reported that she was shot and killed in the home of the University of California at Berkeley Chancellor. Police say that she broke in to "kill the chancellor and his family with a machete."

| **Carol Ann Carlen** | 46 | — |

April 1992. Oakland:

Carol was murdered by her Oakland Police Department husband, who put her body in the trunk of her car, abandoned it in a poor area of town and painted "graffiti" on it to make it look like a gang killing.

| **James Hardeman** | — | — |

January 1, 1992. Santa Clara:

James was shot and killed by police.

| **Mildred Cesardo** | 30 | *Latina* |

November 24, 1991. San Francisco:

Mildred Cesardo was reportedly shot in the head and killed by her SFPD boyfriend. He was arrested for killing her. It is not known whether he was convicted.

| **Richard Dale Collins** | 45 | *white* |

April 14, 1991. San Jose:

According to police, Richard wore military camouflage fatigues and had his face blackened as if for combat when officers shot and killed him. He allegedly rushed them with a grenade. Richard suffered from Post-Traumatic Stress Disorder (PTSD) and flashbacks. **Source:** San Jose Mercury News, 9/21/98

| **William Galen** | 34 | *white* |

February 18, 1991. San Francisco:

William was visiting a friend's apartment when the police made a forced entry. Police shot and killed him when he moved. William was unarmed. No reason was given for the forced entry.

| **Henry Quade** | 56 | *white* |

October 16, 1990. San Francisco:

Neighbors reportedly complained to health officials about a mound of trash behind Henry's house. When Health Department inspectors arrived for a court-ordered inspection, they found the door nailed shut. People who knew Henry called him "a fat Howard Hughes" and a kind recluse. He was half-blind and allegedly threatened to shoot anyone who entered. Police responded by calling in the SWAT team. When he did not respond to negotiators, they broke down the door. Henry Quade allegedly confronted them with a gun. He was shot and killed by the SWAT team in a hail of gunfire. **Source:** San Francisco Chronicle, 7/9/94

| **Philip Lewis** | 16 | — |

May 22, 1990. Sacramento:

Philip and his friend were riding a motorcycle on a residential street in Sacramento when they cruised by a sheriff's car. An officer shouted for them to stop, but the boys continued. The officer sped after them, chasing the teens at speeds of up to 100 mph. While going around a corner, Philip, who was riding as a passenger on the motorcycle, fell off and was killed by the skidding police car. Philip's parents sued police for his death. Andrew C. Clark, a Memphis, Tenn. lawyer said, "You wouldn't want a cop to shoot into a crowd to stop a fleeing jaywalker. Why do we want cops to engage in high speed chases to pursue minor traffic violations?" Judge Harry Pregerson said, "This is not a case in which officers were pursuing dangerous felons. Lewis or Willard, his companion, would have posed no risk to public safety had they gotten away." The California Legislature made police departments "immune from liability" for any deaths or injuries that result from police pursuits.

Damon Lansing   24   *Native American*

November 26, 1989. Santa Rosa:
Police were called about a domestic disturbance. Officer Eric Goldschlag shot and killed Damon when the victim allegedly failed to drop a steak knife he was holding. Officer Goldschlag would later kill Salomon Hernandez on Feb. 15, 1997.

Joel Stephens Limberg   —   *white*

January 28, 1989. San Jose (?):
Joel Limberg of San Jose was described by neighbors as peaceful, but police claim he wielded a knife. Officers shot him 15 times, killing him. He had a history of mental illness. **Source:** San Jose Mercury News, 9/21/98

Peter Vasques Mejïa   —   —

November 28, 1988. San Jose:
Peter was shot and killed by Officers Savage and Norling. He was allegedly "armed" with a screwdriver. A witness said Peter was attempting to avoid police and was never closer that 12 feet when he was shot four times. **Source:** San Jose Mercury News, 11/30/88

Jerry C. Joaquín   —   *Filipino*

May 30, 1988. Richmond:
Police shot Jerry six times and killed him after he reportedly took off all his clothes while in an open field. Jerry had an old saw blade and police said they thought it would result in a fight. Jerry worked and was considered a responsible person. **Source:** James Chanin, Attorney at Law

Silivelio "Tony" Groshe   13   *Samoan*

February 17, 1988. San Francisco:
Tony, a retarded boy, was shot and killed by police while playing with a water gun near his home. Friends and teachers of 13-year-old Tony Groshe said that the boy was so severely retarded that he had trouble with such basic tasks as cooking a can of soup. The seventh grader spent his days with five other autistic children in a cheerful yellow classroom decorated with posters of nature scenes and cartoon heroes. "He would come up and put his head on your shoulder and just hug you. Everyone just loved him," his teacher said. He was learning basic skills like setting the table, putting stamps on envelopes, vacuuming and feeding the fish. His goals for the year were to be able to stack chairs, count money, shop for groceries and cross the street by himself. His extensive family and friends in Portrero Hill Projects watched out for him. The police had stepped up drug raids in Portrero Hill and did not seem to care about the neighborhood and its residents, such as Tony. The Chinese New Year celebration had brought the usual sound of firecrackers to the area and there were volleys of explosions on the hillside below the projects all day. One of many people who knew and loved Tony said he had been playing with a plastic gun (possibly a water gun) in his favorite haunt, a grassy knoll near a huge water tower, when the police arrived: "He was coming up the hill and heard somebody say 'Drop it.' As soon as he turned, they fired. They didn't try to find out nothing about him." **Source:** San Francisco Chronicle, 2/18/88 & 2/19/88

Davin Fuller   14   *Black*

April 28, 1985. San Francisco:
Davin took a Muni bus for a joy ride. He was 5'1", 115 pounds and unarmed. He lived near the Muni station, longed to be a bus driver and had been completing probation for an earlier joy ride by washing buses at the station. Before dawn, Officer Glickman got a call about a stolen bus. He pursued the bus back to the station, where Davin parked it and ran into the garage. The officer yelled "halt," cornered young Davin, then shot him in the stomach from five feet away and killed him. The police found Officer Glickman justified in killing young Davin. Officer Glickman, who had 18 prior citizens complaints filed against him, was reassigned to the Muni detail. The city paid a $35,000 settlement for Davin's life. **Source:** San Francisco Chronicle, 12/30/96

Donald Kizart	—	*Black*

January 1983. Richmond:

Donald was suspected of dealing drugs. While hiding in a closet, police claimed he shot at them. Cops shot and killed him, alleging they were returning fire. But no gun was found and no bullet holes were found to have been made by a gun from inside the closet. This incident occurred the same night the Richmond City Council rejected the case against the police who killed Johnny Roman. Donald's family filed and won a lawsuit. **Source:** James Chanin, Attorney at Law

Johaun S. Hayward	25	*African American*

June 27, 1981. Richmond:

Mr. Hayward was shot 12 times and killed by several officers in front of his mother's residence. The police were there due to a domestic dispute involving a couple in his neighborhood. The victim's daughter, Myesha Hayward, said, "He was a good person and he was robbed of his life and made to be the bad guy in the paper and media. He was falsely represented." Sixteen years later, police shot and killed Myesha Heyward's aunt, Venus Renee Beaird. **Source:** victim's family

Philip Bridges	—	*Black*

1981. Oakland:

An argument ensued between Philip and his wife. When the police arrived, they told Philip to cool off. Philip told police to leave his home, which they did. Then they shot him. Philip died a week later in the hospital. He had three small children. **Source:** James Chanin, Attorney at Law

Charles Briscoe	—	*Black*

1979. Oakland:

Charles had a family and was a member of the Machinist's Union. He was alleged to have fired a gun and was lying in the street. Police arrived and emptied their shotgun and revolver into Charles. There was a mass outpouring of protest at the city council meeting. A justice committee was formed and the lawsuit filed on behalf of Charles' family was won. **Source:** James Chanin, Attorney at Law

Tyrone Guyton	14	*Black*	◉

November 1, 1973. Emeryville:

Tyrone was a ninth grade student at West Lake Junior High School in Oakland. Within a block of his home, Tyrone was shot to death by three Emeryville police officers. He was shot in the back while lying face down on the ground. The community was outraged. The case was transferred to Sacramento and the family won its lawsuit. **Source:** James Chanin, Attorney at Law

Gerard Albanguibet	—	—

Date Unknown. Alameda:

Gerald was shot to death by police.

Abel Giménez	—	—

Date Unknown. Imperial City:

Abel was killed by police.

Don Short	40s	*Native American (Urok/Hoopa)*

Date Unknown. Humbolt County (Eureka or Crescent City):

Don had the original salvage rights to the wreckage of the Gold Rush Era Steamship "Brother Jonathan," which he had discovered. His rights were constantly challenged and he was attempting to fight the matter in court. He was arrested, beaten and left to die in a jail cell. Don's fighting spirit was passed on from his mother, Jessie Short, a leader in the Urok/Hoopa community, who became known in the case of Jessie Short vs. the U.S. Government.

COLORADO

Name	Age	Nationality	Photo

Unidentified Man — mid-20s — —

September 12, 1998. Aurora:
A police officer shot and killed a man while responding to a domestic disturbance call. The man died in the emergency room from multiple gunshot wounds. **Source:** Rocky Mountain News, 9/13/98

Frank Dean Rodríguez — 34 — —

July 13, 1998. Pueblo:
Mr. Rodríguez was shot to death by Officer Thomas Rummel in the early morning hours after a brief car chase. Officer Rummel claimed he saw a car being driven erratically around 12:30 a.m. and suspected that the driver was drunk. After a brief chase, the victim's car crashed into a parked car in the 400 block of West Northern Avenue. He jumped from his car and a foot chase ensued. Police claim Frank pulled a 9mm handgun and started to fire. Officer Rummel allegedly returned fire and hit him in the hip. The cops said more than a dozen rounds were exchanged at a distance of only two or three feet. At this point, the victim supposedly jumped into the driver's seat of the cop's car and the cop fired several shots through the closed window, killing him. Officer Rummel, who was wounded but survived, was placed on paid administrative leave (paid vacation) during the "investigation" into the shooting. Frank had spent seven years in prison for burglary and was allegedly wanted in connection with a recent armed robbery of a store. The newspaper reported that this was the second fatal shooting by the Pueblo police in 1998. **Source:** The Denver Post, 7/14/98

Michael Oliver Lewis — 54 — —

May 7, 1998. El Paso County Jail, CO:
Michael Lewis was a suspect in a child molestation case. He died after being strapped face-down to a one-foot wide board called "The Restrainer" designed to immobilize prisoners. **Source:** Denver Post, 5/10/98

Charles A. Bowyer — 44 — —

May 3, 1998. Denver:
Mr. Bowyer was shot in the chest and killed by Officer Shawn Saunders, who was allegedly responding to a fight between Bowyer and another man around 4 a.m. at the Pleasures Entertainment bookstore at 127 S. Broadway. Cops claim Bowyer "came at" Officer Saunders with an object in his hand as Saunders attempted to mace the two men. Saunders dropped the Mace, pulled his gun and shot and killed Bowyer. Police claim that the object Bowyer was holding was a canister of Mace. The DA declined to press charges against Officer Saunders. **Source:** The Denver Post, 5/4/98 & 6/10/98; Rocky Mountain News (Denver, Co.), 5/4/98

Christopher Trewet — 17 — —

May 2, 1998. Denver:
Christopher was shot and killed by SWAT team members Tom Lahey and Ken Padgett around 2 a.m. in the 200 block of South Lincoln Street. Cops claim Christopher fled a traffic stop, threatened cops with a gun, refused repeated commands to drop the gun and fought with police dogs before the cops opened fire. The DA declined to press charges against the cops who killed Christopher Trewet. **Source:** The Denver Post, 5/4/98 & 6/10/98; Rocky Mountain News (Denver, Co.), 5/4/98

Margaret Hull — 56 — —

May 1, 1998. Aurora:
Ms. Hull died on May 2, 1998, from injuries she suffered the day before in a car crash with alleged gang members who were being chased by police. Authorities charged Queena Quiñonez, the driver of the car they were chasing, with vehicular homicide. A police spokesperson said, "We have a very restrictive pursuit policy in Aurora and this pursuit did fall within our guidelines." Ms. Hull left a husband, John, age 53. **Source:** Denver Post, 5/3/98

Michael Bowers   —   —

April 15, 1998. Greenville County:

Mr. Bowers was suspected of shooting his wife seven times and killing her. Officers flushed him out of the woods. Mr. Bowers allegedly opened fire. Police opened fire, and Mr. Bowers died of numerous gunshot wounds to the head and body.

Abel Lawrence LaCrue   56   —

March 29, 1998. Sheridan:

Mr. LaCrue was killed in a car crash resulting from a police pursuit of a car whose occupants were suspected of stealing a $7.99 12-pack of beer from a convenience store. Mr. LaCrue's wife and mother-in-law were injured in the crash. He is also survived by at least one grandchild. Police claimed the chase was within pursuit protocol. **Source:** Denver Post, 3/31/98

Andrew Gene Alvarez   37   —

March 6, 1998. Adams County:

Andrew Alvarez was shot and killed by Edgewater Police Officer Dave Múñoz after Alvarez allegedly tried to hijack a car from a teenage girl at West 64th Avenue and Pecos Street. Edgewater and Mountain View police were chasing a car that had allegedly been stolen in Denver. The Adams County Sheriff's Department said, "We don't know if they [the cops] rammed it [the allegedly stolen car] or if it ran out of gas." Cops claim that there was a dead body 20 yards behind the car of the teenage girl, who had pulled over to get out of the way of the police cars. Alvarez was a passenger in the supposedly stolen car, whose driver was arrested. Cops claim Alvarez ran to the teenage girl's car, began pounding on the windows, and tried to get in (they don't specify how). A cop yelled that Alvarez had a gun and Officer Múñoz shot him twice. Alvarez supposedly continued to move, so Officer Múñoz shot him five more times, at which point Alvarez fell down behind the young woman's car. No gun was found, only a metal spoon and a syringe. Within a week, the DA had cleared Officer Múñoz of any wrongdoing, finding him to have "acted reasonably in defense of himself and others" and to be "justified in his actions." **Source:** The Denver Post, 3/14/98

Gregory Eugene Rodríguez   32   —

February 7, 1998. west Denver:

Mr. Rodríguez was shot once in the chest and killed by off-duty Officer Raymond Gallardo after he allegedly tried to run over the cop and others outside the Purple Turtle Lounge. Officer Gallardo and Officer Dan Rojas were moonlighting at the bar. The case was compared to the 1996 fatal police shooting of Jeff Truax, which a police spokesman said was justified and that Mr. Rodríguez' case was even more clear-cut. **Source:** The Denver Post, 2/9/98

Lance Kreps   35   —

January 21, 1998. Conejos County (Sanford):

Mr. Kreps was shot to death in an alleged gun battle with sheriff's deputies responding to a domestic violence complaint. Mr. Kreps' father believes that Deputy Chris Monroe fired the shots that killed his son. He filed a petition in court demanding the arrest of Deputy Monroe, one of the three cops at the scene. **Source:** Rocky Mountain News, 3/7/98

Tony Ray Martínez   44   —

January 8, 1998. El Paso County:

Mr. Martínez was shot to death by state patrolman Brian Lyons during a traffic stop. Martínez was pulled over by Officer Lyons on El Paso County 19 for a traffic violation. He stopped but allegedly drove off. He stopped again after a seven-mile chase and pulled over into a field, where he was shot and killed by Officer Lyons. Officer Lyons claimed that Mr. Martínez threw rocks at him, picked up a large rock, and said, "You're going to have to kill me because I'm going to bash your head in with this." Family members questioned this version of events, saying Tony was disabled and walked with a cane as the result of a car accident, so he was not in any condition to put up a fight and even if he did pick up a rock, Lyons could have defused the situation in a non-lethal way. The Colorado Bureau of Investigation cleared Lyons of any wrongdoing. The family filed a federal lawsuit against the Colorado State Patrol, Officer Lyons and other officers. **Source:** The Denver Post, 7/9/98

Unidentified Man — —

January 1998. Pueblo:
The victim was shot and killed by a member of the police SWAT team while cops were serving a search warrant. Authorities claim the man pointed a shotgun at the officer. **Source:** The Denver Post, 7/14/98

Robert Daniel Murphy 37 —

October 31, 1997. southwest Denver:
Cops arrived at the parking lot in response to a call about a suspicious truck. Several witnesses to the beating charged brutality on the part of Officers Mike Rossi, Marco Martínez and Gary Hise during the arrest of Robert Murphy. The official report claimed that Mr. Murphy resisted arrest and tried to swallow the contents of a pill bottle and the bottle itself when confronted by the three cops. Witnesses stated that Mr. Murphy resisted arrest at first but that after he had stopped resisting and was restrained, they saw one officer beat the victim with a leather strap and kick him in the head and body until he was unconscious. Authorities dismissed eyewitness reports because of supposed inconsistencies, while the autopsy claimed that the cause of death was a blocked airway and cocaine poisoning and that the bruises all over his head and body were merely "superficial" and did not contribute to his death. An FBI probe and a protest by the ACLU did not prevent the officers' exoneration. Robert Murphy left behind a wife and brother, who both demanded that the three cops be charged with murder. His brother said, "I don't think it's right to beat somebody to death and get away with it. The criminals are going unpunished because they have a badge." **Source:** Denver Post, 11/8/97, 12/17/97, & 12/18/97; Rocky Mountain News, 12/18/97, 12/23/97, & 12/24/97

Paul Frank Anstett 25 —

September 29, 1997. Boulder County:
Mr. Anstett was shot in the head and killed by police during a high-speed chase. The fatal shot came from a cop's shotgun. Police claimed that Mr. Anstett had robbed a bank a few hours earlier and that they fired on him only after he fired at them while recklessly driving on the highway. Cops did not say how many shots they fired. **Source:** Denver Post, 10/1/97

Dereke Herrera 30 —

September 13, 1997. Denver:
Mr. Herrera was shot and killed by Denver Police Officer Darren Lindsay and Sgt. Brad Lenderick. The press report alleges that police were called to the house after Mr. Herrera, who was supposedly drunk, punched his girlfriend and that he refused to put down his gun despite repeated orders to do so. Officer Lindsay claimed that Mr. Herrera pointed the gun directly at him. The cops fired five shots. No charges were filed against either of them. **Source:** Rocky Mountain News, 12/25/97

Luis McIntire 20 —

August 3, 1997. Boulder:
Luis was killed by being hog-tied and pepper-sprayed at a rave by off-duty cops. Three bouncers took him out of the building (Olympic Bowl, 1740 30th St.) just before 1 a.m. after he "allegedly fondled a female patron." They pushed him to the ground "and restrained him while placing their full weight on top of his body." Sgt. Robert Sullenberger, Officer Scott Adams and Officer Dan Elin, who were working as security guards, pepper-sprayed Luis and hog-tied him. This plus the weight of six people on top of him "caused him to be asphyxiated," killing him. The family filed a federal wrongful death suit against the city, the cops, the bouncers and others. **Source:** The Denver Post, 6/25/98

Bobby Ray Valdez 27 —

July 11, 1997. Denver:
Bobby was shot and killed by two Denver Police Officers James Dempsey and Aaron López, who were called to 3384 Lawrence St. for a domestic disturbance. Bobby was in front of his house. The DA's office claims he was holding a large knife and looked agitated. Cops claim he rushed at the officers, so they shot and killed him, but family members who were present said he did not threaten the officers. The Denver DA declined to press charges against Officers Dempsey and López. **Source:** Rocky Mountain News (Denver, Co.), 10/28/97

Alex Ray Gutiérrez   22   —

May 20, 1997. Denver:

Cops were at Alex's mother's house at 329 Fox Street investigating an earlier report of a domestic disturbance when Alex allegedly showed up carrying a gun and began pounding on the back door. Officer John Sullivan supposedly ordered him to drop the gun, which cops claim he was pointing at his own head. Then, according to police, Alex pointed the gun at Officer Sullivan, at which point the cop fired, hitting Alex in the hand and the abdomen and knocking him down. Supposedly, Alex then fired the fatal shot into his own head, so authorities have ruled the death a suicide. Officer Sullivan was placed on paid administrative leave (paid vacation) pending an "investigation." The newspaper reported that this was the third fatal shooting by Denver police in 1997. **Source:** The Denver Post, 5/21/97; & 6/25/97

James Ace Fleck   22   —

April 19, 1997. Denver:

James was shot and killed by police after he allegedly killed his girlfriend and fired at two cops. **Source:** Rocky Mountain News (Denver, CO), 5/22/97

Eric Younger   52   —

January 21, 1997. Colorado Springs:

Mr. Younger was killed just the city limits in Colorado Springs by one of eight shots fired by Manitou Springs Police Officer John Hayward, who was supposedly returning fire. The cop stopped Mr. Younger on U.S. 24 because his tail lights weren't working and claims that the victim gave several names, at which point the cop decided to take him in. Mr. Younger allegedly agreed to go along. Officer Hayward searched him and put him in the back of his police car without handcuffs. Eric supposedly said he was sick and about to vomit and when the cop pulled over and opened the right rear door, the victim allegedly pulled a gun and fired once, jumped out of the car and fired three more times. The cop fired five times, re-loaded and fired three more times, killing his victim. Officer Hawyard was not injured, even though he was supposedly fired upon repeatedly at close range. **Source:** The Denver Post, 11/22/97 & /23/97

Ernest S. Ackler   44   —

January 12, 1997. Denver:

Mr. Ackler was shot to death at a Denver public housing complex by Police Officer Brian Sides as cops tried to arrest him for allegedly assaulting a security guard. Cops had earlier come to Ernest's apartment in response to a neighbor's complaint that he was too loudly playing his electric guitar. They gave him a ticket and left. A security guard who was a former cop waited by the door to make sure that Ernest complied. The guard claimed that Ernest knew who had called the police and pounded on their wall, shouting obscenities. The security guard knocked on the door and asked him to stop and claims that Ernest attacked him. The guard punched him back, then called the police. The two cops who had come before returned around 12:15 a.m. but Ernest would not open the door. A caretaker unlocked the door and the cops broke through the chain lock. The security guard (the former cop) claims Ackler fired first and that Officer Sides fired back in self-defense. The police claim Ernest fired twice but said they didn't know how many times the cop fired. The district attorney's office ruled the shooting justifiable. The newspaper reported that this was the second fatal police shooting in Denver in the last three weeks (in addition to a non-fatal one). In 1996, the newspaper reported, there were eight police shootings, three of them fatal. **Source:** Rocky Mountain News, 1/14/97, 4/23/97 & 5/22/97

Manuel Moreno Delgado   30   *Salvadoran*

December 22, 1996. Lakewood:

Mr. Delgado was shot and killed around 2 a.m. by off-duty Denver Police Officer Michael Pace. Officer Pace and Officer Karon Price, also off-duty, were driving in separate cars. They claim that Manuel tried to run Officer Pace off the road and then pointed a handgun at him. Officer Pace fired six shots, hitting Manuel twice in the head and once in the chest. Police claim they found a gun in the victim's car that was traced to a previous user. Manuel was returning from a company Christmas party. His family said they never heard of him having a gun (although they reportedly said he was drunk) and retained a civil rights lawyer. They held a press conference Dec. 31, the day of the funeral. The lawyer called the cops "highway hoodlums" and said the case "reeks for justice." Manuel Moreno Delgado, described as a "hard-working immigrant from El Salvador who held two jobs," left behind a wife and two children, ages six years and 11 months. The only witnesses to come forward as of Dec. 31 were the cops. Manuel's family and co-workers called on other witnesses to come forward. **Source:** Rocky Mountain News, 1/1/97

Jeff Truax	25	—

March 20, 1996. Denver:

Mr. Truax was shot and killed while driving a car outside a bar. Sgt. Kenneth Chávez and Officer Andy Clarry emptied their guns, shooting 25 bullets into the victim's car, because they claim they thought he was trying to hit them. Jeff was unarmed. One of his three passengers was shot and wounded. A police spokesperson said the shooting was justified and the Denver District Attorney declined to press charges against the two officers. As of January, 1998, Officer Chávez still remained on the force and had been involved in four non-fatal shootings in addition to the shooting death of Jeff Truax. One year after the incident, Jeff's family and friends held a a vigil to remember their loved one's death and to demand justice. In Nov., 1998, a federal jury awarded Mr. Truax's estate $500,000 in a civil lawsuit filed against the city. **Source:** The Denver Post, 1/3/98, 2/9/98, 5/1/97, & 6/13/97; Rocky Mountain News (Denver, Co.), 3/21/97, 7/9/97, 9/17/97, & 11/13/98

Timothy Watt	—	—

1996. Lakewood:

Mr. Watt died after police arrived at his home to find him hanging from a tree and his wife Gail rushing towards him with a knife. The cops ordered her to drop the knife and detained her in her apartment, preventing her from cutting down her husband. Tim Watt died and Gail sued the officers, charging that her and her husband's constitutional rights were violated when they interfered with her rescue attempt. Judge Clarence Brimmer dismissed the case, ruling that there is no recognized right to be free from interference in rescue attempts and that while "The officers may have been negligent in failing to cut down Mr. Watt from the tree, it cannot be said from the facts pleaded that the officers were reckless in the constitutional sense." **Source:** Rocky Mountain News, 9/4/98

William Abeyta	16	—

January 18, 1995. Denver:

William was shot twice in the back and once in the face and killed by police around 2 a.m. in the 1800 block of South King Street after a short car chase in which William and another youth fled from police in a stolen jeep. The bullet that killed William went through his heart. Cops followed and tried to stop the jeep when they saw a broken wing window and an expired temporary permit. The jeep supposedly rammed two police cars and tried to accelerate away. Three cops fired 12 shots because, they claim, they feared being run over. However, a lawsuit filed by William's family contends that the shots were fired from the rear or the side of the car and that the car was disabled before the fatal shots were fired. In other words, the cops were not in any danger when they opened fire. In May, 1997 or 1998, a federal jury exonerated the three cops — Officers Frank Harrington, Douglas A. Stephens and Angelo Abeita — of using excessive force but awarded the family of the victim $400,000 in damages against the city and $10,000 for wrongful death from two of the three cops. Both sides called this verdict inconsistent. William's friend, Michael Dennis, who was riding with him in the jeep, was wounded but survived. In April, 1997, he settled a $2 million lawsuit against the city for $40,000. The lawsuit contended that the cops violated his civil rights by "shooting him in the back at point-blank range after he surrendered by raising his arms." **Source:** Rocky Mountain News, 4/29/97; Denver Post, 5/1/97 & 5/23/97

Benny Atencio	30	—

1995. Denver:

Benny was shot four times and killed by Officer Scott Blatnick. Benny had allegedly beaten his mother and was supposedly waving knives. Police and the DA's office claim that he lunged at Officer Blatnick, refused repeated orders to drop the knives and told the police to shoot him. Only one witness corroborated the police version and the details of his testimony conflicted with that of other witnesses, who all deny that Benny made any threatening move toward the cops. Benny's mother and other relatives say he was retreating when he was shot. The Denver District Attorney ruled that the shooting was justified and did not press charges; the police chief rejected a finding of the Public Safety Review Commission that Officer Blatnick used unnecessary force. The family filed a $2 million civil rights lawsuit; as of late March, 1998, it looked as if the family and the city would settle the lawsuit for $30,000. **Source:** Rocky Mountain News (Denver, Co.), 3/28/98

| **Steven Gant** | 20 | — |

September 1, 1992. Denver (Capitol Hill):

Steven Gant, an unarmed man, was shot and killed by Officer Michael Blake. Officer Blake was charged and brought to trial but acquitted of second-degree murder and reckless manslaughter. Steven had supposedly had an altercation with his girlfriend and neighbors called the police. He allegedly fled the apartment building at 1032 E. 14th Ave. in Capitol Hill. When cops arrived, they tracked him to a nearby apartment building. Witnesses at the trial said Steven, who had allegedly struck Blake in the chest, yelled "Don't shoot! Don't shoot!" before he was shot. Officer Blake claimed that Steven (who was unarmed) had yelled "You won't shoot. You won't shoot, but I will." A lawsuit filed by the family in 1993 was settled in 1998 for "an undisclosed amount." **Source:** The Denver Post, 6/9/98; Rocky Mountain News (Denver, Co.), 3/28/98

| **Leonard Zuchel** | 26 | — |

1984. Denver (16th Street mall):

Leonard was shot and killed by Officer Frederick Spinharney, who claimed he thought Leonard had a knife. The "weapon" turned out to be a set of nail clippers. Officer Spinharney was not disciplined for this killing, but a federal jury awarded Zuchel's family $499,361 in 1993. In 1998, Officer Spinharney was dismissed after shooting out the tire of a car he was trying to pull over in violation of departmental policy. At the hearing in this incident, Spinharney claimed he thought the driver "was trying to flee in a stolen car" and said, "The impulse just struck me to shoot the tire and incapacitate the car...." The police chief expressed concern about the liability the city could face if it kept Spinharney on the force. **Source:** Rocky Mountain News (Denver, Co.), 4/16/98; The Denver Post, 11/5/97

CONNECTICUT

Name	**Age**	**Nationality**	**Photo**
Victoria Cooper	41	—	

July 13, 1999. North Branford:

Ms. Cooper was shot and killed by North Branford Police Officer Michael Breen. Officer Breen claims he saw Ms. Cooper and a male friend acting "concerned with his movements" in a convenience store so he followed them out, ran a license plate check on their car and discovered that the owner had a suspended license. The cop pulled the car over and the driver reportedly jumped out and ran away into the woods, while Ms. Cooper remained in the passenger seat. Officer Breen chased the driver on foot but failed to catch him. As the cop returned to his own car, Ms. Cooper allegedly jumped from the passenger seat to the driver's seat of her friend's car. Officer Breen claims she tried to run him over and that he fired two shots in self-defense. Friends of the victim disputed that she was trying to run the cop over, saying she had poor night vision, probably did not see the cop and was just trying to drive away. A co-worker at the restaurant where Ms. Cooper worked as a waitress said, "I doubt that she'd hurt anyone. She was probably just very scared." Later, authorities admitted that the fatal shot was fired after Ms. Cooper's car had passed the officer. The victim is survived by her two children. Officer Breen was placed on administrative duty during the investigation. This was the fifth known fatal shooting by police in Connecticut since Dec., 1998. **Source:** The New York Times, 7/14/99, 7/15/99, & 7/20/99

| **Antonio Antolini** | 36 | — |

May 10, 1999. downtown Meriden:

Mr. Antolini had supposedly parked his van in the middle of the street while he argued with a woman inside. When cops approached, he allegedly jumped out of the van and ran before turning toward the cops. Police shot Mr. Antolini twice in the chest, claiming he lunged at them with a knife. He died at the hospital. **Source:** The New York Times, 5/11/99 & 7/20/99

| **Aquan Salmon** | 14 | *Black* |

April 13, 1999. Hartford:

Aquan Salmon was shot once in the back and killed by a white Hartford cop, Police Officer Robert Allen, in the early morning hours. Cops claim that Officer Allen chased and stopped a car after a resident complained she had been beaten and that four young men, including Aquan, jumped out of the car and ran. The article indicates no connection between the beating and the car in which Aquan was riding. The Hartford Police Chief claims the officer thought he heard a gun shot and thought Aquan, who was running away, was reaching for a gun. Officer Allen allegedly ordered Aquan to stop and then shot him. Cops produced a gun-shaped cigarette lighter that they supposedly found at the scene. At a news conference by the police chief that afternoon, Aquan's brother, Mark Barrow, said, "You ain't going to get away with this — killing my brother. You're not going to get away with this." Upon hearing the cops' story, Mr. Barrow shouted, "Thirteen hours to make up this lie? Uh-uh. Nah." The three young men with Aquan in the car were arrested, while the cop who murdered him was put on paid administrative leave. **Source:** The New York Times, 4/14/99

| **Unidentified** | — | — |

March 22, 1999. Hartford:

Cops claim the victim was a larceny suspect who lunged at two police officers with a knife. Police shot and killed him/her. **Source:** The New York Times, 7/20/99

| **Franklyn Reid** | 27 | *Black* |

December 29, 1998. New Milford:

Mr. Reid was shot in the back and killed by a white cop, New Milford Police Officer Scott Smith, after a foot chase and an alleged "scuffle." The victim was unarmed and on his knees when he was shot at close range (possibly point-blank range). Mr. Reid was described in the press as a "convicted sex offender...wanted by police for failure to appear on a number of charges." His family said he planned to turn himself in. Officer Smith justified the shooting, saying he feared for his life when the victim allegedly made a sudden motion. Officer Smith was charged with murder, a first for an on-duty police shooting in Connecticut. He was released on $250,000 bail and put on paid leave until the case is resolved. Mr. Reid is survived by his girlfriend, three children and his parents. His family filed a wrongful death lawsuit. His mother said, "This is a brutal thing. This could have been avoided." His girlfriend said, "He was unarmed; they shot him the back. He was going to turn himself in." Mr. Reid's death was the second fatal police shooting in Connecticut in three days. **Source:** Associated Press, 12/30/98, 1/20/99, & 1/23/99; The New York Times, 12/30/98 & 1/20/99

| **Joseph W. Parsons** | 45 | — |

December 27, 1998. Lisbon:

Mr. Parsons, an ex-corrections officer, was shot and killed by State Trooper John Patterson. Mr. Parsons supposedly pulled a gun on Trooper Patterson and refused orders to drop it as the cop peered in the passenger window of his car (Mr. Parson's car was trapped in a drive-through lane at McDonalds at the time). Trooper Patterson was involved in another fatal shooting in 1996. **Source:** The Hartford Courant, 12/30/98; The New York Times, 12/30/98

| **John Spignesi** | — | — |

November 1998 (?). Danielson:

Mr. Spignesi, an environmental protection worker, was shot and killed accidentally by off-duty Corrections Officer Kevin O'Connell, who was illegally hunting after dark. Officer O'Connell was charged with manslaughter. The victim was on patrol looking for illegal hunters when he was killed. **Source:** UPI-Reuters, 11/26/98

| **Eric "Winky" Richardson** | 32 | — |

August 4, 1998. Hartford (Northeast section):

Mr. Richardson was killed when his car crashed during a high-speed police chase. Cops claim they noticed him and followed his car because he was wanted on several unspecified warrants and that the license plates on his car were stolen. They tried to box him in, but he got away and a chase ensued. Cops claim they were not engaged in a high speed chase when the accident occurred but a lawyer representing the victim's family in a wrongful death lawsuit said that witnesses would testify that the cops were in hot pursuit. The crash occurred on a crowded street, though no one else was injured. **Source:** The Hartford Courant, 8/5/98 & 8/29/98

Yusef Kareem Gause   22   *Black*   👁

November 11, 1997. New Haven:

Yusef Gause, of Bridgeport, CT, was shot in the back of the head and also in the legs by New Haven Police Officer Mark Foster. He died nine days later, on Nov. 20 (his mother's birthday), from his wounds. Cops were supposedly responding to a call of "shots in the area" and claim Kareem, as he was known to his friends, was wearing a bulletproof vest and ran from them when ordered to stop, then pulled out a gun and began firing. Kareem's mother, Dolores Crawford, demanded a medical examination to determine if her son fired a gun but her request went unanswered. She continues to fight for justice. Ms. Crawford said of her son, "...he was a former student of Bassett High School, just starting to get his life in order. He had just completed an application to go to school for computers, he was working on recording a rap song and was particularly close to his 17-year-old brother, his seven-month-old sister and three-month-old daughter. He also loved writing poems and lyrics to rap music." **Source:** letter from victim's family

Bradley Bell   42   —

September 2, 1997. Hartford :

Mr. Bell had reportedly tried to rob someone with a knife. The man fought him off and gained control of the knife. The two men fought. Cops arrived and pepper-sprayed Mr. Bell, who allegedly resisted police, "kicking, spitting and flailing his arms." He died about an hour later after going into cardiac arrest. The medical examiner ruled the cause of death was "mixed drug toxicity," without saying what drugs were in Mr. Bell's system. **Source:** The Hartford Courant, 10/14/97

Christopher Scott   26   —

April 15, 1997. Hartford (Northeast):

Christopher was shot once in the chest and killed by eight to ten cops who arrived with a search warrant around 4:30 p.m. at his apartment on Rockville Street. Police claim that Christopher was a major "middleman" in a marijuana ring. Officers knocked on the back door and announced themselves, then burst into the apartment with guns drawn and came face to face with Christopher, who was allegedly armed with a gun. According to the official account, Officer Jeff Blatter ordered him to drop his gun and the fired twice because he "feared for his life" (although cops declined to say what Chiristopher was doing, justifying the incident by saying, "You are in a split-second situation.") One bullet killed Christopher and the other hit the wall. Cops claim to have recovered a loaded gun from the scene. The cops supposedly didn't realize Christopher was dead, so they maintained a siege for about half an hour and then stormed in, only to find the apartment empty of anyone other than their dead victim. **Source:** The Hartford Courant, 4/17/97

Malik Jones   21   *African American*

April 14, 1997. New Haven:

While driving a car Malik and a friend, Samuel Cruz were pursued by an East Haven police officer. Mr. Cruz reported that when he and Malik stopped the car, they were boxed in by a police car and van. Mr. Cruz said Police Officer Flodquist broke the window on the driver's side where Malik was sitting and shot Malik repeatedly as he sat in the car, unarmed.

Cynthia Cheatham-Hearst   37   —

April 1997. Bridgeport:

Ms. Cheatham-Hearst was killed when a pickup truck being pursued by Trumbull police crashed into her parked station wagon. Her sister was badly injured, "cling[ing] to life in a hospital" seven months later. The chase had begun in Trumbull and had crossed the Bridgeport city line. Ms. Cheatham-Hearst is survived by her husband and three children. Her husband filed a lawsuit against the police, saying they caused her death. The Trumbull police say the cops followed proper procedures. **Source:** The Hartford Courant, 6/8/98, 12/9/97, & 4/30/98

Unidentified Man   —   —

1996. Jewett City:

The man was shot and killed by two state troopers, including Trooper John Patterson, who later shot and killed Joseph Parsons. The man was allegedly armed and the shooting was ruled justifiable. **Source:** The Hartford Courant, 12/30/98

DELAWARE

Name	Age	Nationality	Photo
Clifford T. Manuell	39	*Black*	

August 2, 1999. Seaford:
Mr. Manuell was riding his bicycle around 2:40 a.m. A Seaford police officer stopped him because he was reportedly riding back and forth in an intersection with no lights on his bicycle. A second cop arrived. They demanded Mr. Manuell's identity and his reason for being out at that hour. Mr. Manuell reportedly gave a false name. One of the officers apparently knew his true identity. The cops tried to arrest him for impersonation, and a struggle allegedly ensued. Cops claim the victim broke free, pulled a gun from his waistband, and pointed it at the officers. One of the officers opened fire and killed Mr. Manuell. Authorities did not divulge the identity of the two cops or how many shots they fired. The victim's step-daughter described him as someone who spoke his mind, liked to play basketball, and loved his wife and step-children. She disputed the police version of events, saying, "Everyone knew he never carried a gun." A local minister expressed dismay at the shooting, saying, "I'm from New York City originally. I thought I'd left this behind." **Source:** www.newszap.com, found 8/3/99

FLORIDA

Name	Age	Nationality	Photo
Frank Valdez	36	—	👁

July 17, 1999. Florida State Prison (Death Row):
Mr. Valdez, an inmate on Florida's death row, was beaten to death by up to nine corrections officers during a cell extraction. Mr. Valdez's body had boot prints and broken ribs. The "extraction team" had come for him, armed with stun guns, to search for weapons after he allegedly threatened to kill a guard. After the beating, he was left in a cell without medical attention and pronounced dead several hours later. Guards refused to cooperate with an investigation. The nine guards involved in the incident and two others who may have witnessed it were put on paid leave for their failure to cooperate. Authorities tried to portray the killing of Mr. Valdez as an "isolated incident" even as the newspaper reported that complaints of official brutality from death row inmates are widespread but usually ignored. A letter sent by a death row inmate held in the same wing as Mr. Valdez was received by The Miami Herald two days before Mr. Valdez was killed. It read in part, "The sounds of prisoners screaming in pain and of bodies being beaten keep the inmates on the entire wing up all night. I can hear the officers forcibly take inmates from their cells. The wretched sound of fists and boots striking flesh are unmistakable, as is the sound of some kind of weapon (a stick or a broom handle?) being used. They scream. They whimper. Then there is silence." **Source:** The New York Times, 7/29/99

Jesse Runnels	25	*white*	

March 23, 1999. Miami:
After threatening suicide, Jesse was shot to death in his home by a Miami SWAT officer. Jesse was holding a toy gun when the officer fired. **Source:** The Miami Herald, 3/25/99

Kenin Sherrod Bailey	26	—	

February 15, 1999. Miramar :
Kenin was shot and killed by Miramar police while allegedly fleeing the scene of an attempted robbery at a check cashing store. **Source:** The Miami Herald, 2/16/99 & 2/17/99

Unidentified Man — —

January 24, 1999. Fort Lauderdale:

Around 9 p.m., about ten plainclothes and uniformed Fort Lauderdale police responded to a call from the Fort Lauderdale Mariott Hotel and Marina regarding suspicious men and a burglary. The cops tried to stop a man they considered a suspect on hotel grounds. The man took off in a pickup truck and supposedly hit an officer, who was unharmed. The man continued driving and was boxed in by several police cars a few blocks away. When cops approached the pickup and tried to handcuff the man, he allegedly drove off again, supposedly dragging two officers, who began shooting at him. The man continued to flee but stopped two blocks later, where he died of his wounds. **Source:** Miami Herald, 1/25/99

Unidentified Man — —

January 23, 1999. North Miami-Dade:

Members of the Miami-Dade (county) Crime Suppression Team shot and killed a man during an alleged shootout. The man was reportedly a robbery suspect fleeing the scene of a hardware store robbery in Opa-Locka. Two alleged accomplices were arrested and jailed. **Source:** Miami Herald, 1/24/99 & 1/25/99

Jimmy Sanford 20 —

January 18, 1999. Lauderdale Lakes (Washington Park):

Jimmy Sanford was shot to death by off-duty Broward County Sheriff's Deputy Pete Fortunato in an alleged shootout at Mr. Sanford's grandmother's house. Deputy Fortunato, off-duty at the time, had followed him there after hearing a police bulletin reporting a possible shooting in the area. As dozens of people gathered at the scene, police maced them. When reports of these macings were televised, Sheriff Ken Jenne went to the scene. He denied mace was used. The police summoned a "community relations specialist" to soothe the crowd, which included Mr. Sanford's grandmother. **Source:** The Miami Herald, 1/19/99

Michael Manigoult 35 —

January 9, 1999. Miami-Dade County (in or near Homestead):

Mr. Manigoult was shot to death by Miami-Dade and/or Homestead police after allegedly fleeing the scene of a robbery in Homestead. The truck he was driving crashed. Police claim he was armed when he got out of the truck and that officers ordered him to drop his weapon before they opened fire. **Source:** The Miami Herald, 1/19/99 & 1/11/99

Mark Stephen Bailey 39 —

January 5, 1999. Escambia County Jail:

Mr. Bailey died in a holding cell less than three hours after being brought in on charges of resisting an officer with violence and disguise and battery on an officer. Police say that he appeared drunk. Cops claim that during a procedural check, Mr. Bailey struck a corrections officer and it was supposedly during the attempt to restrain him that the victim lost consciousness. Officials claim jail emergency medical technicians immediately tried to revive Mr. Bailey. The medical examiner, while admitting that there were "some contusions and (Mr. Bailey was) bruised," claimed that asphyxiation, internal injuries or blunt force trauma from a beating were not possible causes of death and said he would await toxicology results before deciding on the official cause of death. Mr. Bailey's family demanded an independent verification of autopsy findings to determine whether he received proper supervision and if excessive force had been used. **Source:** Miami Herald, 1/9/99

Gustavo Molina 25 —

December 7, 1998. Miami:

Mr. Molina was shot to death by off-duty Miami Police Detective Roberto Rodriguez after the victim supposedly attempted to rob a store without displaying a weapon and then walked out with an armload of cigarette cartons. Mr. Molina was reportedly shot once by Det. Rodriguez during an alleged struggle. Police claim Det. Rodriguez was stabbed by Mr. Molina and that the detective then shot the victim to death as the latter attempted to flee in a truck. **Source:** The Miami Herald, 12/8/98 & 12/9/98

Jorge Pérez, Jr.   53   —

November 23, 1998. Miami-Dade County:
Jorge Pérez Jr., was shot to death by Miami-Dade (county) Officer Luis Rubio after Mr. Pérez threatened suicide with a knife at home. His father, Jorge Pérez Sr., had called the police for assistance. **Source:** The Miami Herald, 11/24/98

Unidentified Man   —   —

November 20, 1998. North Miami Beach :
Miami-Dade (county) and North Miami Beach police shot this man to death, possibly during an undercover sting. He was reportedly a drug suspect. Another reported drug suspect may have been wounded in the incident. **Source:** The Miami Herald, 11/21/98 & 2/23/99

José Torres   77   —

October 15, 1998. Miami:
Mr. Torres was shot to death by at least two Miami SWAT officers after he repeatedly cut himself while trying to commit suicide. He was hit by eight bullets from point blank range. He had emphysema and had recently separated from his wife. **Source:** The Miami Herald, 10/16/98 and 3/6/99

Joseph Mule   37   —

October 4, 1998. Hillsborough:
Hillsborough Sheriff's Deputies Larry Parketon, Bob Ura and Kyle Robertson shot Mr. Mule to death when the victim allegedly pulled out a gun after being stopped for driving erratically. All three deputies fired shots. The incident began when the deputies reportedly saw Mr. Mule driving erratically and tried to pull him over for suspicion of drunk driving. Mr. Mule supposedly fled but then pulled into a parking lot. The three deputies surrounded his car. At this point, while still in the car, Mr. Mule allegedly pulled a gun. The three deputies shot and killed him. Friends say Mr. Mule was distraught over the loss of his father, who had died of cardiac arrest about two weeks earlier after spending months in the hospital. Gail Madigan, a neighbor who had known Joseph Mule for ten years, said she last saw him at her home about two hours before he was killed. Ms. Madigan, who was also his employer, said, "We think he just freaked out." She reported that Mr. Mule seemed "confused" after his father's death. Ms. Madigan said of the victim's mother, "She's just been through one death and now she's going through another one." **Source:** St. Petersburg Times, 10/5/98

Unidentified Man   —   —

September 3, 1998. South Dade:
The man was shot in the chest and killed by Miami-Dade Police Officer Cheryl Wiggins. He was reportedly stealing plants from people's yards in the middle of the afternoon when a resident saw him and yelled at him. He ran into a neighbor's garage and the person who had yelled at him called the police. The man supposedly grabbed a shovel from the garage and when the owner walked into the garage, tried to grab his necklace, then went to the front of the house. Officer Wiggins arrived and claims the man lunged at her with the shovel when she ordered him to drop it. Officer Wiggins claims she backed up and that he came at her again before she shot him. **Source:** The Miami Herald, 9/5/98

Ted Leggett   19   —

Aug. 25, 1998 (?). Middleburg:
Mr. Leggett was a passenger in an allegedly stolen car being chased by Clay County sheriff's deputies at speeds of up to 100 mph. He was killed when the driver lost control of the car. All three occupants were thrown out of the car. Mr. Leggett was killed when his body hit a telephone pole, 16 feet above the ground. The two other people in the car were injured but survived. **Source:** States News Service/Florida, 8/25/98 (?)

Unidentified Boy   12   —

August 22, 1998. Miami:
Three undercover narcotics officers chased a woman who had allegedly purchased drugs from them. The fleeing woman drove through stop signs and smashed into another car, killing the boy, leaving his mother unconscious and badly injuring his eight-year-old sister. The driver was charged with manslaughter and possession of cocaine, heroin, and marijuana. **Source:** The Orlando Sentinel, 8/24/98

Steven B. Collins   34   —

August 12, 1998. Fort Lauderdale (Federal Highway):
Mr. Collins was reportedly sitting in his car at a traffic light and did not move even after the traffic light cycled twice. His headlights were off. Pompano Beach police followed him when he started driving. They admit he was not driving fast or breaking any laws. They tried to pull him over, then pursued him when he did not stop. Pompano Beach police claim they stopped pursuit when Mr. Collins left their jurisdiction and entered Fort Lauderdale. He was killed when his car crashed into a tree less than half a mile from where the chase supposedly ended. **Source:** Sun-Sentinel (Fort Lauderdale, FL), 8/13/98

Dennis Michael Leach   37   —

August 8, 1998. Davie:
Police Officers Timothy Albury and Timothy Fitzgerald shot Mr. Leach to death, claiming he was chasing his wife with a knife and stabbing her. But April Leach, age 15, one of the couple's six children, witnessed the whole incident and said that one officer shot her father in the leg first and cops then killed him with three more shots after he was down. She said, "They shot my dad, they shot my dad when they didn't need to." Officers Albury and Fitzgerald were suspended with pay. **Source:** Sun-Sentinel (Fort Lauderdale, FL), 8/9/98 & 8/12/98

Michael Swimmer   27   —

August 1, 1998. Orange County:
Mr. Swimmer was shot and critically wounded outside of his bedroom door around 2:30 a.m. by the Orange County Sheriff's SWAT team, which entered his condominium to arrest him on drug charges. Cops claim he did not respond when they "notified him of their intentions" over a bullhorn and that he pointed a gun at them when they got to his second floor apartment. They supposedly urged him to drop his gun before two deputies opened fire. Police charged that Mr. Swimmer was a dealer of designer drugs and claim to have found drugs, cash and another gun inside his apartment. Mr. Swimmer died in the hospital around 7 a.m., several hours after he was shot. **Source:** The Orlando Sentinel, 8/2/98

Vincent Harris   29   —

July 21, 1998. Pompano Beach:
Mr. Harris was shot in the left thigh by Pompano Beach Police Officer Jason Butler after a car chase and a foot chase. The bullet severed his femoral artery, causing him to "bleed like a faucet," according to one witness. Police did not administer first aid and Mr. Harris bled to death at the scene. The incident began when Mr. Harris and a 15-year-old companion allegedly led police on a chase in a stolen vehicle. The two split up and the 15-year-old was apprehended. Mr. Harris reportedly stole another vehicle, driving through bushes and hitting other cars with police in pursuit. When the car became too damaged to drive, Mr. Harris reportedly fled on foot, then supposedly "confronted" Officer Butler before he was shot. Authorities claim they found a weapon in the area, but witnesses said Mr. Butler was unarmed. Pompano Beach residents were angry that police allowed him to bleed to death. The victim's mother said, "If he did something wrong, he should have been punished. To let him bleed to death, I feel they meant to kill him." Officer Butler was put on paid administrative leave. Mr. Harris' 15-year-old companion was charged with felony murder in connection with Mr. Harris' death on the grounds that if someone dies while committing a crime, accomplices can be so charged. But as the youth's mother pointed out, "My son was already detained in the [police] car when that shooting happened. He was in the car with handcuffs on when he saw them gun down that man." **Source:** Sun-Sentinel (Fort Lauderdale, FL), 7/23/98 & 8/2/98

Carl Williams   29   *African American*

July 15, 1998. Miami (Liberty City):
Carl Williams was shot to death in his own back yard by Miami-Dade (county) Police Officer Mark Bullard. Mr. Williams went into his back yard with a gun because alarm lights had gone off. The police claim that Mr. Williams fired at a possum in a tree and that Officer Bullard and his partner responded to the sound of gunfire, told Mr. Williams to drop his gun and then shot him to death when he allegedly turned towards Officer Bullard while still holding his gun. They say it was a tragic mistake and that Officer Bullard acted to protect himself. Witness accounts do not support this theory. A more likely scenario is that Mr. Williams never fired his gun at anything and that the police themselves tripped the alarm lights by their presence. This killing occurred while Officer Bullard was participating in a police sweep (i.e. a "Jump out") in the area as a member of the Miami-Dade Crime Suppression Team, which conducts such operations in relation to the federal "Weed and Seed" program. This case received extensive publicity in South Florida, in part because Mr. Williams had previously received a medal for saving the life of a police officer. Hundreds of people attended his funeral. His death was an important topic of discussion at a community meeting held on Oct. 22, 1998, the third annual National Day of Protest against police brutality At an inquest held Mar. 18, 1999, no charges were filed against Officer Bullard, despite evidence that the bullets that killed Mr. Williams hit him in the back. **Source:** The Miami Herald, 7/1798 & continuing

Alan Singletary   43   —

July 9, 1998. Geneva:
Alan, a well repairman, was facing eviction when he allegedly pulled a gun on his landlord. Cops claim he killed a sheriff's deputy and wounded two others, then barricaded himself inside his camper-trailer for 13 hours. Cops claim he fired hundreds of shots until 3:24 a.m., when they fired tear gas into the trailer and heard a single return shot. They claim that after six and a half hours of silence, Alan fired two shots, at which point Seminole County sheriff's deputies "responded with gunfire and killed him." **Source:** AP online, 7/9/98

William Carboni   41   —

July 6, 1998. Palm Beach County (Jupiter):
Three people allegedly stole more than $600 worth of designer clothing from a mall, fled in a car and supposedly tried to run down a security guard on their way out of the mall. Martin County sheriff's deputies chased the alleged shoplifters for 30 miles at speeds of up to 110 mph along I-95 and city streets and across the county line into Palm Beach County. At an intersection, the shoplifters' car slammed into a minivan, which hit another minivan and a motorcycle. Mr. Carboni, the motorcyclist, was killed as he waited at a red light. Avonchalene Keisha Liptrot, a passenger in the alleged shoplifters' car, was also killed. Cops claim the shoplifting had been mistakenly called in as a robbery, prompting the chase. A grand jury ruled that the chase was justified. **Source:** Sun-Sentinel (Fort Lauderdale, FL), 7/7/98 & 9/30/98

Avonchalene Keisha Liptrot   24   —

July 6, 1998. Palm Beach County (Jupiter):
Three people, including Ms. Liptrot, allegedly stole over $600 worth of designer clothing from a mall, fled in a car and supposedly tried to run down a security guard on their way out of the mall. Martin County sheriff's deputies chased the three alleged shoplifters for 30 miles at speeds of up to 110 mph along I-95 and city streets and across the county line into Palm Beach County. At an intersection, the shoplifters' car slammed into a minivan, which hit another minivan and a motorcycle. Ms. Liptrot, a passenger in the shoplifter's car, was killed, as was William Carboni, who was on the motorcycle that was hit. A pregnant female passenger in the car being chased was injured, as were two people in the minivans. Cops claim the shoplifting had been mistakenly called in as a robbery, prompting the chase. A grand jury ruled that the chase was justified. **Source:** Sun-Sentinel (Fort Lauderdale, FL), 7/7/98 & 9/30/98

Steve Earl Kerr   25   —

June 27, 1998. Volusia County (Deland):
Mr. Kerr was killed in a crash with a patrol car driven by Volusia County Sheriff's Deputy Charles Lockwood. Authorities claim Mr. Kerr drove his car into the path of the deputy's vehicle as the deputy was on routine patrol duties. **Source:** The Orlando Sentinel, 6/29/98

| **Chester Arthur Weldon** | 79 | — |

June 27, 1998. New Port Richey:

Mr. Weldon was killed and his wife injured when their car was hit by a cruiser driven by Pasco County Sheriff's Deputy Joshua Cooley. Authorities initially claimed that Deputy Cooley had a green light and that Mr. Weldon drove into his path at the intersection of U.S. 19 and Cross Bayou Blvd. But at least two witnesses told the Florida Highway Patrol that Deputy Cooley ran a red light, while the victim had a green light. Mr. Weldon's son said that his father was an extremely careful driver; according to the newspaper, he had a "spotless driving record." Mr. Weldon was an avid fisherman and liked to play the organ. He and his wife had moved to Florida from Minnesota 20 years before and were looking forward to attending a family reunion when he was killed. It was considered unlikely that Deputy Cooley would face any charges. **Source:** St. Petersburg Times, 6/30/98 & 7/7/98

| **Two Unidentified People** | — | — |

June 23, 1998. Homestead:

The two people were shot and killed by plainclothes Homestead police during "a drug sting that went awry." Two cops posed as drug dealers and sold cocaine to several people, who supposedly tried to steal the drugs and fired at the undercover cops. The cops opened fire, killing two and wounding two others. A cop was also reportedly wounded in the incident. **Source:** Sun-Sentinel (Jacksonville, FL), 6/24/97

| **Rickie Allen Austin** | 20 | — |

June 14, 1998. Jacksonville:

Officer Robert Getzan fired seven times at Rickie, hitting him once, after Rickie allegedly pulled a toy gun. The cops reportedly had been called to the apartment complex to investigate a report that a man had threatened another man with a gun in an argument over a woman. They claim Rickie took off running when the police arrived. An assistant police chief justified the shooting, saying, "If somebody is running away from you in the darkness and pointed it at you, it would definitely look like a real gun." Officer Getzan was placed on paid leave (paid vacation) pending an investigation. **Source:** AP online, 6/16/98

| **Joey Summerlin** | 28 | — |

June 3, 1998. Clewiston:

Mr. Summerlin was in a high-speed chase at speeds up to 100 mph through two counties that ended when his pickup truck crashed in the U.S. Sugar Corp. building. Mr. Summerlin then was shot and killed by police. **Source:** Sun-Sentinel, 6/6/98

| **Thomas Scheel** | 33 | *white* |

May 19, 1998. Miami:

Police responded to a 911 call about a naked man masturbating in a parking lot. When cops arrived, Mr. Scheel took off in his pickup and a chase ensured. Authorities claim Mr. Scheel tried to run over an officer. Three cops opened fire, riddling his truck and body with bullets and killing him. The dead Mr. Scheel then fell out of the truck wearing only black lace panties covered by a white apron. His dead body was then handcuffed by police. A police spokesperson defended the fatal shooting and the handcuffing of the dead man. **Source:** Sun-Sentinel (Fort Lauderdale, FL), 5/20/98; Miami Herald, 5/20/98

| **Unidentified Man** | 40 | — |

May 16, 1998. Clearwater:

The man reportedly refused to open the door of his motel room for the manager, so the manager called the police. By the time cops arrived, the man had reportedly barricaded himself in the bathroom. He supposedly told cops he wanted to hurt himself. A negotiator and the SWAT team were called in. Cops sprayed pepper-spray through the keyhole, and when the man did not respond, they broke down the door and claim to have found him dead. They did not release the cause of death but denied that they were responsible, saying, "We did everything to help him help himself." **Source:** St. Petersburg Times, 5/17/98

Jerry Campbell   29   —

May 14, 1998. Pensacola:
Mr. Campbell was shot and killed by Escambia County Sheriff's Deputy Barton Fryer during an alleged struggle. Deputy Fryer began pursuing Mr. Campbell on foot several blocks from the scene of a home-invasion robbery about an hour and 15 minutes after it occurred. Supposedly, Mr. Campbell was a suspect. A coroner's jury voted 6-3 that the shooting was unjustified, a finding that the judge and/or the DA could decide to ignore. In his 11 years on the force, Deputy Fryer had been involved in two other fatal shootings and one non-fatal shooting in which the victim was left paralyzed. All three of the previous shootings were ruled justified. **Source:** St. Petersburg Times, 8/27/98

James Rowlett   43   *white*

May 5, 1998. St. Petersburg:
When James Rowlett, a diagnosed schizophrenic, allegedly threatened a police officer with two champagne bottles, Officer Totz shot him twice and killed him. Reports say that Rowlett had not been taking his medication and was experiencing withdrawal symptoms. **Source:** Tampa Tribune, 5/13/98

Peter Allende   48   —

April 22, 1998. Orlando:
Mr. Allende, a homeless man, reportedly punched another man in the face during an argument, then ran and fell down. A crowd held him until the cops arrived. He died after being arrested by Orlando Police Officers Brett Licciardello and Joe Sommers. Cops claim that he simply stopped breathing, that they unsuccessfully attempted CPR and that the cause of death was unclear. Officers Licciardello and Sommers were put on paid administrative leave. **Source:** The Orlando Sentinel, 4/23/98

Brian Wilson   28   *Black*

April 19, 1998. Daytona Beach:
Shot and killed after he allegedly shot and wounded four officers. The incident occurred during Black College Reunion and according to some was inevitable given the presence of more than 500 police officers. One witness said Brian was shot in cold blood. State Attorney John Tanner announced on July 8, 1998, that the two officers involved, Officer Vincent Del Guercio of the Daytona Beach Police Department and Deputy Loren Smith of Volusia County Sheriff's office, had been cleared of any criminal wrongdoing. **Source:** The Orlando Sentinel, 7/9/98

Lhach Scholes (aka Lawrence John Andrew)   30   —

April 19, 1998. Daytona Beach:
Mr. Scholes was shot and killed by Daytona Beach Police Officer Kenneth Gabrill after reportedly burglarizing a closed supermarket. Officer Gabrill was responding to a silent alarm at the supermarket around 3 a.m. When he arrived, he found the glass door smashed and "a trail of merchandise leading to a darkened area on the north side of the building." Officer Gabrill claims he saw Mr. Scholes hiding in the bushes outside the supermarket and that Mr. Scholes screamed and charged him. He fatally shot the victim during an alleged scuffle, claiming Mr. Scholes refused to stop and that it was too dark to see whether he had a weapon. Officer Gabrill was placed on paid administrative leave during an investigation and cleared of wrongdoing on the grounds of self-defense by the State Attorney's office in December, 1998. Authorities charged that the victim was under house arrest and wearing an electronic monitor when he was killed and that he had a history of arrests, including burglary and for battery on a law enforcement officer. **Source:** The Orlando Sentinel, 4/21/98 & 9/11/98

Unidentified Man   16-20   *Black*

April 14, 1998. Coconut Creek (Tradwinds Park):
The man and a companion were pulled over by a Coconut Creek police officer for allegedly driving erratically around 2:45 a.m. They reportedly got out and ran. The cop ran a license plate check and discovered that the car was stolen. A K-9 unit from the Broward County Sheriff's Office was called in to track the men and picked up their scent. Cops received a 911 call reporting cries for help in a lake. Authorities claim the man drowned while fleeing police. Divers recovered his body around 5:30 a.m. They did not find his companion. **Source:** Sun-Sentinel (Jacksonville, FL), 4/15/98

Dennis Howard Palmer   55   —

April 12, 1998. Pompano Beach:

A prisoner escaped from the Miami-Dade County Prison when his mother and some accomplices rammed a truck through the main gate and two fences and helped him flee. The mother, the driver of the truck, and the driver of the getaway car were arrested that same day. The following day, a Pompano Beach police officer spotted the car containing the escaped prisoner and another accomplice. The cops called for backup and "began following the car discreetly...[in a] low-speed, no-siren pursuit of several miles." The driver noticed that he was being followed and reportedly accelerated to try to outrun the police. Cops turned on their flashing lights and sirens and pursued them. The car being chased ran a stop sign (supposedly within seconds of when the cops turned on their sirens) and hit Mr. Palmer's car. Mr. Palmer was killed in the crash. The driver of the car was charged with first-degree murder and the escaped prisoner, who was a passenger, was charged with escape. **Source:** Sun-Sentinel (Jacksonville, FL), 4/14/98 & 4/19/98

Gilberto Mejía-Leyua   41   *Cuban*

April 5, 1998. Tampa:

Mr. Mejía-Leyua reportedly robbed a Walgreen's by implying that he had a weapon, although store employees did not see one. Cops spotted a stolen car that matched the description of the getaway car. The driver, Mr. Mejía-Leyua, supposedly refused to stop and was chased by police. During the chase, he crashed into a utility pole and died. Authorities claim he was wanted for a total of five robberies in Miami and was a suspect in several robberies in Tampa. This was the second fatal police chase in Tampa in three days. **Source:** The Tampa Tribune, 4/6/98 & 4/12/98; St. Petersburg Times, 4/6/98, 4/7/98 & 4/8/98

Alfonso Watson   31   —

April 3, 1998. East Tampa:

Mr. Watson and his three-year-old daughter Alexis were badly injured when his van crashed during a high-speed police chase. Mr. Watson had reportedly used gasoline to try to set afire his daughter's mother, Linda Wade. When his lighter did not work, he reportedly hit Ms. Wade's sister, grabbed his daughter and fled in Ms. Wade's car. Police said they would have pursued the vehicle even if they knew it carried a young child. Mr. Watson died in the hospital on May 1, almost a month after the crash. His daughter was released from the hospital on Apr. 24 after almost two weeks in a coma. **Source:** The Tampa Tribune, 4/6/98, 4/12/98, & 5/4/98; St. Petersburg Times, 4/7/98

Lionel Bost   18   —

March 28, 1998. Jacksonville:

Lionel drowned in a pond while being chased by police. He and two other teenagers had reportedly stolen a pizza deliveryman's car earlier in the day. They were chased by police, who claimed they abandoned the car and tried to escape by swimming across the pond. **Source:** The Orlando Sentinel, 3/30/98

Lance Adams   50   —

March 27, 1998. Boca Raton (I-95):

Mr. Adams, a developer who built upscale homes in the Bermuda Bay subdivision of Vero Beach, was in the middle of his fourth divorce. He had reportedly strangled his wife, then called a friend, told him he had committed a homicide and said he wanted to buy a gun. The friend agreed to meet him at a Denny's restaurant, then called the Boca Raton police. When Mr. Adams arrived at the restaurant, he saw a police car in the parking lot, apparently became suspicious and fled. Cops chased him north on I-95 at speeds of up to 110 mph. Mr. Adams crossed three lanes of traffic and slammed head-on into a concrete column supporting an overpass. He was partially ejected from the car and died on the scene. Police claim he wanted to commit suicide, that he had slit both his wrists, that they found in his bag a suicide note addressed to his parents and that he drove into the column after "consider[ing] at least two other methods of killing himself...[which] failed." **Source:** Sun-Sentinel (Fort Lauderdale, FL), 3/28/98

Imar Rivera   1   —

March 25, 1998. Ocean Ridge:

One-year-old Imar Rivera was killed when the van driven by her mother, Wendy Susan Peña, crashed during a police chase. Imar was thrown from the back seat into the front seat and the van burst into flames. Ms. Peña was badly injured in the accident. Ocean Ridge Police Sgt. Michael Andrews started chasing the van after it reportedly ran a red light. He told dispatchers he was breaking off pursuit as the van approached speeds of 90 mph, then, shortly thereafter, he reported that the van had crashed. Sgt. Andrews and another officer received commendations from the town commission for rescuing Ms. Peña from the burning vehicle. **Source:** Sun-Sentinel (Fort Lauderdale, FL), 3/26/98 & 5/5/98

James Donald Parker II   —   —

March 24, 1998. Hillsborough County (Brandon):

Mr. Parker was shot twice in the chest and killed by Hillsborough Sheriff's Deputy Charles Alexander. Deputy Alexander arrived in response to 911 calls from Mr. Parker's ex-girlfriend's mother. Mr. Parker had been stalking and harassing his ex. He reportedly beat her and threatened her with a gun before cops arrived. Deputy Alexander claims he ordered Mr. Parker to show his hands and get on the ground but that the latter pulled a gun from his waistband instead. Investigators said they were not sure whether Mr. Parker fired his gun. Mr. Parker was the third (known) person shot to death by law enforcement agents in Hillsborough in six weeks. **Source:** St. Petersburg Times, 3/25/98

Christian Pierre   41   *Haitian*

March 21, 1998. Homestead:

Miami-Dade police officers, responding to a separate domestic dispute in a farmworker housing project, shot and killed Mr. Pierre. They described him as unruly and threatening and carrying a machete. "The police kept saying, 'Put it down on the ground,' but he didn't understand," said his wife. Pierre spoke Haitian Creole. **Source:** Miami Oct. 22 Coalition

Hung Xuan Cao   31   —

March 14, 1998. Tampa:

Mr. Cao, a homeless man who may have been mentally ill, was shot at least twice and killed by Tampa Police Officer Larry Henderson. Officer Henderson claims Mr. Cao hit him on the left forearm with a shovel. The officer had arrived on the scene after someone called police to complain that Mr. Cao was behaving strangely in front of a gift shop. This was the second time in a month that law enforcement agents in Tampa killed a man suspected of having mental problems. **Source:** The Orlando Sentinel, 3/16/98

Jair Salazar   27   —

March 13, 1998. Delray Beach (Duncan Center):

Mr. Salazar had been diagnosed with schizophrenia. He had voluntarily checked himself into the South County Mental Health Center but later walked away from it. Neighbors described him as a quiet young man who often rode his bicycle through the working class neighborhood where he lived. "Sometimes he was friendly and other times he'd walk right by you without saying a word," said one neighbor. Police Officer Peter Cagnina and Auxiliary Police Officer Jeffery Rubenstein responded to a disturbance call at the Duncan Conference Center and claim that Mr. Salazar was bothering people in the parking lot. Officer Cagnina shot Mr. Salazar three times and killed him outside the Duncan Center. Two rounds hit Mr. Salazar in the lower abdomen and a third bullet ripped across his chest and lodged in his right arm. The shooting took place several yards from the center, not in the parking lot. Mr. Salazar's family told a WPTV-Ch. 5 reporter that they had not been told what led to the shooting and questioned why Mr. Salazar had to be shot and killed. Investigators claim that the victim had an object in his hand but refused to say whether it was a weapon. The Florida Department of Law Enforcement (FDLE) alleged that Mr. Salazar charged at Officer Cagnina with a twelve inch ratchet wrench which he pulled from his back pocket and that he was only shot after he refused orders to drop it and continued to charge the cop. State Attorney Barry Krischer wrote in a memorandum, "The officers showed considerable restraint by not firing immediately upon Mr. Salazar reaching behind his back and coming out with a shiny metallic object." A FDLE official said, "Everything he [Officer Cagnina] did was within how we're trained to use force." **Source:** Sun-Sentinel (Fort Lauderdale, FL), 3/15/98 & 5/5/98

| John Tabor | 36 | — |

February 27, 1998. Cocoa:

Cops allege that Mr. Tabor died as a result of ingesting cocaine as officers searched his home for drugs and that he struggled violently with officers trying to get the drugs out of his mouth. They insisted that the cause of death was cocaine poisoning and an existing heart problem, even though toxicology results were not yet available. But civilian witnesses accused officers of using a choke hold on Mr. Tabor. Police admit that no drugs were found inside the home, but said this was because the victim had swallowed them all. Mr. Tabor died at the hospital around 11 p.m. **Source:** The Orlando Sentinel, 3/2/98 & 5/13/98

| Pal Krasniqi | 71 | — |

February 27, 1998. Orlando:

Mr. Krasniqi was shot and critically wounded by the Orlando police SWAT team when they burst into his home. He died in the hospital about two weeks later, on Mar. 11. Cops had reportedly conducted a six month investigation of homes and businesses connected with the Krasniqi family in relation to a series of thefts of safes and ATM machines. **Source:** The Orlando Sentinel, 3/12/98

| Alicia Lewis | 35 | — |

February 26, 1998. Miami:

Lewis, a transsexual inmate at Miami-Dade County jail, died of a rampaging infection after nurses waited 15 hours before getting her treatment. Two days before her death, Lewis complained of abdominal pain. The jail nurse thought a cup of vomit and blood was a trick and sent her back to her cell with a Tylenol. Several others have died in Dade and Broward jails in recent years. Prisoners and relatives complain of delayed or denied medical treatment. Nurses complain of unsafe staffing levels and medical shortages. **Source:** Miami Oct. 22 Coalition

| Carl James Lowery | 21 | *African-American* |

February 24, 1998. South Dade:

When officers from the Cutler Ridge Community Oriented Police unit stopped Carl for an alleged traffic violation, he ran. They caught him, put him face down on the ground and cuffed him. Then he stopped breathing. "My son died for no reason," said his mother, Yvette Mills. **Source:** Miami Oct. 22 Coalition

| Samuel Aaron Studley | 20 | — |

February 13, 1998. Hillsborough County (Brandon):

Samuel Studley had been acting strangely since he was released from jail a week earlier after serving 18 months on robbery and theft charges. He reportedly went to the gas station around 8 a.m., said he was from another planet and asked the cashier a series of bizarre questions. The cashier called the police. Samuel supposedly pushed down Hillsborough County Sheriff's Deputy Sherry Perez when she tried to calm him down. Deputy Paul Duty tried to handcuff him and, after an alleged struggle, sprayed him in the face with pepper-spray. Mr. Studley reportedly ran and Deputy Duty confronted him again. Authorities claim Samuel threw Deputy Duty to the ground and beat, choked, and pepper-sprayed the cop while yelling obscenities. Deputy Perez shot Samuel twice in the back and once in the abdomen. He died at the hospital. Deputy Perez was put on paid administrative leave during an investigation. Within a week, the state attorney cleared her of criminal wrongdoing on the grounds that she feared for Deputy Duty's life. The newspaper portrayed Samuel as a powerful, out-of-control maniac who kept fighting even after he was shot. Cops claim he was 5'9" and weighed 169 pounds, but his driver's license indicated that he was 5'3". The victim's family said he did not have mental problems before being incarcerated but that he had behaved strangely and talked insanely in the week since his release. The victim's mother criticized the cops for shooting him, saying, "He should have been treated like someone who had medical problems. They didn't have to kill him." **Source:** St. Petersburg Times, 2/14/98 & 2/21/98

Zabian J. Anthony	16	—
Erico Christopher Logan	16	—

February 12, 1998. Jacksonville:

Zabian Anthony lost control of his car and crashed into two trees during a police chase. Both he and Erico Logan, his passenger, were killed. Police said they did not know why the two high school students were fleeing from them. The article did not indicate why police were chasing them in the first place. **Source:** Sun-Sentinel (Jacksonville, FL), 2/14/98

James Byrd	74	—

February 10, 1998. Sarasota:

Mr. Byrd reportedly fired a gun at an acquaintance and then set the man's house on fire. He supposedly shot another occupant of the house in the face with birdshot. All the occupants were evacuated and Mr. Byrd was later flushed out by thick smoke. Cops claim he pointed a double-barreled shotgun at them and fired both rounds, grazing an officer. Police opened fire and shot him dead. Mr. Byrd had no criminal record. Cops claim he had another gun and pockets full of ammunition. **Source:** The Tampa Tribune, 2/11/98

Michael Andrew Gregg	29	—

February 2, 1998. Orlando:

Mr. Gregg was shot and killed in an alleged shootout with Florida State Troopers. A resident of a condominium complex in Titusville saw Mr. Gregg asleep in a car parked in a guest spot in the condominium's parking lot. She called the police, who reportedly discovered that the car had been stolen at gunpoint from someone at an ATM machine a month or two before. A cop tapped on the window and Mr. Gregg supposedly sat up, started the car and drove away quickly, almost running over a cop. Sheriff's deputies chased him across four counties at speeds of up to 80 mph. Once in Orlando, Mr. Gregg allegedly began firing at police. The newspaper reported, "seven [Florida State] Troopers encircled his vehicle. Shots rang out. Troopers then cautiously approached the suspect's vehicle and found the man mortally wounded. Paramedics eventually pulled the suspect from the vehicle and attempted to resuscitate him. He was pronounced dead at Orlando Regional Medical Center." Mr. Gregg's car had at least nine bullet holes in the front windshield and four on the left side. No one else was injured, although at least one squad car reportedly had its window shot out. A spokesperson for the Florida Highway Patrol said everything appeared to be in accordance with police guidelines. The woman who called the police to report Mr. Gregg sleeping in his car said he "just looked so peaceful sleeping there, so peaceful to meet such a violent end so quickly." **Source:** The Orlando Sentinel, 2/3/98 & 2/4/98; Sun-Sentinel (Fort Lauderdale, FL), 2/3/98

Samuel Cooper, Jr.	45	*African American*

January 26, 1998. Miami:

Following a failed attempt at the armed robbery of a downtown bank, Mr. Cooper fled with off-duty Police Officer Arturo Beguiristain in pursuit. Both allegedly fired. Mr. Cooper was shot once in the chest and killed. Said homicide Lt. John Campbell: "This is TV stuff. He's shooting someone from a distance of 25 feet in downtown at lunchtime. It's unbelievable nobody got hit." Chief Warshaw said, "It's a really good, clean shooting. I wish they were all like this. There's no muss, no fuss." Beguiristain was present during at least three questionable police shootings in which officials suspect that guns were planted by officers. **Source:** Miami Oct. 22 Coalition; Sun-Sentinel (Jacksonville, FL), 1/27/98

Unidentified	19	—

January 18, 1998. North Dade:

An unidentified Miami-Dade officer shot and killed a fleeing robbery suspect. It was mid-afternoon on a Sunday in a mostly Black residential neighborhood. The brief newspaper account made no mention of a real or suspected gun. Another anonymous police killing. **Source:** Miami Oct. 22 Coalition

Shirley June Ansley   56   —

January 7, 1998. Jacksonville:
Ms. Ansley, a mentally ill woman, was shot four times and killed by Jacksonville Police Officer Terry Shirley in a parking lot. Officer Shirley and two other cops had been trying to issue her a trespass warning elsewhere in the city when she sped away in her van, according to the newspaper. They chased her to the parking lot, where they boxed in her van between police cars and a pickup truck. Officer Shirley claims she drove toward him, but the Jacksonville Sheriff's office board ruled that since she was boxed in when she was shot, the officer could have stepped out of the way instead of shooting and therefore should be disciplined. **Source:** The Orlando Sentinel, 2/22/98

Kathy Kirby   42   —

January 3, 1998. Lady Lake:
Lady Lake Police Sgt. James Kirby shot his wife Kathy three times and killed her before fatally shooting himself. Their teenage daughter found both of their bodies in their bedroom. **Source:** The Orlando Sentinel, 1/4 /98; Sun-Sentinel (Fort Lauderdale, FL), 1/6/98

John Armstrong   39   *African American*

December 12, 1997. Orlando:
Mr. Armstrong was shot through the heart by SWAT officer Bobby Bond. Mr. Armstrong had held two young children hostage for three days when the SWAT team burst in as he slept. "Their intent was to kill him all the time," said Armstrong's brother, Joseph. The children were unharmed. **Source:** Miami Oct. 22 Coalition

Michael Roundtree   17   —

November 29, 1997. Jacksonville:
Michael was shot by a Jacksonville police officer while fleeing after allegedly robbing a fast-food restaurant. He died the next day in the hospital. A companion was wounded but survived. **Source:** Sun-Sentinel (Fort Lauderdale, FL), 12/2/97

Howard Bryan   30's   —

November 8, 1997. South Dade:
Bryan died in police custody following a domestic dispute. Police immediately cited "cocaine psychosis." **Source:** Miami Oct. 22 Coalition

Fernando Louis   22   *Haitian*

October 31, 1997. Miami:
Metro-Dade Police Officer Adrian Cummins shot Fernando after the latter allegedly opened fire on police during an interrupted robbery at a Walgreens. Fernando, whose accomplice had escaped, was supposedly holding two hostages near the back of the store. Cops were searching the aisles and claim he charged forward, firing. Officer Cummins opened fire and wounded Mr. Louis. Cops then dragged Fernando outside to an ambulance. He died at the hospital. **Source:** Miami Herald, 11/1/97; Sun-Sentinel (Fort Lauderdale, FL), 11/1/97; communication from Miami, FL, Oct. 22 Coaliton

Joseph Kevin McGrotha   27   —

October 19, 1997. Jacksonville:
Mr. McGrotha, a construction worker, was shot an estimated 20 times and killed by Jacksonville Police Officer P.D. Soulis. Officer Soulis reportedly saw a suspicious vehicle parked in front of of a closed gas station. The story reported in the newspaper the day after the incident is as follows: Officer Soulis approached the vehicle and Mr. McGrotha, its sole occupant, supposedly "bailed out" and began shooting. Two days after this account, the same newspaper reported that Officer Soulis saw Mr. McGrotha park in the closed gas station, questioned him and was about to return his ID and let him go when Mr. McGrotha began firing. Officer Soulis opened fire, killing Mr. McGrotha. The cop was reportedly shot in the arm, leg and chest (he survived). More police arrived and witnesses saw another officer pointing a gun at the victim's car. The Duval County Medical Examiner's Office said that the victim had a blood alcohol level of .08 when he was fatally shot and police state that there was at least one open can of beer in Mr. McGrotha's car when the shooting occurred. **Source:** Florida Times Union, 8/20/97 & 8/22/97; St. Petersburg Times, 10/21/97; The Orlando Sentinel, 10/21/97

Christopher DeBerry   23   —

October 18, 1997. Broward County:

Christopher fell into a canal and drowned while running away from the police. Family members said he was troubled and frightened of police after he saw his 28-year-old cousin die a week earlier following an arrest in which the two faced alleged drug charges. Cops claim the cousin died from swallowing cocaine, but the official cause of his death remained officially undetermined a week later. After the cousin's funeral, Christopher stopped at a market, bought a soda and went to his car. Broward County Sheriff's Deputy Durden walked out of the market and noticed Mr. DeBerry and a companion sitting in a car. Authorities claim that it appeared as if one of them was rolling a joint, so Deputy Durden approached and asked what was going on. Christopher reportedly became frightened, pushed the deputy and ran. No drugs were found. A witness saw the young man being chased by the deputy and watched as Christopher stopped, tripped and fell into the canal. The witness said, "The officer was yelling 'Get your (expletive) out of the water!'" Christopher came up for air three times and then sank, but Deputy Durden said he would not go into the water to rescue Mr. DeBerry because he did not know what was in the water. A civilian bystander jumped into the water to help but was unable to find the drowning young man. Ten minutes later, rescue workers arrived and pulled Christopher's lifeless body to the shore. "I need to know why they stood there and let him drown," said Mary Louise DeBerry, the mother of the victim. A relative, Alex Johnson, said, "Why is it that a police officer will go in the water for a dog, a deer, or a cat... but for a human life they won't go in because they don't know what's in the water?" A spokesperson for the sheriff's department defended the deputies' actions. **Source:** Sun-Sentinel (Fort Lauderdale, FL), 10/21/97

Mark Samuel Chong   38   —

October 13, 1997. Hollywood:

Mr. Chong, wanted for murder charges in California, jumped two stories and limped away when police surrounded his motel room. When police dog Kimbo caught up with him, Mr. Chong shot the dog and was himself killed in a fusillade of police gunfire. The police department flag was lowered in memory of Kimbo (the dog). **Source:** Miami Oct. 22 Coalition

Andrew Buday   24   —

October 11, 1997. Hollywood:

Mr. Buday was shot once in the chest and killed by Hollywood Police Officer Mike DeJesus. Officer DeJesus was responding to a call from Mr. Buday's girlfriend's brother that Mr. Buday was shouting and pounding on the door of their house. The girlfriend had a restraining order against him. Officer DeJesus claims that Mr. Buday had a six inch knife, refused to drop it and lunged at him. Officer DeJesus was placed on paid administrative leave for a few days. Authorities originally refused to release the cop's name, claiming he had been traumatized by the shooting. **Source:** Sun-Sentinel (Fort Lauderdale, FL), 10/13/97 & 10/14/97

Gerald Houser   36   —

September 30, 1997. Escambia County (Ensley):

Mr. Houser was shot by 11 Escambia County sheriff's deputies as he sat in an allegedly stolen pickup truck on a busy suburban street. He was hit by 15 police bullets. Cops reportedly thought he was a kidnapping suspect. The county medical examiner claimed that an autopsy showed that Mr. Houser had fatally shot himself before the deputies opened fire on him and that the deputies were shooting at a dead man. **Source:** Sun-Sentinel (Fort Lauderdale, FL), 10/4/97

Frank Birch   28   —

September 18, 1997. St. Petersburg:

Mr. Birch, a college student, was shot and killed by six police officers who fired 26 shots, hitting him 12 times. The fatal wound to the abdomen came from a police shotgun. The victim had reportedly been drunk and crashed his car. A neighbor called the police to report seeing a man with a gun and hearing shots fired. When cops arrived, they found Mr. Birch lying face-up in the grass near his crashed car. Cops claim that they noticed he had a gun, that he pointed it at his own head, refused to drop it, gave the cops the finger and yelled, "F*ck you." He supposedly held the gun in the air and pointed it at a cop before the police opened fire on him. Mr. Birch was a student at the University of South Florida. He had a bachelor's degree in criminology, was working on a nursing degree and worked part-time as a bartender. He had reportedly been depressed about the death of an uncle and about how long it was taking him to get his degree. The cops were cleared of wrongdoing by the state attorney and by an internal police department investigation. **Source:** St. Petersburg Times, 10/3/97

Anthony Gerald Stubb   29   *Black*

September 1992 (?). Dade County:

Anthony Stubb was shot in the back and paralyzed. The bullet shifted and he died five years later, on Mothers' Day.

Augusto Meléndez   42   *Dominican*

August 30, 1997. Miami:

Detective Roberto Soler shot Mr. Meléndez for having a toy gun while police were responding to a domestic disturbance call in the area. Det. Soler told him to drop the gun. He allegedly didn't, and Det. Soler fired. Augusto Meléndez died at Jackson Memorial Hospital.

Heriberto Valentín   32   —

August 10, 1997. Orange County:

Mr. Valentín was shot once in the chest and killed by Orange County Sheriff's Deputy Christopher Delabar during an alleged struggle. Cops claim Mr. Valentin stabbed a paraplegic during a burglary and then fought with deputies, refusing an order to surrender. Deputy Delabar and another cop sprayed him with pepper-spray and hit him with a night stick, supposedly with little effect. Mr. Valentín allegedly bit Deputy Delabar's finger and refused to surrender even after the cop drew his gun. The cop justified the shooting by saying that he and his partner were becoming exhausted and feared they would be overpowered. An internal investigation cleared Deputy Delabar in this case but found that, in another incident, he violated policy by shooting an unarmed 18-year-old carjacking suspect who was running away. Deputy Delabar claimed he thought the man was turning toward him during a foot chase, but investigators found that the man was simply running away. **Source:** The Orlando Sentinel, 2/5/98

John A. Edwards   28   —

August 1997. Ft. Meyers (Charlotte Correctional Institution):

Mr. Edwards bled to death while chained to a metal bed in a psychiatric dorm of Charlotte Prison after multiple beatings and an alleged suicide attempt. Guard Robert M. Shepard and two other corrections officers pleaded guilty to federal charges of violating Mr. Edwards' civil rights. **Source:** The Miami Herald, 12/23/98

Ricardo Ponce   37   —

July 22, 1997. Miami:

A barrage of SWAT team assault rifle fire killed this distraught man as he stood in the open doorway of his home. His wife had called 911 saying Mr. Ponce had threatened to kill himself and his family after she had said she was leaving him. The family was out of the house and a negotiating team was present, but they could not communicate over the gunfire. Mr. Ponce was killed on his 37th birthday. **Source:** Miami Oct. 22 Coalition

---

Billy George   30   *white*

July 8, 1997. West Dade:

George was shot 14 times and killed by three Florida Highway Patrol officers at the end of a cross-state ride with his brother David and a hostage, Edith Silver. The brothers had already thrown their guns out of the car. Silver (the hostage) said, "They both thanked me. I think that shows that nobody is all bad." **Source:** Miami Oct. 22 Coalition

---

Julio Mirabal   43   —

July 1, 1997. Hialeah:

Two Dade County police officers shot and killed the Mr. Mirabel, claiming he fired on them first. The two cops were reportedly wounded during the incident. They were in the area around 11 p.m. in response to a call about a body in the trunk of a car. He had allegedly been driving around with the dead body of his girlfriend in the passenger seat of his car. **Source:** Miami Oct. 22 Coalition; Sun-Sentinel (Jacksonville, FL), 7/2/97

Unidentified Man   —

July 1997. Dade County:

The victim, a homeless man, was shot and killed by police in what the newspaper described as a "mistaken police shooting." His death led to a probe of whether police had been stealing and planting guns since 1990. **Source:** Miami Herald, 9/30/97

Michael St. George   17   —

June 23, 1997. Tarpon Springs:

Pinellas County Sheriff's Deputy Stephen Mitchell shot Michael in the thigh and the chest and killed him. The deputy was reportedly peering into an open window of a house and claims he saw Michael with a gun and ordered him to drop it. Michael did not fire any shots, but he sheriffs claim he pointed the gun at the cop before being shot. Deputy Mitchell was in the area responding to a call about two people in a car with drugs and possibly a gun. He was told that the car was at a convenience store, where he found the car and arrested a 14-year-old for loitering and prowling. The other occupant reportedly ran. Deputy Mitchell went back to the house and was supposedly looking for the other occupant of the car when he encountered Michael. Deputy Mitchell was placed on paid leave during an investigation. **Source:** St. Petersburg Times, 6/25/97

Jorge H. Febles, Jr.   46   —

June 20, 1997. Allapattah (Miami):

Six Miami police officers responding to a 911 domestic fight call entered a home in Allapattah. When they left, Mr. Febles Jr. was bruised and not breathing. He died two days later in police custody. Mr. Febles Sr. said it was a typical father-son dispute. Neighbors said the police killed him, for better or worse. The medical examiner cited "cocaine psychosis." **Source:** Miami Oct. 22 Coalition

Edwin Mason   —   —

June 13, 1997. Jacksonville:

Edwin Mason was shot and killed by police after allegedly kidnapping a woman and leading cops on a car chase. **Source:** Florida Times Union, 10/20/97

Fealex Black   24

June 4, 1997. Kissimmee:

Mr. Black was shot and killed by Kissimmee Police Officer Malcom Thompson just after midnight. Authorities claim he fired four shots at the officer before being fatally shot himself, that he had "terrorized a vacationing family and carjacked a maintenance worker" within the past 24 hours and that there was a warrant for his arrest. A review board found the shooting justified but said Officer Thompson could have taken preventative measures to avoid the fatal confrontation. Officer Thompson, who reportedly lost an eye in the incident, was given the department's highest award, the Police Medal of Honor. The head of the review board said the department "allows officers to shoot to kill if someone fires on them or a citizen first," according to the newspaper. **Source:** The Orlando Sentinel, 6/4/97 & 10/30/97

Michael Welsh   —   —

June 2, 1997. Orange County:

Mr. Welsh was shot four times and killed by Orange County sheriff's deputies after a car chase across three counties. One newspaper claims he pointed a gun at a deputy, while another says he was threatening to shoot himself. He was supposedly upset that he would be sent back to jail for violating his probation. The Orange County Sheriff's Office tried to label his death as "suicide by cop." During the previous month (May, 1997), Orange County deputies shot and wounded three people in three separate incidents. **Source:** St. Petersburg Times, 6/3/97; The Orlando Sentinel, 6/4/97

| **Lonnie Causseaux** | 71 | — |

May 16, 1997. Tallahassee:

Mr. Causseaux, an elderly man who suffered from manic-depression, allegedly pointed a shotgun at a code enforcement officer who was taking pictures of his messy yard. The code enforcement officer called the police and about 50 cops responded. After an hour-long standoff, Officer Greg Gibson shot Mr. Causseaux in the head and cops threw a percussion grenade into his house. The victim remained conscious for some time after being shot and died two days later in the hospital. An internal investigation cleared Officer Gibson of wrongdoing. **Source:** The Orlando Sentinel, 5/20/97

| **Vandarell Leon Randall** | 19 | *Black* |

May 7, 1997. Fort Lauderdale:

Vandarell was shot and killed by Fort Lauderdale Police Officer Chuck Morrow, who was trying to arrest him for violating his probation. Vandarell had reportedly eluded capture two weeks earlier by fleeing in his car. Officer Morrow, a member of the department's fugitive task force, knew that Vandarell would be in the area and waited for him to show up. Vandarell reportedly fled in his car after he saw Officer Morrow's unmarked police van. The two vehicles collided and Officer Morrow, thinking that Vandarell's car was immobilized by the collision, got out of his vehicle and tried to arrest the teen. Cops claim that Vandarell drove his car in the direction of Officer Morrow and tried to run him down. The cop opened fire, hitting Vandarell twice, including once in the chest, killing him. The victim's family watched in horror and anger as the cops removed his lifeless, bullet-pocked body from the crashed car. No one official had called them; they only came to the scene after recognizing pictures of Mr. Randall's rented car on TV during the evening news. When relatives got to the scene, they saw his body being loaded on a gurney and placed inside a medical examiner's van. Mr. Randall's grandmother, upset by the scene, wanted to make sure people knew a little something about him: "I want the world to know that he had love behind him. He was not a dog.... He was loved by all." Dozens of relatives and friends gathered to mourn at his family's house. Officer Morrow was suspended during an investigation, but a grand jury cleared him of wrongdoing. Family and friends said that Mr. Randall had told them that he planned to turn himself in to police after celebrating his 20th birthday on May 17. On that day, ten days after Mr. Randall was killed, more than 200 people attending a memorial party for him pelted Fort Lauderdale police with rocks, bottles and possibly bullets when officers arrived in response to reports of loud music. Sixty to 70 police officers, two dozen police cars, the Broward County helicopter and shielded SWAT team members were dispatched to the area. In Oct., 1997, a group of community leaders called for an independent investigation after a grand jury cleared Officer Morrow of any wrongdoing. At Springfield Baptist Church, members carried a sign saying: "Grand jury exonerates police who kill blacks." The Rev. Isom Ross said, "We're just tired of the police coming into the community and stomping on our Black boys." **Source:** Sun-Sentinel (Fort Lauderdale, FL), 5/8/97, 5/19/97, & 10/24/97

| **Felix Pusey** | 13 | — |

April 23, 1997. Delray Beach:

Felix Pusey was a passenger in an allegedly stolen car driven by a 15-year-old friend. Boynton Beach police in an unmarked car saw the youths' vehicle driving on South Federal Highway without headlights in the dark. Cops tried to pull the car over and chased it at speeds of up to 80 mph and into Delray Beach. The driver reportedly ran several red lights, then lost control of the car and crashed. Mr. Pusey was killed. Mr. Pusey's cousin, who was also a passenger in the car, was arrested near the scene of the accident. The driver of the car pleaded guilty to manslaughter, burglary, grand theft and fleeing police officers. **Source:** Sun-Sentinel (Jacksonville, FL), 2/6/98

| **Unidentified man** | — | — |

April 20, 1997. Jacksonville:

Jacksonville Sheriff's Deputy Debra Wickland chased the man down the halls of a motel, then shot and killed him when he allegedly made an "overt action." He was unarmed. The man supposedly whirled around and Officer Wickland fired twice, claiming she thought he was about to fire at her. Officer Wickland was placed on paid administrative leave during an investigation. **Source:** Sun-Sentinel (Jacksonville, FL), 4/22/97

Diego Argáez   21   —

April 17, 1997. Miami Beach:

Mr. Argáez got into an argument with two police officers outside a nightclub. He was shot in the lower back by Metro-Dade Police Officer Shae J. Dunbar, 26, after Mr. Argaez allegedly threw a bottle at the officer's car. Officer Lionel Qualo, 23, also shot at Mr. Argáez. The victim died at Jackson Memorial Hospital.

William "Billy" Collins   43   —

April 15, 1997. Deerfield Beach:

Collins, who had been suicidal, was shot at several times and killed by Broward Sheriff's Office deputy Curt Smith and Pompano Beach police detective Jim Murray on I-95. Media reported that Collins had hijacked a cab and held a knife to the driver's throat.

Corey "C-Low" Footman   19   *African American*

April 8, 1997. Miami:

Corey drowned after Miami-Dade police chased him into Snake Creek Canal at Buccaneer Park where he was picnicking with his family.

Eddie Pepin   49   —

March 30, 1997. Orange County (Lee Road & North Orange Blossom Trial):

Mr. Pepin was riding his motorcycle when he was struck and killed by a teenage driver fleeing from Orange County Sheriff's Deputy Michael Piwowarski. The teenage driver, Joseph Bryant, was also killed in the crash. Deputy Piwowarski began chasing Joseph after the later reportedly ran a stop sign. He was dismissed from the sheriff's office after an investigation concluded that he had lied about the incident, telling dispatchers that he had stopped pursuit when in fact he was still chasing Joseph. The investigation also concluded that Deputy Piwowarski violated a policy which prohibits pursuit in cases involving misdemeanors or traffic violations. Joseph's family filed a lawsuit against the Orange County Sheriff's Office, which they settled for $185,000. The lawsuit charged that Deputy Piwowarski should have been dismissed long ago based on his record. He had been suspended for frisking female suspects without other deputies present and had received no punishment for two physical and oral abuse complaints. The complaint that led to his dismissal was the 18th one filed against him since he became a deputy five years earlier. **Source:** The Orlando Sentinel, 4/25/98 & 7/2/98

Joseph Bryant   16   —

March 30, 1997. Orange County (Lee Road & North Orange Blossom Trial):

Joseph was killed in a car crash as he was being chased by Orange County Sheriff's Deputy Michael Piwowarski. A motorcyclist, Eddie Pepin, was also killed in the crash. Deputy Piwowarski began pursuit after Joseph allegedly ran a stop sign, in violation of rules that forbid chases in cases involving misdemeanors or traffic violations. Deputy Piwowarski also lied about the incident, telling dispatchers that he broke off pursuit when in fact he was continuing the chase. He was dismissed as a result of this incident, his 18th complaint in five years on force. **Source:** The Orlando Sentinel, 7/2/98

Nathan Andrew Kerr   27   —

March 30, 1997. Seminole County (Sanford):

Mr. Kerr was shot in the neck and killed by Seminole County Sheriff's Deputy Andrea Slaby. Deputy Slaby saw Mr. Kerr's wrecked car and stopped. When Mr. Kerr opened the car door, the cop saw him bleeding from the throat and stomach, with a knife sticking out of his stomach. It appeared that he was trying to commit suicide. Rather than try to apply first aid or summon medical help, Deputy Slaby drew her gun and ordered Mr. Kerr onto the ground. Authorities claim he drew the knife (presumably from his stomach) and lunged at the cop. Deputy Slaby fired twice. Mr. Kerr's friends said that he had been upset about an upcoming divorce, but they expressed surprise at the official account of the incident. "Nathan is one of the most laid-back guys I know. I've never heard Nathan yell. He's always a nice guy. Very considerate," said one friend. Nathan Kerr and his friends liked to shoot darts and go fishing together. Before the Florida Department of Law Enforcement completed its investigation, the Seminole County Sheriff was already defending Deputy Slaby, saying, "Until I hear otherwise, her actions were definitely proper." **Source:** The Orlando Sentinel, 4/3/97

Daniel B. Sagers   37   —

March 5, 1997. Osceola County Jail:

Daniel Sagers was arrested for discharging a gun in public on the night of Mar. 4. The following morning, he was beaten in jail by Corrections Officers Gail Edwards, Greg Wilson and Milton Sanitago and Sgt. Michael Bronson. The beating lasted 40 minutes. Several people, including another corrections officer and a trustee, witnessed the incident. Officer Edwards kicked the victim three or four times in the ribs. In a report by the Florida Department of Law Enforcement, witnesses said Sgt. Bronson "patted" the victim's cheek to revive him after he fainted. Mr. Sagers was bleeding from the eyes and nose at the time. Sgt. Bronson then held Mr. Sagers by the legs while Officer Wilson tucked a shirt under the victim's arms to form a sling. Then they dragged the victim, who witnesses said was "folded up like a suitcase, with his pants falling down," about 100 feet to another cell, where he was forced into a restraint chair. Sgt. Bronson was also described by two witnesses as having held Mr. Sagers by the hair while Officer Edwards punched him. Another witness said he saw Sgt. Bronson put a knee to Mr. Sagers' neck. Mr. Sagers died a week later, on Mar. 12, at the hospital. An internal investigation found that Sgt. Bronson used excessive force, supervised the victim's fatal restraint and attempted to cover up his actions. The victim's family filed a $20 million lawsuit against the county. "We will ask the jury to focus on the inhumane and cruel treatment used by the guards in a knowing and indifferent way," said a lawyer for the family. Officers Wilson, Edwards and Santiago were indicted and at least two of them were fired. Officer Edwards, one of the fired guards, pleaded guilty to misdemeanor battery and was sentenced to unsupervised probation. She had been charged with felony aggravated battery. Officer Santiago, who only faced misdemeanor battery charges, was put into a pre-trial diversion program. **Source:** The Orlando Sentinel, 10/24/97, 10/25/97, 11/7/97, 3/8/98, & 4/25/98

Juan Carlos Cortés   31   —

March 3, 1997. Tampa (McDill Air Force Base):

Mr. Cortés was shot to death by five Tampa police officers after a car chase. The cops fired a total of 63 rounds. The newspapers had two different explanations for the chase: that Mr. Cortés ran a red light or, alternatively, that cops saw him driving erratically and believed his truck was stolen. In fact, it belonged to his wife. He had taken it without her permission, but she had not reported it stolen. Authorities claim that he was drunk and had cocaine in his system and that, when they contacted his wife, she said she would press charges for auto theft. Cops continued pursuit even after being ordered to desist by their superiors. They chased Mr. Cortés through residential streets in south Tampa at speeds of up to 100 mph. The chase involved two marked police cars, two unmarked cars and a police helicopter. Cops boxed in Mr. Cortés' vehicle at the McDill Air Force Base. Police claim he ignored orders to get out of the truck and drove toward them. Cops opened fire and killed him. The State Attorney ruled that the use of deadly force was justified and did not press criminal charges against the officers, even though authorities admitted that the car chase that led up to the shooting was problematic. Six officers received letters of counseling as punishment for not breaking off the chase when ordered and a lieutenant and a captain were given written reprimands on the same grounds. **Source:** St. Petersburg Times, 3/28/97, 6/14/98, & 9/5/98; The Tampa Tribune, 4/17/98

Vernon Deon Huewitt   19   —

February 6, 1997. Fort Pierce:

Mr. Huewitt was shot and killed by Fort Pierce Police Officer Antonio Hurtado in a restaurant parking lot. Authorities claim Mr. Huewitt fired at the cop first and that he tried to fire again but his gun jammed. A grand jury cleared Officer Hurtado of criminal wrongdoing. **Source:** Sun-Sentinel (Jacksonville, FL), 2/21/97

Pertti Huhtala   50   —

January 14, 1997. Lake Worth:

Mr. Huhtala was taken into custody after cops received reports that a distraught man was searching for his wife and smashing windows with a pipe. After being handcuffed, Huhtala became ill. Paramedics were called to bring him to the hospital, but he was dead on arrival.

Unidentified Man   30s   —

January 7, 1997. north Tampa:
Two plainclothes sheriff's deputies were sitting in their car waiting to arrest a man selling marijuana to two other plainclothes deputies. Another man reportedly came up to them, spit on their windshield and cursed and yelled at them. When the deputies got out and identified themselves, the man supposedly swung at them with a three- to four-feet long wooden board. Cops claim he engaged them in a scuffle and managed to grab a deputy's gun, although the deputy hit a button that caused the ammunition cartridge to fall out. The deputies knew at that point that the gun was not loaded. The man ran away holding the deputy's gun and supposedly tried to fire it. Plainclothes Deputies Chad Chronister and Thomas St. John, responding to a call for help, supposedly identified themselves and ordered the man to drop the gun. Authorities claim he pointed it at Deputies Chronister and St. John, who opened fire and killed him. The two deputies were put on paid administrative leave during an investigation. Authorities say they do not know why the man confronted the cops in the first place. **Source:** St. Petersburg Times, 1/8/97

Richard Bisaccio   38   —

January 4, 1997. Palm Beach County (Boca Greens):
Mr. Bisaccio was distraught, holding a knife to his ex-girlfriend's daughter's throat. Another woman, Elaine Lines, walked up behind him, began talking to him and was beginning to calm him down. She put her arms around him and she, Mr. Bisaccio and the woman he was holding hostage "fell into a sort of huddle." Shortly thereafter Mr. Bisaccio released the hostage, who ran to her boyfriend. Ms. Lines stayed to talk to the distraught man, trying to get him to drop the knife. But before this could happen, three sheriff's deputies ran up with their guns drawn, yelled at her to get out of the way and, when Mr. Bisaccio allegedly stepped toward them holding the knife, they shot and killed him. One newspaper account claimed that cops had reasoned with him for 30 minutes, that he begged deputies to shoot him and that he lunged with the knife. A sheriff's department spokesperson defended the shooting, saying, "If a man had a knife, I would have drawn my gun. You try to defuse the situation first. But if you're threatened, you shoot for the body. They followed their training." But Ms. Lines, the woman who persuaded him to release the hostage, disagreed, saying the situation could have been resolved non-violently and that, with a little more time, she could have persuaded him to drop the knife. "He would have put the knife back. He was confused, bewildered at what he had done. He needed help." This was the third time in three weeks the Palm Beach County sheriff's deputies killed someone. A sheriff's department spokesperson defended the department, saying, "In all three instances... it appears all the appropriate procedures were followed." **Source:** Sun-Sentinel (Fort Lauderdale, FL), 1/5/97

Roberto Rivera-Román   30   —

January 3, 1997. Auburndale:
Auburndale police went to Mr. Rivera-Román's apartment to question him about a stolen vehicle. Neighbors report that the Mr. Rivera-Román was walking away when a cop pointed a gun at him. Mr. Rivera-Román pushed it away. Cops sprayed him in the eyes with a chemical spray, then shot him once, causing him to fall to the ground. As he was trying to stand, another cop shot him in the chest and killed him. All three neighbors who spoke to investigators said that the victim could have been subdued without being shot. **Source:** St. Petersburg Times, 1/5/97

Fernando Esteban   18   —

January 1, 1997. South Dade:
Called for a domestic dispute, Metro-Dade Officer Al Hernandez shot and killed Fernando. A police spokesman said Fernando was driving toward the officer. **Source:** Miami Oct. 22 Coalition

Kevin Pruiksma   27   —

December 29, 1996. Palm Beach:
Kevin died of heart failure after allegedly fighting with an off-duty sheriff's deputy and paramedics. He'd been handcuffed. He was unarmed.

Lyndon Stark   48   —

December 18, 1996. King's Point:

Mr. Stark died as he fought off five sheriff's deputies trying to take him out of his mother's apartment. Mr. Stark was unarmed. He was found with his feet bound, hands cuffed behind his back, in a prone position in a room clouded with pepper spray.

Matthew Herbert Mills   34   —

December 6, 1996. Tampa:

Mr. Mills was shot twice in the back and killed by plainclothes Tampa Police Sgt. Pete Brevi and Officer Eric Houston. Authorities admit that the victim was laying in the street on his stomach but claim he was pointing a gun "behind him and upward at [the two cops] as they and another officer tried to subdue him," according to the newspaper. Mr. Mills was handcuffed, supposedly after he was shot. Cops described this as "standard procedure." The incident began when Mr. Mills allegedly tried to sell cocaine to an undercover cop from the "QUAD Squad" and an officer tried to arrest him. Authorities claim there was a struggle during which Mr. Mills bit the cop, got control of the cop's gun and fired a shot. But neighbors were angry that the victim was shot in the back as he lay face-down on the ground. More than 100 angry residents gathered, some throwing bottles and rocks at riot police who had been called to the scene. Less than two months later, the state's attorney cleared Sgt. Brevi and Officer Houston of criminal wrongdoing, ruling that the shooting was justified. The victim's mother said, "I'm so mad, I don't know what in the world to do." Later, she filed a wrongful death lawsuit against the Tampa police. The lawsuit charged that the department "permitted and tolerated a pattern and practice of excessive force against the public by (Tampa) police officers." Police tried to trash the victim, saying he had an extensive criminal record, had served time in prison for theft and burglary charges and was under the influence of cocaine and alcohol when he died. **Source:** St. Petersburg Times, 1/23/97 & 10/24/97

Anderson Tate   —   *African-American*

December 3, 1996. Fort Pierce:

Mr. Tate died strapped into a jail chair as he pleaded for help because of an alleged cocaine overdose. White jailers were caught on videotape ignoring and then taunting him for his Muslim chants and cries of "burning up". **Source:** Miami Oct. 22 Coalition

TyRon Lewis   18   *African American*

October 24, 1996. St. Petersburg:

TyRon was shot to death by police during a traffic stop, sparking a two day rebellion. TyRon was the sixth person to be killed by police in 1996. After a grand jury did not return an indictment against the cop who shot him, another rebellion ensued.

Ronald James Turner   26   —

October 4, 1996. Broward County (Wilton Manors):

Mr. Turner was shot and killed by Wilson Manors Police Detective David Jones after allegedly pulling a gun out of a bag and refusing orders to drop it. Mr. Turner had reportedly robbed a bank and was confronted by Det. Jones and another cop ten minutes later on the street. Det. Jones fired two shots. A grand jury declined to indict him. **Source:** Sun-Sentinel (Jacksonville, FL), 4/4/97

Unidentified Man   26   —

July 1996. Tampa:

The man, described in the press as a robbery suspect, was killed in a crash during a police chase. He was from Orlando and was reportedly driving a stolen car. **Source:** St. Petersburg Times, 4/7/98

Donnie Alexander   41   —

May 27, 1996. Riveria Beach:

A homeless man, Mr. Alexander was fatally shot by Police Officer Andrew Scott Cohan. Police claim Mr. Alexander threatened Officer Cohan with a cinder block after the cop stopped him on Blue Heron Boulevard.

Jonathan Storker   24   —

April 20, 1996. Pinellas County (Largo):
Mr. Storker was shot and killed by Pinellas County Sheriff's Deputy Murray Smith after a car chase. Deputy Smith fired 13 shots within three seconds, hitting the victim 12 times. Cops had tried to stop Mr. Storker for driving an allegedly stolen car and after a chase, four cruisers boxed him in in a cul-de-sac. An official investigation concluded that Deputy Smith ordered Mr. Storker at gunpoint to raise his hands but that, "Instead, Storker backed up and hit the deputy's right knee. He then drove toward the deputy, who fired at him." Authorities claimed that Deputy Smith fired so many shots because he did not know whether he had hit Mr. Storker and that Mr. Storker continued driving toward him until his car hit a police cruiser. The victim's family filed a wrongful death lawsuit against the sheriff's office. The family's lawyer said, "The key to this whole thing is the number of shots that were fired. No other officer pulled his gun out. One officer just emptied his gun." The lawyer also questioned whether Deputy Smith was in danger, pointing out that bullets went through the passenger window and the passenger side windshield of the victim's car, indicating that the cop was not standing in front of it. **Source:** St. Petersburg Times, 4/9/98

Unidentified Youth   14   —

April 1996. Tampa:
The young man died when the allegedly stolen car in which he and four other teenagers were riding crashed into a van after a police chase. **Source:** St. Petersburg Times, 4/7/98

Gregory Max Jemison   38   —

February 15, 1996. Deerfield Beach:
Mr. Jemison was shot in the chest by Deputy James Dusenbery after he allegedly raped a woman. It is unclear whether he died or survived.

Mark Anthony Longo   37   —

February 12, 1996. Riveria Beach:
Mr. Longo was shot and killed by Officer David Sissenwein. The officer was allowed into the home by Longo's father to break up a fight between the two of them. Longo had a knife, which Sissenwein claimed he raised above his head in a threatening manner.

Unidentified Man   21   —

February 1996. Tampa:
The man, described in the press as a suspected car thief, was being chased by the police. He was killed in a head-on collision with another car during the chase. **Source:** St. Petersburg Times, 4/7/98

Theopholus Adebisi   —   *Nigerian*

January 1, 1996. Krome Detention Center:
Theo was left to die after he collapsed on the detention center soccer field. Although three INS officials were on the field, none attempted to revive him. When the doctor arrived 35 minutes later, according to one refugee, he approached Theo nonchalantly as if at a dinner party. Other immigrants had been attempting CPR for the previous half hour.

Heinz Baer		*German*
Markus Rossknecht		*German*

December 1995. Tampa (West Shore & Gandy Blvd.'s):

Mr. Baer and Mr. Rossknecht, two German tourists, were killed when their car was hit by teenagers being chased by Tampa Police Officer Michael Skypack. The teenagers' car was allegedly stolen and reportedly ran a red light before hitting the victims' car. In May, 1995, the Tampa Police Department loosened its pursuit policies to allow car chases in cases of suspected auto theft, burglary, firearms and DUI. Previously, cops were only allowed to chase violent crime suspects. The families of Mr. Baer and Mr. Rossknecht sued the city of Tampa, charging that the pursuit policy was responsible for their loved ones' deaths. The mayor justified the pursuit policy, saying, "If you are a decent person and a cop is after you, you stop. People who are eluding the police are criminals." **Source:** St. Petersburg Times, 4/7/98; The Tampa Tribune, 4/12/98

Osiris E. Galán	33	—

December 31, 1995. Miami:

Mr. Galan was shot and killed by Miami Officer Gordon Wing. Police said Galan was armed, but after two days of searches no weapon was found. Mr. Galan had a baseball cap in his hand when he was shot.

Derrick Wiltshire	20	*African American*
Antonio Young	20	*African American*

November 7, 1995. Miami:

Antonio and another young man were shot to death as they tried to flee from police who allegedly saw them trying to rob tourists. Five Miami officers fired at the two young men. Several witnesses heard more than a dozen shots. Investigators were reported as "trying to determine" whether Young and Wiltshire pointed weapons or shot at police first or not. A third youth was charged with their murder. This charge was dropped when the police unit involved was later found to use a planted "throw down" gun and cover-up reports in another case.

Gary Chassagne	40	—

November 5, 1995. Miramar:

Mr. Chassagne allegedly planned to kill his estranged wife, their baby daughter and then himself. He wounded his estranged wife that night. Toward dawn he was shot and killed by a Miramar police officer outside his brother's home.

Catalino (Nick) Sang	42	*Dominican/Chinese*

November 2, 1995. Miami Beach:

Mr. Sang allegedly hijacked a Dade school bus carrying 13 students. He was shot by Sgt. Joseph Derringer and Sgt. José Fernández of the Metro-Dade Police Department's Special Response Team. Shots fired by one of the officers killed him. Mr. Sang had demanded to talk to the IRS, which he thought was persecuting him in a tax dispute. Police said they thought he had "some kind of explosive device," but Mr. Sang was unarmed, carrying only a Bible.

Unidentified Man	—	—

October 30, 1995. Miami Beach:

An unidentified man was shot by police outside a South Beach club. He was allegedly "wielding a gun." It is unclear whether he died or survived.

Kevin Lawler	17	—

October 20, 1995. Liberty City:

Kevin was shot to death by a plainclothes robbery investigator, Officer William Hladky, who allegedly confronted the teen to question him about a robbery. Police claim Kevin pulled a gun and opened fire on Hladky.

Torrey Davon Jacobs   17   *African American*

July 18, 1995. Coconut Grove:

Torrey was shot and killed by Miami Police Officer Chris G. Griffin, who fired five times. The officer claimed that he thought a lighter carried by Jacobs was a loaded gun.

Luis Espinosa Sánchez   26   *Puerto Rican*

June 24, 1995. North Dade County:

Luis was chased by police dogs, then shot and killed behind a vacant house by Metro-Dade Officer Norman Narei. Police claim Luis was wanted in an investigation. They did not say whether or not he was armed.

Mark Rivera   28   *Puerto Rican*

June 9, 1995. Miami:

Mr. Rivera was shot and killed by Officer Andres Capetillo or Officer Tom Gains. Police say Mark was armed with a handgun and suspected of threatening his daughter.

Joseph Ingrassi   36   —

March 1995. Land O'Lakes jail:

Mr. Ingrassi died in his jail cell of medical neglect. He had a history of medical problems, including a prescription drug addiction. He was taking nine medications for heart problems and other illnesses. He coughed up blood. But the jail doctor never saw him. Jail personnel ignored him when he repeatedly told them he was dying. Deputies waited at least 15 minutes after he collapsed in his cell before calling for paramedics, and he died. The deputies were reportedly disciplined for this delay. The victim's family filed a $6 million wrongful death lawsuit against the sheriff's office, which runs the jail, and another wrongful death lawsuit against the jail's medical staff. **Source:** St. Petersburg Times, 10/23/97

Arlene Adams   33   —

February 28, 1995. Miami:

A retired police officer, George Adams, 64, shot and killed his wife Arlene Adams and then killed himself.

Armando Junco   62   —

January 10, 1995. Miami:

Armondo was shot and killed by officer Francisco Casanovas. The officer was part of a task force which stormed into a squatters camp looking for Junco and another man who had escaped from Glades Correctional Institution in Palm Beach County on Jan. 2. A Dade County judge ruled that Casanovas fired in self-defense after Junco allegedly attacked him with a stick.

Two Unidentified People   —   —

1995. South Florida (I-395):

The two people were shot and killed by police on an I-395 overpass. They were allegedly robbers. The victims' families are sure that the case involved "throw down" weapons, where police shoot people and then plant guns on them. Cops claim the families cannot prove this. The case was examined, along with several others, as part of an investigation into whether police in South Florida made a habit of planting guns on people after they shot them. **Source:** Florida Times Union (Jacksonville, FL), 11/30/97

Andrew Robert Tolmie　　　　　　　　23　　　　　—

December 1994. Largo:
Mr. Tolmie was shot and killed by Largo Police Officer John Ferraro. Around 2:30 a.m., Officer Ferraro saw Mr. Tolmie's truck hit a curb and blow a front tire. Mr. Tolmie continued to drive on the rim, veering off the road several times. Officer Ferraro followed him into a parking lot. Police backup arrived and blocked all the exits. Cops claim Mr. Tolmie rammed Officer Ferraro's car and then hit another cop car. Then, his truck stopped, wheels spinning, with all four tires flat. Officer Ferraro got out of his car and fired four shots through the truck's driver's side window, hitting Mr. Tolmie twice. Authorities claim a blood alcohol test performed as part of the autopsy showed that Mr. Tolmie was extremely drunk. The state's attorney found that Officer Ferraro acted "within the scope of state law and Police Department policies and procedures" when he shot and killed Mr. Tolmie. In Feb. 1997, the city settled a wrongful death lawsuit filed by the victim's parents for $25,000. The lawsuit charged that Officer Ferraro had no reason to be afraid of Mr. Tolmie because the latter was unarmed and made no threatening movements. A city memo acknowledged, "There is some question as to why Officer Ferraro placed himself in a position of danger between the two vehicles when the truck was trapped in the parking lot by Largo police vehicles and was disabled to the point that all four tires had been flattened." Mr. Tolmie worked as a cook at a restaurant and also cooked for children at a day care center, where he was called "Mr. Andrew." He had planned to attend culinary school. **Source:** St. Petersburg Times, 2/7/97

Unidentified Man　　　　　　　　　　—　　　　　—

November 29, 1994. Miami International Airport:
An unarmed man was shot and killed by Metro-Dade police officer at Miami International Airport. The officer claimed the man attacked him, hitting him in the face and grabbing at his nightstick.

Arlix Fuentes　　　　　　　　　　　36　　　　　—

September 9, 1994. West of Miami:
Arlix was shot and killed by a member of the Violent Crime Fugitive Task Force of South Florida, a multi-agency team of officers from around the state. Fuentes had escaped from the South Florida Reception Center in April and allegedly pulled a gun when spotted by officers.

Yvon Guerrier　　　　　　　　　　42　　　　　*Haitian*

August 5, 1994. Delray Beach:
Mr. Guerrier was shot and killed by officer John Battiloro in front of a food store. The clerk called police to complain that Mr. Guerrier was harassing customers outside. The officer said Mr. Guerrier reached for his nightstick, so he shot him twice in the abdomen. Mr. Guerrier died ten hours later.

Gustavaus Jody Francis　　　　　　22　　　　　—

July 1994. Riviera Beach:
Gustavaus was shot and killed by police officers Reno Wells, Joel Audate and Cedric Edwards. Gustavaus was in a religious fervor and had cut his own arms with a knife. Family members called police to help him. He ignored police orders to drop the knife. The three officers shot him from a distance of 8 or 4 feet. They claim he lunged at them with the knife.

Unidentified Woman　　　　　　　　—　　　　　—
Egberto Vásquez　　　　　　　　　48　　　　　—
Steve Vásquez　　　　　　　　　　23　　　　　—

May 10, 1994. North Dade County:
All three people were killed during an eight-hour standoff with police. Police went to the house to "check on a complaint" and were held off by Egberto Vásquez, who allegedly had a gun. After police stormed the house and exchanged gunfire with Vásquez, the three were dead.

Jorge Luis Morales   43   —

May 1994. Allapattah (Miami):

A bystander, Jorge was killed by a Miami police Glock 9mm bullet when one of two officers exchanged gunfire with three young robbery suspects in Allapattah. The three robbery suspects, not the officers, were charged with felony murder. The two officers, Ariel Rojas and Jeffery Locke, were soon back on the street. **Source:** Miami Oct. 22 Coalition

Diane Nelson   —   —

March 8, 1994. Pinellas Park (in jail):

Diane was a mother of three who worked as a janitor for four dollars an hour. She was charged with battery and sent to jail, where she died of a massive heart attack, possibly without even having gone before a judge. The jail's practice of treating ill inmates involved ignoring the fact that Diane had previously suffered a heart attack and was in need of medication. It was not provided to her. Diane was suffering from classic heart attack symptoms and lay sick for an entire day after her arrest. As Diane was in the midst of the massive heart attack that killed her, a prison nurse said to her, "Stop the theatrics and get up on the chair. Here we go again, I am really getting tired of this phony bull--." A nurse treating Diane admitted in court documents that before the incident she had joked, "We save money because we skip the ambulance and bring them right to the morgue." A federal court-appointed monitor of the jail at the time of Diane's death said, "It's hard to believe that those kinds of things are still happening in this day and age." **Source:** St. Louis Post-Dispatch, 9/27/98

Alvin Barroso   23   —

March 7, 1994. Coral Gables:

Alvin was shot and killed by rookie officer Carlos Losado. Barroso had asked for extra police patrols to watch his business. Losado and his partner were checking on the business and "may have mistaken (Barroso) for an intruder." A confrontation occurred between Barroso and the officer, who fired several times.

Kiandre Graner   17   —

January 21, 1994. West Palm Beach:

Kiandre was shot in the head and killed by officer Chris Fragakis. Fragakis and another officer entered a rooming house after "watching an unusual number of people entering and leaving." They claimed Garner pointed a gun at them in the stairwell, and they fired at him several times.

Mario Hernández   37   —

Dec. 24 or 25, 1993. Palm Beach County:

Mr. Hernández was struck and killed by a car driven by Palm Beach County Sheriff's Deputy Robert Ferrell Jr., who was returning from a family party. One hour later, Deputy Ferrell's blood alcohol level was tested at .10, then the legal definition for driving while intoxicated. Prosecutors would not charge Deputy Ferrell because they said they could not prove what his blood alcohol level had been at the time of the accident one hour earlier. They said it is possible that the alcohol Deputy Ferrell had drunk had not made its way into his bloodstream when Mr. Hernández was struck and killed. **Source:** The Miami Herald, 2/11/94

Frank A. Seedarnee   54   —

October 26, 1993. Plantation:

Frank was shot at three times by officers Mike Jasinski and Jim O'Haa, who said he pointed a shotgun at them. Police were responding to a 911 call by Seedarnee's girlfriend. It is not known which officer fired the fatal bullet.

Mary Stackton Creamer   —   —

October 18, 1993. Pinellas County:

Ms. Creamer was killed in an accident resulting from a high-speed chase conducted by Pinellas County sheriffs over an expired license plate. It is unclear from the newspaper whether Ms. Creamer was in the car being chased or in another vehicle. The victim's brother said, "[My sister's] life was worth more than an expired tag." **Source:** St. Petersburg Times, 10/27/97

| **Marcillus Miller** | 45 | — |

October 1, 1993. Fort Lauderdale:

A homeless man sleeping in bushes, Marcillus was awakened by an attacking K-9 police dog. After stabbing the dog in self-defense, two Fort Lauderdale officers shot Miller six times, killing him.

| **Roy Maurice Heaton** | 32 | — |

September 5, 1993. Plantation:

Roy was shot and killed by Officer John Mastrianni who said he was "wielding a baseball bat." The police were responding to a 911 call by Heaton's girlfriend. She later said Heaton was verbally but not physically threatening. Another witness said Heaton did not move toward the officer and was not holding the bat in a threatening way. A Broward grand jury ruled the officer was justified.

| **Mariam Burgdorf** | — | — |

September 1993. Miami:

Allegedly wielding a barbecue lighter, Miriam, who the media referred to as a mental patient, was killed because the officer thought she had a gun. **Source:** Miami Oct. 22 Coalition

| **Unidentified Man** | 50s | — |

June 30, 1993. Miami Beach:

A man in his fifties was shot by officers just northwest of South Beach. An officer pulled over his car which they said matched the description of one used in a robbery. The man opened fire and wounded the officer. Other officers pursued the car and shot several times in a residential neighborhood, hitting other vehicles in the area and killing the man. The body lay sprawled on the street for hours.

| **Lawrence "Bo Pete" Johnson** | 17 | *African American* |

June 16, 1993. Miami:

Lawrence was shot in the back and killed by Miami officers. Police claimed that Lawrence shot at them first. A police investigation revealed that someone else may have done the shooting. The officer who fired the fatal bullet could not be identified.

| **Josue Mesidor** | — | *Haitian* |

June 1, 1993. Dade County:

Mr. Mesidor died of treatable pneumonia while held in Dade County jail. After relatives called the police, Mr. Mesidor was arrested for disorderly conduct. He was held for 15 days in a jail cell, naked and without a mattress or blanket, instead of being placed under medical watch for mental illness, as indicated. Other inmates charge jailers with abusing Mr. Mesidor. **Source:** Miami Oct. 22 Coalition

| **Charles Knight** | 38 | — |

April 22, 1993. Miami Beach:

When Mr. Knight, an unemployed roofer, stormed out of his apartment still holding a knife after arguing with his girlfriend, Miami Beach police Sgt. Peter Smolyanski shot and killed him in the hallway. "Charlie walked out the door, and they shot him. No warning. No nothing," said his girlfriend Linda Moulthrop. **Source:** Miami Oct. 22 Coalition

| **Jerónimo Bonilla** | 19 | — |

April 6, 1993. Homestead:

Mr. Bonilla was shot several times and killed by Homestead Police Officer Alfred McClendon. Mr. Bonilla allegedly pointed a gun at the officers after they knocked on his apartment door.

William Dawson — —

February 22, 1993. Lake Park:
William was shot 16 times and killed by Deputy Vincent Tuzeo as he fled in his pickup truck after he set off a burglar alarm at a store. William was unarmed. The State Attorney's Office charged Tuzeo with unnecessary killing to prevent an unlawful act. A jury acquitted the officer in 1994.

Unidentified Man — —

February 15, 1993. North Dade:
An unidentified man who was allegedly brandishing a crowbar was fatally shot by a Metro-Dade police officer outside the elementary school attended by his two children. After attempting to see his daughter's teacher he was asked to leave the school, which he did. No students were present during the shooting.

Robert Barry 23 —

January 20, 1993. Pompano Beach:
Mr. Barry was killed as he chased three burglary suspects by car. Mr. Barry's car was broadsided by a police cruiser. The officer was responding to a 911 call Mr. Barry's wife had made.

María Enriqueta Quintero — *Mexican*

1993. Hillsborough (I-4):
Ms. Quintero, a migrant farmworker, was struck and killed by highway traffic while trying to get away from Hillsborough Sheriff's Deputy Given García, Jr. Deputy García claims he detained Ms. Quintero for possible immigration violations but released her without charges when federal agents declined to take her into custody. After her death, $700 of her money was found to be missing. Deputy García was fired from the sheriff's office but acquitted of theft charges. The victim's family settled a wrongful death lawsuit against the Hillsborough Sheriff's Office and (former) Deputy García. **Source:** St. Petersburg Times, 12/4/97

Fermín Alameda 63 *Puerto Rican*

August 9, 1992. Wynwood:
Mr. Alameda suffered five fractured ribs, a ruptured liver and a dislocated shoulder while being restrained by Miami officers John Collins and Emilio López. Mr. Alameda was arrested for refusing to leave the scene of a fire. He'd been trying to help save merchandise in a burning store owned by people he knew. Witnesses said the officers handcuffed Mr. Alameda, roughly threw him to the ground and kneed him in the back. The Dade County Medical Examiner's Office said pressure, probably from a knee, snapped his ribs and ruptured his liver, causing internal bleeding that killed him. A judge cleared the officers, ruling that Mr. Alameda's death was accidental.

Shelton Wilson 18 *Black*

July 5, 1992. Miami (Little River):
Shelton Wilson was shot and killed by off-duty Officer Reginald Kinchen outside a Little River disco. Mr. Wilson was standing over his own twin brother, who had just been shot and wounded by an unknown assailant. Shelton Wilson supposedly drew his own gun before he was shot and killed by Officer Kinchen.

Anthony Harrell 34 —

February 23, 1992. West Palm Beach:
Anthony was shot and killed by officer David Duncan. Anthony was allegedly chasing a family member. Police said he came toward officer Duncan with a knife. A grand jury ruled the shooting justifiable.

Andrew Morello	16	*Italian American*

February 1, 1992. Miami:

Andrew was shot and killed by off-duty Metro-Dade police officer Laura Russell. Andrew was allegedly waiting for a friend to steal stereo speakers from a parked car when confronted by officer Russell and her husband George, a Miami officer. Russell claimed she fired at Anthony Morello in self-defense because she was afraid he would run over her. But the angle of the bullet and the police 911 tapes of the incident contradict her story. Evidence showed the van was actually backing away.

James Steidley	45	—

January 12, 1992. West Palm Beach:

James was allegedly pointed a gun at officers who were investigating a murder. Officers Kirk Bennett, Khaled Ghumrawi and David Salvador shot him to death.

Two Unidentified Teenagers	teens	—

1992. Tampa:

The two teenagers were killed when the (allegedly) stolen car they were driving crashed into a city bus during a chase by police. In 1996, the Tampa City Council agreed to settle a lawsuit filed by the victims' families for $32,500. **Source:** The Tampa Tribune, 5/29/98

Brad Moffett	34	—

September 10, 1991. Cooper City:

Brad was shot twice in the chest and killed by officer Robert Wallace. Officer Wallace had been dispatched to Brad's ex-girlfriend's home to investigate a report of domestic violence. Brad, who had been undergoing psychiatric treatment and had attempted suicide in the past, allegedly lunged at officer Wallace with a kitchen knife.

Michael Gottlieb	38	—

September 9, 1991. Pompano Beach:

Michael threatened suicide and kept police at bay. He was shot nine times and killed by Sheriff's Deputy Joe Hoffman of a SWAT team. As Mr. Gottlieb sat on the floor behind his bed with his back against a wall, he "made a sudden move." Police said afterward that they later found a loaded pistol behind the bed. Michael had called 911 for help so he wouldn't kill himself. A county grand jury ruled the shooting justified. (Deputy Joe Hoffman has shot and killed four people while on duty, including Herbert Harris, III, 47, who was shot in the back in 1985. Mr. Harris's widow was awarded $209,500 after an appeal overruled an earlier circuit jury that found the shooting justified. Deputy Hoffman's other shootings were declared justified).

Roger Sanford	—	—

August 21, 1991. Deerfield Beach:

Roger was arrested after a domestic dispute and shot by Sheriff's Deputy Daniel Jackowski as Roger sat handcuffed in the locked back seat of a squad car . Police claim Sanford, while handcuffed and after having been frisked, somehow pulled a pistol from his pants, cocked it and pointed it towards Jackowski. Officer Jackowski exited the car and fired through the back window, killing Sanford.

Unidentified Woman	—	—

July 24, 1991. Margate:

A woman was killed by a police bullet in crossfire between police and three people who were allegedly committing a robbery. A grand jury decided not to file charges against the officers.

Reginald Lively   26   —

June 29, 1991. Davie:
Reginald was shot to death by officer Richard Smith when Smith pulled Reginald's van over for having a cracked windshield. Police claim Reginald and his passenger both jumped out of the van and began firing at police. Smith shot Reginald twice in the head.

Homer Davis, Jr.   —   —

April 6, 1991. Pompano Beach:
Homer was killed by two officers. Homer Davis had allegedly abducted a woman and tried to rape her. He allegedly exchanged gunfire with police as he fled.

Brenda Forester   33

February 21, 1991. North Dade County:
Brenda was shot once in the chest and killed. Broward Sheriff's Office deputies had tried to arrest her in a drug sting, and she fled by car. Deputy Ed Madge said his pistol accidentally went off and killed Brenda when he rapped it against her car window. Deputy Madge was later cleared of criminal intent.

Robert "Nutty" Blackledge   —   —

January 30, 1991. Plantation:
Mr. Blackledge was shot to death by four Plantation officers outside a First Union Bank. Mr. Blackledge had gone inside the bank, claimed he was wearing a bomb, and dragged his ex-girlfriend, a teller, outside. He allegedly began firing a gun.

Robert Jewett   34   —

November 24, 1990. West Palm Beach:
Mr. Jewett was beaten to death by Officers Glen Thurlow and Stephen Rollins after they found him staggering in traffic on South Dixie Highway. One officer held him while the other struck him repeatedly with a heavy flashlight. Mr. Jewett died of asphyxiation after his Adam's apple and ribs were broken and his testicles crushed. A jury acquitted the officers of charges of second-degree murder and aggravated assault.

Michael Miguel   33   —

November 18, 1990. West of Miami:
Mr. Miguel was killed by off-duty Florida City Reserve Police Officer Alex Díaz. Officer Díaz said Mr. Miguel was armed and trying to rob him.

Richard Guarine   34   —

November 16, 1990. West of Boynton Beach:
Mr. Guarine was fatally shot in the chest by off-duty, out-of-uniform Sgt. Don West. Sgt. West had followed Mr. Guarine outside city limits on "suspicion of drunken driving." Sgt. West claimed Mr. Guarine had a weapon in his hand. Car keys were found in his hand. Sgt. West was cleared by two grand juries, fired, then reinstated after a five-month suspension.

Two Unidentified Men   —   —

October 25, 1990. Northwest Dade County:
Two men were killed in a gun battle with police and agents from the FBI and the federal bureau of Alcohol, Tobacco and Firearms. They were suspected "members of a home-invasion gang."

George Ellefsen	31	—

October 16, 1990. Pembroke Pines:

Mr. Ellefsen was shot during a fight outside a bar by Miami Police Officer Robert Sadlier, who admitted to drinking ten beers in five hours. Though officer Sadlier deliberately went to his truck for his gun, and never identified himself as a police officer, he was charged only with manslaughter, not second- or first-degree murder. Officer Sadlier claimed to have shot in self-defense after Mr. Ellefsen pulled a bat from his truck.

Angel Arsenio Arencibia	32	—
José Manuel Díaz	33	—
Fred Lawrence Murray	29	—

July 17, 1990. Deerfield Beach:

These three people were shot and killed by seven SWAT team members during a drug sting. The victims allegedly had loaded weapons, but none fired any shots and none had criminal records.

Billy Jo Sizemore	20	—

June 11, 1990. West of Lantana:

Mr. Sizemore was wanted on two warrants from Maryland. He was shot in the chest and killed by Sheriff's Warrants Officer William Sepko. Sepko and another officer, Thomas Neigebauer (both of whom had killed people before in shootings ruled justifiable) said that Mr. Sizemore tried to grab Officer Neigebauer's gun.

James "Jimmy" Perloff, Jr.	—	—

February 14, 1990. Boynton Beach:

An 11th grade runaway from Pennsylvania, Jimmy was shot to death by Florida State Trooper Wallace Dill. Police claim Jimmy fired first.

Huberta Matthews	33	—

February 13, 1990. North Palm Beach:

Huberta was shot and killed by park ranger Capt. John Fillyaw, manager of John D. MacArthur Beach State Park, after she allegedly drew a handgun and began firing at him.

Eduardo Estuardo García	23	*Guatemalan*

January 20, 1990. South Dade County:

Mr. García was shot and killed by Metro-Dade officer James Faurot. Mr. García had allegedly held four people at gunpoint while robbing a Sears store at the Cutler Ridge Mall.

Allan Blanchard	24	*Virgin Islander (St. Croix)*
Clement Lloyd	23	*Black*

January 16, 1989. Miami (Overtown):

Clement Lloyd was fatally shot in the head by Miami Police Officer William Lozano on Martin Luther King Day. Mr. Lloyd was fleeing on a motorcycle after another cop had tried to pull him over for speeding. Officer Lozano, standing a few blocks away, entered the street as the motorcycle approached and fired as Mr. Lloyd passed, killing him and causing the motorcycle to crash. Allan Blanchard, a passenger on the bike, died the following day as a result of head injuries sustained during the crash. A three day rebellion broke out in the community in response to this cold-blooded murder. Officer Lozano claimed he fired in self-defense, that the motorcycle he had jumped in front of was about to run him over. But the bullet the officer fired went into the side of Clement Lloyd's head. Officer Lozano was convicted of manslaughter by a Miami jury. The conviction was overturned on appeal. Lozano was retried in Orlando. He was acquitted on the grounds that an officer has the right to not back off in a confrontation and to defend himself when not backing off. **Source:** "Police Violence is Excessive" by Kevin Brook in Criminal Justice: Opposiing Viewpoints (pp. 173-179), edited by Michael D Biskup. Greenhaven Press, Inc., San Diego, 1993; Miami Herald, 1/17/89 & continuing.

Leonardo Mercado — *Puerto Rican*

December 16, 1988. Miami:

Mr. Mercado, an alleged drug dealer, was beaten to death by Police Officers Pablo Camacho, Andy Watson, Nathaniel Veal, and Charlie Hayners, Jr., all members of a special street narcotics unit. The cops claimed they found the victim injured and dying when they went to his house on a drug raid. A jury acquitted them of criminal charges in 1990, leading to riots in Wynwood, a predominantly Puerto Rican neighborhood in Miami. In 1994, the four cops were convicted in federal court of obstruction of justice and sentenced to 21-30 months in prison. In Sept. 1998, an appeals court upheld their convictions. Their lawyers vowed to appeal. As of Sept. 10, 1998 -- almost 10 years after they killed Mr. Mercado -- none of the officers has spent a day in prison. **Source:** Sun-Sentinel (Fort Lauderdale, FL), 10/10/98

Teresa Mae McAbee 11 —

1987. Lake County:

Eleven-year-old Teresa McAbee was reported missing after going to a convenience store to buy a pencil for school. She was raped and strangled to death by Mascotte Police Officer James Ducett, who was patrolling the area the night she disappeared. Her body was later found floating in a lake. Fingerprint experts found Theresa's prints on the hood of Officer Ducett's car. Investigators testified that they also found tire tracks matching Officer Ducett's patrol car near the spot where the girl's body was found. A hair expert testified that a pubic hair found in Theresa's clothing was similar to Officer Ducett's. In 1988, Officer Ducett was convicted of first-degree murder and rape. **Source:** The Orlando Sentinel, 10/28/97 & 12/18/97

Unidentified Teenager teens —

September 7, 1983. Opa-Locka:

A teenager was killed and another wounded by a Florida Highway Patrol trooper. The trooper chased their car, which was reportedly stolen. They crashed and the officer fired as they ran on foot from the crash.

Wieslaw Skowronek — —

Date Unknown. Clearwater (in custody):

Mr. Skowronek was arrested "after a confrontation with officers outside a building with an image known as the Virgin Mary," according to the newspaper. He was killed by Clearwater Police Officers John E. Smith and Phillip Biazzo while in custody. He suffered a lacerated pancreas and died of internal bleeding by the time he reached a hospital. Officer Biazzo denied several times that either he or Officer Smith had struck the victim. He stuck to that story for five days after the victim's death. Then the officer told a different story. He said that while the victim lay on his back on the ground, Officer Smith, who stands 6'10" and weighs 270 pounds, drove his knee into the victim's stomach. Mr.. Skowronek stopped breathing in the police car and was dead by the time he reached the hospital. Officer Biazzo was fired in the spring of 1997 for lying abut the circumstances surrounding Mr. Skowronek's death. After an arbitration hearing, he was reinstated with full back pay. Officer Biazzo claimed that he did not remember the assault until several days after the incident. The Fraternal Order of Police (FOP) vigorously supported his efforts to be reinstated. Officer Smith was fired after he was arrested on an unrelated charge of buying illegal anabolic steroids. It was the second time that Officer Smith had been fired. The first time, in 1995, he was accused of lying about contact with a woman who filed a sexual harassment complaint against him. An arbitrator ordered Officer Smith reinstated in that case. According to Richard Coffee, a police chief and chairman of Florida's Criminal Justice Standards and Training Commission, "If (a police officer) tells a lie and then retracts the lie in a reasonable period of time, that's not a lie." **Source:** St. Petersburg Times, 2/8/98 & 3/16/98

GEORGIA

Name	Age	Nationality	Photo

Unidentified Man — —

October 22, 1998. Newnan:

Newnan Police Officer Bryan Morgan shot and killed the man after the man allegedly pointed a gun at him. Police claim they received a call about a man carrying a large amount of weapons along railroad tracks. Officer Morgan was put on paid administrative leave during the investigation. **Source:** The Atlanta Journal, 10/23/98

Willie James Williams — Black

September 2, 1998. Valdosta:

Willie was stopped when seen driving on the wrong side of the street. Arresting deputies claim he resisted handcuffing and "fell to the pavement as he was placed in the patrol car." He was taken to Lowndes County Jail. At 9 a.m. the next morning, he was found unconscious and died en route to the hospital. The autopsy indicated that death was caused by "complications of blunt force head trauma." **Source:** Atlanta Constitution, 9/20/98

David Russell McAfee 37 —

May 11, 1998. Marietta:

David was shot and killed by Marietta and Cobb County police officers just after midnight. Cops claim he pulled a gun at a gas station in an attempt to rob it of a six-pack of beer. When cops arrived, David fled in his van and was surrounded in the parking lot of the Crabhouse Restaurant at 2175 Cobb Parkway. David supposedly refused repeated orders to drop his gun, even after he exited his van . David allegedly fired one shot at the cops, who "opened fire, hitting him multiple times," in the words of a police spokesperson. Cops claim to have recovered a rifle and shotgun at the scene. Six Marietta cops were put on paid administrative leave (paid vacation) pending an investigation. David was allegedly distraught over the break-up of his 17-year marriage. He left behind three sons. A co-worker of his at Lockheed Martin Aeronautical Systems said, "He was an extremely nice guy. We are all broken up about the news." **Source:** The Atlanta Journal and Constitution, 5/11/98

Larry Hartstein 28 —

February 22, 1998. Norcross:

Larry collapsed in police custody and died one hour later at the hospital. Police said they picked him up after a report of a man screaming at a house. As he was escorted to a cell at the police station, police said he became completely limp. He was pronounced dead at the hospital. **Source:** Atlanta Constitution, 2/23/98

Alfaigo Terrell Davis 29 Black

February 21, 1998. Augusta:

Neighbors said Alfaigo was surrounded by up to 30 police cars and had his hands up in the air surrendering when he was shot by police and killed. **Source:** Atlanta Constitution, 2/24/98

Edward Cabreja 28 —

February 21, 1998. Norcross:

Mr. Cabreja was arrested for "screaming at a house," according to the newspaper. He was also reportedly wanted on a felony drug warrant. After being handcuffed and taken to the Norcross Police Department, he collapsed and died. Cops claimed he had just smoked crack, but no toxicology results were available. **Source:** The Atlanta Journal and Constitution, 2/26/98

John Robert Vogelle 35 —

February 9, 1998. Douglas County:

Mr. Vogelle reportedly got $15 worth of gas and then drove away without paying. Sheriff's deputies gave chase. Mr. Vogelle drove to a convenience store, ran inside, and allegedly held the clerk hostage with a knife to her throat. He supposedly cut her once and threatened to kill her, but she pulled away. An unidentified sheriff's deputy shot him in the mouth and killed him. **Source:** The Atlanta Journal and Constitution, 2/10/98

Timothy Reed   31   —

December 21, 1997. Cherokee County:

Timothy was shot and killed at point-blank range by two Cherokee County deputies, Craig Ross and Mike Pruner. Deputy Ross fired twice and Deputy Pruner once. Cops claim Timothy had "a history of violence and run-ins with the law;" they do not indicate whether Deputies Ross and Pruner had a history of "run-ins with civilians." Timothy was living with his sister, her two children, and someone else in a trailer. He was allegedly armed with a gun and a knife, and when an argument began, Reed's sister slipped out and called the police. Five deputies arrived. Three burst in the front and Timothy fled through the rear, taking his knife but leaving his rifle. Cops claim they ordered Reed to drop the knife but he turned toward them with it, and Ross and Pruner shot and killed him from less than five feet away. **Source:** The Atlanta Journal and Constitution, 12/23/97

Unidentified Man   —   —

December 11, 1997. Dekalb County:

Police officers chased the man they suspected of attempted auto theft into an office park. Officers claim he turned and lunged at them, so they shot him in the chest. He was tackled by two officers after being shot. As they were taking him into custody, he collapsed and died. **Source:** Atlanta Constitution, 12/12/97

John Albert Jackson   27   *Black*

November 28, 1997. Douglasville:

John was shot and killed by police while driving away from a supermarket parking lot. Police were called to the supermarket because he was suspected of passing a bad check. Two officers shot at him in his car. One bullet hit him in the head, and he was pronounced dead at the hospital. **Source:** Atlanta Constitution, 11/29/97

Unidentified Man   —   —

October 21, 1997. near Byron:

A man was walking north on I-75 when he was picked up by a Dooly County deputy. The man kept telling the deputy that someone was after him, trying to kill him, and that he needed to get back home to Pennsylvania. The deputy decided that the man was paranoid and needed to be in a shelter. The closest suitable shelter was in Macon. The deputy drove to the county line, where the man was transferred to a Houston county deputy. That deputy radioed ahead to Peach County about the transient. When the Houston County deputy met the Peach County deputy, police claim that the man decided that the Peach County deputy was the person who was after him and attempted to kick out the back window. The deputy let the man out and he began to walk down the highway, refusing to let deputies get near him. At that point, Macon State Prison Corrections Officer (and former police officer) Alfonso Tweety pulled his car in between the deputies and the man. Officer Tweety got out, gun in hand, and chased the man, eventually tackling him on the pavement. The two were hit by a tractor-trailer and several other vehicles and killed. **Source:** The Atlanta Journal, 10/23/97

Steven Oliver   17   *white*

October 17, 1997. Forest Park:

Steven was shot and killed in a ball field after being chased on foot by police. Police said he was shot after he "went for one of the officer's guns." An eyewitness said he saw Steven on his back screaming to his mother, "Mama, get them off of me." The eyewitness also said there were three officers over Steven, all with their guns drawn, and they fired as many as seven shots all of a sudden. **Source:** Atlanta Constitution, 10/18/97

Nathaniel Hutchinson   39   —

October 15, 1997. Douglas:

Mr. Hutchinson was shot in the head and killed by a Coffee County sheriff's deputy as he sat in a car with two other men at the Greyhound bus station. Mr. Hutchinson was in the front passenger seat. A half pound of cocaine was reportedly recovered, and the two other men in the car were arrested and charged with cocaine trafficking. Authorities did not reveal the circumstances under which Mr. Hutchinson was shot, and the deputy who killed him was placed on paid administrative leave. The sheriff's deputies had been called to the scene by the Drug Enforcement Agency, which was conducting a drug operation. **Source:** Florida Times-Union (Jacksonville, FL), 10/17/97

| **Clarence Lyons** | 21 | — |

October 9, 1997. southwest Atlanta:

Mr. Lyons was shot and killed by Atlanta Police Officer Scott Priestly after he allegedly pointed a gun at the cop. Officer Priestly reportedly saw Mr. Lyons driving a stolen car and engaged in a car chase. A foot chase ensued when Mr. Lyons and a passenger ran from the car. The cop followed him over a fence and into a church yard where the two allegedly engaged in a scuffle before Officer Priestly shot Mr. Lyons to death. **Source:** The Atlanta Journal and Constitution, 10/10/97

| **Edwin Wingo** | 39 | — |

September 4, 1997. Atlanta:

Edwin died while in the back seat of a police car. Police claim he shot himself in the head with his own gun after having been searched twice before being put in the patrol car. **Source:** Atlanta Constitution, 9/6/97

| **Marquez Hayes** | 4 | *Black* |

August 22, 1997. Atlanta:

Marquez Hayes, a four-year-old child, was playing outside his home. He was killed when he was struck by an Atlanta police patrol car, which threw him 150 feet. The police officer was not on a call or pursuing a suspect. The police spokesperson didn't know if the officer had been speeding. **Source:** Atlanta Constitution, 8/23/98

| **Unidentified Man** | 21 | — |

August 10, 1997. Atlanta:

The man was pepper-sprayed and shot to death in his motel room by Dekalb County police. He was unarmed. **Source:** Atlanta Constitution, 8/11/97

| **Edward James Wolfertz** | 32 | — |

July 28, 1997. Marietta:

Edward was chased by police investigating a report of a suspicious person at a restaurant. He was pepper-sprayed three times and taken to a hospital, where he collapsed and died. **Source:** Atlanta Constitution, 7/29/97

| **Eric William Irby** | 25 | — |

July 19, 1997. Athens (in custody):

Mr. Irby suffocated to death after being hog-tied by Athens police at the conclusion of a car chase. The coroner ruled the cause of death as "positional asphyxia." The District Attorney (DA) refused to prosecute the cops responsible for Mr. Irby's death. He called positional asphyxia the "latest fad" for listing a cause of death . He portrayed cops as the victims, saying they were being unfairly targeted in cases where people die from being restrained. The victim's mother criticized the DA for failing to press charges, saying, "I don't think it's right and I don't understand why (the DA) made that decision." **Source:** The Atlanta Journal and Constitution, 10/11/97

| **Terry Smith** | 26 | — |

July 18, 1997. Lithonia:

Terry was shot and killed by police as he was supposedly holding his estranged wife and stabbing her, with their 2-year-old daughter wedged between them. Cops claim they told Terry to drop the knife and he refused, shouting "Kill me! Kill me!" as he prepared to keep stabbing his wife. The cops fired, killing Terry and wounding his wife (who also had stab wounds) and their daughter. Terry Smith had been Clemson's wide receiver from 1990-1993 and had been signed by the Colts in 1994, although he never played an NFL game. **Source:** New York Daily News, 7/20/97

Adam Jenkins   11   —

June 10, 1997. Holly Springs (on Ga. 5):
Adam was killed in a car accident with a car being chased by police because its license plate light was not working. Adam was a passenger in a car with his mother and grandmother. The driver of the car being chased was allegedly high on methamphetamine. The cops did not know that when they began the chase and drugs was not the reason for the chase. The driver of the car being chased pleaded guilty to vehicular homicide and driving under the influence and was sentenced to 13 years in prison. Adam's parents filed a lawsuit against the Holly Springs police, charging that they acted negligently when they began a car chase over a minor equipment problem. **Source:** The Atlanta Journal and Constitution, 6/11/98

Unidentified Man   25-35   —

February 12, 1997. Jackson (on I-75):
This man was shot and killed by two Butts County deputy sheriffs after he allegedly pulled a gun on them during a traffic stop. The victim was pulled over for speeding on northbound I-75. He supposedly disobeyed an order to get out of the car, instead rolling up his window as the deputy on the passenger side noticed a pistol in his right hand. The victim is believed to be from Daytona Beach, Florida. **Source:** The Orlando Sentinel, 2/13/97

Unidentified Woman   mid-30s   —

January 30, 1997. Clayton County:
This woman was shot in the head and killed by police after a 20-mile car chase. Police claim she waved a pistol at them after she crashed her car. **Source:** Atlanta Constitution, 1/31/97

Joseph Tallent   21   *white*

November 20, 1996. Norcross:
Narcotics officers set up a sting operation at a gas station to try to catch Joseph selling drugs. An undercover officer jumped out of a car with his gun drawn, never identifying himself. Joseph, who was unarmed, turned to run and seconds later was shot in the back of the head and killed. Gwinnett County police say the gun went off accidentally. An autopsy showed that the muzzle of the gun was within six inches of Joseph's head. **Source:** Atlanta Constitution, 8/28/97

Darryl Hobbs   35   —

June 23, 1996. Atlanta:
After a traffic stop, Darryl was pepper-sprayed by Atlanta police and died. **Source:** Atlanta Constitution, 6/25/96

Jerry Jackson   23   *Black*

December 7, 1995. Atlanta:
Mr. Jackson was shot and killed by undercover Atlanta police officers. He was a customer in a motorcycle repair shop when undercover police burst in with guns drawn and didn't identify themselves. He was unarmed. Office workers who witnessed the incident from across the street said Mr. Jackson was shot at point blank range while lying on the ground, apparently pleading for his life. **Source:** Atlanta Constitution, 12/28/95

Edward Wright   20   *Black*

October 10, 1995. Athens:
Edward was killed by police while naked and unarmed in the middle of the street. It took 48 seconds for the police officer to get out of his car, pepper spray Edward, scuffle with him on the ground, and then shoot and kill him. The District Attorney refused to prosecute the police or let a grand jury review the case. A special panel found no violation of departmental policy or training procedure. **Source:** Atlanta Constitution, 4/17/96

William "Wade" Wallace   47   —

July 31, 1995. Cumming:
William died four days after suffering blunt force trauma when he was arrested at the end of a high speed chase by Cumming police. An unidentified sheriff's deputy came forward with information that one of the arresting officers had hit William with a flashlight. **Source:** Atlanta Constitution, 8/17/95

Reginald Roberts — —

August 1994. Warner Robins:

Reginald was at a mobile home park visiting a friend when one police officer drove up and wrestled him to the ground. Another officer beat him unconscious, and then took him to jail. Reginald died in police custody. **Source:** Atlanta Constitution, 7/4/96

Marco Antonio Oliveras   29   *Latino*

June 28, 1994. Norcross:

Unarmed, Marco was shot three times and killed in a field beside a supermarket. The police officer who killed Marco said he did it because Marco challenged him to shoot, threatened to kill him, took off his own shirt as if he were ready to fight, and continued to walk toward the officer. The officer was exonerated of any wrongdoing. **Source:** Atlanta Constitution, 9/23/94

Greg Purvis   33   —

March 26, 1994. Atlanta:

After a chase, Greg was shot and killed while in his car. The officer claimed the car started to move toward him as he approached on foot. The cop fired several shots, then supposedly saw the car moving in reverse toward him. He then fired several more shots. Greg died at the scene. **Source:** Atlanta Constitution, 3/27/94

Gerald Wayne Daniels   25   —

October 24, 1993. College Park:

Gerald was struck with a baton, pepper-sprayed, and shot to death by police in an alley across from the police station. The police intervened in an argument between Gerald and his girlfriend in front of the police station, and claimed Gerald pulled out a box-cutter knife after being pepper-sprayed. **Source:** Atlanta Constitution, 10/26/93

Ronald Gordon   24   *Black*   ◉

July 26, 1993. Atlanta:

Ronald was shot in the back and killed as he fled from undercover cops who never identified themselves, according to witnesses. Ronald was unarmed. The police arrested and severely beat the man Ronald was with. This prevented him from providing key testimony for the first investigation.

Randall W. Castleberry   —   *Black*

September 11, 1992. Avondale Estates:

Randall died after police took him to the hospital for psychiatric observation. He arrived at the hospital unconscious and with brain damage. He had been picked up by police after screaming and trying to take off his clothes on a street. Police used an unauthorized chokehold, then handcuffed and shackled him in the back of the police car. Police said his head accidentally slipped into a seven inch space between the cage and back seat, cutting off his air supply. Six officers were involved. **Source:** Atlanta Constitution, 10/22/97

Henry Lee "Lemon" Cole   35   *Black*

March 13, 1992. Albany:

Henry died in police custody from "neck compression." **Source:** Atlanta Constitution, 3/29/92

Kevin Fee   —   —

December 25, 1991. Atlanta:

Police arrested and jailed Kevin, a gay man in an AIDS-related delirium. He died in police custody. **Source:** Atlanta Constitution, 3/1/92

| **Unidentified Man** | 33 | — |

August 24, 1991. Atlanta:
This man died in police custody shortly after being picked up for "wandering in the street." Cause of death was undetermined, but blood was found in his ear. **Source:** Atlanta Constitution, 8/25/91

| **Unidentified Man** | 30 | — |

May 8, 1991. Atlanta:
This man died in his apartment hallway two minutes after he was "subdued" by two police officers. Police said he apparently suffered a heart attack. **Source:** Atlanta Constitution, 5/9/91

| **Vincent Turner** | 15 | *Black* |

March 12, 1991. Morgan County:
Vincent was shot and killed by police after his car crashed as a result of a high speed police chase. Police claim they were fired on during the chase, but no guns were found and tests indicated Vincent did not fire a weapon. Prosecutors decided not to file charges against the police, even though the Georgia Bureau of Investigation found that police were uncooperative in their investigation, gave evasive answers, or flat out lied. **Source:** Atlanta Constitution, 7/12/91

| **Charles Bonner** | 26 | — |

March 17, 1991. Atlanta:
Charles died at the hospital shortly after police picked him up for creating a disturbance on the street. Three officers were involved in the arrest. Cause of death was undetermined, but he had bruises and cuff marks around his wrists and ankles.
Source: Atlanta Constitution, 3/18/91

| **Alex Davis** | 38 | *Black* |

January 7, 1991. Atlanta:
Alex died in police custody shortly after being arrested on auto theft charges. Police speculated that he had a heart attack.
Source: Atlanta Constitution, 1/8/91

| **Herman Eugene Dyer** | 41 | — |

December 1990. Towns County:
Herman died in police custody four hours after being arrested for public drunkenness. He was hit on the head during or shortly before his arrest. **Source:** Atlanta Constitution, 4/5/91

| **Ronnie Martin** | — | *Black* |

November 14, 1990. Macon:
Ronnie was shot 11 times and killed by Macon police after a 3 1/2 hour standoff at his home. **Source:** Atlanta Constitution, 4/5/91

| **Larry Gene Harrell** | — | — |

October 27, 1990. Decatur County:
Larry was pulled over for suspicion of drunk driving. According to the sheriff's deputy, Larry struggled when being handcuffed and rolled down an embankment with the deputy. Larry climbed back up and got in his car, where he was shot and killed by the officer. The deputy claimed he saw the victim reach for something on the passenger side of the car.
Source: Atlanta Constitution, 6/23/94

Unidentified Woman	—	*Black*

September 23, 1990. Atlanta:

Police shot and killed this mentally ill woman at her home. Police claimed that they were talking with her in her home when she suddenly charged at them with three knives. They ran outside onto the driveway, and the woman allegedly continued to run toward them, so they shot and killed her. Police would not reveal how many shots they fired. **Source:** Atlanta Constitution, 9/24/90

James McCrary	15	—

August 27, 1990. College Park:

James was killed instantly when he lost control of his car during a one-mile high speed chase by College Park police. **Source:** Atlanta Constitution, 8/27/90

HAWAII

Name	**Age**	**Nationality**	**Photo**
Jon Webster Pavao	38	*Native Hawaiian*	

June 10, 1998. Pahoa:

Mr. Pavao was shot twice in the chest and killed by an unnamed Hawaii County police officer responding to a domestic violence call at his girlfriend's house. Cops claim Mr. Pavao pointed a gun at the officer after threatening to kill himself. But three family members who witnessed the incident said that Mr. Pavao did not threaten the officer. They said he had a gun at his side for about two minutes before the officer shot him without provocation. They also said that Mr. Pavao had told the cop that the gun was broken. They offered to match their lie detector test results against the officer's -- an offer that was declined. It was later determined that the victim's gun was not loaded. Mr. Pavao is survived by his wife, his mother, two brothers, two sisters, three children and two grandchildren. His girlfriend, Linda Sadino, described him as a sweet man, happy because he just learned she was pregnant with his baby. **Source:** Honolulu Star-Bulletin, 6/13/98, 6/14/98, & 6/16/98; Hilo Herald, 6/13/98; Honolulu Advertiser, 6/13/98 & 6/14/98

Fortunato "Junior" Barques III	37	*Filipino*

May 5, 1998. Haleiwa:

Mr. Barques was shot twice in the back by Honolulu Police Officer Mark D. Boyce. He was shot after walking away from the cop after a car stop for suspicion of car prowling. The officer alleged that Mr. Barques reached for a gun. Mr. Barques' gun was found still secured in its holster, and a cell phone was lying on the ground near his body. There were no other known witnesses. Mr. Barques died of his injuries on July 5, 1998. Police claimed they recovered marijuana and crystal methamphetamines in his car. His attorney said the drugs were planted by the police. Mr. Barques, who had no criminal record, was a vegetable farmer. Born in Honolulu, he is survived by his wife Jodi, his son, three daughters, his parents, four brothers, three sisters, and both his grandmothers. His family said, "Junior was a kind and gentle man who meant harm to no one. He was a son of Hawaii who loved it, [the] people and the land. He will be missed by those who knew him and loved him." **Source:** Honolulu Star-Bulletin, 5/6/98 & 5/7/98; Honolulu Advertiser, 5/6/98 & 5/7/98; victim's family

Antonio Revera	26	—

April 22, 1998. Honolulu (Oahu Correction Center):

Prison guards beat Antonio while transferring him from the medical unit to his cell. He was later found dead in his cell, and his death was classified as a homicide. No guards have been charged. **Source:** Robert Rees, journalist for Honolulu Weekly

---

Rodney "Banks" Laulusa   30   *Samoan*   👁

January 22, 1998. Honolulu (Palolo Valley Homes):

At least twenty shots were fired at Rodney by three Honolulu police officers; 14 bullets were removed from his body. A community activist described what happened, "...a police car was parked diagonally across Ahe Street blocking my way. Everything around me seemed normal...I asked the nearest person around my car 'What's going on?" This person I later found out was Rodney Laulusa. He answered, "I don't know." I noticed a knife in each hand but didn't give it another thought because he seemed normal and friendly. Also I know a lot of Samoan men cook. The knives looked like kitchen knives to me. I thought he was out of the nearby apartment because he was asking the same question I was asking, 'What's going on.'" As Rodney walked away from the community activist's car, five or six police cars entered Ahe street, parking on the sidewalks and lawns. They moved quickly towards Rodney, who stood nervously in the middle of the street. People were yelling at the cops, "Don't shoot!" The cops ordered Rodney to drop the knives and then opened fire. They continued firing even after Rodney was on the ground. One witness told how police continued to fire into Rodney's back as he lay face down in the street. The cops would not let his family go to help him. It was raining and they didn't cover him. Official reports show it was only three minutes from when the police got a call about a man in the street with knives to when Rodney lay dying in the street. The police claim they tried to disarm Rodney by talking to him but he charged them. Every non-police witness denies this account and says Rodney only came within 10 feet of the cops (within their "kill zone") because the cops moved on him. A statement from the Palolo Tenants Association said, "Mr. Laulusa was not a 'threat' to police until four police officers chose to come within 10 feet of Mr. Laulusa with guns drawn." The media tried to portray Rodney as a criminal, said he was on alcohol or drugs (an autopsy revealed no drugs and a blood alcohol level of .04 - about one beer). The media said Rodney's actions indicated that he wanted to "commit suicide by police." In the days that followed, there were protests by his friends, residents of the Palolo Valley Homes housing project and the Samoan community. The cops who murdered Rodney were back on the street within a few days, and the Honolulu Police Department has vigorously defended their actions. Rodney Laulusa was born in Honolulu and grew up in the Palolo Valley Homes. He is survived by parents, Timo and Filemu; brothers Richard, Randy and Reginald; and sister Cheri-Ann Ramos. **Source:** Revolutionary Worker, 4/19/98; Honolulu Star-Bulletin, 1/25/98 & 1/26/98; Honolulu Advertiser, 1/25/98 & 1/26/98; Honolulu Weekly, 2/25/98

Benedict "Tiki" Manupule   18   *Tongan*

January 1, 1998. Honolulu (Mayor Wright Homes):

Mr. Manupule, a high school student, was shot to death by off-duty Honolulu Police Officer Tenari Maafala. The victim was allegedly drunk and shooting a gun in the air around 1:35 a.m. on New Year's Eve outside his mother's apartment in the Mayor Wright Homes. Officer Maafala claims he ordered Mr. Manupule to drop the gun but that Mr. Manupule responded by firing once at the officer. Officer Manupule fired three times, hitting Mr. Manupule, who died, and another woman, who survived. The cop was not injured. After Mr. Manupule died, his high school math teacher wrote a letter to the editor, saying, "it was clear what a sweet person he was. I have many memories of Benedict and, in every one, his loving nature is apparent. But what impressed me most about him was his ability to reach out to others and show his caring in his own quiet way. He left his loving mark on everyone he knew, and isn't that what we all wish for in our lives? I feel blessed to have had the opportunity to know him. I'll miss his sweet, shy smile." **Source:** Revolutionary Worker, 4/19/98; Honolulu Advertiser; Honolulu Star Bulletin, 1/2/98 & 1/3/98

Benjamin Sotelho   56   *Filipino*

January 1, 1998. Kapaa:

Benjamin was walking along the side of the road when he was hit by a car driven by an intoxicated police officer. The policeman left the scene, and it was classified as a "hit-and-run." Only much later was it revealed that Benjamin was killed by a cop. **Source:** Revolutionary Worker, 4/19/98; Honolulu Advertiser; victim's family

---

Miguel A. Vierra   29   *Salvadoran*

May 19, 1997. Hilo:

Mr. Viera died after police shot him 20 times in an alleged gun battle. He was the proprietor of Miguel's Yard Service and lived in Kurtistown. He is survived by wife, Florence "Cookie" Viera, his mother, his brother, and six sisters. **Source:** Honolulu Star Bulletin, 5/20/97

Jared Fe Benito   16   *Filipino*

June 7, 1996. Pearl City:

Police attempted to stop Jared Fe Benito, along with two 16-year-old passengers, "on a hunch" because they were driving a late-model Honda that was allegedly stolen. After a chase, Honolulu Police boxed in the teenagers' car against a building with four squad cars. The youths allegedly escaped by driving backward quickly and then forward, forcing their way between two cop cars. One of the four officers shot at the vehicle at least five times. The car crashed a half-mile later, with Mr. Benito slumped at the wheel, a bullet in his head. He died a few hours later. Another youth in the car, Chauncey Hata, was shot three times, including once in the face, but survived. The third youth, Sundance Cambra, was not charged in the incident. On Oct. 23, 1996, members of Benito and Hata's crew - Little Pinoys Bad Boys Ilocano - met with Honolulu Mayor Jeremy Harris demanding justice in the killing of Jared Fe Benito and an end to continued police harassment and brutality. One of the youths said afterward, "I thought [the mayor] would be more understanding of the way we feel, but I guess not." The cop who killed Jared Fe Benito was not charged. Jared was from Ewa Beach and attended Campbell High School. He is survived by his parents, Rey and Beverly; brothers Jordan R. Fe Benito and Shawn Martinez; sister Raena J. Fe Benito; grandparents Loretta and Rafael Baclaan and Laureta Fe Benito; great-grandparents Harry and Hattie Morales. **Source:** Honolulu Advertiser, 6/10/96, 6/12/96, & 6/14/96; Honolulu Star-Bulletin, 6/8/96

John Miranda   28   *Native Hawaiian*

February 6, 1996. Honolulu:

Mr. Miranda had reportedly taken a hostage at his former place of employment, resulting in a standoff with police that lasted many hours. Mr. Miranda spoke bitterly of the oppression of the Native Hawaiian people during the standoff. His sister pleaded with police to be allowed to try to talk him into surrendering, but the police, on orders from the FBI in Quantico, VA, refused to allow Mr. Miranda's family to talk to him. Mr. Miranda was shot multiple times and killed by Honolulu police as he allegedly tried to kill the hostage with a shotgun. **Source:** Honolulu Star Bulletin, 2/7/96; Honolulu Advertiser, 2/7/96; victim's family

Jabe LaCorte   22   *white*

December 19, 1995. Waikiki:

Jabe LaCorte was a surfer from the island of Kauai who was temporarily living in a Waikiki apartment building. He was reported to be running naked through the condominium and had supposedly slashed a security guard with a piece of metal. Honolulu police arrived, either in response to this or on a call for a suspected robbery. When the apartment elevator opened, Jabe LaCorte was standing in the elevator naked. The police, who were waiting for the elevator, pepper-sprayed him twice after trapping him in an elevator. Police shot him once in the heart when he allegedly lunged at one of them. Jabe died at the scene. An autopsy showed that he had no drugs in his system. The cop who killed Jabe was not charged. **Source:** Honolulu Advertiser, 12/20/95 & 6/14/96; Honolulu Star Bulletin, 12/20/95; victim's family

Unidentified Male   14   *white*

August 30, 1995. Oahu (Mililani):

A 14-year-old Mililani High School student was shot and killed by the police. The policeman claimed the boy reached into his pocket, and that he believed he was reaching for a gun. The boy was completely unarmed. He only had a soda bottle. The policeman was not charged. **Source:** Honolulu Advertiser, 8/31/95

John Sinapati   30   —

September 1, 1994. Honolulu:

Mr. Sinapati died in an alleged gun battle with Honolulu Police Officer Stan Cook after a traffic stop. Mr. Sinapati supposedly fired 23 times, striking Officer Cook eight times. Officer Cook fired 16 times, striking Mr. Sinapati seven times. The officer survived. Mr. Sinapati died at the scene.

IDAHO

Name	Age	Nationality	Photo
David Zepeda	19 (?)	—	

August 29, 1998. Bonners Ferry:
Mr. Zepeda was killed in a crash at the conclusion of a high-speed police chase. Deputy Steve Short attempted to stop the pickup truck because it was driving erratically. Mr. Zepeda was from St. Maries and was a student at University of Idaho. **Source:** Spokane Spokesman-Review, 9/1/98

Craig Brodrick	30	—	
Doug Brodrick	27	—	

September 20, 1997. Boise:
The two brothers, Craig and Doug Brodrick, were shot and killed by Boise police in an alleged gunfight after a traffic stop for changing lanes without signaling. Cops claim the brothers opened fire on them after being uncooperative. Officer Mark Stall was also killed, possibly by friendly fire, according to the Brodrick family lawyer. Another cop was wounded. Craig Brodrick was struck 12 to 25 times, Doug at least seven, and several of the shots were fired at close range, as indicated by the powder burns on the brothers' skin. The Allegheny County (Penn.) coroner, who did an independent autopsy on the brothers, said, "One bullet that left a powder burn struck Craig just above his right eye, traveled in a downward path through the eye and the into his head. I am at a loss to explain how that could be described as a bullet fired in self-defense." A police audiotape of the incident records someone saying, "Help! Don't shoot us," between volleys of gunshots. Forty five shell casings were found at the scene of the shooting. The brothers had recently moved to Boise from Lucerne Mines, Penn., to find work. The FBI announced that it would investigate the case. Famous lawyer F. Lee Bailey represents their victims' parents, Martin and Patty Brodrick. Bailey said, "The Brodrick's don't understand why their sons died and neither do I. There is no earthly reason why they would take on seven police officers who were wearing bulletproof vests. It was not a level playing field." The parents described their sons, who had applied for jobs with the Pennsylvania Highway Patrol, as respectful of law enforcement. Bailey later reported that civilian witnesses said the brothers were unarmed and trying to surrender when they were killed. In the aftermath of this shooting and continuing community outrage, a police spokesperson said, "There are a small group of young, anti-establishment, anti-authority youth in the community. They're armed. There's also the high blood-alcohol issue. Some of them have an in-your-face attitude. Hopefully, we're seeing a very short violent trend that will end soon." The killings of Craig and Doug Brodrick were the 7th and 8th fatal police shootings in Boise, a city of 370,000, in a period of 20 months. **Source:** The New York Times, 9/22/97; CNN website, 9/21/97; Pittsburgh Post-Gazette, 10/9/97, 10/18/97, & 3/22/97; States News Service, 8/27/98

James "Justin" Atkinson	21	—	

August 31, 1997. downtown Boise:
Mr. Atkinson was shot once in the head and killed by Boise Police Officer Christopher Rogers around 1 a.m. after he allegedly dragged the officer for 3 blocks at speeds of up to 45 mph. The incident started when Officers Bill Smith and Christopher Rogers, on foot patrol, heard Mr. Atkinson "squeal the tires" of the car he was driving in a parking lot. They allegedly ordered him to stop and, when he kept on driving, Officer Smith grabbed his bicep and then jogged alongside the car as it left the parking lot. Justin Atkinson was reportedly drunk. Officer Rogers claims he mistakenly thought his partner was being dragged, so he reached for the emergency brake, knocking his partner away but allegedly getting caught and dragged himself. Officer Rogers claims he only "fell off" the car after fatally shooting Mr. Atkinson in that head and that he warned Mr. Atkinson before firing. At a news conference the next day, the Boise Police Chief said it appeared that Officer Rogers did nothing wrong. A passenger in the car, Rod Page, faced aggravated assault charges in connection with the incident. Justin Atkinson is survived by his parents, Randy and Rheta Atkinson. **Source:** Idaho Statesman, 10/12/97; Pittsburgh Post-Gazette, 10/20/97

| Ramón Aseguinolaza | 26 | *Spanish* |

April 11, 1997. Boise:

Mr. Aseguinolaza was shot seven times and killed around 10 p.m. by Boise Police Officer Bryan Hagler and Cpl. Jerry Lister after a traffic stop for a broken rear brake light that appeared to have been damaged recently. Police alleged that before he was killed, Mr. Aseguinolaza pulled a gun and opened fire on the cops, injuring Officer Hagler and hitting Cpl. Lister's boots and jacket. Cops claim Mr. Aseguinolaza had been drinking and using drugs before the incident. Police said he had been convicted of dozens of traffic violations and other misdemeanors in the last ten years. Boise police refused to release the record of their criminal investigation into the death of Ramon Aseguinolaza because to do so "would interfere with enforcement proceedings." **Source:** SLP form; Idaho Statesman, 10/12/97; Pittsburgh Post-Gazette, 10/20/97

| Scott James Moody | 28 | — |

November 22, 1996. Boise:

Mr. Moody and a friend were driving a van around a neighborhood when they were stopped by Boise Police Officer John Terry. Cops claim the passenger got out of the van and handed over his license while Mr. Moody, the driver, stayed inside. After back-up police officers arrived, Mr. Moldy got out of the van with his hands behind his back. He told Officer Terry he had to scratch himself. He then allegedly reached down, pulled a stolen gun from his waistband, and fired over his shoulder, grazing the cop's hip. A scuffle ensued. Officer Terry broke free and fired his gun, hitting Mr. Moody in the head. Both Mr. Moody and his passenger were then handcuffed. Mr. Moody died of his wounds. Officer Terry was cleared in criminal and internal investigations and awarded the Medal of Honor. Cops claim a search of Mr. Moody's home after his death found a handwritten list of how to rob a bank. Police blacked out witness's names from the report of their criminal investigation into the death of Mr. Moody and withheld 22 pages on several grounds, including to prevent disclosure of "investigative techniques." Mr. Moody is survived by his son and his son's mother. **Source:** Idaho Statesman, 10/12/97; Pittsburgh Post-Gazette, 10/20/97

| Ryan Hennessey | 20 | — |

November 6, 1996. southeast Boise:

Mr. Hennessey was shot once in the heart and killed by plainclothes Boise Police Detective Dave Smith after Mr. Hennessey crashed in an alleged drunk driving accident. Officer Smith allegedly saw Mr. Hennessey speeding and followed him. The officer then approached with his gun drawn when Mr. Hennessey's car crashed. He ordered Mr. Hennessey to keep his hands visible. Mr. Hennessey saw the gun and reportedly asked, "And if I don't, are you going to shoot me?", to which Officer Smith replied, "If I have to." Cops claim the victim resisted being handcuffed, fought Officer Smith, and then crawled out the car window. Police said, "Hennessey refused to stay on the ground when ordered by police and grabbed for the detective's gun." According to Ryan Hennessey's father, John Billington, "witnesses said the officer nudged Ryan in the head with his gun barrel to wake him up because he was unconscious after the accident" and ordered his son from the vehicle. As Ryan was walking away from the vehicle, he turned to tell the officer to leave him alone and was shot in the heart. The victim is survived by his parents, John and Patty Billington, who are now active in Concerned Citizens for Police Accountability. The State Attorney General's office cleared Officer Smith of any wrongdoing, finding that he acted "appropriately and professionally." The police refused to release their internal report on the killing of Ryan Hennessey. **Source:** Idaho Statesman, 10/12/97; Pittsburgh Post-Gazette, 10/20/97

Mario Louis Jaramillo   20   —

June 24, 1996. downtown Boise:
Mr. Jaramillo was shot and killed by Boise Police Officer Clay Christensen as he ran away after an alleged scuffle. Cops had received a tip about a man allegedly carrying a handgun and selling marijuana in a McDonald's parking lot. Two bicycle patrol cops, Officers Scott Mulcahay and Clay Christensen, arrived. They claimed Mr. Jaramillo tried to flee. They tackled him. The three allegedly scuffled on the ground for several minutes. The cops claim they were all trying to get control of Mr. Jaramillo's holstered pistol. Mr. Jaramillo allegedly broke free and aimed his gun at Officer Christensen, although cops say they don't know if he fired. Officer Mulcahay fired three shots at Mr. Jaramillo, and Officer Christensen, thinking that Mr. Jaramillo fired the shots, fired four shots. All seven bullets missed. Mr. Jaramillo then allegedly forced a driver out of her car, drove seven blocks, crashed, fled on foot, fired at a jogger and missed. Officer Christensen claims he caught up with Mr. Jaramillo and ordered him to drop his gun but that he kept running. Officer Christensen shot and killed Mr. Jaramillo with a .223 caliber AR15 rifle, hitting him in the wrist, chest, and head. Officers Mulcahay and Christensen were cleared of any wrongdoing and awarded the Medal of Honor. Mr. Jaramillo was allegedly an escaped prisoner from Nevada. Cops claim he bragged about being a gang member and had 4.2 g of marijuana on him when he was shot and killed. Boise police blacked out witness's names in the report of their investigation of the incident and withheld 19 pages for several reasons, including to prevent disclosure of investigative techniques and procedures. **Source:** Idaho Statesman, 10/12/97; Pittsburgh Post-Gazette, 10/20/97

Lome Edward Stevenson   —   —

January 26, 1996. Boise:
Mr. Stevenson was allegedly a robber holding a hostage at gunpoint. Cops claim he fired at them. He was shot four times and killed by Boise police. **Source:** Pittsburgh Post-Gazette, 10/20/97

Unidentified Man   —   —

December 28, 1995. Lewiston County:
The man was shot and killed by police after an alleged bank robbery. **Source:** Spokane Spokesman-Review, 12/29/95

Vicki Weaver   43   *white*

August 22, 1992. Ruby Ridge:
Vicki Weaver, the wife of white supremacist Randy Weaver, was shot and killed by FBI sniper Lon Horiuchi from 200 yards away while holding her 10-month-old baby during a well-publicized standoff at Ruby Ridge. The standoff began when a federal agent was killed while trying to arrest Randy Weaver on weapons charges. Randy and Vicki Weaver's 14-year-old son was also killed one day earlier. FBI "rules of engagement" in the standoff were "shoot on sight" for any armed male -- rules which a federal appeals court later ruled unconstitutional and which did not apply to Ms. Weaver in any case. The FBI sniper was charged in Idaho state court, but charges were thrown out. He was later charged with involuntary manslaughter in federal court. Vicki Weaver is survived by three daughters and her husband. In Aug. 1995, the US government agreed to pay $3.1 million to the surviving family members. The Weavers were white supremacists, racists. As Stolen Lives shows, police and other law enforcement agents were and are carrying out a program of terror and murder directed predominantly against people of color. The Weavers viewed themselves as "anti-government," but their racist ideology supports this very same program. But this didn't stop the FBI from killing Vicki Weaver. **Source:** Tacoma News-Tribune, 9/4/92 & 8/16/95; Los Angeles Times, 12/17/97

Sammy Weaver	14	*white*	

August 21, 1992. Bonners Ferry:

Sammy Weaver, the son of white supremacist Randy Weaver, was shot and killed by U.S. Marshal Larry Cooper. This reportedly occurred during a firefight with Federal Marshals on Randy Weaver's property after the Marshals shot Sammy's dog. Sammy was shot in the back as he was running away. The federal government said the fatal bullet could have come from Randy Weaver's gun, but the Boundary County Sheriff concluded, "It is clear by the ballistic evidence that Sammy Weaver was killed with a bullet fired by U.S. Marshal Larry Cooper's 9mm Colt." This was the beginning of the now famous "Standoff at Ruby Ridge." The standoff started when a federal agent was killed while attempting to arrest Randy Weaver on weapons charges. The Weavers were white supremacists, racists. As Stolen Lives shows, police and other law enforcement agents were and are carrying out a program of terror and murder directed predominantly against people of color. The Weavers viewed themselves as "anti-government," but their racist ideology supports this very same program. But this didn't stop U.S. Marshals from killing Sammy Weaver. **Source:** Tacoma News-Tribune, 9/4/92 & 8/16/95; Los Angeles Times, 12/17/97; The Orlando Sentinel, 10/24/97

CHICAGO

Name	Age	Nationality	Photo
Kelsey Lamont Hogan	26	*African American*	👁

August 14, 1999. Chicago (South Side):

Kelsey was gunned down in the early morning hours by an off-duty corrections officer. According to the medical report, he was shot 14 times. Police first claimed this was an attempted car-jacking. Later, they claimed that it was an attempted robbery and that Kelsey fired at the corrections officer. Witnesses maintained that there had been an altercation between the officer and Kelsey inside The Other Place Lounge, and that the officer shot Kelsey as the latter attempted to walk away. Witnesses also said that a gun was thrown down on Kelsey's body. No evidence of gunpowder was found on Kelsey's hands. According to Kelsey's wife, Gwendolyn, her husband was "a character and touched a lot of people. He had a social spirit. he was a good person and made people laugh." He was a proud father of a 14-month-old son. **Source:** Chicago Tribune, 8/25/99; Chicago Defender, 8/16/99; victim's family

Devon Nelson	19	—	

July 12, 1999. Harvey (Reservation Apartments):

Mr. Nelson was shot in the back of the head and killed by a Harvey police officer during a random drug sweep in the parking lot of the Reservation Apartments around 1:30 a.m. Six or seven officers surrounded the complex with guns drawn and ordered everyone down on the ground. Mr. Nelson fled. Cops claim he turned and pointed a gun at an officer, who then shot him. But the physical evidence contradicts this. The medical examiner's office found that the police bullet entered through the back of his head. A 13-year-old girl who witnessed the whole incident said that as Mr. Nelson fled, he tripped and was shot as he flailed his arms in an attempt to regain his balance. Then, the cop who shot Mr. Nelson planted a gun on him after the shooting. The witness reported seeing the cop take a gun off his own leg, where it had been strapped with duct tape, put it briefly in the victim's hand, and then lay it next to the victim's body. The mayor of Harvey dismissed out of hand the idea that the gun was planted, saying, "From all indications it was what we call a 'good shot.' The officer was doing his job and responded properly." The victim's family reported that police in the area are overly aggressive and had come through the housing complex looking for drugs the day before. A neighbor who confronted the police right after the incident and accused them of murdering Mr. Nelson was beaten and arrested. Cops broke into his apartment by smashing a patio window and injured his one-year-old daughter when they picked her up by the shirt and tossed her. **Source:** The Chicago Tribune, 7/13/99

Juan Oviedo Torres   41   *Cuban American*

June 18, 1999. Chicago (Area 5 jail):

Mr. Torres was found dead, hanging in his jail cell. Police claimed it was a suicide, but eyewitnesses reported that the police strangled him and then wrapped his shirt around his neck to fake a hanging. No one who knew Mr. Oviedo believes that he killed himself. When his sister went to identify his body, she was only allowed to see his face through a window. She was not allowed to see the rest of his body. Cops also refused to show her the domestic abuse complaint under which he had been arrested. After she appeared on TV to talk about his case, she was contacted by several other families whose loved ones supposedly hung themselves with their own t-shirts in the same lock-up. **Source:** Revolutionary Worker, 7/4/99

Gregory Riley   31   *Black*

June 14, 1999. Chicago (South Side):

Police claim that Mr. Riley was a drug dealer. Cops arrested and handcuffed him. Witnesses report that a cop then put his knee into the victim's back and strangled him with a chokehold. The cops stood around and watched him die. When an ambulance came into view, they started giving him CPR. The mayor defended the police, telling people to "wait for the facts," and said, "Narcotics is the No. 1 issue in the city of Chicago.... Let's allow the Police Department to do their job." The medical examiner's office ruled that Mr. Riley's death was caused by "asphyxia due to compression of the neck and chest." **Source:** Revolutionary Worker, 7/4/99

Robert Anthony Russ   22   *Black*   👁

June 5, 1999. Chicago (Dan Ryan Expwy, near 28th St.):

Mr. Russ was pulled over by Chicago police on a deserted stretch of road around 1 a.m. for allegedly "driving erratically." He was unarmed and on his way to his parents' suburban home. Cops claim he refused to get out of the car, so they reportedly smashed a tinted side window behind his head, reached in, and shot him to death. Later, a secret police report leaked to the press revealed that the cops had opened the unlocked passenger-side door of Mr. Russ's car and had him in full sight when he was shot from the rear. Their story about smashing his rear window to see him was a lie. Authorities claimed he tried to grab the officer's gun and that it went off accidentally during a struggle. Mr. Russ's death was quickly ruled "accidental and justified." The mayor's response was to justify the murder and to call for banning tinted windows. Police and the media also tried to portray the victim as violent because of a previous guilty plea to an assault charge. Cops told Mr. Russ's family that the bullet went through his shoulder and pierced his heart, but family members said that it would be difficult for him to be shot at such an angle during a struggle due to his large size (6'4", 235 pounds). Robert Russ was senior at Northwestern University, an honors student majoring in education, set to graduate in two weeks. He was a football player on Northwestern's Big 10 championship team, and his girlfriend was pregnant with their first child. One of his professors, Martha Biondi, wrote in the Chicago Tribune, "Robert's death sends a message to young people that even if they are fortunate enough to come to a place like Northwestern, it's still not enough to escape the perils of being black.... Because he had a previous encounter with the law, some in the media have used his death to reinforce another paradigm: that of the criminal, less than human, African-American young man. We must resist these responses to Robert's death.... One reason why young black men are dehumanized in these situations is to force the public into identifying with the police... I, and others here at Northwestern, urge the public to see Robert as their son or brother, to affirm his humanity and to demand that the police refrain from shooting unarmed motorists." Robert Russ was killed only six hours after Chicago police killed LaTanya Haggerty, a young unarmed Black woman motorist. These two cases sparked a great deal of public outrage, leading to near-daily demonstrations. Students and professors from Northwestern joined people from the community at a demonstration at city hall a week later. One hundred and forty professors and staff from Northwestern signed a public letter to Chicago's mayor denouncing his defense of police murder. Two weeks after the incident, amid continuing protests, the police commissioner announced that police involved had violated departmental policy by knocking out Mr. Russ's car window with a lug wrench. **Source:** Chicago Tribune, 6/6/99; Revolutionary Worker, 6/20/99 & 7/4/99; The New York Times, 6/19/99

| **LaTanya Haggerty** | 26 | *Black* | 👁 |

June 4, 1999. Chicago (King Dr. & 64th St.):

Ms. Haggerty was a passenger in a car driven by her friend, Ray Smith. She was getting a ride home from her job downtown as a computer analyst. Mr. Smith had pulled over to the side of the road, and cops told him to move on. When he did, cops zoomed up behind him. Mr. Smith stopped, told them that he hadn't done anything wrong and drove off again. Three cops opened fire on the car and then began chasing it. When Mr. Smith pulled over a mile later, cops arrested and beat him. Ms. Haggerty was on her cell phone trying to reach Mr. Smith's mother when cops ordered her out of the car. She was scared and moved slowly. The press initially claimed that she refused to get out. As she got out with her hands in the air, police shot her dead. Cops claimed that they saw the victim "brandish something shiny" and that they thought she had a gun, but she was unarmed. Ms. Haggerty was the first of her working class family to go to college. She was living at home and engaged to be married. She was killed around 5:30 p.m. About six hours later, Chicago police shot and killed Robert Russ, an unarmed young Black man. There was widespread outrage at these two killings, leading to near-daily demonstrations. A protest against police brutality was held at city hall a week later. The mayor of Chicago told people to withhold judgment until they had "the facts," and the police denied that racism played any role in Ms. Haggerty's murder on the grounds that the cop who shot her was also Black. Two weeks after the incident, amid continuing protests, the police commissioner said the cops involved in the case had violated departmental policy by not calling off the pursuit of Mr. Smith's car when ordered to do so. **Source:** Chicago Tribune, 6/6/99; Revolutionary Worker, 6/20/99; The New York Times, 6/19/99

| **Thomas Smith** | 39 | — |

February 27, 1999. Chicago (South Side):

Thomas Smith was shot and killed by police responding to a domestic call involving Mr. Smith and a woman. Mr. Smith allegedly had a butcher knife in his hand when police arrived. Police claim he refused to drop the weapon on command and lunged at a lieutenant. Cops shot him once in the stomach. He died in surgery at the hospital. **Source:** Chicago Tribune, 2/28/99

| **Raynard Anthony White** | 18 | *African American* | 👁 |

February 12, 1999. Harold Ickes Housing Project:

At 10 p.m. on Feb. 11, 1999 witnesses say Raynard ran into 2310 S. State at the Chicago Housing Authority's Harold Ickes housing development. He was chased up to the seventh floor and shot 15 times by police. The Chicago Police Department version of events is that they were "called to the scene, saw a suspect with a weapon, gave chase, trapped the suspect and ordered him to drop the weapon." They claim that Raynard advanced toward police with a 38-caliber revolver before he was shot and killed. The gun Raynard supposedly had in his possession at the time has "yet to be recovered." Raynard's stepfather said, "They hunted my boy down and shot him like a dog and I want to know why... nothing justifies shooting my boy like that." Raynard was outgoing and loved by many people. He loved basketball, football and dancing. Six hundred people attended his funeral. **Source:** Chicago Defender, 2/15/99; obituary; interview with victim's family

| **Milos Kalabza** | 24 | — |

January 26, 1999. Chicago (Portage Park):

Police were called to Linda's Lounge in the 4200 block of N. Milwaukee Ave. to investigate a fight involving Mr. Kalabza and another man. It was reported that the bartender had called for police, warning that "one of the brawlers had a gun". When police arrived, they shot Mr. Kalabza in the head and chest, claiming he fired at a Chicago police sergeant with a .25 caliber pistol. Mr. Kalabza was pronounced dead at the hospital. **Source:** Chicago Tribune, 1/28/99

| **Francisco Morales** | 24 | *Mexican* |

December 18, 1998. Chicago (2137 N. Leamington):

Francisco Morales was shot and killed by Chicago police. Cops were reportedly responding to a domestic dispute call saying that Francisco refused to put down a knife he used to stab his girlfriend. Francisco was from the countryside of Veracruz, Mexico. One and a half years ago, he came to Chicago and worked in a lobster factory. His girlfriend had come to live with him, but when she got to Chicago, she changed her mind. That was when Francisco reportedly attacked her. A friend from Veracruz felt that while Francisco was guilty of trying to attack his girlfriend, the police could have disarmed and detained him without killing him. **Source:** Chicago Tribune, 12/20/98; Chicago Sun Times, 12/20/98

Brennan King   21   *African American*   ◉

November 28, 1998. Cabrini Green Housing Projects:

Chicago police pulled up to a building in the Cabrini Green Housing Projects and tried to question Brennan King. He fled into another building where cops cornered him. Cops claim they shot and killed Brennan in "self defense" because he allegedly slashed the cop with a box cutter. But this was clearly a lie as Brennan was shot in the back. Residents brought out that it was a typical night at Cabrini, where it is routine for police to harass people, especially young men. Brennan just happened to be out there when the cops pulled up. Residents said that the cop cut himself after killing Brennan in order to have a cover story because the young men at Cabrini do not carry box cutters. Women heard Brennan in the stairwell asking the cops not to kill him before six shots rang out. An ambulance soon arrived, but the police would not allow Brennan to be taken to the hospital. Instead, they used the ambulance to smuggle out the police. No box cutter was ever recovered. Residents and activists held press conferences and protest marches the following week. Fifteen hundred people attended Brennan's funeral. Brennan was known and respected throughout the Cabrini Green area, including both sides of the border that divides rival street organizations. He had become active in the movement for social change, marching for Mumia Abu–Jamal, against police brutality and for jobs. He had participated in the October 22 National Day of Protest to Stop Police Brutality only a month before he was killed. At the same time, he shouldered the responsibility of caring for his younger siblings and his own children. **Source:** Revolutionary Worker, 5/13/98; Chicago Defender, 2/4/99 & 2/6/99; interview with victim's family

---

Guillermo Reyes   24   *Mexican*

September 9, 1998. Chicago (25th District holding cell):

Mr. Reyes and a friend were riding their bikes when Chicago police arrested them, claiming that the friend had stolen a car stereo. Mr. Reyes was not charged in connection with the theft but was held to see if he had any outstanding warrants. Other prisoners reported that he was in good spirits. He knew that he had no outstanding warrants and would be out soon. A Black guard was verbally abusive to him and his friend. Later, Mr. Reyes appeared to be in a troubled state and said he wasn't going to get out of the lock-up alive. His family heard nothing of his whereabouts until two days later when they were informed of his death. Cops claim he hung himself with his t-shirt, but his family believes there was foul play on the part of the authorities. **Source:** victim's family

---

Lavell Jones   22   *African American*

September 7, 1998. Chicago (Robert Taylor Homes):

Lavell Jones was shot and killed by police at Robert Taylor Homes housing development. Police claim that he was running toward 5041 S. Federal, then turned and allegedly pointed a 9-mm semiautomatic pistol at the officers. A cop sitting on the passenger side of his squad car fired one shot, killing Lavell. The killing was ruled justifiable because, according to a Chicago Police Department spokesperson, when "somebody pulls a gun on a police officer, (the officer) has a right to use deadly force." **Source:** Chicago Sun Times, 9/8/98

José Luis Contreras   46   *Latino*

August 30, 1998. Chicago (West Side):

Mr. Contreras was fatally shot by Chicago police at El Zacatecas Restaurant after allegedly pointing a gun at two officers. Mr. Contreras was reportedly seen waving a pistol and threatening patrons at a restaurant, demanding to know who had taken his van. As he left the restaurant, tactical officers patrolling nearby claim they heard him fire the gun into the air and arrived to find patrons fleeing the restaurant. Mr. Contreras then got into the passenger side of a truck when police arrived, and the truck drove off. Police followed the truck, stopped it two blocks away and approached with guns drawn. Mr. Contreras, who was in the passenger seat, allegedly pointed his gun at the officers. The cops killed Contreras and wounded the driver of the truck. **Source:** Chicago Tribune, 9/1/98

| Edward Ali III | 33 | — |

July 6, 1998. Chicago (Southeast Side):

Mr. Ali was shot twice in the chest and killed by police after he allegedly grabbed an officer's gun during a scuffle. Cops were responding to a call of a man lying on a lawn of someone's house in the 9100 block of South Paxton Avenue around 7 a.m. Edward supposedly claimed it was his house even though it was not, prompting a neighbor to call the police. Cops claim that Edward refused their order to leave, was "verbally abusive," scuffled with cops, grabbed an officer's gun and pointed it at the cop, at which point the cop's partner opened fire. A preliminary finding determined that the shooting was justifiable as self-defense. **Source:** Chicago Tribune, 7/7/98 & 7/8/98

| Latanya King | 27 | — |

May 16, 1998. Chicago:

Latanya King was shot and killed by her husband, Chicago Housing Authority Police Officer Marvin King, who then shot and killed himself in an apparent murder-suicide. **Source:** Chicago Tribune, 5/17/98

| Jair P. Williams | 20 | *Black* |

May 3, 1998. Burnham:

Jair was shot and killed by police during a "routine traffic stop" of two cars in the 14500 block of S. Hoxie Ave. Cops claim that some of the men in the cars opened fire and a shootout ensued, injuring a cop and killing Jair. The cop's injuries, though only minor, were thoroughly discussed in the newspaper report, while the killing of this young man was only mentioned in passing. **Source:** Chicago Tribune, 5/5/98

| Joe Winfield | 27 | — |

April 30, 1998. Chicago (Washington Park):

Joe was shot and killed by two Chicago police officers after he fled from a traffic stop on foot and then allegedly pointed a gun at the cops. Police stopped the car around 3:30 p.m. near Garfield Blvd. & Prairie Ave. and removed the driver and two passengers when Joe got out of the back seat and began to walk away. When they called for him to stop, he started to run. Two cops chased him on foot while one chased him in a car. Joe allegedly pointed a gun at the cop in the car. The officer took "evasive action" and hit him with the car. Witnesses said that Joe was knocked forward several feet by the impact of the car, causing him to drop his gun. Cops claim that he appeared "combative" and refused repeated orders to drop his gun. Witnesses, however, disputed the police account, saying Joe was not holding a gun when he was shot. One witness said, "The gun was loose from his hands. He didn't try to get up at all. You figure they're trained properly and they could have arrested him without shooting him." Joe's aunt accused the police of harassing her nephew and said they shot him without provocation: "Joe was a kid who had a hard life. He got into some trouble and he tried to straighten out his life. The police kept messing with him. They've harassed him." A friend of Joe's said, "He was a good guy. He wasn't into gang banging. He carried a gun because he wanted to be protected, just like everyone else."
Source: Chicago Tribune, 5/1/98

| Terrance Moses | 17 | *African American* | 👁 |

May 14, 1998. Riverdale (suburb of Chicago):

Police reportedly responded to a 911 call about a man with a gun roaming an apartment building. When they found Terrance in the area, they shot him in the face at close range and killed him, claiming he had a screwdriver. Later, it was confirmed that Terrance had nothing in his hands at all. The victim's family said he had been the target of police harassment and was repeatedly threatened by the police prior to his death. On the night he was killed, police had chased him for some distance before cornering and shooting him. Terrance was a junior at Park Forest Academy and had an 18-month-old daughter. His mother described him as a typical, loving kid and said he did not have a gun. There were a number of rallies at the Riverdale police department and marches through the neighborhood to protest his murder. **Source:** Chicago Tribune; UPI, 5/16/98; interview with victim's mother

Michael Russell   21   *African American*   👁

April 5, 1998. Cabrini Green Housing Projects:

Michael Russell was shot in the back and killed by the Chicago Police Department at the 500/502 W. Oak building in the Cabrini Green housing projects. Police claimed that Michael shot at them first, but no traces of gunpowder were found on his hands and a gun was never recovered. Witnesses strongly dispute police accounts and assert that Police Officer Kenny Knowles executed Michael as he was running, unarmed, into 500 W. Oak. According to witnesses, Officer Knowles had threatened to kill Michael shortly after he had been released from jail two months earlier. As Michael lay bleeding in the stairwell, the cops waved off the first ambulance that arrived on the scene. Another young man shot by the cops at the same time as they shot Michael has been charged with Michael's murder. This murder came the same week as a court hearing in eviction proceedings against the residents of 500/502 W. Oak. Residents are trying to stay in their building in the face of the city's attempt to remove them so the building can be demolished. Officer Knowles had also been strutting around the building the week before threatening people and trying to discourage them from fighting against evictions and the demolition of their building. Michael was the third person killed by the Chicago Police Department that week. Residents staged a three-and-a-half hour protest at the building the next evening to demand justice for Michael. A press conference was held to condemn his murder. **Source:** Revolutionary Worker, 4/19/98; Chicago Tribune, 4/12/98

Tyrus Ellis   33   —

April 3, 1998. Chicago (West Side):

Mr. Ellis was shot after he allegedly tried to run over two Chicago police officers. Officers had pulled over a van in the 5500 block of W. Jackson Blvd. for "suspicious driving," and claim they saw a handgun in the driver's lap. Mr. Ellis drove off. Officers in pursuit reportedly saw Mr. Ellis throw the handgun out the van's window. Officers claimed they recovered the gun. Mr. Ellis' van crashed into several parked cars. As the two officers approached , Mr. Ellis allegedly backed the van towards them "and attempted to run down the officers ... One of those officers fired a single shot into the van, apparently striking the driver in the upper right side." Mr. Ellis continued driving, crashed and was arrested. He died at the hospital. **Source:** Chicago Tribune, 4/5/98

Ernest Hopkins   27   —

April 2, 1998. Chicago:

Chicago police and the Bureau of Alcohol, Tobacco and Firearms (ATF) arranged for an informant to buy guns and heroin across from a high school. When the sellers tried to rob the informant, police and ATF opened fire on the two men, killing one and wounding another. Parents protested to the ATF, saying that the operation put their kids in danger.

Gregory Beck   17   *African American*

April 1, 1998. Chicago (Northwest Side):

Police claim that Gregory was "causing a disturbance" at the Jefferson Park CTA station and then fled. As cops chased him, he allegedly turned and fired one shot at the officers but missed. A plainclothes detective who heard the radio report of the chase pulled alongside Gregory, who was still running. Gregory allegedly shot at the detective and missed. The officer shot and killed him. A .357 caliber handgun was reportedly recovered near his body. **Source:** Chicago Sun Times, 4/2/98; Chicago Tribune, 4/2/98

Jessie Hodges   18   *African American*

February 20, 1998. Chicago:

The alleged stolen car Jessie was driving and the police car chasing it collided in the 100 block of North Hamlin Avenue. Police claim that Jessie sped up to run over a cop when the officer got out of his car and walked towards the front of Jessie's car. Police shot Jessie twice in the head. The victim's family brought out that he had been chased by 15 squad cars, that he was unarmed and that no Black cops were on the scene. Jessie was arrested, and even though he was in a coma for a week and a half until he died on Mar. 3, there was a cop stationed in his hospital room the whole time. Before he died, Jessie was charged with attempted murder and aggravated possession of a stolen vehicle in order to justify this police murder. The shooting took place in the afternoon. **Source:** Chicago Tribune, 2/23/98

Chad Edwards   18   *Black*

February 18, 1998. Chicago (South Side, Chicago Lawn District):

Chad Edwards was shot in the head by Officer Raymond Wilke. Police say they were responding to a call of possible burglary when Chad allegedly burst out of a closet in a neighbor's home holding a pair of pliers. Cops claim that they announced their presence a few times but that the victim did not respond. According to Chad's mother, Chad and his girlfriend were visiting the neighbor's house with permission when the police entered unannounced. Chad was shot when he went to the doorway to investigate the noise. He was unarmed. While hospitalized in critical condition, police charged him with criminal trespass and aggravated assault. The shooting was ruled justifiable homicide. Perhaps the cops felt that filing charges helped justify the shooting of this young man. Chad died three days later, on Feb., 21, of his injuries. **Source:** Chicago Tribune, 2/23/98

Michelle Hollister   25   —

January 29, 1998. Chicago:

Michelle was killed when an unmarked police car pursuing a suspected rapist crashed into her car.

Kevin Morris   18   —   👁

January 18, 1998. Chicago (West Side):

Kevin Morris was shot in the back of his head and thigh and killed by an off-duty Chicago police officer moonlighting as a security guard at a night club. Kevin had been invited to a birthday party at the lounge. The cops claim the killing, which occurred on the street outside the night club, resulted from a fight inside the club. A witness reported that security guards burst out of the lounge just as Kevin was exiting. Kevin got scared and fled to a friend's car. Kevin was chased by the officer and shot as he entered the automobile. The tires of the car were also shot out which prevented his friends from driving Kevin to a hospital. No ambulance was summoned. Twenty four hours later, the Cook County state's attorney's office ruled the incident justifiable homicide. Kevin's father declared, "It's plain murder. He was shot in the back of the head, which means he was running away from them. There was no threat." Kevin's grandfather said a witness to the murder told him that Kevin had no part in the fight and was merely standing with his friends when security guards burst out of the club with their guns drawn. Kevin got scared at the sight of the guns and fled toward a friend's car. Kevin's parents and community activists demanded that the cop, whose name has not been released, be held accountable for Kevin's murder. The cops, however, claim that they do not know who shot Kevin and dismiss the killing as an "isolated incident." In Nov. 1998, Kevin's mother suffered a heart attack as a result of the loss of her son and continues to be in a coma. Kevin had just become a father when he was killed. **Source:** Chicago Tribune, 1/19/98; Chicago Sun Times, 1/15/98

Leroy Reed   30   *Black*   👁

January 16, 1998. Cabrini Green Housing Projects:

Police reports claim that Leroy was shot and killed by a rival gang member, but Leroy's mother disputes that. She maintains that her son was shot and killed by the cops during a police sweep in the Cabrini Green housing development. A witness told her that during this sweep, a police officer had taken notice of Leroy's Michael Jordan sneakers and shouted at him to halt. When he reportedly did not respond, they opened fire. A bullet was recovered by the police, but they have withheld any information about it. In the wake of the killing, a family member reported that police bragged that they had shot Leroy. Leroy's mother reports that witnesses have been intimidated from testifying against the cops. She questions the coroner's motive for burning all of Leroy's clothing. **Source:** Revolutionary Worker, 2/14/99

Robert Taylor   19   *African American*

January 7, 1998. Chicago (in custody):

Robert Taylor was in jail. The family was told that he died of an asthma attack, but when they went to see his body, his face was bruised and swollen as if he had been beaten to death. The autopsy done by the jail ruled his cause of death as "undetermined," and authorities refused to let the family have its own medical expert examine the body. Robert's family is trying to his body exhumed for an independent autopsy. **Source:** SLP Form

---

Jack Brian Richman   34   *white*   👁

November 18, 1997. Skokie:

Jack was the founder of the North Shore Coalition Against Adulticiding, an environmental group that worked to stop the practice of spraying flying mosquitoes. The group believed that this caused cancer and other medical problems for people. Jack was a well-known and well-respected environmental activist and his death was listed as one of the top ten stories in the Pioneer Press, a local newspaper, for two years in a row. After his death, he was given the Citizen Initiative Award by the Citizen Advocacy Center. On the day he was killed, Jack was in court to testify for his mother about a traffic ticket. He got into a dispute with Cook County sheriff's deputies after waiting hours to testify. According to newspaper reports, sheriff deputies pinned him to the ground after he refused to leave the courtroom. He stopped breathing shortly thereafter and died. In a letter, Marcella Richman, Jack's mother, wrote to the Cook County Courthouse saying, "Jack was crippled and compelled to use a cane for support as a result of a leg injury... He was bent over, experienced excruciating pain, having a herniated disc as a result of an auto accident at age 16 and suffered with a severe case of sciatica. He weighed approximately 450 lbs.... He was barely able to walk. He had no record of wrongdoing. He never even received a parking ticket. He did not drink or smoke, nor was he on drugs. I am the tormented mother never to forget the scene. Never to forgive myself for being powerless to help my son, for not blindly attacking the Bailiffs in at least an attempt to help him. Unable to sleep nights, waking up in a cold sweat to cry throughout the night." In another statement to an attorney, she described the events the day her son was killed: "I yelled to that crazy judge that Jack was ill and in pain and that they (the henchmen) would hurt him but he did nothing or said nothing to stop them. The eight [deputies] continued to apply excessive restraint of Jack's body (which does not leave bruises) and continued to attempt to force regular size handcuffs onto his wrists (while he screamed in pain), an action which did badly cut up and bruise his wrists and forearms. He fell to the floor with the eight still on him. Those eight guards used excessive force on a sick crippled person. When I asked one of them the next day, 'I told you he was sick and in pain. Why didn't you leave him alone?', his answer was simply, 'We were following orders!' My comment, 'Orders to kill!'" Jack's mother filed an excessive force complaint against the Cook County sheriffs. **Source:** SLP Form; statements from victim's mother; Pioneer Press, 12/4/97,1/1/98, & 12/31/98; Chicago Tribune, 11/18/98

Andrew Durham   early 20s   *Black*

August 10, 1997. Chicago (West Side):

The Chicago Police Department claims that Andrew was stealing cars when police intervened. They insisted that Andrew grabbed for a policewoman's gun and it "discharged by accident." But eyewitnesses maintain that Andrew was hanging out in a parking lot when cops drove up on them and ordered him and his friend over to the car. Instead, the two took off in opposite directions. The officer chased Andrew, stopped and took aim and shot him in the street. She came up on Andrew, grabbed him, shot him again and was overheard saying, "I shot you, b*tch." Forty five minutes passed before an ambulance came, and by that time Andrew was dead. In the wake of this, a "People's Inquiry" was held at a state senator's office where over 400 people attended. **Source:** Revolutionary Worker, 9/7/97; Standish Willis (lawyer)

Anthony Vegas   20   *Puerto Rican*

June 1997. Chicago (Humboldt Park):

An alleged shoot-out between rival street organizations was interrupted by the police. When the cops yelled freeze, everyone ran away. Anthony Vegas was shot four or five times and killed by the police as he ran away. **Source:** SLP Form

---

Frankie Perkins   37   *Black*   👁

March 22, 1997. Chicago (West Side):

The hospital reported that Frankie died due to strangulation. On her way home one evening, Frankie was crossing an empty lot when she was stopped by the police. Police claimed they had seen her swallow drugs and tried to get her to spit them up. Witnesses state that police killed her, strangling her to death. Pictures show that that there were bruises on her face and rib cage and her eyes were swollen shut. In the wake of this incident, Frankie's mother witnessed many young men in the neighborhood being harassed by police to intimidate them from speaking out about this. Frankie leaves behind three daughters, ages four, six, and 16 years old. **Source:** victim's mother

| **Bernard Solomon** | 19 | *African American* | |

January 13, 1997. Chicago:

After years of police harassment, Solomon was told by police that they would kill him. A few days later he was arrested. He was found hung in his cell at the 2259 S. Damen police station. Although police claim he hung himself with his shirt, when his body was examined by family members, he was found still wearing his shirt on one arm.

| **José A. Méndez Négron** | 22 | *Puerto Rican* | |

November 23, 1996. Chicago:

Mr. Méndez, a mentally disabled man, was beaten, shot five times in the head and killed, as he lay on the floor, by Chicago Police Officer Davila. Cops claimed that Mr. Méndez was attempting to get hold of a weapon and that he refused orders to stop. Officer Davila was not criminally charged or disciplined in any way. He remained on active duty. The victim's sister described her brother as having the mental age of a ten year old. **Source:** e-mail from victim's sister

| **Angel Castro, Jr.** | 15 | *Puerto Rican* | 👁 |

October 23, 1996. Chicago:

After being beaten, abused with racial epithets and told by police that he would be killed if he did not move, Angel Castro's family moved. Angel returned to the neighborhood for a friend's birthday party. After leaving the party, a police car rammed him as he rode his bike. As Angel tried to get on his knees, the police shot and killed him.

| **Bilal Ashraf** | 26 | *African American* | |

September 24, 1996. —:

Two detectives without a warrant came to Ashraf's apartment to question him. According to witnesses and members of his masjid (mosque), the cops jumped Ashraf. Fearing for his life, he grabbed one of the cop's guns and tried to run away. He was shot in the back and leg. As he ran up the back staircase to his apartment, a detective shouted, "Shoot that n★gger!" Bilal dropped the weapon, raised his hands, proceeded to walk down the stairs—and was cut down in a hail of bullets. His body was left for two hours before being taken to a hospital where he was pronounced dead.

| **Eric Smith** | 22 | *African American* | 👁 |

April 9, 1996. —:

Eric's mom pulled her car off to the side of the expressway in order to better communicate with her son, a deaf mute. His grandmother was also in the car. Upset, Eric ran off into traffic and was grazed by a passing car. Two cops from Forest View, a Chicago suburb, pulled up. They trained a gun to Eric's head and brought him to the side of the road. Eric's attempts to sign were not understood. The cops beat Eric with metal batons and then shot him six times—including with hollow point bullets. The final bullet was delivered while Eric lay on his back. Following the shooting, Eric's mother and grandmother were handcuffed and taken to the police station.

| **Angel Paredes** | 18 | *Black/Puerto Rican* | |

April 1996. Chicago (Humboldt Park):

Angel was allegedly selling pot on the corner. When two cops, one Black and one white, came to arrest him, he ran. When they caught up with him, they beat him to death. As they beat him, they called him a "n★gger." **Source:** SLP Form

| **Logan Smith** | 24 | — | |

January 22, 1996. —:

After an early morning argument between Hoffman Estates police and his brother, Mr. Smith was hit by police pepper gas and suffered an asthma attack. Later he was admitted to a hospital, where he died from bacteria contaminated blood. Infected urine had leaked into Mr.. Smith's abdominal cavity from a special intestinal sac that surgeons had created to help with a urinary tract problem. A spokesperson for the coroner didn't discount that the leakage could have been caused by a struggle. Before he died, Mr. Smith had complained of being kicked by cops while in jail.

| **Jorge Guillén** | 40 | *Honduran* | 👁 |

October 3, 1995. —:
Family members called 911 when Mr. Guillén, an immigrant from Honduras, was having schizophrenic hallucinations. When three cops arrived, Mr. Guillén was holding a two-by-four used to keep the door shut. The cops threw him to the floor, beat his head bloody with a flashlight and handcuffed him. One cop stepped on the back of Mr. Guillén's neck. Jorge was asphyxiated as he lay face down in a pool of his own blood. The police department's own Office of Professional Services found the three cops guilty of "excessive and unwarranted" force and recommended short suspensions. The State's Attorney refused to prosecute the cops.

| **Willie Ruffin, Jr.** | 21 | — |

September 29, 1995. —:
Ruffin and his friends had gone over to a wooded area near the back of a Chicago Heights apartment complex where he stayed with his family. Shots rang out and Ruffin was gunned down. He was killed by undercover cops doing drug surveillance.

| **Joseph C. Gould** | 36 | *African American* | 👁 |

July 30, 1995. Chicago:
Mr. Gould, a homeless man, was shot at point blank range by off-duty cop Gregory Becker, who drove away without reporting the shooting as his victim lay bleeding to death in the street. Officer Becker was subsequently charged with involuntary manslaughter, but that charge was dismissed by the judge on the grounds of conflicting witness accounts, including Officer Becker's companions' defense of him. Another witness, however, who knew neither of the men, reported that Officer Becker grabbed Mr. Gould and shot him. Because of sustained community pressure, Officer Becker was subsequently charged with involuntary manslaughter and armed violence and was convicted in Apr. 1997. In May, he was sentenced to fifteen years in prison.

| **Christian Castaneda** | 15 or 16 | *Mexican* |

Summer, 1995. Chicago (near Western & 21st St.'s):
Christian had supposedly shot at some gang members. Police came up on him and shot him dead, claiming he fired first. But witnesses say that he did not. **Source:** SLP Form

| **Kenny Johnson** | 15 | *African American* |

April 15, 1995. —:
After a brief car and foot chase, a Chicago Housing Authority cop caught up with Kenny. The cop claimed that Kenny reached into his belt "as if" going for a weapon. The cop shot three times, hitting Kenny once in the head. Kenny fell to the ground, dead. No gun was found at the scene. Hundreds of people protested the murder.

| **Roger "Bucky" Meyers** | 44 | — |

December 24, 1994. —:
In the middle of a police operation to capture a burglar, Mr. Meyers opened up the basement door of his girlfriend's apartment to look out. He was instantly gunned down.

| **Richie Pack** | 19 | — |

October 16, 1994. —:
With an enlarged heart, cerebral palsy and right-side paralysis from a stroke, Pack was at high risk for "sudden death," according to his doctor. Pack was sitting in his wheelchair in front of his house. Words were exchanged with two plainclothes police who had threatened his dog. The cops struck him in the chest, lifted him out of his wheelchair and threw him into a pillar. Minutes after the cops drove off, Richie was dead.

| Gilberto Cruz | 17 | *Mexican* | |

August 13, 1994. Little Village:

Just after midnight, police showed up while Gilberto and some other youth were spray painting in Chicago's predominantly Mexican-American Little Village neighborhood. Gilberto tried to make a run but was caught and shot to death by cops. The police claimed self-defense. Residents said that Gilberto only had a spray paint can. They also reported that as Gilberto lay dying, the cops did nothing to help him and joked that it was "another Mexican off the streets."

| Jason Collins | 16 | — | 👁 |

July 10, 1994. —:

Running down an alley to avoid police harassment, Collins was shot in the back of the neck. The police claimed Collins drew a weapon but witnesses saw no gun in his hand.

| Stanley Jones | 44 | — | |

July 30, 1994. —:

Standing with his hands up alongside his van, Mr. Jones was shot to death by a Chicago police officer. Mr. Jones had been stopped on suspicion of possession of stolen merchandise. The cop claimed that his gun went off when the van lurched and struck his arm. Witnesses said that Jones was simply shot "point blank in the head." The shooting was ruled a justifiable homicide.

| Darryl Edwards | 18 | — | |

February 18, 1994. —:

Mr. Edwards was chased into the basement of an apartment building and shot to death by detectives. The police first claimed that the officer shot in self-defense. The story became that the officer shot after Mr. Edwards pulled out an object that was later discovered to be a piece of a tire. The police department ruled it justifiable homicide.

| Christoper Keys | 21 | — | |

October 12, 1993. —:

Two plainclothes cops rushed Mr. Keys in his car, mistaking him for a burglar. When Mr. Keys hit the gas, the cops fired nine times and killed him. The police considered it self-defense.

| Tommy Yates | 43 | — | |

October 5, 1993. —:

At a mental health clinic where he went for treatment, Tommy Yates was involved in a confrontation with a cop. After the cop pulled out his nightstick and aimed his revolver, Mr. Yates asked, "What are you going to do, shoot me?" The cop pulled the trigger and killed him. The cop claimed that it was an accident.

| Michael Lowery | 20 | — | |

June 20, 1993. —:

The night of the Chicago Bulls' "3-peat" basketball win, Michael was running through a shopping center when a shot rang out and he fell dead. Witnesses reported seeing the arm of a cop, gun in hand, in motion. The cop was immediately whisked away from the scene in a squad car. The police department labeled Michael's death as "unsolved."

| Thomas Rodríguez | 18 | *Mexican* | |

May (?), 1992 or 1993. Chicago:

Thomas supposedly had a gun. Police chased him after they broke up an alleged gang fight. Cops shot Thomas in the back of his head and in the back and killed him as he fled. **Source:** SLP Form

---

Donnell "Bo" Lucas   28   *African American*

August 7, 1992. —:
Lucas was attacked by a Chicago Housing Authority guard at the Harold Ickes projects. The guard put Bo in a bear hug, body slammed him to the ground, picked him up and then dropped him head first onto the pavement. Though Bo was unconscious, with blood coming from his mouth, the guard handcuffed him—as well as a woman who tried to give Bo CPR. By the time he reached the hospital, Bo was dead. Hundreds protested Bo's murder, and some of the steel doors to the project's locked-down buildings were torn down.

Lavengelist "Fifo" Hightower   20   *African American*

December 7, 1991. Robert Taylor Homes:
During a scuffle at the Robert Taylor Homes, Chicago Housing Authority guards fired their guns into the air. Mr. Hightower tried to run away but was shot in the back by a guard. The guard claims that "Fifo" was reaching for a gun, but no gun was ever found.

Ricky Allen   37   —

June 27, 1991. Hoffman Estates:
Ricky Allen was in the middle of a dispute, chasing a man outside his family's apartment in the Chicago suburb of Hoffman Estates. A cop arrived and killed Mr. Allen with a shot to the neck. The cop claimed that Mr. Allen was about to stab the man. Witnesses, including a paramedic, said they never saw Allen with a knife.

Fred Killingsworth   44   —

April 25, 1991. —:
Fred Killingsworth was reportedly acting erratic, talking to himself and walking into the street in his neighborhood. Police who came onto the scene used force to subdue him. Witnesses saw them strike Mr. Killingsworth with flashlights and put their foot to his neck. The cops left Mr. Killingsworth lying on his stomach, hands and feet both cuffed, with blood coming from his nose and the back of his head. An ambulance was called after he stopped breathing.

Stanley "Rock" Scott   26   *African American*

May 22, 1990. —:
Chicago Housing Authority guards claimed that Mr. Scott was shot while fleeing, after an exchange of gunfire with the guards. Residents who witnessed the incident insisted that "Rock," who was shot in the back, never fired on the guards.

Trinity Bowman   —   *African American*

May 8, 1990. —:
A Chicago Housing Authority guard claimed that he was accompanying a maintenance crew when someone put a gun to his head. The guard said he disarmed the man and then chased him up a crowded staircase. The guard admitted that it was too dark to see the fleeing man's face, but the guard fired his gun anyway and killed Trinity Bowman.

Marshall Levy   31   —

March 1, 1990. —:
Marshall Levy was caught by the police, suspected of trying to pass off a stolen money order. When the cops were finished with him, Mr. Levy's head was bashed in with a cop's revolver. Mr. Levy died shortly after being admitted to the hospital. When asked what happened, a cop told hospital personnel, "Well, he resisted arrest."

Hugh Santee   52   —

December 31, 1990. —:
Hugh Santee lay injured on the street after being struck by a car. Before anyone could help, a police car in a high-speed chase ran over Mr. Santee and killed him. The cop driver, who never stopped, later said that he thought he hit some "garbage."

Leonard "Limbo" Bannister	24	—

September 10, 1989. —:
Police Officer Lowell "Six Point" Hartfield squeezed off two rounds into Leonard's skull while he had his hands held up above his head. Hartfield, who had a notorious reputation for doing shakedowns and brutalizing people, reportedly had it in for Leonard. Five hundred people went out into the streets to fight the police and demand justice for Leonard.

Eugene Davison	16	—

March 1, 1989. —:
It began as a car chase and ended with a foot race, as Davison ran up the back steps of a building in an effort to escape the police over a possible speeding ticket. The cop claimed he was forced to shoot when Eugene turned and lunged with a screwdriver. The medical examiner's report showed that Eugene was shot in the back at close range -- "execution style," in the words of the family's lawyer.

ILLINOIS (OUTSIDE CHICAGO)

Name	Age	Nationality	Photo
Four Unidentified Women	—	—	

1996. Alorton:
These women were killed as a result of a police car chase. The newspaper referred to them as "innocent bystanders."
Source: St. Louis Post-Dispatch, 5/29/98

Her adult daughter		—	
Unidentified Woman	86	—	

1996. Washington Park:
These women was killed as a result of a police car chase. The newspaper referred to them as "innocent bystanders." **Source:** St. Louis Post-Dispatch, 5/29/98

Leland Ray Fulkerson	31	—	

October 17, 1995. Grayville:
Mr. Fulkerson, an oilfield worker, was shot to death by Grayville Patrolman Shane Pritchett during a traffic stop. An Illinois State Police investigation found no wrondgoing on Patrolman Pritchett's part, and a grand jury decline to indict him. The victim's widow filed a $3.5 million wrongful death and civil rights lawsuit against Grayville, its mayor and Patrolman Pritchett. The lawsuit charged that Patrolman Pritchett routinely used excessive force and attacked Mr. Fulkerson without reason. **Source:** Evansville Courier, 10/23/97

INDIANA

Name	Age	Nationality	Photo
Hoover Brown, Jr.	36	—	

October 22, 1998. Indianapolis:

Mr. Brown was shot once in the head and twice in the chest and killed by Indianapolis Police Officers John Waitt, Kurt Greggs and Mark Gregory. He was driving a "bootleg" taxi when cops pulled him over for a broken taillight in the early morning hours. Cops claim he sped off and then rammed a patrol car after a three mile chase. The three cops opened fire when Mr. Brown allegedly tried to back up and run them over. Cops claimed self-defense when, in the newspaper's words, they "fired on the fleeing vehicle." Mr. Brown had no arrest record in Indiana or any other state, and no drugs or guns were found in his car. A neighbor said, "He was such a nice neighbor. He raked my leaves for me, helped me get one of the dead branches out of my tree this week, and he put up a picket fence in my back yard.... He was just a very, very nice person. He was a pretty mellow person. He's not someone I would picture getting real upset. He seemed to be pretty easy-going." Mr. Brown had worked in construction but was out of work for several weeks due to a back injury. The cops were assigned to administrative duties during an investigation, which was described as routine. The two passengers in the taxi were not injured. **Source:** The Indianapolis Star, 10/23/98

Barnie Wayne Nuckels	34	—	
Jesse Nuckels	7	—	

March 31, 1998. Waverly (Morgan County):

Barnie Nuckels was on his way to work when Trooper James Patrick Bartram crashed his squad car into Barnie's pickup truck. Barnie's son Jesse was riding along, excited about going to work with his dad, but they never made it. Barnie Nuckels, Jesse Nuckels, and Trooper Bartram all died in the crash. Dave Nuckels described his brother Barnie as a friendly and outgoing guy and said Jesse was a "good kid." State Police conducted an investigation and concluded that Trooper Bartram was chasing another vehicle, swerved to avoid hitting a Subaru, and instead hit Barnie's truck. Barnie's family criticized the investigation, saying it was so sloppy that 12 days after the crash, they found Barnie's watch at the scene of the accident, still lying on the ground. They also said that the police have not given them any information to help them contact the ten witnesses that cops had interviewed, forcing the family to find its own witnesses to try and determine what happened. One witness the family spoke with said he did not see any lights or hear a siren at the time of the accident. The family is considering a lawsuit. **Source:** The Indianpolis Star, 4/1/98 & 4/17/98

David C. Hairston	29	—	

December 11, 1997. Marion County (Pike Township):

Mr. Hairston was in his house with two friends, Khalalah and Michael Ector, when Officer Myron Powell and his friend, Michael Highbaugh, broke in and attacked them. Mr. Hairston was shot once in the head and killed, reportedly by Officer Powell's friend. Khalalah Ector was stabbed repeatedly, and Michael Ector was shot in the head and hand. Luckily, they survived. Officer Powell, an Indianapolis patrolman who had been suspended seven times in seven years, was arrested while on duty in connection with Mr. Hairston's death. The cop's friend, Michael Highbaugh, was also arrested. He told police that he and Officer Powell had been ripping off drug dealers for more than three years and re-selling the drugs for profit. Mr. Hairston was a suspected drug dealer who apparently "refused to cooperate with Officer Powell's attempt to steal drugs and money." The FBI began investigating possible drug-related corruption within the Indianapolis Police Department. **Source:** The Indianapolis Star, 12/13/97, 12/16/97, 2/7/98, & 2/20/98; The Orlando Sentinel, 12/14/97

Monwell T. Scaife	22	—	

November 29, 1997. Indianapolis (Near Northside):

Mr. Scaife was shot in the head and killed by Indianapolis Police Officers Gary Riggs and Matthew Hall during an alleged gun battle after a car chase and foot chase. He had reportedly escaped from a halfway house where he was serving time for armed robbery charges. Cops claim they pulled over a stolen car he was driving and that he took off, firing shots at pursuing police cars. He reportedly jumped out of the car while it was still in motion and fled on foot, supposedly continuing to fire shots. Eyewitnesses said Mr. Scaife looked confused as he ran from the police. **Source:** The Indianapolis Star, 12/1/97

177

Christopher A. Moreland   30   —

October 25, 1997. St. Joseph County Jail:

Mr. Moreland was found dead in the St. Joseph County Jail's "Drunk Tank" less than eight hours after being arrested. Another inmate, who was processed into the jail just before Mr. Moreland, said he saw officers hitting and pepper-spraying the victim and said, "He [Mr. Moreland] wasn't that drunk. After everything that happened, we were listening for him. He was snoring and when we heard him stop, we started yelling for someone to check on him. They did and he was dead." An autopsy revealed that Mr. Moreland died from a blow to the head inflicted within 24 hours of his death. He had a bump on his head and cuts around his left eye. A videotape from a tavern he had visited that same night showed he had no injuries, indicating that he suffered the injuries in jail. An employee of the tavern said Mr. Moreland only drank a few beers. Authorities admitted pepper-spraying him and placing him in a restraint chair. Four officers from the jail were suspended with pay while his death was investigated. The sheriff said this was routine and that it was not clear that the officers had engaged in wrongdoing. Authorities claimed that the victim's blood alcohol was .14 at the time of his arrest. **Source:** The Indianapolis Star, 10/30/97

Franklin G. Hornsby   32   —

October 16, 1997. Floyd County Jail:

Mr. Hornsby was arrested and held in jail on charges of possessing and dealing marijuana. He had been in the Floyd County Jail for ten days when he died from a blood clot in his lungs. Mr. Hornsby weighed 500 pounds and suffered from serious health problems, but he was not receiving medical care in jail. A lawsuit filed by his mother charges that each day her son was in jail, she called and told jail employees that he needed medical treatment and wasn't getting it. She said each time she called to check on him, even on the day he died, she got the same answer, "He was fine." On Oct. 9, Mr. Hornsby's lawyer said in court that his client was suffering from "high blood pressure, severe arthritic pain, obesity, and other serious problems and needed medical care." Mr. Hornsby went to that hearing barefoot because the jail did not have shoes or socks to fit him, and his feet were "extremely swollen and discolored." By Oct. 10, six days before he died, a prison psychiatrist noted that he was having severe difficulty breathing and appeared to be ill. The jail doctor said he did not treat Mr. Hornsby because the latter didn't ask to be seen. The doctor acknowledged that Mr. Hornsby could have died because his inactivity in the jail allowed blood to pool in his extremities and form clots, which later clogged his lungs. But he tried to blame the victim, saying that such blood clots are a known risk of inactivity and that the jail could not force Mr. Hornsby to exercise. The sheriff also tried to blame the victim, remarking, "The only thing we could have done is when he was young, have someone keep him from eating so much." The lawsuit accuses the sheriff, the county, and the doctor of negligence, of violating the Americans with Disabilities Act, and of violating Mr. Hornsby's civil rights. **Source:** The Courier-Journal (Louisville, KY), 3/11/98 & 10/3/98

Robert Dugger   35   —

1997. in prison:

Mr. Dugger, a mentally ill man, died in prison under what the newspaper termed "suspicious circumstances." **Source:** The Indianapolis Star, 10/4/97

Joshua Christ   17   —

1997. in prison:

Mr. Christ died in prison under what the newspaper termed "suspicious circumstances." **Source:** The Indianapolis Star, 10/4/97

Susan Darwactor   35   —

1997. in prison:

Ms. Darwactor, a mentally ill woman, died in prison under what the newspaper termed "suspicious circumstances." **Source:** The Indianapolis Star, 10/4/97

Joseph W. Love　　　　　　　　　　37　　　　　　　　—

June 14, 1995. Marion County Lockup (jail):

Mr. Love, a mentally ill man, was "violently thrown" into a jail cell by sheriff's deputies minutes before he died. "He is hit, kicked and choked, maybe crushed, until every breath of life expires from his body," said a lawyer for the victim's family. Two forensic pathologists found the cause of death to be "positional asphyxia," while another claimed it was an adrenaline rush and an enlarged heart. Mr. Love had been sent to the jail by a judge who found him mentally incompetent to stand trial on theft, obstruction of justice, and marijuana charges and wanted him committed to a psychiatric hospital. Mr. Love allegedly struggled with deputies as they tried to remove him to the courtroom and was thrown to the floor and sprayed with tear gas. Deputies continued to abuse him at the jail. The victim's family filed a lawsuit against the five deputies who were restraining him when he died. The lawsuit charged that deputies beat and kicked Mr. Love in his padded cell before using their weight to lean on him and stop his breathing. The deputies denied hitting or sitting on him and claimed that they were just trying to remove his clothes as procedure requires for mentally ill or violent inmates. But they were not able to explain why they didn't just ask him to remove his clothes himself, which procedure also requires. The attorney who represented Mr. Love's family, said "Detention should not bring death." The five deputies were cleared of civil liability and family members said they were very disappointed by the outcome. They had hoped to send a message that would prevent any other prisoner from suffering the same kind of death in custody as Joseph Love. **Source:** The Indianapolis Star, 1/27/98, 2/3/98, & 2/4/98

Robert Ellis　　　　　　　　　　31　　　　　　　　—

February 11, 1994. Gary:

Robert was shot and killed by his wife, Gary police officer Myrtle Ellis, during a quarrel at their home. Robert, a firefighter, was shot in the eye, abdomen, arm and thigh. Officer Ellis was found guilty of reckless homicide in Nov. 6, 1997. She faced up to eight years in prison. **Source:** Chicago Tribune, 11/8/97

Unidentified Man　　　　　　　　　—　　　　　　　　—

March 24, 1992. Indianapolis:

A unidentified "drug suspect" was shot in the head and killed by an undercover narcotics officer. The cop claimed to have just completed a drug buy and had started to arrest the victim and his friend when the victim allegedly reached into his waistband for a gun. The victim's family filed a civil lawsuit, claiming the cop's gun went off accidentally and the story about the victim reaching for a gun was made up after the fact as a cover-up. Another cop then erased part of an audiotape of the encounter. A grand jury refused to indict the cop involved in the shooting. The cop who erased the tape received only a 30 day suspension. As of late 1997, both officers were sergeants. **Source:** Human Rights Watch, Shielded from Justice (1998), pp. 192-193.

Edmund Powell　　　　　　　　　—　　　　　　　　*Black*

June 1991. Indianapolis:

Edmund was shot and killed by a white cop, Officer Wayne Sharp, who reportedly had ties to a neo-Nazi group. Edmund had allegedly stolen something from a department store. Officer Sharp chased him with a drawn gun and claimed he fired accidentally when Edmund swung a nail-studded board at him. However, at least one witness said the cop fired at close range as Edmund lay on the ground. Community activists charged that the shooting was racially motivated, and referred to the fact that the same officer had killed a Black man allegedly suspected of burglary ten years earlier. Officer Sharp was cleared by a grand jury in the murder of Edmund Powell, just as he had been cleared in the killing ten years before. Edmund's family filed a civil suit charging that the cop intentionally shot Edmund and won a $465,000 verdict, to which the city litigator responded, "Obviously, we are disappointed by the verdict....Officer Sharp did not do anything wrong." As of Jan.1998, Officer Sharp had been neither disciplined nor re-trained. He remained on the streets and, in the words of the police chief, "has received high accolades and several awards for superior work." **Source:** Human Rights Watch, Shielded from Justice (1998), pp. 190-192.

| Leonard R. Barnett | — | *African American* |

July 9, 1990. Indianapolis:

Mr. Barnett was shot and killed by a white cop, Officer Scott L. Haslar, after a long car chase that ended in a crash. The cop claimed Leonard, an alleged robbery suspect, moved rapidly away from the crashed car (even though he had suffered a broken leg in the accident) and then returned to it quickly. Officer Haslar said he thought the victim was going for a gun so he shot and killed him. The victim was unarmed, and no gun was recovered from the scene. A federal grand jury declined to indict Officer Haslar, who was awarded the medal of valor for the shooting and was later promoted to sergeant. **Source:** Human Rights Watch, Shielded from Justice (1998), p. 190; The Indianapolis Star, 1/21/98

| Michael Taylor | 16 | *African American* |

September 1987. Indianapolis:

Mr. Taylor was shot in the back of the head and killed by a cop as he sat handcuffed in the back of a patrol car. The police and the coroner insisted it was suicide, and the FBI agreed. But there was no residue on his hands or clothes, indicating that he did not fire a gun. It is hard to imagine how someone could shoot themselves while handcuffed. Michael's family won a $3 million judgment against the city in a civil suit which, as of Sept., 1997 (10 years later), was still being appealed by the city. **Source:** Human Rights Watch, Shielded from Justice (1998), pp. 189-190; The Indianapolis Star, 1/21/98

IOWA

Name	Age	Nationality	Photo
Charles Dudley, Jr.	27	—	

June 21, 1997. Des Moines:

Mr. Dudley was shot four times in the back and killed by Des Moines Police Officers Kenneth Brown, Thomas Heller, and Michael McBride, who fired a total of 27 shots. An autopsy confirmed that all the bullets struck the victim from behind. Cops claim they were called to a house by residents who said Mr. Dudley had threatened them. Mr. Dudley allegedly reached into his waistband and brandished a pellet gun that looked like a large black pistol. Police justified the shots in the back by saying that Mr. Dudley ignored their commands to stop and that the officers felt their lives were in danger. In late Oct. 1997, a grand jury cleared the officers of any wrongdoing. A police spokesperson tried to portray the cops as victims, saying the shooting was a tragedy both for them and for Mr. Dudley's family and that it was "time to move on." At an Oct. 22, 1997 protest against police brutality, about 40 people gathered in front of the Des Moines Police Department. Mr. Dudley's mother said, "They shot my son four times in the back. My son died for no reason. What we want is justice, and justice now." **Source:** Des Moines Register, 10/23/97 & 11/1/97

| Eric Shaw | 31 | *white* |

August 21, 1996. Iowa City:

While Eric was in his art studio, the police entered the studio, unannounced, shot and killed Eric the minute they opened the door. They said they were in the building looking for a suspected burglar. The cop who shot him, Officer Jeffrey Gillaspie, first claimed that he thought the phone in Eric's hand was a gun and he was firing in self-defense. But later, the cop changed his story to say that he accidentally fired his gun when he "flinched." The county prosecutor first termed the shooting "unjustified," but after a lengthy investigation, he announced that no criminal charges would be filed against the officer. He said that Officer Gillaspie was guilty of negligence, police malpractice, and that he used deadly force without justification, but that he did not have a willful and wanton disregard for human life.

KANSAS

Name	Age	Nationality	Photo
Mark Orland McKee	38	—	

April 22, 1998. Johnson County:

Mark was shot and killed by police who were responding to a domestic violence complaint. Cops claim Mark threatened to kill them and was acting as if he were holding a gun when an officer shot him. As it turned out, Mark did not have a weapon. **Source:** The Kansas City Star, 5/2/98

| Unidentified Man | mid-20s | — |

November 27, 1997. Kansas City, Kan.:
The man was shot three times and killed by a cop investigating an armed robbery. Police claim the suspect pulled a handgun and shot at the cop, who was trying to question him. The victim was shot twice in the head and once in the abdomen. He was taken to the hospital, where he died. His identity was withheld. **Source:** The Kansas City Star, 11/28/97

| John M. Pannell | 28 | — |

October 27, 1997. Kansas City, Kan.:
John was shot once in the head and killed by a police sergeant as he allegedly held his ex-girlfriend hostage. Cops claim she had called 911 to report that he wouldn't leave her apartment, and that when they arrived, he fired a shot at them. They evacuated four teenagers and a child through a back window. Later on the sergeant shot and killed John who was allegedly using his ex-girlfriend as a shield. **Source:** The Kansas City Star, 10/28/97

| Milton Foster, Jr. | — | — |

October 29, 1994. Bonner Springs:
Milton Foster was shot and killed by off-duty Kansas City, Kan., Police Officer John Cheek. Milton was working as a security guard at a sports bar when he was killed. Officer Cheek was convicted of first degree murder in 1995 and sentenced to 25 years to life in prison. After serving 19 months, the Kansas Supreme Court overturned his conviction. Released on bail, he was re-tried and convicted of voluntary manslaughter in April 1998. He was due to be sentenced in June 1998, and remained free on bond in the meantime. Sentencing guidelines indicated the sentence should be between three years, 10 months and four years, three months, minus credit for time served. The DA asked for a heavier sentence because of three aggravating circumstances: excessive brutality, that the murder "was motivated entirely or in part by race and color;" and that he relied on his status as a police officer "as an excuse for killing his victim." The Justice Campaign of America pushed for federal prosecution for civil rights violations. **Source:** The Kansas City Star, 4/10/98 & 6/26/98

| Gregory Sevier | 22 | *Native American (Creek-Choctaw)* | 👁 |

April 21, 1991. Lawrence:
Gregg was shot six times and killed by Police Officers Ted Boderman and James Phillips. His parents had called 911 because he was depressed and not responding to them. They requested that a trained professional be sent. Instead, police were sent to their house, and within four minutes of the first officer's arrival, their son had been shot dead. One of the bullets went through Gregg and struck his sister Judy in the head as she lay in bed. In February 1996, his family settled a federal civil suit for an undisclosed amount against the police chief and the two cops who murdered their son. The family continues to hold a yearly memorial march for Gregg each year on the anniversary of his death.

KENTUCKY

Name	Age	Nationality	Photo
Unidentified Man	41	*Salvadoran*	

September 5, 1998. Metcalfe County:
Kentucky State Police shot and killed a migrant farmworker, claiming that he was holding his girlfriend at knife-point. Police say they shot him when he raised the knife in a "threatening manner." Carlotta Harris, the man's girlfriend, said "The bullet went right past my shoulder. He died right there.... They just shot him straight in the head." She also said she is very upset with the police. "I didn't think they had to shoot him in the head. I don't think they should have killed him." **Source:** The Courier-Journal (Louisville, KY), 9/6/98

Fidencio Campos-Cruz   30   *Mexican*

June 13, 1998. Louisville:

Fidencio was shot twice (once in the face and once in the chest) and killed by Police Officer Rick McCubbin, who was president of the Fraternal Order of Police, Lodge 6. Officer McCubbin was responding to a report of a fight in the rear apartment of a building at 1511 W. Market St. According to authorities, the officer broke up the fight between Fidencio and another man. The officer was arresting the other man when Fidencio allegedly pulled a knife, struggled with Officer McCubbin, and slashed him across the stomach. The cop was not injured because he was wearing a bulletproof vest. Officer McCubbin then shot Fidencio twice, killing him. The officer was placed on paid administrative leave (paid vacation), which was described as routine. The shooting was still under investigation almost two weeks later. The Mexican Consulate in St. Louis decided to conduct its own investigation, expressing suspicion of the police story, especially since a witness who saw the incident was released and "all of a sudden can't be located." **Source:** The Courier-Journal (Louisville, KY), 6/26/98

Jeremiah Fraley   20   —

May 17, 1998. Fort Wright:

Jeremiah was killed when the car he was riding in crashed while being chased by a Kentucky State Police trooper, who allegedly suspected that the driver was drunk. Jeremiah was a passenger in the car. **Source:** The Rocky Mountain News (Denver, CO), 5/24/98

Charles Collins   37   —

March 23, 1998. Henderson:

Mr. Collins died while handcuffed in the back seat of a patrol car. According to police, he had been involved in a car accident and was "belligerent and very combative" when they arrived. Authorities claim he struggled with emergency personnel before being handcuffed. Cops said he was breathing when they placed him in the patrol car, but a short time later an emergency medical worker noticed he had stopped breathing. He was pronounced dead at the hospital. **Source:** The Courier-Journal (Louisville, KY), 3/25/98

Adrian Reynolds   34   *Black*

January 7, 1998. Jefferson County Jail:

Adrian Reynolds died after being beaten and brutalized by more than six corrections officers in Jefferson County Jail. His family believes he was targeted because he was planning on filing an excessive use of force complaint against the Louisville police officers who arrested him on Jan. 1, 1998. The victim's cousin, Rev. Richard Reynolds, said "This is an example of what is taking place, not just in the corrections facilities here in Louisville on a daily basis, but what's taking place in correctional facilities and police departments around the country." The officers claimed that they were trying to prevent Adrian Reynolds from committing suicide and had no intention of hurting him. But an inmate who witnessed the incident said that he saw Adrian's head bounce twice really hard against the concrete and that Adrian was yelling and screaming "You're hurting me. You're gonna kill me." An autopsy showed that Adrian died of a blunt head injury. Inmates at the Jefferson County Jail have said that many of the officers involved in the killing were known as the "Klan Squad." Officer Timothy Barnes, who stepped on the back of Adrian's neck for 60 to 90 seconds, had been suspended for four days in 1996 for punching an inmate twice in the head with a closed fist while the inmate was shackled to a bed. Officer Mike Durham, who helped pull Adrian out of his cell, was accused in 1995 of abusing an inmate, including slamming his head into a sink and bouncing him off walls. There was major outrage in Louisville when the story of Adrian's death hit the news. Officer Barnes only admitted that he put his foot on Adrian's head after he heard news of inmate eyewitnesses "pointing the finger" at him. The County Jail had been in turmoil for many years and this case highlighted the problem. County Commissioner Russ Maple called the Corrections Department "an absolute snake pit." After an investigation, in which the officers were placed on unpaid leave, the Jefferson County Corrections Department recommended that Officers Barnes and Durham be fired and that six other officers face lesser punishments of demotion and suspension. Officer Barnes was charged with murder. The Louisville Courier-Journal did an investigation of the Corrections Department and discovered that there were 41 cases in which the Department charged officers with abuse or excessive force during the past ten years. Only three officers were fired out of all these cases. **Source:** The Courier-Journal (Louisville, KY), 1/11/98, 1/17/98, 3/14/98, 4/15/98, 4/22/98, & 4/27/98

| Howell Durwood Culver | 42 | — |

December 20, 1997. Louisville:

Mr. Culver was reportedly robbing a drug store. He was shot in the head during a struggle with police after he allegedly took a pharmacist hostage and held a gun to the man's head. Authorities claimed they thought Mr. Culver shot himself but said ballistic evidence was not yet available. They said that two cops and Mr. Culver fired their guns during the incident. Mr. Culver died three days later at the hospital on Dec. 23. **Source:** The Courier-Journal (Louisville, KY) 12/25/97

| Breanna Shane Noe | 17 months | — |

November 26, 1997. Bullitt County (Pioneer Village):

Pioneer Village Police Officer Bart Adkins was off-duty, watching his fiancee's children, Breanna and Blake, while she was at work. Officer Adkins beat Breanna to death. Autopsy results showed that the cause of death was severe head trauma that indicated her head had been slammed into a wall. Blake appeared to be unharmed but later it was discovered that he had suffered severe bone fractures and damaged vertebrae in the months before his sister's death. These are injuries consistent with child abuse. Officer Adkins had been named Officer of the Year the week before he killed Breanna. He was fired from his position two days after her death when he was arrested and charged with murder. But Police Chief Scott McGaha continued to praise (former) Officer Adkins, calling him an "outstanding officer." Breanna's father, Steven Noe, was very upset, stating "I feel a very big loss.... It broke my heart into several pieces. I have every intention of making sure justice is done. It's not going to be another cop getting away with murder." **Source:** The Courier-Journal (Louisville, KY), 12/2/97 & 12/20/97; Cincinnati Enquirer, 11/29/97

| Robert Whitlow | 45 | — |

March 13, 1997. Louisville:

Mr. Whitlow was a former block-watch captain, described as a "good person" by his family and neighbors. Police had a warrant for his arrest based on a complaint by his estranged girlfriend charging that he had kidnapped her in an earlier incident. The SWAT team exploded two "flash bang grenades," which give off a deafening sound and blinding flash, and then entered his house. Detective Rodney Estes, a SWAT team member, fired three shots, hitting Mr. Whitlow once in the back and once in the side and killing him. Det. Estes claims that he only shot Mr. Whitlow after he refused to put down a gun he was supposedly pointing at the detective's "lower extremities." A lawyer for Robert's family said that the police should have used a bullhorn to identify themselves and given Robert a chance to surrender. Robert's brother, Larry, said he believes his brother could not possibly have heard the officer's command after the grenades exploded. Robert's friend, Lynn Sullivan, said "I'm sure they freaked him out, I'm sure he was terrified." A coroner's jury ruled that Det. Estes fired in self-defense and the police department found that he followed proper procedure. The victim's family filed a wrongful death lawsuit charging that police procedure in the case was inappropriate. **Source:** The Courier-Journal (Louisville, KY), 3/5/98 & 4/2/98

LOUISIANA

Name	Age	Nationality	Photo
Cedric Harris	27	*Black*	

July 24, 1998. Shreveport:

Mr. Harris, a wheelchair-bound paraplegic, was shot in the back and killed by Shreveport Police Officer Justin D. Olds. An internal police investigation found that Mr. Harris pointed a gun at Officer Olds before the cop shot him in the back! Cops claim Mr. Harris had a long police record and said the shooting was justified. This was the third highly publicized incident of police brutality against a Black man in Shreveport in 1998 that resulted in protests. The first two were the shooting of Patrick Morris in January and the case of Melvin Lewis in April. Mr. Lewis, a Black man, had is neck broken by police during an alleged scuffle stemming from a traffic stop. He survived but was paralyzed. Internal investigations cleared police of wrongdoing in both of these cases as well. The NAACP and other groups joined in protests against these three incidents. A City Council member representing the predominantly Black district where Mr. Harris was killed said, "There are a lot of unanswered questions here. If it was just harassment, that's bad enough. But when you get people paralyzed and killed, that's just too much." A 46-year-old neighborhood resident said, "They [the police] are harassing everybody, even little kids. They make the kids take off their shoes looking for drugs. They stop people without even saying why they're doing it." **Source:** The Dallas Morning News, 8/8/98

Dion James	32	—
Edwin James	4	—
Bobby Jones	8	—
Brittany Jones	5	—

August 30, 1998. Kenner:

The police were chasing a teenager in a stolen car. The teenager's car hit the car containing the victims, who were on their way to Macedonia Baptist Church for Sunday services. The driver of the car that was hit, Wilmareen James (mother of Dion James), was critically injured, as were three of her surviving grandchildren (the children killed in this accident were also her grandchildren). **Source:** Associated Press online, 8/31/98

Johnnie Mae Mann	73	—

March 22, 1998. New Orleans:

Johnnie Mae Mann was killed as a result of a police chase that ended in a five-car accident. Gretna Police Officer B.T. Clark chased a teenage motorist who was reportedly driving a car with expired license plates. The teenage driver allegedly "crashed through the toll gate on the Crescent City Connection and continued into New Orleans." Also injured in the five-car accident were Mann's two passengers Phil Womble, 68, and his wife, Virginia, 66. The three, all members of the Israel Baptist Church, had just left a dinner with fellow church members and were only seven blocks from Mann's house when their car was struck. **Source:** New Orleans Times-Picayune, 3/24/98

Mevin Cousin	21	—

January 4, 1998. Metairie:

Mevin Cousin was shot and killed in a barrage of 16 shots fired by Jefferson Parish Sheriff's Deputy Frank Francois after an alleged holdup of the Applebee's Neighborhood Bar and Grill. Cops claim Mr. Cousin shot and killed the restaurant's cook and tried to kill the manager, then forced him out of his car at gunpoint. Mr. Cousin was in a his own car fleeing the restaurant, his gun in his back pocket, when Deputy Francois, who was on foot, opened fire on him. Mr. Cousin died at the scene after being hit once in the back of head and once in the shoulder. Sheriff Harry Lee said, "[Mr. Cousin] set into motion the events that lead to his death. These people that choose to live by violence are going to die by violence. . . . Considering the totality of the circumstances, I think it was a good shooting." Joe Cook of the American Civil Liberties Union disagreed, saying "I would question whether that was the minimum use of force necessary. The guy [Mr. Cousin] certainly should have been apprehended. . . . [but] It appears at that particular point in time [when police fired at Mr. Cousin], we don't know that anyone was in danger." **Source:** New Orleans Times-Picayune, 1/6/98

Deborah James	—	—

December 15, 1997. St. John the Baptist Parish (I-10 & US-51):

Deborah James was killed when the car she was driving was struck by a St. John the Baptist Parish sheriff's deputy, Lt. Juan Watkins. An investigation concluded that Lt. Watkins could not have avoided the collision with Ms. James at the intersection of I-10 and US-51. The state contended that Ms. James was at fault. Donald James, Deborah's husband, filed a wrongful death suit against Sheriff Wayne L. Jones and Lt. Watkins. His lawsuit accused Lt. Watkins of negligence, noting that he was speeding with no justification. The suit charged that if Lt. Watkins had been driving slower, the collision would not have happened. **Source:** New Orleans Times-Picayune, 1/29/1998

| Rob Staley | 18 | — |

December 11, 1997. New Orleans:

Rob Staley was a freshman at Tulane University in New Orleans, enrolled in an arts curriculum. He was an honors student, a promising artist and a film maker back in his home town in Iowa. Rob had won numerous amateur film maker awards and played for a club soccer team that won the state championship in 1996. According to his brother, Rob "was well-loved and admired for his humor and creative talent" and had been attracted to New Orleans for its music, art scene and creative atmosphere. In the incident that led to his death, Rob had reportedly taken cocaine. He supposedly grabbed a dog by the throat and started to choke it, then attacked a 38-year-old woman after she told him to leave the dog alone. New Orleans Police Sgt. Frank Vaccarella claims that he found Rob threatening the woman with a broken bottle in the back yard of her apartment building, that he "repeatedly ordered [Rob] to put the bottle down, but he refused." Rob allegedly lunged at Sgt. Vaccarella with the broken bottle. The cop fired twice, hitting Rob once in the chest and rupturing his aorta. Hung Chang, a Tulane student and Rob's campus neighbor, said, "All these things I'm hearing in the media are not like him at all. He would like to joke and stuff. He was never violent." **Source:** New Orleans Times-Picayune, 12/13/97

| Joseph Brown | 40 | — |

December 3, 1997. Gretna:

Joseph Brown, a mentally ill man, was shot three times in the chest and killed by a Gretna police officer. The cop claimed that Mr. Brown came at him wielding an iron pipe as he responded to a routine disturbance call about a fight between Joseph and his brother, Eugene, who lived together. A niece, Brandy Brown, called the police and said that Joseph attacked Eugene with a pipe in his bedroom, and that the brothers' fight spilled into the back yard. The family believes the shooting was unnecessary since the police had quelled similar incidents in the past without gunfire. Relatives said this incident should have been no different since police knew of Joseph's psychological problems. They questioned why the officer fired to kill rather than to immobilize. Toni Evans, a family friend, said, "He only had a stick.... Wound him in the leg. You know he's mentally ill. He's in and out of the hospital constantly. He's on medication." Brandy, the niece who placed the 911 call, said that Joseph was not trying to hit the cop but was merely heading in the cop's direction, trying to leave the yard and carrying the pipe near his knees. This incident marked the second time that year a Gretna police officer shot and killed a civilian. **Source:** New Orleans Times-Picayune, 12/2/97 & 3/24/98

| Patrick Hamilton | 7 wks. | — |
| Dana Jones | 29 | — |

November 30, 1997. Jefferson Parish:

Dana Jones and seven-week-old Patrick Hamilton, the infant son of a family friend, were killed when an alleged shoplifting suspect being chased by Jefferson Parish sheriff's deputies crashed into their car as the family was driving to church. Two of Ms. Jones' children were also injured in the crash. Cops claim the shoplifter refused to surrender to an off-duty deputy who was working as a security guard at the shopping center, then got into his car and tried to run the deputy down. The deputy dove into the car to try to turn it off and the two allegedly struggled for the cop's gun. The shoplifter drove off allegedly dragging the deputy for 20-30 feet before the gun went off and the deputy let go. Another deputy, who was on duty, spotted the shoplifter's car and began the chase which ended in a fatal crash. Authorities said that the chase was conducted in accordance with department policy, which allows deputies to chase suspected felons but not people suspected of misdemeanors. Authorities said they found $1,200 worth of stolen merchandise in the shoplifter's car. Shoplifting becomes a felony when the value of the stolen merchandise exceeds $100. Authorities also said that they considered the shoplifter's struggle with the off-duty deputy a case of attempted murder. The infant's grandmother, Mable Tate, said that deputies overreacted and were now trying to justify their actions. "A life is worth more than that, I think," said Ms. Tate. "It's something that should have never happened." A friend of Ms. Jones said, "I don't think they should have chased him [the shoplifter] for clothes." Dana Jones was described by her relatives and friends as a hard-working, religious mother who loved gospel music. She was employed in the child support enforcement division of the Jefferson Parish district attorney's office. She had high expectations of her children and planned to take in foster children. **Source:** New Orleans Times-Picayune, 12/2/97 & 1/6/98

Charles Pham   17   —

October 30, 1997. Jefferson Parish:

Charles Pham, of Avondale, was killed, and his passenger, an unidentified 14-year-old boy, was injured when their allegedly stolen car crashed during a chase by State Police Trooper Darryl Thomas. The chase began when Trooper Thomas allegedly saw the car run a stop sign and then flee when he tried to stop it. A license plate check reportedly showed that the car was stolen. The state trooper said he saw the car spin out of control as it passed over a small bridge with a slight incline. The car left the road and flipped over several times, ejecting the driver (Mr. Pham) and front-seat passenger, who was listed in critical but stable condition at the hospital's Pediatric Intensive Care Unit. **Source:** New Orleans Times-Picayune, 10/31/97

Unidentified   —   —

June 1997. Gretna:

A Gretna police officer officer shot and killed a person who allegedly robbed a McDonald's at gunpoint and pointed a gun at officers during a chase. **Source:** New Orleans Times-Picayune, 3/24/98

Edmore Green   —   *Black*

February 15, 1997. Alton:

Edmore Green was shot to death by St. Tammany Parish sheriff's deputies who "swarmed" his house after his girlfriend reportedly called the police and said her boyfriend had a weapon and that her nine-year-old son was inside the house. State Rep. Avery Alexander, D-New Orleans, condemned Mr. Green's death as a racist killing on the part of the police, saying that cops meant it as a warning "that in St. Tammany Parish, a Black man had better not take up with a white woman." "Mr. Green was a gentle man. He took in a white women and her two children because they were living on the streets.... They argued; she called the police and more than 30 of them rushed the house and they shot him down. If it had been a Black woman and Black children and a Black man, maybe one deputy would have gone," said Rep. Alexander. Cops claim Mr. Green came out of the house with a shotgun and fired once at four deputies before two of the deputies opened fire on him. But Rep. Alexander said this was untrue, that Mr. Green was unarmed. Civil rights activists, calling themselves the "Pilgrims of Dr. Martin Luther King," marched through Slidell's Olde Towne in St. Tammany Parrish to protest the murder of Mr. Green. In front of the police department, Elwin Gillum, a longtime member of the Souther Christian Leadership Conference, talked about racism: "White Slidell officers harass Black and white people in poorer Slidell neighborhoods [many of which] police have declared a drug zone.... I can't walk out at night in those areas to visit a friend without being stopped as a drug suspect.... That is not happening in the higher-income white areas of the city." **Source:** New Orleans Times-Picayune, 3/13/98

Richard Curtis   —   —

August 1995. New Orleans:

New Orleans Police Officers David Singleton and Renard "Zoo" Smith kidnapped Richard Curtis on an Algiers street "under the guise of a traffic stop." They used their police lights to pull him over. They handcuffed him and drove him to a meeting with a "drug kingpin" with whom the two cops were collaborating. Two months later, Mr. Curtis' "skeletal remains" were found deep in the woods in Mississippi. The drug kingpin was charged with his murder. Officer Smith was assigned to desk duty two years later, in June, 1997, when he came under investigation in connection with the case. He resigned two months later rather than answer questions from his supervisors, and Officers Smith and Singleton were charged with kidnapping Mr. Curtis. In 1991, the two had been acquitted of shaking down drug dealers in a high profile federal trial. This time around, Officer Singleton and his brother, Ronald, also a New Orleans police officer, pleaded guilty to federal drug trafficking charges and left the force. As part of his plea bargain, (former) Officer David Singleton agreed to testify against former Officer Smith in the latter's trial on charges of kidnapping Mr. Curtis. Former Officer Smith faces a life sentence if convicted. **Source:** New Orleans Times-Picayune, 8/8/98

Unidentified Man (brother)	—	*Vietnamese*
Unidentified Woman (sister)	—	*Vietnamese*

March 4, 1995. east New Orleans:

This man was shot and killed execution style by Police Officer Antoinette Frank around 1 a.m. as he lay begging and pleading for mercy on the floor of the Vietnamese restaurant that his family owned. Officer Frank, who had moonlighted as a security guard at the restaurant, also killed an off-duty cop who was working there as a security guard at the time. After the incident, she responded to the call for help as if she had not been involved. Officer Frank, who was not disguised, was recognized by a brother and a sister of the victims who had hid in a cooler. She was convicted and sentenced to death in Sept., 1995 -- which is virtually unheard of in a police brutality case. Perhaps it was the death of the off-duty cop which affected the sentence. **Source:** Human Rights Watch, Shielded from Justice (1998), pp. 255-256.

Kim Groves	—	—

October 13, 1994. New Orleans:

Kim was killed on the orders of New Orleans Police Officer Len Davis when he learned that she had filed a brutality complaint against him. Federal agents, who were surveilling Officer Davis for suspected drug dealing, overheard the conversation where he ordered the murder, talking about the "30" he would be taking care of (30 is a police code for homicide) and saying, "Get that whore!" Afterwards, he talked about "N.A.T." -- police jargon for "necessary action taken." Officer Davis was known as "Robocop" in the Desire housing project. He had a long list of brutality complaints. Another cop told a reporter, "He's got an internal affairs jacket as thick as a telephone book, but supervisors have swept his dirt under the rug for so long that it's coming back to haunt them." Activists reported a "chilling effect" that this murder had on people coming forward to complain about police brutality. On Nov. 6, 1996, a federal court sentenced Officer Davis to death for ordering the murder of Kim Groves. This type of sentence is virtually unheard of in police brutality cases. **Source:** Human Rights Watch, Shielded from Justice (1998), pp. 254-255.

Mitchell Ceasar	—	—

April 23, 1994. Lower Coast Algiers:

Mitchell Ceasar was shot with about six bullets "execution-style" and killed in a field by Patrolman Weldon Williams and his half-brother, George Gillam, then 16. Gillam was told by a neighbor that Mr. Caesar's roommate, Willard Storey, had broken into his apartment and stolen money, clothes and jewelry. Gillam told his brother, Patrolmen Williams, about the alleged break-in. The two brothers went to the apartment that Mr. Storey and Mr. Ceasar shared. Officer Williams ordered the two men into the car and drove to the field. Officer Williams ordered the two captives to lie face-down on the ground. Gillam said to his brother, "Let's do this." Mr. Storey was hit in the shoulder, arm and leg before stumbling into the darkness, with Caesar's last screams echoing in the background. Mr. Storey hid in a ditch where Gillam tracked him down, stood over him, and pulled the trigger, but the gun jammed. Officer Williams was fired, convicted of first-degree murder and sentenced to life in prison. Gillam also received a life sentence. **Source:** New Orleans Times-Picayune, 11/7/97

Adolph Archie	—	*African American*

March 22, 1990. downtown New Orleans:

Adolph was beaten to death by police on his way to the hospital. Archie had allegedly killed a white cop and was himself injured in a shootout. Cops took 12 minutes to transport Archie from the site of the shooting to the hospital seven blocks away, then decided not to enter the hospital because they thought there might be a lynching by the approximately 100 cops waiting there. They drove Archie to the police station, where he allegedly got into a scuffle with the cops. At the hospital where he was eventually brought, X-rays showing his injuries disappeared. Throughout the incident, cops were broadcasting death threats for Archie over the police radio. The coroner eventually called Archie's death "homicide by police intervention." The city settled with Archie's family for $333,000, one-third of which was for the family of the dead cop. Within hours, all the cops involved were cleared of departmental violations, and there were no criminal prosecutions. The cop who arrested Archie was "vilified" by other cops for not executing him on the spot. **Source:** Human Rights Watch, Shielded from Justice (1998), pp. 251-253.

MAINE

Name	Age	Nationality	Photo

Jerzy Sidor — 43 — —

December 29, 1998. Monmouth:

Cops claim Mr. Sidor charged out of his house, attacked a trooper with a sword and refused to drop it. State Trooper Don Armstrong fired 3 shots, hitting Mr. Sidor at least twice and killing him. Mr. Sidor had a long history of mental illness. State troopers and a mental health worker had gone to his house to take him for a mental evaluation, although it is not clear what prompted them to do so. Trooper Armstrong was placed on paid administrative leave while the attorney general's office investigates the shooting. The victim is survived by his mother and sister. **Source:** Associated Press, 12/30/98

Joshua Williams — 18 — —

October 11, 1997. near Standish:

Josh Williams was being chased at high speeds by Cumberland County sheriffs when his car crashed into a van, killing him and the couple in the van (Richard & Phyllis Ham) and injuring Josh's passenger, 16-year-old Ryan Selby. Cops claim they began pursuing Josh for driving erratically at high speed, forcing other drivers to swerve and avoid him. After half a mile, he crashed into a stop sign, then allegedly backed up and tried to hit an approaching deputy (he missed), then took off again at high speeds. Police deny reports that a deputy pulled a gun on Josh. Cops also claim they stopped the pursuit when speeds reached 85 mph, but continued following him for 11 miles. However, these same cops arrived at the scene of the crash 30 seconds after it occurred, and another cop who started pursuit when he saw Josh go by arrived 10 to 12 seconds after the crash, indicating that the pursuit was still on. Josh reportedly ran a red light and hit the couple's van. He died later at the hospital. He may have been worried about getting stopped because his license was suspended for failing to pay a ticket. Josh, a senior at Portland High School, was described by an assistant principal as "a friendly, outgoing student who stood by his friends.... Joshua certainly was a giving sort of person, always rooting for the underdog. This really is a terrible tragedy." The assistant principal said Josh would stop by his office from time to time "to ask him to be patient and tolerant with students having problems." **Source:** Portland Press Herald (Portland, ME), 10/13/97; The Indianapolis Star, 10/13/97; Boston Globe, 10/18/97

Phyllis Ham — 58 — —
Richard Ham — 58 — —

October 11, 1997. near Standish:

Mr. and Mrs. Ham were killed when Joshua Williams, a teenager being pursued by police in a high-speed chase, allegedly ran a red light and hit their van. The Ham's were from Indianapolis and were visiting family in Maine. They would have celebrated their 38th wedding anniversary two days later. They were described by their son as "very family-oriented, devoted to their 3 children and 9 grandchildren." **Source:** Portland Press Herald (Portland, ME), 10/13/97; The Indianapolis Star, 10/13/97; Boston Globe, 10/18/97

Dorothy Applebee — 65 — —

September 3, 1997. Ellsworth (Rte. 172):

Ms. Applebee was killed when her car was broadsided by State Trooper Daniel Ryan's cruiser as he traveled at least 64 mph (14 mph above the speed limit) to a non-emergency call. Ms. Applebee was backing out of a friend's driveway after an evening of playing cards and was killed instantly. A witness whose car Trooper Ryan passed about a half mile before the crash estimated the cop was going 75-85 mph. On Oct. 21, 1997, the Hancock County DA announced that he was not charging Trooper Ryan with anything, not even speeding, saying that the accident would have occurred even if the cop had obeyed the speed limit. A friend of the victim criticized the investigation, saying, "He [Trooper Ryan] was not in control of his vehicle that night. Nothing will make me believe that man was in control." She also questioned why he had not even gotten a speeding ticket. **Source:** Bangor Daily News, 10/22/97

| Michelle Theriault | 31 | — |

May 18, 1997. Scarborough:
Scorborough police began chasing an allegedly speeding car in which Ms. Theriault was a passenger. She was thrown from the car and killed when the driver lost control and crashed during the high-speed chase. **Source:** Portland Press Herald (Portland, ME), 10/12/97

| David Foster Davis, Jr. | 26 | — |

July 13, 1995. Gardiner:
Mr. Davis crashed his car and died as he was being chased by Gardiner police. The victim was from Randolph. **Source:** Portland Press Herald (Portland, ME), 10/12/97

| Henry Seekamp | 22 | — |

July 13, 1994. —:
Mr. Seekamp, of Scarborough, was being chased by state police when he crashed into a tractor trailer at 60 mph. He was killed in the accident. Cops claim he was trying to commit suicide. **Source:** Portland Press Herald (Portland, ME), 10/12/97

| Sandra Chase | 54 | — |

April 21, 1994. Androscoggin County:
Ms. Chase was killed when an Androscoggin County deputy who was chasing 2 speeding cars crashed into the car in which she was riding, killing her. Ms. Chase was from Poland, ME. **Source:** Portland Press Herald (Portland, ME), 10/12/97

| Katherine A. Hegarty | 51 | *white* |

May 26, 1992. Dennistown Plantation:
Kathy confronted some campers who were trespassing on her land and asked them to put out their camp fire, which posed a forest fire hazard in the dry climate. When they ignored her repeated requested, she got a rifle and fired 7 shots into the air. The campers went and complained to the police, and five officers went to her cabin around 12:30 a.m. When she refused to come out, they kicked in the door and shot her dead.

MARYLAND

Name	Age	Nationality	Photo
Lucas Fitigu	late 20s / early 30s	*Ethiopian*	

July 27, 1999. Beltway (near MD-VA border) (?):
Cops in Virginia reportedly saw Mr. Fitigu driving 52 mph in a 35 mph zone near the Virginia-Maryland border and tried to pull him over. He allegedly tried to outrun the cops and figured that if he crossed the state line into the Maryland, the police would stop chasing him. Virginia police chased him at high speeds across the state line until he crashed into a wall. A fireman pulled him out of the car, injured but very much alive. Then, in front of witnesses, a cop shot him point blank in the head and killed him. The authorities claim Mr. Fitigu had a gun and that he shot himself in the head. Police refused to do an autopsy, and the victim's family tried to get custody of the body to have their own independent autopsy done. Police tried to ruin the victim's reputation, claiming they found $1000 cash and 1 1/2 pounds of marijuana in his car. A friend of the victim's brother said that this was probably a lie and that this was not the first time Lucas Fitigu had been falsely accused of criminal activity. In an earlier incident, he was accused of being involved in an extortion racket and a case of arson, even though he was in Ethiopia at the time. The Philadelphia Inquirer printed a front-page apology when this inconsistency was exposed, but media have reportedly resurrected these charges in an attempt to further smear the victim's reputation and to justify his death. **Source:** friend of victim's brother

Unidentified Man	—	—

September 9, 1998. Prince George's County:

An unidentified man was stopped by U.S. Park police for speeding. While still in the driver's seat, he allegedly turned and opened fire on two cops who approached the car. The motorist was shot dead at the scene. **Source:** The Washington Post, 9/10/98

James Hill	29	—

September 7, 1998. Baltimore:

Baltimore police approached James Hill, of Park Heights, to search him. He allegedly reached into his waistband for a semiautomatic handgun. Cops shot him in the shoulder and the stomach. He died at the hospital. **Source:** The Baltimore Sun, 9/8/98

Bryan Steven Howser	23	—

August 17, 1998. Glen Burnie:

Mr. Howser was allegedly involved in a domestic dispute. He was shot twice in the chest and killed by Police Officer Peter Scarpetta, who claimed that Mr. Howser brandished a "long kitchen knife ... in a threatening manner." Mr. Howser's wife, their son, and infant child were in the home when Mr. Howser was killed. **Source:** The Baltimore Sun, 8/19/1998

Parrish Michael Spinoso	22	—

June 7, 1998. Howard County Detention Center:

Parrish died alone in his jail cell 42 hours after being arrested on charges of selling heroin to undercover cops. Parrish, an asthmatic, relied on an inhaler. Thin, quiet and cooperative, he described himself as a community college student when arrested. **Source:** Baltimore Sun, 6/9/98

Gary Leonard Sanford	42	—

May 20, 1998. Prince George's County:

Gary was shot once in the abdomen and once in the upper leg and killed by a Prince George's County Police Officer, Cpl. Joseph M. Palmieri, at the Citgo gas station at Baltimore Ave. & Madison St. around 2:15 a.m. He was unarmed. Cops later said they found a half-empty beer can and urine outside the van, hardly capital offenses. Cpl. Palmieri saw two men standing near a van at the closed gas station and asked them to show their hands. Gary complied, but police say he then appeared to reach behind his back. Cpl. Palmieri fired two shots. The officer was placed on paid administrative leave (paid vacation) pending an investigation, but a police department spokesperson said it appeared that Cpl. Palmieri acted properly. Gary's family expressed anger at the killing and accused the cops of being trigger-happy. His girlfriend said, "I feel it was wrong. The police were the ones with the guns, the ones in the position of power. They were armed, and Gary wasn't. He must have just been reaching for his wallet. That's the first thing most people would do." Gary's daughter said, "If he [the cop] didn't see a weapon, he shouldn't have fired. I don't think he had a reason to shoot to kill. He could have used other means. Just because you're a police officer, it doesn't mean you always need to shoot." In response to the suggestion that maybe warning shots or shots not aimed to kill could have been fired, a police spokesperson said that such "tactics" were "ineffective." **Source:** The Washington Post, 5/21/98

Vicky Lee Austin	30	—
Jessica Elaine Morgan	5	—

April 13, 1998. Harford County:

Vicky Austin and her daughter, Jessica, were shot and killed in their home by Ms. Austin's boyfriend, Baltimore City Police Officer Michael Edward Thompson. Officer Thompson was indicted on two counts of first-degree murder and other related charges. He was held without bail and suspended without pay from his job pending an administrative investigation. Ms. Austin was remembered by family and friends as a devoted single mother who worked as a dancer in a Baltimore nightclub to support her daughter. Jessica Elaine Morgan was described as an energetic kindergartner who was to return to class from spring break at Hickory Elementary School. **Source:** The Baltimore Sun, 4/15/98 & 5/5/98

| Unidentified Man | — | *Ethiopian* |

April 1998. Gaithersburg:

The victim, who had been in a mental institution, was shot and killed by Police Officer George Boyce, a white cop with a history of racism and hostility toward mentally impaired people. **Source:** Lyrad Productions

| Unidentified Man | 34 | — |

March 31, 1998. West Baltimore:

A group of children told a cop that they had seen a man and a woman allegedly trying to force a "cocaine like substance" in a crying baby's nose. Cops went to rowhouse and reportedly saw the couple fleeing with the baby. They caught the man in an alley, and he supposedly engaged them in a violent struggle. More cops were called to the scene. Civilian witnesses reported that the cops were kicking the victim, who was down on the ground. Police admit an officer placed her foot on the victim to "keep him down." Police allege he suffered a seizure. He died at the hospital. **Source:** The Baltimore Sun, 4/2/98

| Unidentified Man | — | — |

February 1998. Lochearn:

Police Officer Dana S. Austin killed his ex-girlfriend's boyfriend, held his ex-girlfriend hostage for 16 hours in her home, and then fatally shot himself. **Source:** The Baltimore Sun, 4/15/98

| Yohannis Wondim | — | *Ethiopian* |

January 31, 1988. downtown Baltimore:

Mr. Wondim was shot and killed by a security guard, Kevin Scott. It is reported that the guard had an "ongoing dispute" with the victim. Mr. Wondim's body was found dead in the parking garage office. **Source:** The Baltimore Sun, 2/2/98

| Blanche H. Baker | 50 | — |

January 26, 1998. Baltimore (Govans):

Ms. Baker, a mentally ill woman, was shot at least twice and killed by Baltimore police after she allegedly attacked them with a knife as they answered a call about an armed woman roaming the area. Cops claim the victim had a history of run-ins with the police and was not stopped by their pepper spray. They called her death "unavoidable." **Source:** The Baltimore Sun, 1/26/98

| Derek McIntosh | 25 | — |

January 13, 1998. West Baltimore:

Derek McIntosh was shot and killed by Baltimore City Police Officer Shane C. Stufft. Authorities allege that Officer Stufft saw Mr. McIntosh selling drugs from the trunk of a car. A chase ensued and the two supposedly engaged in a struggle, at which point Derek McIntosh was fatally wounded. A crowd gathered at the scene to protest and condemn the shooting. **Source:** The Baltimore Sun, 1/14/98

| Kevin P. Ferguson | 43 | — |

December 6, 1997. Glen Burnie:

Kevin P. Ferguson was killed by a single police bullet that struck him in the back of the neck. Cops claim Mr. Ferguson drove a stolen Mercedes-Benz through a police roadblock around 6 a.m., rammed three cruisers, drove onto a sidewalk and ran from them. Police did not divulge how many shots were fired. **Source:** The Baltimore Sun, 12/10/97

| **Frank Julius Bochnowicz** | 76 | — |

October 29, 1997. northeast Baltimore:

Mr. Bochnowicz, a retired steelworker, was killed when his station wagon was broadsided by a car being chased by police. Cops had stopped the car for allegedly having license plates from a stolen truck, then began pursuit when the car sped away. Mr. Bochnowicz was in the process of helping a relative keep an appointment with a doctor when he was killed. The victim's only son, Frank Bochnowicz, Jr., was not informed by the police that his father's death was the result of a police chase. Cops claimed they had stopped chasing the car two miles before the crash. The teenage driver of the car being chased was charged with felony vehicular manslaughter. **Source:** The Baltimore Sun, 10/30/97

| **Lucio Rodas** | 33 | *Salvadoran* |

October 12, 1997. near Hagerstown:

Lucio Rodas died when Maryland State police officers subdued him as he rode a Greyhound bus bound from Cleveland for Washington. Around 3 a.m., he reportedly began pacing the aisle and speaking in Spanish, which no one else on the bus understood. He allegedly tried to pry open the door, grabbed the steering wheel form the driver, tried to kick out side windows, and tried to kick and bite passengers attempting to restrain him. The driver pulled into a parking lot and summoned the police. When they restrained him, he went limp and vomited. CPR was unsuccessful and he died. Authorities claimed he had no visible injuries and did not appear to be a victim of excessive force, so the officers involved remained on regular duty during the investigation. **Source:** The Baltimore Sun, 10/13/97

| **Dwayne K. Waiters** | 21 | — |

October 10, 1997. Prince George's County:

Dwayne K. Waiters was shot several times in the upper body and killed by two Prince George's County police officers, Cpl. Robert P. Hettenhouser and Officer Corey Joyner, who had been summoned to his apartment. Cops claim that Mr. Waiters was choking his father when they arrived at the apartment and that they only shot him when he reached for a kitchen knife. **Source:** Washington Times, 10/11/97

| **Christina Hopper** | 31 | — |

August 31, 1997. Laurel:

Christina was shot and killed by her ex-boyfriend, a Prince George's County police officer, Cpl. Paul David Lancaster. Cpl. Lancaster claims he shot Christina in self-defense after she attacked him with Mace and a knife. Cpl. Lancaster was indicted for first-degree murder by a special grand jury that reviews all police shootings in Prince George's County. **Source:** The Washington Post, 4/17/98

| **Ronald Wilson** | 32 | *white* |

September 1997. Port Deposit:

County sheriff pursued Ronald and claimed to have engaged in a struggle to the death. Eyewitnesses say he was raising his hands to surrender when he was shot. Wilson's family said he was a frequent victim of police harassment.

| **James Quarles III** | 22 | *African American* |

August 9, 1997. Baltimore (Lexington Market):

Mr. Quarles was shot dead by one of four cops surrounding him as he stood in a marketplace holding what cops claimed was an eight-inch knife. In fact, it was a 3" pocket knife. According to his sister, bystanders said he was using the knife to reopen a pack of socks which he bought wholesale in order to resell. The cops claim he lunged at them, but witnesses and a videotape clearly contradict this account. James was setting the knife down when he was shot. The cop who shot him, Charles Smothers, was allowed to work and carry his gun even though he was on probation for shooting at a car occupied by his former girlfriend. Officer Smothers said he was sorry he shot Quarles but added, "I know it had to be done." No charges were filed against Officer Smothers despite protest marches and demands that he be charged with murder. The State's Attorney did not even bring the case before a grand jury. However, the city settled a lawsuit filed by his family for an undisclosed amount. Unity for Action, Concerned Citizens for Police Accountability, and the Baltimore ACLU took up the case. **Source:** The Baltimore Sun, 8/17/97 &9/10/97; Unity for Action (anti-police brutality group)

Andre Boone   23   —

March 21, 1997. Columbia:
Marine Cpl. Andre Boone was shot and killed by his stepfather, former Maryland State Trooper James M. Harding, Jr. Trooper Harding was convicted of second-degree murder and sentenced to 25 years in prison. During his trial, Trooper Harding claimed that when he fired his pistol-grip shotgun, he meant only to scare Mr. Boone., who had allegedly threatened to burn down their house. Andre Boone's mother recalled his recent appointment as a noncommissioned officer as part of the Marine Corps unit that guards the president at the White House. **Source:** The Baltimore Sun, 4/25/98

Daniel Edward James   33   —

February 18, 1997. Carroll County (Baltimore?):
Daniel was shot and killed by a state police sniper around 8:30 a.m. outside his parents' house on the 6500 block of Day View Drive after a 9 1/2 hour standoff when he allegedly shot at (but missed) the cops. His parents were away at the time. Daniel, who had "a long history of mental health problems," was wearing camouflage gear and supposedly had a rifle, a shotgun, a 24-inch machete and other weapons. According to the authorities, he had refused to talk to police negotiators throughout the standoff as his parents house burned down. Cops claim they only fired after Daniel raised his rifle, fired at them and then refused to drop the weapon. **Source:** The Baltimore Sun, 5/1/97

Tiffani Carrington   19   —

December 1996. Charles County:
Ms. Carrington, a volunteer firefighter, was killed while on a coffee run from the firehouse just after midnight when he car was struck by a cruiser driven by Charles County Deputy Sheriff Jody Powell. Ms. Carrington's passenger, Ann Damon, was injured but survived. Deputy Powell caused the accident by driving through a red light while trying to join a police pursuit of a drunk driver. Ms. Carrington's family filed a wrongful death lawsuit against the state and the county, charging that Deputy Powell was negligent and failed to follow procedures by not stopping at the red light. Firefighters held a reception to mark the one-year anniversary of their colleague's death and expressed anger about the case, saying that the sheriff should have apologized and instituted new safety procedures. Deputy Powell was placed on three weeks administrative leave and fined but cleared of criminal charges. **Source:** The Washington Post, 12/27/97

Julie Mead   16   *white*

November 21, 1996. Laurel:
Julie called 911 saying she was going to commit suicide. She walked outside with a pellet gun, and the cops shot and killed her. **Source:** SLP form

Cochise Ornandez Daughtry   18   *Black*

September 2, 1996. Annapolis (Robinwood):
Cochise was shot and killed, and his friend, Vernon Eugene Estep, Jr., (age 19, also Black), was shot and critically injured, both by Annapolis Police Officer David W. Garcia, who fired four shots allegedly to stop the pair from beating a 40-year-old Black man. In January 1997, a protest of over 100 people at City Hall was organized by the Black Political Forum and Friends of Black Annapolis. They said called it a case of "young Black men dying at the hands of zealous white police officers." **Source:** The Baltimore Sun, 1/14/97

Keith Devi Hill   26   *Black*   👁

January 26, 1996. Salisbury:

Mr. Hill was shot in the chest by Maryland State Police Cpl. Michael A. Lewis. Cpl. Lewis pulled him over on the highway, reportedly for speeding, and claims he smelled marijuana. He ordered Mr. Hill out of the car and noticed a bulge in his pocket. Mr. Hill emptied his pocket, pulling out a large amount of cash. The cop claims he saw some marijuana. Mr. Hill allegedly started fighting when the cop tried to arrest him. Cpl. Lewis maced the victim, who then allegedly got into his car, refused orders to get out, and supposedly tried to run down the cop. Cpl. Lewis opened fire, hitting Mr. Hill, allegedly in self-defense. Mr. Hill allegedly drove away, was forced off the road by a tractor-trailer, and later died at the hospital. Cpl. Lewis was put on paid administrative leave during an investigation. Mr. Hill is survived by his wife, his parents, his four children, several siblings and large extended family. He worked as a systems analyst and was a manager for the rapper "Smooth The Hustler." His funeral program described him as "a soft spoken distinguished gentleman at all times. He made his dreams a reality." **Source:** The Daily Times, dates unknown; victim's funeral program

---

Unidentified Woman   —   —

1996. Baltimore:

The victim, a mentally ill woman, was shot and killed by police after she allegedly attacked them with a knife and did not "succumb to pepper-spray." **Source:** The Baltimore Sun, 1/26/98

Michael Donald Reed   32 (?)   *white*

February 1995. Prince George's County:

Michael Reed was shot to death by Prince George's County Police Officer Wang Cheney 20 months after the same officer shot and killed Archie "Artie" Elliott, III. Officer Cheney claimed he thought Mr. Reed was reaching for a gun, but no gun was found, and he turned out to be unarmed. Even after committing two murders, Officer Cheney remained on the force. **Source:** communication from Lyrad Productions; www.afamerica.com/elliott/

Donovan M. Morant   18   *African American*

August 29, 1994. Hagerstown Correctional Facility:

Donovan had an asthma attack and did not receive emergency treatment. He was given no medicine and as a result died in jail. Other inmates say he was wheezing and a guard said, "Well, he should know how to act." Donovan had been in jail for 7 months and was due to be released in only 22 days when he died. **Source:** SLP form

---

Thappanika Ang   24   *Cambodian*

February 26, 1994. Prince George's County:

D.C. Police Officers Keith DuBeau and James Sulla and two other cops opened fire on Mr. Ang's car after a chase that began in Virginia, went through D.C. and ended in Maryland. According to the medical examiner, the victim's car was hit with 39 police bullets, including 13 in the trunk. The victim was hit five times, with the fatal shot hitting him in the back. Although Mr. Ang's car was boxed in by five D.C. police cars, cops claim he "started moving, ramming cars and scattering the officers," according to the newspaper. Officer DuBeau emptied his clip, firing 18 shots, and Officer Sulla fired eight to ten shots as the car drove away from them, allegedly toward other police cars. Mr. Ang worked as a baker and had left home after a fight with his family a few days earlier. Authorities claimed he had cocaine in his blood. An internal investigation found that the shooting was unjustified because the cops fired their guns after the threat to them had passed. Officers DuBeau and Sulla got five day suspensions as punishment. Their attorney complained that this was too harsh. In July 1996, the city settled a lawsuit filed by the victim's family for $10,000. **Source:** The Washington Post, 1998

Archie "Artie" Elliott III	24	Black	👁

June 18, 1993. Prince George's County (Forestville):

Mr. Elliott was driving a car when he was stopped for weaving by Prince George's County police. He was wearing only shorts and sneakers (no socks or shirt), and when searched, was found to be unarmed. He was intoxicated but very cooperative. The police handcuffed him behind his back and put him in the front seat of a police car with the windows rolled up. Cops claim that the handcuffed, unarmed Mr. Elliot then pointed a gun at them. Officers Jason Leavitt and Wang Cheney fired 22 shots, hitting Mr. Elliott 14 times and killing him. A grand jury concluded that the officers acted in the line of duty. Twenty months later, Officer Cheney shot and killed Michael Donald Reed. As of Mar. 17, 1999, Joe Madison, a Washington DC talk-show host, was engaged in a hunger strike to demand that the police involved in the murder of Archie Elliott be prosecuted. This case was cited as an important example of the "epidemic of police brutality" at a national news conference held in March 1999 by national Black leaders calling for a National March for Justice on Apr. 3, 1999. **Source:** Seattle Medium, 3/17/99; communication from Lyrad Productions; www.afamerica.com/elliott/.

Becky Garnet	18 (?)	Black	

Date Unknown. Gaithersburg:

Ms. Garnet was shot in the back of the head and killed by Officer Christopher Albrecht as she sat in her car during a traffic stop. The cop allegedly thought she had a gun. It turned out she had a bag of potato chips. **Source:** Lyrad Productions

MASSACHUSETTS

Name	Age	Nationality	Photo
Unidentified Man	—	—	

September 12, 1998. Auburn (Worcester suburb):

This man was shot and killed by police after being pulled over in his car near a busy shopping mall. Cops approached his car with guns drawn and shouted for him to keep his hands visible. They opened fire when he allegedly reached for or pulled a gun (another police account, earlier in the newspaper account, claims he was waving a gun and refused to put it down). A witness reported that the man was shot in the neck. Cops claimed the man was a suspect in a recent murder in Millbury. **Source:** The Boston Globe, 9/13/98

Unidentified Man	—	—	

September 5, 1998. Groton (Rte. 40):

The victim lost control of his motorcycle and crashed while being chased by a Westford police officer who was trying to stop him for traffic violations. The man was killed. A female passenger was injured. **Source:** The Boston Globe, 9/7/98

Robert J. Albanese	47	—	

July 1, 1998. Haverhill (Rte. 125):

Robert was killed on his 25th wedding anniversary in a head-on collision with a driver fleeing from police. He was returning from New Hampshire, where he had gone to buy a Powerball ticket. The driver of the other car, Elias Jabour, was also killed. **Source:** The Boston Herald, 7/3/98

Elias J. Jabour	48	Lebanese	

July 1, 1998. Haverhill (Rte. 125):

Elias was being chased by police after someone called to complain about his driving. He got into a fatal head-on collision that killed himself and Robert J. Albanese, the driver of the other car. Cops claim that when they tried to pull Elias over, he dragged a cop six feet when the officer tried to pull him from his car. Cops say they do not know why Elias, who had no criminal record, was fleeing from them, and speculated that he may have been drunk. The cops also claim they broke off the pursuit 30 seconds before the accident occurred. Elias' landlady described him as "a very nice man." He left behind his girlfriend, with whom he lived, and their 4-year-old son. **Source:** The Boston Herald, 7/3/98

| **Errol Williams** | 32 | — |

May 23, 1998. Dorchester:

Errol was shot and killed by Boston police patrolman James Griffin around 3 a.m. on Bowdoin Ave. near Mallon Rd. Officer Griffin fired several shots at Errol's gray Ford Escort, shattering the driver's side window, hitting the windshield and killing Errol. Cops claim they found a .45-caliber semi-automatic handgun, cocked and loaded with hollow-point bullets on the victim's body as they dragged him from his car, allegedly to give first aid. But the police say the gun was not why they shot Errol. Rather, they claim it was because he accelerated his car toward Officer Griffin as the two cops, Officer Griffin and his partner, Vadan Scantlebury, approached. Cops claim to have found, either on the victim or in his car, thirty-three $20 bags of crack, $500 in cash and some Jamaican money. They claim that Errol had an "extremely violent history," had been arrested many times in Boston and "was believed to be at the center of a crack-cocaine ring that was thriving in the area." Police Department spokespeople put out a press release, which the media dutifully reported, that both cops had "great reputations" and were "devout members of their respective churches." The Police Department and the media also tried to paint Officer Griffin as the victim, reporting how distraught and traumatized he supposedly was over the shooting. Officers Griffin and Scantlebury were placed on paid administrative leave (paid vacation) during the investigation of the shooting. This was described as "standard procedure." **Source:** The Boston Globe, 5/24/98 & 5/28/948

| **Travis Flanagan** | 23 | — |
| **Frank Gonsalves** | 17 | — |

May 16, 1998. Falmouth:

An unnamed officer attempted to pull a car over for violations and gave chase. The officer gave up the chase and found the car crashed a few moments later. Travis and Frank, both passengers in the car, were killed. The car's driver and another passenger were injured. **Source:** Associated Press, 5/16/98

| **Unidentified man** | — | — |

April 27, 1998. New Bedford:

This man was shot and killed by a police SWAT team at a McDonald's where he was allegedly holding about fifteen hostages. The man and an accomplice had allegedly been robbing the restaurant when police arrived around 9:30 p.m. on April 26, prompting a 2 1/2 hour standoff that ended shortly after midnight when the SWAT team stormed in. None of the hostages were injured. The other suspect managed to escape in a car and reportedly had a hostage with him. Cops claim the pair fired at them from inside the restaurant. **Source:** The Boston Globe, 4/27/98 & 5/11/98

| **Royford Lewis, Jr.** | 21 | — |

February 22, 1998. Boston (Dorchester):

A man fleeing from police in a high-speed chase crashed into Royford's car at 4:15 a.m. at Dorchester's Four Corners, killing him. Police engaged in pursuit because the car had allegedly run some stop signs and a license plate check showed that it was stolen. The driver of the car being chased was charged with motor vehicle homicide. Police claim that the chase had been called off when the accident occurred. The chase began in Roxbury (Boston). **Source:** The Boston Globe, 2/24/98; AP, 2/23/98

| **Michael Revoredo** | 26 | — |

December 25, 1997. Fall River:

Michael was shot once in the abdomen and killed by police around 4 a.m. on Christmas day. Michael had supposedly been thrown out of a party on the third floor of a building on High Street. A friend let him into a second-floor apartment to clean up and then called 911 when Michael allegedly grabbed a knife from the kitchen. Michael was trying to get back into the party when cops arrived. Cops claim he threatened them with the knife and they shot him. He died several hours later at the hospital. Michael's aunt said, "There were five cops around and they had to kill him? Police are supposed to be trained to do a job -- they had to kill him?" Another aunt said that that "[someone] who knew Michael wanted to come down and help talk him into dropping the knife, but the police wouldn't let her. So they shot him." **Source:** The Boston Globe, 12/27/97

Michael Clougherty   30   —

December 21, 1997. Boston (Dorchester):
Mr. Clougherty, a laborer, was shot and killed by Boston Police Officer Jose Ruiz outside the China Pagoda restaurant on Dorchester Ave. Cops claim the victim was armed with a meat cleaver and lunged at another man. Mr. Clougherty was reportedly drunk. **Source:** The Boston Globe, 4/21/98 & 5/24/98

Gary Michaels   —   *Black*

November 30, 1997. Walpole State Prison:
Described by his family as very strong in both character and beliefs, Gary was put in Departmental Disciplinary Unit (lockdown). These units have slick walls and no devices where someone could hang themselves. Despite this, he was "found hanging." **Source:** Article from Holbrook Teter

---

Shawn Mottram   24   —

October 11, 1997. Rte. 213 (near Metheun Mall):
Shawn was shot in the back and killed as he ran away from State Trooper Joseph Stone. Cops claim that Shawn was driving a car erratically and a license plate check showed it was stolen. A car chase ensued. Cops claim that Shawn rammed two police cruisers that had been chasing him, then got out of the car and ran, leaving Frederick J. Mottram, his father, in the car. Frederick Mottram was arrested. Shawn allegedly ran away and scaled a fence with Officer Stone in pursuit. Cops originally said that Officer Stone's gun was never drawn. Later they were forced to admit that his gun was drawn but claimed that he fired it accidentally when it got snagged on the fence. One of Shawn's cousins disputed this, saying, "There's no doubt about it. They [the police] wanted him off the street. They didn't like him....He knew the cop didn't like him. He seen the cop. He turned around and went the opposite direction." She also said that Shawn did not have a gun. Police refused to comment on this. Shawn's father was informed of his son's death by a priest while in jail. The media published Shawn's arrest record , reporting that he used to be in a car thief gang. Shawn's cousin explained that that was no longer the case. The media portrayed both him and Officer Stone as victims, saying Stone was "distraught" and "devastated" by the shooting. Officer Stone was placed on paid administrative leave (paid vacation). Shawn is survived by his fiancee, his father, his cousin and other family members. **Source:** The Boston Globe, 10/15/97; The Boston Herald, 10/13/97

Clifford P. Buchanan   49   —

October 4, 1997. Hanover Mall (Rte. 53):
Mr. Buchanan was struck and killed by a speeding car being chased by police as he crossed Rte. 53 in front of the Hanover Mall. Cops claimed they had called off the chase several minutes before the accident occurred. The driver, who was reportedly drunk, later crashed into a police car and was charged in connection with Mr. Buchanan's death. The victim was described as "a nice person, very loved," "a good guy who never hurt anyone," who spent much of his time caring for his elderly parents who had recently been injured when they were hit by a car. **Source:** The Boston Globe, 10/6/97 & 10/7/97; The Boston Herald, 10/6/97

Abel Remy   36   *Haitian*

August 1, 1997. MCI-Walpole Prison:
Mr. Remy, a musician and gospel singer, was serving a prison sentence for indecent assault. He was in the process of appealing his conviction when he died on Aug. 12, 1997 -- 11 days after he was severely beaten by prison guards. Authorities maintained that he died of natural causes. The official cause of death was listed as cardiac arrest resulting from a blood clot in the leg. An autopsy report cited dehydration as the cause of death. But Haitian activists and members of the victim's family contend that he was murdered and that there was a cover-up. They demanded an investigation. It was known that Mr. Remy "clashed frequently with prison officials.... [and] was beaten by guards on several occasions." A lawyer involved in the case said, "We are here because it is up to the prison authorities... to ensure that the death penalty will not be administered in prisons.... The fact that after there was a beating on Aug. 1... and then he died on Aug. 12 - that alone ought to have triggered an independent investigation." **Source:** The Bay State Banner, 9/25/97

Reggie Regan — —

August 1997. Walpole State Prison:

Regan was put on suicide watch, meaning that he was under constant surveillance. He was put naked in a cell with only a mattress and a blanket, but he was somehow "discovered hanging." **Source:** Article from Holbrook Teter

Benjamin J. Schoolfield — *Black*

February 1994. Springfield (downtown):

Ben, who was unarmed, was shot and killed by a white cop, Officer Donald J. Brown, after being stopped at a downtown intersection for driving a van that was falsely reported as stolen. Cops claim Ben was accidentally shot after a struggle, but witnesses said that no struggle occurred. In 1994, a grand jury refused to indict Officer Brown, finding no evidence of criminal behavior. Fellow cops then held a congratulatory party for Officer Brown and presented him with a ham. Black leaders in Springfield commented that this reflected the Ku Klux Klan practice of rewarding whites who murdered Blacks. Ben's family filed a civil suit in federal court against the city of Springfield and Officer Brown. On June 15, 1998, the jury found that Officer Brown had used excessive force and had violated Ben's civil rights. The city was found liable for negligence. The jury awarded the family $2 million, which the judge reduced to $1.1 million; $100,000 from the city (reduced from $1 million due to a state law) and $1 million from Officer Brown. Officer Brown and the city of Springfield said they planned to appeal the verdict. Officer Brown remained on the force. Springfield has a history of tension between police and communities of color. **Source:** The Boston Globe, 6/22/98

Rev. Accelyne Williams 75 —

1994. Boston:

Rev. Williams died of a heart attack when the Boston Police SWAT team burst into his home to carry out a drug raid on what turned out to be the wrong apartment. **Source:** The Boston Globe, 1/11/98 & 5/11/98

Unidentified Man 47 —

August 1993. Boston (?):

This man was shot an killed by a cop. Police allege that he confronted the cop with a knife. **Source:** The Boston Globe, 5/24/98

Cristino Wilfredo Hernández 38 *Salvadoran*

July 16, 1993. Worcester:

Cristino was arrested for disturbing the peace. In the process of the arrest, the two arresting officers pepper-sprayed, beat, dragged and threw Cristino down the stairs to the ground floor. They sat on him and twisted his shackled hands backward past his head. Cristino lost and never regained consciousness, dying ten days later. The cops were placed on administrative duty and, as of June 1998, have not been sanctioned by the Police Department or the City of Worcester. A wrongful death civil suit has been filed by Cristino's family after an inquest failed to find criminal fault with police conduct. **Source:** SLP form (via e-mail)

Hector Morales 19 *Latino*

November 1990. Boston (near Egleston Square):

Hector was shot and killed by Officers Thomas Gomperts and Darrin Greeley. The two cops approached Hector, an alleged gang member, and asked "What's up?" Hector supposedly fired several blasts of birdshot from a shotgun, at which point the cops shot and killed him. The cops, who were wearing bulletproof vests, suffered only minor injuries. Hector was a self-taught artist and a talented musician who had "shown signs of wanting to break out of the gang life." **Source:** The Boston Globe, 3/4/98

MICHIGAN

Name	Age	Nationality	Photo
Brian Hangsleben	49	—	

May 6, 1999. East Grand Forks:
Mr. Hangsleben was shot and killed by police after allegedly threatening them with a knife. Cops claim he had killed his mother and seriously wounded his father. **Source:** New York Daily News, 5/7/99

Janice Harrison	45	—	

February 21, 1999. Detroit:
Janice Harrison was shot and killed by her husband, a Detroit police investigator, who then fatally shot himself. According to police, Officer Harrison, who worked out of the second precinct, was depressed because he had cancer. **Source:** Detroit Oct. 22 Coalition

James Anthony Thomas	27	—	

February 7, 1999. Detroit-Canadian Ambassador Bridge:
Mr. Thomas tried to drive his pickup truck off the Detroit-Canadian Ambassador Bridge into the water but failed. He began walking toward the U.S.-Canadian border. Cops claim that when they arrived, Mr. Thomas momentarily turned toward them with a gun in his hand. Three cops opened fire. Mr. Thomas died of multiple gunshot wounds. **Source:** Detroit Oct. 22 Coalition

Darryl Paul Gates	21	—	

February 5, 1999. Detroit:
Mr. Gates was shot and killed by police during a prostitution sting in which one officer was reportedly killed and another wounded. **Source:** Detroit Oct. 22 Coalition

Demetrius Posey-Horsely	19	*African American*	

December 5, 1998. Detroit:
Witnesses say Demetrius was shot to death immediately after exiting his car during a traffic stop by Detroit police from the ninth precinct. Although not a suspect, Demetrius was killed the same night that a ninth precinct officer was shot to death and two other officers wounded in what police termed an ambush shooting. **Source:** Detroit Oct. 22 Coalition

Theodore Laroque	28	*Latino*	

September 14, 1998. Detroit:
Mr. Laroque was shot four times and killed by Police Officer Anthony Goree, a member of Mayor Dennis Archer's security detail, after a verbal altercation resulting from a traffic incident outside the officer's house. The cop was presumably off-duty. The victim was unarmed. **Source:** Detroit Oct. 22 Coalition

Bernard Salazar	21	*Latino*	

September 1998. Detroit (southwest side):
Mr. Salazar was shot in the head and killed by police who broke into his home on Homer Street under the pretense of conducting a drug raid. According to friends, Mr. Salazar was given no chance to explain or to surrender after police broke down his door. All over Detroit, similar drug raids were conducted and continued at least through Aug. 1999. They resulted in an unknown number of injuries and fatalities, including the shooting of a 16-year-old honor student at Mackenzie High School in October. **Source:** Detroit Oct. 22 Coalition

Cora Bell Jones	79	*African American*

August 15, 1998. Detroit:

Someone did a drive-by shooting on Ms. Jones' house. About 20 cops arrived, stormed into the house, and started beating her great-grandson, who was allegedly coming down the stairs with a gun to protect his family from whomever did the drive-by. Ms. Jones, who had Altzheimer's, was partially blind and deaf, and was confined to a wheelchair. She confronted the police, yelling at them to stop beating her great-grandson. The cops maced her. Her son begged the police to let him deal with her, but they shot her in the chest at point-blank range and killed her instead. Cops claim she had a knife. Her family said she might not have even known that the people beating her great-grandson were cops. The police called the shooting a "proper use of force." Homicide Inspector William Rice said, "A shot was fired and it went where it was directed." **Source:** Detroit Oct. 22 Coalition

Wanda Katrell	39	—

August 1, 1998. Detroit:

Ms. Katrell and her fiance were crossing the street when they were knocked down by a Detroit police car. Ms. Katrell was put in a coma and died several weeks later. Her fiance went through the windshield of the cop car but survived. As of Aug. 26, 1998, Ms. Katrell's family said they had not yet heard from the police regarding the accident. **Source:** States News Service/Yahoo Michigan, 8/26/98

Wayne Garrison	47	—

July 26, 1998. Detroit:

Mr. Garrison was shot and killed in his apartment building on W. Chicago Blvd. by police. Neighbors reported that he was a peaceful, Bible-reading man who had recently been treated for depression. According to news accounts, he was unclothed and hiding in a closet when he was shot. **Source:** Detroit Oct. 22 Coalition

Tong Kue	36	*Laotian*

June 18, 1998. Detroit:

Mr. Kue was killed by police. **Source:** SLP form (via e-mail)

Mark Gaydos	37	—

June 10, 1998. Redford Township:

Mr. Gaydos was shot and killed by Redford Township Police Sgt. James Turner after being pulled over for squealing his tires. He was reportedly driving with a suspended license. Cops claim that as they were about to search him, he ran down the block, pulled out a gun, and shot Sgt. Turner's partner in the thigh. Officer Turner chased him and fired at him, then returned to help his wounded partner. Mr. Gaydos supposedly returned and fired more shots before Sgt. Turner shot him dead. **Source:** The Detroit News, 6/12/98 & 6/14/98

David Allen Dowd	40	—

June 6, 1998. Southgate:

Mr. Dowd was shot to death by Southgate Police Officers Bernard Priest and Mark Allen Farrah. Cops claim that Mr. Dowd tried to run them down when they attempted to stop him for not having a license plate light. Mr. Dowd's companion, Nicole Rittenberry, was shot in the leg and wounded. **Source:** Detroit Oct. 22 Coalition

Charles Prins	42	—

May 8, 1998. White Cloud:

According to police, Charles Prins shot and wounded two Ionia County deputies when they tried to serve him with a misdemeanor warrant. A week-long manhunt followed. Tracking dogs picked up his scent, and a short foot chase ensued. Charles is alleged to have fired one shot at the pursuing cops. Police fired three shots, hitting him once. Charles died immediately from a shot to the head. **Source:** AP, 5/8/98

| **Unidentified Male** | — | — |

April 27, 1998. Detroit (eastside):
An unidentified male was shot and killed by an off-duty Detroit police officer who works days patrolling the fifth (Jefferson) precinct. The officer claimed that the man tried to rob him. **Source:** Detroit Oct. 22 Coalition

| **Dante Foster** | 21 | — |

March 27, 1998. Royal Oak:
Dante was shot and killed by a cop after allegedly trying to buy a car with phony identification at Diamond Lincoln Mercury. He was unarmed. Police claim they chased him through downtown until he jumped behind the wheel of a 1997 Pontiac Grand Am. Cops claim that the shooting was accidental and that the cop's gun went off during a struggle as Dante was trying to escape from the car. But witnesses disputed the police version of events. In early June, Dante's family's lawyer said that the cop should be charged with murder but the report of the investigation of the incident contained no recommendation for prosecution. **Source:** Chicago Tribune, 3/30/98; The Detroit News, 6/4/98

| **Robert Villareal** | 29 | *Latino* |

March 15, 1998. Detroit:
Mr. Villareal was shot multiple times and trampled in a massive police assault. Police claimed that the victim was attempting to escape out the front door after three officers had been shot. But a friend told the Detroit Oct. 22 Coalition that Mr. Villareal was trapped in the kitchen of the house, where he was summarily executed by the police. The autopsy report showed numerous footprints over his body. **Source:** Detroit Oct. 22 Coalition

| **Amir Saleh** | 31 | *Ethiopian* |

March 12, 1998. Oak Park Jail:
Mr. Salah died of an epileptic seizure in jail as a result of deliberate medical neglect. Jail videotape and testimony from other inmates confirm that he begged for medication that would have saved his life, but the cops at the jail ignored him. Mr. Salah had been taken into custody after being arrested for allegedly exposing himself to two girls and resisting an officer. He had a history of mental illness. He was awaiting a decision on whether to be released to his family or sent to a psychiatric facility. Earlier in the day a judge found him mentally incompetent to stand trial for a previous charge of indecent exposure and resisting arrest. Given this record, Mr. Saleh should not have been brought to jail in the first place. The victim's family filed a $75 million lawsuit against the City of Oak Park and its Public Safety Department. **Source:** Detroit Oct. 22 Coalition

| **Damian Solomon** | 26 | *African American* |

February 12, 1998. Detroit:
Damian Solomon and two companions were stopped by police for allegedly loitering in a vacant lot. Residents in the area said that no one had complained about their presence. Police Officer Marlon Benson shot Mr. Solomon three times at point-blank range in the heart and killed him, supposedly after a chase during which Officer Benson was shot in the hip. Police claimed Damian had a gun, but residents observed cops searching through the area for a weapon after the killing. Residents also complained of constant police harassment. **Source:** Detroit Oct. 22 Coalition

| **Johnny Lee Henderson** | 22 | — |

December 29, 1997. Humphreys County Jail:
Johnny, a burglary suspect, died of appendicitis while in jail. The staff was criticized for not getting help. The sheriff said Johnny did not ask for help. This incident is the second at the jail being investigated by the Department of Justice.

Jimmi Ruth Ratliff   47   *African American*

December 9, 1997. Detroit:

A beautiful professional woman who worked at Blue Cross for 22 years, Jimmi Ratliff was shot to death by police in her apartment at 1300 E. Lafayette. The shooting took place after a horrific assault on her building by an army of police including a SWAT team using tear gas and the latest in modern assault weapons. The police were called by the apartment manager simply because Ms. Ratliff would not allow building staff into her apartment. Although police claim she fired a gun, her sister said that the gun she owned had only been fired twice, at a practice range. Family members called to the scene were not allowed to see or talk to Ms. Ratliff. While guarded by police, they heard Police Chief Benny Napoleon and others cold-bloodedly plan her killing. Ms. Ratliff was shot through the wall of her bedroom by a rifle with an infrared sight. As of Aug., 1999, no justice has been obtained. **Source:** Detroit Oct. 22 Coalition

---

Germaine Brittman   23   —

October 26, 1997. downtown Detroit (near Detroit-Windsor tunnel):

Mr. Brittman hailed a cab, then held the cabdriver at gunpoint. The taxi drove along city streets and, in downtown Detroit, the driver deliberately hit the curb and blew a tire. Mr. Brittman jumped out, reportedly running through traffic and shooting a motorist, who was wounded in the leg. Then, Mr. Brittman allegedly fired shots at law enforcement agents. He died in a hail of gunfire from a Detroit police officer and U.S. Customs and immigration agents. **Source:** The Detroit News, 10/28/97; Houston Chronicle, 10/27/97

Jeffrey Eggart   34   —

October 7, 1997. Auburn Hills (Oakland County) (I-75):

Mr. Eggart was shot in the neck or the head and killed by an Oakland County sheriff's deputy whom he had allegedly dragged with his car for over a quarter of a mile at speeds of up to 45 mph. Cops claim that Mr. Eggart sped away when they pulled him over and tried to administer a sobriety test. He pulled over two miles later, but supposedly took off again, dragging the deputy, after the latter tried to reach into the car to turn off the ignition. **Source:** The Buffalo News, 10/9/97; The Detroit News, 10/8/97

Jesse Smith   35   —

September 18, 1997. Macomb County (Warren):

Jesse was shot and killed by a Warren police officer as he allegedly drove a stolen Jeep Cherokee at the cop. The cop, who was not identified, fired three shots. One of them hit Jesse in the head. Cops claim they spotted the car, which had been reported stolen, on Hoover and followed it onto Dorothy Lane, south of Common. This is an entrance to a condominium complex. It is the only way out. The cop blocked the driveway with his car and then got out to stop Jesse, who allegedly "spun around" and sped at the cop, causing the cop to fire. Jesse lost control of the car, traveling at high speed across several streets and hitting a street sign, a light pole, and a fence before coming to a stop. He died 13 minutes later at the hospital. The Macomb County Prosecutor's office said a week later that the shooting appeared to have been justified, an act of self-defense. The cop who shot Jesse was placed on desk duty pending the outcome of the investigation. **Source:** The Detroit News, 9/25/97

Damita Morton   43   —

September 1997. Wayne County (Highland Park):

Ms. Morton was killed when her car was broad-sided by a reportedly stolen vehicle being chased by Highland Park police. She was on her way to a niece's birthday party. The victim was survived by her seven children and five grandchildren. **Source:** The Detroit News, 10/3/97 & 3/5/98

Dalon Gunn   24   *African American*

July 19, 1997. Detroit:

Dearborn Police Officer Michael Christoff was chasing a suspect who reportedly drove off in a police car. The cop chased the suspect at speeds of up to 90 mph without sirens, crossing the city line into Detroit. Officer Christoff crashed into Ms. Gunn's car and killed her. The State Police found the cop at fault, but Wayne County prosecutors refused to bring charges against him. Ms. Gunn left behind a three-year-old daughter. **Source:** Detroit Oct. 22 Coalition

---

Roy Hoskins   14   *African-American*

April 20, 1997. Detroit:

Roy was shot in the back by Detroit Police Officer James Woods. The cop shot him from inside the police car while Roy was standing still, arms raised, with his back to the officer. He was unarmed at time of death.

Derek Womack   13   —

December 9, 1996. Macomb County:

Thirteen year old Derek Womack was killed when State Troopers James Hanson and David Jeffries, driving separate vehicles, hit a car they were chasing for erratic driving. The car they rammed was knocked off the road and into Derek, killing him. The victim's parents filed a $10 million lawsuit against the two state troopers, charging that they hit the car deliberately in a needless effort to end the chase. The family's attorney said that the police had no pressing reason to capture the man they were chasing and that they could have simply arrested him later. "This was not a bank robber. This was not a kidnapper. This was not a car-jacker. You know who he was. You know where he lived. You know what he did. That's the tragedy of this case: There was no reason to stop him the way they did, and a boy lost his life." The lawsuit also charged that the two cops "did nothing to assist the 13-year-old boy who lay dying on the side of the road." Derek was reportedly alive at first but died waiting for the ambulance. The lawyer also called it offensive that the two cops did nothing for a 12-year-old friend of Derek's who observed the whole incident and, while unhurt himself, saw his friend get killed. The driver of the car being chased was charged with second-degree murder. The cops denied hitting his car deliberately, but from witness descriptions of the crash, it appeared that the cops hit the car in a deliberate maneuver. **Source:** The Detroit News, 3/30/98

Lamar Wayne Grable   20   *Black*

September 21, 1996. Detroit:

Lamar was shot eight to eleven times and killed by Police Officer Eugene Brown, who is Black, and Police Officer Vicki Yost, who is white. The autopsy showed that he was shot twice in the back, once in the shoulder, and three times in the chest area at such close range that powder burns were left on his skin. The Police Department ruled the shooting a "justifiable homicide," claiming Lamar shot at Officer Brown, who subsequently received an award because he was wearing a safety vest while chasing Mr. Grable on foot. The mayor justified the shooting. No one saw the gun police claim to have removed from the scene. Lamar's body was removed from the scene before investigators arrived and taken to the hospital even though it was obvious that he was dead. The crime scene was not secured. A toxicology report revealed that no drugs were in Lamar's system. The Police Department refused to turn over evidence to the Gable family's attorneys or to let them have an independent medical examiner look over Lamar's clothing. They also tried to conceal the identities of the cops involved in the shooting. **Source:** SLP form; flyer put out by family; autopsy report

---

Vickey Finklea   41   *African American*

September 1996. Detroit:

Off-duty Wayne County Sheriff Anthony Binion and his cousin shot Vickey Finklea, a Black woman, to death after arguing with her in her driveway.

William Ruehle   39   —

August 16, 1996. Detroit:

William Ruehle was shot and killed by three Grosse Pointe Park police officers as he wandered in the street with a shotgun. Ruehle had unsuccessfully tried to commit suicide, was bleeding from slashed neck and wrists and was disoriented. Witnesses say that he did not threaten police with the gun, and that he was trying to kill himself.

Bobby Mitchell   51 (?)   *African American*

August 9, 1996. Ecorse:

Bobby Mitchell, a Black man, was shot and killed by Ecorse police in front of the municipal complex. Police say that Mr. Mitchell threatened them with a knife. However, it was well-known in Ecorse, to the people and the police, that he had mental problems. He was well-liked and harmless. The "weapon" was a carpet cutter which he was proud of and liked to show to people. Ecorse residents denounced the killing and accused the police of racism.

Lou Adkins   32   —

August 5, 1996. Detroit:
Lou Adkins was shot three times and killed by Detroit police after they stopped him for a domestic dispute. Adkins was unarmed when he got out of his pickup truck and no gun was found in the truck. Police say that he was shot in a struggle over one of their weapons. The police department ruled the killing justifiable.

Crystal Lujan   —   —

June 5, 1996. Ann Arbor:
Crystal died of asphyxiation in jail. According to the Washtenaw County Sheriff Department, the asphyxiation was self-induced.

Unidentified Detroit Youth   —   —

June 4, 1996. Detroit:
An undercover Metropolitan Airport police officer working in Detroit as part of a drug operation killed a young man who he said tried to car-jack him. The cop was placed on administrative leave.

Kurt Eugene Remmers   21   —

May 20, 1996. Macomb County (Clinton Township):
Mr. Remmers died while being chased by police when his vehicle went airborne and ejected him. **Source:** The Detroit News, 3/5/98

Edward Swans   —   *African American*

February 2, 1996. Lansing (in custody):
Mr. Swans died after being left hog-tied in his cell. A jail video showed police sitting on and standing over an inert Mr. Swans inside the cell. The Swans family won a $13 million lawsuit against the City of Lansing. **Source:** Detroit Oct. 22 Coalition

Rex Bell   —   *African American*

February 1996. Lansing (in custody):
Rex Bell died under suspicious circumstances in the custody of Lansing police. He had been beaten unconscious by bouncers at a club known for racist incidents. Instead of taking him to a hospital, police handcuffed and arrested him. He died shortly thereafter in his cell. There were protests for months afterwards demanding justice for his death. **Source:** Detroit Oct. 22 Coalition

Charles Antoine Clarence Cooper   20   *African American*

January 9, 1996. Detroit:
Charles Cooper, a Black youth from Kalamazoo, was arrested on the east side by Detroit police after a car chase ended in a shooting, leaving one cop dead. Cooper did not look hurt when he was arrested. He died in the jail elevator while in police custody. The official police story is that Cooper was shot before he was arrested, but for unexplainable reasons he did not tell them he was hurt. Police said because of his thick coat, they did not realize Charles had been shot until he collapsed.

Rahaab White   21   *African American*

December 9, 1995. Detroit:
Mr. White left his mother's house late at night after having dinner. He was planning to meet a friend who worked near the Union Street restaurant on Woodward. Moments later, he lay dying on Woodward, shot twice in the chest by off-duty Detroit Police Officer Thomas Phillips. Officer Phillips and a parking lot valet claimed Mr. White had tried to rob them of $40 in receipts at gunpoint. Rahaab White was planning to get married and go to Wayne State University the following month. He had just completed a year of study in Africa. He had no reason to commit a robbery and did not own a gun. Contradictory statements about the incident were given to the police by parking lot attendants and other witnesses. Officer Phillips was assigned to a desk job during an investigation.

Unidentified Man   —   —

November 29, 1995. Detroit:

Off-duty cop Carl Morris killed an unidentified man who Morris said he found inside the business where he moonlighted as a security guard. Morris fired a number of shots which hit the man. Morris admitted that he had not identified himself as a police officer, but the man had made a motion "as if he were armed with a gun." No charges were filed.

Unidentified Man   —   —

October 18, 1995. Detroit:

A man was shot and killed by a Detroit cop in a bar. Police say he had a gun and that when they told him to drop it, he turned around and pointed it at them.

Charles Ledell Clay   13   *African American*

August 25, 1995. Detroit:

Off-duty Detroit cop Archie Ard shot and killed 13-year-old Charles Clay, a Black youth, claiming that Clay was trying to break into a car and pointed a "shiny object" at him. No weapon was found.

Aaron Phillips   19   —

August 1995. Detroit (west side):

Mr. Phillips was a passenger in a patrol car with two Detroit police officers. While pursuing a car for erratic driving, their patrol car collided with another police car. Mr. Phillips was killed, as were the two cops in the car with him. It is unclear why Mr. Phillips was in the police car in the first place. **Source:** The Detroit News, 3/5/98

Lou Ann Allaer   41   —

August 1995. Macomb County (Eastpointe):

Ms. Allaer died in a head-on collision with an allegedly stolen truck being chased by St. Clair Shores and Eastpointe police. Her family filed a $17.5 million lawsuit against the two cities. **Source:** The Detroit News, 3/5/98

Unidentified Man   —   —

May 25, 1995. Detroit:

An undercover Inkster cop working a drug sting shot and killed a man who police say was trying to buy drugs from them. He was shot in the head when he tried to get away in his car.

Tana Snell   29   *Black*

May 15, 1995. Detroit:

Tana's cop husband threatened to kill her for months. She felt trapped. When friends suggested that she seek help, she replied, "Who am I supposed to call, the police? He is the police and they all stick together." He forced his way into a friend's house where Tana was with her mother and two children. He attacked Tana, putting his foot on her neck. When Tana's mother tried to pull his foot away, he shot her twice in the face (she survived). Tana fled. He shot her in the back, killing her. He then killed himself. The two young children (approximately ages 2 and 6) witnessed all of this.

James Johnson   —   —

1995. Detroit:

Off-duty Detroit cop Jimmie Wheeler shot James Johnson to death, claiming he mistook a hand-held VCR remote control unit in Johnson's pocket for a gun.

Mikey Hill   teens   *white*

July 1994. Detroit:

Mikey Hill, a white teenager, was killed in southwest Detroit after police were called about a disturbance. Police claimed that they shot Hill because he was threatening them with a weapon. Witnesses, however, say he was shot in the back while he was face first against a wall. Police painted Hill as a gang member, as if that justified shooting him in the back.

Marcel Washington	20	*African American*

April 2, 1994. Grand Rapids:

Mr. Washington was visiting his girlfriend and became involved in an argument with neighbors. At the suggestion of his girlfriend, he decided to leave for home to avoid further problems. Neighbors called the cops and said he had a gun. Police arrived and cornered him a few blocks away. Cops claim Mr. Washington pointed a gun at them. They shot him in the head and killed him. **Source:** Detroit Oct. 22 Coalition

Freddie Vela	11	*Chicano*

1994. Detroit:

Freddie Vela was shot and killed by a drunk off-duty Detroit cop who had rammed his car into a tree after leaving a bar. The cop tried to shoot a resident of the neighborhood who reached to turn off the car's alarm. The shot hit Freddie. Freddie's family were Chicanos from Texas who had come to Detroit to seek a better life.

Floyd Johnson	—	—

December 25, 1993. Ann Arbor:

Floyd died from ketoacidosis while in jail, according to the Washtenaw County Sheriff Department. Ketoacidosis usually occurs when diabetics do not get the insulin they need.

James Monroe Johnson	21	—

November 2, 1993. Detroit:

Mr. Johnson was shot and killed by Detroit police. He was a mental patient. Police claim they mistook his VCR remote for a gun. **Source:** Detroit Oct. 22 Coalition

Gary Glenn	—	*African American*

July 8, 1993. Detroit:

Detroit police killed Gary Glenn, a Black youth, saying he pointed a gun at them. Glenn was shot in the hand and head. Police claim that after he was shot in the hand, Glenn continued to threaten them with the gun. However, doctors who examined the body said that the first shot so badly damaged Glenn's hand that he would have been unable to hold a gun. Witnesses say he had no gun at the time. No charges were ever filed against the cops, despite protests.

Ronald Lee Allen, Jr.	27	*African American*

April 13, 1993. Detroit:

Ronald Allen was shot in the chest and killed by Detroit police. His brother, Eugene Lee Allen, was shot in the shoulder by police during the same incident but survived. **Source:** Detroit Oct. 22 Coalition

Ricardo Gordy	21	*African American*

March 24, 1993. Detroit:

While handcuffed, Mr. Gordy choked to death in the back of a police car near his home on Seyburn. Witnesses stated variously that police either refused to help him when he choked, or intentionally used a "death choke." The police officers responsible for his death were not punished or reprimanded, although a small legal settlement was obtained by his family. **Source:** Detroit Oct. 22 Coalition

Johnnie Junior Thacker	42	—

February 16, 1993. Melvindale:

Mr. Thacker was shot and killed by Melvindale police. They claim he wounded a police officer with the officer's own gun. **Source:** Detroit Oct. 22 Coalition

William Leon Ferguson   —   —

January 27, 1993. Taylor:
Ferguson was shot and killed by Taylor police. They claim he was trying to run them down with his car. **Source:** Detroit Oct. 22 Coalition

Willie Cornelius Stanley   39   —

January 22, 1993. Detroit:
Mr. Stanley was shot several times in the chest at close range and killed by Detroit police. They claimed he came at them with a knife. **Source:** Detroit Oct. 22 Coalition

José Itturalde   —   *Cuban*   ◉

1993. Detroit:
Two undercover cops confronted José Itturalde, a Cuban immigrant, after he spoke to them in Spanish. When he reached to get his I.D., Mr. Itturalde was shot dead. The cops claimed he was reaching for a weapon. No weapon was found.

Malice Green   —   *African American*   ◉

November 1992. Detroit:
While a number of fellow police stood guard, Detroit cops Nevers and Budzyn, known by the people in the neighborhoods as "Starsky and Hutch" because of their brutality, beat Malice Green, a Black man, to death. They beat him with a flashlight for the "crime" of refusing to open his hand in which he clutched a piece of paper. Officers Nevers and Budzyn were tried and convicted of second degree murder. They appealed the verdict.

Sara Pantke   20   —

September 7, 1991. Oakland County (Pontiac trial):
Ms. Pantke was killed when her car was hit by a vehicle being chased by Walled Lake police at 93 mph. Cops claim they were about a quarter mile behind the car they were chasing and therefore were not in "hot pursuit." **Source:** The Detroit News, 3/5/98

Pamala Lavern Frowner   21   *African American*

April 18, 1991. Detroit:
Pamala gave a neighbor a ride to pick up a friend at a bar. She was pursued by the police shortly after driving away from the bar with the two men. One of the men had supposedly robbed someone in the bar. He allegedly held a gun to Pamala when police pulled behind her. The cops fired 13 shots. Pamala was shot in the back of the head and killed by police. She was survived by her one-year-old son. Both men were sentenced to prison. Pamala's family received a small out-of-court settlement. **Source:** Detroit Oct. 22 Coalition

DeShawn Wright   —   —

March 31, 1990. Ypsilanti City:
DeShawn died when his car crashed while being chased by the police.

Lee Floyd Berry   26   *African American*

June 23, 1987. Detroit:
Detroit Police Officer Joseph Hall chased Mr. Berry for allegedly speeding. Mr. Berry got home where he was shot in the back and killed in his own driveway, three to ten feet away by Officer Hall. Mr. Berry was unarmed. Officer Hall claims that the victim attacked him. Mr. Berry's family won a $2.5 million lawsuit against the city, which was overturned on appeal. **Source:** Detroit Oct. 22 Coalition

Carlos Walker	26	*African American*	

March 11, 1971. Detroit:

Carlos Walker was running away from a bar when he was shot in his stomach with a sawed-off pump shot gun by a STRESS (Stop-Theft-Robberies-Enjoy-Safe-Streets) unit officer. This controversial police unit employed to deter crime in 1970-1971 killed many Black men. The first official action of the late Mayor Coleman Alexander Young was to end STRESS. **Source:** Detroit Oct. 22 Coalition

MINNESOTA

Name	Age	Nationality	Photo
Unidentified Baby Boy	6 months	—	
Unidentified Woman	35	—	

December 4, 1998. Minneapolis:

The woman and child both died from injuries sustained when a police van ran them over on the sidewalk. The police van was looking for intoxicated people at a holiday parade when it careened out of control, hit a squad car, and then plowed into a crowd of parade goers. Ten other people were injured. **Source:** USA Today, 12/5/98

Casanova Hamilton	33	—	

October 22, 1998. St. Paul:

Mr. Hamilton, a father of two, was described by his girlfriend as the kind of person who would do anything for anyone. But not anymore. He died hours after a car being chased by the police ran a red light and hit his car. Police claim they did not exceed speeds of 40-45 mph, but Tammy Morse, Mr. Hamilton's girlfriend, said she did not believe that a low speed impact could have thrown the 235 lb. man into the back seat of his car. She said "I would suspect a higher speed chase....I'd like them to do something about police chases." **Source:** Star Tribune (Minneapolis, MN), 10/23/98

Artis Graham	35	—	

October 12, 1998. St. Paul:

A St. Paul police officer who was arresting Mr. Graham struck him three times in the head with a flashlight. The third blow "brought Graham to the ground." The cop claims he struck the first two blows when Mr. Graham grabbed the butt of the officer's holstered gun. He struck the third blow after Mr. Graham allegedly "raised both hands as if to surrender but instead lunged forward and attempted to head-butt the officer." Mr. Graham was taken to the hospital that night when he started having convulsions but was discharged. He died six days later on Oct. 18 of a blood clot in his lung. The victim's mother, Oprah Keaton, said her son told her he did not resist arrest and was hit on the head after being handcuffed. She said, "He told me to make sure that I try to get something done about this because they did him wrong." Spike Moss, a community activist, said "He wouldn't have had a blood clot if he hadn't been beaten." Mr. Graham's family filed complaints with the St. Paul Police Dept. and the State Dept. of Human Rights. **Source:** Pioneer Press, 10/20/98; Star Tribune (Minneapolis, MN), 10/23/98

Unidentifed Woman	—	—	

August 24, 1998. downtown Minneapolis (Lowry Hill tunnel):

Police began chasing a motorist for reckless driving in the early morning hours. A total of five squad cars chased the driver through downtown Minneapolis. The driver's van ran into two cars inside the Lowry Hill tunnel, killing one woman and badly injuring another. **Source:** Yahoo! State News, 8/24/98

Troy Senesac	38	—	

July 30, 1998. Plymouth:

Mr. Senesac was being chased by Plymouth police when his motorcycle crashed into a tree. He died the next morning at the hospital. The chase began after the officer stopped him for an equipment violation and he reportedly fled. **Source:** Star Tribune (Minneapolis, MN), 8/1/98

Michael Max Truchinski   41   —

July 24, 1998. Crosby:
Six Crow Wing County Sheriff's Deputies entered Mr. Truchinski's home in a "no-knock raid" around 11:30 p.m. to search for drugs and stolen property . Deputies claim Mr. Truchinski had a gun, refused to drop it and pointed it at them. Deputy Dennis Lasher shot him once in the chest. He died two days later in the hospital. Deputy Lasher was placed on paid administrative leave during a routine investigation. Within four days authorities were already saying the killing appeared justified. **Source:** Star Tribune (Minneapolis, MN), 7/28/98

Ronald J. Carlson   34   —

July 18, 1998. Byron (outside Rochester):
Mr. Carlson was struck and killed by a pick-up truck driven by Olmsted County Sheriff's Deputy Eric B. Thompson. Deputy Thompson was off-duty when he rammed his pick-up truck into Ronald Carlson and his wife Terry (who was injured) as they were walking home on the gravel shoulder of the highway facing on-coming traffic. The deputy then drove away but was arrested for criminal vehicular operation several hours later. Shortly before the accident, he had been seen at a street party where beer was being served from a keg. Police refused to disclose Deputy Thompson's blood-alcohol level, even though they did tested him hours after the accident. **Source:** Star Tribune (Minneapolis, MN), 7/21/98

Jennifer Beumer   15   —
Dale Hays   18   —

May 24, 1998. County Road 53 (outside Becker):
Dale was killed when their car crashed as they were being pursued by the police. According to authorities, a cop tried to pull them over for undisclosed reasons and they sped up to avoid being caught. After a chase of undisclosed length, their car went off the road and flipped into a ditch. Three other people in the car were injured. **Source:** Star Tribune (Minneapolis, MN), May 25, 1998

Teng Xiong   30   —

May 12, 1998. St. Paul:
Teng was shot to death by police after he allegedly stabbed his wife and then dragged a cop with a car. **Source:** Star Tribune (Minneapolis, MN), May 15, 1998

Thomas D. Peterson   40   —

February 25, 1998. Bloomington:
Mr. Peterson died shortly after being chased in his car and arrested by a state trooper for allegedly having an expired license plate. After being chased for a couple of minutes, Mr. Peterson pulled over and was ordered out of his car at gunpoint. He was forced to lie face-down on the ground, handcuffed and was put into the squad car. When other state troopers finally arrived, they noticed he wasn't breathing and called paramedics. Police claim he coughed up a plastic bag that may have contained drugs, though this has not been verified. An autopsy was reportedly inconclusive. The state troopers involved were put on paid leave during the investigation. **Source:** Star Tribune (Minneapolis, MN), 2/27/98

Gerald Lehn   30   —

October 21, 1997. St. Michael:
Mr. Lehn was shot twice in the chest and killed after being chased in his car and then on foot by Hennepin County Sheriff's Deputy Gary Johnson. Mr. Lehn had been pulled over for driving erratically and having license plates that did not belong to the car. Mr. Lehn reportedly sped off and, after a chase, crashed his car, got out and ran away. Deputy Johnson claims he ordered Mr. Lehn to stop and raise his hands, but Mr. Lehn allegedly came at him and tried to grab his gun, supposedly forcing the deputy to fire in self-defense. Deputy Johnson was placed on routine administrative leave with pay during the early phases of the investigation, but was soon returned to duty. In Dec. 1997, a grand jury declined to indict him. In Jan. 1998, less than three months after the incident, Deputy Johnson was given the department's highest medal of honor for killing Mr. Lehn. **Source:** Star Tribune (Minneapolis, MN), 10/23/97, 12/10/97, & 1/9/98

Gary Westby	51	—

October 15, 1997. Paynesville:

Gary was killed when his van was hit by a Paynesville police officer involved in a car chase. The cop was cleared by a grand jury. The man he was chasing got 10 years in prison for vehicular homicide (even though it was a cop car that collided with Gary's van and killed him). **Source:** Star Tribune (Minneapolis, MN), 10/17/97 & 5/22/98

Brian Feist	38	—

August 11, 1996. Minneapolis:

Mr. Feist, a limo driver, was killed in a car crash with a teenager being chased by police in the middle of the afternoon. The police were chasing the 19-year-old driver the wrong way on the freeway at speeds of up to 40-50 mph. A cop pulled the teenager over and approached with his gun drawn. The teenager reportedly "uttered an obscenity and sped away." Cops claim both the driver and a passenger were making "obscene gestures" at them during the chase. The teenage driver, who also suffered injuries in the accident, pleaded guilty to third degree murder in connection with Mr. Feist's death. Dorothy Feist, the victim's mother, filed a wrongful death lawsuit against four of the officers involved and the city of Minneapolis. **Source:** Star Tribune (Minneapolis, MN), 8/8/98

Thomas Kantor	—	—

1996. Benton County:

Mr. Kantor was shot and killed by Benton County Sheriff's Deputy Nancy Wiggin on the same night that a St. Joseph police officer was also killed. Mr. Kantor was allegedly a suspect in that killing. Deputy Wiggin was later found to have post-traumatic stress disorder and did not work for eight months. A bill passed by the Minnesota State House awarded her $23,000 - in essence for killing Thomas Kantor. **Source:** Star Tribune (Minneapolis, MN), 3/14/98

Richard LeGarde	—	*Native American (Anishinabe)*

November 6, 1994. Anishinabe Reservation:

Richard, an Anishinabe rights activist, was illegally arrested and then returned him to his home by Deputy Kevin Penner, who was the last person to see him alive. The victim's family charges that Deputy Penner killed him. Deputy Penner was charged in state court for the illegal arrest as well as multiple sexual assault charges against Native women.

MISSISSIPPI

Name	Age	Nationality	Photo

Charanjit S. Aujla	—	*Indian (South Asian)*	

December 4, 1998. Jackson:

Mr. Aujla was shot twice in the head and killed by four to six Hinds County sheriff's deputies. The deputies had conducted an undercover operation against alcohol sales to minors at the convenience store where the victim worked as a clerk. A minor working with the undercover operation made an alcohol purchase at the store, and the deputies then came to issue a warrant to Mr. Aujla. Authorities claim that the deputies were in uniform and that the victim fired four shots at them. The deputies fired a total of 7 shots, killing the victim, who had been inside bulletproof plexiglass when the deputies entered the store. While there were no known civilian eyewitnesses to the shooting, several civilian witnesses say the deputies were in plain clothes. Community members questioned why so many cops were needed to serve a warrant that could have resulted in nothing more than a fine. They speculate that the deputies were conducting an undercover raid and the victim pulled a gun because he feared the store was being robbed. Authorities deny this and claim the victim was facing the cops when he was shot, even though the autopsy said he had been shot in the back. Community members also questioned why cops shot him in the head when he was in a bulletproof enclosure with deputies blocking his only means of escape. Mr. Aujla is survived by his wife and two children. He had a master's degree in education. Members of the local Indian community continue to fight for justice. **Source:** India Aborad Center for Political Awareness

| **Clinton J. Byrd** | 21 | — |

May 6, 1998. Long Beach:
Clinton Byrd showed up at the home of his former girlfriend wearing fatigues and allegedly waving an assault rifle. Police were called. Clifton's girlfriend and her mother got away. Supposedly, Byrd went outside and ambushed two cops who were pulling up to the house, killing them. An off-duty cop who lived in the neighborhood then shot and killed Clinton Byrd. **Source:** AP, 5/6/98

| **Eddie Bassett** | 46 | — |

October 22, 1997. Jackson:
Mr. Bassett was allegedly drunk, armed with a shotgun, and making threats around 4:30 a.m. when his girlfriend called the police. Cops from the tactical unit arrived and claim that as they were attempting to "make contact" with him, Mr. Basset came outside, fired 2 shots and killed a cop, then retreated back into the house. Cops then fired tear gas into the house and tried to enter. Mr. Bassett was forced out of the house by the tear gas and allegedly came out holding a shotgun, and made a "threatening motion at officers after ignoring repeated orders to drop [it]." Cops fired at least 6 shots, hitting Mr. Bassett in the chest. He died later at the hospital. **Source:** The Commerical Appeal (Memphis, TN), 10/23/97

| **Bobby Everett** | 19 | Black |

February 1993. Jackson City Jail:
Bobby was found hanging from a bedsheet in the Jackson City Jail. He was included on list of 24 Black men that have died in police custody in Mississippi between 1990 and 1993. Mississippi authorities have ruled all the deaths were suicide by hanging, but local activists are suspicious and suspect foul play. **Source:** Atlanta Constitution, 3/17/93

| **Unidentified Male Youth** | 14 | Black |

February 1993. Jackson (in custody):
He was found hanging from a shoelace in the bathroom of a Jackson youth detention center. He was included on list of 24 Black men that have died in police custody in Mississippi between 1990 and 1993. Mississippi authorities have ruled all the deaths were suicide by hanging, but local activists are suspicious and suspect foul play. **Source:** Atlanta Constitution, 3/17/93

| **Andre Jones** | — | African American |

August 22, 1992. Simpson County Jail:
Andre, the son of Jackson NAACP President Esther Jones Quinn and Nation of Islam Minister Charles X Quinn, was murdered in jail, despite claims of local law officials that he committed suicide. A second autopsy clearly shows that Andre was murdered while in custody of Simpson County authorities.

| **Johnny Griffin** | 37 | Black |

April 1990. Jackson:
Johnny was killed in cold blood by two police officers. A man who was with Mr. Griffin at the time was forced to stand behind a tree so he could not be a witness. A second person said that Mr. Griffin had already dropped a gun retrieved earlier to ward off a local gang. Officers fired two shots at Mr. Griffin, who had been standing passively with his hands in the air. **Source:** "Police Violence is Excessive" by Kevin Brook in Criminal Justice: Opposiing Viewpoints (pp. 173–179), edited by Michael D Biskup. Greenhaven Press, Inc., San Diego, 1993.

| **David Scott Campbell** | — | Black |

1990. Neshoba County Jail:
David was found hanged in Neshoba County Jail. The sheriff claimed he committed suicide. The Black community believes he was killed for dating the daughter of a white deputy sheriff in a nearby county. He was included on list of 24 Black men that have died in police custody in Mississippi between 1990 and 1993. Mississippi authorities have ruled all the deaths were suicide by hanging. **Source:** Atlanta Constitution, 3/17/93

MISSOURI

Name	Age	Nationality	Photo

Carol A. Kerns — 37 — *white*

January 12, 1999. Kansas City, Mo.:

Ms. Kerns was shot in the lower left side of the chest and killed by a traffic police officer. The officer claimed that she sped at him with her car as he attempted to give her traffic tickets for running a red light. According to the officer, Ms. Kerns handed over her ID after he pulled her over and he went back to his car to run a check. When he returned, she allegedly rolled up the window, locked the door and refused to get out. She then "bumped" the cop in the legs with her car but he did not require medical attention for any injury. The cop drew his gun and ordered her out of the car. A male passenger got out with his hands up, but Ms. Kerns supposedly started to drive again. The cop shot her through the driver's side window, indicating that he was not in the path of the vehicle and was thus in no danger of being run over when he opened fire. Another shot hit Ms. Kerns' front tire. Authorities refused to disclose how many bullets the cop fired. Ms. Kerns drove off, injured, crashed into a pickup truck, and was taken to the hospital where she died. This incident led the Kansas City Police Department to propose new rules which would prohibit officers from firing into a vehicle. Ms. Kerns was pregnant when she was killed. **Source:** The Kansas City Star, 1/13/99, 1/14/99, & 1/27/99

Unidentified Man — — — —

November 10, 1998. St. Joseph:

The man was shot and killed by police after allegedly opening fire from the window of an apartment building and then walking onto the street still firing randomly at passersby. Authorities claim he shot and killed the first officer who tried to stop him, and kept firing at other police who cornered him behind a church. **Source:** Associated Press, 11/10/98

Timothy Wilson — 13 — *African American*

November 9, 1998. Kansas City, Mo.:

The pickup truck Timothy was driving had become stuck in the mud after a police chase. Four cops fired 11 shots and killed him, claiming his truck "lurched backward," struck a cop and hit a police car, allegedly putting officers in fear for their lives. But a police diagram of the scene shows that none of the six cops on the scene were standing directly in front of or behind the truck. They were not in danger of being run down. The medical examiner's report showed that based on where the bullets hit Timothy and his vehicle, it appears that he was either shot outside the truck or by a cop standing to the side. In either case, there would be no danger of an officer getting run over. The Kansas City Board of Police Commissioners issued a statement supporting the cops, and a grand jury declined to indict them. This case, along with the fatal police shooting of Carol Kerns, set off a great deal of anger in the community. **Source:** The Kansas City Star, 1/8/99 & 1/27/99

William Lattin, Jr. — 33 — —

November 8, 1998. St. Joseph:

Cops claim they shot and killed William Lattin, Jr., as he strolled up a city street firing at random. Police claim that William killed a police officer and wounded three bystanders before being fatally shot himself. They claimed he was carrying an assault rifle with 300 rounds of ammunition and a 12-gauge shotgun. **Source:** San Francisco Chronicle, 11/12/98

JNA Crawford — 22 — —

August 11, 1998. St. Louis:

Cops claim Mr. Crawford approached a car containing two undercover detectives, lifted his shirt, and showed a pistol in his waistband. He allegedly ran when cops identified themselves and supposedly pulled a pistol during the chase. One of the detectives fired two shots, striking Mr. Crawford in the chest and killing him. **Source:** St. Louis Post-Dispatch, 8/13/98

Michael Tramble III	2	—
Reginald Sublet, Jr.	12	—
Michael Tramble, Jr.	32	—
Rosalind Tramble	33	—

July 11-14, 1998. Ballwin:
Reginald Sublet, a former Dallas police officer, killed his ex-wife (Rosalind Tramble), her new husband (Michael Tramble, Jr.), her son from himself (Reginald Sublet, Jr.) and her son from her new husband (Michael Tramble III). The former couple had been in a "bitter custody dispute." After the killing, (former) Officer Reginald Sublet killed himself. Police would not say how everyone was killed. The bodies were found on July 14.

Richard A. Lay	23	—

June 15, 1998. St. Louis County:
Richard was shot several times and killed by two St. Louis County police officers around noon in the 11800 block of Kingsfont Drive. The authorities say paramedics went to the Heatherton Apartments, where Richard lived, in response to a 911 call about an injury. They claim Richard cut a paramedic with a butcher knife and ran out of the apartment. The paramedics locked themselves in the apartment and called the police. They reported a "mentally disturbed individual with a knife... [who was] acting irrational." The paramedic suffered a minor cut on the abdomen which was treated at the scene. When cops arrived, Richard was in the parking lot of the apartment complex, allegedly still carrying the knife. Cops claim they tried to talk him into dropping the knife and he appeared to relax. Then, the cops allege, Richard suddenly raised the knife and lunged at them, at which point they shot and killed him. **Source:** St. Louis Post-Dispatch, 6/16/98

Richard L. Conrad	34	—

April 19, 1998. Franklin County:
Mr. Conrad reportedly drowned while trying to swim across a river to escape police pursuit. Cops began chasing his pickup truck based on a tip that one of three young children traveling with him might be ill or in trouble. After a chase for several miles, Mr. Conrad stopped, waited for the sheriff's car to stop, then allegedly put his truck in reverse, rammed the police car, and drove off. Cops used spikes to flatten Mr. Conrad's tires. He reportedly drove into a field and took off on foot with the children. According to authorities, he left the children in a clearing and dove into the river. Police said he died of drowning or hypothermia. Cops claim they later found out that the truck he was driving was stolen and that he had served three years in prison for motor vehicle theft, receiving stolen property, and tampering. **Source:** St. Louis Post-Dispatch, 4/30/98

Tracy Patterson	22	—

April 11, 1998. St. Louis:
Tracy was on her way to visit her son at her parent's home when her car was hit by a police car. She died. Witnesses say the cop car was speeding and in a chase. Police deny this. The police have failed to explain the accident to Tracy's parents.

Robert Rebstock	23	—

March 27, 1998. St. Louis:
Cops were searching for Robert, who authorities suspected for a series of auto thefts and burglaries. The police found out he was staying at the Super Inn of America at 1100 North Third Street, just north of downtown. Cops arrived around 8 a.m. to arrest him. They claim he threatened to shoot himself and that he had boasted that he would never be taken alive. A two-and-a-half hour stand-off ensued. Hostage negotiators were supposedly talking to Robert until shortly before 10:25 a.m. when cops claim he opened the door of his room on the third floor balcony and fired one shot at them. According to the newspaper, "one of the four officers, who wore military-style uniforms and carried assault rifles, then fired a short burst at Rebstock's head." A police department spokesperson said, "Sometimes you have to do this." Robert is survived by his girlfriend, their three kids, ages 1-5, his mother, his grandmother, and other relatives. **Source:** St. Louis Post-Dispatch, 3/28/98

Thai Pham   33   *Vietnamese*

March 14, 1998. Kansas City, Mo.:

Mr. Pham, a mentally impaired man, was shot in the heart and left lung and killed by an unidentified police officer who had come to the house with other cops to arrest the victim's brother, Thuan, on a theft charge. Thuan Pham had had a wage dispute with his boss and had taken two nail guns from his place of employment to ensure that the money would be paid. He returned one nail gun, but his boss called the police anyway. Cops came to the Pham house with Thuan's boss and asked for the nail gun. Thuan turned it over and was arrested. Thai Pham, his brother, did not understand what was going on as a result of his diminished mental capacity and allegedly pushed an officer. Another cop tried to arrest him. The two supposedly "struggled," and the cop pepper-sprayed Thai. Police claim that Thai then grabbed two knives, ignored orders to drop them, and advanced toward the cops, at which point the officer fired two shots. Thai's family disputed the official account, saying that Thai was mentally impaired, could not understand English, and in any case would not have lunged at police with knives. They said that he probably went to the kitchen to wash the pepper-spray out of his face, not to grab knives. Thai Pham was five feet five inches tall and weighed 130 pounds. Neighbors described him as "loud and excitable – but never violent or erratic," according to the newspaper. Five members of his family had drowned in the late 1970's as they tried to leave Vietnam and their boat capsized in a storm. Thai was unemployed and received disability payments but tried to keep busy, often mowing neighbors' lawns and doing other chores for them. One neighbor said, "I'd try to pay him because he worked so hard. But he would not take my money. He always said, 'No. We're friends.'" The neighbor said Thai was friendly and would talk to anyone, despite his limited English: "He would talk loud. His English wasn't very good, so if he thought you couldn't understand him, he would just talk louder. Some people were afraid of that. But that was his way to communicate." Another neighbor described how Thai came over one evening and cooked them a Vietnamese dinner. The police spokesperson justified the shooting, and in response to questions of why cops didn't shoot Thai in the arm or the leg, said, "We teach officers to shoot for the center mass, the chest. That's the best way to stop the action that caused them to shoot in the first place." The officer was placed on paid leave during the investigation. On Apr. 22, he was cleared of any wrongdoing by a grand jury, which ruled the shooting justified. Thai's cousin said, "It's a case of excessive force or police brutality." **Source:** The Kansas City Star, 3/17/98, 4/12/98, & 4/23/98

Jason Larrimore   23   —

December 6, 1997. Kansas City:

Mr. Larrimore was a passenger in an allegedly stolen car being pursued by police. Cops chased the vehicle until the driver lost control of the steering wheel and hit a stone wall. Mr. Larrimore was declared dead at the scene, and the driver was charged with murder under a state law allowing for such a charge when someone is killed in the course of a felony. **Source:** The Kansas City Star, 12/18/97

Shawn H. Garner   26   —

December 3, 1997. St. Louis County:

Mr. Garner was shot in the chest and arm and killed in an alleged shootout with an undercover officer during a drug bust. According to the police, several officers knocked on the door of Mr. Garner's hotel room that night. When he opened the door and saw it was the police, he supposedly tried to close the door and began firing, striking a cop in his bulletproof vest before being shot himself. **Source:** St. Louis Post-Dispatch, 12/5/97

Ravone Thompson   26   —

December 1, 1997. St. Louis:

Ravone was shot in the back and killed by Pine Lawn Police Officer Bryan Hubbard, who stopped him on the street on suspicion of armed robbery of a beauty salon. The police later conceded that Ravone was not involved in the robbery. Ravone allegedly "bolted and ran." Officer Hubbard chased him over the city line into St. Louis. Officer Hubbard claimed that he fired when he saw Ravone reach for something in his waistband. No weapon was found. Police claim they cannot find any witnesses to the shooting. Ravone's parents held a press conference demanding that the St. Louis DA charge Officer Hubbard or submit the case to a grand jury for a murder or manslaughter indictment. His mother said, "I feel like my son was executed. He was shot in the back. He was running away." His father said, "We want justice." The DA refused to charge Officer Hubbard, saying he acted in self-defense. Officer Hubbard was placed on paid leave (paid vacation). **Source:** St. Louis Post-Dispatch, 12/2/97, 12/17/97, & 12/21/97

| Kaleb Lewis | 11 months | — |

November 1997. Hickory County:

Kaleb was killed when the minivan driven by his mother, Rebecca Lewis, crashed into a creek after a high-speed chase. Police began pursuing the van when they reportedly clocked Ms. Lewis at 52 mph in a 35 mph zone. Rebecca Lewis allegedly led the police on a chase through rural backyards, forcing several cars off the road. The incident touched off widespread criticism of police high-speed pursuits. Critics believe a case of slight speeding, like that of Ms. Lewis, was not serious enough to warrant such a dangerous chase. In 1996, 377 people nationwide were killed in accidents involving high-speed police pursuits, according to the newspaper. Groups that study police pursuits put the death toll much higher.
Source: St. Louis Post-Dispatch, 2/8/98

| Larry Turks | — | — |

September 9, 1997. Dellwood (in custody):

Mr. Turks was arrested for allegedly abusing his teenage son, and cops claim he hung himself with a blanket while in custody. He was taken to the hospital and died several months later, on Feb. 15, 1998. But Larry's wife, Sandra Turks, contends her husband was brutalized, citing a picture of her husband in his hospital bed with a bump and several bruises on his head that were not there before he was arrested. She also said her husband, who had tried to hang himself before, should have been placed on suicide watch in any case. Civil rights groups picketed the Dellwood police station. Cops claimed Larry Turks hanged himself to get sympathy from his family. The Dellwood Police Department instituted a policy of not allowing prisoners to have blankets in their cells, ostensibly for safety, but inflicting hardship and punishment. **Source:** St. Louis Post-Dispatch, 4/5/98

| Robert Green | 36 | *Black* |

June 11, 1997. St. Louis:

Robert was shot and killed outside his home in the 5900 block of Wells Avenue just before 1 a.m. by a white officer. Three detectives from the North Patrol Division allegedly saw Robert walking briskly down the street with a pistol in his hand. Police say they got out of their car, identified themselves, and ordered him to drop it. Robert allegedly turned around and pointed the gun at them. Police fired two shots at him as he started to run. Robert was shot in the left rear side. Cops claim they recovered a loaded gun at the scene. Robert's family disputed the police version of events and said the shooting was racially motivated. They said that Robert "runs every time he sees the police. They beat him [four or five year ago]." Robert worked at a recycling center and left behind his girlfriend, who was pregnant, and four daughters. **Source:** St. Louis Post-Dispatch, 6/12/97

| Duane Cain | — | — |

March 27, 1997. Republic:

Duane was shot and killed by police after he allegedly broke into the home of a former Miss Missouri and beat her bloody with a gun. Cops claim that when they ordered Duane to drop his gun, he pointed it at them and opened fire. **Source:** Chicago Tribune, 3/28/97

| Randolph Vance | 47 | — |

October 20, 1996. St. Louis:

An autopsy report claimed Mr. Vance died of "agitated delirium," which is often caused by drug use. But the victim's family and friends charge police brutality and a police cover-up. Protests against police brutality were held in the aftermath of his death. **Source:** St. Louis Post-Dispatch, 1/26/97

Walter Bynum   45   —

October 16, 1996. St. Louis:

A woman who lived on the same block as Mr. Bynum's mother had called the police to say she was afraid that her children's father was coming over and that he would be violent. St. Louis Police Detective Charles Burton, a member of the Domestic Abuse Response Team, was patrolling the block to look out for the abuser. Meanwhile, Walter Bynum had just left his mother's apartment. It was around 1 a.m. Det. Burton stopped and questioned him, then told him to be on his way when he realized that Mr. Bynum was not the abuser. Mr. Bynum reportedly "berated" Det. Burton, then supposedly grabbed for the cop's holstered gun. After an alleged struggle, Det. Burton shot Mr. Bynum in the chest and killed him. The police chief said the shooting appeared justified, and Det. Burton was later cleared of criminal wrongdoing. After Mr. Bynum's death, police released his criminal record, including non-conviction arrests, to damage his reputation. The victim's mother recalled how her son had kissed her on the cheek and said, "I love you, Mom," moments before he was killed. In addition to his mother, Mr. Bynum leaves behind ten children and seven grandchildren. **Source:** St. Louis Post-Dispatch, 10/17/96 & 1/26/97

Garland "Lil' Goo" Carter, Jr.   17   *Black*

January 8, 1996. St. Louis (Carr Square Village):

Mr. Carter was shot and killed by St. Louis Police Officer Eddie Sanchez in the Carr Square Village public housing complex. Patrolman Sanchez, whose name was initially withheld by the authorities, had gone to the housing complex to arrest Mr. Carter as a robbery suspect. He stopped a car in which Mr. Carter was riding. Mr. Carter ran and Patrolman Sanchez opened fire. One bullet hit Mr. Carter in the back of the neck and came out through his mouth. Another bullet hit him in the left buttock, showing he was running away when he was shot. Patrolman Sanchez claimed Mr. Carter pointed a gun at him, but every civilian witness disputed this, saying Mr. Carter was unarmed. The victim's fingerprints were not found on the gun allegedly recovered from the victim's hand, and his family and friends charged that Patrolman Sanchez planted it. Patrolman Sanchez was suspended about a week after the shooting when detectives found a .22-caliber gun, a tear-gas gun, and a toy pistol, widely believed to be "throw-down weapons," in a briefcase in the trunk of his patrol car. A grand jury declined to indict the officer, sparking protests organized by the victim's family, but he later resigned from the force right before a departmental trial was about to begin. The murder of Garland Carter sparked anger in the Carr Square Village housing complex where he lived. One youth described routine police harassment: "The police are always messing with us. They plant drugs and guns on us. They killed my homey. They got to stop messing with us." A motorcade of several dozen cars carrying Mr. Carter's coffin circled police headquarters for 15 minutes before proceeding to his funeral service. Cops complained that some people in the motorcade made shooting motions at cops and said this was "hostile and unnecessary." But Carr Square residents reported that Patrolman Sanchez had driven through the housing complex making shooting motions at them after killing Mr. Carter. A family friend said, "This is the only way we can show how we feel. The police are preying on the kids in our area. A lot of them are being harassed and we just want some justice." Police trashed the victim as a high school dropout and a "troublemaker" with a criminal record who was allegedly known to carry a gun. But his grandmother said, "The police didn't like him because he spoke up for himself." Another grandmother said, "He always respected me. He liked to play and tease." The victim's father told of how his son loved his 17-month-old daughter and described him as "a typical teenager trying to find his way." Patrolman Sanchez had been involved in another shooting about a year earlier. That shooting was ruled justified. **Source:** St. Louis Post-Dispatch, 1/9/96, 1/10/96, 1/13/96, 1/18/96, 1/20/96, 1/23/96, 1/25/96, 2/3/96, 2/6/96, 2/8/96, 2/9/96, 2/18/96, 3/22/96, 4/29/96, 4/30/96, 5/1/96, & 5/7/96

Paul Tinsley   26   —

December 25, 1995. St. Louis:

Mr. Tinsley was shot and killed by St. Louis Patrolman Owen Hill during an alleged struggle. Cops claim Mr. Tinsley was driving a stolen car and had a criminal record. **Source:** St. Louis Post-Dispatch, 12/27/95

Gerard Cartwright	31	—

August 2, 1994. St. Louis (downtown):
Around 1 a.m., cops tried to question Gerard Cartwright about why his Wall Street Journal delivery van did not have any license plates. His brother was in a nearby building making a delivery. Gerard allegedly rolled up the windows, locked the door, refused to talk and then began eating ID cards from his wallet. Cops broke a window and doused him with pepper spray. He drove off, then crashed the van as he tried to make a U-turn. Cops pepper-sprayed him again. Police claim he pulled a pistol, fired one shot at them and then sped away. As he fled, cops opened fire. Seven officers fired about 60 shots, hitting Mr. Cartwright six times and killing him. Police sources said the shooting appeared justified, although some cops might face discipline over their handling of the initial arrest. The victim's mother said, "The police murdered my son," and criticized delays in the investigation and the lack of information made available about the shooting. She said that her son carried a gun for protection because he worked downtown in the early morning hours but that he would not have started a gunfight with police. He had no drugs or alcohol in his system and his police record consisted only of driving-related offenses. **Source:** St. Louis Post-Dispatch, 10/23/94

Lugine Short	32	—

February 12, 1994. St. Louis:
Mr. Short was shot in the groin and killed by St. Louis Police Officer Kevin Dabney during an alleged struggle. Officer Dabney claims he caught Mr. Short burglarizing a house and ordered him to halt. Mr. Short supposedly jumped him. Mr. Short ran off but died a block away from his wound. Cops reportedly recovered two bags of stereo equipment taken from the house. Homicide detectives said the shooting appeared justified and within police guidelines. **Source:** St. Louis post-Dispatch, 2/14/94

Ellen "Honey" Ross	46	—

1993-1998. Vandalia (in prison):
Ellen died in a Missouri prison, apparently of a stroke. Her friend and fellow prisoner, Bonita Holley, said that Ellen had told her the night before the stroke that "Her medicine was switched and she said, 'I don't want to die in here.'" When Ellen was found slumped in her cell, an officer radioed for help but none came. Ms. Holley, ran to an area off-limits to prisoners to get a stretcher. An officer called for someone to drive the emergency vehicle but no one at the prison knew how to operate it. Ms. Holley was so shaken by Ellen's death that she has written to advocacy groups and the governor. The Department of Public Safety in Missouri has the authority to examine a prisoner's death. But their investigator stated that since he took the job in 1993, he has not looked into the death of a single prisoner. 167 people died in Missouri prisons between 1994 and 1997. **Source:** St. Louis Post-Dispatch, 9/27/98

Unidentified	—	—

Date Unknown. St. Louis Workhouse:
An inmate in the St. Louis Workhouse died from complications of asthma after treatment was delayed. **Source:** St. Louis Post-Dispatch, 9/27/98

MONTANA

Name	Age	Nationality	Photo
Ramsey Edward Jay IV	14	—	

November 30, 1998. Anaconda:
Mr. Jay died as a passenger in a car that crashed while being pursued by Montana Highway Patrol Officer Joe Wyant. The victim was from Colorado Springs, Colorado.

Michael Kamp	28	—

October 14, 1998. Kalispell:
Mr. Kamp was being pursued by Montana State Police as an assault suspect. He allegedly shot at the police who were chasing him. Cops fired on him, and his car crashed. He was killed. Police claim Mr. Kamp shot himself in the head before his car crashed. Mr. Kamp was from Colburn, Idaho.

NEBRASKA

Name	Age	Nationality	Photo
Kirk W. Collins	34	—	

September 3, 1998. Cherry County (near Valentine):

Mr. Collins died during a routine traffic stop by a state trooper. An ambulance was called, but he was pronounced dead at the scene. Authorities refused to divulge any information about the cause of Mr. Collins' death or the circumstances surrounding it, although a grand jury was assigned to investigate the case. Mr. Collins was from Palisade, Neb., and ran a dog kennel with his longtime girlfriend, Karla Doetker. **Source:** Omaha World-Herald, 9/9/98

Tracy Pollock	43	*white*	

May 16, 1998. Omaha:

Tracy was shot and killed by five police officers who had been called to the Rinky Dink Tavern at 2001 S. Sixth St. to investigate a disturbance. Cops claim Tracy fled from them, speeding away from the tavern in a car with his lights off (it is not indicated why cops were chasing him in the first place). Tracy supposedly rammed a police car and fired at the cops before they shot him to death. The five cops involved in the shooting - Sgt. Gerald L Hawley, Sgt. Gerald D. Baggett, Officer Warren V. Walter, Officer Angela K. Baker, and Officer Timothy R. Rhoades - were cleared of any wrongdoing by the Police Department, the DA's office, and a grand jury. **Source:** Omaha World-Herald, 6/13/98, 6/30/98, & 7/2/948

Marvin Ammons	33	*Black*	

October 26, 1997. Omaha:

Marvin was shot multiple times and killed by a white cop, Omaha Police Officer Todd Sears, near 63rd St. & Hartman Ave. According to the newspaper, Officer Sears and his partner, Officer Troy Kister, were responding to a report of "a traffic accident involving a disturbance." On their way to the accident, the cops saw two vehicles stopped in the road. One vehicle drove away as the cops arrived. Police claim that Marvin approached the cruisers to talk to the cops and that the cops saw a gun in his waistband and told him to keep his hands in the air. They claim that Marvin initially raised his hands but then reached down and was shot as he pulled his gun. However, the gun was later found to still be in its holster. (Marvin's cellular phone was later found in the back seat of Officer Kister's car; cops have not explained how it got there). Protests and rallies were organized to demand justice for Marvin, and his family, religious leaders, the local chapter of the NAACP, and community members participated. A grand jury indicted Officer Sears for manslaughter as town leaders fretted about the damage this case of police murder had done to race relations. The Omaha Police Union defended Officer Sears and, in its newsletter, attacked the movement demanding justice for Marvin Ammons with what amounted to charges of reverse racism. A non-profit national group called the "Law Enforcement Legal Defense Fund" sent out a letter which contained a racist appeal for funds to help with Officer Sears' defense. Recipients of this group's generosity in previous years include the cops who beat Rodney King in Los Angeles in 1991 and a Michigan cop who beat and maced a man he was arresting. **Source:** Omaha World-Herald, 10/30/97, 12/8/97, 1/23/98, 1/30/98, 2/27/98, 6/13/98, & 7/2/98

Mario Velez	49	*Mexican*	

October 3, 1997. Alda:

Mr. Velez was shot and killed by an undercover police officer during an alleged struggle after a staged drug buy conducted by members of the Tri-Cities Drug Task Force. Authorities, who refused to divulge the cop's identity, claim the undercover officer bought one kilogram of cocaine and one pound of heroin from from Mr. Velez. They also claim that Mr. Velez pulled out a gun before being shot by the officer. Mr. Velez was supposedly a convicted drug dealer who had served time in prison and had twice been deported to Mexico. **Source:** Omaha World-Herald, 10/6/97

Guadalupe Vallesillo — —

August 7, 1997. Omaha:
Police were called because Mr. Vallesillo was sitting on top of a garage. He fell or dropped off the garage before the cops arrived, then allegedly tried to flee when he saw them. Omaha Police Officers Alan M. Reyes and Brian A. Heath tackled him in a nearby yard. Mr. Vallesillo died. An autopsy supposedly showed that the victim died of "acute bronchial asthma." An internal police investigation cleared the officers of using excessive force, and a grand jury chose to believe the autopsy report, clearing the cops of criminal wrongdoing. **Source:** Omaha World-Herald, 10/31/97

Randy Tabler — 17 —

May 8, 1996. Omaha (13th & William St.'s):
The stolen car Randy was driving was being chased by the police when he crashed into a mail truck, killing himself and a postal worker, Joseph Bobor. **Source:** Omaha World-Herald, 6/22/98

Joseph Bober — 30 —

May 8, 1996. Omaha (13th & William St.'s):
Joseph Bobor, a postal worker, was killed when the mail truck he was driving was hit by a stolen car being chased by the police. The driver of the stolen car was a teenager, Randy Taber, who was also killed. Joseph's family sued the city for over $1 million but agreed in June, 1998, to settle for $719,000. The suit contended that the police should have stopped the chase once it became clear that the risk of injury outweighed the need to catch the suspected car thief. **Source:** Omaha World-Herald, 6/22/98

Kristal L. Bradshaw — 24 —

November 25, 1994. Omaha (43rd & Lake St.'s):
Ms. Bradshaw was killed when a car being chased by police for allegedly running a stop sign ran into her car. The 16-year-old driver of the car being chased was charged in connection with her death. Ms. Bradshaw is survived by her three young children. **Source:** Omaha World-Herald, 10/18/97

Joan Sagendorf — —

1994. Omaha:
A car being chased by police crashed into a parked car. The parked car spun around and hit two women: its owner, Vicki Wilkerson, and her friend, Joan Sagendorf. Ms. Wilkerson was injured. Ms. Sagendorf was killed. The city paid a $497,500 settlement to Ms. Wilkerson in Oct., 1997, but refused to change its police pursuit guidelines. **Source:** Omaha World-Herald, 10/9/97

Arden Westcott — —

October 29, 1986. Omaha:
Mr. Westcott was shot and killed by Omaha Police Officer Joseph Crinklaw after he allegedly tried to burglarize a Keystone Pharmacy. In 1996, a jury found that the shooting involved excessive force, then awarded the victim's wife one dollar. The US Court of Appeals ordered a new trial, saying the one dollar reward "amounts to a plain injustice or a shocking or monstrous result." **Source:** Omaha World-Herald, 1/10/98

NEVADA

Name	Age	Nationality	Photo

Kaylyn Cotton-Dobie — 34 — —

March 24, 1999. Reno:

Officers claim that Kaylyn became angry and attacked them when they responded to a disturbance call at her apartment complex. She was supposedly distraught and threatened to kill herself and her daughter. Cops allege that Kaylyn had concealed a knife in her coat pocket until one of the cops, Officer Matt Dellavella, reached out to grab her arm. Both Officer Dellavella and Officer Pam Cercek pulled out their guns and shot Kaylyn. Both officers allegedly suffered stab wounds, but none were life threatening. Kaylyn, however, died during surgery from her gunshot wounds. **Source:** Los Angeles Times, 3/26/99

Mike Smith — 20 — —

December 3, 1998. Elk:

Mr. Smith was shot in the head and killed by Officer Mike Smith (same first and last name, no relation) as he allegedly lunged at the officer with a ballpoint pen. He had supposedly been using the pen to hold his girlfriend hostage on a Greyhound bus. Mr. Smith was from Terre Haute, Indiana.

Lonnie James — 51 — —

October 20, 1998. Las Vegas:

Mr. James was shot 3 times and killed by Las Vegas Police Officer Dennis Devitte after a standoff in which Mr. James allegedly wielded a knife. Mr. James was reportedly afraid that he would be going back to prison for a sex crime. The incident was captured on videotape, which supposedly showed that Officer Devitte chased Mr. James with pepper-spray. But the pepper-spray didn't work, and Mr. James then walked toward Officer Devitte with his jacket over his head blindly and wildly swinging the knife, at which point Officer Devitte opened fire. Cops claim Mr. James had previously called the police department and told them that he was "going to kill the first person who comes near me." Police called this killing a "classic suicide by cop" case. A coroner's jury ruled that the shooting was justified.

Darryl Daniels — 30 — —

August 5, 1998. Reno:

Mr. Daniels died while in police custody, about six hours after a Reno police car and foot pursuit. The police claim that it was a combination of cocaine and exertion that killed him. An autopsy result is pending.

Steven Schaaf — 40 — —

April 2, 1998. Carson City:

Mr. Schaaf, a prisoner, slipped out of his restraints during a visit to an outside doctor in Carson City. He was shot and killed by Corrections Officer Charles Looman when he was running away. Mr. Schaaf was serving time for an attempted murder conviction.

Eric Payton — 40 — —

February 27, 1998. Las Vegas:

Police responded to a call from Eric's wife. Eric was shot to death during a struggle with two police officers. His wife contends the shooting was not justifiable. **Source:** Las Vegas Review-Journal, 3/12/98

James McClintic — 45 — —

September 20, 1997. Las Vegas:

Mr. McClintic was shot and killed by a SWAT team after a two and a half hour standoff in which he allegedly wielded a shotgun. Police claim they only shot him after he pointed the shotgun at one of the cops.

Laxma Reddy	41	—

March 19, 1997. Elko:
Laxma was shot and killed by Elko County Sheriff's Deputy Jim Pitts during a traffic stop after the victim allegedly pulled a gun on the cop. Laxma was wanted by Massachusetts authorities for killing his wife, daughter, and father-in-law in Brookline, a Boston suburb. **Source:** Chicago Tribune, 3/20/97

John Paiva	37	*white*

April 4, 1992. Reno:
Three officers came to the door of John's house for routine questioning about a disagreement with a neighbor. Police described him as "polite, calm and respectful." Yet, when he tried to end the interview by slowly closing the door, one cop stuck his foot in the gap. John asked him to remove his foot and tried once again to close the door. The cop went off, pulling out his gun and shooting John. The other two cops also began shooting. Eighteen shots were fired. John closed the door and went inside to die. Five hours later John's body was found in a pool of blood. Two guns were found on his body and one was placed in his right hand. John was left handed. All evidence of the crime, including a videotape, statements of the cops, bullets, the door and even the clothes John was wearing were destroyed by the Reno PD before a trial could take place.

Charles Bush	—	*Black*

July 1990. Las Vegas:
Mr. Bush was killed by three Las Vegas police officers who entered his apartment without a warrant. He died in a struggle with the officers. Afterward, the police department paid his relatives $1.1 million.

Jacqueline Reich	40	

October 19, 1994. Reno (Washoe County Jail):
Jacqueline was a homeless woman who suffered from mental illness and diabetes. She was jailed for allegedly obstructing a sidewalk. Three days later, she was dead from ketoacidosis, a condition that results from not getting enough insulin. Jacqueline wore a Medic Alert bracelet for her diabetes and had informed jail officials she was an insulin-dependent diabetic. A nurse gave her a shot and put her on a diabetic regimen when she was brought into the jail. Dr. Warren Gilbert, who never saw Jacqueline, canceled these orders. Jacqueline quickly began exhibiting symptoms of insulin deficiency and was found semi-conscious, lying in her own urine. She died later that day. "It was a dirty, rotten deal," said her son, Jeremy Reich. "They should have taken a lot better care of her." Correctional Medical Services, Inc., the prison health provider, settled a lawsuit with Jacqueline's family for an undisclosed amount. Seven nurses had their licenses revoked or suspended as a result of her death. The Nevada State Board of Medical Examiners held Dr. Gilbert responsible for her death. Dr. Gilbert disputed the charges, saying that he was not told of the need for a special diet. **Source:** St. Louis Post-Dispatch, 9/27/98

NEW HAMPSHIRE

Name	Age	Nationality	Photo
Unidentified Man	40s	—	
Unidentified Woman	40s	—	

September 17, 1998. Manchester:
The two victims were driving an allegedly stolen pickup truck being chased by police when they crashed into a dump truck. The chase began in Hopkinton and went through Dunbarton and Goffstown before ending in Manchester. Cops claim they had stopped pursuit in Dunbarton, six minutes before the crash, due to excessive speed. Witnesses said Goffstown cops arrived on the scene within minutes. They admit they knew about the truck but denied they were chasing it. The driver of the dump truck was injured and hospitalized. The two people in the pick-up truck being chased were killed. **Source:** Associated Press, 9/17/98

Spencer Moon 16 —

April 9, 1997. Lyndeborough:

Spencer was shot in the neck and killed by State Trooper Jeffrey Long, a member of the State Police SWAT Team. Spencer and another 16-year-old were allegedly burglarizing a house whose owner, a gun collector, kept over 150 firearms in his home. The gun collector called the police when he called home to check his messages and heard noises in the back yard. (Evidently, his answering machine had a function allowing him to hear background noises). The SWAT team was sent because of the extensive weapons collection. Cops claim that Spencer came out holding a rifle in one hand and a revolver in the other and that he pointed the rifle at State Trooper Long and threatened to shoot the cops and himself. The only shot fired was the shot by Trooper Long that killed Spencer. Spencer did not fire any shots. The Hillsborough County DA's office said the shooting appeared justified, but one of Spencer's friends said, "They could have just shot him in the leg or something. He was just a kid." **Source:** The Boston Globe, 4/11/97

Justin Poster 21 —

January 16, 1997. Concord:

Justin was shot and killed in the kitchen area of a Friendly's restaurant on Louden Road by Sgt. Glenn Wasp. Justin Poster, also known as Justin Greenwood, was wanted on two arrest warrants and was reportedly "armed, dangerous, and possibly wearing a bulletproof vest." Three cops, acting on a tip, came to the restaurant. Justin supposedly ran to the back, hid in the bathroom, and refused to surrender. Cops claim Justin was pulling a handgun from his waistband when he was shot. The Concord police chief and the state attorney general said the shooting seemed justified. **Source:** The Boston Globe, 1/17/97

Robert Cushing — —

June 1, 1988. Hampton:

Mr. Cushing was shot to death in his home by off-duty Police Officer Robert McLaughlin. Officer McLaughlin was convicted of first-degree murder and sentenced to prison, the only police officer in the history of New Hampshire to be convicted of first-degree murder (as of July, 1999). **Source:** statement from victim's family

NEW JERSEY

Name	Age	Nationality	Photo

Joel Figueroa Ramos 30 —

June 23, 1999. South Hackensack (Rte. 46):

Mr. Ramos was at a shopping mall. He allegedly picked up a knife, threatened to kill everybody there, said he was not a crack head, put down the knife, and left. South Hackensack and Little Ferry police arrived on the scene, confronted him, and caught him after a short foot chase. Civilian witnesses said Mr. Ramos first appeared calm and shook hands with the police, then panicked, ran across the highway, and threw himself onto the ground. Two cops jumped on him, kicking and punching him. "It was in the back of the neck, the back of the head. You could hear the punches," said an eyewitness. A total of eight or nine cops jumped on Mr. Ramos, kicking, beating, punching, and stomping him for several minutes, killing him. The witnesses reported that cops noticed that the victim had stopped breathing and rolled him onto his back. His face was blue and his hands were cuffed. Police reportedly tried but failed to revive him. A county prosecutor ignored the eyewitness accounts, claiming that the cause of death was undetermined and that the results of the autopsy were not "consistent with beatings or kickings." But the prosecutor admitted that the autopsy showed that the victim was in handcuffs and "being held down... [while] struggling." He also claimed that the victim had cocaine and marijuana in his blood, six partially dissolved plastic bags in his stomach, and an enlarged heart and liver, and only six cops were on the scene, rather than eight or nine. **Source:** The New York Times, 6/26/99

Ronald Van Thomas 45 —

June 6, 1999. North Bergen:

Mr. Van Thomas, a bouncer at a nightclub, was shot between the eyes and killed by off-duty Newark Police Officer Rasheen Peppers, who was working with him as a bouncer at the club. The cop allegedly mistook the victim's flashlight for a gun in the parking lot, where patrons of the club were having fistfights and where one patron had reportedly fired a shot. Officer Rasheen remained on duty while the case was investigated. **Source:** The New York Times, 6/8/99

Stanton L. Crew	31	*Black*	👁

June 3, 1999. Parsippany-Troy Hills (I-80):

Mr. Crew, an unarmed man, was shot and killed by four police officers from several jurisdictions. Police had boxed in his car with their vehicles and he allegedly tried to escape by maneuvering around them. Mr. Crew had gone to a bar to pick up a white female friend who had been drinking and then called him for a ride. His driver's license was suspended for lapsed insurance, and as he drove home, a cop tried to pull him over for "driving erratically." Reportedly afraid that he would not be able to afford the fines for driving an uninsured car, Mr. Crew allegedly sped up, going 70-80 mph for ten miles. He then crossed the median and drove five miles in the other direction before being boxed in. Police claim they feared that Mr. Crew was going to run them over. Cops fired 27 shots at his car, killing Mr. Crew and wounding his passenger. A neighbor of the victim said, "I'm mad because somebody I grew up with and knew got killed. But I'm also mad because these guys [the cops] are supposed to be trained to handle this in a benign way. Twenty-seven shots? The kid's never been in trouble, ever." The assistant manager at the restaurant where Mr. Crew worked as a waiter said, "He was a great employee. He was one of the most honest people I ever met." The Morris County Prosecutor said he would investigate the case. While refusing to say whether he considered 27 shots excessive, he claimed that the shooting was not racially motivated on the grounds that, while Mr. Crew was a Black man, his passenger was a white woman. This shooting came in the wake of a scandal in which the governor herself was forced to admit that New Jersey State Troopers routinely engage in racial profiling, pulling over and searching Black and Latino motorists based on their race and in vast disproportion to their numbers on the road. **Source:** The New York Times, 6/3/99 & 6/8/99

Earl Faison	27	*Black*	

April 11, 1999. Orange:

Mr. Faison was arrested by police as he hailed a cab outside his girlfriend's house, one block away from where an Orange police officer was shot and killed the previous week. Although cops already had a suspect in custody, they decided that Mr. Faison "bore a resemblance" to a composite sketch of the man they were seeking for shooting the officer. He allegedly fled, and when caught, was supposedly found in possession of a gun. That same night, he was beaten to death in police custody. Cops claim he had a seizure or asthma attack as he was being taken into a detective's office for questioning. But photographs of his body showed he was covered with bruises (family members were not allowed to see the actual body). The victim's father, Earl Williams, said, "I'm a war vet. I know trauma when I see it. My son was beaten badly." Meanwhile, another man charged with killing the cop showed up to court with a black eye from being beaten in custody, presumably by cops. Some cops expressed doubt that this suspect was the right man, and he was released a week after his arrest. Mr. Faison's girlfriend said he was with her on the night the officer was killed. An Essex County prosecutor, whose office is "investigating" the death of Earl Faison, said, "It is my understanding that the Orange police officers did nothing wrong in this situation." Mr. Faison was an aspiring rap singer. **Source:** The New York Times, 4/13/99 & 4/14/99; WCBS (Channel 4, NYC) TV, 4/12/99

Thomas Spranger	49	—	

March 13, 1999. Chatham:

Mr. Spranger was shot twice and killed by Chatham Police Sgt. George Petersen after allegedly leaping from the bushes with a large kitchen knife and refusing orders to drop it. Mr. Spranger's estranged wife had told a friend that she was concerned about her ex-husband. The friend became worried when he was unable to reach her by telephone. He drove by her house, saw Mr. Spranger's car parked in her driveway, and called the police. After the shooting, cops entered the house and found Mr. Spranger's estranged wife and eight-year-old son dead and his three-year-old son injured with numerous knife wounds. Authorities believe that Mr. Spranger killed his ex-wife and son before the police killed him. **Source:** The New York Times, 3/15/99

James Rusell Stiptek   48   —

December 28, 1998. Hackensack:

Mr. Stiptek had reportedly stabbed his roommate several times (the roommate survived). Two plainclothes detectives arrived in response to a call about the stabbing and allegedly saw Mr. Stiptek running toward them. They pulled their guns and ordered him to stop, but he supposedly kept coming, shouting, "I'm going to kill you." Cops claim he tackled one of the detectives and wrestled for the detective's gun, still shouting, "I'm going to kill you." The other detective, James McMorrow, hit Mr. Stiptek on the head with a police-issued flashlight. Mr. Stiptek allegedly kept fighting until he was handcuffed by a third cop. He stopped breathing and died at the hospital. The medical examiner claimed that his death was unrelated to the blow to his head, but did not offer an alternative explanation. **Source:** Associated Press, 12/29/98

Michael Howard   19   —

November 25, 1998. Elizabeth:

Mr. Howard was shot and killed by police after he allegedly smiled at them and "began shooting wildly" in what authorities called a "suicide by cop." Mr. Howard had allegedly shot and killed a bicyclist in Maryland, robbed a bank, shot and wounded another man in Plainsfield, NJ, . He then pulled up to a cop car in Plainsfield, honked his horn, and shot and wounded the two cops inside. Police chased Mr. Howard to Elizabeth, where he allegedly opened fire on them before they killed him. **Source:** Associated Press, 11/26/98

Adrian Howell   27   —

November 24, 1998. Newark (West Ward):

Mr. Howell was shot and killed by Newark Police Detective David Foster. Mr. Howell's girlfriend had filed a domestic violence complaint against him. Det. Foster was escorting the girlfriend home when Mr. Howell reportedly opened fire on them and wounded the officer before the officer shot and killed him. **Source:** The New York Times, 11/25/98

Damon Washington   42   —

November 18, 1998. Bayside State Prison:

Damon complained of chest pains early Tuesday morning, Nov. 17, 1998. Prison officials say nurses gave Damon some antacid medication and checked his vital signs, which seemed to be normal. Yet the next morning, at around 6:37 a.m., Damon was found dead in his cell. The preliminary cause of death is said to be a heart attack. The union representing prison workers, the Communications Workers of America, has stated that the company operating the prison's privatized medical services since 1996, Correctional Medical Services Inc., has lowered the quality of care to cut costs. Mary Ellen Bolton, the department's chief of staff, said that a doctor did not see Damon. Bayside has been the focus of at least two other investigations, State and Federal, over the treatment of inmates. A class action lawsuit of about 500 inmates, including Damon, has been filed in Federal court stating physical brutality by correction officers. **Source:** Philadelphia Inquirer, 11/20/98

Samuel Lorde   44   —

Englewood. Sept. 3, 1998:

Police arrived in response to a call that Mr. Lorde was tearing up the apartment he shared with his girlfriend and her child. Cops claim that when they knocked on the back door, Mr. Lorde broke the glass window on them and said, "Shoot him." Patrolmen Thomas Loschiado and Herman Savage entered the apartment and handcuffed him, then placed handcuffs on his ankles when he allegedly tried to kick them. Mr. Lorde began vomiting on his bed, went into cardiac arrest, and died. Cops claimed he seemed drunk, smelled of alcohol, and had heart disease. No criminal charges were filed against the cops. The victim worked as a machinist at the Marcal Paper Co. **Source:** Associated Press, 9/4/98

Giodimuray Sulaymanov   35   —

July 18, 1998. Paterson:
Cops claim Mr. Sulaymanov died from a single blow to the head after falling down the stairs at a slaughterhouse while being chased on foot by police after a traffic violation. Police claim they handcuffed Mr. Sulaymanov after he fell down the stairs. But a security guard saw the victim in handcuffs moments after hearing him land, implying that he had already been handcuffed before falling down the stairs and that the cops may have pushed him. An independent autopsy paid for by Mr. Sulaymanov's employer found that he died of multiple skull fractures. The case aroused much anger in Paterson's Muslim community, of which Mr. Sulaymanov was a member. Police Officers Vincent Acquaviva and Willie Palmer, who had chased Mr. Sulaymanov, had been members of a special anti-gang unit that had recently been disbanded after some of its members were indicted on brutality charges. **Source:** The New York Times, 7/24/98

Franklin Pettiford   47   *Black*

April 24, 1998. Paterson:
Franklin was pepper-sprayed to death by five police officers. According to police accounts, Pettiford was seen buying drugs by undercover narcotics officers. Detectives followed his car, pulled him over, and claim they saw him swallowing a bag of marijuana. At 10:23 p.m. they smashed the window of his locked car and pulled him out through the window. Cops allege that Franklin resisted (they do not say how), so they pepper-sprayed him, handcuffed him, and placed him face down on the pavement. He began having trouble breathing and died a short while later at the hospital. Police claim the cause of death was choking on the bag of pot. Franklin's family does not believe this account. His father, a well-known minister, said that his son didn't do drugs and was not a violent person. Even the newspaper admitted that it is extremely rare for people to try to swallow marijuana to hide the evidence as the penalty for possession is only a $200 fine and no jail time. **Source:** Bergen Record, 4/28/98

Aamira Edwards   20   —
Darryl Elliot   21   —

April 11, 1998. Newark:
A driver trying to get away from police crashed into a metal pole, splitting the car in two. Aamira and Darryl, both passengers in the back seat, were killed. The driver was injured, as was a woman who had supposedly been waving her arms and screaming from the front passenger seat, which cops said prompted the chase. **Source:** Associated Press, 4/12/98

Jennie Hightower   14   —

March 27, 1998. Trenton:
Jennie was a passenger in an allegedly stolen car in a high speed chase with police. The driver supposedly sped toward police, and cops fired 20 rounds, killing Jennie with a shot to the back of the head and seriously wounding the 16-year old driver, Hubert Moore, with a shot to the neck. Officers James Letts, Chris Drew, and Joseph Gachetti fired ten, seven, and three shots respectively at various times. They claim they thought the driver was giving up and they approached the car only to see it start moving toward them. The car supposedly hit Officer Drew in the leg and injured him. A grand jury declined to indict any of the three cops. The prosecutor refused to disclose any details, such as who fired the fatal shot. Jennie's brother, speaking for her mother, who is deaf-mute, denounced the findings of the grand jury, saying, "The cops acted out of hand, and we wanted the Prosecutor's Office to do something. The officers should have been punished for their actions." Meanwhile, Hubert Mercer, the driver, has been charged with manslaughter for Jennie's death. **Source:** Associated Press, 3/28/98 & 5/13/98

Guy Walsifer   40   —

January 15, 1998. Cedar Grove Police Headquarters:
Guy was shot and killed by two detectives at the headquarters of the Cedar Groves Police Department. Cops claim Guy was completing a statement about a burglary for which he'd been arrested when he struck a detective, took away his 9-millimeter pistol and pointed it at the same detective. Two other detectives, Charles Lagattura and Andrew McPhail, fired several shots at Guy, killing him. All this allegedly took place in a basement interrogation room. **Source:** The New York Times, 1/17/98

| **Unidentified Man** | 20s | — |

November 6, 1997. Princeton:

This man was shot and killed by police as he allegedly held a woman hostage while robbing the Sovereign Bank on Nassau Street around 6:30 p.m. Police claim that when they arrived at the scene, the man came off the elevator wearing a ski mask and holding a gun to a woman's head. He supposedly said his life was over, pointed the gun at the woman, and started to count, at which point the police "had no choice and fired." A preliminary investigation by the Mercer County Prosecutor found that the cops acted appropriately. **Source:** New York Newsday, 11/8/97

| **Dannette "Strawberry" Daniels** | 31 | *African American* |

June 7, 1997. Newark:

Police claim they arrested Strawberry for drug dealing and that she was shot after a scuffle broke out in the squad car. People on the scene say Strawberry, who was pregnant, wasn't buying any drugs. Protests erupted on the spot as cops were pelted with rocks and bottles.

| **Michael Byrd** | 21 | — |

January 30, 1997. Elizabeth:

Michael was shot 38 times in an apartment building by members of the FBI Violent Crimes Task Force. He was unarmed. The FBI originally claimed that he fired at them first. A grand jury refused to indict.

| **Carolyn "Sissy" Adams** | — | *African American* |

September 10, 1996. New Brunswick:

Sissy was shot to death by white police officer James Consalvo after he stopped to question her about alleged prostitution.

| **Jan Vida** | 42 | — |

August 1996. Garfield:

An unemployed laborer, Jan was pepper-sprayed to death by cops who came to his apartment because they heard he was causing a disturbance. Cops claim he attacked them, at which point they held him on the floor and pepper-sprayed him, supposedly with no effect. However, Jan went into cardiac arrest and died an hour later. The cops were cleared of any wrongdoing. His brother filed a lawsuit against three cops, saying Jan posed no threat and that the officers used excessive force. The lawsuit also named the manufacturer of the pepper spray, the town of Garfield, and the Garfield police department as defendants. **Source:** Associated Press, 12/8/97

| **Scott Tofano** | — | — |

July 1996. Ramsey:

Scott was pepper-sprayed and wrestled to the ground by police. He died a few hours later. The cops were cleared of any wrongdoing. **Source:** Associated Press, 12/8/97

| **Catherine Falzarano** | 42 | — |

June 10, 1996. Woodbridge:

Catherine was married to a police officer and suffered from depression. She allegedly pointed a handgun at three officers in an 11-minute standoff. She was shot seven times and killed. Her gun was empty. Cops claim she left a note saying she "didn't have the guts" to do it herself. **Source:** Associated Press, 4/25/98

Bobby Rodriguez　　　　　　　　　　　24　　　　　　　　—

July 19, 1995. Jersey City:
Jersey City police officers Hazecamp and Wolfe pulled Bobby over, allegedly for running a stop sign. Police claim that the unarmed Rodriguez then jumped out of his van and ran into a vacant lot. The officers gave chase. Wolfe said he scuffled with Rodriguez and lost control of his weapon. Wolfe's gun went off three times. Hazecamp then shot Bobby four times, and he died on the spot. The two cops each suffered a minor wound. Witnesses contradicted the police account. Several people who ran to the vacant lot when they heard the shots arrived to see Bobby lying face down in a pool of blood, with the cops removing handcuffs from behind his back. The cops deny this, but cannot explain why he would have fled and braved police gunfire over a traffic violation. As it turned out, Bobby had been driving home to pick up his companion to take him to work. His companion was Jose Torres, the prisoner being transported in the back of Chiusolo's car the night that Maximino Cintron was killed. Jose Torres told the press that ever since he testified to the grand jury in 1991, Jersey City police had continually harassed him and Bobby Rodriguez.

Julio Tarquino　　　　　　　　　　　22　　　　　　　*Bolivian*

May 7, 1995. Jersey City:
Julio, his fiancée, and a friend went to a gas station convenience store to buy some food around 3:30 a.m. Two white men began taunting and insulting them and Julio and his friends headed to their car to leave. As they were leaving, Officer John Chiusolo (who killed Maximino Cintron four years earlier) drove up. He was off-duty and out of uniform. He handcuffed Julio and beat him to the ground, kicking him repeatedly in the head. Julio's finacée attempted to reason with Chiusolo and was also beaten. Julio was arrested for assaulting an officer, then taken to Christ Hospital in Jersey City and treated. He was released back into police custody at 6:30 a.m. "coherent and even joking," according to hospital personnel. Six hours later, Julio was returned to jail – a time lapse that has never been accounted for. Fifteen minutes later, he was found slumped over in his cell, convulsing. He died on May 11 of skull fractures. Julio was a housepainter and a contractor, a good-natured and hardworking person, engaged to be married. Community protests followed, and another man, German Barrantes, came forward so say that Chiusolo had beaten him at a traffic stop a few days before the murder of Julio Tarquino. In September, 1995, Chiusolo was indicted for second-degree manslaughter. As of September, 1997, he remains free on bail with no trial date set.

Khary Grimes　　　　　　　　　　　18　　　　　　　　—

between September 1994 & July 1995. Jersey City:
Khary was killed by police who claim he stole a car and threatened an officer with a b.b. gun. No witnesses other than the police were present. **Source:** Revolutionary Worker

Unidentified Man　　　　　　　　　　—　　　　　　　　—

between September 1994 & July 1995. Jersey City:
This man was shot and killed by police who claim he pointed a gun at them. No witnesses other than the police were present. **Source:** Revolutionary Worker, Fall, 1997

Armando Lopez　　　　　　　　　　—　　　　　　　　—

June 12, 1994. Jersey City:
Armando was found hanging in his cell while in custody of the Jersey City police.

Maximino Cintron	23	*Puerto Rican*

July 16, 1991. Jersey City:

Maximino was tinting the windows of a friend's car in the early evening. Two plainclothes cops transporting a prisoner (Jose Torres) to jail stopped to write Maximino a ticket for "illegally repairing a car in the street." Maximino took the ticket, said he'd "put it with the rest of his collection," tore it up, and threw it on his windshield. Police claim he threw the ticket at them and then 20 people attacked them, but witnesses contradict this account. Officer John Chiusolo became enraged, attacked Maximino, and put him in a headlock. Maximino struggled out and the two stood facing each other. Chiusolo pulled his gun, and Maximino began backing up, saying "All right, all right, what are you going to do, shoot me?" Chiusolo fired into Maximino's upper abdomen, severing his aorta. While he bled to death in the street, the first ambulance on the scene transported Chiusolo and his partner to the hospital for treatment of bruises. Maximino left behind his wife, Maria, and their 1-year-old son, "Little Max." Community protests followed, including a march of over 400 people. Information about Officer Chiusolo's background started to come out. At the time, Chiusolo was facing numerous brutality complaints and a civil action for assault. Officer Chiusolo, however, remained on the force, and four years later, he arrested and assaulted a man who died in custody.

Phillip Pannell	15	*Black*

April 10, 1990. Teaneck:

Phillip was chased by a white Teaneck officer. Police reported that the officer fired one shot that missed Phillip while he was attempting to climb over a fence, and that Phillip turned and ran toward the officer. One grand jury absolved the officer of any criminal wrongdoing. A second grand jury indicted him when it was discovered - after lining up the bullet hole in the youth's jacket with the entry wound from the second shot fired - that Phillip was shot in the back and killed while his arms were raised. According to witnesses, Phillip never got the chance to turn and face the officer, but was shot while attempting to surrender. At the officer's second trial, an all-white jury deliberated for a little over 8 hours before returning a verdict of not guilty.

NEW MEXICO

Name	**Age**	**Nationality**	**Photo**
Abelino Montoya	18	—	

February 14, 1998. Las Vegas, NM:

Mr. Montoya, a high-school honors student, was shot and killed by Las Vagas Police Sgt. Steve Marquez and Officer Joseph Mantelli after they followed him in his truck into a dead-end street. The officers claim they saw him driving the wrong way on a one-way street, lost him, and then saw him later that night. They say they opened fire only after Mr. Montoya backed into their patrol car and refused orders to get out of the truck. Officer Mantelli fired 3 times, hitting the victim once in the head and once in the torso, with the 3rd bullet striking the truck. Sgt. Marquez fired once and hit the truck. A toxicology test supposedly showed that Abelino Montoya was legally drunk. Both cops were charged with second-degree murder, manslaughter, and several lesser charges, but were allowed to remain free on unsecured bond of $50,000 for Marquez and $100,000 for Mantelli. That same night, Officer Mantelli assaulted another allegedly drunk driver, Gene Gonzales, in an unrelated incident and put a gun to the un-resisting man's head. Mr. Montoya's family filed notice of their intention to file a civil suit against the city of Las Vegas and its police department. **Source:** Albuquerque Journal, 10/23/98

Tommy Martinez	34	*Latino*

September 9, 1996. Albuquerque (Menaul & Wyoming):

Tommy allegedly robbed the Village Inn with an 8-10" knife around 1:30 a.m. Police chased him one block where he supposedly charged at an officer who was 10-12 feet away. Officers Jeffrey Stone and Brian Dennison fired a total of six shots, hitting Tommy three times and killing him. **Source:** Vecinos United (Albuquerque, NM)

Orlando Barranca — —

November 6, 1995. Albuquerque (1200 Polomas SE):
Cops arrested Orlando at the residence of a friend on a misdemeanor warrant. He died in the back seat of the patrol car while being hog-tied. Police were responding to a call about a loud party. The medical examiner called in accidental death by asphyxiation. The Albuquerque Police Department said it would stop hog-tying people following this incident. **Source:** Vecinos United (Albuquerque, NM)

Larry Harper　　　　　　　　　　　　　　　　33　　　　　　　　*white*

October 14, 1995. Albuquerque (Elena Gallegos picnic area):
Larry's family sought help because he was threatening suicide. He ran away from police prior to the incident but asked to speak to his family. Cops would not allow this. When Larry allegedly pointed a gun at the SWAT team officers who had surrounded him, he was shot and killed. He was hit twice, once after he was down. He died on the scene, around 2 a.m. A grand jury found no criminal wrongdoing by police. **Source:** Vecinos United (Albuquerque, NM)

Richard Lee Nicholds　　　　　　　　　　　41　　　　　　　　*white*

September 16, 1995. Albuquerque (2200 block of Garfield SE):
Richard allegedly cocked and pointed a gun at a police officer. He was six feet inside his apartment when the cop fired through the screen door. Richard supposedly went for the gun again after he was down, at which point he was shot and killed by Albuquerque Police Officer John Bode. Richard was hit several times in the chest and abdomen. The incident happened around 4 p.m. Witnesses said that the police did not announce themselves or tell Richard to drop the gun before killing him. The cops initially denied this, but were reported to have later changed their stories. A grand jury found no criminal wrongdoing by police. **Source:** Vecinos United (Albuquerque, NM)

Russell Dean Wells　　　　　　　　　　　　37　　　　　　　　—

March 28, 1995. Albuquerque (200 Espanola NE):
Russell was shot four times, once in the head, and killed by Albuquerque police officers who were responding to a report of a possible stolen vehicle. Cops claim Russell tried to run them down, so they shot and killed him. The incident happened around 9:15 a.m. A grand jury found no criminal wrongdoing by police. **Source:** Vecinos United (Albuquerque, NM)

Jay McAllister　　　　　　　　　　　　　　25　　　　　　　　*white*

March 1995. Albuquerque (600 Elk Drive):
Members of Jay's family called paramedics to their residence in the Four Hills Mobile Home Park, 600 Elk Drive, because Jay was suicidal. Six Albuquerque Police Officers also responded. The victim emerged from his home and allegedly pointed a gun at the cops. He was shot twice, in the chest and the hip, and killed. Cops claim the victim fired shots, but there is no evidence of this. An elderly neighbor was almost hit by police bullets. The incident happened around 10 a.m. A grand jury found no criminal wrongdoing by police. **Source:** Vecinos United (Albuquerque, NM)

Allen Chris Hensley　　　　　　　　　　　45　　　　　　　　—

August 24, 1994. Albuquerque:
Police responded to a report of a man on the Bridge SW at the Rio Grande River with a gun around 3:50 p.m. Officer Ralph Gonzales fired three shots and Officer Thomas Paul Jacobo fired six shots. Allen was hit in the neck and killed. Cops claim he fired four rounds at Officer Jacobo. A grand jury found no criminal wrongdoing by police. **Source:** Vecinos United (Albuquerque, NM)

Renee Lee Holms　　　　　　　　　　　　38　　　　　　　　—

August 18, 1994. Albuquerque (I-25 & Gibson):
Renee was shot in the neck, head, and chest and killed around 11 p.m. by police, and possibly SWAT team officers, responding to a report of a possible stolen truck. Cops claim Renee fired on them from his pick-up truck. A grand jury took less than ten minutes to find no criminal wrongdoing by police. **Source:** Vecinos United (Albuquerque, NM)

Leo Kampa   64   —

July 29, 1994. Albuquerque (8401 Spain NE):
Leo was shot once in the back and killed by SWAT team officer Stan Grey. Leo was allegedly suicidal and asking police to shoot him. He had a gun to his own head, but never pointed it at the cops. Police, who were responding to reports of gunfire at the apartment complex, initially claimed the victim came towards them, but witnesses said that Leo was walking back into his apartment and was no threat to anyone. The police bullet severed Leo's spinal cord. A grand jury took 15 minutes to decide there was no criminal wrongdoing by police. **Source:** Vecinos United (Albuquerque, NM)

Miguel Dominguez-Flores   43   *Mexican*

October 7, 1993. Albuquerque:
Miguel was shot once in the head and killed by Albuquerque police at the United New Mexico Bank at Pennsylvania & Montgomery NE during a botched bank robbery that led to hostage taking. None of the hostages were hurt. Miguel was allegedly robbing the bank, and was a suspect in other robberies. Newspapers reported that he was armed with a gun and a fake bomb. The fatal shot was fired by SWAT Officer Steve Rodriguez in what was his fourth fatal shooting in his 12 years on the force. A grand jury found no criminal wrongdoing by police. **Source:** Vecinos United (Albuquerque, NM)

Bernard Saiz   23   *Latino*

September 5, 1993. Albuquerque (1200 Commerical SE):
Bernard was shot once in the chest and killed by Officer Felipe Rael who was one of two cops responding to a report of shots fired. Police claim the victim fired at them and said they found cocaine, crack and marijuana. Witnesses reported that the cops did not identify themselves. A grand jury found no criminal wrongdoing by police. **Source:** Vecinos United (Albuquerque, NM)

Randy Stewart Libby   30   —

March 20, 1993. Albuquerque (12600 Copperwood NE):
Randy was at a friend's house when cops came to serve an arrest warrant for a 1990 parole violation on an arson charge. He was depressed, suicidal, and allegedly threatening to kill the officers and telling them to shoot him. He supposedly said he was armed, but he wasn't. He came out of his friend's house around 3 a.m., after a 4 1/2 hour standoff, holding a cologne bottle shaped like a train. Police allegedly mistook it for a gun and fired five or six shots, hitting Randy three times (in the head, chest, and back) and killing him. He was shot by SWAT officers Howard Terry and Steve Rodriguez. A grand jury found no criminal wrongdoing by police, but in Feb.1996, his family settled a lawsuit for $100,000. Randy's girlfriend and a neighbor were both critical of the police, saying the victim posed no threat when he was gunned down. **Source:** Vecinos United (Albuquerque, NM)

David Holly   mid–30s   —

January 22, 1993. Albuquerque (6101 Central NE):
The Albuquerque Police Department and the Secret Service were conducting an investigation into counterfeit money, illegal gun sales, and false ID crime rings. When they arrived at the room at the Economy Inn, David allegedly pointed a gun at them. He was shot twice and killed by Office Augustin Salcido. A grand jury found no criminal wrongdoing by police. **Source:** Vecinos United (Albuquerque, NM)

Alejandro Torres   50   *Latino*

December 25, 1992. Albuquerque (3400 Eastern SE):
Alejandro was shot four times and killed by Albuquerque Police Officers Jan Dickerson and Eric Hammond. Cops were responding to a report of shots fired outside the apartment building. They allegedly saw a man run into the building and were in hot pursuit. Cops claim they fired after Alejandro pointed a gun at them. Witnesses dispute the police version of events, saying Alejandro did not point a gun at the cops and that the officers did not announce themselves. Alejandro was hit in the eye, shoulder, hand, and back. A grand jury found no criminal wrongdoing by police. His family settled a civil rights violation and wrongful death lawsuit for $400,000 in March, 1995. **Source:** Vecinos United (Albuquerque, NM)

Marshall Smith, Jr.   late 20s   *African American*

December 2, 1992. Albuquerque (I-40 Rio Grande Bridge):
Marshall was allegedly threatening to commit suicide by jumping off the bridge or to throw his 11-month-old daughter off the bridge. He was shot once and killed by SWAT officer Steve Rodriguez of the Albuquerque Police Department. Marshall was unarmed. His daughter was not hurt. A grand jury ruled that it was justifiable homicide. **Source:** Vecinos United (Albuquerque, NM)

Roy Hilton   46   —

October 7, 1992. Santa Fe (New Mexico State Penitentiary):
Roy, an inmate serving 18 months for possession of a firearm by a felon, had a history of heart problems. He died of heart failure when prison health officials failed to provide surgery to replace a heart valve. A cardiac surgeon who examined Roy said that he had a 100% chance of death in the near future. Roy requested heart surgery twice, in writing, as required by prison protocols. His requests were denied, and he filed a grievance. Roy wrote, "If I don't get medical attention very soon, I will surely die." Ten days later, he had a heart attack and died. Despite Roy's repeated pleas and the fact that several cardiologists stressed he would die soon without immediate treatment, health officials at the New Mexico penitentiary where Roy was incarcerated unnecessarily delayed the surgery. Dr. Lambert King, a court appointed monitor for the state's prisons said that, "The death of this patient reflects egregious systemic deficiencies in the quality of care." The correction department's own medical director said that "cost consideration" was a factor in the decision to delay surgery. **Source:** St. Louis Post-Dispatch, 9/27/98; Independent, 7/1/98

Kevin Dale Odom   34   —

October 23, 1991. Albuquerque (200 Adams NE):
Kevin was shot and killed at his girlfriend's home by Albuquerque Police Officer Steve Devoti after he allegedly brandished a toy Uzi. Police had come to serve Kevin with a Texas felony arrest warrant. A grand jury found no criminal wrongdoing by police. **Source:** Vecinos United (Albuquerque, NM)

Gary D. Bodiford   36   *white*

July 20, 1991. Albuquerque (4600 Central NE):
Cops were responding to reports of shots fired at the Zia Motor Lodge at 4600 Central NE. Gary, who was visiting from Florida, had gotten into an altercation with a transvestite, at whom he allegedly fired a gun, in his motel room. Officer Duffy Ryan arrived and, without identifying himself, shot and killed the victim. A grand jury found no criminal wrongdoing by police. **Source:** Vecinos United (Albuquerque, NM)

Christopher McKissick   19   —

May 22, 1991. Albuquerque (I-25 & Coal):
Christopher was shot and killed when cops responded to an attempted suicide call. Police claim the victim lunged at them with a 2-3" knife. Witnesses said the police used unnecessary force and that Christopher was retreating when he was shot. A grand jury found no criminal wrongdoing by police. **Source:** Vecinos United (Albuquerque, NM)

John Sollars   36   —

May 21, 1991. Albuquerque (149 Alcazar NE):
John was shot multiple times in the chest, abdomen, arm and possibly the back by Albuquerque Police Officers Martin Porath, Thomas Martin, Joe Romero, and Michael Fox, who fired a total of 11 shots. Cops responded to a call about a family fight. They shot and killed John when he allegedly threatened them with a Buck knife. John reportedly had mental problems and supposedly told officers to shoot him. John's family and neighbors dispute the police account, saying the four officers were kneeling with their guns pointed and that another cop mocked the dying man. A grand jury found no criminal wrongdoing by police. **Source:** Vecinos United (Albuquerque, NM)

Grant Montoya	28	*Latino*

February 13, 1991. Albuquerque (2100 Wisconsin NE):
Grant had a long history of mental illness and was going through a crisis. The Albuquerque Police responded to a call for help from his family, the second such call that week. Grant's family supposedly told cops that he had left his mother's apartment carrying a hatchet. When Grant allegedly lunged at police with the hatchet, he was shot twice in the chest and killed by Officer Mark Lillie. A grand jury found no criminal wrongdoing by police. **Source:** Vecinos United (Albuquerque, NM)

Manual Rameriz	26	*Latino*

October 12, 1990. Albuquerque:
Cops executing a narcotic search warrant used a tow truck and cable to rip off the front door. Manual allegedly pulled an unloaded gun on SWAT team members when they entered his house at 3414 Thaxton SE to execute the warrant around 6 a.m. He was shot twice in the chest and killed by SWAT team officers Stan Grey and David Bertrum. Navy SEALS accompanied the Albuquerque Police Officers in the search. No explanation for this was given and the city claimed that the SEALS were not on duty. A synopsis of a police report says no drugs were found, while a newspaper reported that cops found two marijuana cigarettes on the premises. The victim's 16-year-old niece was forced to change her clothes in front of male officers. Others inside the residence said police did not announce themselves. Manual's survivors settled a lawsuit for $275,000 in May 1993. **Source:** Vecinos United (Albuquerque, NM); The Boston Globe, 1/11/98

Carlos Lucero	46	*Latino*

August 30, 1990. Albuquerque (4640 10th NW):
Carlos allegedly confronted Officers Richard Rohlfs and Kenny Salazar with a fork and a steak knife when they responded to a call about a family fight in his home while he was eating dinner. He was shot once in the head and killed by police. He supposedly told officers to shoot him. A grand jury determined that it was justifiable homicide. **Source:** Vecinos United (Albuquerque, NM)

Jackie Gonzales	31	*Latino*

August 4, 1990. Albuquerque (3515 Cypress SW):
Cops responded to a call about a suicidal person, Jackie Gonzales. His wife denies that he was suicidal. Jackie allegedly waved a gun at the officers as he sat in a pick up truck in his back yard. He was shot in the shoulder and hand and killed by the police. The victim did not fire any shots. His wife and a neighbor dispute the police version of events. A grand jury determined that no criminal charges should be brought against the police. **Source:** Vecinos United (Albuquerque, NM)

NEW YORK CITY / WESTCHESTER / LONG ISLAND

Name	**Age**	**Nationality**	**Photo**
Richard Watson	32	*Black*	

September 1, 1999. Manhattan (Harlem/Washington Heights):
The day before he was killed, Mr. Watson had been arrested for selling heroin on the corner of Broadway and 137th Street. He was released from jail downtown on the morning of Sept. 1. He hailed a cab and took it back to the spot where he was arrested, reportedly to pick up his car. When he arrived at his destination, he allegedly jumped out of the cab without paying the fare. The cab driver called the police. Cops tried to question Mr. Watson, who reportedly ran, hid under a van, and then dove head first into the open window of a livery cab that was stopped at a red light. As cops tried to pull him out by his feet, New York Police Officer Foster Gilkes shot him once in back and killed him. Officer Gilkes said the shooting was accidental. He did not explain why he had his gun drawn in the first place. Residents in the predominantly Dominican neighborhood gathered to condemn the shooting, chanting "Policía - Asesinos" (police - murderers). This was the second fatal shooting by New York police in three days **Source:** New York Newsday, 9/2/99; The New York Times, 9/2/99

Gidone "Gary" Busch   31   *Jewish*   ◉

August 30, 1999. Brooklyn (Borough Park):

Mr. Busch, an emotionally disturbed man, was shot 12 to 19 times and killed by four New York City police officers. Earlier in the day, someone had called 911 to report that Mr. Busch had been dancing in the streets, clothed only in a colorful bath towel, singing a religious song, and waving a hammer. Later, in response to another call, cops went to his home, and he reportedly answered the door with a hammer in his hand. Six cops surrounded him and ordered him to drop the hammer. He reportedly said, "You can shoot if you want but I'm not putting my hammer down." He started rapping on the steps with the hammer and the cops maced him. Cops claim he lunged at them with the hammer and hit a sergeant before they opened fire. One TV station reported that cops said he had been arrested the day before for hitting someone with a hammer. But another TV station reported that he had never been arrested. One neighborhood resident said on TV that Mr. Busch was known to dance around the neighborhood holding a hammer and wearing a prayer shawl. This shooting sparked intense outrage in Borough Park's large Hasidic Jewish community. People pointed out that cops knew Mr. Busch was mentally ill and that they could have dealt with him less forcefully. That same night, an overwhelmingly Hasidic crowd held an angry demonstration in the streets near the scene where Mr. Busch was killed, chanting "No Justice, No Peace." Flyers were distributed calling the cops "Nazi pigs" and warning people that they could be killed by the police for holding a hammer. A supervising sergeant who was involved in the fatal shooting of Mr. Busch had been involved in another shooting several years earlier. That earlier shooting was ruled justified. It is unclear whether or not it was fatal. **Source:** FOX-Ch. 5 News (New York), 8/30/99; WNBC-Ch. News (New York), 8/30/99; WABC-Ch. 2 News (New york), 8/30/99; New York Daily News, 8/31/99; New York Post, 8/31/99; The New York Times, 8/31/99

Unidentified Man   35   —

August 27, 1999. Bronx (Melrose):

This unidentified man was shot in the head and killed by retired New York Police Detective Donald E. Pagani, Sr., during an alleged shootout. Former Det. Pagani was working as a security guard. He was on his way to deliver cash to the bank when the unidentified man and one or two companions supposedly tried to rob him at gunpoint. In the ensuing altercation, both the unidentified man and former Det. Pagani were killed. **Source:** The New York Times, 8/28/99

Larry Cobb   30   *Black*

August 18, 1999. Manhattan (Upper East Side):

Mr. Cobb was shot in the chest and killed by New York Police Officer Douglas Grant around 4 a.m. The officer's gun was loaded with the deadlier hollow-point bullets that had recently become standard issue for the NYPD. The incident began when Officer Grant and his partner saw a parked Jeep with a broken passenger window. They reportedly saw Mr. Cobb hiding under a nearby car and ordered him to come out, which he did. Cops claim Mr. Cobb began struggling with Officer Grant and that the officer's gun went off accidentally during the struggle. Mr. Cobb ran, then fell down and died less than a block away. On his person, police reportedly recovered items stolen from the jeep. The victim's family questioned the police version of events, saying that Mr. Cobb was not violent and was afraid of guns. His brother said, "My brother was never a violent person. If you look at his history, he did not do violent crimes. There was no excuse for them to kill him." Authorities admitted that while the victim had a drug problem and a history of convictions for minor crimes, mostly breaking into cars, he had no record of violent crimes. The authorities maintained that the shooting was accidental but also that it appeared justified. This was the third fatal shooting by the NYPD in a ten day period. **Source:** The New York Times, 8/19/99; Fox Ch. 5 News (New York, NY), 8/18/99

Angel Reyes   47   —

August 15, 1999. Manhattan (East Harlem):

Mr. Reyes was shot in the abdomen and critically wounded by police during an undercover drug operation. He died the following day in the hospital. Cops claim Mr. Reyes threatened an officer with a 34-inch machete. But a witness reported that the victim was running away when he was shot. The cops who were chasing him were wearing civilian clothes. A neighbor said that the victim, a building superintendent, did not speak English. Cops claim Mr. Reyes had a history of drug arrests and was facing an attempted murder charge. The incident took place at 110th St. & Lexington Ave., right near where Sherly Colon was pushed off the roof of a housing project by the police on Apr. 24, 1997. **Source:** The New York Times, 8/16/99 & 8/17/99

Robert Striker   54   —

August 9, 1999. Manhattan (Financial District):

Mr. Striker went into a bank that he had allegedly robbed a few months before. A teller told a security guard that she recognized him. The security guard called the police and followed him outside and into another bank, then back to the first bank. At about the same time, police arrived. Officer Bernadette Batignani opened fire on him. Cops claim Mr. Striker took out a handgun, pointed it at the officer and refused orders to drop it. Mr. Striker was wounded and ran outside. More cops shot him. He continued running, then collapsed and died. Cops fired a total of 35 shots, wounding a bystander and sending lunch-time crowds ducking for cover on the busy, narrow streets of downtown Manhattan. Authorities admit that the victim probably did not fire any shots. They also claim that some civilian witnesses were under the mistaken impression that Mr. Striker had fired shots. Authorities used that to argue that it was also reasonable for cops to believe that Mr. Striker had fired, and that this would have prompted the cops to keep firing. Referring to the fatal shooting, a police official said, "It looks like this was justified." **Source:** The New York Times, 8/10/99

Jatrek Hewitt   17   —

August 5, 1999. Staten Island (New Brighton):

Mr. Hewitt was shot twice in the chest and killed by off-duty Irvington (New Jersey) police Sgt. Dwayne Mitchell. Sgt. Mitchell claims that Mr. Hewitt and two other youths approached him around 3 a.m. and that Mr. Hewitt pointed a "long-barreled pistol" at him in an attempted robbery. A Daisy air pistol was reportedly recovered from the scene. Sgt. Mitchell was not charged in the shooting. The Staten Island DA's office said they were investigating. **Source:** The New York Times, 8/6/99

Unidentified Man   —   —

August 2, 1999. Long Island (Massapequa):

The man had allegedly robbed a bank around noon by brandishing a gun, which turned out to be a toy. As he left the bank, retired New York City Police Officer Emil Florie chased him across the street, where the man climbed into a taxi. Former Officer Florie confronted the man at the taxi's rear door and claims the man ignored an order to drop the gun and pointed a "realistic-looking toy gun" at him. Former Officer Florie shot and killed him. **Source:** The New York Times, 8/3/99

Delano Maloney   32   —

July 24, 1999. Brooklyn (Flatbush) (in custody):

Mr. Maloney was arrested on drug possession charges and died in police custody. Several witnesses said police beat him before he died. Cops claim he choked on a bag of drugs, which they supposedly found in his throat when he suffered "medical distress" on the way to the station house. An official preliminary autopsy supposedly found no bruises consistent with a beating. The victim's family said they would conduct their own autopsy. **Source:** The New York Times, 7/26/99

Renato Mercado   63   —

June 28, 1999. Manhattan (Upper West Side):

Mr. Mercado, a mentally ill man, was shot once in the chest and killed by police in his apartment building as he stood outside the super's apartment allegedly holding a machete. The victim reportedly had a long-running dispute with the super. The super called the police to report that a tenant was trying to break into his apartment. Police claim that Mr. Mercado was wielding a machete when they arrived, so they shot him to death. Cops claim they recovered a machete at the scene. But at least one neighbor did not believe the police account, saying that Mr. Mercado often walked around with a butter knife in his mouth, especially when he was not taking his medication to treat his mental illness. She described Mr. Mercado as troubled but harmless, saying "He was an old man. He walked with a cane. All you had to do was push him.... If he had a machete, I don't know, but I saw him every day and he always had a butter knife." Another neighbor said of the victim, "He was a very nice man. He always said hello." Authorities withheld the name of the cop who killed Mr. Mercado. **Source:** The New York Times, 6/29/99; New York Daily News, 6/29/99

| **Rodney Mason** | 38 | — |

May 25, 1999. Queens (South Jamaica):

Six months before he was killed by police, Mr. Mason, a mentally ill man, had been released from a psychiatric hospital. His mother became concerned that he was behaving strangely and had stopped taking his medication. A mental health team from the hospital was on its way but called Mr. Mason's mother to say they would be late. Mr. Mason overheard the conversation and reportedly "became distraught and then violent, grabbing the phone from his mother," so a hospital official called 911. Cops arrived and allegedly found Mr. Mason brandishing a four-inch folding knife. They charged up the steps at him and engaged in a "ferocious struggle," during which the cops were reportedly "driven down the stairs." One cop was supposedly stabbed twice and slashed once. The cop's partner, New York Police Sgt. Edward Heim, shot Mr. Mason once in the chest and killed him. **Source:** The New York Times, 5/26/99

| **Amadou Diallo** | 22 | *Guinean (West African)* | |

February 4, 1999. Bronx (Soundview):

Amadou Diallo came to New York from his homeland in Guinea, West Africa, to work and study. He worked long hours as a street vendor, selling socks and videotapes on Manhattan's 14th Street. On the night he was killed, he got home from a long day of work around midnight and then stepped out again, possibly to get something to eat. Four white cops, New York Police Officers Sean Carroll, Kenneth Boss, Edward McMellon, and Richard Murphy fired 41 bullets at him as he stood in the narrow vestibule of his building, hitting him 19 times and killing him. Officers McMellon and Carroll emptied their clips, firing 16 shots each. Officer Boss fired five shots and Officer Murphy fired four. Bullets penetrated deep into the building, going through the walls of an occupied apartment. Amadou was unarmed. All that was found on him were his wallet and his beeper. The cops were members of the Street Crimes Unit (SCU), which is notorious for stopping and searching large numbers of Black and Latino men without probable cause. The SCU's slogan is "We own the night," and members of the unit were known to wear t-shirts bearing an Ernest Hemingway quote about the thrill of hunting human beings. Massive community outrage followed the murder of Amadou Diallo. His funeral was attended by thousands, and his coffin was carried through the street outside the mosque after the service. There were weeks of near-daily demonstrations around the city, and over 1,200 people demanding murder indictments of the four cops were arrested in acts of civil disobedience in front of police headquarters. Large numbers of people of diverse ethnic and socio-economic backgrounds were outraged at this cold-blooded murder and the city's failure to arrest the cops. Under intense community pressure and almost two months after killing Amadou Diallo, the four cops were indicted by a grand jury for second-degree murder. Outside the hearing where the indictments were unsealed, several hundred off-duty cops held a demonstration supporting the four cops who murdered Amadou Diallo, saying, "It could have been any one of us." After their indictments, the four cops were arrested, but released on bail almost immediately. They were suspended without pay for 30 days, but then returned to work on desk duty. Through their lawyers, the cops suggested that perhaps they thought Amadou had a gun, perhaps he made a suspicious movement, perhaps he did not obey their order to stop. But as of Aug., 1999, they have not offered a concrete explanation for why they shot Amadou so many times. Outrage mounted when it came out that cops searched Mr. Diallo's apartment after they killed him, looking for drugs or something they could use to defame his reputation and thereby justify his death (they didn't find anything). An autopsy showed that at least one bullet hit Amadou in the bottom of the foot, showing that the cops kept shooting after he was down. In the wake of the shooting, the city speeded up its plan to arm cops with deadlier hollow-point bullets on the grounds that the number of shots fired showed that police lacked adequate "stopping power." Officer Boss had previously shot and killed another Black man, Patrick Bailey, on Oct. 31, 1997. Two of the other cops who killed Amadou Diallo had previously been involved in non-fatal shootings. **Source:** The New York Times, 2/8/99, 2/10/99, 2/11/99, 2/18/99, 2/20/99, 2/22/99, 2/25/99, 2/26/99, 3/4/99, 3/5/99, 3/9/99, 3/17/99, 3/18/99, 3/25/99, 3/26/99, 3/27/99, 3/29/99, 4/16/99, & 5/4/99; New York Post, 2/7/99, 2/13/99, & 2/14/99; New York Newsday, 2/7/99, 2/12/99, & 2/15/99; The Daily Challenge (New York, NY), 3/9/99; Caribbean Life (Brooklyn, NY), 3/2/99; New York Daily News, 2/14/99

Thomas Pizzuto   38   *white*   ☞

January 8, 1999. Long Island (Nassau County Jail):

Mr. Pizzuto, a part time delivery man for New York City schools, was serving a 90-day sentence for traffic violations. A recovering heroin addict in a methadone maintenance program, Mr. Pizzuto was not given his methadone, despite repeatedly asking for it. On Jan. 8, his second day in jail, guards became angry with his repeated requests and his refusal to be quiet. Four guards entered his cell and beat him and stomped him, rupturing his spleen and breaking his ribs. A guard with a metal chain wrapped around his fist punched Mr. Pizzuto in the face, leaving chain link marks. He was left in his cell for three days without medical treatment and forced to sign a statement saying his injuries resulted from falling in the shower (he was threatened with further beatings and continued denial of methadone if he refused to sign). Mr. Pizzuto was finally taken to the hospital, where he died of his injuries on Jan. 13. On his death bed, he said, "Two guards did it." His relatives condemned the guards for covering up the murder. The victim's mother was twice prevented by guards from seeing her son. The victim's father said, "Tommy went in for a traffic ticket. He got the death penalty." The victim's brother said, "These people [the guards] are murderers...and we want them arrested." In addition to his parents and brother, Mr. Pizzuto leaves behind his wife and their 14-year-old son, who has Down's Syndrome. The murder of Thomas Pizzuto sparked numerous exposures of brutality and abuse at the Nassau County Jail as victims came forward to tell their stories and the press began to report on them. **Source:** The New York Times, 1/21/99, 1/22/99, & 1/23/99; Associated Press, 1/23/99

Kenneth Banks   36   *Black*

October 29, 1998. Manhattan (Harlem):

Kenneth was riding his bicycle in Harlem. New York Police Officer Craig Yokemick claims that Kenneth was involved in what he thought was a drug transaction, then swallowed vials of crack to destroy evidence and went riding away. That is when Officer Yokemick hurled a 2-pound radio at him. It struck Kenneth in the head, and knocked him off his bike onto the pavement. He died 11 days later on Nov. 10, after slipping into a coma at the hospital. While in police custody on Oct. 29, Kenneth suffered three seizures, and was later diagnosed with a skull fracture and bleeding of the brain. The victim's family attorney, Jonathan Abady, said that Kenneth's death is another example of how people of color are being mistreated by the police department. He added, "Kenneth Banks was not posing any threat to the physical safety of any member of the New York Police Department." Officer Yokemick was placed on modified assignment. **Source:** Associated Press, 11/12/98

Kevin Cerbelli   30   —

October 25, 1998. Queens (Elmhurst):

Mr. Cerbelli, a mentally ill man, was shot four times and killed by police in the 110th precinct station house. The fatal bullet was to the victim's back. Mr. Cerbelli reportedly walked into the station house bare-chested and barefoot, carrying a rosary and a screwdriver. Cops claim he tried to stab a sergeant in the back with the screwdriver and refused orders to drop it before they opened fire. Mr. Cerbelli suffered from schizophrenia and, according to his mother, was still delusional when he was discharged from a psychiatric hospital two months before he was killed. She filed a lawsuit against the police and the mental health system. "I loved my son so much and I tried so hard," she said. "No one would help me." **Source:** The New York Times, 8/18/99

Yvette Marin Kessler   36   *Puerto Rican*

September 30, 1998. Manhattan (Central Booking):
Two days before her death, Ms. Kessler was arrested on drug possession charges, which were later dismissed. She was held on a warrant from Norfolk, VA, for three hours of community service which she had been unable to complete because she was pregnant. At 2:30 a.m. on the day she died, Ms. Kessler was taken to the hospital with stomach pains, then released back into police custody at 5:00 a.m. with no drugs in her system and no bodily trauma. Three hours later, she was found dead in her jail cell. Photos shown to her family showed a large contusion on her forehead, her nose bent to one side, and face, ears, and lips that were swollen and red. Her family reported, "The sight of her face and body convinced us that she had been the victim of foul play. No answers or cooperation and cover-ups from police officials then led us to believe that they were responsible for her death. Then eyewitnesses started coming forward with their stories of police officers beating Yvette." The medical examiner's office tried to claim that her death was caused by an acute drug overdose, and the police commissioner claimed her injuries were self-inflicted. Cops tried to trash her reputation by saying she had a history of drug abuse. But as her family pointed out, "How did Yvette manage to get drugs, enough to cause death while she beat herself up in the process and all without police awareness and supervision?" She had tested negative for drugs in the hospital, and her blood tests, x-rays and other medical records showed that she was in fine health when she left the hospital. Ms. Kessler is survived by her six children and other family members. A statement from her family read in part, "We believe that her death was indeed caused by police misconduct and we will not rest until her death is avenged. We must demand an end to these police crimes so our children can feel free to walk our streets again without fear of police picking on them because of the color of their skin or because the neighborhood they live in has been chosen as the target of the week." **Source:** victim's family

---

Cristian Sepulveda, Jr.   26   —

September 17, 1998. Brooklyn :
Mr. Sepulveda was shot and killed by a member of the New York Drug Enforcement Task Force during a raid. Cops claim Mr. Sepulveda fired at them first and that one cop was hit in his bulletproof vest, although he was not injured. Authorities allege that Mr. Sepulveda was part of a drug gang that specialized in robbing narcotics from other drug gangs. Police had set up a warehouse to look like a rival gang was storing cocaine there. The victim's father and four others were arrested and charged with conspiring to commit armed robbery and distribute cocaine. **Source:** Associated Press, 9/18/98

Joseph Gasparro   29   —

September 6, 1998. Queens (Astoria):
Mr. Gasparro, his wife, and a friend, had allegedly robbed a stationary store and drove away. They were stopped by police, and cops claim that a scuffle ensued when they tried to arrest the three of them. Mr. Gasparro was shot by police when he supposedly jumped into a police car and tried to drive off during the altercation. He died at the hospital. **Source:** The Buffalo News, 9/8/98; Associated Press, 9/7/98

Ronald Johnson   23   —

August 28, 1998. Bronx (Morrisania):
Mr. Johnson was killed when police officers who were waiting for him began chasing him as he left his apartment. He was climbing a drainpipe to get away. It broke and he fell to his death. He was wanted on alleged armed robbery charges. **Source:** The New York Times, 8/29/98

| **Federico Hurtado** | 62 | — |

April 26, 1998. Queens (Queens Village):
In a fatal traffic accident, off-duty Police Officer Robert Bolson, driving his car, collided with a car driven by Mr. Hurtado. Mr. Hurtado was killed, and his wife was seriously injured. One witness said that Mr. Hurtado had stopped his car at a stop sign. When he then edged into the intersection, Officer Bolson's car collided with his car with a great impact, crushing the driver's side of the car. According to a report from the hospital, Officer Bolson's breath smelled of alcohol, but the police prevented a Breathalyzer test at the hospital because they said that their colleague was too badly injured. However, a routine hospital blood test showed that the cop was intoxicated when driving. Police Commissioner Howard Safir said he is trying to determine if ranking police officials prevented accident investigators from giving Officer Bolson a Breathalyzer test. Officer Bolson was put on modified duty assignment 9 days after the accident when the result of the hospital blood test was released. Originally the police public information office did not disclose that Officer Bolson was a cop. **Source:** New York Daily News, 5/6/98; The New York Times, 5/7/98

| **Bryan Stewart** | 24 | — |

August 10, 1998. Nassau County (East Meadow):
According to the police account, Mr. Stewart abducted his ex-girlfriend, Caryn Lieber, from her home at gunpoint. Ms. Lieber had been able to call 911 prior to being abducted, and when the police arrived, her mother and brother told them about the abduction. When Mr. Stewart saw two police cars in pursuit, he reportedly pulled off the road. Cops claim that when they approached the car, Mr. Stewart shot Ms. Lieber. Three officers fired eight shots, killing Mr. Stewart. One newspaper reported that it was unclear whether Ms. Lieber had been shot by her ex-boyfriend or by the police. She was brought to the hospital and listed in critical-but-stable condition. **Source:** New York Newsday, 8/12/98; New York Daily News, 8/12/98

| **Freddie Rivera** | 17 | *Puerto Rican* | 👁 |

August 4, 1998. Bronx:
Freddie Rivera was shot in the chest with dum-dum bullets and killed by an unidentified cop. The cop did not identify himself or yell "Freeze!", "Police!", "Put your hands in the air!", or any such thing. His family described him as a bright kid, always looking forward to the future. Freddie was about to start college in September. **Source:** SLP form

| **Alex Santos** | 23 | — |

August 4, 1998. Bronx (Longwood):
Alex was shot and killed in the hallway of a building by undercover cops in a "buy-and-bust" operation. Police claim that two undercover cops went to Raul Morales Terrace, 834 East 161st St., at Prospect Avenue, just after 6 p.m. to buy cocaine from Alex and Jorge Ortega, age 15. Cops claim that the two youths "brandished weapons" and tried to get away with the money without handing over any drugs. The cops pulled their guns and fired, killing Alex and wounding Jorge. Police would not say whether any guns were recovered at the scene, nor did they release the names of the cops involved in the shooting. They did, however, release the rap sheet of the victim. Cops sealed the block and did not allow residents to return to the building. According to the newspaper, this is the third time cops have shot and killed someone in an undercover drug operation in New York City in 1998. **Source:** The New York Times, 8/5/98

| **Christopher T. Johnson** | 29 | — |

July 31, 1998. Long Island (North Bellport):
Suffolk County police officers Robert A. McGee, Jr., and Samuel Barretto spotted Chistopher, who was wanted on charges of driving without a license (a misdemeanor), on Provost Avenue. The cops stepped out of their car and tried to arrest him at 9:43 p.m. Chris "fled into the woods, and the officers chased after him," according to the police. He was sprayed with pepper Mace while being arrested, handcuffed, and brought out of the woods. He died as he was being transported to Brookhaven Memorial Hospital for treatment for the pepper Mace. Chris was an automobile mechanic, a married man with three children ranging in age from 15 months to 13 years. His family said he had no history of respiratory or other medical problems. His lawyer said, "Mr. Johnson was not a rapist or a murderer, or anything of that nature. His only crime was using his car to get back and forth to work and getting food for his family." The police say they are investigating. The family said they would probably seek an independent autopsy. **Source:** The New York Times, 8/1/98

| **Paul Anthony Maxwell** | 28 | *Black* | 👁 |

July 31, 1998. Nassau County (Hempstead):

Mr. Maxwell was shot five times and killed by police officer John Zoll, who claimed Mr. Maxwell struck several police officers with a baseball bat and was standing above an officer with the bat in his hand. According to Paul Maxwell's father, Roy Maxwell, neighbors called the police to report that his son was walking naked down the street with a bat in his hand and wearing only a knapsack. The victim's father pointed out that the police knew his son had a history of emotional problems and should have handled him differently. Moreover, he pointed out that Paul "didn't have a knife, he didn't have a gun. Is this a man the police should have shot five times?" Paul Maxwell had graduated from Moorehouse College in Atlanta and was working as a substitute teacher when his mother died of breast cancer in 1996. His brother called him a "born writer" and a genius. According to a newspaper article, neighbors knew him as "a gentle soul who remembered people's names and had a talent for making them feel special, especially children. He loved children." Paul took his mother's death hard and developed emotional problems, spending a week in a psychiatric hospital. A witness to Paul's murder told the NAACP that he was shouting "My mama is dead! I want you to leave me alone," as he swung a bat at the squad car when police approached. The witness said that Paul was swinging the bat one-handed in a radius around himself when he hit the two cops, hardly a life-threatening situation. **Source:** New York Newsday, 8/6/98; friend of victim

| **Christopher Malone** | 24 | *Black* |

July 19, 1998. Westchester County (Ossining):

Christopher was shot multiple times and killed by three white cops at 3:40 a.m. Cops were allegedly responding to a report of a man with a gun. They chased Chris and claim he turned and pointed a gun at them, at which point they opened fire. A protest march of over 150 people, mostly Black, occurred that evening, with protesters marching and chanting "No justice, no peace." Five cops were placed on paid administrative leave (paid vacation). The three cops involved in the chase were Officers Daniel Slater, Raymond DeBenedictis, and Richard Damiano. The other two who joined them at the scene were James C. Montague and Lisa Gallagher. Portraying the cops as victims, the mayor of Ossining said that the shooting was "the biggest nightmare of a police officer's life." In Sept., 1998, a grand jury refused to indict any of the cops. **Source:** The New York Times, 7/20/98, 7/21/98, 7/23/98, & 9/19/98

| **Jose Luis Zarete** | 22 | *Mexican* |

July 18, 1998. Bronx:

Jose Zarete, his brother, and Jose Alcala, all workers at a Bronx restaurant, expelled several unruly patrons. Those patrons then called in three friends with baseball bats and a fight began. Alcala called the police. Two narcotics cops, Officers William Maher and David Powers, claim that Zarete had a gun in his right hand and that they repeatedly ordered him to drop it. When he allegedly did not, they shot and killed him. The 2 cops admitted that Zarete was not pointing a gun at them when they opened fire. The police claimed that Zarete obtained the gun from his brother, Hugo, who was arrested and charged with criminal possession of a weapon. Mr. Alcala, age 42, disputed a key fact. "He [Jose Zarete] was trying to throw the gun away because he was scared of the police," Alcala said. He emphasized that the gun was not pointed at the police when Zarete was shot. Alcala also said that Zarete was struggling with another man when ordered to drop the gun. He added that the gun was found two feet from Zarete's body, next to a car, indicating that Zarete was trying to get rid of it. The officers did not face disciplinary charges. **Source:** New York Newsday, 7/20/98

| **Christopher Jackson** | 28 | *Black* |

July 1998. Long Island (Nassau County Jail):

Mr. Jackson suffered from sickle-cell anemia. While awaiting trial on a minor drug charge, he became ill and asked for treatment, which was denied. He was not hospitalized until three days later when his mother urged officials to get her son a blood transfusion. He lapsed into a coma and died. **Source:** The New York Times, 1/23/99

| **Sterling Robertson** | 69 | — |

June 22, 1998. Manhattan (Upper West Side):

Mr. Robertson was staying at the YMCA at 5 West 63rd St. and allegedly left a threatening note at the front desk on the day he was supposed to leave. Security guards went to his floor and claim that he pulled a knife and acted confused and disoriented, according to YMCA officials. The guards called the police, who claim that when they arrived, the man had barricaded himself in his room. After "fruitless negotiations," the police tossed in a stun grenade, then entered the room. They claim that Mr. Robertson slashed a cop's badge with his knife as the cop approached, causing another cop (Sgt. Cory Coneo) to fire two shots, both of which pierced the victim's chest, killing him. According to the press, Robertson was from Los Angeles and the knife turned out to be a seven-inch kitchen knife. **Source:** The New York Times, 6/23/98; New York Daily News, 6/23/98; Manhattan Spirit, 7/2/98

| **Steven Soma** | 37 | — |

June 16, 1998. Suffolk County (Holtsville):

Police claim they spotted Mr. Soma driving on a street at 11 p.m. without his headlights but within the speed limit. As cops tried to pull him over, he reportedly fled, eventually driving onto a side street and jumping out of the car. Police allege that he then ran and attempted to cross the Long Island Expressway on foot, where he was hit and killed by a passing car. Cops say they do not know why Mr. Soma fled. **Source:** New York Newsday, 6/18/98

| **Gloria Ambrosovitch** | 70 | — |
| **Melinda Podesta** | 40 | — |

June 11, 1998. Westchester (Tarrytown):

Retired Mamaroneck (Westchester) Police Officer Anthony Ambrosovitch shot and killed his wife and his daughter and wounded his daughter's boyfriend. A long-time family friend, Greenburgh (Westchester) Police Officer Ellen Lewitt, claimed that Gloria Ambrosovitch's death was meant as a mercy killing but had no explanation for the other two shootings. Former Officer Ambrosovitch said, "This was premeditated...I did it intentionally, and I want it to be known that it was intentional." When asked if he really hated his disabled wife that much, he replied, "What the f*ck hasn't she done to ruin my life?" He was charged with two counts of second degree murder. **Source:** New York Daily News, 6/13/98

| **James Crawley** | 52 | — |

May 30, 1998. Bronx (Kingsbridge):

James was shot once in the chest and killed by Officer Ray Ledda in an apartment on East 223rd Street in Kingsbridge around 3:30 a.m. Cops were responding to a 911 call from his former girlfriend who lived in the apartment. The newspaper reported that James had a history of assaulting her and that she had an order of protection against him. Cops claim that when they arrived, James was threatening the woman and her daughter with a knife. He allegedly refused an order to drop the knife and instead lunged at police, at which point he was shot and killed. **Source:** New York Newsday (Queens Edition), 5/31/98

| **Jose Serrano** | — | — |

May 26, 1998. Brooklyn (East Flatbush):

Jose was shot and killed in his apartment by Officer Anthony Mosomillo, who was also shot and killed, allegedly by the victim. Jose Serrano was confronted by cops from the 67th Precinct who were attempting to arrest him on a parole violation. Officer Mosomillo and Officer Miriam Sanchez-Torres arrived at Jose's basement apartment at 523 East 34th Street just after 8 a.m. His girlfriend let the cops in while Jose allegedly hid under the floorboards of a closet. Police claim that when they found Jose, he and his girlfriend struggled with the cops and managed to get Officer Sancez-Torres's gun away. Jose then allegedly used this gun to shoot Officer Mosomillo, who shot back with his own gun, killing Jose. Jose's girlfriend was arrested and charged with second-degree murder. The media talked about what a great guy Officer Mosimillo was, how hard this was on his family, etc., but said nothing about the family of Jose Serrano. The mayor and the police commissioner spoke about the fact that Jose Serrano was on parole (for a non-violent drug offense) and used his case to call for abolishing parole. The newspaper claimed that cops and residents of East Flatbush generally enjoyed a good relationship. In this neighborhood police murdered Keshawn Watson, on June 13, 1996, sparking a week of angry protests. **Source:** The New York Times, 5/27/948

Daniel Vereline   36   —

April 13, 1998. Manhattan:

According to the police, Daniel Vereline was spotted driving a stolen van. The police chased him from the Bronx into Manhattan, where he got away. Cops claim he was spotted later by another police car and as they started to pursue him, he smashed his van into a wall. As police approached, he allegedly climbed over the wall and jumped 40 feet in an apparent attempt to avoid capture. He was taken to the hospital, where he died of injuries. **Source:** New York Daily News, 4/14/98

Maxine Cardoza   61   —

April 9, 1998. Brooklyn:

According to a police spokesperson, three men were fleeing from a burglary in a stolen car and were being chased by a police car through a residential and shopping area during the afternoon. The cars were traveling at speeds up to 100 mph when the car being chased jumped the curb, hit Ms. Cardoza on the sidewalk, and killed her. The cops caught the three men and charged them with burglary, auto theft, and murder. A police department spokesman said that an investigation did not indicate any violation of police procedures. **Source:** New York Daily News, 4/11/98

Cesare Mollo   —   —

March 30, 1998. Bronx (Parkchester):

Mr. Mollo was shot in the head and killed by (presumably off-duty) Westchester County Police Officer James DiMaria. Officer DiMaria arranged to meet him at a Bronx home, lured him into driving to another location and, during the trip, shot him, dumped his body in the street, and drove away. He was caught 11 days later. In Jan., 1999, Officer DiMaria was convicted of second-degree murder and criminal possession of a weapon. He received consecutive prison terms of 25 years of life and four to eight years. Officer DiMaria claimed that Mr. Mollo was a mob enforcer trying to collect a $40,000 debt and that he shot him in self-defense. **Source:** The New York Times, 1/22/99

Unidentified Man   —   —

March 25, 1998. Queens (Little Bay):

New York State police claim that they spotted the man driving a stolen car and chased him for miles onto the Throgs Neck Bridge, where he stopped his car and was pursued on foot by the state troopers. He then allegedly jumped off the bridge about 120 feet in what appeared to be an attempt to elude the cops. He was pronounced dead when his body was recovered. **Source:** New York Newsday, 3/26/98

Steven Service   20   —

February 27, 1998. Brooklyn (Bed-Stuy):

Steven was shot in the head, torso and leg and killed by police during a "buy-and-bust" operation at 325 Franklin Avenue, near Clifton Place. NYPD investigators say a total of 11 shots were fired by three of the four cops on the scene. No non-police weapons were recovered. Police claim that "suspects" (including Steven Service) and cops were grappling in the hallway during the raid. A sergeants gun was allegedly grabbed and fired by one of the "suspects," and two of the three backup officers rushed in and opened fire, killing Steven Service. Cops claim they fired to save the life of the sergeant leading the raid, who ended up being wounded, probably by friendly fire. Police claim that two other suspects were arrested and that one got away. The investigation of the incident is focusing on how the sergeant was wounded and expresses no concern about the death of Steven Service. Mayor Giuliani said the cops did "an excellent job." This incident made the newspapers because the sergeant was wounded. **Source:** The New York Times, 2/28/98

Clayborne Parks   51   —

February 10, 1998. Manhattan (midtown):

An Amtrak spokesman claims Mr. Parks was being loud and abusive outside Penn Station, so he called the police. According to the report, when Mr. Parks refused an order to move, the police arrested him and charged him with disorderly conduct. The police admit that he did not resist arrest. After spending 12 hours in a police lockup, cops report he began having seizures and was taken to a hospital where he died about an hour later. Police claimed Mr. Parks had a criminal record. **Source:** New York Daily News, 2/11/98

Fred Pilataxi   20   —

February 9, 1998. Queens (South Richmond Hill):

According to police reports, an unidentified off-duty transit police officer was returning home from the subway early in the morning. The police claim that Mr. Pilataxi approached the off-duty cop with a pellet gun altered to look like a .44 caliber Magnum revolver. The officer fired twice. Pilataxi was pronounced dead at the hospital. **Source:** New York Newsday, 2/10/98

Unidentified Man   —   —

February 6, 1998. Bronx (South Bronx):

According to the police, a security guard discovered two armed burglars in the basement of a supermarket very early in the morning. The police said the guard shot and killed the unidentified man, and the other alleged burglar fled. Police said they were considering charges against the security guard because his shotgun was not licensed. **Source:** New York Newsday, 2/2/98

Vladimir Santana   19   —

February 5, 1998. Queens (Elmhurst):

Vladimir was shot and killed by six cops, who fired over 20 shots while he was allegedly robbing a sandwich shop at 86-55 Broadway, near Queens Blvd. Cops claim they walked by as Vladimir, armed with a 30-round semi-automatic pistol, was robbing the shop and that he had already shot and wounded an employee. Cops supposedly told Vladimir to drop the gun. Police then used pepper spray and night sticks on him. Vladimir fell onto and broke a neon sign. Some of the cops got electric shocks from the broken sign and lost their grip on Vladimir. Vladimir allegedly fired a shot at the cops, which hit the floor. Then he was killed in a fusillade of police bullets. **Source:** New York Daily News , 2/6/98; New York Newsday (Queens Edition), 2/6/98

Margaret McGivern   94   —

February 1, 1998. Queens (Jackson Heights):

Ms. McGivern and a friend were crossing the street in front of McGivern's house at 11 a.m. when a police car traveling in reverse on their one-way street struck Ms. McGivern. "They never even blew horns or sirens," said Margaret Taylor, a friend of the victim. "I didn't know they were there until they came upon us." Ms. McGivern was taken to the hospital where she was treated for a fractured shoulder and back injuries. Ms. Taylor said that Officers John Kilpatrick and Denise Torres, who were in the police car, "didn't even come to the hospital with me," nor did they inquire about their condition. According to Eileen Steward, executor of Ms. McGivern's estate, Ms. McGivern had been living alone, doing her own shopping. She was very energetic. After the accident, however, she needed two nurses to watch her 24 hours a day. Ms. Steward said the victim was in constant pain after the accident and had difficulty breathing. She died six weeks later on Mar. 16, 1998, and the death certificate said she died of natural causes. When Steward, Taylor, McGivern's lawyer, and New York Newsday all tried to find out why the police car was backing up on the street, they were given no answer. **Source:** New York Newsday (Queens edition) 4/17/98

Lawrence Elie   26   —

February 1998. Manhattan (Harlem):

Mr. Elie was shot and killed outside a social club by two members of the NYPD's Street Crimes Unit, Sgt. Patrick Buttner and Officer Vincent DeQuieroz. The two cops fired 13 shots, hitting Mr. Elie four times. Mr. Elie had allegedly fired a gun at another man during a dispute, and cops claim he fired on them when they identified themselves. **Source:** New York Daily News, 2/14/99

Richard Austin   22   —

January 26, 1998. Brooklyn (Canarsie):
Richard was shot and killed by police who claim he refused an order to stop. Police claim that they saw two men approach a third man on the sidewalk at East 80th Street and Flatlands Avenue in Canarsie. Police decided to stop and investigate. Richard allegedly began to run away and one cop jumped into the patrol car and drove ahead of Richard while the other officer followed him on foot. They said Richard was holding a gun in his hands as he ran, and that when the patrol car stopped ahead of him, he turned around and began running back toward the officer who was following him on foot. That officer fired four times, hitting him twice in the upper chest and once in the left shoulder, according to the Medical Examiner. **Source:** The New York Times, 1/27/98

Leon Smith   33   —

January 19, 1998. Bronx (Morris Heights):
Leon was shot and killed by a cop during a "buy-and-bust" operation that went bad in a Morris Heights apartment building. Cops claim that Leon shot and killed Det. Sean Carrington before being fatally shot himself. Another alleged suspect was arrested and charged with second-degree murder. **Source:** New York Newsday (Queens Edition), 1/24/98

Scott Warne   31   —

January 16, 1998. Bronx:
Police claim that two cops were told that a man in a nearby car was armed. When the officers approached the car, the woman driving it allegedly sped away. The officers pursued. They claim that when the car got stuck in traffic, Scott jumped out and fired at them. They claim Scott was killed when they fired back. **Source:** The New York Times, 1/17/98

Miguel A. Valoy-Núñez   40   *Dominican*   👁

January 4, 1999. Manhattan (Varick St. INS Detention Center):
Mr. Valoy-Núñez was sent to the INS detention center to await deportation. He'd served seven months in jail on a misdemeanor drug charge stemming from an incident where cops found a tiny amount of heroin in his home. A Dominican immigrant who had not become a U.S. citizen, he faced deportation under a 1996 immigration law that mandates deportation for non-citizens convicted of even minor drug offenses. Mr. Valoy-Núñez died of pneumonia and a viral infection a week after being admitted to the detention center. When he complained of chest pains and a persistent cough, he was given over-the-counter cold medicine. He was not seen by a doctor for two days, and authorities refused requests by him and his wife to take him to the hospital. Two days later, a doctor saw him and ordered blood work and an X-ray, but it was too late. Mr. Valoy-Núñez died. His wife blamed medical neglect for her husband's death, saying, "He didn't get the right treatment, that's all. He belonged in a hospital and they refused to listen." As early as 1992, the ACLU had written a report exposing deficiencies in the medical care provided to inmates at the Varick St. Detention Center. That was before the center became more overcrowded as a result of the 1996 immigration law. Authorities said they were "baffled" by Mr. Valoy-Núñez's death and denied that it was caused by medical neglect. **Source:** The New York Times, 2/9/99

William J. Whitfield   22   *Black*   👁

Dec. 25, 1997 (Christmas Day). Brooklyn (Canarsie):
Police officers from the 63rd precinct heard gunfire from the roof of an apartment building in the Glenwood Houses. They were in the area to investigate a domestic dispute. They saw Mr. Whitfield running along Ralph Avenue and assumed he had fired the shots. They chased him in their car. He allegedly ignored an order to stop and ran into a grocery store. Cops followed him into the shore and claim that he rose suddenly from behind some shelves with a blue knit cap in his hand (at other times, cops said he was holding a key chain). They claim to have mistaken the (blue) cap (or the key chain) for a gun. Officer Michael J. Davitt shot him once in the chest, killing him. Officer Davitt, had discharged his weapon in eight separate incidents prior to this, more than any other active-duty NYPD cop. Officer Davitt also had 12 civilian complaints, none of them substantiated, during his 14 years on the force. William Whitfield, who lived in the Glenwood Houses, was going to use a pay phone in front of the grocery store since he did not have a phone in his apartment. He was going to call his mother to tell her that he was bringing his two kids over for Christmas. He was unarmed. Cops tried to paint Whitfield as a criminal, with an "anonymous investigator" telling the media that the dead man had a record of arrests for robbery, larceny, and assault (although "it was unclear whether he had been convicted," according to the same investigator.) The article which made this allegation did not contain the name of the cop who killed Whitfield, as this information had not yet been released. A grand jury cleared Officer Davitt.

Reginald Bannerman   35   *Black*

December 19, 1997. Brooklyn (Crown Heights):
Reginald sometimes worked at the BBB Cafe on Bedford Avenue near Crown Street as a cleanup man, although he was off duty on this particular night. He asked a group of six undercover narcotics detectives, who were being loud and disorderly, to quiet down. They complied, but half an hour later encircled him outside the club. They repeatedly kicked and beat Reginald, then fired on him as he fled on foot. Less than two hours later, Reginald was hit by a train in a subway station about half a mile away. It is unclear whether he was chased onto the tracks by the cops or whether he fell into the tracks as a result of his injuries. The city claims his death was a suicide. The family disputes that. The cops were placed on desk duty for failing to report their involvement in the incident.

Moshe Pergament   19   *Jewish*

November 14, 1997. Long Island
According to press reports, Moshe, a Nassau Community College student, bought a toy gun, got in his car and started driving erratically on the Long Island Expressway. When cops pulled him over, he allegedly got out of his car and charged them with the toy gun in his hand. The cops shot him dead on the spot. The press published a copy of a note Moshe had supposedly written: "To the Officer who shot me!...It was a plan. I'm sorry to get you involved. I just needed to die." If this note is real, it is significant that Moshe knew the cops would kill him and that they would not be punished for it. The authorities called Moshe's death "suicide by cop." The two cops who killed Moshe were Officers Thomas Pollack and Anthony Sica. Cops claim Moshe's "suicide" was a result of gambling debts. **Source:** New York Daily News, 11/17/97; Revolutionary Worker, 12/14/97

Patrick Bailey   20   *Jamaican*

October 31, 1997. Brooklyn (East New York):
Police claim they confronted Mr. Bailey in front of his apartment building at 731 Sheffield Ave. after a resident told them that Bailey had threatened him with a gun. Cops claim that Mr. Bailey fled into a nearby apartment building as they approached, then spun around to confront them in the hallway. Officer Kenneth Boss fired, hitting Mr. Bailey twice, once in the leg and once in the buttocks. The leg wound severed an artery. Cops claim they recovered a shotgun at the scene. The family says cops chased Mr. Bailey into the basement, shot him, and left him to bleed to death while they rounded up and arrested his friends. This killing took place on Halloween night. Cops had been saying that gangs were supposedly going to carry out slashings and other attacks and "initiation rites" on Halloween. Many parents kept their kids home from school in fear of such attacks. Police were later forced to admit that no such "gang attacks" occured on Halloween. Officer Boss was cleared of wrongdoing and remained on the force. On Feb. 4, 1999, he was one of four cops who shot and killed Amadou Diallo. **Source:** Village Voice (New York, NY), 7/7/98 & 3/9/99; New York Daily News, 11/2/97

Oswaldo Andrew   43   —

October 18, 1997. Bronx:
According to a police spokesperson, two cops from the 44th precinct broke down Mr. Andrew's door around 6 a.m. because Andrew was attacking his wife with a knife. Cops allege they ordered him to drop the knife and then maced him. He allegedly kept attacking his wife, refused a second order to drop the knife and lunged at the cops. One of the officers shot Mr. Andrew once in the chest, killing him. Oswaldo Andrew's wife, Iris Ruiz, was taken to the hospital where she was listed in serious but stable condition. **Source:** The New York Times, 10/19/97; New York Daily News, 10/19/97

Karem McDonald   20   —

October 15, 1997. Bronx (Hunts Point):

Mr. McDonald was shot six times and killed by police in a schoolyard just as school was letting out. Ariel Coporal, 18, was shot twice and ended in the hospital. Reggie Des, 18, was held for questioning. The undercover police were conducting a drug "buy-and-bust" operation outside the school. According to witnesses, shots suddenly rang out at 3:07 p.m. Barbara Farrow, a Head Start teacher, said she was leading students back to school when the shooting began. She said that also in the area were many children from a nearby elementary school and a junior high. Ben Rodriguez, director of a local community facility, said the cops "couldn't have picked a worse possible time" for an undercover drug operation. Police Commissioner Howard Safir said the shooting was "a result of the fact that an undercover officer was being assaulted by three people." Detective Lafferty was running and shooting when he was shot in the thigh. But no weapons were found on the victim or any of the other youths, making it appear that Det. Lafferty was shot by friendly fire. The seven cops fired 52 shots although they were not threatened by weapons. **Source:** New York Daily News, 10/16/97, 10/17/97; New York Newsday (Queens edition), 10/19/97

Alcadio Guerrero   54   *Dominican*

October 13, 1997. Manhattan (Harlem):

Alcadio was shot and killed during a shootout between cops and a civilian. He was killed by a stray bullet. An immigrant from the Dominican Republic, Alcadio worked as a porter. He was sweeping the sidewalk when, cops claim, a man in a livery cab pulled a gun on a woman who had rejected his advances. The cab driver pulled in front of a police car and the man jumped out of the cab as the cops emerged from their car. Police claim the man fired first. Officers chased him about 100 feet along 137th Street toward Riverside Drive (he was later caught and arrested). The newspaper said "10 to 12 shots whizzed up and down the block." Police claim it is not clear whose bullet killed Alcadio Guerrero. The newspaper reported that, "While cops said they had no choice but to fire, some area residents thought the cops should have held back." **Source:** New York Daily News, 10/14/97

Unidentified Man   20-40   —

October 5, 1997. Bronx (Morrisania):

The man and an associate had allegedly tried to rob a bodega and exchanged gunfire with the owner before fleeing empty-handed. The bodega owner called 911, and Officers Damian Colon and Anne Santos responded. They saw a man they thought resembled the gunman. When they went to question him, he ran and the cops pursued on foot. The man allegedly pointed a gun at them. It jammed, he threw it away and ran again. He plunged off the roof of a six story building and fell to his death. Cops claim that no officers were on the roof when the man went over the edge. **Source:** New York Daily News, 10/7/97

Ahmed Zia   19   *Iranian*

August 16, 1997. Long Island (North Babylon):

Ahmed was shot and killed by an off-duty New York City cop. Authorities say Ahmed allegedly robbed a McDonald's when he was shot and killed. Cops claim he entered the McDonald's at 4:45 p.m. wearing a ski mask, went around the counter and pointed a gun (which turned out to be a pellet gun) at an employee. He was shot and killed by the cop. The police implied that Ahmed had been involved in two other robberies of McDonalds' in the area. Ahmed was a student at Nassau Community College. He was on the wrestling team and had worked for two years at another McDonald's. He immigrated from Iran with his family and attended Elmont High School, where he was on the football and wrestling teams. His college wrestling coach said he was "a hard-working kid," and a friend said he was a "nice guy." The officer who killed Ahmed Zia was not named because he allegedly works undercover. A "preliminary investigation" ruled that the shooting was justified. Ahmed was killed on Saturday. His family reported him missing on Sunday. His body was not positively identified until Tuesday. **Source:** New York Daily News, 8/21/97

Unidentified Man　　　　　　　　　　　—　　　　　　—

August 6, 1997. Manhattan (West Side):

One man was killed and another wounded by plainclothes DEA agents during an undercover drug sting at a McDonald's. Two undercover agents were at the McDonald's to meet some men who allegedly believed the pair wanted help laundering money. The authorities claim that four men got out of a car and starting shooting at the undercover agents, intending to steal the money they were supposed to launder. Two other federal agents rushed in and a shootout ensued. A federal agent was also wounded, and two men were arrested. **Source:** Los Angeles Times, 8/8/97

Antonio Orengo　　　　　　　　　　　44　　　　　　—

July 17, 1997. Brooklyn (Bushwick):

According to a police spokesperson, two foot- patrol police officers in the Bushwick Housing Project responded to reports of gunshots. They went to the third floor of a building where they found a woman who had been shot to death. The report alleges that they saw Mr. Orengo across the street holding a handgun to his head and a shotgun with the barrel pointed inside his mouth. The report claims that backup officers and a member of the police hostage negotiation team arrived on the scene to try to negotiate a peaceful end to the situation. Instead, they claim, Mr. Orengo turned one of his guns on the officers, so the cops shot and killed him. The police spokesman claimed the dead woman was Mr. Orengo's girlfriend and had been killed by him. **Source:** New York Newsday (Queens Edition),

Robert Merle　　　　　　　　　　　56　　　　　　—

June 20, 1997. Suffolk County (Smithtown):

Mr. Merle was married but his wife and left him and he'd been laid off from his electrical engineering job. He had a long history of mental illness. Cops claim he called the police precinct 50 times on the day of his death, finally threatening them with a shotgun if they came to his home. Neighbors had also reportedly lodged complaints against him. Robert Merle's brother John, a retired Nassau County police lieutenant, had been on the telephone with him when the police arrived at his home to serve a warrant for making harassing phone calls to the precinct. The police claim they knew he had a shotgun, and when they tried to break down the door, he allegedly picked it up and pointed it at the door (cops supposedly saw this through a window next to the door). Five officers fired a total of seven shots, and Robert Merle died later at the hospital. His brother said that police knew Robert was mentally unbalanced and questioned why they did not proceed more cautiously. **Source:** New York Newsday, July 6, 1997

Unidentified Man　　　　　　　　　　　—　　　　　　—

June 12, 1997. Manhattan (Harlem):

According to a police spokesperson, two undercover police officers were executing a search warrant when a man emerged from an apartment. Cops claim he was carrying a .44 magnum and exchanged shots with them. The unidentified man was hit. He was declared dead on arrival at a hospital. Neither cop was injured. Police claimed that the building was a known drug location, that they had received 32 complaints about it that year, and that they had arrested 150 people there during the same period. **Source:** New York Daily News, 6/13/97

Bliss Verdon　　　　　　　　　　　25　　　　　　—

June 10, 1997. Queens (Jackson Heights):

Ms. Verdon was shot three times in the chest and killed by her former boyfriend, New York City Transit Police Officer Rodney Dilbert, as she spoke on a pay telephone. Officer Dilbert then shot and killed himself. The victim had filed an aggravated harassment complaint against Officer Dilbert about two weeks before she was killed. **Source:** New York Daily News, 6/12/97

Jose Santos　　　　　　　　　　　22　　　　　*Puerto Rican*

June 9, 1997. Rikers Island (jail):

Jose was hung in jail while sitting on a chair with two sheets tied to the window sill. He was beaten before he was hanged. The authorities claim it was a suicide. His family disputes this. Federal authorities refused to investigate, citing a lack of witnesses. The Santos family believes that witnesses - other inmates - were intimidated into not speaking up. They apparently feared retaliation. **Source:** victim's family

Unidentified Man　　　　　　　　　　　　　about 30　　　　　　—

June 6, 1997. Bronx (Tremont section):
The unidentified man had allegedly robbed three people. One of them flagged down a police car and reported the robbery. According to police, Officers Washington Zerita and Robert Caralyus saw a man running, and they chased him into a building. The cops claim they asked if they could speak with him but that he drew a handgun and fired, hitting Officer Zerita in the hand. Officer Zerita also fired and hit the man in the torso. The man died later that evening while undergoing surgery in a hospital. Police claim they found a .380 handgun at the scene of the shooting. **Source:** New York Newsday (Queens edition), 6/7/97

Sherly Colon　　　　　　　　　　　　　33　　　　　　*Latino*　　　　　　　　　　👁

April 24, 1997. Manhattan (East Harlem):
Sherly was pushed off the roof of the Clinton Houses, a housing project in East Harlem, by the police. She landed in a playground outside the building. Witnesses said the police threw a sheet over her body and then removed handcuffs from behind her back. The cops claim they were removing her bracelets. Police claim she committed suicide by jumping, but neighbors and her mother do not believe this. There were several protest marches from the Clinton Houses to the 23rd Precinct in the week after Sherly was killed. She left behind two children, ages 5 and 14. Sherly was a community leader, well-known, well-liked, and respected in the community.

Kevin Cedeno　　　　　　　　　　　　16　　　　　　*Trinidadian*　　　　　　　　👁

April 6, 1997. Manhattan (Washington Heights):
Police claimed Kevin Cedeno came at them with a machete but an autopsy report revealed that he was shot in the back. Witnesses said that cops shot him in the back without warning or ordering him to stop from at least 15 feet away. Cops then claimed that Kevin was running away from the cop who shot him, Officer Anthony Pelligrini, but toward another cop, and that they thought the black handle of the machete was a gun. After he was shot, a cop stood on Kevin's back and handcuffed him. Police stripped him of his clothes. The cop who murdered Kevin, Officer Anthony Pelligrini, was voted "Officer of the Month" by his fellow cops in the 34th precinct. **Source:** New York Daily News, 4/10/97; The New York Times, 4/9/97

Deonarimec Matan　　　　　　　　　　40　　　　　　—

March 23, 1997. Queens (Woodhaven):
Police officers fatally shot Mr. Matan at his family home after being called because of a domestic dispute. The police claim that Mr. Matan charged them with a 12-inch knife. **Source:** The New York Times, 4/9/97

Donald Davidson　　　　　　　　　　48　　　　　　—

March 21, 1997. Bronx (Tremont section):
According to the medical examiner's report, Mr. Davidson died after the police shot him once in the arm, twice in the back and four times in the abdomen. The police allege that they opened fire when Mr. Davidson approached them with a knife. According to Davidson's daughter, Adrianne Matthews, she called the police to the apartment because her father had become argumentative. She said her father was a schizophrenic. She hoped the police would take him to the hospital. The police later admitted that Davidson had a history of psychiatric problems. Ms. Matthews also said the officers provoked a confrontation by shoving her father as he got dressed and then sprayed him with pepper spray. She said her father ran to get a kitchen knife only after the officers had shot him twice in the back. According to Ms. Matthews' lawyer, Michael Barnes, reported that two other civilian witnesses saw the officers shoot Mr. Davidson twice in the back. **Source:** New York Newsday (Queens edition), 3/24/97; The New York Times, 4/9/97

Shante Gadson　　　　　　　　　　　21　　　　　　—

March 18, 1997. Bronx (Morris Heights):
Shante was allegedly threatening customers with a gun in a donut shop. A witness flagged down a police car and drove back to the shop with them. Cops claim that Shante drew a gun when Sgt. James Griffen ordered her up against a wall. The sergeant shot her in the abdomen. She died later at the hospital. Police said her weapon was not loaded. **Source:** New York Daily News, 4/19/97

Donald Owens   21   —

February 28, 1997. Brooklyn (East New York):

Cops allege that Donald Owens and a friend threatened a grocery store worker with a knife after another friend stole some beer from the grocery store. Police Officers Michael Murray and Richard Pavese claim they saw the confrontation and ordered Mr. Owens to drop the knife, but that he moved toward the police instead. Officer Murray shot the victim in the chest, killing him. **Source:** New York Daily News, 2/28/97

Jose Antonio Sanchez   56   *Dominican*   👁

February 22, 1997. Queens (Corona):

Jose Sanchez, a recent Dominican immigrant, was shot and killed when five plainclothes cops from the vice squad and social club task force charged into the El Caribe restaurant where Sanchez worked as a cook. Cops claim Sanchez would not put down his kitchen knife. Witnesses say cops did not identify themselves. The incident started when Sanchez saw some men in civilian clothes beating up a customer. He intervened on behalf of the customer and pulled one of the attackers off (he did not know they were cops). A cop then pushed him back roughly. He returned to the kitchen and retreated behind a table that was always in the middle of the kitchen floor. He was shot over this table, making the cops' story that he lunged at them with a knife impossible. No one but the cops was allowed in the kitchen for half an hour after the shooting, and when they were able to enter, the table had been moved to the side to make the cops' story seem plausible. Sanchez, known to his friends as "Librado," was always cracking jokes and making people laugh. Several protests organized by his family and friends followed. The Queens DA reluctantly brought the case to a grand jury which did not return an indictment against Richard Soto, the officer who killed Librado Sanchez. **Source:** "Killed by NYPD" poster in Revolutionay Worker, 3/30/97; victim's family

James Burch   20   —

February 17, 1997. Brooklyn (East Flatbush):

James Burch had reportedly been involved in an altercation at a club the previous week. When he arrived with his brother Daron and friends, the club refused them admittance and called the police. A sergeant arrived, no arrests were made, and James, his companions and the sergeant left. Cops claim that 20 minutes later, James and Daron returned and that James was carrying a 12-gauge shotgun. Officer Daniel Reefer, who was off-duty and working illegally at the Brooklyn nightspot as a security advisor, claims that James pumped the shotgun, leading Officer Reefer to approach him. Claiming James pointed the shotgun at him, Officer Reefer fired 3 shots. James was declared dead at the hospital. James' brother, Daron, was wounded in the leg, but no explanation was offered as to how he was shot. The police department suspended Officer Reefer for working at the club illegally. **Source:** New York Daily News, 2/19/97

Lutten Murrell   27   —

February 9, 1997. Brooklyn:

Lutten was arrested in the hospital after a domestic dispute in which he was stabbed in the chest. Lutten spent two days in police holding cells (with only a two hour hospital visit) before police took him in restraints to Kings County Hospital. He was dead on arrival. **Source:** "Killed by NYPD" poster, first published in the Revolutionary Worker, 3/30/97.

Lori Leitner   26   *European American*

February 1, 1997. Manhattan (Washington Heights):

Lori was shot and killed while sitting inside a four by four car. Police claim she got out of the vehicle and drew a toy gun on them. Bullet holes in the passenger window indicate she was still inside the vehicle when she was shot. **Source:** "Killed by NYPD" poster

Dion Hawthorne   17   —

January 25, 1997. Queens:

Dion was killed when an off-duty cop intervened in what police claim was a gun fight between two groups of youth. Police claim the victim was armed, but no gun was found at the scene. **Source:** "Killed by NYPD" poster

Richard Singleton	18	*African American*

January 20, 1997. Bronx:
Richard died in police custody. Police claim he went into a coma from drugs and alcohol when they were about to interrogate him for a stabbing. He died ten days later. **Source:** "Killed by NYPD" poster

Anthony King	44	—

December 24, 1996. Queens (Jamaica):
According to police, Anthony King called 911, said he was having trouble breathing and that "he would kill the first police officer that arrived." Cops claim they found Anthony with a pistol and knife. They shot and killed him. **Source:** "Killed by NYPD" poster

Charles Campbell	37	*African American*	◉

October 4, 1996. Westchester (Dobbs Ferry):
Charles was shot and killed by an off-duty NYPD cop, Officer Richard DiGuglielmo, because Charles parked in a spot in front of his father's delicatessen. Charles had to defend himself from assault by the cop's father for parking in his father's favorite parking spot. Charles, who was Black, had parked his car outside the father's deli (the family is white) and ran across the parking lot to buy a slice of pizza. Weekly protests led by Charles' family at the site of the murder followed. Diguglielmo Jr. (the cop) was indicted for second-degree murder while his father and a cousin were indicted on assault charges. The father and cousin were acquitted, but DiGuglielmo Jr. was convicted of second-degree murder and sentenced to 20 years to life in prison. **Source:** "Killed by NYPD" poster; victim's family

Joseph Stevens	20	*African American*

September 18, 1996. Harlem:
Joseph was shot dead by a cop while walking down the street with his bicycle. **Source:** "Killed by NYPD" poster

John Cochran	26	*African American*

August 18, 1996. Manhattan:
John was shot five times and killed because he was holding a cigarette lighter shaped like a gun. **Source:** "Killed by NYPD" poster

Oliver Campbell	18	—

July 4, 1996. Brooklyn:
Oliver was shot and killed by police after a grocery store robbery. **Source:** "Killed by NYPD" poster

Emilio Eucdea	40	*Latino*
Menellio Eucdea	30	*Latino*

July 4, 1996. Brooklyn (Sunset Park):
Emilio and Menellio were shot and killed when confronted by police who had flooded the area in response to what cops said was a gang shooting earlier in the evening. **Source:** "Killed by NYPD" poster

Nathaniel Gains	26	*African American*

July 4, 1996. Bronx (subway):
Nathanial was shot in the back and killed by a transit cop on a Bronx subway platform. His family waged a fight for justice, and several protests were held. The cop was convicted of second-degree manslaughter. **Source:** "Killed by NYPD" poster

Unidentified	—	—

June 30, 1996. Bronx (Morris Heights):
The victim was shot and killed by police in a chase after a drug bust setup. **Source:** "Killed by NYPD" poster

Carmine Capone	25	—

June 29, 1996. Queens (Rockaway):
Carmine was shot and killed during an undercover sting operation police say was set up to buy weapons. **Source:** "Killed by NYPD" poster

Steve Excell	37	*African American*

June 19, 1996. Jamaica, Queens:
Steve was shot in the back of the head and killed as he ran away from police who were called to break up a domestic dispute. **Source:** "Killed by NYPD" poster

Aswon "Keshawn" Watson	23	*African American*	👁

June 13, 1996. Brooklyn (East Flatbush):
Aswon was shot at 24 times and hit by 18 police bullets while sitting in his car with his hands in the air. According to witnesses, undercover cops in an unmarked car rammed Keshawn's car as he pulled out of a parking space. After the first shot, one cop said, "You're a dead n*gger," and continued firing. Cops claim he "made a motion" of going for a gun, but no gun was found. The victim died on the scene. A grand jury refused to indict the cops. Protests over the shooting took place in the neighborhood. **Source:** "Killed by NYPD" poster; eyewitness accounts

Dwight Oliver	33	—

May 1996. Long Island:
Dwight was shot and killed by an off-duty New York City housing police officer moonlighting at a gas station during an alleged robbery. **Source:** "Killed by NYPD" poster

Diógenes Paolino	32	*Dominican*

January 22, 1996. Manhattan (Washington Heights):
Diógenes was shot and killed by police outside a pool hall. An immigrant from the Dominican Republic who spoke little English, Diogenes did not understand when police officers told him to "put down the weapon." **Source:** "Killed by NYPD" poster

Patrick Heslin Phelan	39	*Irish*	👁

January 21, 1996. Bronx:
Mr. Phelan was shot in the head and killed by a drunk off-duty New York City cop named Richard Molloy. Police claimed Mr. Phelan committed suicide by grabbing the cop's gun and shooting himself. Before he killed Patrick Officer Molloy had shot and killed Granson Santamaria in 1993, and had shot at someone else in 1994. But he still remained on the force through both these incidents. Officer Molloy was eventually indicted for killing Mr. Phelan. In the spring of 1999, he was convicted of second-degree manslaughter. He faced a five to 15 year sentence and, following his conviction, was finally dismissed from the force. **Source:** The New York Times, 9/19/97; "Killed by NYPD" poster

Leonard Lawton	25	*African American*	👁

January 20, 1996. Manhattan (Harlem / Washington Heights):
Leonard was shot once in the face and murdered by a police officer. Police claim the victim was armed, but no gun was found at the scene. **Source:** "Killed by NYPD" poster

| **Frankie Arzuaga** | 15 | *Puerto Rican* | 👁 |

January 12, 1996. Brooklyn:

Frankie was shot and killed when three cops from the 90th precinct approached the car he was a passenger in. Police claim they fired when the car tried to drive off, but no weapon was found at the scene. Young Frankie was shot in the head. The following Mother's Day, cops called the family, cursed them, and taunted his mother about Frankie's death. The family knows it was the police who called because *69 rang the 90 precinct. In August, 1997, the commander of the 90th precinct was transferred to the 70th precinct after the infamous plunger rape and torture of Haitian immigrant Abner Louima by cops in the 70th precinct. He was allegedly transferred there to help clean up the precinct. It was under his watch in the 90th precinct killed Frankie Arzuaga and then called and taunted his family. **Source:** "Killed by NYPD" poster; victim's family

| **Perry Walker, Jr.** | 36 | *Black* | |

January 6, 1996. Manhattan

Perry was shot five times and killed by Paul Ruine, a retired or off-duty police officer, during a traffic dispute. Perry allegedly got out of his car and yelled at former Officer Ruine for cutting him off, at which time Ruine shot and killed Walker. Ruine was convicted of second-degree murder on April 1, 1998 and sentenced in June to 15 years to life in prison. The prosecutor said that former Officer Ruine fired out of "anger, rage and fury and hatred for a black man" and that he cursed the dying man with racial epithets. The judge said it was clear that Ruine was "not a bad person" and that he would not object to his placement in an early-release program. **Source:** The New York Times, 6/26/98

| **Christopher Wade** | 28 | *African American* | |

December 31, 1995. Nassau County (Elmont):

Mr. Wade was shot and killed by Nassau Officer Anthony Raymond, who fired 16 shots and reloaded once, hitting the victim 9 times. Four of the shots hit Mr. Wade in the back. Scarring on his knees indicates that he was shot while kneeling. Cops claim Mr. Wade pointed a gun at the officer but admit that he never fired a shot. Nassau police ruled the shooting justified, and a grand jury declined to indict officer Raymond. Mr. Wade is survived by his girlfriend, Vera Padgett (who was pregnant at the time of his death) and their 3 children. Ms. Padgett filed a $560 million suit against the county, calling her boyfriend's death a "violent execution" and charging a pattern of brutal police practices against people of color. **Source:** New York Newsday, 4/10/97

| **Richard Butler** | 40 | *African American* | |

December 23, 1995. Brooklyn (Bushwick):

Richard died in police custody after being chased and arrested by police. **Source:** "Killed by NYPD" poster

| **Mohammed Assassa** | 55 | *Arab* | |

December 7, 1995. —:

Mohammed died of cardiac arrest after being pepper-sprayed and beaten while in police custody. **Source:** "Killed by NYPD" poster

| **Dario Diodonet** | 35 | *Latino* | 👁 |

November 9, 1995. Manhatten (East Harlem):

Dario was going to his girlfriend's sister's house. In a statement read at the precinct to his mother, police claim they "chased him to the 2nd floor and stopped at the 3rd floor" and that he threw himself off the roof. His mother saw the body and found a close-range bullet wound in the stomach, but this was not reflected in the autopsy report. His mother also saw handcuff marks of his wrists - another indication that the cops' story is a lie. Police stomped him because there were also boot marks on him. He suffered a crushed pelvic bone and received multiple fractures to his right side. He was also placed in an illegal choke hold and tortured with a stun gun. A witness said Dario was taken to the hospital alive. The hospital performed open heart surgery for no apparent reason. This procedure makes no sense in light of his injuries. The police have refused to give Dario's mother a copy of the police report. In response to a Freedom of Information suit his mother filed, she was told that there was no indication that Dario was even dead and she was referred to the Missing Persons Bureau. **Source:** victim's mother

Roberto Ramírez	43	*Latino*

November 4, 1995. Brooklyn (Red Hook projects):
Roberto was shot five times and killed by the police. **Source:** "Killed by NYPD" poster

Calvin Edwards	20	—

October 30, 1995. Long Island (West Islip):
Calvin died in police custody while handcuffed—supposedly of seizures caused by a drug overdose. **Source:** "Killed by NYPD" poster

Abe Richardson	22	—

October 13, 1995. Manhattan (Lower East Side):
Mr. Richardson was shot and killed by six police officers during a drug arrest at a Lower East Side housing project. He was fleeing on a bicycle when he was shot. A grand jury declined to indict the cops. **Source:** The New York Times, 12/17/95

Timothy Griggs	26	—

October 8, 1995. Queens:
Timothy was shot dead after being chased by police. **Source:** "Killed by NYPD" poster

María Rivas	25	*Latina*

September 17, 1995. Manhattan (Washington Heights):
María was killed by a stray bullet fired by a drunk off-duty cop harassing customers in a restaurant in Washington Heights. **Source:** "Killed by NYPD" poster

Fausto Vásquez	—	*Latino*

August 28, 1995. Queens:
Fausto was shot and killed outside a nightclub by an off-duty Transit cop. **Source:** "Killed by NYPD" poster

Annette Pérez	—	—

August 19, 1995. —:
Annette Pérez was shot and killed by her boyfriend, a New York City cop. **Source:** "Killed by NYPD" poster and victim's mother.

David McIntosh	28	—

August 13, 1995. Queens:
David died after being taken into police custody. **Source:** "Killed by NYPD" poster

Raymond Murray	20	—

June 22, 1995. Queens College:
Raymond, a student, was shot and killed by an off-duty police officer who says he wouldn't drop his air gun when confronted by the cop. **Source:** "Killed by NYPD" poster

Unidentified	—	—

June 10, 1995. Queens:
The victim was shot and killed by police after a robbery. **Source:** "Killed by NYPD" poster

Joseph Orlando	29	—

May 16, 1995. Brooklyn (Bay Ridge):
Joseph was shot twice in the chest and killed by police after being pulled over for driving a stolen car. Police claim someone in the car was making a motion "as if they were going for a gun." No gun was found. **Source:** "Killed by NYPD" poster

Julio Núñez	32	*Latino*	

May 13, 1995. Bronx:
Julio was shot and wounded by police who crashed into his apartment. He fell out the window of his apartment to his death. **Source:** "Killed by NYPD" poster

Gregory Legrier	19	—	

May 11, 1995. Manhattan:
Gregory was shot and killed by police after a robbery in a clothing store. **Source:** "Killed by NYPD" poster

Roger Eppes	26	*African American*	

April 28, 1995. Harlem:
Roger died of asthma attack after police chased him. As he raced to the hospital for treatment, they pursued him into hospital and held him at gunpoint. He died from the delay in treatment. **Source:** "Killed by NYPD" poster

Morris Duncan	27	—	

April 14, 1995. Manhattan:
Cops responded to a call about an emotionally disturbed man with a knife. They allegedly found Mr. Duncan crouching down and brandishing a screwdriver. Mr. Duncan died after being taken into police custody. His family charged that he was beaten into a coma by arresting officers and that he might have suffered a heart attack or a broken bone from a choke hold. Upon identifying her son's body in the morgue, his mother saw a broken tooth, a bruised right side, a badly lacerated eye, a bruised forehead, and skinned knees. **Source:** New York Amsterdam News, 4/25/95

Kuthurima Mwaria	25	*Kenyan*	◉

April 13, 1995. Manhattan (Harlem):
Kuthurima was shot and killed by two cops outside his West Harlem home. **Source:** "Killed by NYPD" poster; victim's mother

Benjamin Núñez	—	*Puerto Rican*	

April 9, 1995. Bronx:
Benjamin was shot and killed by an off-duty corrections officer during a fight at Jimmy's Bronx Cafe. **Source:** "Killed by NYPD" poster

Yong Xin Huang	16	*Chinese*	◉

March 24, 1995. Brooklyn (Sheepshead Bay):
Yong was a ninth grade honors student who was shot in the head and killed by a police officer who first threw him into a glass door. **Source:** "Killed by NYPD" poster

Michael Wayne Clark	31	—	

March 8, 1995. Brooklyn (subway):
Michael died of a heart attack in police custody after seven cops pepper-sprayed, handcuffed and carried him to the police station. He was accused of urinating on a subway platform. **Source:** "Killed by NYPD" poster

Mitchell Edey	32	—

February 1995. Manhattan (Washington Heights):
Mr. Edey shared an apartment with his brother and mother. He was 5'8" and weighed 130 pounds. His mother, Chrysanthe, called the police because her son was acting irrationally. He had not left the apartment for months and was refusing to eat. Five cops from the Emergency Service Unit arrived with a court order to take him for a psychiatric examination. The police allege that Mr. Edey attacked them with a hammer, a knife, and a gas-powered chain saw, all at the same time. Cops admit dousing him with a water cannon and pepper spray and then firing six taser stun-gun darts into him. Mr. Edey was killed. The police never mentioned firing any shots, but two days after the killing, the medical examiner revealed that the victim had also been shot four times in the back. No action has been taken against the police. **Source:** New York Daily News, 4/10/97

Anibal Carrasquillo	21	*Puerto Rican*	

January 22, 1995. Brooklyn (Flatbush):
Anibal was shot in the back by police because he was supposedly "peering into car windows." According to a friend, the cops had stopped him, frisked him, and found nothing. Cops claim he took a "gun stance," but he was unarmed. He was shot in the back as he was running away. The police bullet punctured his spine, aorta, colon, and liver and exited from the front. He also had blunt impact injuries to the head, torso, chest, and extremeties and abrasions on the face and hands. No officers were indicted. **Source:** "Killed by NYPD" poster

Sean McGovern	24	—

January 18, 1995. Brooklyn:
Sean was shot and killed by a cop who claimed he was being beaten by Sean with his own nightstick. **Source:** "Killed by NYPD" poster

Anthony Rosario	18	*Puerto Rican*	⬤
Hilton Vega	21	*Puerto Rican*	⬤

January 12, 1995. Bronx:
The two cousins were shot repeatedly while laying face down on a floor by two former bodyguards of Mayor Giuliani, Detectives Patrick Brosnan and James Crowe. Anthony was shot 14 times. Hilton was shot eight times. Both were killed. Freddie Rivera, a friend who accompanied them, was shot but survived because he lay still and played dead. Mayor Giuliani called the detectives that night to congratulate them for a job well done. The parents of Anthony Rosario later found their car torched outside their Bronx home. Lettering on the car read: "Anthony Rosario - Killed by Cops." When Anthony's mother, Margarita Rosario, confronted Mayor Giulliani on his call-in radio show concerning her son's death, he said she was to blame for not bringing him up right. **Source:** victims' family

Unidentified	40s	

December 23, 1994. Brooklyn (Prospect Park):
The victim was shot and killed by police. **Source:** "Killed by NYPD" poster

---

Anthony Baez   29   *Puerto Rican*   👁

December 22, 1994. Bronx:
Anthony was killed in an illegal choke hold by police officer Francis X. Livoti after Anthony's football accidentally hit a parked patrol car. After repeated protests led by the family, Livoti was indicted for second-degree manslaughter. The indictment was dismissed because of a typographical error. Further protests followed, and the Bronx DA's office re-indicted Livoti, this time for criminally negligent homicide (a lesser charge, in which he faced a maximum of four years in prison). Livoti was found not guilty in a non-jury trial. Further protests followed and the federal authorities indicted Livoti for violating Anthony's civil rights. He was convicted in June, 1998, by a jury and sentenced to seven and a half years in prison. In between the state acquital and federal conviction, Livoti was dismissed from the police force by the political establishment which had earlier defended him. In the time between the two Baez trials, he was also convicted of misdemeanor assault charges for choking (but fortunately not killing) Steven Resto, a 16-year-old Puerto Rican youth who was allegedly driving a go-cart recklessly in the street. Livoti was sentenced to seven months. Livoti had a long record of brutality complaints and was under observation by a seargent on the night he killed Anthony Baez. Fellow cops who covered up for Livoti's crime face federal perjury charges. The victim's family settled a wrongful death lawsuit against the city for $3 million. **Source:** victim's family

---

Wen Ping Hsu   —   *Asian*

December 18, 1994. Queens (Rego Park):
Wen was hit by at least 35 bullets of the 250 rounds police fired at him in a shoot-out ... the largest number of shots ever recorded by the NYPD (to date). He was killed. **Source:** "Killed by NYPD" poster

---

Laakhraj Dalipram   31   *Trinidadian*

December 18, 1994. Queens (Rego Park):
Laakhraj was shot and killed by police bullets after police unleashed 250 rounds on a Queens street trying to kill someone else (Wen Ping Hsu). **Source:** "Killed by NYPD" poster

---

Eric Pitt   27   *African American*   👁
Donald Taylor   31   *African American*

December 7, 1994. Queens:
Eric and Donald were shot in the head and killed while sitting in a car after being forced to a stop by police. Police claim someone in the car was making a motion "as if they were going for a gun." No gun was found. **Source:** "Killed by NYPD" poster

---

Richard Larrier   30   *African American*

December 2, 1994. Brooklyn:
Richard was a part-time street vendor killed by police in a bicycle store robbery. **Source:** "Killed by NYPD" poster

---

Keith Richardson   34   *African American*

November 25, 1994. Brooklyn (Crown Heights):
Keith was shot and killed by plainclothes cops on bicycles. **Source:** "Killed by NYPD" poster

---

Abdo Al Qotaini   29   *Yemeni*

November 25, 1994. Brooklyn (Crown Heights):
Abdo was a grocery clerk. He was shot and killed by police patrolling on bicycles who were aiming at (and also killed) another man (Keith Richardson). **Source:** "Killed by NYPD" poster

---

Larry Shin   23   —

October 25, 1994. Brooklyn:
Larry was shot and killed by police after the driver of the car he was in sped away from a traffic stop because he did not have a license or registration. **Source:** "Killed by NYPD" poster

---

Anthony Merisier   25   *African American*   👁

October 24, 1994. Brooklyn:

Anthony was shot in the chest and killed after he and the driver of the car were pulled over by police. Police claim someone in the car was making a motion "as if they were going for a gun." No gun was found. **Source:** "Killed by NYPD" poster

---

Jason Nichols   27   *African American*   👁

October 17, 1994. Queens (Jamaica):

Jason was pinned face down on the ground, shot in the head, and killed by a Department of Corrections police officer who mistook him for someone they were looking to return to jail. **Source:** "Killed by NYPD" poster

---

Nicholas Heyward, Jr.   13   *African American*   👁

September 27, 1994. Brooklyn (Gowanus Houses):

Nicholas was 13 years old when he was shot and killed by Housing Police Officer Brian George in the housing complex where he lived with his family. Nicholas was playing a game of cops and robbers, using a bright orange plastic toy gun, with his friends, ages 11 to 14. His friends said that when Nicholas realized a police officer was present, he dropped his toy gun and said, "We're only playing, we're only play..." The cop shot him in mid-sentence. Nicholas died eight hours later after being taken, not to the nearest hospital in Brooklyn, but to Manhattan. Officer George had a history of patrolling the buildings of the Gowanus Houses with his gun unholstered. The shooting was labeled an accident. Brooklyn District Attorney Charles Hynes closed the case on the grounds that the officer, who was supposedly responding to a 911 call, feared for his life when he heard a clicking sound in the dimly lit stairwell. Officer George allegedly thought the clicking sound was a gun misfiring, so he fired into the darkness. After the case was dismissed, Officer George made statements that contradicted this version of events. He said that he was on routine patrol, not responding to a 911 call. He said that when he opened the stairwell door, no one was there and that Nicholas jumped from the stairs and suddenly appeared. Officer George had a flashlight in one hand and a gun in the other. He claimed that Nicholas jumped back up the steps, pointed the toy gun at him and clicked it four times, and that this is when he opened fire. In other words, this was not a "split-second decision." Two years before Nicholas was killed, cops placed the then 11-year-old boy in a police line-up against his parents' protests. When Nicholas also protested, police threatened that he would not live to be 15. **Source:** victim's father

---

Lemiel Brand   39   —

July 7, 1994. —:

Lemiel died in police custody after being maced and handcuffed. He was arrested for entering a building and acting erratic. **Source:** "Killed by NYPD" poster

---

Carlos García   28   *Latino*

June 21, 1994. Brooklyn:

Carlos was shot and killed by a correction officer in a Brooklyn hospital clinic. **Source:** "Killed by NYPD" poster

---

Robert Rotella   34   —

June 2, 1994. —:

Robert died in police custody after his father called police to report he was emotionally disturbed. **Source:** "Killed by NYPD" poster

---

Israel Alicia, Jr.   35   —

May 31, 1994. Brooklyn (East New York):

Israel was chased off a roof by police. He fell to his death. Police say they mistakenly thought he was wanted for fleeing work release. **Source:** "Killed by NYPD" poster

---

José Fuentes   15   *Puerto Rican*

May 29, 1994. Bay Shore:

José was shot in the chest and killed by an off-duty cop who claimed he was attempting a robbery. **Source:** "Killed by NYPD" poster

Frank Pérez   28   —

May 24, 1994. Queens:

Frank was shot in the chest and killed during a traffic dispute with a cop. **Source:** "Killed by NYPD" poster

Unidentified   —   —

May 22, 1994. Manhattan:

The victim was shot and killed after a robbery and a chase by police. **Source:** "Killed by NYPD" poster

Miguel Rodríguez   38   *Puerto Rican*

May 16, 1994. —:

Miguel was shot in the head and killed while sitting in a car as he reached down to open the door. He was unarmed. **Source:** "Killed by NYPD" poster

Ernest Sayon   22   *African American*

April 29, 1994. Staten Island:

Ernest died after police put him in a chokehold while handcuffed. His murder outraged the residents of the housing projects where he lived, and many people from around New York City protested his killing. No cops were charged in connection with his death. **Source:** "Killed by NYPD" poster

Willie Lucas   20s   —

April 25, 1994. Brooklyn (East New York):

Willie was shot and killed by police in a drug bust setup. **Source:** "Killed by NYPD" poster

Anthony Boatwright   —   —

March 21, 1994. Bronx (Grand Concourse):

Attorney General Janet Reno has given permission to prosecute John Cuff and seek the death penalty for the murder of Mr. Boatwright and seven other persons. Cuff was a New York City housing cop from 1981 through 1986. Investigators claim that during Cuff's years as a policeman, he also worked as a driver for Clarence (The Preacher) Heatley, a drug dealer in Harlem and the Bronx. Officer Cuff reportedly would use his police badge if cops stopped Heatley's car when he was driving. According to the prosecutors, when Cuff left the police force, he became one of Heatley's top lieutenants. According to the charge, Cuff lured Boatwright to an apartment building basement where he shot him in the head and killed him. Then, the charge continues, he had his underlings cut Boatwright's body up with a circular saw. The indictment said that Boatwright was a member of a rival drug operation. **Source:** New York Daily News, 12/18/97; New York Newsday, 12/19/97

Raymond Antonio Azcona   30   —

March 5, 1994. Brooklyn:

Raymond was shot twice in the chest and killed after police claim he pointed a shotgun at them. **Source:** "Killed by NYPD" poster

Roberto Blanco   —   —

March 3, 1994. —:

Roberto was shot and killed by police who responded to a 911 call from his mother. **Source:** "Killed by NYPD" poster

Sima Gonik   81   *Ukrainian*

January 29, 1994. Brooklyn (Coney Island):

According to reports from the Brooklyn District Attorney's office, Ms. Gonik was killed in a fire set by Auxiliary Police Sgt. Robert Campanella and a former auxiliary police officer, Richard Keenan. The report said Sgt. Campanella and Officer Keenan set fire to a car in the basement of Ms. Gonik's building, and the fire spread to her apartment, killing her. An investigation found that the two had set more than 10 fires in Coney Island. They were charged with murder and arson in 1997. **Source:** New York Newsday, 10/15/97; New York Daily News, 10/15/97

Michael Argenio   29   —

January 25, 1994. Babylon:

Michael was shot and killed by a police officer after the driver of van he was riding in hit some trash cans in the cop's neighborhood. **Source:** "Killed by NYPD" poster

Shu'aib Abdul Latif   17   *African American*

January 11, 1994. Brooklyn:

Shu'aib was shot and killed by police in the basement of his apartment building in Brooklyn. Police claim the victim was armed but no gun was found at the scene. **Source:** "Killed by NYPD" poster

Hector Cabot   41   *Latino*

November 4, 1993. Bronx (Fordham):

Mr. Cabot was shot once in the back of the neck and killed by New York City Police Officer Stephen Phipps during a traffic stop. Mr. Cabot reportedly hit a light pole and then drove off. He was followed by police and stopped five blocks away when his car stalled. Four cops approached, and one yelled, "He's reaching for something," at which point Officer Phipps fired. After they killed Mr. Cabot, police searched his car and allegedly found a starter's pistol, crack, marijuana, and open alcohol containers. A passenger in the car was arrested and charged with drug possession. The victim's mother described her son as a regular churchgoer who played the keyboard in a local salsa band and gave piano lessons to kids. **Source:** New York Newsday, 11/5/93

Lester Steven Yarborough   34   *Black*

October 13, 1993. Westchester (Mount Vernon):

Firefighters arrived at Mr. Yarborough's apartment in response to a report of a stove fire. Authorities claim Mr. Yarborough brandished a fork and barricaded himself in the kitchen with the open refrigerator door and folding chairs. When three cops approached him, he allegedly threatened to turn on the oven and ignite a $100 bill. Police pepper-sprayed him. He went into cardiac arrest and died. Mr. Yarborough leaves behind his wife and four children. He had a history of heart problems and had just come out of the hospital after a four-day stay. He had no known history of mental illness, and neighbors did not believe the official account of his behavior. They also charged that police had handled him too roughly. **Source:** The New York Times, 10/15/93

Johnnie Cromartie   —   *Black*

May 25, 1993. New York City:

Johnnie died in police custody in a hospital. He was admitted to the hospital after suffering from epileptic seizures following an arrest on weapons charges. He had waited in the emergency room for nearly 30 hours without incident, handcuffed to a bed. Police claim that when he was transferred to another room and a handcuff was removed to allow him to use the bathroom, he announced his intention to leave the hospital. Cops claim a violent struggle followed. Five officers tried to restrain him. He was placed face down on a stretcher, handcuffed behind his back with his ankles tied together with velcro straps. He went into cardiac arrest 15 minutes later.

Bekim Ahmeti   20   —

March 20, 1993. Manhattan (Chelsea):

Mr. Ahmeti was shot three times in the back and killed by police outside a diner around 5 a.m. Another shot went through his left hand, and police admit firing a total of six shots. The initial police report claimed that Mr. Ahmeti had turned toward police holding a gun and was shot three times in the chest and stomach. But the city medical examiner found that the three shots were to his back. Witnesses said that while he was in possession of a gun, the gun had remained in his pocket throughout the encounter with police. After he was shot, Mr. Ahmeti got up, turned to cops, and said, "Why did you shoot me?" before collapsing again. A friend who saw the whole incident said, "There was nothing in his hands. They [the police] were just trying to kill him." Mr. Ahmeti had pulled his gun when he and a group of friends were threatened with a stick and a knife by other patrons inside the diner. But he had put the gun away after the people who threatened him left. He was shot down by police as he and his friends left the diner to avoid trouble if the people who had threatened them returned. Mr. Ahmeti's girlfriend, who was there when he was killed, said, "I want it to be known they [cops] shot a retreating figure and they have to be punished." **Source:** New York Newsday, 3/22/93

Granson Santamaria   —   —

March 3, 1993. New York City:

Granson was shot and killed by Officer Richard Molloy. Molloy claimed that he thought Santamaria was reaching for a gun, but no gun was found. No action was taken against Officer Molloy, who remained on the force. Three years later, he shot and killed Patrick "Hessy" Phelan. Between these two incidents, he shot at another person. **Source:** The New York Times, 9/18/97

Lenas Kakkouras   30   *Greek Cypriot*

February 26, 1993. Westchester (Mount Vernon):

Dr. Kakkouras, a medical doctor, was sitting in his car on a deserted, industrial street when he was shot and killed by plainclothes Mount Vernon Police Det. Anthony Rozzi. Dr. Kakkouras was on his way to Yonkers for a date and got lost. He had pulled over to get his bearings. Det. Rozzi and his partner blocked his car with their unmarked vehicle. According to an attorney for his family, Dr. Kakkouras had been chased by muggers several weeks earlier and probably thought the plainclothes cops were robbers, so he tried to drive off. Police claim that they displayed their badges and that Dr. Kakkouras put his car in reverse, hit Det. Rozzi's partner, and was driving at Det. Rozzi when the cop fired four shots. Later, authorities changed their story to say that Dr. Kakkouras got out of his car and struggled with Det. Rozzi after the latter had fired three shots, and that the fatal fourth shot was fired during the alleged struggle. The police murder of Lenas Kakkouras sparked widespread anger in the Greek-American community, in his native Cyprus, and among colleagues at the hospitals where he worked. Friends described him as a shy, sensitive, quiet man who was respectful of others and had a special affinity for children. He had been in the U.S. only 2 1/2 years. He worked with disabled children and planned to return to Cyprus to open a clinic. **Source:** New York Newsday, 3/20/93

Aurea Bonnie Vargas   41   —   👁

January 29, 1993. Manhattan (Upper West Side):

Four men had reportedly robbed a bank, then split up as they ran away. They were chased by police. One of the men, Mujahid Muhammed, allegedly shot and wounded a transit cop, then grabbed Ms. Vargas as a hostage as she stepped out the door of her apartment building. While holding her hostage, Mr. Muhammed allegedly fired three shots and wounded another cop in the foot. A lawyer for Ms. Vargas' family said that 20 to 30 cops were surrounding the pair and were shouting confusing messages and that Mr. Muhammed only fired when an officer stood up from behind a car to fire at him. Cops opened fire, killing both Ms. Vargas and her captor. Police estimated that the robbers fired a total of 16 shots. Police fired 46 shots, 19 of them while Ms. Vargas was being held hostage. Three shots hit Ms. Vargas, including the fatal shot to her chest. Ms. Vargas was killed by police bullets within 90 seconds of being taken hostage. A grand jury declined to indict the cops, and Mr. Muhammed's alleged accomplices, who were not even present when Ms. Vargas was killed, were convicted of murder in connection with her death. Ms. Vargas' family filed lawsuit against the police and in July, 1999, a jury awarded them $5.7 million in damages. Ms. Vargas' brother, who had criticized the police for not negotiating with Mr. Muhammed, said of the verdict, "I'm very happy. We proved that the police did something wrong." The city maintained that the cops did nothing wrong and vowed to appeal the verdict. **Source:** The New York Times, 1/31/93, 2/5/93 & 7/21/99

Mujahid Muhammed   24   —

January 29, 1993. Manhattan (Upper West Side):

Mr. Muhammed had reportedly robbed a bank with some accomplices and fled. He was pursued by police, got separated from his accomplices, and allegedly shot and wounded a cop, then grabbed Auera Bonnie Vargas as a hostage as she stepped out of her apartment building. While holding Ms. Vargas hostage, Mr. Muhammed allegedly fired three more shots and wounded another cop. A lawyer for Ms. Vargas' family said that 20 to 30 cops were surrounding the pair and were shouting confusing messages and that Mr. Muhammed only fired when an officer stood up from behind a car to fire at him. Police fired 19 shots, according to their own estimates, killing both Mr. Muhammed and Ms. Vargas within 90 seconds of when he took her hostage. Mr. Muhammed was hit 12 times. A grand jury declined to indict the cops, and Mr. Muhammed's alleged accomplices, who were not even present when Ms. Vargas was killed, were convicted of murder in connection with her death. **Source:** The New York Times, 1/31/93, 2/5/93, & 7/21/99

Unidentified Man   —   —

January 22, 1993. Manhattan (Upper West Side):

The man was shot in the chest and killed by off-duty Transit Police Officer Anna Mendez. He allegedly threatened her and tried to rob her with an "Uzi type" machine gun, which turned out to be a toy, in the elevator of her apartment building. Officer Mendez, who was returning from work, reportedly flashed her badge, identified herself as a cop, and pulled her gun. She claims the gun went off during a struggle. **Source:** The New York Times, 1/23/93

Dagoberto Pichardo   —   *Dominican*

July 6, 1992. Manhattan (Washington Heights):

Mr. Pichardo was pushed to his death off the roof of a six-story building by police during the Washington Heights rebellion, which broke out after a cop murdered José "Kiko" Garcia two days earlier. **Source:** Revolutionary Worker, 8/9/92

José "Kiko" Garcia   —   *Dominican*

July 4, 1992. Manhattan (Washington Heights):

Kiko Garcia was beaten and then shot to death in the lobby of a building by New York Police Officer Michael O'Keefe, sparking a week-long rebellion against police brutality in Washington Heights. At its peak, the rebellion covered an 80-block area, and over 3,000 police were brought in to suppress it. Officer O'Keefe was widely known and feared throughout the predominantly Dominican neighborhood for brutality, for framing people on drug charges, and for reselling drugs he confiscated from dealers. One witness reported that Officer O'Keefe had beaten Kiko with his walkie-talkie aand then shot him as he lay semi-conscious on the ground. Other witnesses confirmed that the victim was on the ground when he was shot. Mr. Garcia was shot twice, once in the stomach and once in the back. Officer O'Keefe claims he fired the shot to the stomach only after Mr. Garcia punched him and pulled a gun on him. He claims the second shot to the victim's back occurred when Kiko "spun around to shoot [him]." But medical experts said this was impossible and that the shot to the stomach "probably would have paralyzed him." Authorities falsely claimed that Kiko was a drug dealer and refused to release the autopsy results to the victim's family. Officer O'Keefe spent some time on paid leave. It took the DA's office 11 days to question him. O'Keefe was never punished for the murder of Kiko Garcia. **Source:** Revolutionary Worker, 8/9/92

Earl Black   42   —

May 27, 1992. Brooklyn (Flatlands):

This emotionally disturbed man was shot and killed in his parents' apartment by two police officers, John Petrullo and Max Goldman, who claim Earl lunged at them with a knife. According to police, Earl's mother, Ivy Black, called Coney Island Hospital to request treatment for her son. The hospital sent a mobile crisis team consisting of a psychiatrist, two nurses, and a medical student. Cops allege that when they arrived, Earl lunged at them with a knife. In addition to killing Earl, they shot and wounded his mother, Ivy Black, in the upper chest. The cops, who fired a total of 12 shots, were cleared by a grand jury, and their account of the incident was backed up by the psychiatrist, Dr. Saul Gorman. However, the police hid the identiy of the medical student, Joseph Accetta, for three years and only revealed his identity after a contempt of court ruling. At the trial in the civil case brought by Earl's family, Accetta testified that Earl Black did not have a knife. The jury found that a conspiracy existed and awarded the family $6.7 million in June, 1997. A Deputy Police Commissioner called the jury's verdict "outrageous" and urged the city to appeal. Earl's mother, Ivy Black, said "My reaction to the verdict is that money cannot buy life and my son should not have died. I am happy to know that they could prove that these policemen killed my son without just cause. I called them to help get medication for my son. Instead, they killed him and shot me in my breast. I could have been killed, too." **Source:** The New York Times, 6/10/97

Douglas Orfaly   29   *white*

March 3, 1992. New York City:

Douglas was shot and killed as he sat in his car by a housing cop. The officer, who had been responding to a burglary report, said he thought Douglas fit the description of the burglar. As he approached the car, Douglas allegedly made a sudden movement and the officer shot him through the window, striking him in the head. It was later revealed that this cop had been the target of two police brutality lawsuits. In August, 1995, he was convicted of criminally negligent homicide and sentenced to one-to-four years, the first New York City police officer to be convicted of an on-duty homicide since 1977.

Hector Rivera   —   *Puerto Rican*

December 29, 1991. Brooklyn:

Hector, an unarmed man, was shot in the chest and killed when two cops were called to a domestic dispute outside his home. The cops say they shot him after he put his hand into a paper bag when told to freeze. The bag turned out to contain a can of beer. The cop was indicted for second-degree murder but a judge dismissed the indictment, ruling that the prosecutor's instructions to the grand jury regarding self-defense had been in error. A second grand jury refused to indict.

Grady Alexis   26   *Haitian*

May 1991. Manhattan (Greenwich Village):

Grady and his friends were crossing the street and brushed into an off-duty officer's jeep. A fight ensued and Grady was punched in the head several times by the officer and the officer's friend. He received a fatal blow to his head. The officer's friend left Grady dying on the pavement. They were later arrested on misdemeanor assault charges when the jeep's registration number was traced to the officer. The charges were dismissed and then reinstated. The officer was acquitted by a judge on the grounds of self-defense. His friend was convicted of third degree assault and sentenced to weekends in jail for four months plus community service.

Frederico Pereira   21   *Puerto Rican*

February 5, 1991. Queens:

Frederico was killed by five white police officers in the early morning hours as they dragged him from a stolen car in which he had been sleeping. The NYC Medical Examiner ruled the death a homicide and concluded that Frederico had died form traumatic asphyxia associated with compression of the neck. The autopsy also noted multiple blunt force injuries, including lacerations above the eye, abrasions to his head and knees, and contusions, all of which occurred shortly before death. The cops claimed that Frederico had violently resisted arrest and his injuries were caused by his banging his head against the pavement. Two civilian witnesses came forward to say they saw the cops use a choke hold on Frederico as he lay face-down and handcuffed on the ground. The cops denied this and were cleared in an internal inquiry. The five cops were indicted on charges of second degree murder, manslaughter, assault, and criminally negligent homicide in March, 1991, but all charges were dismissed against four of the cops and reduced to manslaughter and criminally negligent homicide against the fifth at the request of a new DA. This officer was acquitted by a judge in a non-jury trial in March, 1992. Frederico's family settled their wrongful death suit against the city for $175,000 in 1995.

Mary Mitchell   41   *Black*

November 1990. Bronx:

Mary was shot dead by a white police officer in her apartment. The cops had been called to investigate a fight between Mary and her daughter. An officer apparently tried to barricade Mary in a room during the fight. However, the door opened and the officer dropped his nightstick. He shot Mary once in the chest, according to the officer, after she grabbed the nightstick and started swinging it at him. A grand jury charged the officer with second-degree manslaughter. He was acquitted in a non-jury trial when the judge ruled that Mary had been a deadly threat when she was shot. Her family maintains that at least eight cops were at the scene at the time she was shot, that less lethal methods could have been used to restrain her, and that she may have been treated differently if she were white.

Frank Olsen   49   *white*   ◉

October 16, 1990. New York City:

Frank was released from a psychiatric hospital. He ran away from an after-care home and was living on the streets. He got into a fight with two plainclothes cops over a supposed knife. A cop fired five bullets. One struck Frank in the neck. He died six months later on Apr. 17, 1991. He was not known to be violent. **Source:** SLP form

---

Luis Allende   —   *Latino*

August 9, 1990. Bronx:

Luis was shot dead by a transit cop. He was unarmed. Police received a report of a chain snatching and saw Luis, who flagged down a cab, supposedly in an attempt to escape. The cops surrounded the cab and ordered Luis, who was sitting in the back seat, not to move. He was shot once in the head, allegedly after turning toward one of the officers who was opening the cab's door to arrest him. The shooting was ruled within police guidelines on the grounds that the cop thought Luis might have been reaching for a weapon, even though he turned out to be unarmed. The family filed a civil suit, stating he posed no immediate threat to life when he was shot as the car was surrounded and he was in plain view.

David Cotto   20   —

March 1, 1990. Brooklyn:

David was shot dead with 11 bullets by police in his parents' apartment. According to his family, he had been in a fight with a neighbor over a card game and was in the apartment washing blood out of his mouth when the cops arrived. His sister said the police were abusive to David, who they knew, and pushed him to the ground, which led to a violent struggle. David then ran into the kitchen and picked up two knives which he allegedly held to his own throat, threatening to kill himself. According to his sister, he dropped the knives after one of the cops maced him. Two cops fired as he was rubbing his eyes and stumbling forward. Based on eyewitness accounts and the autopsy report, it appears that he was shot nine times by two cops while standing and shot twice while he was lying on his back on the ground. A grand jury did not indict any of the cops involved, and neither of the two cops who shot him were disciplined. The third cop present, a sergeant, reportedly got a mild reprimand for failing to follow the required procedure for dealing with an emotionally disturbed person.

Jose Luis Lebron   14   *Latino*

January 31, 1990. Brooklyn (Bushwick):

An unarmed youth, Jose Luis Lebron, was shot dead by a cop from the 83rd Precinct around 5:30 pm after a man in a police car identified him as one of two youths who had robbed him of $10. One of the suspects was captured. Lebron ran away but was cut off by a patrol car. When he turned around to go back the other way, he was shot in the back of the head by a cop who said he thought Lebron was reaching for something in the front of his jacket. Two eye-witnesses denied that Lebron had reach into his jacket. They said that the officer said "freeze" and then immediately fired two shots in quick succession when Lebron kept on walking. In March, 1990, a grand jury indicted the officer for second-degree manslaughter. In September, 1990, a judge dismissed the indictment. The DA brought the case to a grand jury again in 1992 but the grand jury did not indict. Lebron's attorney said that the DA did not call or seek the eye-witnesses when he presented the case the second time. Lebron's family filed a civil suit. Amnesty International wrote to the Police Department to ask if disciplinary charges had been brought against the officer but received no reply. Lebron was the second unarmed teenager fatally shot by police within a week in Bushwick.

Louis Liranso   17   —

January 27, 1990. Brooklyn (Bushwick):
Louis was shot in the back and killed by a cop who was holding him with his hands raised at gunpoint after a drunken brawl near a Chinese restaurant. The cop claimed that her gun went off when Louis turned around and grabbed her arm. Witnesses, however, say that he simply tripped as the officer was ushering him into the restaurant at gunpoint. An earlier police report also contradicted her testimony, saying that Louis was shot as he lowered his hands and started to turn toward the officer. Louis was unarmed. A grand jury refused to indict the cop who shot Louis Liranso.

Dane Kemp   28   *Black*

January 1, 1990. Brooklyn:
Dane died in a holding cell in the 69th Precinct. He was arrested after a woman accused him of assaulting her. The Emergency Services Unit was called to the precinct supposedly because Kemp, who had one hand handcuffed to the cell bars, was kicking at the mesh of his cell and threatening to kill his accuser. He died while being restrained by five officers who strapped his legs together with a Velcro strap, tied his hands behind his back, and placed him face-down on a stretcher. A grand jury indicted one of the cops for criminally negligent homicide. A judge dismissed the indictment.

Kevin Thorpe   31   *Black*

July 10, 1989. Brooklyn:
A mentally disturbed man, Kevin died of asphyxia in his mother's apartment after at least four cops lay on top of him while he was face-down on the floor, handcuffed behind his back with his legs strapped together. The police were called to the apartment after Kevin Thorpe became violent after failing to take his medication. Four witnesses said they saw the cops hit Kevin with their nightsticks and fists after he was handcuffed on the ground. Bruises were noted in the autopsy report.

Richard Luke   —   *Black*

May 1989. New York City:
Richard died in the custody of NYC Housing Police. The cops had responded to a call for medical assistance from his mother's apartment and Luke was arrested, supposedly after a violent struggle. Cops claim that he began to strike his head against the bars, floor, and wall of his cell, so they removed him from his cell, placed him in a restraining blanket, and took him to a local hospital. He died on the way. The NYC Medical Examiner said the death was caused by cocaine intoxication, but the New York State Commission of Corrections Medical Review Board concluded that he had choked on vomit while lying face-up in a restraining blanket.

Lydia Ferraro   32   *white*

April 27, 1988. East Harlem:
Lydia, an unarmed woman, was shot dead after six cops fired 16 bullets into her car following a car chase. A grand jury refused to indict any of the cops, and her son settled a civil suit against the city for $300,000 in August, 1993. According to a summary of the court-agreed settlement, police began to follow her after she made an illegal turn, believing that she had come to East Harlem to buy drugs. They were joined by another police car, and Lydia's car was eventually cut off and stopped. The cops approached her car with their weapons drawn. The City claimed that as one cop opened the door, Lydia pulled away from him and an officer shot at her. Other cops then opened fire, killing her with multiple gunshot wounds. A departmental investigation found that the police had acted within proper police guidelines and only one officer was disciplined for firing at her car while it was still moving. He had also reportedly tried to cover up his role in the shooting by replacing the three spent cartridges he had fired at the car.

Juan Rodriguez	40	Latino

January 30, 1988. Bushwick (Brooklyn):

An emotionally disturbed man, Juan died in police custody after being arrested by cops from the 83rd Precinct for allegedly breaking doors and windows in his apartment building. An autopsy report found that he suffered "blunt injuries" to his head and body and died of a heart attack. Four cops were indicted, and an assistant DA said that the officers had struck Juan with "police instruments" including their radio, "punching him in the head a striking him about the body." The police claim Juan became violent when they tried to handcuff him. The cops were acquitted by a judge in a non-jury trial and have returned to full duty. They did not face disciplinary charges. Juan's family settled their civil suit for $275,000 in September, 1994.

Hector Mendez	47	Puerto Rican	👁

1988. Bronx:

Hector was beaten to death by nine police officers. **Source:** SLP form

Michael Tebbs Nunn	18	white	👁

October 3, 1987. Manhattan (Old Fulton Street):

Two witnesses saw police officers in their police car following closely behind Michael, who was "striding briskly" down Old Fulton Street towards the East River. Witnesses say police were whistling the theme of Close Encounters over their PA system. It is unclear how Michael ended up in the East River but according to one eyewitness, "The police definitely weren't trying to help him." His body was found five days later with severe bruising on his head and face. The officers denied the whole scenario and called Michael's death a suicide. They later changed the cause of death to accidental drowning. The DA ruled Michael's case a homicide and subpoenaed the police and all related police records. The police never responded to the subpoena. **Source:** written statement from victim's family

UPSTATE NEW YORK

Name	Age	Nationality	Photo
Gregory Lee Richardson	42	—	

June 28, 1999. Colonie (Albany County Jail):

Mr. Richardson, a mentally ill man who suffered from paranoid schizophrenia, was restrained face down and given haldol by corrections officers. He was found unconscious in his jail cell and later pronounced dead at the hospital. In violation of jail policy, he was not kept under constant supervision while under restraint. Mr. Richardson was from Brooklyn, New York City. He was in jail on misdemeanor reckless endangerment charges stemming from a police car chase on June 10. Within a month of his death, it was announced that the guards would not face criminal charges. **Source:** The New York Times, 7/20/99

Leigh Edelman	21	—	

June 12, 1999. Woodstock:

Mr. Edelman was shot twice in the chest and killed by New York State Trooper Robert Klein. Cops claim Mr. Edelman pointed a gun at the Woodstock Police Chief and said, "Come on, do me. I want to get this over with," before he was shot. The incident started when cops were called to a cabin around 1 a.m. over a dispute Mr. Edelman had with his girlfriend and a cousin. By the time cops arrived, the girlfriend and the cousin had left the cabin. Police allegedly found Mr. Edelman screaming and firing shots. He supposedly fired 30 shots toward the cops, but no cops were injured. A 90 minute standoff ensued before Mr. Edelman was killed. Forty cops from the Woodstock Police Department and the New York State Police were involved in the standoff. **Source:** The New York Times, 6/14/99

Christopher Colberg	37	—

April 1, 1999. Sullivan County:
Mr. Colberg was shot to death by his father, retired State Police Commander Carl Colberg. The younger man had reportedly gotten into an argument with his parents when he came home from drinking with his friends. Former Officer Colberg fired four shots. He was arrested and charged with first-degree manslaughter. Before he retired, Officer Colberg was a state police commander for a five-county region. **Source:** The New York Times, 4/5/99

Ashley Fitzgerald	7	—
Leeanne Fitzgerald	38	—
Shane Fitzgerald	4	—

September 25, 1998. Orange County (Greenville):
Officer Patrick Fitzgerald, a veteran New York City cop, used his gun to kill his wife and two children at their home in Orange County and then killed himself. According to the police, Officer Fitzgerald's seven-year-old daughter, Ashley, called 911 and said, "My daddy is trying to kill my mommy." Relatives of Leeanne Fitzgerald said she had previously warned the New York Police Department that her husband was abusive, but the department took no action. A baby-sitter for the family also said that Leeanne had called the 34th Precinct where her husband worked to complain, but "the Police Department closed its eyes." **Source:** New York Daily News, 10/1/98

Norma Roman	30	—

May 1, 1998. Buffalo:
Juan Roman, a guard at Erie County Holding Center, shot and killed his estranged wife, Norma, at their children's elementary school. He also wounded a teacher's aide. Officer Roman reportedly used a handgun taken from the locker of a fellow guard. He had been seen arguing with his wife outside the school when she was dropping off her two children. He was charged with second-degree murder, assault, and weapons possession. **Source:** The Buffalo News, 5/9/98; The Orlando Sentinel, 5/2/98

Pierina R. Pascucci	77	—

January 28, 1998. Olean:
Ms. Pascucci, a retired waitress, was out for her daily exercise walk. While she was crossing the street, a car driven by Olean Patrolman James J. Kolkowski struck her. Patrolman Kowalski was off-duty and according to police reports, a breath test detected alcohol in him. District Attorney Edward Sharkey claimed that Patrolman Kolkowski's blood alcohol level was .04, well below the legal limit of .10 for intoxication. The DA also claimed that speed was not a factor in the accident and blamed the victim, saying that the problem was Ms. Pascucci's dark clothing and hooded jacket and the fact that she was stopped in the street outside the marked crosswalk when she was struck. Ms. Pascucci suffered a fatal head injury and died. After an investigation by the police department, no charges were brought against Officer Kolkowski. **Source:** The Buffalo News, 2/3/98, 3/12/98, & 5/19/98

Stanley Washington	41	—

January 8, 1998. Buffalo (in custody):
Cops claim Stanley and his brother, Douglas Washington, were arrested when they resisted the cops' efforts to break up a "violent fight" between the two of them at Northland Ave. & Schuele St.. Douglas asserts that there was no such fight. The family says that cops severely beat Stanley on the face and head, but the autopsy performed by the Erie County medical examiner supposedly found no brain damage. Cops admit pepper-spraying Douglas, but the Erie County medical examiner ruled that Stanley was not pepper-sprayed, and claim that he died of a fatal heart attack that could have resulted from exhaustion, cocaine abuse, or two pre-existing heart ailments, as well as from head, neck and abdominal injuries. The medical examiner claims toxicology tests found traces of alcohol, marijuana, and cocaine in Stanley's blood. A month later, the DA still needed two or three weeks to decide whether to present the case to a grand jury. **Source:** The Buffalo News, 2/9/98

| **Nerrow Black** | 24 | — |

November 2, 1997. Schenectady (in custody):

Cops claim Mr. Black hanged himself in a Schenectady police holding cell, and the county coroner's upheld the police version of events. But the dead man's family does not believe the police explanation, saying that Mr. Black's body had bruises on the arm and neck They ridiculed the official story that he used a T-shirt and a sock in his suicide. The victim's mother charged the police with killing her son, saying, "I think he got down there and started acting up. They couldn't take what he was dishing out. I don't care what they say." Mr. Black was arrested when a friend called police when Mr. Black was acting strangely and would not leave after a party. The friend said she only wanted help getting him to leave, that she did not want him arrested and felt guilty that he was dead. Mr. Black was found hanging only 20 minutes after police had booked him on charges of seventh-degree criminal possession of a controlled substance and second-degree harassment. Police had Mr. Black under an active suicide watch because he had refused to answer questions about his state of mind. Under the watch, he was to be checked every 15 minutes. According to police records, he was booked at 2:47 a.m., placed in his cell at 3:15 a.m., checked at 3:20 a.m., and discovered hanging at 3:35 a.m. This was the third alleged suicide reported in a Capitol Region jail in 1997. Later that week, 100 people held a protest on the steps of City Hall to demand a full, independent investigation. "We have to be afraid of the people who protect us, and that's a shame," said a spokesperson for the victim's family. The victim's father said, "Nerraw had a volatile relationship with the Police Department. He was very outspoken. It is not surprising that a physical confrontation occurred. I think, yes, they used excessive force in restraining and silencing him. And, yes, they caused his death." **Source:** Albany Times Union, 11/3/97, 11/4/97, & 11/5/97

| **Timothy Sousie** | 17 | — |

October 28, 1997. Troy:

Police allege Mr. Sousie was in a stolen car, weaving back and forth on the highway. Trooper Richard Bango gave chase. Mr. Soursie's car overturned. He was ejected and killed. **Source:** The Buffalo News, 10/30/97

| **Antwon Thomas** | 18 | — |

August 26, 1997. Buffalo:

Mr. Thomas was killed around 3 a.m. during a high-speed police chase into the city of Buffalo. Mr. Thomas, who was a passenger in the allegedly stolen vehicle that cops were chasing, was either thrown from the car or jumped from it as the car was about to crash into a concrete porch. The car bounced backwards and ran over Mr. Thomas, killing him. The 19-year-old driver of the car was convicted of criminally negligent homicide and other charges stemming from this incident. **Source:** The Buffalo News, 4/28/98

| **Daren Alexis** | 38 | — |
| **Ronald Russell** | 46 | — |

May 26, 1997. Buffalo (Kensington Expressway):

Mr. Russell and Mr. Alexis, two cousins, were killed in a motorcycle crash with a police car driven by Officer Thomas Bluff. Police initially said that Mr. Russell's motorcycle rammed into Officer Bluff's parked police vehicle, which was supposedly parked on the highway to investigate an earlier fatal crash. But Mr. Russell's family contends that the two cousins were killed when Officer Bluff was driving and pulled his police car in front of Mr. Russell as they were riding on the highway. The family filed a negligence and wrongful death lawsuit, charging that the cops had been trying to reconstruct the scene of a fatal crash that had occurred three days earlier and had failed to set up warning markers. Mr. Russell, an 18-year firefighter, was a past president of a local motorcycle club and was an experienced motorcycle rider. His cousin, Daren Alexis, was a car mechanic. **Source:** The Buffalo News, 2/11/98

| **Jonah Drisdom** | 47 | *Black* |

May 1997. Niagara Falls:

Jonah had a history of emotional illness. He was shot to death by an off-duty Niagara Falls police officer while leaving the hospital. Police claimed he had a knife. A butter knife was found.

Paul Skinner   34   —

November 30, 1996. Ashford (Rte. 219):

Lackawanna Police Lt. Stanley J. Janus was driving his sport-utility vehicle on Rte. 219 when he crossed the center line and struck the car being driven by Paul Skinner, who died at the scene of the accident. Lt. Janus was indicted for criminally negligent homicide and for traffic violations. Eleven years earlier, Lt. Janus had struck a Buffalo resident with his patrol car, severing the man's right leg. The City of Lackawanna settled that case for $1.5 million. Two weeks after Mr. Skinner was killed, Lt. Janus was elected the treasurer of the Police Captains and Lieutenants Association of Erie County. In June, 1998, a judge concluded that in the Skinner case, Lt. Janus was not intoxicated on the grounds that his blood alcohol was .07, below the legal limit of 0.10, and that he probably fell asleep. The judge accepted a guilty plea and set a fine of $600 with no jail time. As part of the plea bargain, Lt. Janus promised to resign from the police force and agreed not to appeal his conviction. The victim's family sued Lt. Janus for $20 million. **Source:** The Buffalo News, 6/23/98

Jermaine Vayton   25   *African American*

July 3, 1996. Buffalo:

Jermaine was beaten and pepper-sprayed by police who claimed he tried to jump a fence and broke his neck. A 911 call said the victim had a gun, but a gun found after the incident had no fingerprints on it.

Mark Virginia   38   *white*

March 14, 1996. Buffalo:

Mark was chased, beaten, pepper-sprayed and killed in police custody.

Kenneth Arnold   29   *African American*

April 27, 1995. Buffalo:

Kenneth was beaten and pepper-sprayed by police and was dead on arrival at hospital.

Felix Jorge, Jr.   24   *Dominican*   👁

July 28, 1994. Clinton Dannamora Correctional Facility:

Felix was beaten up in prison by guards, then tied up. Guards stuffed 15 yards of toilet paper into his nose and mouth, causing him to die of suffocation. They did not inform his mother of what happened. **Source:** SLP form

---

Eric Szczerbiak   16   —

December 7, 1992. Cheektowaga:

Cheektowaga Police Officer Michael Pilat was responding to what turned out to be a phony emergency call when he struck Eric Szczerbiak with his patrol car and killed him. Eric was riding his bicycle and trying to cross the street with a group of other children when the accident occurred. Officer Pilat claims he glanced down to turn on his emergency lights and headlights, and it was then that he struck Eric. A defense expert claimed the cop was going no more than 39 mph at the time, although a witness said he was driving at least 55 mph. The appeals court, agreeing with the lower court, said that more than "a momentary judgment lapse, such as the officer momentarily looking down, is required to satisfy the 'reckless disregard' test," meaning he had not shown reckless disregard for the safety of others. The court ruling threw out a negligence lawsuit filed by the victim's parents. **Source:** The Buffalo News, 10/25/97

Donald Fleming   31   *African American*

October 16, 1992. Buffalo:

Donald was kicked and beaten to death by police who may have also used an electric prod.

Keith Harrier	21	—
Teri Sisson	26	—

August 30, 1992. Portville:

State Police Troopers Joseph J. Mecca, Jr., and Eugene L. Garitot were chasing a pickup truck driven by Michael Sweeten at high speeds when the truck slammed into Ms. Sisson's car, killing Ms. Sisson and her passenger, Keith Harrier. Mr. Sweeten was also killed in the accident. The troopers claim they spotted Mr. Sweeten passing another car in a no-passing zone and driving 52 mph in a 35 mph zone on the highway. When they tried to stop him, he allegedly drove off at 110 mph, changed lanes, and slammed into the Ms. Sisson's car. Ms. Sisson's husband filed a $7.5 million wrongful death lawsuit against the state police. His attorney said that eyewitnesses disputed the troopers' contention that they slowed down upon entering the town of Portville. One eyewitness said the cops were going so fast that they "narrowly missed crashing into other vehicles at the scene of the accident." **Source:** The Buffalo News, 1/14/98

Michael Sweeten	27	—

August 30, 1992. Portville:

State Police Troopers Joseph J. Mecca Jr. and Eugene L. Garitot claim they saw Mr. Sweeten pass another car in a no-passing zone as he drove at 52 mph in a 35 mph zone on the highway. When they tried to pull him over, he allegedly sped away at speeds of up to 110 mph, changed lanes, and crashed into another car. Mr. Sweeten died in the accident, as did Teri Sisson and Keith Harrier, who were in the other car. Cops claim they slowed down upon entering the town of Portville, but one eyewitness said they were going so fast that they "narrowly missed crashing into other vehicles at the scene of the accident." **Source:** The Buffalo News, 1/14/98

Unidentified Person	—	—

1992. Buffalo:

The police shot and killed an unidentified car-theft suspect. **Source:** The Buffalo News, 1/29/98

Paul Mills	19	*African-American*

December 5, 1991. Buffalo:

Paul was shot by police on Dec. 5, 1991. He died in custody five days later, on Dec. 10, 1991.

Mark A. Spano	20	*white*

April 16, 1978. Onondaga County:

According to Mark's father, Mark was unknowingly chased by Officer Edward McAvoy, who did not have his emergency lights on. When McAvoy came up to Mark's car, he shined a spotlight into Mark's rearview mirror and then pushed Mark's car into a tree with his police car. Mark died immediately after hitting the tree. The police claim there was a high speed chase and they thought Mark (who is white) was a Black murder suspect. Based on the distance from where McAvoy began chasing Mark to the crash site, and the time between the two points, Mark's father does not believe that his son was speeding.

NORTH CAROLINA

Name	Age	Nationality	Photo
Jerry Hendricks	48	—	

February 2, 1999. Oconee County (Seneca):

A preliminary examination suggested Jerry Hendricks died of a "massive stroke." He died shortly after midnight in Oconee Memorial Hospital after having been picked up by the Seneca police and taken to a "drunk tank." Police reportedly found Mr. Hendricks slumped over his car's steering wheel. A lab test showed that no alcohol was in his system. The victim's nephew said, "He wasn't drunk. He had had a stroke. Instead of hauling him to jail, they should have called an ambulance."
Source: Charlotte Observer, 2/5/99

Ronald Francis Pool   57   —

November 2, 1998. east Charlotte:

Mr. Pool was shot and killed by Charlottle SWAT Sgt. Glen Neimeyer after he allegedly called 911 saying he "wanted to take out the SWAT team before they could kill him." When cops arrived at his home, Mr. Pool allegedly came out firing a semi-automatic assault rifle and wounded a cop. Sgt. Neimeyer was sent to the scene to determine if a SWAT team was needed. Sgt. Neimeyer got out of his car, walked quietly through several yards, and fatally shot Mr. Pool with a department-issued shotgun. After Mr. Pool's death, police searched his home and reportedly seized "medicine, booze, ammo," according to a newspaper headline. Cops claim they recovered 11 bottles of medication, five liquor bottles, 29 live rounds of ammunition, a pistol, a bayonet, a holster, a scope, and a gun case. A neighbor described Mr. Pool as "a good neighbor. Very kind. Seemed very gentle." Sgt. Neimeyer was placed on administrative leave, a routine measure while the shooting was investigated. investigation. This was the third fatal police shooting in Charlotte in two months. **Source:** The Charlotte Observer online, 11/3/98 & 12/15/98; Charlotte (NC) Record, 11/24/98

Douglas Arthur Hutchinson   —   —

September 21, 1998. Charlotte:

Police claim that Mr. Hutchinson threatened them with knives. He was shot by a Charlotte police officer and died two weeks later from his injuries. **Source:** The Charlotte Observer online, 11/3/98

Charles Irwin Potts   56   —

September 4, 1998. west Charlotte (Wingate):

Mr. Potts was shot in the chest during a drug raid and killed by Charlotte-Mecklenberg Police Officer James D. Guard, a member of the SWAT team. The SWAT team was carrying out two simultaneous drug raids, but a police sergeant said he did not think any drugs were found, although cops supposedly seized a gun from the house where Mr. Potts was killed. Officer Guard claimed Mr. Potts pointed a gun at him, but a man in the house said that Mr. Potts was unarmed: "They just shot him for nothing. He didn't reach for nothing." Officer Guard was placed on desk duty while the police investigated the case. The next day, 40 people held a candlelight vigil in the victim's memory and circulated a petition saying he was wrongfully killed. Mr. Potts is survived by his son, his fiancee, his brother, and his sister, Evelyn Carter. Ms. Carter, a pastor, described her deceased brother as a friendly, quiet man: "He liked to play cards, and he was in that house playing cards. He wasn't no rowdy man." **Source:** The Charlotte Observer, 9/6/98; The Charlotte Observer online, 11/3/98

Jack Allen Crooks   28   —

April 10, 1998. Greensboro:

Jack Crooks was shot and killed by a Greensboro police sniper after a 6 1/2 hour standoff. Mr. Crooks was barricaded on the roof of the Sherwin Williams paint factory where he worked. He had been sought by police in connection with the killing of his estranged wife. After negotiations broke down, Jack allegedly fired "at least two shots" at the cops with his rifle. The police sniper then shot and killed him. The sniper who killed Mr. Crooks was put on desk duty pending an investigation. According to the newspaper, this was the first "police-related shooting in Greensboro in almost four years." **Source:** Associated Press, 4/10/98; unidentified newspaper, 4/14/98

Derrick Kenyatta Warner   36   —

March 30, 1998. Gaithersburg:

Mr. Warner, a mentally ill patient in a group home, supposedly grabbed a gun from one of the police officers who had come to serve him with a "petition for an evaluation." Police claim they ordered Mr. Warner to drop the gun several times but that he refused. Officer George Boyce fired, hitting Mr. Warner in the head and killing him. A grand jury declined to issue indictments in the death of Derrick Kenyatta Warner. State's Attorney Robert L. Dean said, "We consider the matter . . . closed." **Source:** The Washington Post, 4/17/98

Joseph Anthony Brown — Black

February 7, 1998. Red Springs:

Mr. Brown died after a traffic stop as police attempted to arrest him. The state medical examiner said he suffocated on a plastic bag containing cocaine. While conceding that there was head trauma, they said this did not contribute to Joseph's death. The police who stopped him, Officers Daniel Pickler and Victoria Bartch and Sgt. Ronnie Patterson, were cleared of any wrongdoing by the Robeson County DA. Two were back in uniform, and one was cleared to return to duty, within two and a half months. The police chief had expressed certainty that the cops would be cleared shortly after the incident. Witnesses, however, said that Officer Patterson used excessive force while arresting Joseph. Family members say Joseph was beaten before he died. This was the third time that Officer Patterson had been investigated by the State Bureau of Investigation in five years. A lawyer for the family is conducting his own investigation. Two days after Joseph's death, 200 people from the Black community held a vigil outside the police station. **Source:** Fayetteville (N.C.) Observer-Times, 2/10/98 & 4/28/98

Damon Kearns teen- —

December 25, 1997. Davidson:

Officers Mark Swaney and Charles McLean went to "a quiet neighborhood [near Davidson College] to investigate reports of gunfire." Police allege that Damon Kearns fired on them as they tried to break up a fight, and they returned fire. Damon was killed, as was Officer Swaney. Officer McLean was wounded. A newspaper account does not indicate whether the cops were shot by Damon or by friendly fire. **Source:** Sun-Sentinel (Fort Lauderdale, FL), 12/27/97

Warnie Lee Patton 36 —

October 25, 1997. Winston-Salem:

Warnie Lee Patton died while in the custody of Winston-Salem police. The victim had been talking to some people in a car and allegedly began yelling when they drove away. Police arrested him for disorderly conduct. Officers Kerry Israel and Horace Bryant used pepper spray to subdue Mr. Patton, whom they claimed was "combative." On route to the hospital with police, Mr. Patton slumped over in the police car. Efforts to revive him at the hospital were unsuccessful. **Source:** Greensboro News Record, 10/27/97

Donald Lee Moseley Jr. 38 —

October 24, 1997. Rocky Mount:

Mr. Moseley, a motorist, was shot and killed by Detective Jeff White. Police claim that Mr. Moseley approached Det. White's car with a "weapon," which may have been a pair of scissors. **Source:** News & Observer (Raleigh, NC), 10/25/97

Movell Daniels — —

October 20, 1997. Spencer County:

An alleged standoff began Sunday night, Oct. 19, 1997, when two Spencer County police officers went to the home of Movell Daniels to serve warrant papers on his brother, Marty Burke. Marty Burke and another brother, Randy, jumped behind a couch when the shooting began and came out with their hands up when ordered to do so by the cops. Mr. Daniel's mother and two of his nephews, ages 10 and 11, were also in the house when the shooting began. Mr. Daniels was shot and killed. Two cops were reportedly wounded, one critically. A robotic camera showed the body of Movell Daniels in his mother's home. The victim's mother said cops might have mistaken him for his brother. The State Bureau of Investigation is investigating the case. **Source:** Greensboro News Record, 10/21/97

Jackie Linwood Gearheart 61 —

September 23, 1997. Winston-Salem:

Jackie Linwood Gearheart was shot by an off-duty Winston-Salem police officer for allegedly assaulting Sgt. J.K. Dorn with a "large stick." Mr. Gearheart died five days later, on Sept. 28. **Source:** News & Observer (Raleigh, NC), 10/4/97

David Michael Sivak   32   *white*

August 29, 1997. Hoke County:
David Sivak was shot and killed in a hail of sheriff's gunfire after he drove away from being stopped for driving while intoxicated (DWI). His wife said, "He just didn't want to get that DWI ticket. But he shouldn't have had to die for not wanting a ticket." **Source:** Atlanta Constitution, 11/28/97

Carolyn Sue Boetticher   48   *Black*

April 8, 1997. Charlotte (west):
Ms. Boetticher was shot in the back of the neck and killed by one of 22 bullets fired by two white cops, Officers Donn Belz and Shannon Jordan, after the car in which she was a passenger refused to stop and drove through a driver's license checkpoint. Fourteen police bullets hit the rear of the car. The driver of the car, who was white, had allegedly stolen it and refused to stop at the checkpoint. Police claim that when Officer Jordan stepped out into the road to stop the car, the driver sped up and headed toward him. The FBI investigated the case as a possible civil rights violation. Both cops were given administrative duties while internal and criminal investigations were conducted. Officer Blez was suspended for 30 days and Officer Jordan was fired over the incident. In Feb., 1999, the DA announced that the officers would not be prosecuted. A spokesperson for the local NAACP criticized the DA's decision, saying, "A life was lost, and that life was lost as a result of the officers shooting at the rear of the vehicle...after the danger had passed." **Source:** The Houston Chronicle, 4/12/97; The Charlotte Observer online, 2/17/99

Joseph Hoffman   35   —

February 6, 1997. Burlington:
Joseph allegedly robbed a bank with a pellet gun. When apprehended by police, he supposedly aimed it at them. Joseph Hoffman was shot ten times and killed. According to police, he left a note indicating he wanted to die. **Source:** Associated Press, 4/25/98

Henry Brown   32   —

January 6, 1997. Shelby:
Henry Brown, a security guard, took two guns to the police station. He stood outside and allegedly begged police to shoot him. Police claim they tried for 40 minutes to talk to him to get him to calm down. Then one of Mr. Brown's guns reportedly discharged and a police marksman shot him through the heart, killing him. **Source:** Associated Press, 4/25/98

Malachiah McQueen   36   —

January 3, 1997. Anson County (Lilesville):
Malachiah McQueen was gunned down in the backyard of his home. Deputies were allegedly trying to serve a warrant on him for threatening his sister, Janis Little. Ms. Little filed a civil lawsuit against Anson County Deputies Mike Smith, David Morton and Tony Martino, as well as the Anson County Sheriff. The lawsuit states that Ms. Little obtained a "commitment order" for her brother, who she thought needed a mental evaluation based on threats made to her earlier that day. The magistrate issued a warrant for Mr. McQueen's arrest for disturbing the peace. Ms. Little accompanied the deputies back to her home. She reminded the deputies that her brother suffered from "paranoia and other mental problems." Deputy Morton then told her that shooting Mr. McQueen might be their only option. Ms. Little again reminded the deputies that her brother was mentally ill. "Officers fired a series of shots at close range and Mr. McQueen hollered out in pain and fear," the suit contends. "The bullets that eventually killed (him) pierced his chest and neck." The deputies reported that they used pepper spray to stop Mr. McQueen, who they supposedly thought was pointing a handgun at them. It was a pipe. The sheriff said, "In my opinion...they certainly had a legitimate cause to use deadly force." **Source:** unknown newspaper, 1/12/99

James Willie Cooper   —   *Black*

November 1996. Charlotte:
Mr. Cooper was shot and killed by Police Officer Michael Marlow during a traffic stop. Officer Marlow was cleared of wrongdoing in criminal and internal investigations. **Source:** The Charlotte Observer online, 2/17/99

Daryl Howerton	19	Black	👁

September 8, 1994. Greensboro:

Daryl Howerton was shot six times and killed by Greensboro Police Officers Charles Fletcher and Jose Blanco outside a Phillips Ave. barber shop. Two of the shots were fired as he lay on the ground. A total of nine shots were fired. The owner of a tire store called 911 when Daryl failed to heed his warnings to stop feeding his vicious guard dog. The tire store owner told the 911 operator that "a man [is] eating with the dogs....he needs help...someone should come and take him to the hospital." When cops arrived, Daryl was holding a steak knife he had used to cut meat for the dogs. The cops ordered him to drop the knife several times, then pepper-sprayed him. When he raised his hands to wipe the pepper-spray out of his eyes, police shot him to death. Cops claim Daryl had raised the knife to stab his friend, Jamie Moore. Mr. Moore says Daryl did not threaten him or anyone else. Daryl, who was upset about the murder of his brother the previous year, had gone to the barber shop to talk to Mr. Moore, who worked there. Daryl was shot within 42 seconds of the police arrival at the scene. In the course of the shooting, two bystanders were wounded and two cars were hit by police bullets. The shooting was found to be in accord with departmental policy. **Source:** communication from victim's family; flyer from North Carolina Racial Justice Network

Unidentified Man	—	—	

mid-1993. Concord:

The man died after being maced or pepper-sprayed by police. He was asthmatic and the medical examiner determined that the chemical spray contributed to his death. **Source:** The New York Times, 10/15/93

Unidentified Woman	—	—	

1992. Oak City:

The victim, a cleaning woman, was shot and killed by a police paramilitary-unit sharpshooter as she ran from a bank robbery in which she had been held hostage. **Source:** The Boston Globe, 1/11/98

Vinson Harris	31	Black	

March 4, 1986. Raleigh:

Vinson was on a federal prison bus, wearing leg-irons, waist-chains, and handcuffs, travelling to Lewisburg, PA. An hour into the trip he asked to use the bathroom, but the guards wouldn't let him. He argued with them, was beaten, and then chained to his seat. When the bus stopped at a federal prison outside Raleigh, he was gagged and his head was completely covered and sealed with an ace bandage and tape. As the guards watched, Vinson convulsed, collapsed, and died. A state medical examiner said he died of asphyxiation.

CLEVELAND, OH

Name	Age	Nationality	Photo
Steven Singler	41	white	

September 5, 1998. Cleveland:

Mr. Singler, of Lakewood, Ohio (a suburb of Cleveland), was gunned down by Cleveland Municipal Housing Authority Police Officers Tyrone Cooper and Jack Justice. Mr. Singler reportedly went up to an undercover cop and allegedly got into some kind of altercation. Police grabbed him, but he got away. He got into his truck and drove off, supposedly dragging one of the officers. Police shot and killed him. They were not charged in connection with his death. **Source:** Cleveland Plain Dealer; friend of the victim

| **James Harris** | 51 | *African American* | 👁 |

August 15, 1998. Cleveland (Outhwaite Housing Projects):
James and his wife, Lorene, were arguing over a music tape, and they could not seem to stop. At one point, Lorene called the Cleveland Municipal Housing Authority police to calm her husband down. Two white cops, Officers Derrick Keidel and Michael Lewis, approached James as he was trying to get into his apartment with a knife since he had left the key inside. The cops saw him at his door and shot him down as he raised his arms. As he fell, the cops kept shooting. As James lay dying, his wife was handcuffed and put in a police car for hours, from where she could see her husband dying. She was then taken downtown for questioning. The city claims that James lunged at the police with his knife. But he was twenty feet away and was shot down as soon as police saw him. No charges were brought against the cops. **Source:** victim's wife

| **Dennis Tate** | 22 | *Black* |

August 7, 1998. Cleveland (9th & St. Clair):
The police began chasing a car driven by a 13-year-old girl after she cut through the parking lot of a Shell gas station to avoid a traffic light. Police chased her at speeds of up to 80 mph until her car crashed into another vehicle being driven by a friend of Dennis Tate. Dennis Tate, a passenger in the struck vehicle, was ejected through the car window, thrown through a bus shelter window, and killed. The 13-year-old driver was given an eight year sentence in a youth prison. But the police were not charged or disciplined. The family of Dennis Tate blames the police for killing their son. **Source:** Cleveland Plain Dealer

| **Correy Major** | — | *Black* |

July 2, 1998. Cleveland:
The Cleveland police narcotics unit was passing by on its way to an assignment when they saw Mr. Major talking to a girl. The cops jumped out, and Mr. Major ran. He ran up the stairs of a building where someone he knew lived. According to witnesses, Mr. Major had just opened the door of an apartment when Officer Robert Clark tried to grab him. Mr. Major reportedly shot and killed the cop. Another officer shot and killed Mr. Major. **Source:** Associated Press, 7/2/98

| **Andre Tony** | 27 | — |

June 14, 1998. Warrensville Heights:
Mr. Tony was shot and killed by Warrensville police. He was an out-of-town psychiatric patient staying in a local motel.

| **Hassan Haamid** | 60 | *Black* | 👁 |

April 11, 1998. Warrensville Heights:
The police were called to Mr. Haamid's home on a domestic dispute. According to a neighbor, Mr. Haamid came out of the house pleading for help. Police may have claimed he was threatening them with a gun, but eyewitnesses said he was not threatening police. After a short time, cops shot and killed him near his home. **Source:** victim's family

| **Josh Nicholas** | 13 | — |

April 1998 (?). Cleveland:
A stolen car carrying three teenagers sped past a police cruiser. Police started a chase but refused to say how fast they were going. The teenagers' car hit a utility pole. Josh, a passenger, was thrown from the car and killed. The driver and another passenger, both age 15, were injured, one critically. **Source:** Associated Press, 4/98 (via Michael Novick)

| **Richard Jacobs** | 28 | *white* |

July 14, 1997. 32nd & Clark Avenues:
Richard Jacobs was shot and killed by an off-duty county sheriff. Richard had supposedly stolen some toiletries from the Walgreen store. The off-duty deputy chased him and fatally shot him in the back when Richard was cornered against a wall with no place to go.

Darnell Davis	28	*African American*	

June 11, 1997. 102nd & Colonial St.:
Darnell was beaten and maced after a minor traffic accident at 3:30 pm. Police sprayed pepper gas into his mouth and nose, causing a fatal heart attack. It was ruled "justifiable homicide."

Adolph Boyd, Jr.	30	*African American*	👁

April 14, 1997. 118th & Buckeye Ave.:
Adolph was shot at least 12 times in the back and killed by one or two Cleveland cops as he was walking toward Wendy's. Although police say he was brandishing a gun, none has been produced.

James Rhodes	26	*African American*	👁

February 19, 1997. 107th & St. Clair:
James was brutally beaten and then shot to death by a Cleveland cop, Earl Holcomb. Before the beating and shooting, James had been nearly run down by the police car while standing around with some of his friends. The cop was cleared by the County Grand Jury of any wrongdoing.

Paul Cavins	35	*white*	

February 10, 1997. East 78th:
Paul was gunned down by police without warning in front of his house.

Stephen Horton	41	*African American*	👁

January 1, 1997. Cleveland (4th District Jail):
Stephen was arrested but never booked on disorderly conduct charges. After being taken to the Fourth District jail on Dec. 31, 1996, another inmate called Stephen's parents and Stephen yelled to them that he wanted them to come to the jail to see what was going on. In another call to a friend Stephen asked a friend to pick him up as soon as e was released. He said that his shoelaces and belt had been taken and that detectives were harassing him. Stephen stated that he was not going out like that. Stephen's parents got a call in the early hours of Jan. 1, 1997 from Detective Gunsh. The detective told them their son had committed suicide by hanging. The Horton's were in shock, knowing their son, at 41, was not depressed and was very much in control. A few hours later, the Horton's asked to see the cell where Stephen had allegedly hung himself. Their request was refused. They were not allowed to view the body for identification at the city morgue (They were told the police had already done that). After getting a lawyer, the Horton's were able to see their son's body at the morgue, more than a day after his death. But even then, they were only allowed to see him through glass. Stephen's body was also wrapped in gauze from his chin to his toes, obscuring the condition of his body. When Stephen's father saw pictures of his son taken at the morgue, he could see they had been doctored. When he took pictures at the funeral home, bruises were visible. Many questions remain unanswered. For example, why was Stephen taken directly from the jail to the morgue when a hospital is a few blocks away from the jail? Two years after Stephen's death, with the city still refusing to investigate, the Horton's had Stephen's body exhumed. An autopsy was performed by their own medical examiner. Another shock: seven body parts were missing, including parts around the throat area and Stephen's testes. The Horton's grieve and also continue to fight for justice for Stephen. The victim's father described his son, saying he "had a firm handshake, a magnetic personality, very intelligent, he was a magnet for all people of all races and nationalities. All Stephen had to do was open his mouth and it looked as if people just gravitated toward him." **Source:** victim's family

Danny Harmon	38	*white*	👁

November 1996. Cleveland (westside):
Danny was coming out of a housing project to meet his sister. As he approached her car, two cops jumped out to grab him. Danny ran and the cops ran after him. They also took the keys out of his sister's car and kept them so that she couldn't follow and check on her brother's safety. The police returned after aan hour and a half but without Danny. One cop said Danny went into the river and the other cops said he didn't. The city refused to search the river. After weeks of Danny's friends and relatives searching the area, his body was found in a shallow pool of water surrounded by ten foot walls. He'd been clearly beaten and thrown into this pool. The police involved continued to work. The authorities claimed Danny had been in the wrong place (i.e., he was a white man in a mostly Black and Latino housing project). They also said it was wrong to run from the police.

Steven Harms   29   *white*

August 16, 1996. Cleveland:
Steven was shot and killed by a Cleveland cop who came right into his house after a routine domestic violence call. A cop came into his house as he had his head on the kitchen table, tired from drinking. Steven had no weapon and was shot twice after he was told to wake up after being passed out. Steven left behind a wife and two daughters. The officer was cleared on the grounds of justifiable homicide.

Michael Thomas Smolira   23   *white*

July 26, 1996. Cleveland:
After a routine traffic stop, Michael was beaten up badly before he was shot and killed. The police claimed he tried to kill an officer.

Edward V. Uhnak   34   *white*

May 1, 1996. Cleveland:
Mr. Uhnak was killed by police when they told him to drop what they thought was a gun. It was actually a metal rod covered by a blanket.

Granville Caudell, Jr.   46   *African American*

April 30, 1996. Cleveland:
Graanville was beaten and his ribs broken before being arrested. The coroner ruled it was homicide because his injuries provoked a heart attack while in jail that led to his death. The grand jury cleared the cop(s).

Shirley Jackson   30   *African American*

1996. Cleveland (in custody):
Ms. Jackson died of a heart attack while in police custody. She had no health problems before she was put in jail.

Sylvester Tate   39   *African American*

August 19, 1995. Cleveland:
Sylvester was shot and killed by police as he sat on a couch in his living room. According to police, he had a gun.

David Cardenas   35   *Latino*

December 30, 1994. Cleveland (westside):
The police were called because David was drunk and allegedly came out on his porch swinging a bat and hit the porch railing. As he stood on his porch, a cop shot him dead. The cop was cleared of any wrongdoing.

Harvey Burton   24   *African American*

October 26, 1994. I-90 (highway):
After a low-speed chase on I-90 in an EMS (Emergency Medical Service) truck he had stolen, Harvey had already stopped when the police walked up to the window and shot him in the head. Harvey was unarmed.

Spencer Calhoun   28   *African American*

August 20, 1994. Cleveland:
Spencer Calhoun was stopped for a minor traffic violation. He was taken to the 4th district but not charged. He was taken to Cleveland Heights for a past traffic violation. After being in the Cleveland Heights jail for several hours, Calhoun had an apparent seizure and was taken to Huron Hospital where doctors noticed bruises on his body and massive internal head injuries. The cops in the Cleveland Heights jail said Spencer got his injuries from falling off a cell bench. He died a week after being beaten.

| **Rebecca Miller** | 22 | *African American* |

June 6, 1994. Cleveland:

Rebecca was shot and killed at close range in the hallway of her apartment. The police had been called in on a domestic squabble with her boyfriend. Allegedly, Rebecca would not drop the knives she had in her hand. She was killed with her 2-year-old son by her side.

| **Zobeyda Rivera** | 19 | *Latina* |

May 13, 1994. Bay Village (Cleveland suburb):

Ms. Rivera was killed execution-style by the Cleveland Police when she ran out of a stolen car after a 30 minute car chase. She weighed 90 pounds. She was thrown to the ground with police on top of her. Her jacket was put over her head and she was shot in the back of the head. The officer was not charged.

| **Michael Smith** | 33 | *African American* |

March 23, 1994. Woodhill Ave.:

Michael was shot 5 to 7 times and killed by two 4th district vice detectives as he got off the bus. He had a beer bottle in his hand.

| **Everett Dismuke** | 20 | *African American* |

November 28, 1993. Lee Road:

Everett was brutally gunned down on Lee Road. The police claimed he grabbed at the cop's gun, but eyewitnesses say that didn't happen.

| **Walter Dobzansky** | 54 | *white* |

mid-Nov., 1993. West 11th St.:

Walter was gunned down by two cops in his own house on West 11th Street. The police were called there about a burning chair in the basement. The police say Walter drew a gun on them, but no shots were ever fired.

| **Darnell Baker** | 16 | *African American* |

October 5, 1993. Cleveland:

Darnell was gunned down by a Cleveland detective as he supposedly tried to steal her car.

| **Michael Pipkins** | 23 | *African American* |

December 28, 1992. Cleveland (131st & Miles):

Michael Pipkins was choked to death by two cops, thrown in the police car, taken to the Fourth District, and put into a cell dead. Even though the coroner ruled his death was caused by the police, the cops were never charged, and officials refused to present it to a grand jury. Michael was being arrested on suspicion for driving a stolen car. But there was no stolen car, and Michael was not even in a car at the time. He was just hanging out with a friend, enjoying Christmas week. The only "punishment" the two cops who killed Michael received was one day of paid leave each.

| **Larry Thomas** | 28 | *African American* |

September 12, 1992. dwontown Cleveland (Palace Theater):

A homeless man, Larry was choked to death by police when he was getting in out of the cold at the Palace Theater.

| **Ronnie Williams** | 28 | *African American* |

October 29, 1991. Cleveland (eastside):

Ronnie was chased by a bounty hunter and the FBI in cars. Ronnie jumped out of his car and tried to run inside his mother's house. He got to a yard next door. He threw his hands up and threw his gun away. They riddled him with bullets in front of his mother and neighbors.

| Dwayne Harris | 31 | *African American* | 👁 |

September 14, 1991. Cleveland (eastside):
While stopped at a traffic light, a relative of a friend in the car asked for $2 to borrow. Two unmarked police cars came up to the front and back of Dwayne's car. A cop got out, came up to Dwayne's car and shot through the window, killing him.

| Napoleon H. Woods III | 25 | *African American* | |

May 28, 1990. Cleveland (eastside):
Napoleon was shot in the face with a shotgun blast and killed after he and his girlfriend had a struggle with the police. The police claimed that they'd been threatened.

| Audrey Marshall | 34 | *African American* | |

Easter, 1990. Cleveland (eastside):
Audrey was killed by two officers in her kitchen after the police had chased her as she was trying to protect her baby. The officer was cleared and said he shot in self-defense.

OHIO (OUTSIDE CLEVELAND)

Name	Age	Nationality	Photo
Colico Smalls	21	*Black*	👁

August 4, 1999. Canton:
Around 2:30 a.m., Mr. Smalls allegedly went into a bar wearing a ski mask, pulled a gun, and tried to rob somebody. Police were called. Mr. Smalls left the bar by the time cops arrived. People inside the bar heard a single shot. Police had shot Mr. Smalls once in the chest and killed him, claiming he pulled a gun on them. **Source:** The Canton Repository, 8/5/99; friend of victim's family

| Michael Demonn Carpenter | 30 | *African American* | 👁 |

March 19, 1999. Cincinnati (Northside):
Mr. Carpenter was shot 5 times and killed by police officers Michael B. Miller II and Brent McCurley during a traffic stop. The victim had the top of his head taken off by a bullet fired by Officer McCurley and was also hit in the right arm. The cops had seen him at a convenience store where he bought a soda and then panhandled for gas money. They followed him when he drove away and stopped him, allegedly for expired license plates. Police said he was "acting suspicious." Police claim he refused to give his name or get out of the car, so they shot him dead. Cops searched the car after his death and supposedly found a utility knife in the glove compartment. They tried to use this to justify the shooting (although they couldn't have known about the utility knife when they opened fire). The family's lawyer filed a civil rights complaint against the officers. A protest rally was planned for Apr. 17, 1999. **Source:** communication from local anti-police brutality activist

| Robert Williams | 17 | — | |

May 11, 1998. Arlington Heights:
Robert was killed when the alleged stolen jeep he was driving crashed during a police chase. He was being pursued by an Arlington Heights cop, supposedly for speeding. **Source:** The Rocky Mountain News (Denver, CO), 5/24/98

| Anthony Carmichael | 18 | — | |

April 1998 (?). Trotwood (Dayton suburb):
According to police, Anthony was shooting at a man in a mall parking lot around 8 pm. When cops arrived, Anthony allegedly threatened them. The police opened fire, killing Anthony. **Source:** Associated Press, 4/98 (via Michael Novick)

Daniel T. Williams   41   —

February 2, 1998. Cincinnati:

Daniel was shot in the head and killed by Officer Kathleen Conway. Police claim Williams approached Officer Conway and shot her four times in a random attack as he stood outside her cruiser. Authorities say he then opened the door and pushed the cop over, at which point she pulled her gun and shot him in the head, killing him. Officer Conway, who is expected to recover fully from her wounds, was portrayed as a hero in the press. **Source:** The Columbus Dispatch, 2/6/98

Derrick Calhoun   21   —

January 20, 1998. Columbus:

Derrick was shot and killed by undercover cops who claimed they had bought several thousand dollars worth of crack from Derrick and 16-year-old Desmond Johnson in a "buy-and-bust" operation at a Sunoco gas station. The pair fled in a car, with Derrick driving, when cops tried to arrest them. The police allege that Calhoun's and Johnson's vehicle hit two cop cars (although the cops were not injured) and that Desmond Johnson began firing from the window, hitting Officer Ronald M. Moss once (Officer Moss, who supposedly bought the drugs from them, was expected to recover quickly). Three other cops returned fire, hitting Derrick at least once and killing him. Derrick's car then crashed, and Desmond Johnson was arrested and charged with, among other things, involuntary manslaughter. Apparently the cops are holding Johnson legally responsible for the fact that one of their own killed his associate. Prosecutors want to try him as an adult. **Source:** The Columbus Dispatch, 1/222/98

Dr. Margo S. Prade   —   —

November 26, 1997. Akron:

Dr. Prade was shot and killed by her former husband, Akron Police Department Capt. Douglas E. Prade. Her body was found inside her van at her family practice office. Investigators say Prade killed her because he could no longer control her after their divorce. **Source:** Beacon Journal, 5/98

Daniel L. Pratt   23   —

August 10, 1997. Madison County (Rte. 29):

Daniel was shot multiple times and killed by state troopers Jeffrey Reynolds and Daniel Finnel. Cops claim Daniel opened fire on them after he was pulled over. They claim they "returned fire" and killed him. The authorities claim Daniel was wanted for two counts of attempted murder and first-degree assault in his hometown (Jamestown, NY) and that he was driving a stolen pickup truck. Law enforcement sources from Ohio and New York discussed the dangers facing state troopers and how violent the public has become. They said that the incident showed that, "right now, the training that we have seems to be doing the job," and "I'm glad they [the cops] were on their toes." "Details" of the shooting are being "withheld" by police investigators until they "review the case" with the Madison County Prosecutor. Both cops were put on paid administrative leave (paid vacation), but they returned to full duty shortly afterwards. In December, a grand jury cleared them of any wrongdoing. **Source:** The Columbus Dispatch, 8/12/97 & 12/11/97

Lorenzo Collins   30   *African American*

February 28, 1997. Cincinnati:

Lorenzo escaped from a psychiatric ward at the University of Cincinnati Hospital. He was shot and killed by Cincinnati police officers and University police officers.

Mike Hill	—	*white*

June 28, 1995. Frazeysburg (Muskingum County):

Mike Hill, a member of the Ohio Unorganized Militia, was shot and killed by Officer Matt May, a member of Frazeysburg's three-member police department. Officer May pulled Mr. Hill over because the latter's car allegedly had militia license plates instead of the official Ohio state license plates. Mr. Hill allegedly pulled a pistol, and Officer May fired in self-defense, according to the Muskingum County sheriff's office. The controversy that resulted from this shooting included moves (ultimately unsuccessful) to disband Frazeysburg's three-member police department. In Dec., 1997, Frazysburg's newly-elected mayor commented "Matt [Officer May] was involved in a couple of things before that (Hill shooting). In my opinion, he should have been terminated long before he killed Mr. Hill. It's the cop attitude, which in today's society is not helpful." It is worth noting that such official reaction against a police murder is virtually unheard of in most cases. **Source:** The Columbus Dispatch, 12/12/97

Unidentified	—	—

December 31, 1995. Columbus (Oak Street):

This person was shot and killed by Officer Ronald M. Moss, who was serving a search warrant during a drug raid at the victim's house. The victim supposedly shot at Officer Moss, though the bullet lodged in his helmet, causing no serious injury. Officer Moss said he "returned fire," killing the "suspect." He received the Medal of Valor for the shooting. **Source:** The Columbus Dispatch, 1/22/98

Walter E. Brown	—	*Black*

1991. Cincinnati (Corryville):

Mr. Brown was shot to death by Cincinnati police in a hallway outside his apartment. The Office of Municipal Investigations found that the cops had used excessive force, but police investigators cleared them of wrongdoing. **Source:** Cincinnati Post, 5/21/99

Ervin Fanning	—	—

1991. Cincinnati:

Mr. Fanning choked to death after being restrained by Cincinnati police. The Office of Municipal Investigations found that cops had improperly applied restraints, causing the victim to vomit and choke. Police investigators cleared the cops of wrongdoing. **Source:** Cincinnati Post, 5/21/99

OKLAHOMA

Name	Age	Nationality	Photo
James Travis Laucks	26	—	

June 24, 1999. Checotah:

Mr. Laucks was shot twice and killed by Deputy Jimmy Hamm, who claimed that the victim charged him. Mr. Laucks had supposedly given Deputy Hamm permission to search his house. The deputy claimed Mr. Laucks attacked him when he "saw what he thought were methamphetamines in the garage." **Source:** The Daily Oklahoman, 6/25/99

Fernando Gonzales-Ceniceros	35	*Mexican*	

June 20, 1999. north Tulsa:

Mr. Gonzales-Ceniceros was shot and killed in a bar by Tulsa Police Officers Mike Brown and Jason Wheeler. The cops had arrived in response to a 911 call. Mr. Gonzales-Ceniceros allegedly began cursing when they tried to talk to him. Cops claim he "became extremely agitated and began making gestures with his hands, pulled the gun out, and pointed it at the officers." The two cops fired a total of 17 shots. Police evacuated the bar and called in the Special Operations Team and sharpshooters. They were reportedly not sure if Mr. Gonzales-Ceniceros was hit. Police fired tear gas into the bar in an attempt to flush out the victim. About two and a half hours later, they went inside and found Mr. Gonzales-Ceniceros sprawled on the floor, dead from police bullets. **Source:** The Oklahoma Eagle, 6/24/99 & 7/13/99

Clyde McSlann   17   —

February 16, 1999. Okmulgee County:

Clyde McSlann was shot three times in the back and killed by Okmulgee County Deputy Elbert Fuller. Deputy Fuller claimed he was attacked with a knife that Mr. McSlann had hidden up his rectum. Police claim Mr. McSlann retrieved the knife while his hands were cuffed to waist chains and shackled to his ankles in the police car, which had turned over three times. Deputy Fuller also alleged that Mr. McSlann had attempted to cut the deputy's throat and afterwards attempted to escape, at which time the cop shot him three times in the back, killing him. **Source:** Curtis Mullins, Coalition Against Police Brutality and Harassment

Michael Bonner   22   —

January 16, 1999. Oklahoma County Jail:

Authorities claim that Michael Bonner, an inmate in the Oklahoma County jail, attacked two guards and engaged them in a scuffle when they came to give him breakfast. The guards knocked him to the ground and handcuffed him. Michael lost consciousness and died. The sheriff claimed a preliminary autopsy showed that the victim had died of a heart attack caused by a combination of the psychotropic medication he was taking and physical activity. The sheriff told investigators that the guards did nothing wrong, that "While it is unfortunate the Mr. Bonner died, I am also pleased our officers appeared to conduct themselves in a professional manner." **Source:** Oklahoma City Oklahoman, 1/18/99

Edwin Levall Vines   —   —

November 1998. Tulsa:

Tulsa police claim Mr. Vines reached down as he was running and pulled a gun out of his sock. Officer Jeff Little shot and killed him. **Source:** Andree Smith, mother of Justin Smith

Unidentified Man   —   —

September 5, 1998. Shawnee:

The man had allegedly robbed a bank and fled in a car, holding a bank official hostage with a gun. Shawnee police pursued him about eight miles through town and flattened his car tires with "stop sticks." He stopped, but supposedly held a pistol to the bank official's head. A Shawnee police officer shot and killed the alleged robber. The bank official was unharmed. **Source:** newspaper clipping, 9/5/98

Justin H. Smith   24   *Black & Native American*   👁

August 14, 1998. Tulsa:

While handcuffed in police custody, Justin was brutally beaten by several officers after being pursued by Tulsa (Okla.) sheriffs and police on a 30-minute high speed chase. Police came up on Justin while he was driving on a deserted road allegedly for having faulty bright lights on his car. Justin pulled over once he reached a residential area, then got out of the car and ran. Police beat him. A witness said that when Justin spit in his attacker's face, the police beat him to death. Rather than call an ambulance to the scene where witnesses were present, officers transported his lifeless body to a nearby gas station, supposedly to buy gasoline en route to the jail. Emergency medical assistance was called to the gas station, but Justin could not be resuscitated. He was pronounced dead at the hospital. The medical examiner's report stated that Justin died from "acute cocaine intoxication (312 ng/ml in his blood and 905 ng/g in his brain) and the vigorous physical exertion related to his apprehension and arrest." His mother questions the validity of the cocaine report. The only official explanation for the large bruises on his body was for "handcuff injuries." No possible explanation was given for a dark bruise on his temple, where witnesses said he was kicked by police, or for other severe bruises on his neck, chest, and back. His mother requested the assistance of the NAACP. "The Tulsa County Medical Examiner covered up for the cowards who killed my son and lied about their murderous actions," said his mother, Johnsye Andree Smith. "There is no conceivable way the examiner could ignore Justin was beaten. To do so was irresponsible and immoral. This has happened time and time again in Tulsa, as in the case of Herrod Boyd, who was sadistically tortured, sexually assaulted and murdered by the TPD in 1992. America can no longer continue to cover up these criminal acts by killer cops. I am pleading with every parent, family or loved one of everyone killed by this country's paid assassins called police to contact each other and get organized. Coming together is the only way we can collectively survive our never-ending agony, get justice for our loved ones and help insure that one day our streets will be safe from the most God-forsaken, heartless killers this country has ever produced." **Source:** SLP form filled out by Andree Smith, victim's mother

Gerald Coleman   16   —

October 20, 1997. Lawton:
Gerald Coleman and two other teenagers had allegedly broken into a woman's house to rob it. The woman called 911 and was hiding in her bedroom with a gun. She fired when the three teenagers supposedly pointed guns at her. The woman was uninjured. The teenagers fled the house and encountered Lawton Police Officer Gerald Nooner, who fired nine shots at them, killing Mr. Coleman and injuring one of his companions. Cops claim all three teenagers fired their guns. Police admitted that the fatal shots were probably fired by Officer Nooner, but Mr. Coleman's two surviving companions were charged with first degree murder on the grounds that "if someone is killed during commission of a felony, those responsible for the felony may be charged with murder," according to the newspaper. **Source:** Daily Oklahoman (Oklahoma City, OK), 10/22/97 & 10/23/97

Charles Guffey   39   —

October 15, 1997. Tulsa (in custody):
Charles Guffey, a divorced father of two, had been in a Tulsa jail on a drug charge for only ten days when he died of a perforated ulcer. Nurses ignored his pleas for help concerning severe abdominal pain. During those ten days, Charles lost 23 pounds and often lay in his own vomit and diarrhea. Several times guards brought him to the medical unit, once on a stretcher because he was too weak to walk. On the evening before his death, inmates who shared Charles' dorm complained that he had open sores and was vomiting and having bowel movements. Charles was moved to a private cell where he screamed, "I'm dying, I'm dying. I can't breathe." Guards called a nurse who sat outside Charles' cell for five minutes. He had quit screaming so she never entered the cell. Five hours later, a guard found Charles' body. Rigor mortis had already set in. Charges of manslaughter and preparing false evidence have been brought against a prison nurse and former nursing director. "He was a person crying for his life and no one caring," said one of Charles' dorm mates. **Source:** St. Louis Post-Dispatch, 9/27/98

Wendell Oliver Niles   43   —

October 5, 1997. Oklahoma City:
Police Sgt. Mary Rowland tried to stop Mr. Niles for a traffic violation. He allegedly sped away and Sgt. Rowland pursued. Mr. Niles crashed during the chase and died at the scene. Sgt. Rowland claimed that the victim's car was a mile ahead of her and that she had lost sight of him at the time of the crash. **Source:** Daily Oklahoman (Oklahoma City, OK), 10/6/97 & 10/7/97

Kenneth Michael Trentadue   45   —

August 21, 1995. Oklahoma Federal Prison:
Kenneth was arrested for a minor parole violation and was expected to spend two days in jail. Federal prison guards placed him in a suicide proof cell. They sabotaged all the surveillance cameras. Then they beat him with a metal baton from head to foot, tasered him, tortured him, slit his throat, and stomped on him with boots. Kenneth suffered a smashed skull, boot marks on his face, tearing, and large cut marks on his throat. They cleaned up the blood and placed the body in a different cell which was clean of any blood. Then they claimed that Kenneth had died of suicide. However, they refused to allow any medical staff or investigators to enter the jail. They tried to coerce Kenneth's family to sign a permission form to allow the guards to cremate the body, which would destroy the body as evidence. The family refused. When the body was finally examined, the guards could not explain how Kenneth could have received such injuries without the use of a taser, knife, boots, or the metal baton which crushed his skull. Nor could they explain how Kenneth could have torn a gash in his own throat with his bare hands after slicing his own throat. They could not explain the absence of blood in the cell where they claimed that the "suicide" took place. The clean-up job at the true murder scene was sloppy and small blood stains were found. The guards could not explain that either. No arrest was made, no charges filed, no punishment of any kind given. Attorney General Janet Reno has stonewalled attempts to investigate Kenneth's murder. **Source:** SLP form; The Oregon Observer, 6/97; flyers from U.S. Citizens Human Rights Commission

Phillip Wayne Bailey   41   —

November 14, 1994. Tulsa:
Mr. Bailey was shot and killed by Tulsa police at 2541 E. Oklahoma St. **Source:** Andree Smith, mother of Justin Smith, police brutality victim

Randy Smith   31   *Black*

July 2, 1994. Tulsa:

Mr. Smith was shot and killed by the police. He was not charged with a crime and was not under arrest. As he walked away from Tulsa Police Officer Buckspan, he was shot once in the back, then twice in the chest when he turned around. Curtis Mullins, a local anti-police brutality activist, said, "[Tulsa Police] Chief Palmer let his body lay uncovered on the ground in the Ridgeview Apartment Complex in full view of many children for several hours." A member of Randy's family said that police would not let them examine him at the scene and told family members to "shut the f*ck up and get the f*ck out of here" when they voiced concern for his welfare. One white female police officer at the scene equated Randy's death with retribution for the killing of Officer Gus Spano a year earlier. Randy Smith had no connection with Officer Spano's death. **Source:** Curtis Mullins, Coalition Against Police Brutality and Harassment; Andree Smith, mother of police brutality victim Justin Smith

Ralph Edward Boaz, Sr.   38   *Black*

February 5, 1994. Tulsa:

Mr. Boaz was shot and killed by Tulsa police at 135 E. Haskell St. **Source:** Andree Smith, mother of Justin Smith, police brutality victim

Bobby Henry Rogers   29   —

October 2, 1993. Tulsa:

Mr. Rogers was shot and killed by Tulsa police at 1904 E. 51st St. **Source:** Andree Smith, mother of Justin Smith, police brutality victim

Harrod Boyd, Jr.   24   *Black*

October 2, 1992. Tulsa:

Mr. Boyd was beaten and tortured to death by Tulsa police. An object was forced into his rectum. No one was ever charged with his murder. **Source:** Curtis Mullins, Coalition Against Police Brutality and Harassment

Perry Stuart   35   *Black*

1992. Tulsa County Jail:

Sheriffs claim that Mr. Stuart committed suicide in custody by shooting himself in the back of the head while his hands were cuffed behind his back. Given the impossibility of such a scenario, one can only conclude he was shot to death by the sheriffs. Curtis Mullins, a local anti-police brutality activist said, "Mr. Stuart was assassinated." **Source:** Curtis Mullins, Coalition Against Police Brutality and Harassment

Kevin Young   17   —

September 11, 1991. Tulsa:

Mr. Young was shot and killed by Tulsa police at 7005 E. 89th Place. **Source:** Andree Smith, mother of Justin Smith, police brutality victim

Tommy Ottis Glidewell   42   —

August 29, 1989. Tulsa:

Mr. Glidewell was shot and killed by Tulsa police at 8787 E. Admiral. **Source:** Andree Smith, mother of Justin Smith, police brutality victim

Royce A. Owings   25   —

April 15, 1989. Tulsa:

Mr. Owings was shot and killed by Tulsa police at 3341 E. 31st St. He had allegedly committed a robbery and pointed a gun at cops before he was shot. **Source:** Andree Smith, mother of Justin Smith, police brutality victim

Ray Peters   —   —

Two Unidentified Men   —   —

July 6, 1980. Oklahoma City:

Mr. Peters and two other men were shot and killed while playing pool at a motel. Clifford Henry Bowen, a professional poker player with a history of burglary, was charged with the three murders and sentenced to death. Two years later, a lawyer for Mr. Bowen received information indicating that a South Carolina police lieutenant had committed the murders. The lieutenant's physical description matched the killer's. He was known to carry a .45 caliber automatic loaded with unusual silver tipped bullets (the weapon used in the murder), and Ray Peters' ex-wife, who was now married to the lieutenant, had reportedly been slapped and threatened by her ex-husband. The lieutenant had been in Oklahoma on the day of the shooting and returned to South Carolina later that day. Prosecutors knew all this at the time of Mr. Bowen's trial but concealed it. In response to Mr. Bowen's well-supported alibi that he was at a rodeo 300 miles away a few hours before the murder, the prosecutor contended, with no evidence, that he had taken a private jet to get to Oklahoma City. Mr. Bowen's conviction was thrown out by a federal appeals court after he had spent five years on death row. **Source:** Chicago Tribune series on prosecutorial misconduct

OREGON

Name	Age	Nationality	Photo
Jose Luis Calbaren Dominguez (?)	—	*Latino*	

Jan. 20, 1992 (?). Woodburn:

Mr. Dominguez was shot four times and killed by Woodburn Police Officer Dave Hussey outside a house after an early morning chase from a convenience store. Mr. Dominguez was allegedly armed. Friends of the victim were outraged because they felt the shooting was racist. The Northwest Treeplanters and Farmworkers United Union questioned the police investigation of the shooting. **Source:** Salem Statesman Journal, 1/21/92, 1/22/92, 1/23/92, 1/24/92, 6/12/92; Oregonian, 1/21/92

Marvin Donald Free	64	—	

January 23, 1999. Lane County (near Creswell):

Mr. Free was shot three times and killed by Oregon State Trooper James Hawkins during a traffic stop. The victim's wife was driving the pickup truck in which he was a passenger. She was pulled over for speeding and supposedly failed sobriety tests. Cops claim that Marvin Free pulled a rifle from the cab of the truck, ignored repeated orders to drop it, pointed it at Trooper Hawkins, and fired a shot (which missed) after the officer handcuffed his wife. Trooper Hawkins fired at Mr. Free, hitting him three times and killing him. Mr. Free was reportedly drunk at the time. **Source:** The Oregonian, 1/24/99; Associated Press, 1/28/99

Peter C. Gilbaugh	44	—	

December 31, 1998. downtown Portland:

Mr. Gilbaugh was shot and killed by Officer William D. Blazer after he allegedly assaulted Officer Blazer's partner, pinned her down, and grabbed her gun. Cops were originally called to the scene at the low-income residential hotel when another tenant called to complain that the victim had urinated on her door. Mr. Gilbaugh at first opened the door, then closed it with the cops still outside, and was so drunk they had to remind him to unlock the door as he attempted to re-open it. He then let the officers into his room, denied the urination incident, and supposedly became "increasingly aggressive." The cops decided to take him in for detoxification, which is when the scuffle broke out. Mr. Gilbaugh was a successful used car salesman, well respected by his colleagues, but he had a drinking problem, and had lived in the same small furnished room for four years. A grand jury cleared Officer Blazer of wrongdoing within a month, ruling that he feared his partner's life was in danger. **Source:** The Oregonian, 1/22/99; Associated Press, 1/1/99

Roosevelt Wesley Harris III   14   —

December 14, 1998. Portland:

Mr. Harris was killed at the conclusion of a police chase when his car hit a utility pole. He had taken his parents' car without permission. A 15-year-old girl in the car with him suffered a head injury and was hospitalized. Mr. Harris was from Beaverton and was a freshman at Westview High School. He is survived by his mother Karen Preston, father Roosevelt Wesley Harris Jr., and grandmother MaryAnn Heldt. His mother said, "He loved cars. He liked to go fast." **Source:** Oregonian 12/16/98.

Lewis Stanley McClendon   63   —

October 30, 1998. Tiller:

Mr. McClendon was killed, allegedly in a firefight with Douglas County sheriff's deputies at his home. Two deputies were supposedly wounded in the shooting. The sheriffs were there to serve a search warrant for suspected marijuana growing. Police were the only witnesses. **Source:** Oregonian, 10/31/98

Richard C. Dickie Dow   30   —

October 20, 1998. Portland:

Mr. Dow was beaten and restrained by Portland police. A coroner's report said that he died from "positional asphyxia." Police officers attempted to detain Mr. Dow, a paranoid schizophrenic. He became distraught, and started struggling and yelling to his mother for help. His mother, who witnessed the incident, described what happened: "I said, 'Just don't hurt him, he has a mental problem, let me calm him down.' And suddenly, the street was full of policemen and they came out of their cars swinging billy clubs and kept swinging and swinging." Up to eight police officers participated in beating and subduing Mr. Dow with batons and pepper-spray. The autopsy found that he had numerous abrasions and two broken ribs. Mr. Dow collapsed and stopped breathing. Police did not administer first aid and refused to allow Deborah Howes, a neighbor, to give CPR. Richard Dow's mother and stepfather were arrested and detained for five hours. They were released at 3:30 a.m. and told only that their son was in intensive care. When they arrived at the hospital, he was dead. Neighbors were disturbed about the way police handled the situation. One said, "His parents could have definitely defused the situation if they were allowed to." Another said, "You want to know why that man died? They choked him to death. That's beyond excessive force. It's straight murder. If it'd been one of us, we'd be in jail." The victim's mother said, "I'm not a doctor, but my son had no marks on him when the police first had hold of him, and when I saw him seven hours later, I could not recognize him as my own son. The only conclusion I can draw is that they literally beat him to death." In contrast, the coroner concluded that he had simply suffered from "sudden death syndrome." On Nov. 13, 1998, a grand jury ruled that the killing was justified. Mr. Dow is survived by his mother and stepfather, Barbara and Ted Vickers. **Source:** Oregonian, 10/21/98, 10/22/98, 10/24/98, & 11/14/98; Salem Statesman Journal, 10/21/98; Vancouver Columbian, 10/25/98; Associated Press, 10/22/98

Daniel Jordan Ogburn   46   —

October 19, 1998. La Grande:

Mr. Ogburn was shot to death after he allegedly attacked an officer with a knife. Officers had been called because Mr. Ogburn had violated a no contact order by visiting the home of his victims, a woman and her three children, in an upcoming case for assault, rape, sodomy, and sexual abuse. Mr. Ogburn supposedly chased the officers out of the house with the knife when they arrived, then attacked one of them. **Source:** Oregonian, 10/21/98

Richard Dennis Lee   —   —

Sept. 30, 1998 (?). Eugene:

The newspaper headline read, "Man died of illness, not acts by police: Probe: One expert says intervention by the officers prolonged the victim's life." Mr. Lee may have been mentally ill. Pepper-spray was involved, and the headline implied that police used pepper-spray on Mr. Lee. It is not uncommon for "natural causes" to be listed as the cause of death when supposedly non-lethal agents like pepper-spray are involved. **Source:** Eugene Register Guard, 10/16/98

Luthur Danzuka	42	*Native American*

August 5, 1998. Warm Springs:

Mr. Danzuka was bitten by a four-foot rattlesnake. His friend William Wainanwit called 911 for help. Tribal police and ambulance personnel arrived quickly but refused to believe that Mr. Danzuka had been bitten. They said he was drunk and arrested him. He was taken to a hospital four hours later, but it was too late and he died. An autopsy confirmed the cause of death as untreated rattlesnake bite. The FBI announced that they would investigate the case. Mr. Danzuka is survived by his girlfriend of 17 years, Arlene "Leta" Smith, and at least two children. Ms. Smith said of him, "He had a good sense of humor. He was always smiling. He was always happy." **Source:** Oregonian, 8/13/98; Salem Statesman Journal, 8/13/98

Timothy Jay Fight	29	—

July 26, 1998. Beaverton:

According to the police account, Beaverton police stormed Mr. Fight's house, breaking down the door, to arrest him on a felony warrant after observing him drive erratically earlier. He then supposedly shot at them three times but missed. Police returned fire, striking him multiple times and killing him. **Source:** Oregonian, 7/28/98 & 7/30/98; Salem Statesman Journal, 7/28/98

Donald Hupp	—	—

July 18, 1998. Turner:

The newspaper reported on July 18: "Armed standoff in Turner: police shoot, kill sniper suspect. The Silverton man allegedly fired at family and police." On July 30, the newspaper reported: "Turner area death ruled suicide. An armed man turned his Uzi on himself, grand jurors find." Mr. Hupp died from multiple gunshot wounds, which makes the suicide scenario seem implausible. **Source:** Salem Statesman Journal, 7/19/98, 7/20/98, 7/21/98, 7/24/98, & 7/30/98

Unidentified Male	—	—

May 31, 1998. Portland:

A young Tacoma man was chased by Portland police. He stripped off his clothes and climbed onto a police car. When he was handcuffed, he ran away. Police tackled him and "hobbled" him. Sweating profusely, the youth soon died. **Source:** Portland Copwatch

David Charles Fackler	41	—

March 29, 1998. Albany:

The headlines read, "Outside agencies probe shooting by Albany officer [Ben Atchley]: Apparently suicidal man killed in police confrontation." On May 1, the Linn County District Attorney ruled that the shooting was justified. **Source:** Corvallis Gazette-Times, 3/30/98, 3/31/98, & 5/2/98; Salem Statesman Journal, 3/31/98

William Paul Kincaid	43	—

February 27, 1998. Central Point:

Mr. Kincaid was shot to death by three officers in his home during a domestic violence call. He allegedly pulled a gun out of his pocket in front of the officers and his girlfriend. He was shot 5 times. On Mar. 10, 1998, an inquest jury ruled that the shooting was justified. **Source:** Medford Mail Tribune, 2/28/98 & 3/11/98; Salem Statesman Journal, 3/12/98

Donald Alton Rozelle	33	—

February 13, 1998. Medford:

Mr. Rozelle was shot to death by Medford police officers Philip Eastman and Ken Dickerson after a short foot chase. Police say that they grappled with him and pepper-sprayed him. Then he allegedly walked toward them with a hunting knife and a car jack, telling the officers that they would have to shoot him. Officer Eastman shot him twice in the chest. Police were originally called because he had "caused a disturbance" on a bus on which he had been riding as part of a community service work crew. He was put off the bus, and police arrived shortly thereafter. An inquest jury ruled on Feb. 26, 1998, that the shooting was justified. Mr. Rozelle's sister, Jodie Kramer, who lived with him, said that her brother suffered from depression and alcoholism. She also said, "Don was a wonderful person and we loved him very, very much. He's going to be missed more than anyone can imagine." **Source:** Medford Mail Tribune, 2/14/98, 2/16/98, 2/26/98, & 2/27/98

Eric Allen Shannon	33	—

January 28, 1998. Pendleton:
Mr. Shannon was shot to death by state and local police in a Pendleton gas station at the conclusion of a car chase in which he allegedly fired at the officers for an hour. The chase started after he and his girlfriend grabbed his five children out of a foster home and took off in their car. At the conclusion of the chase, he supposedly "started ranting and raised his gun," forcing the officers to fire. Mr. Shannon was from Pilot Rock. **Source:** Oregonian, 2/1/98; LaGrande Observer, 1/30/98; Seattle Times, 1/30/98

Unidentified Male	—	—

January 27, 1998. Portland:
Police claim that a suspect wearing body armor fired on police just before midnight on North Albina Avenue. Police shot him, and he died hours later. This incident happened just before midnight, hours after an unrelated shootout in which someone had fired on Portland police, killing Officer Waibel and wounding 2 other cops during a drug raid. The killing of this unidentified man was not reported in its own right, but was referred to in press coverage of Officer Waibel's death. **Source:** Oregonian, 1/29/98 & 2/1/98

William Hoge	31	—

January 15, 1998. Portland:
Mr. Hoge's car was rear-ended by a teenager fleeing the police in a stolen car. Mr. Hoge was killed in the accident when his car struck a utility pole. Police claim that they had called off the chase before the accident occurred. **Source:** The Oregonian, 1/22/98; Salem Statesman Journal, 1/16/98.

John Millman Napier	77	—
Gene Amos Tawney	55	—

December 26, 1997. Portland:
Mr. Napier and Mr. Tawney were killed when a car being chased by Portland police ran a stop sign and hit their car. Mr. Napier's 60-year-old wife, Jeanette Napier, survived but was severely injured in the crash. Police allege that the car they were chasing was stolen. The driver of the car being chased was convicted and sentenced for their deaths. **Source:** Salem Statesman Journal, 12/28/97

Reginald B. Gafford	29	—

October 11, 1997. Portland (Multnomah County Jail):
Mr. Gafford died after he was injected with Ativan, a tranquilizer, and strapped to a backboard in the Multnomah County Jail. According to authorities, it took about five minutes for deputies to secure him to the backboard, which prevents all movement. When they finished, they noticed he had stopped breathing. Sheriff Dan Noelle said, "The autopsy showed he had scuffs, abrasions and bruising, injuries that should not have caused even serious injury. The guy shouldn't have died." **Source:** Salem Statesman Journal, 10/14/97; Oregonian, 10/24/98

Bill Utton	65	—

September 23, 1997. Portland:
Mr. Utton was shot and killed by Portland police after a five hour standoff. Cops claim he had two guns and had fired at them numerous times before he was killed. **Source:** Salem Statesman Journal, 9/24/97

Judith Irene Hinch	—	—

September 11, 1997. Gresham:
Ms. Hinch was shot to death by police after allegedly making threats. **Source:** Salem Statesman Journal, 9/12/97

Edward Vincent Wyatt	—	—

April 21, 1997. Forest Grove:
"Cyclist's death ends high-speed [police] pursuit. After missing a curve on Highway 47, the rider is thrown 68 feet into a thicket," according to the newspaper report. Mr. Wyatt was from Hillsboro. **Source:** Salem Statesman Journal, 4/22/97

Luis Carrasco-Flores   45   *Mexican*

February 28, 1997. Salem:

Mr. Carrasco-Flores died when police broke down his bedroom door down at 5:15 a.m., startling him awake, and he reached for a pistol under his pillow. Officer Larry Roberts shot him five times, the last shot from point blank range. Salem attorney Brian Whitehead said that plenty of other people might have reacted the same way if they were awakened suddenly with a flashlight in the face and forced to decide in seconds whether it was an intruder or police. There had been a robbery and murder at the neighboring apartment nine months before, which might explain why Mr. Carrasco-Flores was armed. Although 20 other people were arrested from the apartment complex, police said that there was no evidence against Mr. Carrasco-Flores. The autopsy found no drugs or alcohol in his system and said that he died from gunshot wounds to the chest. On Mar. 5, the District Attorney announced that the shooting was justified and that Officer Roberts had acted in self-defense. This was the second Salem police killing of a Mexican man during a drug raid in seven months. Neither of the victims were suspects. Mr. Carrasco-Flores worked in a nursery. He is survived by 12 children who live in Mexico. **Source:** Oregonian, 3/6/97; Salem Statesman Journal, 3/2/97, 3/5/97, 3/6/97, 3/9/97, & 4/2/97

E. Jean Amerson   69   —

December 1996. Portland:

A "drug felon" fleeing from police in a high speed chase ran a stop sign and hit Ms. Amerson's car. She was thrown through the window and killed. She had been on her way to shop for Christmas. Police claim they called off the chase before the accident occurred. **Source:** The Oregonian, 1/22/98

Lance Sterling Alexander   —   —

October 3, 1996. Salem:

Mr. Alexander was shot to death by a police sniper in an overturned car on Interstate 5 after a 100 mph police chase, as he allegedly held a gun to the head of a kidnapped seven-year-old girl. Mr. Alexander had supposedly killed someone before he kidnapped the girl. **Source:** Vancouver Columbian, 10/6/96; Salem Statesman Journal, 10/4/96 & 10/9/96; Eugene Register Guard, 10/4/96; Tacoma News-Tribune, 11/29/96

Unidentified Man   —   —

September 29, 1996. Portland:

The man was shot to death by Portland police on the Interstate 205 bridge after a high-speed car chase. **Source:** Vancouver Columbian, 9/30/96

Anthony Charles Reece   —   —

Aug. 18, 1996 (?). Salem:

"Quarrel leads to fatal shooting: a Salem security guard [Elliot Carlson] fires in self defense, police say." "Police [said] guard in shooting was lucky," according to the newspapers. A grand jury considered evidence about the shooting, but the result is not known. **Source:** Salem Statesman Journal, 8/19/96, 8/20/96, & 8/24/96

Mark Andrew Lawson   30   —

August 4, 1996. Medford:

Mr. Lawson was shot in the head and killed by Medford police officer Keith Mak after a car chase and then a foot chase. The chase had been initiated when Mr. Lawson fled the scene of an attempted drug bust. According to Officer Mak, he was pursuing Mr. Lawson on foot when Mr. Lawson suddenly turned and faced the officer. Officer Mak alleged that he thought Mr. Lawson was armed and about to shoot. He shot Mr. Lawson in the head. The victim was unarmed. He died later at the hospital. The victim was from southern California and is survived by his wife, Susan Lawson.

Salvador Hernandez   63   *Mexican*

August 2, 1996. Keizer:

Salvador Hernandez, a farm worker, was shot five times in the chest and killed while he was preparing breakfast for his three children. Salem Police Officers Ken Gilbert and John Manitsas fired the fatal shots during a drug raid on his house. Police claimed that Mr. Hernandez came at them with a knife, but Mr. Hernandez's son and daughter-in-law say that he was just cooking breakfast. They say that he either did not understand their orders to "get down" in English, or did not hear because he was hard of hearing. Witnesses said that he did not have a knife in his hand after he was shot, and that he had just turned toward the refrigerator to get some sausage when he was shot. The raid on the house involved 47 officers. Mr. Hernandez was not even a suspect in the drug raid. After a grand jury cleared the officers of wrongdoing on August 7th, the victim's family denounced the decision and the shooting as racist. On Aug. 16, The FBI announced that it would investigate the shooting. On Nov. 6, the FBI decided not to prosecute the officers due to "insufficient evidence." The family intends to sue. Mr. Hernandez is survived by a large family, including at least three children, 21 grandchildren, and one great-grandchild. **Source:** Salem Statesman Journal, 8/8/96, 8/10/96, 8/17/96, 8/21/96, 3/9/97, 11/6/97, & 11/7/97

Lynn M. Kibbee   31   —

June 1996 (?). Portland:

Mr. Kibbee was shot to death by Portland Police Officer Thomas Newberry. His wife, Chandra Kibbee, filed a $1 million civil suit against the officer and the city of Portland.

Marvin Young   43   *white*

March 13, 1996. Eugene:

According to police and autopsy accounts, Mr. Young was shot once in the back as he drove away from plainclothes Eugene Police Officers Larry Crompton and Randy Berger. They had been following and watching Mr. Young and a female passenger. He allegedly attempted to drive away as the police were moving in to interrupt a drug deal and arrest him, forcing Officer Berger to shoot. Mr. Young died from loss of blood. It is not clear what medical treatment he received, if any. He was unarmed. Officer Berger later changed his story to say that his gun went off accidentally when he used it to try to break the car window. Police have not released the name of the female passenger in Mr. Young's car. Officer Berger also shot Brad Alan Smith to death less than a year earlier in Aug., 1995. Mr. Smith was the person most recently killed by the Eugene police. On Mar. 21, the District Attorney ruled that the shooting was accidental and declined to prosecute. On July 18, a police panel said that Officer Berger should be punished for the shooting death of Mr. Young. **Source:** Oregon Daily Emerald, 3/18/96; Eugene Register Guard, 3/14/96, 3/15/96, 3/17/96, 3/22/96, 4/4/96, 5/16/96, 7/15/96, & 7/19/96

Deontae Keller   20   —

February 28, 1996. Portland:

Mr. Keller was shot in the back and killed by Portland police. A grand jury found that, although Mr. Keller was fleeing at the time he was shot, the shooting was justified because he was armed. He is survived by his father, Joseph Keller, who has been active in the October 22nd Coalition to Stop Police Brutality. **Source:** Oregonian, 10/25/98

Edward Davis (?)   —   —

Feb. 16, 1996 (?). Nesika Beach:

A man, presumably Mr. Davis, was shot to death by a state police detective (possibly Det. David Gardiner) at a residence. Mr. Davis was supposedly drunk. The autopsy determined that he died from a bullet to the heart. A public inquest was held, and the jury deadlocked over whether the shooting was justified. On Apr. 30, the Curry County District Attorney decided the shooting was justified. The DA's office stated, "[The] detective will not be charged because he felt threatened and acted in self-defense." **Source:** Coos Bay World, 2/17/96, 2/24/96, 4/26/96, & 5/1/96

Unidentified Woman   —   —

January 1996 (?). Portland:

The newspaper reported, "Officer John Aichele killed his wife. Her family says the police chaplain could have stopped him." **Source:** Willamette Week, 2/28/96

George Edward Ferrell   42   —

December 4, 1995. Eugene:

The newspaper reported, "High-speed [police car] pursuit leaves one man dead." **Source:** Eugene Register Guard, 12/5/95

Archie Michael Murray   —   —

November 11, 1995. Dallas:

Mr. Murray was shot and killed by police after a disturbance at a Safeway grocery store. He was reported to be mentally ill and had previously been a Salem Hospital psychiatric in-patient. Police were called because Mr. Murray had allegedly assaulted customers at two grocery stores. On Nov. 15,1995, a grand jury found that the shooting was justified. **Source:** Salem Statesman Journal, 11/12/95, 11/13/95, & 11/16/95

Bradley Alan Smith   31   —

August 1995. Eugene:

Mr. Smith was shot and killed by Portland police officer Randy Berger during a foot chase, allegedly after an attempted armed robbery. Officer Berger claimed that Mr. Smith had turned and pointed a gun at him. Mr. Smith was homeless and a long time resident of Eugene. **Source:** Oregon Daily Emerald, 3/18/96; Eugene Register Guard, 8/13/95

Terrence Turner Rea   —   —

July 21, 1995. Corvallis:

Mr. Rea was shot and killed in a standoff with Benton County Sheriff's Civil Emergency Response Team (CERT) deputies after he allegedly kidnapped his wife at gunpoint. His wife escaped unharmed. Mr. Rea was killed three hours later. On Aug. 9, the newspaper reported, "Deputy cleared in shooting." In Aug., 1997, Mr. Rea's wife, Raven Wing Rea, sued police for his death. **Source:** Tacoma News-Tribune, 7/22/95; Salem Statesman Journal, 7/22/95 & 8/14/97; Corvallis Gazette-Times, 8/9/95

Jacob Dewitt   14   —

April 23, 1995. Salem:

Mr. Dewitt died in a fiery crash at the conclusion of a Marion County sheriff's deputies' high-speed car chase. Four others were injured. It is not clear if the victim was in the vehicle being chased or in another vehicle, but it is clear that he was a passenger. Mothers of some of the victims and many others criticized the Sheriff's Department after the incident. On May 23, 1995, police announced numerous charges, including manslaughter, against the teenage driver of the car. **Source:** Salem Statesman Journal, 4/23/95, 4/26/95, 4/27/95, 4/29/95, 5/6/95, & 5/24/95

Unidentified Person   —   —

Dec. 12, 1994 (?). Milwaukie:

The newspaper reported, "Officer fatally shoots suspect in doghouse." **Source:** Salem Statesman Journal, 12/13/94

Gale Moody   52   —

August 24, 1994. Portland:

Portland police shot and killed Ms. Moody, a mentally ill woman, as she allegedly pointed a fake handgun at them. This was the second of two (known) fatal police shootings of mentally ill women in the Portland area in one week. **Source:** Salem Statesman Journal, 8/26/94; Human Rights Watch, Shielded from Justice (1998), pp. 340-341

Janet Marilyn   —   —

Aug. 21 (?), 1994. Gresham:

Ms. Marilyn, a mentally ill woman, was shot and killed by Gersham police as she allegedly wielded a knife while threatening to kill her cat. This was the first of two (known) fatal police shootings of a mentally ill woman in the Portland area in one week. **Source:** Salem Statesman Journal, 8/22/94 & 9/1/94; Human Rights Watch, Shielded from Justice (1998), pp. 340-341

| Paul L. Froats | 35 | — |

August 6, 1994. North Bend:

"Deputy gets threats after shooting suspect [to death]," according to the newspaper. **Source:** Salem Statesman Journal, 8/10/94

| Evan Espinoza | 15 | — |

June 18, 1994. McMinnville:

Mr. Espinoza died in a police chase. It is not clear if he was in the vehicle being pursued. **Source:** Salem Statesman Journal, 6/19/94 & 6/22/94

| John Steven Nardi (father) | 26 | — |
| Richard L. Nardi (son) | 11 months | — |

June 12, 1994 (?). Dallas:

"Dallas man died from multiple shots.... [Dallas] police officer [Dennis Tiernan] who shot Dallas man [as he was fleeing] identified. The 20-year veteran was placed on leave, as was his partner who did not fire her gun," according to the newspaper. On July 7, the paper reported, "Jury clears officer in Dallas case. The fatal shooting of a fleeing suspect is ruled justified, ending the investigation." On Oct. 20, the newspaper declared, "Baby dies [on Oct. 15, 1994] three months after father fatally shot." Officer Tiernan had also been involved in a police shooting in 1980. **Source:** Salem Statesman Journal, 6/13/94, 6/14/94, 6/15/94, 7/7/94, 7/8/94, & 10/20/94

| Unidentified Man | — | — |

Feb. 22, 1994 (?). Eugene:

The newspaper reported, "Police officer kills gunman." This was apparently a shooting. **Source:** Eugene Register Guard, 2/23/94

| Joe Gene Barton | 44 | — |

November 26, 1993. Springfield:

Mr. Barton was shot seven or eight times by Springfield Police Officers John Slimak and Joe Zito after he allegedly refused to put down his gun and yelled "shoot me!" The officers fired at least 27 rounds. Mr. Barton died on the way to the hospital. The shooting occurred in the back yard of a house where officers were called by someone reporting neglected children. No children were found. There were no warrants for Mr. Barton's arrest, and police did not know if he had fired at them. **Source:** Eugene Register Guard, 11/27/93; Salem Statesman Journal, 11/28/93; Tacoma News-Tribune, 11/28/93

| Unidentified Person | — | — |

Aug. 28, 1993 (?). Coos Bay:

"State trooper cleared in fatality. He shot and killed a knife-wielding motorist in Coos Bay," according to the newspaper. **Source:** Salem Statesman Journal, 8/29/93

| Ramona Pearl Heinze | 39 | — |
| Keith Randall James | 36 (?) | — |

August 25, 1993. Clackamas County:

The newspaper reported, "Head-on crash kills two during Clackamas [police] chase." **Source:** Salem Statesman Journal, 8/26/93 & 9/3/93

| Jay R. McDonnell | 32 | — |

March 3, 1993. Salem:

The newspaper reported, "Motorists, shoppers watch Salem police give chase: many witness the death of a knife-wielding man near Lancaster Mall." The fatal shooting by Officers Rodger Greenfield and Leroy Shrum was ruled justified on Mar. 12, 1993. Mr. McDonnell was from Redmond. **Source:** Salem Statesman Journal, 3/4/93, 3/5/93, & 3/13/93

Nicholas Kirschder — —

November 12, 1992. Canby:
Mr. Kirschder was shot and killed by a Canby police officer after a car chase. Cops claim he was armed. **Source:** Oregonian, 11/13/92

Steven Clark Foster 41 —

October 13, 1992. Oregon City (Clackamas County Jail):
Mr. Foster was shot, supposedly during an escape attempt from Clackamas County Jail. He had allegedly confessed to murder the day before. He died of his injuries three weeks later on Nov. 5, 1992. **Source:** Tacoma News-Tribune, 11/6/92

Aimo Kallio Savuno 78 —

October 5, 1992. Portland:
Mr. Savuno was shot and killed by Officer Henry Groepper after trying to flee and then allegedly pointing a pistol at the officer. **Source:** Salem Statesman Journal, 10/6/92; Oregonian, 10/6/92

Allen Robert Peterson 41 —

September 13, 1992. Portland:
"Police [shoot and] kill man during family fight," according to the newspaper. **Source:** Oregonian, 9/14/92; Social Security Death Index

Unidentified Person — —

Sept. 7, 1992 (?). Warrenton:
"[Police] shooting, heart attack end coast car chase [in death of suspect]," according to the newspaper. **Source:** Salem Statesman Journal, 9/8/92

Jerry Edwin Albin (?) — —

June 11, 1992 (?). Salem:
The victim, reportedly Mr. Albin, was shot to death by Salem Police Officer Marc Leeder at Union Street Pizza. He was supposedly armed. Police said Mr. Albin was a transient. **Source:** Salem Statesman Journal, 6/12/92, 6/13/92, 6/14/92, & 6/16/92; Oregonian, 6/13/92

Mark Wayne DeVoe 35 —

May 29, 1992 (?). Salem:
Three deputies shot and killed Mr. DeVoe after a chase. Afterwards, a neighbor said he was "puzzled" by the incident, saying that Mr. DeVoe was helpful and friendly and never caused any problems. Police alleged that the victim might have been mentally ill and that he threatened them with a toy gun. Mr. DeVoe was from Salem. The shooting was ruled justified on June 11, 1992. **Source:** Oregonian, 5/31/92; Salem Statesman Journal, 5/30/92, 5/31/92, 6/1/92, 6/11/92, & 6/12/92

Fred Thor Goodmanson — —

May 27, 1992 (?). Portland:
Mr. Goodmanson was shot to death by Portland police in his apartment for allegedly wielding a pellet gun. **Source:** Oregonian, 5/28/92; Salem Statesman Journal, 5/28/92

Unidentified Man — —

Apr. 26, 1992 (?). Reedsport:
A man was shot eight times and killed by a Douglas County sheriff's deputy at the Loon Lake resort. The names of the parties involved were David Maddux and Roger Loomis; it was not clear from the newspaper account which was the victim and which was the cop. A grand jury ruled that the shooting was justified on May 19, 1992. **Source:** Eugene Register Guard, 4/28/92 & 5/21/92; Oregonian, 4/27/92; Salem Statesman Journal, 5/20/92

Robert Harvey Rinehart   48   —

March 25, 1992. Beaverton:

The newspaper reported, "Transient dies after shootout with police." Mr. Rinehart was from Oregon. **Source:** Oregonian, 3/26/92; Salem Statesman Journal, 3/27/92; Social Security Death Index

Nathan Thomas   12   —

January 16, 1992. Portland:

Nathan Thomas was being held hostage in his home by Bryan French, an intruder who was allegedly threatening to kill him and then supposedly began cutting his throat. Five Portland police officers opened fire, killing both Nathan Thomas and Bryan French. Mr. French was reportedly suicidal. A grand jury found that the shooting was legal, though not necessarily justified. Nathan's parents asked for an independent investigation on July 16, 1993. **Source:** Tacoma News-Tribune, 1/24/92; Willamette Week, 12/7/94; Oregonian, 1/17/92 & 1/18/92; Salem Statesman Journal, 1/17/92, 1/18/92, 1/24/92, 3/30/92, 1/18/93, & 7/17/93; Human Rights Watch, Shielded from Justice (1998), p. 341

Bryan French   20   —

January 16, 1992. Portland:

Bryan French was killed as he allegedly held 12-year-old Nathan Thomas hostage. Five Portland police officers opened fire, claiming Mr. French was cutting Nathan's throat, and killed both of them. Mr. French, who was reportedly suicidal, had allegedly broken into a home and taken Nathan Thomas hostage. A grand jury found that the shooting was legal, though not necessarily justified. Nathan's parents asked for an independent investigation on July 16, 1993. **Source:** Tacoma News-Tribune, 1/24/92; Willamette Week, 12/7/94; Oregonian, 1/17/92 & 1/18/92; Salem Statesman Journal, 1/17/92, 1/18/92, 1/24/92, 3/30/92, & 1/18/93; Human Rights Watch, Shielded from Justice (1998), p. 341

Unidentified Man   —   —

December 15, 1991. Portland:

The unidentified man was shot several times and killed by Portland Police Officer Robert King after the officer stopped a car that was supposedly involved in a shoplifting incident. The victim was a passenger in the car who allegedly stabbed Officer King in the shoulder before he was shot. **Source:** Oregonian, 12/16/91; Seattle Times, 12/16/91

Unidentified Person   —   —

Oct. 22, 1991 (?). Portland:

"Sheriff's deputy shoots, kills [cocaine] suspect," according to the newspaper. **Source:** Oregonian, 10/23/91; Salem Statesman Journal, 10/24/91

Brian R. Byrd   23   —

Sept. 17, 1991 (?). Irrigon:

"Irrigon man dies after police chase," according to the newspaper. **Source:** Salem Statesman Journal, 9/18/91

Michael Patrick Malloy   —   —

Aug. 7, 1991 (?). Portland:

Mr. Malloy, of Portland, had allegedly taken Sheryle Bennet and her daughter hostage, and had supposedly made repeated threats to kill Ms. Bennet. He was shot to death by police. **Source:** Oregonian, 8/8/91

Terry Schmidt   —   —

July 20, 1991 (?). Corvallis:

Mr. Schmidt was shot to death by Officer Brad Sharpton for allegedly "wielding" a knife near the Timber Hill Shopping Center. The shooting was ruled justified on Aug. 9, 1991. **Source:** Oregonian, 7/21/91 & 8/10/91; Salem Statesman Journal, 7/22/91 & 7/23/91

Unidentified Man — —

May 16, 1991 (?). Portland:

"Police shooting kills man." The Gang Enforcement Team and a "drug house" were somehow involved. **Source:** Oregonian, 5/17/91

Michael Henry 19 —

April 13, 1991. Portland:

Mr. Henry died in what was supposedly a shootout with police after a three and a half-hour standoff at a bank in which he held two hostages. He freed one of the hostages after 90 minutes. Two police officers were wounded and Mr. Henry was killed when they rushed the bank to free the second hostage. The hostage was not injured. It was determined later that Mr. Henry did not fire at the officers. They were hit by "friendly fire" from other cops. Mr. Henry said that he was sexually abused by his parents and that he took the hostages "to show the system up" because he had not received justice. He was reportedly suicidal. **Source:** Salem Statesman Journal, 4/14/91 & 4/15/91; Oregonian, 4/14/91; Seattle Times, 4/14/91; Tacoma News-Tribune, 4/14/91, 4/20/91

Unidentified Man — —

Feb. 27, 1991 (?). Salem:

An ex-cop from Sacramento was arrested for shooting and killing a Salem man. In Nov., 1991, a jury found him not guilty in the roadside shooting. **Source:** Salem Statesman Journal, 2/28/91 & 11/22/91

Sineth Yin — —

January 15, 1991. Hood River:

Mr. Yin was shot to death by Hood River Police Officer Robert Lunyou while allegedly robbing Smith's Outdoor Adventure gun store. Two other suspects were arrested and nine escaped. Police claimed that Mr. Yin was a member of the Portland "Red Cobra" gang. **Source:** Oregonian, 1/16/91 & 1/17/91; Seattle Times, 1/16/91

Mari Lyn Sandoz 29 —

December 4, 1990. Portland:

Ms. Sandoz was shot 22 times and killed by Portland Police Officers Michael Barkley and Craig Bonnarens. She allegedly had threatened suicide, then pointed a pellet gun at the officers. A county grand jury ruled that the shooting was justified. **Source:** Seattle Times, 12/6/90, 12/9/90, & 12/23/90; Salem Statesman Journal, 12/7/90

James Raymond Talley 22 —

Nov. 5, 1990 (?). Milwaukie:

Mr. Talley was shot and killed by deputies, who claim they were returning fire. The incident occurred at a home. **Source:** Salem Statesman Journal, 11/6/90; Oregonian, 11/6/90; Social Security Death Index

Unidentified Man — —

October 31, 1990. Medford:

The man was surrounded by six police officers and shot to death after an alleged attempted bank robbery. Police said the man threatened them. **Source:** Salem Statesman Journal, 11/1/90; Seattle Times, 11/1/90

Russell E. Rice (?) 30 —

Sept. 27, 1990 (?). Josephine County:

"Josephine deputies kill gunman," according to the newspaper. This was apparently a shooting. **Source:** Oregonian, 9/28/90

Darlene Marie Barrientes	teenager	—
Tasha Marie Nathan	15	—
Jason Summerford Purvis	teenager	—
Dale James Saunders	25	—

Sept. 13, 1990 (?). Florence:

The four victims died when their allegedly stolen car tumbled into a small reservoir during a high speed police chase. Tasha Marie Nathan's mother Judith initiated a lawsuit against police in Sept. 1992. **Source:** Oregonian, 9/14/90; Eugene Register Guard, 9/14/90 & 9/20/90; Salem Statesman Journal, 9/16/90 & 9/17/92; Social Security Death Index

John Rhodes Huber	50	—

July 14, 1990. Camas Valley:

Mr. Huber was shot to death by Oregon State police after a 13-hour siege in which he allegedly held a woman hostage in a camping bus at Bear Creek campground. Authorities claim he had shot and killed a woman in Columbia, Penn., on July 6, another woman in Scottsburg on July 11, and a man who had tried to stop him at the campground on July 13. **Source:** Eugene Register Guard, 7/16/90; Seattle Times, 7/16/90

Kevin McCoy	—	—

June 10, 1990. Portland:

Mr. McCoy was shot to death at his house by Portland Police Officer John H. Payne as he allegedly wielded a knife. Cops claim Officer Paune asked the victim to drop the knife, but that he threw the knife onto the front lawn and then lunged for the officer's gun. **Source:** Oregonian, 6/11/90; Salem Statesman Journal, 6/11/90; Seattle Times, 7/29/90

Larry Wayne Helberg	52	—

January 15, 1990. Union:

Mr. Hellberg was killed by police during a drug raid at a farmhouse. Two other "suspects" were arrested. This was apparently a shooting. **Source:** Salem Statesman Journal, 1/19/90; Oregonian, 1/19/90 & 2/1/90; Social Security Death Index

Gary R. Tull	48	—

January 10, 1990. Jefferson:

Mr. Tall was shot to death by Salem police during a raid. An inquiry cleared the cops, saying Mr. Tall was pointing a rifle at them. On Mar. 17, 1994, a jury found the officers not liable in a wrongful death civil lawsuit. **Source:** Salem Statesman Journal, 1/11/90, 1/20/90, & 3/18/94; Oregonian, 1/11/90; Social Security Death Index

CENTRAL PENNSYLVANIA

Name	Age	Nationality	Photo

John David Hirko, Jr. 　　　　　　　　22 　　　　　*white*

April 23, 1997. Bethlehem:

Mr. Hirko was shot at least eleven times, mostly in the back, and killed by heavily armed, masked police dressed in "black Ninja suits." They threw a percussion grenade into the house he shared with his girlfriend and then burst in and shot him dead, never identifying themselves as police. The stun grenade set the house on fire, and John's body was allowed to burn beyond recognition. Some witnesses said the cops delayed firefighters from putting out the fire. Police claim they were carrying out a search warrant in response to reports of drug sales at the residence (three $10 sales of heroin and cocaine, to be exact). They also claim that John had a handgun. The only weapons found were an unloaded shotgun and hunting rifle among other hunting equipment. Police claim to have found some marijuana and heroin that miraculously survived the fire. An un-singed bag of marijuana seeds was supposedly found "on the same floor where the heat reached temperatures hot enough to melt two-inch metal," according to the family's lawyer. Cops questioned John's girlfriend for eight hours without a lawyer present, without reading her rights, and then released her with no charges. Several weeks later, after her lawyer publicly questioned the police version of events, she was arrested on a variety of drug charges. The prosecutor requested high bail because she was not living in an "established residence" and was thus a flight risk. Her "established residence" had been burned down by the police on the night her boyfriend was killed. Three months later, no police report or official autopsy results had been made public. John's family filed a wrongful death lawsuit, and their lawyer called for criminal charges to be filed against the cops responsible for John's murder. The Police Commissioner said the killing was "an unfortunate event," and that he was "confident the actions of the officers were 100% correct under the circumstances." **Source:** SLP form; High Witness News, 10/97; Media Bypass Magazine, 9/97

PHILADELPHIA / EASTERN PENNSYLVANIA

Name	Age	Nationality	Photo

Stephen "Kuado" Opaku 　　　　　　— 　　　　　*Ghanian (West African)*

November 1998. Philadelphia:

Mr. Opaku was involved in a car wreck. Philadelphia Police Officer George Morris arrived on the scene, approached the car, and shot out the window in what he claimed was an attempt to rescue Mr. Opaku. The bullet set the car on fire, and Mr. Opaku was killed in the blaze. **Source:** Revolutionary Worker, 8/1/99

Donta Dawson 　　　　　　　　　　18 　　　　　*Black*

October 1, 1998. Philadelphia:

Mr. Dawson was sitting in his car in the middle of an intersection when officers approached him. When he lifted up one of his hands, Officer Christopher DiPasquale shot him in the right eye and killed him. None of the other nine or more cops at the scene claim to have seen anything in Mr. Dawson's hand. The District Attorney concluded that Officer DiPasquale used excessive force, and as of Nov. 20, 1998, he is facing criminal charges of voluntary and involuntary manslaughter. Officer DiPasquale has faced 11 other complaints of police misconduct during his eight years with the Philadelphia Police Department. This is the first time in six years that a Philadelphia police officer has been criminally charged with homicide. Mr. Dawson's family says that Officer DiPasquale should face more severe charges. The victim's mother, Cynthia Dawson, said, "I think he should be charged with murder. Any citizen out here would be charged with murder immediately." His sister Antoinette said, "If it was one of us killing a cop, we'd have a life sentence or be on death row." **Source:** The Philadelphia Inquirer, 11/20/98

| **Phillip McCall** | 50 | *African American* | 👁 |

May 18, 1998. West Philadelphia:

Three white U.S. marshals came to his daughter's house, and Mr. McCall's four-year-old granddaughter let them in. They ran to the backyard, surrounded Mr. McCall, and Deputy Michael Garwood opened fire, killing him with a bullet through the heart. Mr. McCall had a history of mental health problems and was on parole. He was unarmed. He was the father of seven daughters and a grandfather. When Mr. McCall's brother heard about the murder on TV, he was distraught and went to a bar to have a drink. He was charged with violating his parole, and he was thrown back in prison. **Source:** flyer from National People's Democrtic Uhuru Movement

| **Kenneth Griffin** | 26 | *African American* | |

September 26, 1997. Philadelphia:

Mr. Griffin was shot in the back and killed by state parole officers while lying naked in bed in his mother's home at 6 a.m. with his girlfriend and two children.

| **Anthony DiDonato** | 62 | — | |

July 8, 1995. Philadelphia:

Mr. DiDonato was manic-depressive and was taken to be committed for treatment. Police beat him, striking him 15 to 20 times in the face with a nightstick, dragged him down 23 steps face first while handcuffed and shackled, and then dragged him across 30 feet of pavement. He was then thrown toward an ambulance gurney and missed, landing face first. He died two weeks later.

| **Moises DeJesus** | — | — | |

August 21, 1994. Philadelphia:

Mr. DeJesus' family had called 911 because he was having a seizure. Police came and beat him to death with batons and flashlights.

| **Unidentified Man** | — | — | |

March 24, 1991. Philadelphia:

The man was shot and killed by Officer Rodney Hunt, who was off-duty, at a party around 3 a.m. Officer Hunt claims two men fired on him, so he shot back and killed one of them, wounding a female bystander. Officer Hunt was the same cop who killed Sean Wilson about six months before. He had been allowed to keep his gun during the "investigation." After this second killing, Officer Hunt was indicted in the shooting of Sean Wilson and dismissed. Prior to the indictment, he had received perfect performance ratings. Officer Hunt was acquitted of murder charges, but Sean Wilson's mother got a $900,000 settlement from the city. Officer Hunt challenged his dismissal, charging that it was "political" and that the shooting was justified. In 1994, he was reinstated with back pay and, as of Aug., 1997, he was still working as a police officer. **Source:** Human Rights Watch, Shielded from Justice (1998), pp. 324-325

| **Sean Wilson** | — | — | |

November 4, 1990. Philadelphia:

Mr. Wilson was shot 12 times, twice while on the ground bleeding to death, by off-duty Police Officer Rodney Hunt. Six months later, Officer Hunt was fired "never to be a police officer again," but four years later, he was back on the job.

Conrad Africa	—
Delicia Africa	—
Frank James Africa	—
Katricia Africa	—
Phil Africa	—
Raymond Africa	—
Rhonda Africa	—
Theresa Africa	—
Thomaso Africa	—
Zenetta Africa	—
Vincent Leaphart	—

May 13, 1985. Philadelphia:
Eleven members of the predominantly Black organization, MOVE, were massacred after city officials approved and launched a massive police raid on MOVE's home. Police fired 10,000 rounds in 90 minutes. Water deluge guns pounded the house with thousands of gallons of water. Explosive charges blew out walls. A bomb consisting of FBI-supplied, military explosive C-4 was dropped on the house. Fire erupted and police gunfire prevented MOVE members from exiting the burning house. Over sixty homes in this Black community were also burned to the ground. No city official or police officer was ever charged with a crime. But the sole adult survivor, Ramona Africa, spent seven years in jail for the "crime" of surviving. MOVE had been and continues to demand the release of nine members unjustly convicted of killing a police officer in a 1978 confrontation.

PITTSBURGH / WESTERN PENNSYLVANIA

Name	Age	Nationality	Photo
Devon Grimmit	—	Black	

December 1998. Pittsburgh:
Mr. Grimmit was shot and killed by a Pittsburgh police officer. According to the Pittsburgh Post-Gazette, the cop who killed Mr. Grimmit is the "Blue Knight," a police officer who repeatedly posted threatening e-mail messages to a website dedicated to the fight for justice for Johnny Gamage. Mr. Gammage was murdered by police in the Pittsburgh suburb of Brentwood in 1995. The cop was criminally charged in connection with the killing of Devon Grimmit. **Source:** local anti-police brutality activist

Merle Africa	47	Black	👁

March 13, 1998. Cambridge Springs Correctional Institution:
Merle Africa, a member of the MOVE organization, fainted after a short bout with a stomach virus. Forty-five minutes later she was taken to an outside hospital where she died. MOVE says she "died under very suspicious circumstances." Ms. Africa was in fine health on Mar. 5 when her family visited her. She was serving a 30 to 100 year sentence stemming from the police raid on the MOVE compound in Powelton Village, Philadelphia, in 1978.

Joey Benton	21	—

December 20, 1997. Garfield:

Mr. Benton was shot and killed by four Pittsburgh cops around 3 a.m. in the 5200 block of Kincaid Street, near Atlantic Avenue. According to police, they were responding to a 911 report of shots fired when they saw Mr. Benton holding two guns. Seven to nine officers surrounded him and ordered him "multiple times" to drop the guns. Cops claim he fired seven shots at them, and four of the officers fired a total of 23 shots at him, hitting him four times: twice in the head, once in the chest, and once in the leg. None of the cops were injured. Police claim they found two stolen guns and ammunition on Mr. Benton, and "preliminary findings" by the coroner's office supposedly indicated that he was firing both guns at once. Mr. Benton's girlfriend did not believe the police version of events, saying that she did not think her boyfriend "had the nerve to fire at police and end his life." The newspaper article claims that this was only the second shooting involving Pittsburgh police in 1997. **Source:** Pittsburgh Post-Gazette, 12/22/97

Gerald Potter	—	—

March 1997. Homewood:

Gerald Potter was shot and killed by an off-duty Pittsburgh cop, Officer Fred Crawford, Jr. The officer was working as a security guard at a Homewood bar. The coroner's office ruled the shooting justifiable. The newspaper claimed this was the first shooting in 1997 involving Pittsburgh police. **Source:** Pittsburgh Post-Gazette, 12/22/97

Jerry Jackson	40s	*African-American*

1997. Pittsburgh (Hill District):

Mr. Jackson was shot and killed by a Housing Authority police officer while driving an allegedly stolen car in the Armstrong Tunnel. The victim's car was in motion when he was shot. The cop who was pursuing him claims that Mr. Jackson turned around in the tunnel and drove in his direction. But this is impossible for several reasons. The narrowness of the tunnel meant that if Mr. Jackson had somehow managed to turn around, his car would have been damaged, and it was not. Tire marks in the tunnel showed that Mr. Jackson's car did not turn around. And the evening news showed the police cruiser crashed into the passenger side of the victim's car; if he had been turning around, the cop car would have hit the driver's side. And both cars were facing the same direction (out of the tunnel) in any case. **Source:** Renee Johnson, anti-police brutality activist

Craig L. Guest	—	*African American*	👁

June 26, 1996. Homewood:

Craig Guest was killed by a policeman being dragged by a car. He was shot at point blank range as he sat in the back seat of the car. On Apr. 1, 1999, the DA re-opened the case. **Source:** victim's mother

Maurice Hall	—	*African-American*

1996. Homewood:

Maurice Hall was killed by a policeman being dragged by a car. **Source:** Urban Center for Peace and Justice

Lawrence Powell	—	*white*

1996. Pittsburgh:

Lawrence Powell was killed by off-duty housing authority police. **Source:** Urban Center for Peace and Justice

Johnny Gammage	31	*African American*	👁

October 12, 1995. Brentwood:

Mr. Gammage was killed in struggle with white officers after an alleged traffic violation, i.e., "driving erratically." He was pulled over, beaten, and choked by five police officers in the predominantly white community of Brentwood. None of the cops were convicted, and one was later promoted. **Source:** Urban Center for Peace and Justice

Askia Muhammad (Rodney Webster)	—	*African-American*

August 1994. Northside:

Mr. Muhammad was shot and killed by two officers. **Source:** Urban Center for Peace and Justice

Anthony Starks	—	*African-American*

1994. East Liberty:
Anthony Starks died in a struggle with police. Even though Mr. Starks had apparently been beaten, authorities claimed his death was the result of a drug overdose. **Source:** Urban Center for Peace and Justice

Maneia Bey	—	*African-American*

November 1993. East Liberty:
Maneia Bey was shot 15 times, 14 times in the back, and killed for alleged suspicion of selling drugs. No drugs were ever found. **Source:** Urban Center for Peace and Justice

'Streeter'	—	*African-American*

1993. Hill District:
The youth was strangled to death by housing authority police, who claimed he died of an overdose. **Source:** Urban Center for Peace and Justice

Dwayne Dixon	—	*African-American*

February 21, 1992. Wilkinsburg:
This killing is surrounded by misinformation. Mr. Dixon was shot by one officer and mysteriously shot in the head by his own gun. **Source:** Urban Center for Peace and Justice

Darryl Dean	14	*African-American*

Date Unknown. Garfield:
Darryl Dean was shot in the face by a cop on a bike and killed. **Source:** Urban Center for Peace and Justice

Anthony Walton	—	*white*

Date Unknown. Pittsburgh:
Anthony Walton, an intoxicated white motorist, was shot and killed by an off-duty Black police officer. The case went to trial, and the officer won. **Source:** Urban Center for Peace and Justice

RHODE ISLAND

Name	**Age**	**Nationality**	**Photo**

Two Unidentified Men	—	—	

July 1997. —:
The two men were killed when their car crashed during a high-speed police chase. The newspaper article implies that the chase began in Massachusetts. **Source:** The Boston Globe, 10/6/97

SOUTH CAROLINA

Name	**Age**	**Nationality**	**Photo**

Benjamin A. Williams	—	*African American*	

September 8, 1998. Greenville County:
Mr. Williams was shot and killed by a South Carolina State Trooper while allegedly fleeing arrest. **Source:** Efia Nwangaza, attorney, Coordinator of South Carolina Malcolm X Grassroots Movement for Self-Determination

Clyde Harvey	54	*African American*	

September 8, 1998. Greenville County:

Mr. Harvey, an emotionally disabled homeless man, was shot three times and killed by sheriff's deputies "investigating a burglary in progress." **Source:** Efia Nwangaza, attorney, Coordinator of South Carolina Malcolm X Grassroots Movement for Self-Determination

Tyrone Napolean Salters	—	*African American*	

April 29, 1998. Greenville County:

Mr. Salters was shot and killed by a sheriff's deputy. He was a passenger in a car that was stopped for "improper lane change." The deputy fired into the car when he supposedly thought the driver was about to run him over. The shooting was ruled justified by the Sheriff, and a grand jury refused to indict. **Source:** Efia Nwangaza, attorney, Coordinator of South Carolina Malcolm X Grassroots Movement for Self-Determination

Michael Ross Bowers	—	*African American*

April 15, 1998. Greenville County:

Mr. Bowers was shot and killed by sheriff's deputies. **Source:** Efia Nwangaza, attorney, Coordinator of South Carolina Malcolm X Grassroots Movement for Self-Determination

Timothy Scott Fowler	29	*African American*

October 10, 1997. Greenville County:

Mr. Fowler was shot in his bed and killed by a vice officer serving a warrant. Cops claim that the victim sat up in bed and fired at them. **Source:** Efia Nwangaza, attorney, Coordinator of South Carolina Malcolm X Grassroots Movement for Self-Determination

Jamel Radcliff	21	*Black*

August 21, 1997. Greenville:

Mr. Radcliff died of asphyxiation after four guards wrestled him to the floor as he was being booked in the county detention center. He had been picked up by police at the restaurant where he worked for not paying a $378 fine. One jail guard applied a chokehold while another held Mr. Radcliff in a bear hug. They slapped his head onto the cement floor, causing blood to fly everywhere, then put him unconscious into a holding cell. Mr. Radcliff was the fifth person to die in the detention center in two years. One inmate fell 18 feet over a railing, another died from medical problems, a third was found hanging, and a fourth died of alcohol withdrawal. **Source:** Atlanta Constitution, 10/2/97

David Burrell	42	—

July 2, 1997. Clover:

David Burrell, an alcoholic suffering from severe depression, was threatening suicide. Family members called the police. When they arrived, Mr. Burrell walked outside with a gun pointed to his head. Cops claim he then pointed the gun at them, so Officers Gary Love and Leon Mosley shot him twice, in the arm and leg. He died six days later, on July 8, from his injuries. Mr. Burrell's wife, Brenda, filed a federal civil lawsuit against the two cops, charging them with unnecessary, unreasonable, and excessive force and with causing Mr. Burrell "severe and extreme mental and physical pain and suffering form the time of the gunshot wounds until his death." An inquiry by the State Law Enforcement Division cleared the officers of any wrongdoing. **Source:** The Herald (Rock Hill, SC), 10/18/97

Frederick Cory Ellis	33	*African American*

June 23, 1997. Greenville County:

Mr. Ellis was shot and killed by a deputy sheriff during a traffic stop. He had allegedly tried to run over a deputy. **Source:** Efia Nwangaza, attorney, Coordinator of South Carolina Malcolm X Grassroots Movement for Self-Determination

---

Chinue Tao Hashim   20   *African American*

February 20, 1997. Greenville County (Greer):

Chinue Tao Hashim was shot between the eyes and killed by a sheriff's deputy while surrendering in a drug bust. The Sheriff ruled his death "accidental," but the deputy was indicted for manslaughter. **Source:** Efia Nwangaza, attorney, Coordinator of South Carolina Malcolm X Grassroots Movement for Self-Determination

---

Dennis Richard Mickel   44   *white*   👁

October 28, 1996. Greenville County Detention Center:

Mr. Mickel died in custody of a heart attack. He had been denied permission to keep his heart medication with him. **Source:** Efia Nwangaza, attorney, Coordinator of South Carolina Malcolm X Grassroots Movement for Self-Determination

---

Donald Williams   41   *African American*

November 6, 1995. Greenville County:

Mr. Williams was shot in the neck and killed by sheriff's deputies after being subdued, with his hands cuffed behind his back. His death was ruled justifiable homicide. His family filed a lawsuit. **Source:** Efia Nwangaza, attorney, Coordinator of South Carolina Malcolm X Grassroots Movement for Self-Determination

---

Douglas Fischer   24   *Black*

July 20, 1995. Spartanburg:

Douglas Fisher, a student at Georgia State University, was choked to death by security guards at Best Buy when the guards accused him of trying to buy computer equipment with a phony credit card. Douglas left the store empty handed. Two security guards ran after him. One guard, Ricky Coleman, choked Douglas while another guard, Tom Davies, sat on his back. Douglas was down on the ground, his hands behind his back, spitting up blood and "obviously couldn't breathe." Coleman continued to choke him and said, "Quit fighting or I'll break your f*cking neck." Police arrived and did not arrest the security guards. The security guards said they would have stopped choking Douglas if the store manager had told them to. Douglas' father continues to fight for justice. **Source:** victim's father

---

Harvey Lee Duke, Jr.   38   *white*   👁

May 8, 1995. Greenville County Detention Center:

Mr. Duke died in jail of multiple organ failure shortly after being released from restraints. He had been in restraints for five hours. His death was ruled justifiable. **Source:** Efia Nwangaza, attorney, Coordinator of South Carolina Malcolm X Grassroots Movement for Self-Determination

---

Brenda Faye Cooper   23   *African American*

March 16, 1995. Greenville County:

Ms. Cooper was shot and killed by a sheriff's deputy when she allegedly "threatened him with a knife and refused to surrender" during an altercation at a local motel. Her death was ruled justifiable homicide. **Source:** Efia Nwangaza, attorney, Coordinator of South Carolina Malcolm X Grassroots Movement for Self-Determination

---

Humberto Eddie Rodriguez   38   *Puerto Rican*

October 17, 1994. Greenville County:

Mr. Rodriguez was shot 30 times and killed by five members of the Sheriff's SWAT Team during a brief standoff. The victim had escaped from prison to dramatize his chronic untreated medical and emotional condition. He barricaded himself in his house, allegedly with a 9mm pistol. His death was ruled justifiable homicide. **Source:** Efia Nwangaza, attorney, Coordinator of South Carolina Malcolm X Grassroots Movement for Self-Determination

| Kenneth Brian Fennell | 23 | Black | 👁 |

August 30, 1993. Guilford County (I-85):

Mr. Fennell was shot four or five times and killed by State Highway Patrolman Richard Stephenson after being pulled over for allegedly driving 70 mph in a 65 mph zone. Two of the shots were fired from less than five feet away. Trooper Stephenson told several stories, variously claiming that Mr. Fennell had pulled a gun or was "going for" a gun. According to the story, the gun then flew from the victim's hand when the cop shot him and was supposedly found in the underbrush. But all three civilian witnesses denied seeing any gun, it was unclear which cop found the gun, and the Deputy Industrial Commissioner who investigated the shooting said, "the handgun that was found at the scene was placed there by someone other than Fennell." Mr. Fennell's lawyers contend that the traffic stop itself was illegitimate and pretextual, that it was part of a pattern of troopers stopping young Black men on that stretch of the highway for DWB ("Driving While Black") and then searching their cars on the grounds that they appeared "nervous." **Source:** report from lawyers for victim's family

TENNESSEE

Name	Age	Nationality	Photo

| Unidentified Man | — | — | |

May 14, 1998. Nashville:

Described as a "suspected bank robber" in the press, the victim was shot and killed by a police SWAT team member in the woods after a two-hour standoff. Cops claim that the victim robbed a bank and fired on police, grazing a cop's foot and killing a police dog. Cops chased him and, after a standoff, killed him. While the police released the name of the dead police dog, they did not release the name of the human being whom they killed. **Source:** The Orlando Sentinel, 5/15/98

| Kevin McCoullough | 27 | Black | |

May 8, 1998. Chattanooga:

Mr. McCoullough was shot and killed by police at Choo Choo Customs (a van detailing company), where he worked. Cops came up with several stories to justify the shooting. First, they claimed that he "threw or ran at them with a tire iron with studs attached" (although the only thing in his hand was a toilet rod). Then, they claimed that he had a loaded gun in his locker (which was never produced), and finally, they claimed that he was a rape suspect. However, numerous co-workers described the shooting as nothing but a police execution (a carefully placed bullet to the heart). More importantly, Mr. McCoullough predicted his own murder when he told co-workers and his supervisor days before that he had been threatened by the police. He was suing the city for a 1992 case of unjust imprisonment, was known to have a "bad attitude" toward the cops, and had been convicted of a number of shootings, mostly during his teenage years. More recently, Mr. McCoullough had gotten out of that scene, turned his life around, was holding down a job and raising a family. The cops, however, maintained their vendetta against him. Local activists have speculated that "a police death squad is at work getting rid of young Black men with criminal records in a bid to 'clean up the streets.'" **Source:** BLNS (Lorenzoa Komboa Ervin) via Michael Novick

| Nathan Pillow | 21 | Black | |

May 7, 1998. Columbia:

In the early morning hours, Mr. Pillow was shot in the head and killed by a white Columbia police officer after spending the previous evening on a date with the cop's daughter. The cop had previously warned his daughter and a Black man (not Nathan Pillow) who had fathered her child that he was going to kill the "n*gger baby's daddy." Police ruled Mr. Pillow's death a suicide, claiming that his car was involved in two hit-and-run accidents with other vehicles and that they later found the car with the victim dead in the driver's seat from an allegedly self-inflicted gunshot wound. Police denied reports that they had been chasing Mr. Pillow's car shortly before his body was "discovered." **Source:** Columbia Herald, 5/7/98; Police Report; local anti-police brutality activist

Montrail Collins   22   *Black*

May 1, 1998. Chattanooga:
According to police and the white press, Mr. Collins was a "Crips gang leader" who was shot and killed in a gunfight after trading fire with an officer, who was also shot. Yet community eyewitnesses said Mr. Collins was shot in the back and then shot again by cops who reportedly had a grudge against him stemming from the drug trade. **Source:** BLNS (Lorenzoa Komboa Ervin) via Michael Novick

Andre Stenson   34   —

January 9, 1998. Knoxville:
Mr. Stenson was stopped by Knoxville police for driving with his headlights off. He ran from police, was caught in a vacant lot, and allegedly fought with officers before being handcuffed. He died en route to the hospital. An autopsy report claimed he died of a congenital heart defect. Meanwhile, police falsely reported that crack was found in his car and in the lot where he was caught, an allegation they were forced to retract. Officer Scott Coffey, one of four cops put on paid administrative leave as a result of Mr. Stenson's death, was seen carrying his weapon in a City Council meeting. That meeting was held to discuss the creation of a civilian review board in the wake of Mr. Stenson's death. Officer Coffey had come with a group from the Fraternal Order of Police (FOP) to oppose the civilian review board. **Source:** Knoxville News-Sentinel

Stephen Lamont Weaver   23   —

October 18, 1997. Morgan County Jail:
Authorities claim that Mr. Weaver was arrested on suspicion of possession of cocaine for resale and evading arrest after fleeing from a police stop stemming from an expired license plate. It was also alleged that the badly shaking Mr. Weaver refused the services of the Anderson County Ambulance Service. He was taken to Morgan County Jail, and after his arrival, EMS was called. Mr. Weaver was taken to the hospital, where he died. **Source:** The Commercial Appeal (Memphis, TN), 10/10/97

Juan Lorenzo Daniels   25   —

October 17, 1997. East Knoxville:
Mr. Daniels called 911, saying he had been assaulted and his house vandalized by a longtime friend, Stephanie Means, whom he had referred to as his sister for years. A few minutes later, Ms. Means called 911 saying Mr. Daniels had assaulted her and broken her car mirror. Mr. Daniels had a history of mental illness and was receiving counseling from a local mental health center. His roommate said he had occasional violent outbursts, usually directed at inanimate objects. Knoxville police showed up at Mr. Daniels' apartment and found him in the dark basement holding a knife to his own throat. Mr. Daniels responded to police orders to drop the knife with "Why? So you can shoot me? Well, you might as well shoot me now." According to Mr. Daniels' roommate, Chris Goudlock, police would not allow him, Mr. Daniels' mother, or Mr. Daniels' caseworker to talk with the distraught man, even though at one point, Mr. Daniels was yelling, "Chris, help me!" Cops claim that after about an hour and 20 minutes of fruitless negotiations, Mr. Daniels lunged out at them with a knife. Officer Bobby Soloman, who the police chief called one of his "most experienced negotiators" and Officer Chris Caulpetzer opened fire, shooting Mr. Daniels six times in the chest, once in the stomach, once in the leg, and once in the hand, and killing him. Stephanie Means' grandmother, who Mr. Daniels called "granny," said "They didn't have to kill him. They could have shot him in the leg." She also criticized the cops for refusing to let her talk with Mr. Daniels, saying "What went wrong last night, I don't know, but I think I could have got him to come out." The cops were placed on administrative leave with pay during criminal and internal probes. **Source:** The Knoxville News Sentinel, 10/18/97

James Madison Foster, Jr.   56   —

October 9, 1997. East Memphis (Shelby County):

On Oct. 8, two fugitive squad officers walked through the open door of Mr. Foster's home and searched his house because he had failed to show up in court on misdemeanor traffic charges. Cops claim that "when they engaged him, he pointed a rifle" and fired twice at them. The deputies fired three shots. Later that day, the SWAT team surrounded his house and cut off power to the house and the surrounding street lights. After attempts to negotiate reportedly failed, the SWAT team stormed in and supposedly found him dead on his bed. Cops claimed he had died of a heart attack, and the medical examiner ruled that his death resulted from "natural causes." Mr. Foster was said to have a history of resisting warrants and fighting with police. His house was filled with various inventions he had made over the years, and one of his lawyers referred to him as a "genius," saying he had encouraged his client to contact NASA about one of his inventions. Cops claim they found up to 100 pounds of gunpowder and over 10,000 rounds of ammunition in the dead man's house. **Source:** The Commercial Appeal (Memphis, TN), 10/10/97

Ricky Terry   17   —

September 30, 1997. Memphis (Village Woods):

Mr. Terry was shot and killed by off-duty Memphis Police Officer Troy Sawyer. A police spokesperson claims Mr. Terry and another man were attempting to get into the officer's car when the officer came out of his apartment and shouted at them. At least one of the men allegedly responded with gunfire. The officer shot and wounded Mr. Terry several times, and the two men ran to a brown Buick and drove off. Mr. Terry was dead when he arrived at the hospital. The officer was relieved of duty with pay pending the outcome of the investigation. **Source:** The Commercial Appeal (Memphis, TN), 10/1/1997

Leon R. Fisher   23   *Black*

August 10, 1997. Nashville:

Mr. Fisher was shot and killed by police after they stopped his car for speeding. Police claim he violently resisted arrest. According to bystanders, Mr. Fisher had already been handcuffed when he was shot. Police claim they handcuffed him after he was shot because he was still moving. The shooting occurred near the Sam Levy Homes housing project. A rebellion broke out in which people threw rocks and bottles at the police and burned down and looted a department store, Dollar General, nearby. Press coverage focused mostly on the damage to the store. Police waited before trying to resuscitate Leon. The mayor justified the shooting. **Source:** The New York Times, 8/17/97; ?

Geraldo Moreno   28   *Mexican*

June 25, 1997. Nashville:

Mr. Moreno was fatally shot by two security guards at Metro General Hospital. The guards claim they shot in self-defense after Mr. Moreno pulled a three-inch knife. They allegedly ordered him to drop the knife, but he did not understand English. When he didn't drop the knife, the guards shot him even though they also had batons and pepper spray available. The Counsel for the Mexican Government in Nashville said, "We believe there was an abuse of power." **Source:** Nashville Banner, 7/3/97

5 other men   —

David Speakman   34   *white*

April 1997. —:

Mr. Speakman was in a prison van being sent from Michigan back to Orlando for violating parole on a DUI charge. He and five other men were burned to death, handcuffed and shackled in an iron holding cage as the van burst into flames due to poor maintenance. "He had a drinking problem," said his mother Rosemary Bonifacio. "But he was loving, passionate and harmless." **Source:** Miami Oct. 22 Coalition

Roger Dean Lansdown   —   —

February 8, 1997. Gassville:
Mr. Lansdown, a mentally ill man, died in a fire in his home. On the day he died, he had gotten gasoline from a station and driven off without paying. As the disturbed man poured the gasoline on the family home, Gassville Police Officer Bill Chadwick waved an assault rifle at him. After a fire broke out, Officer Chadwick refused to allow a neighbor to enter the home to help Mr. Lansdown, nor would he go in himself. Law officers placed crime scene tape around the home while the fire was still blazing in an attempt to prevent firefighters from saving Mr. Lansdown. Baxter County Sheriff's Deputy David Osborn even attacked one fire fighter who inadvertently broke the tape. Later that year, Mr. Lansdown's father filed a suit against Gassville Police Officer Bill Chadwick, Baxter County Sheriff Charlie Garrison, and Sheriff's Deputies David Osborn and Ken Hopman. **Source:** The Commercial Appeal (Memphis, TN), 10/2/97

Bobby J. Russell, Jr.   41   —

1995. near Arlington:
While driving an unmarked police car, Officer James Michael Williams struck Mr. Russell, an off-duty firefighter, as the victim trimmed weeds by the side of the road. The accident threw Mr. Russel 50 feet, causing multiple injuries and killing him. Officer Williams was acquitted of vehicular homicide and drunken driving and reckless driving in May, 1997, but sentenced to two years in prison for leaving the scene of an accident involving death. As of Oct. 7, 1997, the sentence was on hold while the conviction was being appealed. **Source:** The Commercial Appeal (Memphis, TN), 10/7/97

TEXAS

Name	Age	Nationality	Photo

Reginald LaVergne   18   *Black*   👁

April 17, 1999. Tennessee Colony (Texas Dep't of Criminal Justice):
Mr. LaVergne died while in prison lockdown (administrative segregation). Prison authorities claim he had been depressed and probably committed suicide by eating his mattress. But the victim's family disputed this account and charged that he was murdered by prison authorities. When the family saw the body, they noted that his weight had dropped from 175 lbs. to 100 lbs. in five months (since Dec., 1998). They also noticed that his body had bruises on the shoulders and chest and holes on the bottom of the feet that looked like they were made with nails. All of his internal organs were missing. Mr. LaVergne had been sent to prison at age 15 for allegedly stealing a pair of shoes. An aunt described him as shy, sweet, kind, and full of jokes. **Source:** SLP form

Donnie DeWayne Jackson   23   —

January 14, 1999. Harris County:
Police arrested Mr. Jackson for possession with intent to deliver crack cocaine and booked him into the city jail. About six hours later, an ambulance was called when Mr. Jackson allegedly fell. He was pronounced dead at the hospital an hour later. The medical examiner claims he found a gram of cocaine in his stomach and ruled that the cause of death was a cocaine overdose. But the victim's relatives said they suspected foul play after viewing the body because they noticed several head wounds. The medical examiner claims this happened when Mr. Jackson fell.

Derek Jason Kaeseman   24   *Anglo*   👁

October 25, 1998. Houston:
Mr. Kaeseman was shot and killed by seven Houston police officers who were surrounding his truck, which had hit a guardrail after a short chase. The police fired 59 rounds, hitting the victim 14 times as he sat in his truck. Cops claim they saw him holding a "shiny object," which later turned out to be a can opener. None of the civilian witnesses saw the "shiny object." In Dec., 1998, a grand jury cleared all seven officers of criminal wrongdoing. Derek Kaeseman had started a landscaping business with a friend. He liked working outside with his hands and being close to nature. Mr. Kaeseman also loved good food and had gone to culinary school. He was known as someone always willing to help out friends and family. His mother said, "His light will always shine brightly in our family." **Source:** The Houston Chronicle, 12/21/98 & 4/8/99; SLP form; statement from victim's family

Stephanie P. Ryne   35   —

October 3, 1998. Houston:

Ms. Ryne was shot once in the chest and killed by Houston Police Officer J.D. Hudson. She was reportedly "intoxicated, despondent, and threatening to kill herself." Cops claim that she fired a pistol once into the ground as they tried to talk to her in the back yard, that she followed them as they retreated, and that she pointed a cocked gun at Officer Hudson and refused an order to drop it. **Source:** The Houston Chronicle,10/5/98

Charley Edward Cook   23   —

October 2, 1998. Fort Worth:

Mr. Cook was shot and killed by Fort Worth police officers after he allegedly fired on them, wounding a cop and killing a police dog. Mr. Cook was being sought for a non-fatal shooting of a state trooper during a traffic stop the day before. Texas Rangers and Fort Worth police heard he was hiding in a wooded area and went to find him. A shootout allegedly ensued. The headline of the newspaper article about this incident referred to the dead police dog. Mr. Cook's death was mentioned in passing several paragraphs later, while most of the article talked about the police dog that was killed and the trauma suffered by cops when they lose a police dog. **Source:** The Dallas Morning News, 10/4/98

Russell Robertson   27   —

October 1, 1998. Dallas County (Farmers Branch):

Mr. Robertson was shot once in the chest by Farmers Branch police in the home he shared with his girlfriend and her mother. He died a short time later at a local hospital. Three unidentified police officers were responding to a 911 call from Mr. Robertson's father, who said his son was suicidal and may have fired a gun. When cops arrived and knocked on the door, they got no response. After ten minutes, they entered through the unlocked front door and saw a body lying motionless under a sheet. Cops claim that "when they announced their presence, Mr. Robertson moved from under the sheet, revealing a shotgun pointed at his head," according to the newspaper. As police approached, he supposedly sat up in bed with the shotgun and said, "Just shoot me." Cops claim that when they tried to grab the gun, which they admit was not pointing at them, a struggle ensued, during which the gun was supposedly pointed at the cops several times, "perhaps in a threatening manner." Authorities claim the cops only shot Mr. Robertson because their lives were in danger and said the shooting appeared justified. **Source:** The Dallas Morning News, 10/3/98

Unidentified Man   —   —

September 26, 1998. Fort Worth:

The man, who was driving a van, was shot twice and killed by Fort Worth Police Officer B.W. Randolph as he allegedly dragged the cop alongside his van. The officer approached the van in front of a "known drug house" and ordered the passenger out while he questioned the driver. The cop allegedly saw crack cocaine in the driver's hand and ordered him to drop it, which he did. But the driver supposedly refused to turn off the engine, and when Officer Randolph reached in to do so, the driver allegedly took off, dragging the cop. **Source:** Fort Worth Star, 9/28/98

Erick Costilla   20   —

September 24, 1998. San Antonio:

San Antonio Police Officer Albert Marin shot and killed Erick Costilla. Officer Marin claims that Mr. Costilla lunged at him with a three-and-a-half inch knife. This was Officer Marin's second fatal shooting in the last six years. Mr. Costilla's family described him as a caring person. "The guy's a real compassionate kid," said Scott McCrum, the family's attorney. **Source:** Express News via Michael Novick

Unidentified Man   40   —

September 17, 1998. Dallas:

Police were on the scene in response to a report that a man was exposing himself. The cops saw the man expose himself and tried to arrest him, but he reportedly resisted and locked his car windows, keeping the police outside. One cop smashed a window with his baton and grabbed the man, who allegedly broke away and ran about 30 feet. Other cops caught him. One sprayed him with tear gas while another placed him in a neck hold. Cops handcuffed him, and the man stopped breathing and died. Cops allegedly tried to revive him using CPR. **Source:** The Dallas Morning News, 9/18/98

Richard Jason Anderson 29 —

September 1, 1998. Dickinson:
Dickinson Police Officer John Wilson shot and killed Mr. Anderson because the latter allegedly "made a move" after a lengthy foot chase. Officer Wilson chased Mr. Anderson after another man said he caught Mr. Anderson trying to break into his house. **Source:** The Houston Chronicle, 9/4/98

Edward Bradford 30 —

August 20, 1998. Northwest Houston:
Mr. Bradford was reportedly a drug addict, wanted for killing his mother several months before. His brother-in-law went with police to the now-abandoned house where Mr. Bradford had lived with his mother. Houston Patrolman David J. Hilbert reportedly went around to the back while the brother-in-law waited in the front. The cop said he heard a gunshot, came around the house, and saw that the brother-in-law had been shot. Officer Hilbert shot Mr. Bradford in the head and killed him, claiming Mr. Bradford fired at him first. He was placed on administrative duty during an investigation. **Source:** The Houston Chronicle, 8/21/98

Santos Rijos 35 —

August 20, 1998. southeast Houston:
Mr. Rijos was shot in the chest and killed in his home by a Texas Department of Public Safety Officer, O. Garcia, during an undercover drug operation conducted jointly with the federal Drug Enforcement Agency (DEA). Authorities claim Mr. Rijos showed undercover Officer Garcia a kilo of cocaine for sale, then supposedly pulled a gun and fired at the cop when the latter signaled the DEA team to enter and arrest Mr. Rijos. Officer Garcia, who was not injured, claimed he was returning fire when he shot Mr. Rijos. **Source:** The Houston Chronicle, 8/22/98

Unidentified Man & Woman — —

August 18, 1998. Fort Worth:
An unknown man and woman died in a fiery crash after a high speed chase involving dozens of police cars. Cops had reportedly been called to the couple's house by a family member saying the man and woman were having a domestic dispute. When police arrived, the couple was not there, but cops allegedly saw a pickup truck pull up and saw the man striking the woman inside it. The man, who was driving, then drove off, leading to the fatal chase. **Source:** The Dallas Morning News, 8/19/98

Reginald Wayne Smith 32 —

August 18, 1998. Northeast Dallas:
Mr. Smith was shot and killed by Detective Alan Foster as cops executed a search warrant of his home. Police claim that they identified themselves before forcing open the front door and that the victim fired one shot at them before Det. Foster fired on him. Authorities said that department policies were followed. Det. Foster shot another man in 1986. He claimed that this man (who was wounded but survived) had also opened fire on him. **Source:** The Dallas Morning News, 8/20/98

| Robert "Jack" Williams | 29 | — |

August 10, 1998. Richmond:

Robert "Jack" Williams was shot at least six times and killed by Fort Bend County Sheriff's Deputy Tony Woody. He was unarmed. The deputy claimed Mr. Williams' jeep was weaving, so he followed him and pulled him over. Mr. Williams allegedly attacked Deputy Woody, who claims he fired in self-defense. But members of the victim's family, who were with him shortly before he was killed, said he was never even near the Riverwood subdivision where the deputy supposedly started following him. The family also questioned how police could justify the number of shots fired, asking, "Why would you shoot an unarmed man that many times?" Another family member found eight shell casings on the scene, indicating that the deputy fired at least eight shots. Deputy Woody was placed on paid leave during the investigation. He had previously been the subject of an excessive force complaint, for which he was exonerated. In that incident, deputies followed a young man home late one night. When his father went out to ask what was going on, Deputy Woody told him to "get your ass back in the house right now," then ran up behind him and choked him, forcing him to the ground. Mr. Williams is survived by a large family, including many brothers and sisters with whom he was very close. He had been out shooting pool with some of them the night he was killed. He worked six days a week as a cable installer for a cable TV company. His sister said, "We're family oriented. He's not a violent person. It [the shooting] is unjustified, no matter what they say." **Source:** The Houston Chronicle, 8/12/98

| Paul Watson | 41 | — |

July 22, 1998. Houston:

Mr. Watson was shot and killed by a Houston police SWAT team sharpshooter during a standoff that was broadcast live on TV. Mr. Watson had reportedly killed his ex-wife and was holding his two young daughters hostage. Police were negotiating with him, but Mr. Watson got angry as he repeatedly saw SWAT officers creeping closer to his house on live TV. When the TV showed cops on a nearby roof, Mr. Watson allegedly fired two shots, one through his own roof, before the police sharpshooter shot and killed him. **Source:** The Houston Chronicle, 7/24/98

| Pedro Oregón | 23 | *Mexican* | ◉ |

July 12, 1998. Houston (Gulfton Barrio):

Mr. Oregón was shot twelve times and killed around 1:30 a.m. by Houston police officers from the gang task force. Cops stormed into the apartment complex where Mr. Oregon lived, allegedly to look for a drug dealer, and busted into his apartment without a search warrant. They began beating his brother, demanding to know whether he was "Julio." Mr. Oregón told them they had the wrong man. A cop fired a shot that hit another cop, leading cops to spray the apartment with bullets. Mr. Oregón was hit three times in the initial blast and shot nine more times in the back, execution style, as he lay on the floor saying, "I'm not Julio. I'm innocent. Don't kill me." Cops fired a total of 31 bullets, some of which went as far as three apartments away. Pedro Oregón worked as a landscaper. He left behind a wife and two daughters. He was well known and loved in the community. No drugs were found in his apartment and a toxicology test showed no traces of drugs or alcohol in his blood. Cops supposedly found a pistol, which they admitted did not belong to Mr. Oregón (they traced the owner but refused to divulge his/her identity) and which was not fired. Outraged residents of Gulfton Barrio, a Central American/Mexican neighborhood in southwest Houston, held an angry protest two weeks later demanding justice for Pedro Oregón. **Source:** Revolutionary Worker, 8/16/98

| Emile Duhamel | — | — |

July 9, 1998. Ellis Death Row Prison:

Mr. Duhamel died in prison from exposure to extreme heat. He was taking a medication for mental illness which makes people sensitive to heat. The extreme temperatures on Death Row ranged from 105 to 130 degrees over the summer. **Source:** e-mail from Texas Coalition to Abolish the Death Penalty, 8/12/99

| Ernest Moore | 25 | — |

July 1998. San Benito:

Mr. Moore, the son and brother of police officers, had reportedly committed a double homicide. While making a get-a-way, he allegedly became engaged in a shootout and killed two Border Patrol agents. He was also killed in the shootout. **Source:** Associated Press, 7/10/98

Gabriel Demoise Ledet   22   —

June 28, 1998. Southeast Houston:

Police report that Mr. Ledet was killed as he fell beneath a moving train as they pursued him. Officers claim Mr. Ledet was a suspected car thief and gave this as the reason for chasing him. **Source:** The Houston Chronicle, 6//29/98

Dominigo Artea   24   —

June 6, 1998. East Fort Worth:

Mr. Artea was shot in the neck and chest and killed by Police Officer C.L. Sadler and Police Lt. A.J. Allcon. Cops claim Mr. Artea tried to rob Officer Sadler at gunpoint and fired a rifle at them. They also charge that Mr. Artea and another man had robbed several people that evening. After Officer Sadler shot him, Mr. Artea allegedly tried to force two people out of their pickup truck, so Lt. Allcon shot him. Both officers remained on duty while Mr. Artea's death was investigated. **Source:** The Dallas Morning News, 6/7/98

William Euell Poynor   96   —

May 29, 1998. Gorman:

Police responded to a 911 call from Mr. Poyner's wife about a domestic dispute. When officers arrived, they fired ten shots, four of which hit the victim, killing him. Mr. Poyner was 96-years-old, half-deaf, nearly blind, and "known for his friendly disposition and storytelling at the local gas station." His wife filed a civil suit saying county officials covered up the facts of the shooting. **Source:** The Houston Chronicle, 6/26/98; Associated Press, 7/9/98

Richard Young   72   —

May 5, 1998. Houston:

Police went to an apartment complex in response to a call about a man with a gun. When they arrived, Richard Young allegedly threatened to kill himself and any cops who came into his apartment. A four hour standoff ensued. The elderly Mr. Young was reportedly suicidal and despondent over his ill health. After four hours, he reportedly laid down the 12-gauge shotgun. Cops claim Mr. Young grabbed the gun and pointed it at them as they rushed into his apartment. Two Houston SWAT police officers opened fire and killed him. Authorities refused to reveal the names of the cops who killed Mr. Young on the grounds that they did not know which officer fired the fatal shots. **Source:** The Houston Chronicle, 5/6/98

Wilbert Martin Guidry   22   —

May 5, 1998. Fort Bend County (Fresno):

Mr. Guidry was killed in a fatal car crash while being pursued by police. Five other people in two other vehicles were injured in the crash. Cops had stopped Mr. Guidry for speeding, and a license check reportedly showed a "drug suspension." The chase began when Mr. Guidry allegedly drove away after being asked to step out of his car. **Source:** The Houston Chronicle, 5/6/98 & 5/7/98

Minh Nguyen   26   —

May 2, 1998. Southwest Houston:

Mr. Nguyen was killed in a car crash while being pursued by Houston police. Before he died, he was charged with evading police and possession of a pistol. A passenger in his car and the driver of a car he hit were injured in the accident. **Source:** The Houston Chronicle, 5/4/98

Unidentified Male   —   —

April 30, 1998. near Floresville:

Wilson County Sheriff's deputies were called to a location near Floresville because a man was threatening to kill himself. According to police, when the man leveled his rifle at the deputy, a deputy shot and killed him. Police did not release the name of the victim or the cop who killed him. **Source:** UPI, 5/1/98

Korey Lavale Rawls   24   —

April 23, 1998. southeast Houston:

Mr. Rawls was shot and killed by Police Officer Scott X. Pena after the former allegedly opened fire on another officer during a drug operation in an apartment complex. This occurred in the 9200 block of Nathaniel Street around 10 a.m. Undercover cops claim they bought three kilograms of cocaine from Mr. Rawls. Another "suspect" was shot and wounded. According to police, the victims ran from the apartment after the undercover cops identified themselves and then supposedly shot back into the apartment at the officers. The officers opened, killing Mr. Rawls and the other man. **Source:** The Houston Chronicle, 4/24/98 & 4/25/98; UPI, 4/23/98

Unidentified Man   —   —

April 18, 1998. Harris County (Humble):

The man was shot once and killed by an unidentified Humble police officer while allegedly robbing a Home Depot with two companions around 5 a.m. The cop claims that the man pointed a pistol at him and that he ordered the man to drop the pistol before shooting him. **Source:** The Houston Chronicle, 4/19/98

Kelvin Dewayne McDowell   25   —

April 3, 1998. Houston:

Mr. McDowell was shot in the chest and killed by Houston Police Officer R.L. Morris. The victim was allegedly on a balcony firing a weapon at a party when police came. Cops claim he refused an order to drop his weapon and made a threatening move. Children were in the apartment when police shot and killed Mr. McDowell. **Source:** The Houston Chronicle, 4/4/98

Brendan John Hightower   34   —

April 3, 1998. Mesquite:

Mr. Hightower, described as "gravely ill with diabetes," was killed by police gunfire after first being doused with pepper spray. The unidentified cop alleges that he shot in self-defense, claiming Mr. Hightower hit him over the head with a flashlight. Family members dispute that Mr. Hightower was threatening police. The victim's brother said, "The effects of the diabetes were that he couldn't stand on his feet for more than two hours. They [the police] screwed up." Police had been called to the apartment to prevent Mr. Hightower from committing suicide. **Source:** The Dallas Morning News, 4/5/98

Gregory Ruiz   32   —

March 28, 1998. Fort Bend County Jail:

Mr. Ruiz was reportedly pounding on the doors of people's homes in the pre-dawn hours, yelling for help and shouting "they got guns" and "laser sights." Fort Bend County sheriff's deputies arrested him for public intoxication. He allegedly struggled with them as they tried to book him and suffered a heart attack. Mr. Ruiz died in the hospital. Cops claim he had cocaine in his system. **Source:** The Houston Chronicle, 3/31/98

William Saldana   32   —

March 23, 1998. El Paso:

Mr. Saldana was shot and killed by an unidentified Border Patrol agent. The agent was chasing Mr. Saldana and claims the victim tried to run him over. **Source:** The Houston Chronicle, 3/26/98

Salvador Solis   17   —

March 21, 1998. Dallas:

Salvador Solis was killed when the truck in which he was a passenger got into an accident while being chased by police. The truck reportedly ran a red light, hit another vehicle, and then hit a lamp post during the chase. Mr. Solis and the truck's driver were supposedly suspects in an aggravated assault, and a 911 caller allegedly said they were waving or firing guns. The driver of the truck, who was injured in the crash, was expected to be charged with manslaughter for his companion's death. Two people in the vehicle they hit were also injured. A Police Department spokesperson said, "There doesn't seem to have been any violation of departmental policy." **Source:** The Dallas Morning News, 3/22,98

Dolores Gallegos   17   —

February 8, 1998. Dallas:
Officer Francis Crump was speeding at over 70 mph (twice the speed limit) to another officer's call for help when he struck Ms. Gallegos' car, killing her. She died at the scene. Officer Crump was not using his flashing lights or sirens, which is permitted in some cases under department policy. Ms. Gallegos was a junior in high school and left behind an infant daughter. Her mother and the father of her daughter each filed a wrongful death lawsuit against the city. A grand jury declined to indict Officer Crump for manslaughter. He was suspended without pay for four weeks in June 1998, after over four months on paid administrative leave (paid vacation) since the accident. This was described as one of the most serious punishments a cop has received in the five years that the current chief has headed the Dallas Police Department. **Source:** The Dallas Morning News, 3/7/98 & 6/20/98

Julian Garcia   23   —

January 24, 1998. Pasadena:
Julian Garcia was killed when a Pasadena patrol car driven by Police Officer B.C. Kelldorf collided with his Nissan. Officer Kelldorf was reportedly on his way to investigate a fight at a restaurant when the accident occurred. Authorities refused to say whether Officer Kelldorf was driving with lights and sirens on or to release any other information about the circumstances of the crash. The cop was treated and released at a local hospital. **Source:** The Houston Chronicle, 1/25/98

Rodney Paul Wickware   31   —

January 23, 1998. Austin:
Mr. Wickware died after allegedly fighting with five police officers who were trying to arrest him for weaving through traffic on foot. Cops claim Mr. Wickware stopped breathing suddenly during the fight. He was taken to the hospital with two broken ribs and a bruised throat and died the following morning. The five officers were put on administrative duty. **Source:** The Houston Chronicle, 1/29/98

Brian Cloud   4   —

January 23, 1998. Houston:
Police officers with Houston's North Patrol gang unit tried to stop a speeding car. The driver of the car reportedly refused to stop and sped away, and police gave chase. The driver of the car being chased ran a stop sign and slammed broadside into a another vehicle that had just entered the intersection. Brian Cloud, age four, was ejected from the second vehicle and sustained massive injuries. He later died at a local hospital. His aunt, who was driving, was hospitalized with broken bones and bruises. **Source:** The Houston Chronicle, 1/25/98

Christopher Molina   32   —

January 4, 1998. northwest Houston:
Mr. Molina was arrested after he allegedly smashed the window of an apartment and then struggled with one of its occupants. When police arrived, they found neighbors holding Mr. Molina down. According to the newspaper, police reported that "shortly after handcuffing Molina, the man quit breathing." An autopsy was scheduled, and the police department and the District Attorney's office said they would investigate his death. **Source:** The Houston Chronicle, 1/5/98

Darnell Solomon   15   —

December 11, 1997. Dallas (Marvin D. Love Freeway):
Darnell Solomon, a ninth-grader, was struck by a pickup truck and killed as he fled across a highway during a police chase. He and a friend had been pursued by Dallas police as suspected car thieves. The car they were driving crashed through a fence near the highway and stopped. Darnell reportedly jumped out and started running. He was struck moments later. His friend was arrested at the scene and charged with unauthorized use of a vehicle, evading arrest, cocaine possession, and vandalism. Darnell's mother said, "My baby wouldn't do nothing like this – he had to be influenced into this. He was a wonderful kid." The principal at his high school described him as a "pleasant kid" who was good at drawing and aspired to be an architect. Classmates observed a minute of silence in Darnell's memory and hung a banner with messages to him in the school's hallway. **Source:** The Dallas Morning News, 12/13/97

Oliver Rodriguez, Jr.   33   *Latino*   👁

November 29, 1997. east Houston:

Oliver Rodriguez, Jr., was shot once in the chest and killed by Houston Police Officer A. Munoz. The shooting occurred in front of the victim's parents, sister, and other family members, including children, at a family barbecue. Police were summoned by a 911 call reporting a domestic disturbance at the Rodriguez home. When Officer Munoz arrived, Mr. Rodriguez came out of the kitchen holding a knife, but his sister said, "[T]he knife was never meant for the police. He was cutting up ribs when the officer came." She added, "He had got into an argument with our dad, but he had not touched a soul. The officer was only there a few seconds when he shot my brother." A Houston police spokesperson said cops are trained to shoot in the torso in "life-threatening situations." This amounts to a shoot-to-kill policy. Officer Munoz claims Mr. Rodriguez refused an order to drop the knife and lunged at him before being shot. **Source:** The Houston Chronicle, 12/4/97; SLP form

Joel Marquez   18   —

November 3, 1997. southeast Dallas:

Joel Marquez, a passenger in an allegedly stolen vehicle, was killed during a police chase at speeds of up to 70 mph. The 15-year-old driver of the car failed to make a sharp left turn and crashed into a tree near an intersection. Mr. Marquez died on the scene from a broken neck. The 15-year-old driver was hospitalized. He was charged with manslaughter and other offenses. Police said it appeared that proper procedures were followed and that they began chasing the car when they saw it stopped at an intersection and noticed that there were no keys in the ignition. **Source:** The Dallas Morning News, 11/4/97

Rose Marie Treadway (a.k.a. Melody Ann Carson)   43   —

October 30, 1997. Houston (U.S. 59):

Ms. Treadway was shot at least twice and killed by Houston Police Officers J.R. Johnston and Matthew Lem. Railroad workers found her sitting on the tracks. She allegedly brandished an eight-inch knife at them, and they flagged down a cop. Authorities claim Ms. Treadway pulled a knife on the officer as he tried to talk to her, then jumped into the patrol car, which had the keys in the ignition, and drove off. She contacted a police dispatcher on the cruiser's radio, reportedly "ranting and raving." She crashed the patrol car into a concrete barrier on the highway and allegedly threatened another motorist who stopped to help her. Officers Johnston and Lem claim Ms. Treadway charged at them with the knife and refused several orders to drop it before they opened fire. Neighbors, who knew her as Melody Ann Carson, said she was a friendly person and a devoted mother who lived with her boyfriend and 12-year-old son and worked at a grocery store. "She was a good mother," said a neighbor. "When she came home from work, she would either read a book or if her son wanted to swim, she went out to the pool to watch him." Another neighbor said she was "real quiet... a normal person. I never saw any signs of instability.... I thought I was having a nightmare when I heard about what happened. I couldn't believe it. I thought I would wake up from it." **Source:** The Houston Chronicle, 10/31/97 & 11/3/97

Paul Dickson Voncolditz   53   —

October 30, 1997. Montgomery County:

Mr. Voncolditz, an ostrich rancher, was shot and killed by Montgomery County police when he allegedly fired shots at arson investigators who were trying to arrest him for setting a fire at his Magnolia home. Cops claim he fled into an office and fired a pistol at police as they forced their way in and that they were returning fire when they killed him. **Source:** The Houston Chronicle, 11/4/97

Leonard Lewis — — —

October 28, 1997. east Fort Worth (I-30):

According to his sister, Mr. Lewis had been acting erratically for several days. The newspaper account portrayed an apparently disturbed person and captured his erratic behavior. After an argument between Mr. Lewis and his sister, he jumped off a second story balcony and headed off. Minutes later, he was injured by a tractor-trailer. Then, he reportedly went up to a pickup truck stuck in traffic, demanded a ride, climbed in the back, and told the occupants that he had a gun. The occupants of the pickup truck managed to attract the attention of the police and pulled over next to an Arlington police officer waiting on the side of the road. The cop claims that when he ordered Mr. Lewis, who was lying down, to get up, Mr. Lewis allegedly jumped out of the truck, waved a hatchet at the cop, jumped into the officer's patrol car, and drove off. Other police chased him in rush hour traffic along the center shoulder of the highway near the guardrail at speeds of over 100 mph for about five miles. Just across the Fort Worth City line, Mr. Lewis crashed head-on into a concrete bridge support. The car exploded instantly, killing him. **Source:** The Dallas Morning News, 10/29/97 & 10/30/97

Phillip Raymond Garcia — 27 —

October 26, 1997. Dallas:

Mr. Garcia was shot twice and killed by Cockrell Hill Police Officer Anthony Hogan, who claims Mr. Garcia pointed a gun at him and pulled the trigger after a routine traffic stop. The officer tried to pull Mr. Garcia over for driving without lights and pursued him across the city line into Dallas. Mr. Garcia's 15-year-old fiancee, who was a passenger in his car, said in an affidavit that Mr. Garcia got out of the car with a handgun and pointed it at Officer Hogan. The cop repeatedly warned him to put the gun down before firing one shot, which struck Mr. Garcia in his left leg below the knee. The fiancee ran to Mr. Garcia's aid and pushed the gun about eight feet away and into the street. She repeatedly asked the two cops to get the gun lying in the street. When the wounded Mr. Garcia tried to roll over on the pavement, Officer Hogan shot him again, hitting him in the side and killing him. Officer Hogan was cleared of criminal wrongdoing by a grand jury. The victim's family said they might file a lawsuit against Officer Hogan and the city of Cockrell Hill. An uncle said, "We want to take this as far as we can because this is wrong. We're not going to stop right here." He added that the family thinks the first shot to Mr. Garcia's leg was justified but that the second shot constituted excessive force. "We think that Phillip should be in jail right now with a bullet wound to his leg, maybe on charges of attempted murder. But he shouldn't be dead. It's the second shooting that we say shouldn't have happened." **Source:** The Dallas Morning News, 10/28/97 &12/9/97

Darrell Barnett Britton — 44 —

September 17, 1997. Houston:

Mr. Britton was shot in the head, face, and neck and killed by off-duty Police Officer Christopher Allen in a park near his home. Mr. Britton was reportedly threatening to hit his six-year-old nephew with a chunk of concrete and then a wooden board if the child did not go home. Officer Allen went to his car, got his badge and gun, and confronted Mr. Britton, reportedly identifying himself as a cop and telling Mr. Britton to calm down. Mr. Britton supposedly said, "Today's a great day to die," then allegedly lunged at the cop and grabbed his arm. Officer Allen shot and killed him. The victim's sister said she was upset that the cop brought his gun into the park, which was filled with children, and killed her brother in front of their nephew instead of trying to restrain him physically. Mr. Britton is survived by his wife and small son. A civil suit was filed on their behalf. Officer Allen remained on active duty, and a grand jury declined to indict him. An autopsy showed that the victim had water on his brain, a condition that can cause erratic behavior. **Source:** The Houston Record Chronicle,5/20/98 & 3/21/98

| **Robert Lee Castillo** | 36 | — |

August 11, 1997. Fort Worth (North Side):

Mr. Catstillo was shot once in the chest and killed by Officer D.P. Shipp at his house on Oscar Avenue. His relatives had called 911 after an argument in which, according to one family member, "He went crazy," had been drinking, and was possibly high on cocaine. Cops claim that Mr. Catstillo came out of the house with large kitchen knives in each hand and several more stuck in his waistband, waved the knives, "made threatening statements" to the cops, and went back inside. This supposedly happened three or four more times, and the cops pepper-sprayed him. The pepper spray presumably had no effect. According to police, Mr. Catstillo came out of the house again holding a large barbecue fork instead of a knife in one of his hands, and held it to his own neck as if he were going to stab himself. Cops claim that when they told him to put it down, he pointed it at them and lunged, at which point they shot and killed him. The family disputes the police version of events, saying that the knives were only in his waistband, that his hands were empty, and that the barbecue fork never left the sink inside the house. Mr. Catstillo's niece said, "The barbecue fork was inside the house in the sink. I had just used it to cook steaks. He [Robert Castillo] didn't lunge at anybody. He was walking toward them [the cops], but slow." His sister said she had begged the cops not to kill her brother and if they had to shoot, to shoot him in the leg. Police officials felt that this request was unreasonable. According to a Police Department spokesperson, cops are trained to shoot at a suspect's trunk in "life-and-death" situations. "These are high-stress situations and to control a weapon and hit a small target like a moving hand or leg is asking too much of a human being," according to the police spokesperson. Cops claimed that other non-police, non-family witnesses confirmed that Castillo lunged, but they did not specify who these witnesses were (if they even really exist). The police department spokesperson portrayed Officer Shipp as a victim, saying "It [killing someone] is a tremendous stressor in their lives. Officers commonly have nightmares, second-guess themselves, and question if they did the appropriate thing. It's a grieving process not too dissimilar to the loss of a loved one." **Source:** The Dallas Morning News, 8/13/97

| **Randy Redd** | 38 | — |

July 8, 1997. Odessa:

Randy Redd, a mentally ill man, was shot and killed by police in his front yard when he allegedly came out of his house swinging a metal pipe after a standoff. A grand jury declined to indict the cops. The victim's family filed a $2.75 million wrongful death lawsuit against the police department and two officers. **Source:** The Houston Chronicle, 12/18/97

| **Willie K. Friday** | 34 | — |

June 6, 1997. San Antonio:

San Antonio Police Officer Ernest Trevino shot and killed Willie Friday after the victim allegedly made a "sudden movement" which the police chief claimed put Officer Trevino and his partner in fear for their lives. Mr. Friday was unarmed. Cops claim he refused their orders to move his left hand from behind his back. They also claim hospital staff later found 19 grams of crack in his underwear. The incident is being "investigated," but the police chief said that Officer Trevino followed procedures in this fatal shooting, his second (that we know of) in his four years on the force. Six months earlier, Officer Trevino was one of four cops who shot and killed Tony Reyes. The media reported that Mr. Friday's death was, so far, the second fatal police shooting in San Antonio in 1997 (in addition to two non-fatal ones) and that in 1996, there were seven police shootings in San Antonio, three of them fatal. **Source:** Associated Press, 6/8/97

| **Esequiel Hernandez, Jr.** | 18 | *Chicano* | ◉ |

May 20, 1997. Redford:

Out herding his family's goats after school, Mr. Hernandez was stalked for 20 minutes by four camouflaged, heavily-armed U.S. Marines patrolling the border. He was carrying a .22 caliber rifle handed down from his grandfather to protect the goats from wild animals. Mr. Hernandez was shot in the back from 200 yards away by one of the Marines with an M-16. The Marines claim he pointed his rifle at them and fired several shots, but Mr. Hernandez was shot in the back and probably did not even know he was being stalked. A grand jury refused to indict his killer, citing military "rules of engagement."

Mike Matson   48   *white*

May 5, 1997. Fort Davis area:
Mr. Matson was a member of the Republic of Texas, a right-wing militia group seeking independence for Texas. After a week-long standoff with law enforcement agents in which members of the group held two hostages, most of the group surrendered but Mr. Matson and an associate escaped into the woods. Two days later, Mr. Matson was shot and killed in an alleged gun battle with police. His associate escaped and was arrested several months later. **Source:** Kansas City Star, 10/25/97

Brian Daniel Arledge   22

April 16, 1997. Houston:
Mr. Arledge was shot in the abdomen and killed by Hedwig Village Police Officer Scott Ashmore. Cops reportedly stopped Mr. Arledge for suspicion of drunk driving and discovered that he had a suspended license and an outstanding assault warrant. Mr. Arledge allegedly broke away while being handcuffed and ran into a residential back yard. Officer Ashmore claims he saw a "glint" of something shiny, so he opened fire. Officer Ashmore was not suspended and remained on active duty. The killing occurred just over the city line in Houston. **Source:** The Houston Chronicle, 4/17/97

Edwards Seth Rogers, Jr.   —   —

April 7, 1997. Corpus Christi:
Mr. Rogers, a mentally ill man, was shot four or five times and killed by three police officers while walking in his neighborhood around noon. Cops claimed he had a gun, but no gun was found, nor was Mr. Rogers running away. Police say they pursued him at a "fast walk." A toy gun was later recovered a block away by police. The three police officers were suspended with pay pending an internal investigation. **Source:** The Houston Chronicile (3 Star Edition),4/9/97

Gary Lee Crenshaw   —   —

January 25, 1997. west Texas Prison:
Mr. Crenshaw's family says he was brutally beaten by prison guards and then denied medical care for over ten minutes. He died from the beating. Part of the incident was recorded on videotape. **Source:** Dallas Morning News (AP), 6/16/98

Eli Montesinos Delgado   44   —

January 1, 1997. San Antonio:
Mr. Delgado suffered fatal injuries during an alleged struggle with off-duty San Antonio Police Officer James A. Smith, who was working as a security guard at a Dillard's department store. He died five days later on Jan. 6. A grand jury declined to indict Officer Smith. **Source:** Express-News (San Antonio, TX), 10/31/97

Tony Reyes   —   —

December 1996. San Antonio:
San Antonio Police Officer Ernest Trevino was one of four officers who fired at Mr. Reyes after he allegedly came to the door with an assault rifle. Mr. Reyes was shot and killed. An "investigation" cleared Officer Trevino of wrongdoing, and he returned to active duty. Six months later, he shot and killed Willie Friday. **Source:** Associated Press, 6/8/97

Joe Lee Calloway   —   *Black*

October 7, 1996. Grand Prairie:
Mr. Calloway, a mentally ill man, was shot and killed by Grand Prairie Police Officer Blake Hubbard. Officer Hubbard, who claims he thought Mr. Calloway was lunging at another cop with a pocket knife, was charged with murder but was acquitted in Aug. 1997. Officer Hubbard was placed on indefinite suspension and filed a civil service complaint about this. His complaint was settled with the following terms: the city paid Officer Hubbard $150,000, and he was allowed to resign with a clean employment record. The city originally tried to keep the terms of the settlement secret. This was the first time in 24 years that a Dallas County police officer was charged with murder for on-duty actions, according to the newspaper. The victim's family filed a lawsuit charging excessive force. **Source:** The Dallas Morning News, 3/4/98,7/7/98 & 11/3/97

Herbert Caldwell   —   —

August 26, 1996. Arlington:

Mr. Caldwell was shot in the stomach and killed by Arlington Police Sgt. Jeff Petty. Sgt. Petty and Sgt. Tom Wood were allegedly responding to a 911 call from a gas station reporting that Mr. Caldwell was harassing customers. Cops claim they tried to restrain him and only shot him after they were unable to subdue him. But the victim's family says he was merely using a pay phone when the cops confronted him and demanded ID. When he refused, police pepper-sprayed him and Sgt. Wood struck him with his baton. Mr. Caldwell tried to run away and was struck again, then shot when he struggled with the cops. The two officers were placed on administrative leave for three days. They were cleared of wrongdoing by an internal police investigation and were not criminally charged. Sgt. Petty was later promoted to supervisor. The victim's wife and daughter filed a wrongful death lawsuit against the police and the city of Arlington, charging excessive force and lack of probable cause. **Source:** The Dallas Morning News, 8/27/98

Otis Charles Cooks   21   *Black*   👁

August 8, 1996. Houston:

Mr. Cooks was in a vacant apartment with some other people when police arrived and shouted for everyone to come out. Others left, but Mr. Cooks did not hear the cops and remained inside. When police ordered everyone out a second time, Mr. Cooks looked out the window and saw the cops outside. He put his hands up. It is unclear whether he had left the apartment or remained inside when the fatal encounter occurred. Police Officer L.C. Thompson shot Mr. Cooks to death as the victim stood with his hands raised. **Source:** SLP form

Katherine Findley   18   —

Megan Jones   18   —

February 17, 1996. northeast Dallas:

Senior Police Cpl. Tommy Ames was speeding to the call of another officer without using flashing lights or a siren when he slammed into the victims' jeep, killing both of them. A grand jury declined to indict the officer. An autopsy supposedly found that Katherine Findley, the driver, was legally drunk at the time of the crash. Megan Jones' family filed a wrongful death lawsuit against the city. **Source:** The Dallas Morning News, 3/7/98

Matthew Morgan   29   —

August 15, 1995. Houston:

Mr. Morgan, a mentally ill man, was shot in the abdomen and killed outside his parents' house by Houston Police Officer Steven C. Riegle, a member of the special weapons team. Mr. Morgan, who was manic-depressive, reportedly had an "emotional outburst" and began destroying his parents' property shortly after discontinuing his medication. Cops arrived and a three hour standoff ensued as the victim allegedly "paraded up and down the driveway carrying an ax" and "shout[ed] obscenities and [told] officers to shoot him." Cops claim Officer Riegle shot Mr. Matthew only when the latter supposedly raised the ax over his head and charged another officer. The victim's parents filed a wrongful death lawsuit, which was dismissed by a federal judge, who ruled the shooting justified because an officer's life was presumably in danger. **Source:** The Houston Chronicle, 8/7/98

Travis O'Neill Allen   17   *Anglo American*   👁

July 15, 1995. Bellaire:
Mr. Allen was shot in the back and killed as he lay on the floor under arrest by Bellaire Police Sgt. Michael Leal and Officer Carle Upshaw. The officers found him injured and bleeding on the floor of a house after he had allegedly smashed through the patio door. Mr. Allen's parents filed a $25 million lawsuit against the two cops and the city. They charged that Sgt. Leal shot their son twice in the back while Officer Upshaw held Travis down on the floor with his foot. The victim's parents said their son was under the influence of LSD but that he obeyed police commands and laid down before he was shot. He weighed 126 lbs. and was unarmed. Cops claim Mr. Allen was resisting arrest and put his hands in his pockets, which the police took as a "threatening move." Cops testified that they shot him because he gave them a "target stare" as he rolled to the side with his hand in his pocket, even though they said he never raised a hand nor said a word. The physical evidence showed that he was totally face down when shot with his right hand under his chest. A grand jury declined to indict the cops, but two jurors later said they felt pressured not to indict by a "politically connected fellow juror." The city and the two cops tried to get the parents' lawsuit dismissed, but the judge ruled it would go to trial on Aug. 18, 1998. The cops were never charged by the state or federal government. And the cop who killed Travis was later given a promotion.
Source: The Houston Chronicle, 7/1/98; SLP form

Francisco Javier Campero   20   *Mexican*

November 8, 1994. El Paso:
Unarmed as he started to flee on foot back to Mexico, Mr. Campero was shot twice in the back and died. A Customs agent said he fired on Mr. Campero after he tried to drive his truck through the Juarez/El Paso border checkpoint.

Chanel Andrade	1	white American
Jennifer Andrade	19	white American
Katherine Andrade	24	white American
George Bennett	35	Black (British)
Susan Benta	31	Black (British)
Mary Jean Borst	49	white American
Pablo Cohen	38	white (Israeli)
Abedowalo Davies	30	Black (British)
Shari Doyle	18	white American
Beverly Elliot	30	Black (British)
Doris Fagan	51	Black (British)
Yvette Fagan	32	Black (British)
Lisa Marie Farris	24	white American
Raymond Friesen	76	white (Canadian)
Dayland Gent	3	white American
Page Gent	1	white American
Sandra Hardial	27	Black (British)
Diana Henry	28	Black (British)
Paulina Henry	24	Black (British)
Phillip Henry	22	Black (British)
Stephen Henry	26	Black (British)
Vanessa Henry	19	Black (British)
Zilla Henry	55	Black (British)
Novellette Hipsman	36	Black (Canadian)
Floyd Houtman	61	African American
Sherri Jewell	43	Asian American
Chica Jones	2	white American
David M. Jones	38	white American
Little One Jones	2	white American
Serenity Jones	4	white American
Bobbie Lane Koresh	2	white American
Cyrus Koresh	8	white American
David Koresh	33	white American
Rachel Koresh	24	white American
Star Koresh	6	white American
Jeffery Little	32	white American
Nicole Gent Little	24	white (Australian)
Livingston Malcolm	26	Black (British)
Anita Martin	18	African American
Diane Martin	41	Black (British)
Lisa Martin	13	African American
Sheila Martin, Jr.	15	African American

Wayne Martin, Sr.	42	*African American*
Wayne Martin, Jr.	20	*African American*
Abigail Martinez	11	*Mexican American*
Audrey Martinez	13	*Mexican American*
Crystal Martinez	3	*Mexican American*
Isaiah Martinez	4	*Mexican American*
Joseph Martinez	8	*Mexican American*
Julliete Martinez	30	*Mexican American*
John-Mark McBean	27	*Black (British)*
Bernadette Monbelly	31	*Black (British)*
Melissa Morrison	6	*Black (British)*
Rosemary Morrison	29	*Black (British)*
Sonia Murray	29	*African American*
Theresa Nobrega	48	*Black (British)*
James Riddle	32	*white American*
Rebecca Saipaia	24	*Filipino*
Judy Schneider	41	*white American*
Mayanah Schneider	2	*white American*
Steve Schneider	43	*white American*
Clifford Sellors	33	*white (British)*
Floracita Sonobe	34	*Filipino*
Scott Kojiro Sonobe	35	*Asian American*
Aisha Gyrfas Summers	17	*white (Australian)*
Gregory Summers	28	*white American*
Startle Summers	1	*white American*
Hollywood Sylvia	1	*white American*
Lorraine Sylvia	40	*white American*
Rachel Sylvia	12	*white American*
Michelle Jones Thibodeau	18	*white American*
Margarida Vaega	47	*Asian (New Zealander)*
Neal Vaega	38	*Somoan (New Zealander)*
Mark H. Wendell	40	*Asian American*

April 19, 1993. Waco:
After a 51-day siege that began with a raid by federal agents, 74 people, including 22 children, were killed in the now-infamous Waco incident when the compound of the Branch Davidian religious sect was attacked by federal agents from the FBI and the Bureau of Alcohol, Tobacco, and Firearms (ATF). Tanks knocked holes into the walls of the compound and inserted tear gas. Wind helped dissipate the gas but fanned flames that broke out inside the compound. Authorities blamed the Branch Davidians for setting the fires, but survivors of the raid deny this, and many people believe that federal agents are responsible for the fires. The deaths of the 74 Branch Davidians resulted from several causes, including gunshot wounds, smoke inhalation and asphyxiation from the fire, and falling debris from either the tank assault or the fire. No law enforcement agents or government officials were held accountable for the deaths resulting from the initial raid or the final assault on the compound. Eight surviving Branch Davidians were convicted of charges including voluntary manslaughter. Seven were sentenced to 40 year terms, one got five years, and another received a three year sentence after testifying for the government. For over six years after the incident, the FBI strenuously denied that they had used any potentially flammable devices in their final assault on the compound. Finally, faced with mounting and increasingly public evidence to the contrary, FBI spokespeople and Attorney General Janet Reno admitted, in late Aug.

1999, that pyrotechnic military CS gas canisters were fired at the Branch Davidian compound. But they continued to insist that these canisters, which are known to explode and cause fires, did not cause the fire at Waco. They insisted that the canisters were fired six hours before the fire broke out and that they bounced harmlessly off the roof of the compound and fell into a puddle. They continued to insist that the Branch Davidians had set the fires themselves. The newspapers reported that Attorney General Reno was upset about the six years of deception because it damaged her credibility. **Source:** www.pbs.org/wgbh/pages/frontline/waco/timeline3.html Frontline's "Waco: The Inside Story"; The New York Times, 8/27/99; CNN on-line, 8/26/99

Cody Underkofler	13	—

March 23, 1993. Dallas (west Oak Cliff):
Mr. Underkofler was run over and killed by a speeding police car being driven by Officer Alfred Nunez on a darkened street. Officer Nunez was not using his flashing lights or siren. A grand jury refused to indict Officer Nunez. **Source:** The Dallas Morning News, 3/7/98

Winston Blake	28	*Black (British)*
Peter Gent	24	*white (Australian)*
Peter Hipsman	28	*white American*
Perry Jones	64	*white American*
Michael Schroeder	29	*white American*
Jaydean Wendell	34	*Native Hawaiian*

February 28, 1993. Waco:
Federal agents from the Bureau of Alcohol, Tobacco, and Firearms (ATF) arrived at the compound of the Branch Davidian religious sect to serve arrest and search warrants as part of an investigation into possible illegal possession of weapons. A gun fight erupted. The feds claim the Branch Davidians fired first. But one ATF agent initially reported that an agent may have fired first when he shot and killed a dog at the compound (he later retracted this). The Branch Davidians maintain that they fired in self-defense after the federal agents fired at them. Six Branch Davidians were shot and killed by ATF agents during the raid. Four federal agents were killed and 16 were wounded. David Koresh, the leader of the Branch Davidians, was wounded. This was the beginning of the now-infamous Waco incident. A 51-day siege ensued. The compound was surrounded by federal and local law enforcement agents and patrolled by tanks. Authorities cut the phone lines, permitting access only to negotiators. They cut the electricity, shone bright lights, and played loud music at all hours of the night. The siege ended on Apr. 19 when federal agents assaulted the compound, killing 74 people. **Source:** www.pbs.org/wgbh/pages/frontline/waco/timeline3.html Frontline's "Waco: The Inside Story."

Wendell Baker, Jr.	21	—

March 1992. Galveston:
Mr. Baker, of Waller, was shot and killed by Galveston Police Officer Mike Putnal. The cop claims he only shot Mr. Baker after the latter allegedly fired a pistol into the air on a crowded beach, re-loaded, and pointed the gun at him. In Jan. 1998, a federal lawsuit over Mr. Baker's death was settled for an undisclosed amount. **Source:** The Houston Chronicle, 1/28/98

Julio Cesar Galicia	26	*Mexican*

November 5, 1990. Lower Rio Grande Valley:
Mr. Galicia was shot to death by the Border Patrol.

UTAH

Name	Age	Nationality	Photo
Andrew Vialpando	19	—	

January 9, 1998. Emery County:
Mr. Vialpando was allegedly driving a stolen jeep with four passengers. They were chased by cops for 35 miles, then ran from the jeep. The four passengers were arrested. Mr. Vialpando was chased off a 400-foot cliff and fell to his death. Cops claim he slipped on the "rocky and steep" terrain. The victim's uncle said, "It doesn't make sense that in the middle of the afternoon that he would jump off a 400-foot cliff. With a 400-foot cliff, you're not going to make it." Andrew Vialpando had been wounded in the 1997 Cinco de Mayo shooting spree in Denver. **Source:** The Rocky Mountain News (Denver, CO), 1/11/98; The Denver Post, 1/10/98

Bryan Larry Davis	26		

January 4, 1998. Salt Lake County:
Mr. Davis was shot and killed by Salt Lake County Sheriff's Deputy Stacey Rawlings. He had allegedly tried to bash out of a ring of police cars with a stolen sports car, but became stuck on a decorative railway tie. Deputy Rawlings fired two shots through the front windshield as Bryan shifted the car back and forth from first gear to reverse, trying to rock it off the railway tie on which he was caught. Cops claim they felt their lives were in danger. Mr. Davis' father said, "He was stuck, he didn't move, and they murdered him. I don't care if they didn't think he was worth anything. He was worth something to me. No one knew him like I did. He had a good heart." The Salt Lake County District Attorney's Office cleared Deputy Rawlings of any wrongdoing, allowing him to return to work. **Source:** The Salt Lake Tribune, 1/21/98 & 12/22/98

Alicia Avila	17	—	

December 19, 1997. Salt Lake County:
Cops began chasing a stolen car in which Ms. Avila and two male friends were riding. When the car got stuck in a snowbank, the three got out of the car and ran, chased by Salt Lake County Deputy Mike Anderson. When cornered, Ms. Avila's two friends climbed a fence and got away. Ms. Avila was shot and killed by Deputy Anderson, who claimed she turned to fight him and raised her arm in a "threatening gesture," making him think she had a weapon. She was shot once at close range in the chest or throat. A hairbrush was recovered from the scene. The Salt Lake County DA's Office cleared Deputy Anderson of any wrongdoing. **Source:** The Salt Lake Tribune, 1/22/98 & 12/22/98

John R. Dinsmore	49	—	

November 24, 1997. Mohab:
Mr. Dinsmore was allegedly wielding a knife and threatening to kill himself. He was shot and killed by Mohab Police Officer Mike Wiler. **Source:** interview with newspaper reporter

Michael Valent	29	—	

March 20, 1997. Salt Lake City (Utah State Prison):
Mr. Valent collapsed and died immediately after being released from a restraint chair in Utah State Prison. He had been there for 16 hours. The chair caused blood clots, which had traveled to his lungs and caused a fatal pulmonary embolism. Mr. Valent was a schizophrenic who had been tied to the chair because he refused to remove a pillowcase from his head. The state denied wrongdoing but paid a $200,000 settlement in a lawsuit filed by the victim's mother and agreed to discontinue use of the restraint chair. Restraint chairs and a similar type of restraining board have been referred to as "medieval" and "barbaric" by the American Civil Liberties Union (ACLU), which is challenging the use of such devices in the prison systems of several states. **Source:** Salem Statesman Journal, 3/27/97; Philadelphia Inquirer, 11/19/98; The Dallas Morning News, 1/11/98

| **Dorothy Stevens** | 89 | — |

March 19, 1997. I-84 (near Morgan):
Deputy Tony Pierson negligently rammed Ms. Stevens' vehicle as he turned to chat with three prisoners he was transporting. Cops claimed that Ms. Stevens was zig-zagging at 10 to 20 mph across the highway in a 75 mph zone and that she lurched in front of Deputy Pearson's car as he briefly turned his head when a prisoner's chain rattled. The jury, most of whom knew Deputy Pierson, acquitted him of negligent homicide. **Source:** Standard-Examiner, 1/14/98

| **Blaine Tripp** | 67 | — |

February 8, 1997. Murray:
Mr. Tripp was severely intoxicated. He allegedly grabbed a loaded 357 Magnum and got into a fight with his granddaughter. When his wife intervened, Mr. Tripp reportedly shot and killed her and shot his granddaughter in the hand as she was calling 911. When police arrived, they shot and killed Mr. Tripp. **Source:** interview with newspaper reporter

| **George White** | — | — |

July 28, 1996. Salt Lake County:
Cops claim Mr. White barricaded himself in his home and tried to ambush two SWAT team members, Salt Lake County Sheriffs Deputies John Stowe and Tim Langely. The two deputies shot and killed him. Both deputies went on to commit various crimes, in Stowe's case, repeated domestic violence and in Langely's case, putting a loaded gun to the head of a handcuffed drug suspect. Both cops portrayed themselves as victims and blamed their behavior on trauma that resulted from their killing of George White. Langely lost his job as a sheriff's deputy after entering a "plea in abeyance" to a reduced misdemeanor charge, which will be dismissed if he stays clean for a year. Stowe may work as a Deputy again after his wife requested, and the Salt Lake County DA agreed, to drop most of the domestic violence charges against him. **Source:** Salt Lake Tribune, 5/98.

| **Unidentified Boy** | 15 | — |

May 14, 1996. Salt Lake City:
The boy, despondent over the recent deaths of three friends, allegedly shot and wounded a school bus driver and then drove off in the empty bus. During a high-speed police chase, the bus crashed into a house. The boy was found dead in the wrecked bus. Police had thought the youth was holed up inside the two-story house after the crash, and surrounded it with SWAT teams. They also fired tear gas into the bus. **Source:** Vancouver Columbian, 5/14/96

| **Wade Ward** | 33 | — |

Date Unknown. Wellington:
Police were called for a domestic dispute. Sheriff Mark Watkins shot and killed Wade Ward when the victim allegedly tried to grab his baton and engaged him in "hand-to-hand combat." **Source:** interview with newspaper reporter

VIRGINIA

Name	**Age**	**Nationality**	**Photo**
Darnell Lee Tinsley	24	—	

August 8, 1998. Alexandria (Burtonsville):
Darnell Lee Tinsley was shot and killed by off-duty Alexandria Police Detective Eric Ratliff after he allegedly pulled a "silver-colored handgun" from his waistband and aimed it at the officer. Det. Ratliff claims he ordered Mr. Tinsley to drop the weapon, then opened fire when he refused. Cops claim Mr. Tinsley was a serial rapist and that his clothes matched the description from several sexual assault victims, some of whose property was allegedly found on his person and in his car. A female jogger had called the police to say that someone who matched the description of the serial rapist was in her building. When police arrived, they did not find anyone, but as they were leaving, they saw Mr. Tinsley, who ran. Cops gave chase. Det. Ratliff, who was off-duty, joined in, caught up with Mr. Tinsley, and shot him dead during the encounter. **Source:** The Washington Post, 8/11/98

Brian Cox	25	—

December 12, 1997. Dumfries:

Mr. Cox was shot seven times and killed by two cops as he lay in his own bed. Cops claim he pulled a rifle on them when they were in his town house, allegedly looking for a burglar. (It appears as if the cops surprised him in bed and he shot in self-defense. It is not clear that Mr. Cox knew the two strangers in his house were cops). In Jan. 1998, a spokesperson for the Prince William County police department, which conducted the "investigation" into the shooting, said it was "entirely justified" and "consistent with police department policy." Mr. Cox's widow criticized the investigation and requested that it be conducted by a "more objective authority," but the DA refused. Meanwhile, the FBI said they had begun a preliminary inquiry to see if the cops had violated Brian's civil rights. **Source:** The Washington Post, 1/17/98

Jack L. Palmer	62	—

October 5, 1997. Wise County (Coeburn):

Mr. Palmer, a disabled man, was shot and killed by Wise County Sheriff's Deputy Joel Marcum and off-duty Police Officer Scott Brooks as he drove his motorized wheelchair along US 58, a four-lane highway, allegedly pointing a handgun at passing motorists and threatening to shoot anyone who came within ten feet. Mr. Palmer had reportedly shot and killed his wife, who was seeking a divorce, then drove his wheelchair a half mile to the highway. After a low-speed chase, cops tried to tip over his wheelchair with their car. Police claim they only opened fire after Mr. Parsons fired on them, shouting "I'm going to shoot you, I'm going to kill you." Deputy Marcum was allegedly shot in the chest and wounded in the course of the incident. **Source:** Richmond Times, 10/7/97; Milwaukee Journal-Sentinel, 10/7/97; News and Observer (Raleigh, NC), 10/7/97

Melvin L. Stith, Sr.	32	—

October 1997. Petersburg:

While driving to his estranged wife's home, Mr. Stith reportedly hit another car. When he arrived, he reportedly rammed his car into her front door in an effort to get in and, once inside, shot her several times. Mrs. Stith, another woman, and three children ran from the apartment. Mr. Stith then allegedly engaged police in a gun battle. Cops evacuated the neighborhood and tried to contact him unsuccessfully for three hours. The standoff ended when his car, which had sat idling on the lawn, blocking the front door, suddenly cut off and rolled back about ten feet, revealing the legs and shoes of the dead Mr. Stith in the doorway. Cops claimed Mr. Stith shot and killed himself with his own handgun, and an unofficial autopsy report called his death a suicide. A distant cousin of the deceased described him as friendly and hard-working. The manager of the funeral establishment, where he had worked for about a year, described him as "reliable and hard-working." **Source:** Richmond Times-Dispatch, 10/9/97

Kennith "Kenny" Harris	31	Black	●

August 2, 1997. Arlington (I-66):

Mr. Harris, an unarmed man from Vienna, Va., was shot eight times and killed after a routine traffic stop by Arlington County police officers. Police fired a total of 13 shots. One of the shots was to his back, and he was also doused with two cans of pepper spray. Cops claim they opened fire after he rammed patrol cars while trying to flee. They also claim he was drunk and had a history of resisting arrest. The DA held that the shooting was justified. No one from Mr. Harris' immediate family, including his mother, was allowed to identify the his body. Mr. Harris' mother, cousin, and other family members continue to fight for justice. **Source:** www.afamerica.com/harris; The Washington Post, 1/8/98

David Jerome Pryor   youth   *Black*

December 31, 1997. Danville (Piedmont mall):

David Jerome Pryor was shot in the left side of the chest and killed by Danville Police Officer Dewey Joseph Hancock, Jr. The victim and another man had been arrested on suspicion of shoplifting at the Belk-Leggett department store in the Piedmont Mall. According to authorities, it took three security guards to handcuff Mr. Pryor. Police arrived and asked security guards to remove the handcuffs. Mr. Pryor identified himself as "Frederick Douglas" and insisted he was a juvenile. He was about to be placed under arrest when he allegedly ran from the office and across the mall parking lot, jumped a six foot fence, and crossed a busy road. Cops and security guards chased him but lost him as he cleared the fence and headed toward a nearby shopping plaza. They called for assistance, and Officer Hancock joined the search. Officer Hancock saw Mr. Pryor running near the rear of a store in the plaza and, over his car's loudspeaker, ordered him to stop. Mr. Pryor continued to run, and Officer Hancock jumped out of his car to chase him. The officer caught him when he tripped and fell, and a struggle allegedly ensued. Officer Hancock claims that when he tried to use pepper spray, Mr. Pryor got control of the canister and sprayed him in the face, then tried to take the cop's gun out of its holster. Claiming he was blinded by the pepper spray, Officer Hancock shot and killed Mr. Pryor. Rev. Keen, president of the Danville chapter of the Southern Christian Leadership Conference (SCLC), said white Danville cops have "shot four black men in the chest in the last seven years, killing two." Rev. Keen presented a laundry list of questions, including why Officer Hancock had not waited for backup before confronting David Pryor and why authorities had been so slow in identifying Mr. Pryor, even though they had his fingerprints from an earlier arrest. Members of David Pryor's family, who came to Danville from New York, said they had been given no information, not even a copy of the autopsy report. L. A. Andrews, an aunt, said, "David Pryor was a handsome young man but at his funeral he had a face that was beaten on before he was shot." Officer Hancock was placed on paid administrative leave for about two months, then returned to duty when a special prosecutor found that he acted reasonably when he shot and killed Mr. Pryor. A local civil rights leader said, "It was a paid vacation; he [Officer Hancock] rested up for a month. And if there is nothing done, another white officer will shoot a Black man." **Source:** Richmond Times-Dispatch, 10/21/97

Bruce Vincent Quagliato   28   —

March 1997. Virginia Beach (Little Creek Naval Amphibious Base):

Mr. Quagliato, an unarmed motorist, was shot and killed by eight members of the Virginia Beach Police Department after a car chase which began when the victim allegedly "refused to accept a traffic ticket" and "rammed a police vehicle." The eight cops fired a total of 60 rounds. Twelve other cops were present but did not fire. The city only released the names of the officers involved in Mr. Quagliato's death in response to a request under the state Freedom of Information Act. The cops were suspended, but all were cleared of criminal wrongdoing. The victim's family filed a notice of intention to sue the city and the Navy. **Source:** The Washington Post, 10/11/97

Kevin Arnold   —   —

July 24, 1995. —:

Kevin Arnold, an ex-cop who had become a bank robber, was shot and killed by two FBI agents, Special Agent Joseph White and Special Agent Anthony Caruso, who later received medals for the shooting. The pair was trying to arrest Mr. Arnold on charges of robbing a dozen banks when, according to authorities, he pretended to reach for a weapon and then repeatedly tried to grab the FBI agents' guns. Mr. Arnold then got into his car. Agent White grabbed the keys and was supposedly dragged by the car, at which point he shot the victim once and killed him. When giving out the awards, FBI Assistant Director Timothy McNally said, "I truly admire men like this." **Source:** The Orange County Register, 1/24/97

Otis Kelley   24   *Black*

March 16, 1995. Alexandria:

Otis Kelley was shot 16 times by Police Officer Scott Ogden. He was unarmed and running away. He died the next day (Mar. 17) from his injuries. **Source:** SLP form

---

Jerone J. Walton   28   —

1994. Norfolk City Jail:

Mr. Walton died because Correctional Medical Service (CMS) simply forgot to schedule him for crucial dialysis treatment. **Source:** Independent, 7/1/98

Henry Simmons   —   —

Date Unknown. (in prison):
Henry Simmons died in a Virginia prison of a heart attack when tests ordered by a doctor were not administered. **Source:** St. Louis Post-Dispatch, 9/27/98

WASHINGTON, D. C.

Name	Age	Nationality	Photo

Patrick Joseph Hill, Jr.   36   —

August 21, 1998. Southeast Washington (I-295):
Mr. Hill was reportedly behaving "erratically and in a bizarre way." Police claim he smashed a parked car with a tire iron and nearly sideswiped an off-duty cop's car before fleeing on I-295. Mr. Hill's pickup truck was boxed in by police. He allegedly ignored orders to get out and supposedly began ramming a civilian car in front of him and a police car behind him. D.C. Police Officer Jacques Doby fired 38 shots, reloading twice, according to an official police report. He killed Mr. Hill, claiming he feared for the lives of other motorists. Mr. Hill was unarmed. Officer Doby was placed on administrative leave with pay. Authorities said it was unclear whether he fired at Mr. Hill or at his tires. Mr. Hill was married and worked odd jobs. A friend said, "He was a nice guy. He had a good sense of humor [and was] easygoing." **Source:** The Washington Post, 8/23/98 & 11/16/98

Unidentified Person   —   —

August 10, 1998. Washington, D.C. (400 block of Q St. NW):
The unidentified victim was shot and killed by two D.C. police officers in an alley around 1 a.m. Cops claimed s/he was an armed robbery suspect and that they opened fire after the victim allegedly confronted them. **Source:** The Washington Post, 8/10/98 & 8/13/98

Unidentified Man   —   —

June 1, 1998. Northwest Washington:
D.C. Police Officer Adrian Owens and his partner reportedly encountered a man who said he had jumped from a second-story apartment to escape an armed intruder who had robbed a woman still inside the apartment. The cops went up to the apartment, opened the door, and allegedly saw an armed man turning his weapon on them. Officer Owens shot him once in the chest and killed him. He was placed on paid leave during an investigation. **Source:** The Washington Post, 6/2/98

Wendell Fleming   37   —

May 16, 1998. Benning Park:
Mr. Fleming was shot to death in the early morning hours in the 5300 block of E Street SE by Police Officer George Thomas, Jr. Officer Thomas claims that he was trying to arrest Mr. Fleming for selling crack when the latter tried to flee and then allegedly grabbed a flashlight and began beating the cop on the head. Officer Thomas fired four shots. The newspaper reported that the cop was "forced to shoot and kill" the victim, and gave prominence to police officials justifying the shooting. They also worried over the health of the cop, who was allegedly injured in the scuffle. Mr. Fleming's mother and daughter expressed outrage that cops had not bothered to come to their house, only a few blocks away from where the shooting occurred, to explain how he had been killed. His mother also disputed the police account, saying, "His face was swollen. His right cheek was really big and he had a little cut. They beat my boy....People told me he was just taking a walk; he wasn't selling no drugs. But even if drugs [were] involved, drugs don't give you no reason to shoot somebody....What's wrong with shooting people in the legs or something? That's just dog-style, what they did to him." Mr. Fleming worked as a guard at Constitution Hall. He had come by his mother's apartment to pick up his uniform. Officer Thomas was put on paid administrative leave (paid vacation) pending an investigation, a procedure that was described as routine. **Source:** The Washington Post, 5/17/98

Unidentified Homeless Man	30-40	—	

March 7, 1998. The Pentagon:
A body was found lying in a road near the Pentagon's river entrance. A security guard (a contract employee of a firm that provides some security services to the Pentagon) reported that his weapon had discharged. It was not clear if it was intentional.

Eric Antonio Anderson	18	—	

June 9, 1996. Washington D.C. (50th St. & C St. SE):
Mr. Anderson was shot and killed by D.C. Police Officer Terrence Shepherd after being stopped at a roadblock set up to make sure people had valid driver's licenses and were wearing seat belts. He was unarmed. The cop's bullet passed through the victim's left shoulder, aorta, and esophagus and stopped in his right shoulder blade. His car went into reverse, backed up 50 feet, and struck a tree. He was taken to a hospital, where he died. The cop who initially stopped Mr. Anderson, Lt. Stewart Morris, said he asked Mr. Anderson to turn off his engine based on "a bad feeling" that the latter would flee. Mr. Anderson responded, "What do I got to do that for?" and Lt. Morris shouted, "I think we have got a problem here." The next thing Lt. Morris knew, Officer Shepherd had come up behind him and opened fire on Mr. Anderson. Officer Shepherd originally said his gun went off by accident and was put on paid administrative leave during a criminal investigation. But he later told prosecutors that he had begun questioning Mr. Anderson and fired deliberately because he feared for his own and Lt. Morris' safety. This contradicted both his own initial account and Lt. Morris' account. Powder marks on the victim's clothes indicated that he had been shot from less than 24 inches away, not the three to four feet that Officer Shepherd claimed, and ballistics tests showed that the car was not moving when the victim was shot, again contradicting Officer Shepherd's account but confirming the accounts of Lt. Morris and several other officers on the scene. Officer Shepherd was fired from the police department over a year after the incident but faced no criminal charges. He had previously been involved in at least one fatal shooting and a non-fatal shooting at a car. Both of these shootings were ruled justifiable. **Source:** The Washington Post, 11/16/98

Edward Thomas	20	—	

March 21, 1996. Martin Luther King Jr. Ave. & Fourth St. SE:
Four D.C. police officers on foot shot and killed Mr. Thomas when he allegedly "swerved at them" after driving away from the scene of a shooting, pursued by police cars directed by a police helicopter. Cops claimed Mr. Thomas had fired at them during the car chase, but no gun was recovered from his car and no evidence that he fired on police could be produced. The cops fired 46 times at Mr. Thomas. No criminal charges were filed against the four cops, although one received a ten day suspension for making false statements about the shooting. The victim's mother filed a lawsuit contending that her son was "in a stationary vehicle" when he was shot. **Source:** The Washington Post, 1998

Joseph N. Cooper, Jr.	21	*Black*	👁

November 11, 1995. near Robert Kennedy Memorial Stadium:
There was a fight near the stadium between Mr. Cooper and a white male. Mr. Cooper was unarmed and seemed to need help. Sgt. Gerald Neil was off duty and riding in an unmarked police car near the stadium. He shot and killed "Lil Joe."

Anteneh Getachew	30	*Ethiopian*	👁

October 14, 1995. Northeast Washington:
Mr. Getachew was shot and killed by off-duty D.C. Police Officer Jonathan G. Jackson. The circumstances surrounding his death are mysterious, and groups in the community called for "an open and complete investigation." **Source:** victim's family

Damon Henry   18   —

August 20, 1995. Washington, D.C. (Naylor Road SE):
Mr. Henry was a construction worker. He and a friend were driving to a liquor store, trying to get there before it closed at 2 a.m. Around 1:50 a.m., they swerved to avoid another car and hit a utility pole, flattening a tire. They drove to the liquor store, had someone buy them liquor, and drove off. Meanwhile, off-duty D.C. Police Officer Rodney Daniels was checking the utility pole for damage. When he heard a car with the flattened tire coming back down the road, he raised his badge, took out his gun, and reportedly yelled, "Police! Stop the vehicle!" three times. Officer Daniels claims Mr. Henry slowed down 30 feet away but then sped toward him. The cop fired 11 shots, hitting Mr. Henry in the spine and paralyzing his legs. Mr. Henry remained unable to wash or dress or care for himself. On Feb. 5, 1997, he died of septecemia due to infections caused by his injuries. Mr. Henry was initially charged with assaulting a police officer with a dangerous weapon (a car). But both his friend who was with him at the time and his mother said he didn't realize that Officer Daniels was a cop. Almost two years after the incident, an internal police investigation found that the shooting was not justified, and Officer Daniels' received a nine day suspension as punishment (he served only four of them). The victim's family filed a lawsuit against the city. **Source:** The Washington Post, 11/16/98

Kedemah Dorsey   16   —

May 15, 1995. Washington, D.C. (Florida Ave.):
Mr. Dorsey was allegedly driving the wrong way on a one-way street outside Banneker Senior High School, which he had attended before dropping out. D.C. Police Officer Vernell R. Tanner claims Mr. Dorsey was speeding and that two young women told him they had nearly been run over, so he began pursuit. Because he was working on foot, he used his own, unmarked car. He was unable to pull over Mr. Dorsey without lights or sirens and was ordered by supervisors to break off pursuit, but he persisted, pulling up behind Mr. Dorsey in a line of rush-hour traffic. Officer Tanner got out of his car to confront Mr. Dorsey. The cop claimed that he only pulled his gun after Mr. Dorsey backed up and rammed his car, and that he only fired because he feared being run over. But Doug Sparks, a lawyer sitting in traffic a few cars behind them, said, "That's not what I saw. That kid didn't have to die." He said that Officer Tanner was standing next to the driver's side door talking to Mr. Dorsey, that the cop fired the first shot as Mr. Dorsey began to pull out of the line of traffic and fired the second shot as he "sidestepped" to keep up with the victim's car as it moved across the lane of oncoming traffic. A lawyer for the victim's family pointed out, "It's somewhat difficult to use the car as a weapon when it is wedged in rush-hour traffic and the officer is standing to the side of it, not in front of it." The first shot hit Mr. Dorsey in the chest at close range, according to a police investigation, and the second shot hit him in the back. He died on the scene. Officer Tanner claimed not to remember firing the second shot. Mr. Sparks said he did not realize that the man with the gun was a cop and said, "It was basically at point-blank range. I thought, here's someone getting murdered in front of me. I thought it was some kind of drug shooting." Mr. Dorsey worked at Roy Rogers and was scheduled to begin his shift two hours after he was killed. His father said, "I want someone to explain to me how an officer walks up to a car for a traffic violation - and a child gets killed." Officer Tanner was put on paid administrative leave. He was not criminally charged, but the police department found the shooting unjustified and began proceedings to remove him from the force. The city also settled a lawsuit filed by the victim's family for $150,000. **Source:** The Washington Post, 11/16/98

James Madison McGee, Jr.   26   *Black*

February 7, 1995. Southeast Washington:
Mr. McGee, a Black off-duty motorcycle cop, was shot twice and killed by Police Officer Michael Baker, an on-duty white cop. Mr. McGee, wearing civilian clothes, had jumped out of a sports car with a gun in his hand in an attempt to stop a taxi robbery. Officer Baker was cleared of wrongdoing, and "racial tensions inside the police station reached a rancorous pitch," according to the newspaper. **Source:** The Washington Post, 2/8/98

Antonio Williams   18   —

February 7, 1995. Lincoln Heights:

Mr. Williams was shot seven times and killed by D.C. Police Officer Kristopher Payne at the mouth of an alley in the early morning hours. Five bullets hit his left side, one went through his left cheek, and the other through the back of his head. But Officer Payne claims he only opened fire when Mr. Williams turned to his right and pointed a gun at him. A witness saw the cop stand over the victim's prone body and fire finishing shots into his head, and ballistics tests done by the police showed that one or both bullets to the head were fired from 24 to 30 inches away. But the shooting of Mr. Williams was eventually ruled justified. No criminal charges were filed, and Officer Payne returned to active duty. Mr. Williams was allegedly armed and on drugs. He had supposedly threatened the mother of his best friend with a gun, which she grabbed from him and found to be unloaded. When he reportedly grabbed it back and ran, she called the police. Officer Payne found Mr. Williams and pursued him on foot before shooting him down. Officer Payne had a history of brutality, including several cases in which people filed (and won) police brutality lawsuits against him and a non-fatal shooting a month before Mr. Williams was killed (it was ruled justified). Police supervisors knew that the officer, who worked the midnight shift, routinely stopped and searched people without writing the proper reports and sometimes removed his name tag, thus preventing people from identifying him. When they confronted him, Officer Payne declared that there was "a war being fought in the streets." A former supervisor said some of Officer Payne's fellow cops "characterized him as some kind of overzealous brute." But the newspaper reported that supervisors "saw Payne's aggressiveness as an inner-city virtue." The former supervisor said, "Yeah, he used force, and sometimes his tactics may have seemed a little overbearing to some people. But if you're going to be a street officer...in this day and age, you have to have Kris Payne's approach. Anybody that doesn't is less an officer than Kris Payne." The victim's family filed a lawsuit against the city. **Source:** The Washington Post, 11/17/98

Roland Antonio Wells   21   —

January 14, 1995. Livingston Road SE:

Mr. Wells was shot once in the right knee and once in his left abdomen by off-duty Police Officer Melvin Key. He died six months later of his wounds. Officer Key was driving with his younger brother when the latter said he saw a boy holding a gun in a woman's face. The cop made a U-turn and saw a young man with what he thought was a gun (it was a BB gun), but no woman was present. He ordered Mr. Wells to drop the gun. Mr. Wells supposedly "just kept looking at [Officer Key] as if he was going to do something," then "suddenly" raised both arms. Officer Key claims he feared he was about to be shot, so he opened fire, shooting four bullets and knocking Mr. Wells to the ground. Two boys who were with Mr. Wells and witnessed the whole thing said his hands were in the air and he was putting the gun down when he was shot. Police did not even interview these witnesses until weeks later, when Mr. Wells' family's attorney called federal prosecutors. Officer Key was involved in four shootings in just over a year, of which this was one. In July, 1998, the city settled a lawsuit brought by Mr. Wells' father. Officer Key was promoted to sergeant in March 1997. **Source:** The Washington Post, 11/17/98

Terrence Hicks   31   —

August 16, 1994. Southeast Washington:

Mr. Hicks, described in the press as a drug user, was shot and killed by the D.C. Police Emergency Response Team (ERT) as he allegedly held his 70-year-old mother hostage with a 9 1/2 inch kitchen knife. Police fired at least 23 shots, hitting Mr. Hicks 13 times. Twelve of those shots hit him in the back. The victim's mother filed a lawsuit against the cops for wrongfully shooting her son, and her attorney charged that the cops fired "finishing shots" at Mr. Hicks as he lay prone underneath the coffee table. City lawyers claimed that he still posed a threat because he was moving and could reach the knife. One cop initially admitted that Mr. Hicks had dropped the knife during the incident, then changed his story to say that he held onto it until the end. A jury awarded the victim's mother's estate $6.1 million in May, 1998 (she died of unrelated causes prior to the verdict). Lawyers for the city appealed the verdict. **Source:** The Washington Post, 11/17/98

Sutoria Moore   19   —

July 15, 1994. Washington, D.C.:
Mr. Moore, an unarmed motorist, was shot in the back of the neck and killed by Det. Roosevelt Askew, who allegedly feared that the victim was about to run over Sgt. William Middleton with his car during a traffic stop. Det. Askew later pleaded guilty to filing a false statement, admitting that there was no danger to Sgt. Middleton and that he lied to cover-up the incident. He claimed that his gun discharged accidentally. He agreed to resign from the police force, and was sentenced by a federal judge to two years probation (no jail time) and a $5,000 fine. Other cops aided in the cover-up. Pointing fingers over who first had the idea to cover-up the incident, Sgt. Middleton said in a deposition that Det. Askew had said, "Come on, Sarge, help me out," moments after the shooting. The sergeant also contended that the shooting was not accidental. A lawsuit filed by the victim's mother against the city was settled for $375,000. **Source:** Human Rights Watch, Shielded from Justice (1998), pp. 381-382; The Washington Post, 1/6/98 & 11/16/98

Dion Hinnant   —   *Black*

May 26, 1994. near Atlantic Terrace housing complex:
Mr. Hinnant was shot in the back and killed by D.C. Police Officer Jack Yezzi after a traffic stop followed by a foot chase. Officer Yezzi and three other cops pulled over Mr. Hinnant's car on a "sketchy, day-old tip that someone in a gold Acura was carrying drugs into the area," according to the newspaper. Mr. Hinnant allegedly grabbed a gun from the car and ran with three officers in pursuit (the fourth one arrested Mr. Hinnant's passenger). The newspaper said Mr. Hinnant was on probation and may have run to avoid being caught with a gun in his car. Officer Yezzi claimed that Mr. Hinnant ignored several orders to stop, continued running, and "twist[ed] his torso to the left, lifting his left arm and curling his right hand beneath it, so the gun was pointed at the officers." Officer Yezzi shot Mr. Hinnant and claims the victim staggered a few steps before falling down. But three civilian witnesses disputed the police account, saying either that Mr. Hinnant dropped the gun before Officer Yezzi shot him or that they never saw him with a gun. Ballistic evidence also contradicted the police account. The gun was recovered 31 feet behind the victim's body, showing that he dropped it before he was shot and not simply before he "staggered four steps" after being shot. No drugs were found on or near Mr. Hinnant or his car, and his passenger said they were going home from a pickup basketball game. Police covered up the murder, initially writing that the gun was "recovered from Mr. Hinnant," not from 31 feet behind him, and that he was stopped for "possible narcotics violations" without saying that no drugs were found. At various times, cops changed their stories about what had happened. But an internal investigation ruled the shooting justified, and Officer Yezzi was later promoted to sergeant. In May 1995, the victim's family filed a lawsuit against the police. **Source:** The Washington Post, 11/17/98

Adesola Adesina   34   —

March 23, 1994. Greyhound Bus terminal, First St. NE:
Mr. Adesina, a cab driver, was shot and killed by off-duty D.C. Police Officer Troy Ray, who was working as a security guard at the bus station. Officer Ray tried to arrest Mr. Adesina for failing to display a taxi license and ran 35 feet to block him from fleeing at an exit ramp. The officer claimed that the taxi was driven towards him and that he feared being run over. He fired one shot into the windshield as the cab supposedly came at him and two more into the driver's window after the cab allegedly hit him. The bullet deflected off Mr. Adesina's arm and went into his chest, killing him. The U.S. Attorney's office declined to prosecute, ruling that the shooting was justified. **Source:** The Washington Post, 1998

Unidentified Man   —   —

1994. Washington, D.C.:
The man was shot and killed by off-duty D.C. Police Officer Terrence Shepherd. Officer Shepherd claimed the man threatened him with a knife, and the shooting was ruled justified. About two years later, Officer Shepherd shot and killed Eric Antonio Anderson while on-duty. **Source:** The Washington Post, 11/16/98

Nathaniel "Bud" Mitchell   38   —

May 18, 1993. Marshall Heights:

D.C. Police Officers Lawrence D. Walker and Dwayne Mitchell fired 23 shots at the victim, hitting him four times, including three from behind. Bud Mitchell fled to a relative's apartment, then collapsed on the couch and died. The newspaper referred to the victim as "an unemployed sometime panhandler who had served time for robbery in the 1980's." Officers Walker and Mitchell claimed they saw Bud Mitchell threaten his drinking partner with a toy gun. He allegedly ran as they approached, then supposedly turned and pointed the toy gun at them as they chased him up a hill. After shooting Bud Mitchell, the two cops picked up and passed around the toy gun in violation of departmental rules concerning handling of evidence. Police did not test the two cops' blood alcohol level even though they admitted drinking a beer earlier that evening. Officer Walker later claimed that he was still in his car when the victim first pointed the gun at him, and said he did not mention this earlier because, "I forgot, I guess." Officer Walker was involved in five shootings, two of them fatal, in a ten-month period in 1992 and 1993, and a sixth shooting the following year. Two months before killing Bud Mitchell, he shot and killed someone else. As of Nov. 1998, Officer Mitchell remained on the force and had been involved in four additional shootings since 1994. The four additional shootings came out during a deposition in a lawsuit filed by a woman who charged that Officer Walker had brutalized her during an arrest. **Source:** The Washington Post, 11/17/98

Telulope Awonie   41   —

April 8, 1993. Shepherd St. NW (900 block):

D.C. Police Officer Daniel Hall approached a car parked in an alley. He claims that the driver, Mr. Awonie, tried to pull away and hit him. Officer Hall fired 14 times, killing Mr. Awonie and hitting nearby garages, cars, and apartment windows. Officer Hall was put on administrative leave with pay. Four years later, the U.S. Attorney's office announced that the cop would not be prosecuted. **Source:** The Washington Post, 1998

Unidentified Person   19   —

March 1993. Washington, D.C.:

D.C. Police Officer Lawrence D. Walker shot the victim in the back and killed him. The victim was allegedly an "armed drug suspect." Officer Walker was involved in five shootings, two of them fatal, in a ten month period in 1992 and 1993, and a sixth shooting the following year. All six shootings were ruled justified. Officer Walker and his partner, Officer Dwayne Mitchell, were put on routine administrative leave after this killing but received permission from their supervisors to continue carrying their guns for protection. Two months later, they shot and killed Nathaniel "Bud" Mitchell. As of Nov. 1998, Officer Walker remained on the force. He had been involved in four more shootings since 1994. **Source:** The Washington Post, 11/17/98

WASHINGTON STATE

Name	Age	Nationality	Photo

Eric A. Larsen   23   —

March 24, 1999. Graham:

Mr. Larsen was shot and killed during an alleged shootout with Pierce County Police Officer Corey Olson after a traffic stop. Cops claim the victim was wanted for a killing in Tacoma a month earlier. The shooting was ruled justified on Apr. 8, 1999. Mr. Larsen was from Spanaway. **Source:** Seattle Post-Intelligencer, 3/26/99 & 4/9/99

Karl Eugene Walton   37   —

March 18, 1999. Lynden:

Mr. Walton was shot to death by a Blaine police officer outside a barn at a dairy farm. Police had been called because Mr. Walton had allegedly threatened someone at the farm. The victim was shot when he supposedly refused to get down on the ground and appeared to grab something at his waist. He was unarmed. Mr. Walton was from Ferndale. **Source:** Seattle Times, 3/19/99

Max Martinez   39   —

March 12, 1999. Federal Way:

Mr. Martinez was shot to death by two police officers after a traffic stop when he allegedly threatened them with a handgun. **Source:** Seattle Times, 3/16/99

Sovate Sou   14   —

March 11, 1999. Spanaway:

Sovate Sou, a 14-year-old boy, died when his car hit a tree while being chased by police. Cops claim the car was stolen. There were two boys in the car, and it is unclear if the victim was the driver or the passenger. He was from Tacoma. **Source:** Seattle Post-Intelligencer, 3/12/99; Tacoma News-Tribune, 3/13/99

Nicholas Ryan   23   —

February 23, 1999. Kingston:

Mr. Ryan was shot to death during an alleged gun battle with State Trooper Jason Linn after a traffic stop of a car in which he was a passenger. Mr. Ryan was allegedly wanted on a burglary warrant. **Source:** Seattle Post-Intelligencer, 3/26/99

Kenneth Maurice Boyd   24   *Black*   👁

January 4, 1999. Tacoma:

Mr. Boyd was shot in the head by Tacoma Police Officer John Bair while he allegedly dragged the officer with his car. Mr. Boyd died later at the hospital. The officer, who claimed to have been investigating suspected drug activity, said that he reached into Mr. Boyd's car and was pinned against the door when Mr. Boyd drove off. The car crashed after about a block and a half when the officer shot Mr. Boyd. Cindy Clinton, a witness, said the police then pepper-sprayed, beat, and kicked the surviving passenger, Everett Watkins, and arrested him for allegedly assaulting them. Ms. Clinton said, "That was the worst thing that I'd ever seen." Mr. Watkins, the passenger, said that he thought Boyd had driven off because he was startled when the officers suddenly opened the doors on both sides of the car without warning and that the shooting of his friend was not justified. The Tacoma Ministerial Alliance met with the Tacoma police chief the next day asking for an explanation. On Mar. 2, 1999, friends and relatives of Mr. Boyd crammed the Tacoma City Council meeting and demanded justice in this case. Mr. Boyd's obituary referred to his large extended family and read, in part, "Kenneth always put family and friends first. Kenneth is survived by his common-law wife, Allyson Waller, his daughter, 5-year-old Ki-ondra Denise Boyd, of Tacoma.... His hobbies included playing basketball, football, and rapping." **Source:** Seattle Times, 1/5/99; Tacoma News-Tribune, 1/6/99, 1/7/99, 1/8/99, 1/9/99, & 3/3/99

Patrick Raimond   39   —

December 28, 1998. Everett:

Mr. Raimond was shot to death by three Snohomish County sheriff's deputies on the front porch of his home. The deputies, who were allegedly trying to serve an arrest warrant on Mr. Raimond's former roommate, claim Mr. Raimond answered the door with a gun, thus sparking the shooting. **Source:** Seattle Times, 12/31/98

Michael R. Ealy   35   *Black*

December 28, 1998. Seattle:

Mr. Ealy supposedly died of a heart attack after struggling with ambulance personnel and police. Police said they subdued him in the ambulance, but would not say how. Afterward he was "unresponsive" and died five hours later on Dec. 29, 1998. Mr. Ealy was initially taken to the hospital because he was "acting bizarrely" on Dexter Avenue North near downtown Seattle. According to inquest testimony, he was attempting to stop cars and asking for help. Autopsy results, released on Jan. 14, 1999, did not determine an official cause of death, but stated that there was "evidence of neck and chest compression" and then went on to point to heart disease and cocaine intoxication as factors. Mr. Ealy's family's attorney, Lembhard Howell, said, "This is not a case of an OD or a man with a bad heart. His injuries [from police] caused his death." An inquest found the killing justified on Mar. 31, 1999. The family has vowed to get justice in this case and many community activists have taken up the case. **Source:** Seattle Times, 12/31/98, 1/15/99, & 4/1/99; Tacoma News-Tribune, 12/30/98, 1/30/99

David Lewis Lambertsen   31   —

November 25, 1998. Lakewood:
Mr. Lambertsen was shot by Pierce County Sheriff's Deputy Joe McDonald. He died at the hospital. Authorities claim Mr. Lambertsen's wife called 911 to report that her husband was threatening to shoot himself and police with his shotgun. Police arrived and shot him, claiming he refused to drop the shotgun and aimed it at the officers. The prosecutor ruled the shooting justifiable. Mr. Lambertsen is survived by his wife, Sue Marie Lambertsen. **Source:** Tacoma News-Tribune, 11/27/98, 12/4/98, & 12/23/98

Horace Register   74   —

October 26, 1998. Pasco:
Mr. Register died, allegedly in a shootout with police in a grocery store parking lot. Cops claim he was a suspect in the shooting death of another man. **Source:** Tacoma News-Tribune, 10/27/98

John Henry Ashley   49   —

September 10, 1998. Seattle (King County Jail):
Mr. Ashley died in the King County Jail. Jail officials alleged that he died from heroin withdrawal and a stroke. Although he had been in jail for three days for suspicion of possession of heroin, he was not treated for heroin withdrawal. An inquest was ordered on Dec. 4, 1998. Mr. Ashley was from Kent and worked for the Department of Transportation. He is survived by his long-time girlfriend, Karen Conley, a 12-year-old daughter, and one other child. **Source:** Tacoma News-Tribune, 12/4/98; South County Journal, 12/7/98

Samath Mom   18   *Vietnamese*

August 29, 1998. Tacoma:
Samath Mom allegedly hanged himself with a sheet two and a half hours after being booked into Pierce County Jail as a suspect in the Tacoma Trang Dai restaurant massacre. He died in the hospital the next day. His family suspects foul play. He is survived by his sister, Saoeun Mom, brothers, Tum Mom and John Phet, and father, Mom Phet. **Source:** Tacoma News-Tribune, 8/30/98

Mary Millard   88   —

July 18, 1998. Tacoma:
Ms. Millard was injured when the van she was driving was struck by a car driven by Anthony Jay Huver, who was being pursued by police for an alleged forgery. She died two days later at the hospital. **Source:** Tacoma News-Tribune, 7/21/98

Howard L. Aga   17   —

June 22, 1998. Seattle:
Mr. Aga died when his car struck a pickup truck at the conclusion of a Seattle Police car chase. His car was allegedly stolen. **Source:** Tacoma News-Tribune, 6/24/98

Michael Valentine   39   —

June 21, 1998. Tacoma:
Mr. Valentine was shot to death by Tacoma Police Officer Christine Coulter after police responded to a domestic dispute at his sister-in-law's house. Officer Coulter claimed that Mr. Valentine fired at her and she returned fire. Mr. Valentine was from Sedro-Woolley. He is survived by his wife Brenda Valentine, two sons, ages seven and 16, and his parents in Lakewood. **Source:** Tacoma News-Tribune, 6/30/98

Douglas J. Lefebvre   41   —

June 12, 1998. Chewelah:
Mr. Lefebvre was shot by a Spokane County Sheriff's Department SWAT Team after a six-hour standoff. There is videotape of this incident, which reportedly shows police shooting the suspect as he retreats. Mr. Lefebvre was in a Spokane hospital in critical condition. It is not clear if he survived. He was supposedly wanted for a robbery and a carjacking. **Source:** Vancouver Columbian, 6/13/98

Kevin Rangitsch   36   *white*

June 9, 1998. Bothell:

Kevin Rangitsch was shot four times and killed after a car chase by King County Sheriff's Deputy Orford and Police Trainee Naylor. Many other area police were involved in the chase. The chase, which started over an alleged cracked windshield, violated King County Police policy of not engaging in high-speed pursuit for traffic violations. Information obtained through public disclosure law by a member of the October 22 Coalition proves police misread Mr. Rangitsch's license plate near the beginning of the pursuit and jumped to the mistaken assumption that his car was stolen, thereby intensifying the chase. At the conclusion of the chase, police rammed the driver's side of Mr. Rangitsch's car, then shot him when he allegedly pointed a shotgun at them. The two police officers took several days and consulted with a police guild representative before writing their statements about the incident. Nevertheless, their statements contradicted each other in important aspects. After Mr. Rangitsch's death, the press ridiculed him, saying "Kevin Rangitsch did dumb things in cars," because he had been earlier convicted of five counts of vehicular homicide stemming from a 1983 car crash, for which he served 13 years in prison, ending in 1996. The passenger in Mr. Rangitsch's car, James Foote, who survived the incident, has retained a lawyer and announced his intention to file a lawsuit. He reported that, while Mr. Rangitsch tried to remove the shotgun from a case in the back seat of the car, he was not able to, and that he never came close to pointing it at the officers. At least one of the shots hit Mr. Rangitsch in the back. He was shot more than once and then crawled onto Mr. Foote's lap, where he was apparently trying to get out the passenger's side door of the car. Mr. Foote reported that Mr. Rangitsch looked him in the eye and said, "I'm dying," as another shot ripped open his throat. Mr. Foote was covered in his friend's blood and has not been able to work since the incident. According to police reports, Mr. Rangitsch then crawled out the driver's side window, where he staggered and fell face first on the ground. Police handcuffed him, but did not administer first aid as he lay bleeding to death. He allegedly died later at the hospital. No inquest was held and the police were not prosecuted. Mr. Rangitsch had three children and was married when he went to prison in 1983. After his release, he was an aspiring author, who was trying to sell several books he had written. He worked in electronic repair. He is survived by his mother, Lillian Rangitsch, who lives in Montana, at least one sister, and his girlfriend. **Source:** Seattle Times, 6/11/98; extensive police reports obtained through public disclosure requests; eyewitness account

Trent Lincoln   38   —

April 30, 1998. Centralia:

Mr. Lincoln died when his car crashed into a house at the end of a police chase for suspected drunk driving. **Source:** Everett Herald, 5/1/98

Christopher Kraft   35   —

April 28, 1998. Spokane:

Mr. Kraft died when his motorcycle crashed while being chased by Spokane police for a traffic violation. **Source:** Spokane Spokesman-Review, 5/22/98

Anthony Tyrone "Smurf" Davis, Jr.   16   —

April 12, 1998. Tacoma:

Tacoma police pursued Mr. Davis, who was driving a car that police claim was stolen. His family, however, insisted that the car was not stolen. In the resulting high-speed chase, Mr. Davis crashed and died. He is survived by his grandmother and his father who raised him. Leslie Campbell, his father's fiancee, said of him, "He had a lot of friends who really loved him. He was really close to his family. We're trying to raise money to get the funeral together. We love you, Smurf!" **Source:** Tacoma News-Tribune, 4/14/98

Unidentified Man   19   —

March 28, 1998. Spokane:

The man died when his motorcycle crashed while being chased by Spokane police. The pursuit lasted about a minute before the crash. **Source:** Spokane Spokesman-Review, 3/29/98

Shannon M. Bradley	28	—

February 22, 1998. Longview:
Ms. Bradley died in a car crash after being chased by a Washington State Patrol trooper. Her car was allegedly stolen.
Source: Vancouver Columbian, 2/23/98

Shaun Rutledge	20	—

February 7, 1998. Tacoma:
Mr. Rutledge was killed as he walked on the sidewalk near his home. He was struck by a car driven by William Rosemond, who was being pursued by Pierce County sheriffs deputies for a traffic violation. Mr. Rutledge worked at a Tony Roma's Restaurant and had planned to attend school locally. He is survived by his two roommates, Julie Rosing and Tom Horstmann, his mother and his girlfriend who both live in Olympia, and his father who lives in Portland. Mr. Rosemond, the driver of the car being chased, also died in the accident. **Source:** Tacoma News-Tribune, 2/8/98 & 2/9/98

William Rosemond	32	—

February 7, 1998. Tacoma:
Mr. Rosemond was being pursued by Pierce County sheriffs deputies for a traffic violation. His car struck and killed a pedestrian, Shaun Rutledge, and then crashed into a convenience store wall, killing Mr. Rosemond as well. **Source:** Tacoma News-Tribune, 2/8/98 & 2/9/98

Elsie Delos Reyes	80	—

February 2, 1998. Renton:
Ms. Reyes was killed when her car was struck by a car driven by another car being pursued by Renton police for an alleged burglary. The driver of the car being pursued was reportedly a candidate for "Three Strikes You're Out" life incarceration.
Source: Tacoma News-Tribune, 2/4/98

Robert Wayne Guy, Jr.	19	*Black-Latino*	👁

December 29, 1997. Seattle:
Mr. Guy, also known as "Junior," was killed by King County Jail guards. According to inquest testimony, after an alleged "drug delirium," Mr. Guy was subdued by eight to 12 guards, bound hand and foot, pepper-sprayed, gagged, strapped face down to a "restraint board," then denied CPR for at least eight minutes after his pulse and breathing stopped. He was revived, but lapsed into a coma and later died. His family was not notified for another 16 hours. When they did see him, they could see that he had been severely beaten. The Nov. 1998, inquest absolved the guards of all charges. Relatives formed the "Justice for Junior Memorial Task Force" and continue to demand an end to police and guard brutality and justice in this case. Junior was from Yakima. He is survived by loving family and friends. **Source:** Tacoma News-Tribune, 2/11/98; Seattle Times; victim's family and supporters

Aaron Lee Ahern	25	—
Michael Judson Brock	24	—

October 17, 1997. Vancouver:
"Two men died in a shootout with police and a third man escaped following two bank robberies that were committed one after the other...," according to newspaper reports. **Source:** Associated Press, 10/18/97; Vancouver Columbian, 10/26/97

Theresa Henderson	24	*Black*

October 2, 1997. south Seattle:
According to friends and family, Ms. Henderson died in south Seattle after police choked her when she tried to swallow a small amount of cocaine. This case has never appeared in newspapers or any "official record." **Source:** friends and family of victim

Emily Milonas   78   —

September 20, 1997. Tacoma:
After a "scuffle" with police, Ms. Milonas allegedly suffered a heart attack and died while handcuffed in the back of a Tacoma Police patrol car. Her 70-year-old male companion was also violently arrested and accused of vandalizing cars in the Tacoma Central Cinemas parking lot. He also suffered a heart attack later in jail, but survived. Cops claim the elderly couple were strongly resisting them. Ms. Milonas was from Spanaway. The following appeared in Tacoma News-Tribune on Sept. 20, 1998: "It's been a year since we lost you, Mom. We love and miss you. Your loving family - daughter Barbara, son Lee, grandchildren Gary, Laura, Bill, and all who knew and loved you." **Source:** Tacoma News-Tribune, 9/22/97 & 9/23/97

Michael David Oakes   30   —

July 13, 1997. Vancouver:
Mr. Oakes was shot to death by Vancouver police as he allegedly threatened them with a hatchet. **Source:** Vancouver Columbian, 7/14/97

Unidentified Man   39   —

July 6, 1997. Vancouver:
The man was shot by Clark County sheriff's deputies after he allegedly drove into an officer with a truck and then tried to knife one of them. He died later in a Portland, Oregon hospital. **Source:** Tacoma News-Tribune, 7/7/97

Nicholas Struckman   19   —

June 13, 1997. Spokane (in custody):
It appears that the authorities claim this was a suicide in custody. Mr. Struckman's father has come forward to question the police version of events. **Source:** Spokane Spokesman-Review, 10/31/97

James J. Willis   34   —

June 4, 1997. Lake Stevens:
Mr. Willis was shot to death by off-duty Snohomish County Deputy Michael Mansur after a traffic stop for "reckless driving." The officer claimed that Mr. Willis had a knife while standing 15 feet away and that he had "no choice" but to fire. Witnesses said that he was not threatening the police when he was shot. According to the Seattle Times, his wife had just filed for divorce and he had lost his job shortly before the incident. A July 14, 1997 inquest ruled that the shooting was justified. Afterwards, Mr. Willis' wife, Angela Willis, said, "Justice wasn't done." **Source:** Seattle Times, 7/15/97 & 7/17/97

David L. Seago   35   —

May 28, 1997. Lakewood:
Mr. Seago was shot three times and killed by Pierce County Deputy Robert Glenn Carpenter after he allegedly fired two shots at the deputy with an assault rifle. Mr. Seago was reportedly drunk and had supposedly shot at and fled a bail bondsman earlier. Prosecutors ruled the shooting was justified. Mr. Seago was from Tillicum. **Source:** Tacoma News-Tribune, 5/31/97 & 6/10/97

Joe R. Lawson   41   —

April 15, 1997. Spokane:
Mr. Lawson was shot to death by Spokane Police Officer Patrick Dobrow after he allegedly charged at them with a knife during a domestic violence call at his home. The Spokane County prosecutor ruled that the shooting was justified. **Source:** Spokane Spokesman-Review, 4/16/97 & 5/1/97

Amy Sue Deines   35   —

April 11, 1997. Auburn:

Ms. Deines died as the result of a high-speed police chase of a car in which she was a passenger. The Auburn police allege that they were chasing the driver of the car, Richard Martin, on suspicion of burglary. The chase ended when Martin's car struck another car head on, killing Ms. Deines. Martin and two passengers in the other car were seriously injured. Ms. Deines was from Seattle. **Source:** Tacoma News-Tribune, 4/13/97 & 4/14/97

Laurence Buck   44   —

April 4, 1997. Tacoma:

Mr. Buck was shot in the head and killed by security guard Hans Allard at Tacoma Boat - where Mr. Buck had recently been laid-off after working there for 17 years. Police arrived within minutes and exonerated the guard. After allegedly breaking into his former workplace to steal copper wire, Mr. Buck had been hiding with an accomplice when they were discovered by the guard. The guard claimed that Mr. Buck charged him with a pipe. However, no pipe was found and the other suspect said that Mr. Buck complied with the guard's command to stop, but was shot anyway. This testimony was disregarded by police, and the guard was never prosecuted. Mr. Buck is survived by his wife Gloria, three children Holly, Eric, and Angie, and an 18-month-old grandson Connor. **Source:** Seattle Times, 7/27/97

Michael Ray Mitchell   22   *Native American*

March 13, 1997. Tacoma:

Mr. Mitchell was killed in his home by Tacoma Police Officer Mark Fedderson. His parents called the police because they were concerned that he was suicidal. The officer claimed that Mr. Mitchell charged at him with a knife and he had no choice but to fire. Mr. Mitchell's parents said that their son was shot and killed after he walked toward the officer with his arms spread, saying, "Shoot me, shoot me." He was allegedly armed with a folding pocketknife. The shooting was ruled justified by police. Officer Fedderson had earlier killed Rot Nguyen on Jan. 29, 1993. Mr. Mitchell attended Chief Leschi Schools and had recently returned to Tacoma from a cross-country Native American Youth Run organized by Native American leader Dennis Banks. Native American activists organized a memorial and protest walk and relay run for Mr. Mitchell on June 7, 1997. Mr. Mitchell is survived by his parents, William and Earline Mitchell. **Source:** Tacoma News-Tribune, 3/14/97, 6/5/97, & 6/8/97

David McClure   —   —

December 31, 1996. Kalama:

Mr. McClure was shot to death by a Washington State Patrol trooper as two Kalama police officers and 2 state troopers were serving arrest warrants on him at his home. **Source:** Vancouver Columbian, 1/2/97

Tama T. Ava   43   *Samoan*

December 20, 1996. Federal Way:

Mr. Ava was killed by "police restraint" in Federal Way after a traffic stop of the van his wife was driving. Police decided to arrest Mr. Ava because he refused to talk to them. They do not allege that he broke any law. One witness testified that police gave each other "high fives" after Mr. Ava was subdued. An inquest ruled on Apr. 24, 1997, that "he wouldn't have died if he didn't struggle and didn't have a heart condition," but that officers "contributed to Ava's death by restraining him." The officers were not prosecuted. The victim's wife had warned the police of her husband's heart condition while they were assaulting him. Mr. Ava is survived by his wife Masina, daughter Christline, brother Asofaatasi Vala Vala, and other family. The family filed a $5.5 million lawsuit. **Source:** Seattle Times, 4/25/97; Tacoma News-Tribune, 4/22/97

Robert K. Mills   54   —

December 8, 1996. Twin Lakes:

Mr. Mills was killed at his home in an alleged shootout with Kootenai County sheriff's deputies. **Source:** Spokane Spokesman-Review, 12/11/96

| **William Scott Scurlock** | 41 | *white* | |

November 27, 1996. Seattle:

Mr. Scurlock allegedly shot himself in the head and died in a camper trailer after fleeing from a shoot-out with police after a Seattle bank robbery. Witnesses at the scene, however, reported over 30 rounds fired by Seattle police at the camper before his body was found, and police reported that the body contained numerous bullet wounds. He is survived by his parents, William and Mary Jane Scurlock of Olympia, cousin Stuart Scurlock, and sister Debbie. Mr. Scurlock was alleged to be the famous "Hollywood bank robber" and was from Olympia. **Source:** Tacoma News-Tribune, 11/29/96, 11/30/96, & 11/21/97

| **Ralf C. Sanjurjo** | 32 | — | ◉ |

November 15, 1996. Everett:

Mr. Sanjurjo was shot four times and killed by a Washington State Trooper after a traffic stop. He was unarmed. His family, who was not allowed to see his body after the killing because the police said it was "evidence," is demanding an inquest and/or prosecution. So far, they have been ignored. Mr. Sanjurjo graduated from Mountlake Terrace High School and joined the Navy. He had recently been working as a fisherman and had been living with his fiancee and her children in Marysville. He is also survived by his father, Antonio Sanjurjo-Manso, and stepmother, Julie Sanjurjo, of Mountlake Terrace. **Source:** Seattle Times, 12/13/96; Tacoma News-Tribune, 11/17/96; victim's family

| **Patty DiBartolo** | 39 | — | |

November 2, 1996. Spokane (South Hill Park):

Ms. DiBartolo was shot to death by her estranged husband, 18-year veteran Spokane County Sheriff's Deputy Thomas A. DiBartolo. Officer DiBartolo faked a robbery and shot his wife and then himself with her gun to cover-up the murder. He claimed that two Black men had mugged them in a park and shot his wife in the head and then himself during a struggle over the gun. This was proved false. The motive was reportedly insurance money. At a bail hearing after his father's arrest, Patty's 17-year-old son Nick spoke strongly against his father's release on bail, saying he feared his father would kill him or others in the family. He was released anyway. Officer DiBartolo was convicted of first-degree murder on Dec. 12, 1997, and sentenced to 26 years in prison. In an unusual development, a man that DiBartolo had tried to frame for his wife's murder and another who backed out as a key defense witness at the last minute were each killed in separate shooting incidents within two months of his conviction. On learning of the second death, Thomas DiBartolo's attorney, Maryann Moreno said, "My mouth fell open for about a minute... to have this happen to two people whose only link was as persons of interest in the DiBartolo murder seems totally bizarre." In addition to her son Nick, Patty DiBartolo is survived by her daughter Michelle Robinson, 20, and three other children. **Source:** Seattle Times, 2/14/97; Spokane Spokesman-Review, 2/18/98; Tacoma News-Tribune, 11/5/96

| **Shane L. Lowry** | 26 | — | |

October 3, 1996. Parkland:

Mr. Lowry was struck and dragged to his death as he walked across Pacific Avenue South by a squad car driven by Pierce County Deputy Kristine Elkins. Officer Elkins was driving at high speed with no emergency lights or sirens. Officer Elkins was punished by a two day suspension without pay. **Source:** Tacoma News-Tribune, 10/4/96, 12/16/96, 1/1/97, & 1/18/97

| **Bodegard Mitchell** | 84 | *Black* | ◉ |

September 30, 1996. Seattle:

Mr. Mitchell was killed by Seattle Police SWAT team after a five hour stand-off that started when a repairman came into his house and was kicked out by Mr. Mitchell. Police shot him multiple times in the chest. It was found that the gun he allegedly wielded actually contained non-lethal birdshot shells. Police evacuated the area before the killing, so there were no civilian witnesses. They did not videotape the confrontation. A news reporter witnessed police delay medical attention for Mr. Mitchell ten to 15 minutes while attending to minor injuries of one of the officers. An inquest later found the police were justified. In 1999, a scandal erupted when it was revealed that police at the scene had stolen (later returned) $10,000 in cash found in Mr. Mitchell's home after they killed him. **Source:** Tacoma News-Tribune, 10/1/96, 10/2/96; Seattle Medium; Seattle Post-Intelligencer, 3/26/99

Douglas Reagan   35   *white*   👁

September 30, 1996. Everett:

Mr. Reagan was detained and killed by Everett police after walking naked outside of his apartment due to disorientation from the use of a small amount of cocaine. After he was handcuffed and detained, he climbed out of the open police car and crawled along the ground. Police threw him headfirst to the sidewalk and repeatedly pepper-sprayed his face and mouth. Mr. Reagan yelled that he was unable to breathe. Police responded by sticking a towel in his face, kneeling on his back, and hog-tying him. Witnesses reported that he was dead at the scene. Hospital workers reported that the pepper spray on Mr. Reagan was so thick and toxic that they had to wear masks during the examination. The coroner, while admitting that the amount of cocaine in Mr. Reagan's system was "minimal," nevertheless went on to claim that the cause of death was cocaine toxicity. The official cause of death was listed as "undetermined." The Snohomish County Sheriff's Department found no wrongdoing. So far, they have not ordered an inquest. Doug Reagan is survived by his father Ken, mother Betty, wife Perna, daughter Melissa, and six brothers and sisters. His parents are seeking justice for his death.

Stanley Chambers   17   *Black & Native American*

September 22, 1996. Tacoma:

Mr. Chambers was shot in the back of the head and killed by Tacoma Police Officer Paul Strozewski. Mr. Chambers was shot while fleeing after a domestic violence incident with his girlfriend. The police claimed that they told him to stop and put up his hands and then shot him when he reached for his gun. They said that when they reached his body, he had his hand on his gun. However, Mr. Chambers' girlfriend's father, who witnessed the incident, said he heard no order to raise his hands and the body was found with one hand behind his back and another over his head. There was no mention of a hand on the gun. Furthermore, Mr. Chambers' gun was found to be unloaded. The shooting was ruled justified by the prosecutor. Mr. Chambers' sister had been killed in front of him in a drive-by-shooting four years earlier. After his death, he was remembered and honored by friends and family in a Native American healing ceremony. Mr. Chambers is survived by his mother Judy Matz, seven sisters and brothers, and his girlfriend, Tricia Boardman, who was 11 weeks pregnant with his child at the time of his death. **Source:** Tacoma News-Tribune, 9/24/96, 9/26/96, 10/4/96, & 10/7/96

Andre Rufus Stapleton   33   *Black*

September 1, 1996. Seattle (85th & Aurora):

Mr. Stapleton, a homeless man, was killed by Seattle Police at a convenience store in Seattle. Police claim that they don't know why he died. His death was captured on the store security videotape, and Seattle October 22nd Coalition activists were able to obtain a copy. The tape is unclear, but shows that Mr. Stapleton was physically alert before police arrived, and that when they arrived, he complied immediately with their order to "get down." He died in the ensuing one-sided "struggle." It is widely believed that Mr. Stapleton died from either a chokehold or pepper-spray. The Coroner's report, released on Sept. 26, 1996, said that death resulted partly from "restraint." Local and national media have not aired this shocking videotape, though it has been made available to them. An inquest was ordered, but the result is not known. **Source:** Seattle Times, 9/26/96 & 10/8/96; videotape of incident

---

Stacey Lee Mattice   21   *white*

August 17, 1996. Bonney Lake:

Mr. Mattice died in a car wreck while being chased by Pierce County Sheriffs for a traffic violation. **Source:** Tacoma News-Tribune, 8/19/96

Fred Muir   51   —

August 11, 1996. Sumner:

Mr. Muir was shot and killed in his home by Pierce County Police SWAT team sniper Eugene Allen after a nine hour standoff in which he allegedly shot at police. The shooting was ruled justified. Mr. Muir is survived by his wife, Susan Muir, and a daughter. **Source:** Tacoma News-Tribune, 8/12/96, 8/13/96, 9/28/96, & 10/1/96

James Bradley Wren   35   *white*

August 10, 1996. Preston:
Mr. Wren was killed by King County Police Sgt. Mathias Bachmeier. Sgt. Bachmeier, a decorated 25 year veteran officer, burned his own house down to collect on insurance, reportedly to raise money to join the professional bowlers tour. Later, when the investigation started to focus on him, he was allowed to continue to work as a police officer and he took the following actions. While responding to a domestic violence call alone, he kidnapped ("arrested") Mr. Wren from his home, tortured him until he signed a phony confession to setting the fire at Sgt. Bachmeier's house, killed him, and dumped the body on Cougar Mountain. Then, using this "confession," he protested his innocence in the arson fire investigation! Officer Bachmeier was convicted of first degree murder on June 13, 1997, and sentenced to life without parole. Sgt. Bachmeier had earlier killed Guadalupe Rios in 1988. Mr. Wren had earlier sued the police for a beating he received on June 8, 1990, and won $17,000. He had been working in construction, but since the beating, had only been able to do odd jobs. He was in the Air Force from 1979 to 1983, where he worked as a mechanic. James Wren is survived by his brother, Terry Wren, and mother, Shirley Wren, who lives in Malaga, and his step-father, Rex Wren. Rex and Shirley Wren filed a wrongful death suit against King County in federal court on Feb. 5, 1998. They charge that the county is liable because of their inaction in the earlier killing and that it has "paid substantial money settlements to settle brutality claims and other wrongful acts committed" by Sgt. Bachmeier. **Source:** Tacoma News-Tribune, 6/14/97 and others

Matt Acheson   25   *white*

August 3, 1996. Gold Bar:
Mr. Acheson was killed in Gold Bar when a man in a pickup truck being pursued by Snohomish County sheriffs and Gold Bar police for having expired license plate tabs crossed the centerline and struck Mr. Acheson's car head on. Originally, police falsely told the public they were chasing the truck because they thought it was stolen. The accident happened right after the police attempted to cut off the suspect vehicle. Attorney Tony Shapiro represented Mr. Acheson's parents and one of the injured passengers in the suspect vehicle in a lawsuit against the county and the town of Gold Bar. They received $600,000 in a settlement on Mar. 17, 1998. Jerry Sheehan of the Washington American Civil Liberties Union (ACLU) said, "We've been watching the issue of high-speed chases for about three years now, and we've realized that this is just another example of the use of deadly force." The officers involved were not reprimanded or charged with wrongdoing. Mr. Acheson was from Shoreline. He was a student at the University of Washington in Seattle. He is survived by his parents, James and Margaret Acheson. **Source:** Seattle Times, 3/18/98

Elmer L. Ingram   21   —

June 27, 1996. Colville:
Mr. Ingram was shot to death by Stevens County sheriff's deputies, allegedly in a shootout after a burglary of a gun store. **Source:** Spokane Spokesman-Review, 12/3/96

Chen Thach   30   *Vietnamese*

April 30, 1996. Tacoma:
Mr. Thach's car was struck broadside shortly after he left his brother's house at 1:00 a.m. by a Tacoma police car that was traveling at high speed without emergency lights or sirens, according to witnesses and police. The police said they never saw him. He died at the hospital a few hours later. No charges were filed against the police. Mr. Thach is survived by his girlfriend, four-year-old son, and three-year-old daughter, brother Dien Thach, who is a Buddhist monk, and many friends and family. He and his brother had moved to the U.S. in 1989 for a better life. He worked at a furniture company in Seattle. **Source:** Tacoma News-Tribune, 5/1/96 & 8/13/96

Christine Wetrich   14   —

April 24, 1996. Tacoma:
Ms. Wetrich died at the hospital after being found unconscious in her cell at the Remann Hall youth detention facility in Tacoma. She was jailed for running away from a foster care home. The victim died from untreated (and apparently undiagnosed) acute leukemia. A Remann Hall representative, Dan Erker said, "I don't believe that we did anything inappropriately given our information." A DSHS administrator said, "We all thought she had the flu." Her mother, Cindy Wetrich, said that the Remann Hall staff believed her daughter was faking. **Source:** Tacoma News-Tribune, 4/25/96

| **Terry Grubham** | 33 | — | |

March 27, 1996. Renton:

Mr. Grubham died when his car was hit head on by a station wagon driven by two Renton teenagers being chased by Renton police. The teenagers were supposedly wanted for a burglary earlier that day. Mr. Grubham, who was from Kent, is survived by his nine-year-old twins and family who live in Idaho. **Source:** Tacoma News-Tribune, 3/28/96

| **Scott Waterhouse** | 30 | — | |

January 23, 1996. Spokane:

Mr. Waterhouse died after being arrested on a warrant after a traffic stop by Spokane police. Police say that they don't know why he died. Mr. Waterhouse was from Fairfield, CT. **Source:** Spokane Spokesman-Review, 2/1/96

| **Unidentified Woman** | 39 | — | |

January 22, 1996. Spokane:

The woman was shot to death at her home by two Spokane County sheriff's deputies after she allegedly shot a third deputy in the chest with a shotgun. The deputy was not seriously injured. **Source:** Spokane Spokesman-Review, 1/23/96

| **Michael Dries** | 38 | — | |

January 22, 1996. Bellevue:

Mr. Dries was shot to death in Bellevue after a traffic stop by the Washington State Patrol. Police claim that he had a felony warrant, ran from them, then approached them with a knife, forcing them to shoot. There are no other known witnesses. **Source:** Tacoma News-Tribune, 1/28/96 & 1/29/96

| **Edward Anderson** | 28 | *Black* | 👁 |

January 15, 1996. Seattle:

Mr. Anderson's wife allegedly called police for domestic violence at her house. Responding officers chased Mr. Anderson into the back yard, where he tripped over a fence. According to police testimony at the inquest, Officer William Edwards approached Anderson with his gun drawn as Anderson was lying on his back, hands raised, his feet still up in the air hung up on the fence. He wasn't wearing a shirt and was unarmed. The officer shot him in the throat from 18 inches away, killing him. After the shooting, the officer at first claimed that the gun "went off by itself". Later, after the gun was tested and this was found to be impossible, he changed his story and said, "maybe my finger slipped." The inquest found that this was justified. Many witnesses were angry and protested immediately after the killing, calling it "an execution." Only one of these witnesses testified at the inquest, and he contradicted the police version of events. Later, some of the officers who were on the scene when Mr. Anderson was killed upheld the shooting because they said that Mr. Anderson was a criminal. Eddy Anderson was well-known in the Central Area of Seattle, nicknamed "Steady Eddy." He lived in Seattle most of his life. He is survived by his family. Less than two years later, Officer Edwards was present at the scene of the shooting of another young Black man, Alfred Lewis, on Aug. 25, 1997. In that case, Officer Edwards testified in court that he "was attempting to get in position" to shoot Mr. Lewis when he was shot by other officers. Mr. Lewis survived that incident, but was seriously injured. **Source:** Seattle Times, 5/24/96; Tacoma News-Tribune, 1/16/96; victim's family; witnesses

| **Unidentified Man** | — | — | |

December 28, 1995. Spokane:

The man was shot and killed by police after a car chase stemming from an alleged bank robbery. Another person in the car was not injured. **Source:** Spokane Spokesman-Review, 12/29/95

| **Don Stowell** | 41 | — | |

December 13, 1995. Spokane:

Mr. Stowell was shot four times and killed after a high-speed car chase by Spokane County police. Police allege that he was armed and suicidal and that he might have shot himself as well. **Source:** Spokane Spokesman-Review, 12/14/95

Carl Bolton   31   —

October 29, 1995. Spokane:

Mr. Bolton was shot to death by Spokane police after he allegedly threatened them with a pellet gun. **Source:** Spokane Spokesman-Review, 10/30/95

Unidentified Man   28   —

September 3, 1995. Spokane County Jail:

The newspaper reported, "A 28-year-old Spokane man died at the Spokane County Jail Sunday morning, less than ten minutes after being restrained [by five officers] and placed in a holding cell. The cause of death has not been determined." **Source:** Spokane Spokesman-Review, 9/4/95

Tisha Ann Storm   18   —

June 7, 1995. Cascade Park:

Ms. Storm died in a crash at the conclusion of a police car chase from Oregon to Washington State. She flashed a peace sign at the officers during the chase. Police were attempting to pull her over for a traffic violation. Three other people were also injured in the crash. Ms. Storm was from Hubbard, Oregon. **Source:** Vancouver Columbian, 6/8/95

Thomas Roy Smith   27   —

May 26, 1995. Puyallup:

Mr. Smith supposedly tried to carjack someone and drove the wrong way on the freeway during a desperate police car chase. Puyallup police officer Dalan Brokaw shot him to death when he allegedly pointed a gun at the officer. Mr. Smith was a candidate for a "Three-Strikes-You're-Out" life sentence. Pierce County decided not to do an inquest, because "there are no disputed facts." Smith's aunt-in-law, Gloria Rowland of Tacoma, said despite his problems, Smith had a good heart. She recalled when he visited her in the hospital a few years ago when her son was sick: "Tommy came in to a special room at the hospital that they'd set up for me so I could stay. He said, 'I came to sit with you. You need people too,' and he would not leave me," Rowland said. "He was a wonderful boy. He did some bad things, but that doesn't make him bad." **Source:** Tacoma News-Tribune, 5/27/95, 6/7/95, & 6/20/95

Steven Roy Brink   30   —

May 20, 1995. Bonney Lake:

Mr. Brink "died Sunday after he was subdued by Bonney Lake police so paramedics could treat him." According to Bonney Lake police, Mr. Brink's girlfriend called paramedics to her home because he was agitated and having trouble breathing. Before he was treated, police spent five to ten minutes subduing him. He then "grew lethargic and stopped breathing". Police say there is no reason why he would have died, that maybe it was a drug overdose. Autopsy results stated that he died of "acute methamphetamine intoxication" and the death was ruled "accidental." His parents filed suit in May 1996 charging that officers handcuffed, beat, pepper-sprayed, and brutalized their son. They say their son died from "positional asphyxia" when a Bonney Lake police officer knocked him to the floor, pinned him face down and struck him several times. His parents said that Mr. Brink had worked as an informant for the Bonney Lake Police Department. He is survived by his girlfriend, his parents, four siblings, and a grandmother. **Source:** Tacoma News-Tribune, 5/23/95, 7/1/95, & 5/25/96

Nolan L. Davis   38   —

May 3, 1995. Stanwood:

Mr. Davis was shot and killed at his home by a Snohomish County Sheriff's SWAT Team after he allegedly refused to put down a rifle. Cops claim he had previously shot and killed his father. **Source:** Tacoma News-Tribune, 5/4/95

Antonio Silo Dunsmore   31   *Filipino*   👁

April 22, 1995. Seattle:

A "man with gun" call to police led to a confrontation outside the Garfield Community Center in Seattle. Mr. Dunsmore was shot by eight different officers and was hit at least 19 times. The "gun" turned out to be a water pistol. An inquest later determined the shooting to be justified. At least two of the officers who shot Mr. Dunsmore later participated in the killing of Edward Anderson on Jan. 15, 1996. Mr. Dunsmore is survived by his mother Lourdes Dunsmore, who filed a federal wrongful-death lawsuit on Apr. 22, 1998. **Source:** Seattle Times, 4/24/98; Tacoma News-Tribune, 4/23/95

Viniamin Polevoy   20   —

April 8, 1995. Shoreline:

Mr. Polevoy was killed when he crashed his pickup at the end of a Lake Forest Park police chase. Two passengers in another car and Mr. Polevoy's 11-year-old brother were also injured. Officer Tim Langan was chasing him for alleged traffic violations. Mr. Polevoy was from Kirkland. **Source:** Tacoma News-Tribune, 4/10/95

Christina Varner   15   —

March 22, 1995. Tacoma:

Ms. Varner died in a crash after police pursued the van she and her boyfriend had allegedly taken from her father without permission. **Source:** Tacoma News-Tribune, 3/23/95

John Porter   43   —

March 10, 1995. Auburn:

Mr. Porter was killed during an Auburn police SWAT-team raid on an apartment building. He was parked in an alley behind the building and supposedly tried to drive off during the raid, allegedly dragging Officer Scott Near, who tried to stop him. Then, he was shot by Officer William Pierson. An inquest ruled that the killing was justified. His mother, Iris Brown, filed a lawsuit against the police in May 1997. She charged that the cops had no reason to stop her son and no warrant, that they brutalized him after the shooting, tearing his ear off, dragged him from the vehicle, handcuffed him, and left him to bleed to death face down on the ground with no medical attention. **Source:** Tacoma News-Tribune, 7/11/95, 7/12/95, 4/22/95, & 7/18/95

Unidentified Man   —   —

March 9, 1995. Vancouver:

The man died in a fiery crash at the conclusion of a chase by Vancouver police. The police alleged that his car was stolen. **Source:** Vancouver Columbian, 3/9/95

Blaine Dalrymple   38   —

March 8, 1995. Spokane:

Mr. Dalrymple was shot to death by three Spokane police officers after he allegedly lunged at them with a shard of glass. He was shot five times. Police said that he was mentally ill. The newspaper reported, "It was the fifth time in two years city police have shot to death an armed suspect." **Source:** Spokane Spokesman-Review, 3/9/95

Dennis Rice   56   —

February 18, 1995. Port Townsend:

Mr. Rice was shot to death by a police officer after he allegedly fired at the officer. Several cops had been hiding outside a bar he was in and jumped out to arrest him for an alleged earlier assault when the shooting occurred. Mr. Rice was from Cape George. **Source:** Tacoma News-Tribune, 2/20/95

Unidentified Man   40   —

January 1, 1995. Spokane:

The man died while being held in his home by Spokane police. Police identified the man to the press only as "a major drug dealer" and would not say why he died or what happened, pending an autopsy. **Source:** Spokane Spokesman-Review, 1/3/95

Patricia Ann Borgman   39   —

December 17, 1994. Spokane:
Ms. Borgman was shot and killed by police responding to a domestic violence call after she allegedly pointed a gun at one of them. **Source:** Spokane Spokesman-Review, 12/18/94 & 12/19/94; Tacoma News-Tribune, 12/18/94

Antonio Jackson   25   *Black*

December 14, 1993. Federal Way:
Mr. Jackson was chased down and choked to death by Safeway grocery store clerks Donald Carrick and Scott Elston and two bystanders in Federal Way after allegedly shoplifting a pack of cigarettes (no cigarettes were found). King County Police Officers Michael L. Rayborn and Jeff A. Nicolai, arriving on the scene, handcuffed Mr. Jackson face down in the mud while he was unconscious, did nothing to revive him, and, according to witnesses, stopped Mr. Jackson's friend, Mona McKoy, after she had begun CPR and threatened to arrest her. Their stated reason was that they thought Mr. Jackson or his friends had a gun, and "a strong possibility" that Mr. Jackson was "faking." In the words of Officer Rayborn, "My main and number one concern is to keep myself safe." The King County medical examiner ruled the death to be a homicide. After many delays, an inquest jury found criminal negligence on Feb. 3, 1995. Nevertheless, on Mar. 23, 1995, King County prosecutor Norm Maleng announced his decision not to prosecute. Previously, on June 10, 1994, the US Civil Rights Division announced that their investigation into the officers was closed. There is videotape of this incident. Mr. Jackson was from Pacific and is survived by his mother, grandfather, brother, wife, and children. **Source:** Tacoma News-Tribune, 6/10/94 & 1/26/95

Kai Michael Blesko   24   —

November 23, 1994. Kent:
Mr. Blesko, who was unarmed, was shot during an altercation with King County Deputy Robert Nix outside his girlfriend's house. The police claimed that he tried to grab the officer's gun, then took the officer's pepper-spray away from him and sprayed him with it. The officer recovered and shot Mr. Blesko as he fled. Mr. Blesko then drove himself to the hospital, but died in the emergency room. An inquest ruled that the officer was justified. **Source:** Tacoma News-Tribune, 11/24/94, 1/5/95, 3/14/95, & 3/17/95

Lisa Marie Hensley   33   —

November 15, 1994. Tacoma (Pierce County Jail):
Ms. Hensley died in the Pierce County Jail, allegedly from internal bleeding from a head injury. She had been a passenger in a car that was pulled over in Milton for "erratic driving" after a brief chase. During the traffic stop she allegedly "fainted a couple of times" and assaulted an officer. She was arrested for third-degree assault and resisting arrest by Milton police and state patrol. The driver was not arrested. After her arrest, Ms. Hensley was placed alone in a jail holding cell and left there for 12 hours. At the end of that time, she was found dead. It was not determined where she suffered the head injury, but it was possibly during the arrest or car chase. She apparently never received medical attention or supervision after the fainting. Her mother, Barbara Burns, flew to Tacoma from Florida and stayed in a motel for at least three weeks investigating the incident. Ms. Hensley is survived by her mother and eight-year-old son Jonathan. Her mother said, "I'm having fits of crying now and then. I'm not getting help from anyone, and that's frustrating." She said that her daughter was trained in interior design and flamboyant by nature and that the two were close and shared much. "I can't allow myself time to grieve," her mother said. "If I do that, who is going to be here to pick up the pieces?" **Source:** Tacoma News-Tribune, 12/12/94

Bikram Singh   31   —

September 19, 1994. Seattle (North Rehabilitation Facility jail):
Mr. Singh died after being subdued by staff at the Seattle North Rehabilitation Facility jail. An inquest was scheduled for Feb. 1995. The result is unknown. **Source:** Tacoma News-Tribune, 9/21/94 & 2/7/95

Anthony Varela   31   —

September 6, 1994. Spanaway:

Mr. Varela was shot to death in his car at the conclusion of a chase by Pierce County sheriff's deputies for a traffic violation. Cops claim that they had no choice but to shoot him because they blocked him in with three cars and he started ramming their cars to try to get out. Mr. Varela was unarmed. The name of the officer(s) who shot Mr. Varela have not been released. **Source:** Tacoma News-Tribune, 9/13/94 & 9/16/94

Sidney McDermott   42   —

August 28, 1994. Spokane:

Mr. McDermott died in a gun battle with police when an officer followed him home after a traffic violation. His wife filed a $9 million wrongful death lawsuit against the police in May 1997. He is survived by his wife, Lois McDermott, daughter Jessica McDermott and four other children. **Source:** Spokane Spokesman-Review, 8/29/94

James C. Whitney   36   —

August 26, 1994. Port Orchard:

Mr. Whitney was shot and killed by Washington State trooper Kent Hitchings after he allegedly shot at the officer. Mr. Whitney had supposedly called 911 and asked police to come pick him up on a warrant, then shot at the patrol car when it arrived. Mr. Whitney was from Bremerton. **Source:** Tacoma News-Tribune, 8/27/94

Randy Green   35   *Black*

June 28, 1994. Seattle:

Mr. Green died while in police custody. Friends learned of the death, but were not allowed to see the body. They feel police probably killed him and covered it up. **Source:** friends of the victim; Social Security Death Index

Denny Allen   33   —

May 24, 1994. White Salmon:

Mr. Allen was shot to death by Klickitat County Sheriff's Deputy Steve Shields. Officer Shields alleged that Mr. Allen, who was unarmed, was stopped for drunk driving and that he threatened the officer's life. Officer Shields reported that he then pulled his gun and that Mr. Allen made a lunge for it, forcing the officer to fire, striking Mr. Allen in the face and killing him. After this incident, Officer Shields was demoted and put on paid leave. He returned to work in 1995. An inquest found that the shooting was justified, but a Deadly Force Review Board found that the officer had violated policy and recommended that he be fired. He was fired on June 19, 1996. After an appeal of that decision and a favorable arbitration ruling, the officer was reinstated again on Dec. 1, 1998. Mr. Allen was from Yakima. **Source:** Everett Herald, 11/28/98

Gertrude Barrow   41   —

May 16, 1994. Purdy (Washington Corrections Center for Women):

"The Pierce County medical examiner's office ruled Gertrude Barrow died at 5:30 a.m. Monday from a perforated chronic peptic gastric ulcer and acute peritonitis," according to the newspaper. She had been half way through a 31 month sentence for a drug crime at Washington Corrections Center for Women. Based on medical records, it appears that the prison ignored Ms. Barrow's persistent complaints of intense pain, refusing to prescribe pain medication and dismissing her problem as not life threatening. Her condition was not diagnosed until after she died. The press reported, "The dying woman couldn't eat or drink, and frequently vomited dark ooze, [fellow] inmate Bonnie Miller said. Ms. Barrow fainted shortly before she died, Ms. Miller said. Those symptoms - the pain, the bloody vomit and the collapse - were clues Ms. Barrow should have been rushed to the hospital [according to Dr. James Wagonfeld, a Tacoma ulcer specialist].... She should have been taken to an operating room, where doctors could mend the hole in her stomach and drain the infected fluid from her abdomen...When an ulcer perforates...patients suffer horribly, Wagonfeld said. 'People describe it as the worst pain they've ever experienced,' Wagonfeld said. 'They will often have a sense of doom. They know this is something that they've never experienced, and they know they may die from it.'" Ms. Barrow, who was part of a class action lawsuit against the prison medical system, is survived by a husband and four children. She left behind a box full of hand-made cards from her children, family photographs and carefully kept certificates of achievement she received in the prison school. Ms. Barrow was from Vancouver. **Source:** Tacoma News-Tribune, 5/19/94 & 5/20/94

Shawn Bradley Cottrell   19   —

March 31, 1994. Federal Way:
Mr. Cottrell was shot seven times and killed by King County Sheriff's SWAT Team member Zsolt Dornay during a drug raid at his apartment. Police claim Mr. Cottrell was pointing a loaded 9 mm handgun at the officer. The suspect in the drug raid was Mr. Cottrell's roommate. A next door neighbor reported that he never heard police identify themselves during the raid. An inquest determined the shooting to be justified. Mr. Cottrell is survived by his mother, Paula Horvath. **Source:** Tacoma News-Tribune, 10/14/94, 2/2/95, & 2/7/95

Ross Linear   53   —

February 24, 1994. Seattle:
Mr. Linear was allegedly causing a public disturbance when Seattle police officers attempted to restrain him. According to the press, he "died of hypoxia induced by acute cocaine intoxication and the stress and positioning of his body while officers were attempting to get him under control, the county medical examiner decided." An inquest into the death was convened on Feb. 6, 1995, but the result is unknown. **Source:** Tacoma News-Tribune, 10/14/94 & 2/7/95

Larry Dawson   51   —

February 4, 1994. King County:
Mr. Dawson died as a result of a King County police car chase of a 23-year-old man, whom police tried to stop for having a broken tail light and expired license plate tabs. The fleeing driver tried to pass Mr. Dawson, whose station wagon collided with the suspect's vehicle. The two were then struck by the officer's vehicle. Mr. Dawson was fatally injured in the crash. **Source:** Tacoma News-Tribune, 2/10/94

Deborah A. Cooper   38   —

January 30, 1994. Des Moines:
Ms. Cooper died as a result of a crash at the end of a Des Moines police chase of a car in which she was riding. Police believed the vehicle to be stolen. Ms. Cooper was from Seattle. **Source:** Tacoma News-Tribune, 1/31/94

William Melanson Jr.   24   —

January 25, 1994. Kent:
Mr. Melanson was shot to death by police as he tried to drive away from a police stakeout. He was unarmed. Police claimed that he tried to run them over. Mr. Melanson's sister and several other witnesses said that police continued to fire even after he was slumped over the wheel. They estimated that up to 20 shots were fired and one witness described police approaching the pickup and firing multiple times from short range into Mr. Melanson's motionless body. An inquest later found that the shooting was "unnecessary but reasonable." The police were not punished or prosecuted. **Source:** Tacoma News-Tribune, 1/26/94 & 2/11/95

Ernesto Carlos Mata   17   *Latino*

December 19, 1993. Bellevue:
Mr. Mata was shot and killed by Bellevue police after a car chase for a traffic violation. Police allege that one of the four passengers in his van fired at officers before the officer returned fire and killed Mr. Mata. An inquest found the police justified. Mr. Mata was from Quincy. **Source:** Tacoma News-Tribune, 12/20/93, 12/21/93, 12/24/93, & 2/7/95; Seattle Times, 12/20/93

Josef Bosch   17

November 1, 1993. SeaTac:
Mr. Bosch was shot several times and killed by King County Police Officer Gary Yetter when he allegedly pointed a gun at the officer. Josef Bosch and his brother, Jason Bosch, were stopped for investigation of a robbery in the early morning hours. Subsequently, they were accused and Jason was prosecuted for a string of motel robberies. The boys' mother, Sue Bosch, said her sons were wearing masks because it was Halloween. **Source:** Tacoma News-Tribune, 11/3/93, 11/4/93, 11/9/93, & 2/23/94

Eric Alexander Valdez   24   —

October 17, 1993. Kent:

Mr. Valdez was shot to death by Kent police officers Jon Straus and Todd Durham after he allegedly charged at them with a BB gun pistol in each hand. The officers were called after Mr. Valdez allegedly broke a car window outside his home, apparently upset that his parents were about to have him involuntarily committed to a psychiatric hospital. He was reported to be manic-depressive and supposedly had talked about getting the cops to kill him. The officers fired 27 times, striking Mr. Valdez 15 times. Officer Straus reloaded during the shooting, firing 16 shots. On Jan. 28, 1994, an inquest ruled that the shooting was justified, and the officers were not prosecuted. **Source:** Tacoma News-Tribune, 1/29/94, 2/10/94, 1/26/95

Dennis Wayne Bowerman   50   *white*

October 8, 1993. Seattle:

Mr. Bowerman was suspected of bank robbery by Seattle police. They shot him to death because he allegedly refused to comply with an officer's order to drop a pipe wrench and advanced on them in a threatening manner. Dennis, who was also known as "Big Frank" to his friends on the streets, was a homeless man from Michigan. Friends said he was well-read, educated, and not aggressive. **Source:** Tacoma News-Tribune, 10/9/93

Paul Rushing   42   *Black*

October 8, 1993. Seattle:

Mr. Rushing collapsed in the old Doghouse restaurant in Seattle, but fled when paramedics arrived, fearing that they were police. Thirty minutes later, witnesses saw him across the street surrounded by police, paramedics, and others. Mr. Rushing was placed on a gurney while hog-tied, his face pressed into the mattress. Police lifted his head to take a picture and noticed that he was unresponsive, then took him away in an ambulance. The next day a small notice appeared in the paper saying that he died of a drug reaction. Mr. Rushing's family is from Michigan. **Source:** Seattle Times, 10/10/93; witness account

David Lopez   —
Bobby Woods   31   —

September 30, 1993. Pierce County:

Mr. Woods and Mr. Lopez both died when their car crashed while being chased by Pierce County sheriff's deputies. The men were allegedly fleeing the scene of an armed robbery. Both victims were from Tacoma.   **Source:** Tacoma News-Tribune, 10/2/93

Michael P. Spence   18   —

September 27, 1993. Kitsap County:

Mr. Spence crashed and died on his motorcycle after a brief chase by a county deputy. The chase was initiated for a traffic violation. Mr. Spence was from Port Orchard. **Source:** Tacoma News-Tribune, 9/28/93

Unidentified Man   —   —

August 6, 1993. Spokane:

The victim was shot and killed by Spokane Police Officer Jeffrey Harvey, who arrived with his partner as the man left an Army Surplus store where he had allegedly been threatening the customers with a knife and a hatchet. Police alleged that he pointed a rifle at them, forcing Harvey to shoot. Two independent witnesses reported that the man was unarmed - a report that was "angrily challenged" by the Spokane police chief. Officer Harvey had been disciplined twice previously for unauthorized use of force. **Source:** Tacoma News-Tribune, 8/7/93

Ted Rathbun   29   —

July 29, 1993. College Place:

Mr. Rathbun was shot after he allegedly ran from an officer and then threatened him with a shovel. The officer was attempting to arrest him on felony warrants. Mr. Rathbun died two hours later at a Walla Walla hospital. **Source:** Tacoma News-Tribune, 7/30/93

Jeffrey Williams   13   —

July 26, 1993. Seattle:

Mr. Williams was killed when he hit another car head on while being chased by Seattle police. Police suspected the car of being stolen. Four cars and a police car were involved in the crash and eight people were injured. **Source:** Tacoma News-Tribune, 7/27/93

Peter Badewitz   25   —

June 25, 1993. Seattle:

Mr. Badewitz was shot to death by a state trooper in an alleged gun battle on the side of Highway 520 near Lake Washington. He had supposedly been shooting at cars after his van stalled. His ex-girlfriend, Melene Brekke, described him as depressed and volatile since his father had committed suicide the year before. He is survived by his ex-girlfriend and their two-year-old son. **Source:** Tacoma News-Tribune, 6/28/93

Roger C. Lawhorne   25   *white*

April 30, 1993. Seattle:

Mr. Lawhorne was suspected of robbing two hotels. Seattle police shot him to death after he allegedly fired on them from a commandeered taxicab. **Source:** Tacoma News-Tribune, 5/1/93

Elwood Rayvon Lee   34   —

February 27, 1993. Spokane:

Mr. Lee was shot to death by Spokane police when cops came to his home unexpectedly and he allegedly answered the door with a rifle in his hands. Police claim that he ignored their orders to drop the rifle and pointed it at one of them. He was shot once in the head by Officer Benjamin Estes. Mr. Lee's wife and two children were standing outside at the time and witnessed the shooting. Mr. Lee's wife, Joan Lee, filed a lawsuit against the city of Spokane. **Source:** Spokane Spokesman-Review, 8/11/94; Tacoma News-Tribune, 2/28/93

Rot Nguyen   17   *Asian*

January 29, 1993. Tacoma:

Mr. Nguyen was shot and killed by Tacoma Police Officer Mark Fedderson, who later killed Michael Mitchell on Apr. 9, 1997. The following is from the police account: Mr. Nguyen and a friend were "hiding in the bushes" when Police Officer Fedderson and his partner, James F. Smith, arrived to investigate a car prowling. The two youths ran and the police chased them. The officers claimed that Mr. Nguyen tried to shoot at the police but his gun misfired and there was a struggle over the gun. Mr. Nguyen then allegedly hit Officer Fedderson with his own baton, at which point Officer Fedderson shot three times, striking Mr. Nguyen once and killing him. The other youth was tracked with a dog and arrested for "suspicion of theft." The police are the only known witnesses. The shooting was ruled justified. Mr. Nguyen was from California. **Source:** Tacoma News-Tribune, 1/31/93 & 2/12/93

Kurt Ridener   34   *white*

December 20, 1992. Seattle:

Mr. Ridener was shot four times and killed by Seattle Police Officer Bernard Patton after allegedly pointing a gun at the officer. Mr. Ridener's gun turned out to be empty. **Source:** Tacoma News-Tribune, 12/22/92

Stephen Paul Marthaller   36   —

December 15, 1992. Renton:

Mr. Marthaller was shot four times by King County Police Officers Glenn R. Edmondson and Howard W. Gordon as he fled an alleged video store robbery. He died of his injuries two weeks later on Dec. 30, 1992. He had been under police surveillance at the time of the robbery. An inquest ruled that he died because of incompetent first-aid, "not police bullets." **Source:** Tacoma News-Tribune, 1/2/93 & 3/6/93

Robert Allen   38   —

October 31, 1992. Vancouver:

The coroner reported that Robert died of shotgun wounds after being shot by police. **Source:** Oregonian, 11/2/92

Unidentified Man   —   —

October 20, 1992. Lynnwood:

Police were called after the man allegedly set a small fire in his house and then stood in front of a church with a gun. The man supposedly "confronted deputies with a weapon. A shot was fired. The man was fatally wounded." **Source:** Tacoma News-Tribune, 10/21/92

Richard Martin   —   —

September 1, 1992. Tacoma:

Mr. Martin was shot to death at his home by Tacoma Police Officer Chris Pollard after a domestic violence call. Police claimed that Mr. Martin was drunk and threatened his family with kitchen knives. They said they shot him because he ignored their commands to drop a knife and came "real close to the door" of the house in which his infant granddaughter was sleeping. Officer Pollard was not prosecuted. In an unsuccessful 1997 lawsuit against the officer, the family said that the granddaughter had already been removed from the house, the door was locked and had no outside doorknob, and Officer Pollard unilaterally escalated a situation that three fellow officers already had under control. Mr. Martin's ex-wife Vicki Dennison, who witnessed the shooting, said, "It was flat-out cold-blooded murder, and they'll get away with it because they're the police." **Source:** Tacoma News-Tribune, 9/2/92, 9/3/92, 9/18/92, 3/7/97, & 3/29/97

Jon Sanders   27   —

August 21, 1992. Redmond:

Mr. Sanders died in a crash at the end of a police car chase on Washington 520. His female passenger and the drivers of two oncoming cars were also injured in the crash. Mr. Sanders was being pursued for allegedly trying to pass a stolen check at a Redmond bank. He was an extra in the 1983 Seattle homeless documentary "Streetwise." He is survived by good friend and former girlfriend Andrea Flamming. **Source:** Tacoma News-Tribune, 8/22/92 & 8/23/92; Seattle Times, 8/23/92

Yoshihiko Tanabe   71   *Japanese*

August 9, 1992. Fife:

Mr. Tanabe was killed when a patrol car driven by Milton police officer Mike McMullen struck his car at high speed. Mr. Tanabe's passengers, Antonio Moreira and Tak Sagae, were also injured in the accident. Officer McMullen was involved in a car chase of a domestic violence suspect. No disciplinary action was considered against the officer. Mr. Tanabe is survived by his wife, Fumi, whom he met at a World War II internment camp in Idaho, daughters Crystal and Cheryl, 41, son Rick, 34, and five grandchildren. Rick Tanabe had taken over the family farm, but Crystal Tanabe said her father still "helped out every day." Yoshihiko Tanabe was known as an advocate for local farmers and was elected twice to the Pierce County Committee on Agricultural Stabilization and Conservation, which disburses federal funds to area farmers. He served on the committee the past eight years. He also was an active member of the Japanese-American Citizens League and the Tacoma Buddhist Church. "He was always good-natured, very humble and well-respected in his family, in the Japanese American community and in the farming community," Crystal Tanabe said. **Source:** Tacoma News-Tribune, 8/11/92 & 10/17/92

Jon Otis   48   —

July 22, 1992. Summit:

Mr. Otis was shot four times by Pierce County sheriff's deputies after he allegedly pointed a shotgun at them and threatened suicide outside his art studio. He died later at the hospital. He had called the suicide crisis line several times before he was killed and asked them not to send police, but they did anyway. The prosecutor ruled that the shooting was justified. Mr. Otis was a teacher and an artist. He is survived by his ex-wife, Jeanne Otis, and their three children. His ex-wife said, "My daughter… feels bad that she will never get to see him again. They all took it hard…. They loved him." **Source:** Tacoma News-Tribune, 7/23/92, 7/24/92, & 7/31/92

Anthony P. Scontrino   17   —

July 3, 1992. Issaquah:
Mr. Scontrino fell to his death from the Snoqualmie Falls observation deck while being chased by Washington State Patrol Officer Todd Blue. The car and foot chase developed when Officer Blue attempted to stop Mr. Scontrino for a broken tail light in Fall City. A security guard at Salish Lodge near the falls reported that the officer fired several shots at Mr. Scontrino before he fell. Police disputed that account, saying no shots were fired. The King County executive requested an inquest, but the result is unknown. **Source:** Tacoma News-Tribune, 8/12/92

Heather L. Steven   23   —

May 18, 1992. Kent:
Ms. Steven died in a four car crash caused by Amandeep Singh, a teenage driver fleeing police in a high-speed chase. The newspaper reported, "A 15-year-old Kent youth was driving a stolen car at an estimated 90 mph when it crossed the center line in the 9000 block of the Kent-Kangley Road, hit one car, then hit Ms. Steven's car on the driver's side door." **Source:** Tacoma News-Tribune, 5/19/92

Robin Marie Pratt   28   *white*

March 28, 1992. Everett:
Ms. Pratt was shot and killed by Snohomish County Sheriff's SWAT team member Anthony Aston during an early morning raid on her house. The police raided the house looking for "dangerous armored car robbers" based on a tip. Flash grenades were thrown into the bedroom window, and a battering ram was thrown through the sliding glass living room door where her niece and six year old daughter were sleeping. Ms. Pratt then ran down the hall from her bedroom toward her daughter and niece in the living room. Deputy Aston shot her once in the neck from a range of two feet with his MP-5 assault machine gun. She was then handcuffed. It turned out that the family had nothing to do with the armored car robberies. At the inquest, Deputy Aston testified that he "fired a round or something like that" and that he didn't know how he shot her. Outside the inquest, protester Pat Dickinson of Lynnwood said, "They're trying to cover up what happened in that apartment." The inquest jury split, with three of six jurors saying the shooting was "an intentional criminal act" and another one saying it was criminal negligence. Later, a Sheriff's Review Board found that the shooting was unintentional and the state Attorney General's office announced on Aug. 7, 1992, that it would not prosecute the officers involved. In July 1992, Ms. Pratt's family filed damage claims against Snohomish County and three cities for $87 million. Ms. Pratt is survived by her husband, Larry Dean Pratt, five-year-old daughter Tanya, and four-year-old niece Jessica Craig. **Source:** Tacoma News-Tribune, 8/8/92 & 7/21/92

Mark Overby   16   —

March 15, 1992. Olympia:
Mr. Overby died when he lost control of his car during a chase by the Washington State Patrol and the Lewis County Sheriff's Office. According to the Seattle Times, "Overby had argued with his parents, then drove off in the family car without a driver's license. His father called police and reported Overby as a runaway. A state trooper and two Lewis County deputies located Overby and chased him down a narrow, two-lane road. Overby lost control going through a curving underpass and hit a tree at 90 mph." **Source:** Tacoma News-Tribune, 9/27/94; Social Security Death Index

John Bernard McDonald   70   *white*

February 28, 1992. Seattle (University District):
Mr. McDonald, a retiree, allegedly threatened police with a knife. Officer Howard Hadfield shot him dead in the hallway of his apartment building. **Source:** Seattle Times, 10/24/96

Anthony Neiggale Lyons   24   *Black*

February 21, 1992. Seattle (Capitol Hill):
Mr. Lyons, a laborer, allegedly attempted an armed robbery at 2:00 a.m. at a Capitol Hill gas station. Seattle Police Officers Richard Atkins and James Cooper jumped out of a back room from behind Mr. Lyons, who turned around in surprise and was shot dead. **Source:** Seattle Times, 10/24/96

Benjamin Buell   6   —

January 18, 1992. Bellevue:

Benjamin was killed and his eight brothers and sisters, aged three months to 14 years, were injured when a car driven by his mother crashed after a Bellevue police chase. His mother, Lettie Buell, was in critical condition in the hospital. The chase started when Ms. Buell drove off while her husband was talking to a police officer during a traffic stop. **Source:** Tacoma News-Tribune, 1/19/92

David Allen Whitford   26   —

September 15, 1991. Tacoma:

Mr. Whitford was shot ten times and killed in his brother's home by Tacoma Police Officers Dawn Bennett and Steven J. Reopelle. A third officer was also present. The cops were responding to a domestic violence call. They allege that Mr. Whitford, who was drunk, ran into the kitchen for a knife, forcing them to fire. **Source:** Tacoma News-Tribune, 9/16/91 & 9/17/91; Seattle Times, 9/16/91

Steven Smith   32   —

August 29, 1991. Seattle:

Mr. Smith, unarmed and supposedly drunk, was shot and killed by State Patrol Officer Lane Jackstadt during an alleged struggle after a traffic stop. Officer Jackstadt was later fired and prosecuted for a separate incident in which, while on duty, he kidnapped a couple on their way to a women's clinic, then forced them to drive to a fundamentalist family counseling center and watch anti-abortion videos. The couple was paid $175,000 by the state of Washington. After Mr. Smith's death, an inquest cleared Officer Jackstadt of responsibility in the shooting. Mr. Smith was from England. **Source:** Seattle Times, 11/1/91 & 11/2/91; Tacoma News Tribune, 10/4/94

Jacqueline "Crys" Williams   38   —

August 16, 1991. Renton (?):

Ms. Williams was working on her job as a construction flagger when she was struck and killed by a car driven by Scott Alan Pechman, who was being chased by King County police. Pechman was being pursued for alleged drunken driving. Two of Ms. Williams' co-workers were also injured in the accident, one seriously. The victims of the accident sued the King County police and the bar where Pechman drank. Ms. Williams was from Marblemount and had five children. **Source:** Tacoma News-Tribune, 1/1/94

Kelly A. Miller   30   —

August 15, 1991. Spokane:

Ms. Miller was shot and killed in her home during a Spokane police shootout with accused killer John Chavers, who had taken refuge in her house. Six officers were reported to have fired over 50 shots, and Ms. Miller was shot by police through a wall of her home. Her two young sons witnessed the shooting. Her husband, Rod Miller, filed a $5 million claim against the city of Spokane. **Source:** Spokane Spokesman-Review, 12/2/94; Seattle Times, 8/17/91 & 10/20/91

Rodney A. Lucht   34   —

June 28, 1991. Tacoma:

Mr. Lucht was shot and killed by four Tacoma police officers after he allegedly lunged at them with a knife. He was reportedly wanted in connection with a crime spree. On July 5, the Pierce County prosecutor said that officers showed "great restraint and discipline" and that the killing was justifiable homicide. Mr. Lucht was from Eatonville. **Source:** Tacoma News-Tribune, 6/29/91, 8/12/91, & 9/26/91; Seattle Times, 7/7/91

Michael Darwin Hull   33   —

June 23, 1991. Tacoma:

Mr. Hull was shot and killed by two Tacoma police officers during a traffic stop when he allegedly shot at the officers. The officers shot him at least six times, claiming he shot once at them before his gun jammed. **Source:** Tacoma News-Tribune, 6/25/91, 8/12/91, 9/24/91, & 9/26/91; Seattle Times, 6/24/91

Glenn Graves   21   —

June 20, 1991. Stanwood:
Mr. Graves was shot by Stanwood Police Chief Bob Kane after he allegedly pointed a gun at one of the other four officers who confronted him. He fell to the ground and then supposedly shot himself in the head. The officers claimed that Mr. Graves had begged them to shoot him. The death was ruled a suicide by the prosecutor's office. **Source:** Seattle Times, 6/22/91

Alvin Euell   34   —

June 8, 1991. Auburn:
Mr. Euell choked while being subdued and arrested by four Auburn police officers after a foot chase. He allegedly choked on a bag of marijuana swallowed some time during the chase. Officers did not seek medical attention for him until they arrived at the jail. He died of his injuries three days later in the hospital. Police chased Mr. Euell in error; they had thought he was his brother. In August, an inquest ruled that officers were not responsible for his death. **Source:** Tacoma News-Tribune, 8/9/91 & 8/10/91

Natividad Valdez Corral   22   —

May 23, 1991. Wenatchee:
Mr. Valdez was shot to death by Yakima County Sheriff's Major Ruben Garcia during a drug raid on his motel room. The police allege that Mr. Valdez pulled a pistol and pointed it at the officers when he was shot. An inquest cleared the officers, but the victim's brother, Alfonso Valdez, was not satisfied with the verdict, pointing out that only police witnesses had been asked to testify. **Source:** Tacoma News-Tribune, 5/25/91; Seattle Times, 6/2/91

Jeffrey E. Orris   20   —

March 17, 1991. Puyallup:
Mr. Orris was killed in a crash at the conclusion of a Puyallup police chase of a pickup truck in which he was a passenger. He was thrown from the bed of the truck where he was riding. Police said that they chased the vehicle because they saw the occupants "drinking alcoholic beverages and acting in a disorderly manner" at a park. Mr. Orris was from Tacoma. **Source:** Tacoma News-Tribune, 3/18/91 & 3/19/91

Carl Pruitt   28   —

January 10, 1991. Auburn:
Mr. Pruitt was killed when he was run over by a car being pursued by police. He was an electrical worker. His co-worker was knocked off a utility pole and severely injured. Mr. Pruitt was from Seattle. **Source:** Tacoma News-Tribune, 1/12/91

Sourisack Simmavong   20   *Asian*

December 25, 1990. Seattle:
Mr. Simmavong was shot to death by Seattle police officer Eric Besel during an alleged gun battle in Stan Sayres Memorial Park on Lake Washington. Mr. Simmavong was a press operator from Auburn. An inquest later found the shooting justified. **Source:** Tacoma News-Tribune, 12/26/90, 1/11/91, & 3/6/91

Robert Good   16   —

December 17, 1990. Toppenish:
Mr. Good, of Tacoma, was shot to death by police at the conclusion of a car chase by Yakima County and Yakima tribal officers near Toppenish. He and another youth, Ted Oreiro, had escaped from Pierce County's Remann Hall juvenile detention facility on Dec. 15, 1990, and allegedly stolen a car. Police shot at them during the car chase. Yakima County Sheriff's Sgt. Max James shot at the youth four times with a shotgun at the conclusion of the car chase as they emerged from the car. Mr. Good died from wounds to his back, and Mr. Oreiro survived. The youth were unarmed and allegedly attempting to surrender. Mr. Good's family sued Yakima County. A Tacoma court awarded them approximately $1 million, which the county appealed and then settled for $500,000 on Feb. 16, 1994. Ted Oreiro received $10,000. The officers were not disciplined. **Source:** Tacoma News-Tribune, 1/7/91, 4/14/93, 7/30/93, & 2/17/94

Donald Davis 29 —

December 13, 1990. Fife:

The newspaper reported, "Tacoma man, 29, Dies After Smashing Through Plate-Glass Window During Confrontation With Fife Police." **Source:** Tacoma News-Tribune, 12/14/90

Rodney Ray Anderson 32 —

October 18, 1990. Seattle:

Mr. Anderson died after a police car and foot chase from the scene of a fight. At the conclusion of the chase, he allegedly tried to swim away from officers in Echo Lake, north of Seattle, but drowned. An inquest found the officers justified. Mr. Anderson was from Seattle. **Source:** Tacoma News-Tribune, 2/2/91

Unidentified Man — —

October 16, 1990. Tacoma:

The man was shot and killed by an off-duty Tacoma police officer as he allegedly tried to rob a restaurant. **Source:** Tacoma News-Tribune, 6/29/91

Chad Martinson 18 —

September 3, 1990. Tacoma:

Mr. Martinson was killed when a vehicle being chased by Pierce County Sheriffs hit his vehicle. **Source:** Tacoma News-Tribune, 3/18/91

Dwight Dwigans — —

August 4, 1990. Puyallup:

Headline: "Man who died after police tackle didn't get quick aid: off-duty Kent police tackled Dwigans Aug. 4 to prevent him from attacking others. For a time, Dwigans was semiconscious or unconscious at the scene." The Pierce County prosecutor's office later ruled that Mr. Dwigans' death was "excusable homicide." **Source:** Tacoma News-Tribune, 8/14/90

Lorenzo Walker 39 *Black*

July 25, 1990. Seattle (King County Jail):

Mr. Walker died of undetermined medical causes in the King County Jail. Jail officials claimed Mr. Walker was given proper medical care, but inmates said care was delayed even after repeated requests were made. Fellow inmate Michael Ryan said that Mr. Walker had been vomiting blood for two days and then was given a paper cup of Pepto-Bismol six hours after he asked for help. In the morning, a guard ignored him while he lay in the cell covered in blood and dying. It took medics 20 to 30 minutes to arrive, and guards did not help give CPR when the nurse got tired and stopped. After his death, Dr. Bud Nicola and other jail officials implied that the death was drug related. They mentioned that he had been arrested previously on drug charges, but then refused to comment on Mr. Walker's specific medical condition, saying that "patient's medical records are confidential." The county coroner did not announce the cause of death. The Seattle NAACP protested the death. **Source:** Seattle Times, 7/25/90 & 7/26/90

Daniel Lewis Jones 44 —

July 10, 1990. Tacoma:

Mr. Jones was killed in an alleged shootout with Tacoma Police Officers Denny Martin, Larry Smith, and Larry Stril. Mr. Jones had been in and out of mental hospitals and was mentally ill. When confronted by officers at Point Defiance Park, he supposedly refused to put down his shotgun, and instead shot one of them. A police review board determined that the killing was justified. In 1991, Tacoma Catholic Worker activists opened the "Lewis Jones House," a house for homeless psychiatric patients. The activists said of Mr. Jones, "He was a man with a great deal of dignity and he tried to find ways to protect that." **Source:** Seattle Times, 7/10/90, 7/11/90, & 7/21/90; Tacoma News-Tribune, 1/30/91

Jesse Jerome   20   *Native American (Chippewa)*

July 4, 1990. Taholah:

Mr. Jerome was shot to death by Quinault Indian Nation Police Chief Robbin Rhoades. Police Chief Rhoades, who is also a former Seattle Police undercover narcotics detective, shot four or five times into a group of people, claiming that they were beating him and that he feared for his life. Mr. Jerome was killed and another man was injured. Police admit that neither Mr. Jerome nor anyone else was armed. Witnesses reported that Rhoades, who was not in uniform, had stopped his truck and gotten out to confront the three men after they insulted him as he drove by. According to the newspaper, "The shooting raised a furor in Taholah, where tribal headquarters are located. Two days afterward, about two dozen young people marched to protest the shootings. Teenagers kept vigil at the shooting site and mounted a three-foot-high wooden cross adorned with candles, flowers and feathers." U.S. Attorney Mike McKay declined to prosecute. Mr. Jerome was from Moclips. **Source:** Tacoma News-Tribune, 4/19/91; Seattle Times, 7/5/90, 7/6/90, 7/8/90, & 8/26/90

William Nelson Stewart   65   —

April 5, 1990. Longview:

After several hours of unsuccessful negotiations, Longview Police Lieutenant Charles Harper ordered Officer Harry Hackett to shoot Mr. Stewart. Cops claim Mr. Stewart had been firing his own gun at the interior walls of his house and would not stop. Officer Hackett shot Mr. Stewart through the back door window, killing him. **Source:** Seattle Times, 4/5/90

David Zaback   33   —

February 3, 1990. Renton:

Mr. Zaback died in a gun battle with Renton Police Officer Timothy Lally and store clerk Danny Morris as he allegedly tried to rob a leather store. Cops claim Mr. Zaback fired three times. He was shot four times, and an inquest determined that the shooting was justified. Mr. Zaback was from Renton. **Source:** Tacoma News-Tribune, 2/4/90; Seattle Times, 5/10/90

Brian Edmond Hull   21   —

January 18, 1990. Seattle (King County Jail):

Mr. Hull died of untreated appendicitis when his appendix burst, four days after he had initially requested treatment, while he was imprisoned in the King County Jail. He was serving a 15 day sentence for possession of a stolen car. Guards and medical staff ignored urgent requests for help for four days before he was taken to the hospital, where he died. An inquest found that Mr. Hull had not received proper medical treatment. King County later paid his mother, Doris Hull, $322,500 in a settlement. The jail staff was not prosecuted. Mr. Hull was from Maple Valley. **Source:** Tacoma News-Tribune, 2/25/90, 5/1/90, 5/4/90, & 1/6/91; Seattle Times, 1/23/90, 5/4/90, 6/7/90, 6/11/90, 6/12/90, 6/13/90, 7/17/90, 7/25/90, 7/26/90, 8/1/90, & 8/8/90

Bryce Rae   19   —

Jan. 3, 1990 (?). Port Orchard:

Mr. Rae died in a collision with a truck after fleeing police on his motorcycle. **Source:** Tacoma News-Tribune, 1/4/90

Samuel Johnson   41   —

December 14, 1989. Auburn:

Mr. Johnson was shot to death by Auburn Officer Robert Michnick after a car chase from the scene of an alleged burglary. Officer Michnick claimed that after Mr. Johnson's van crashed he charged at the officer with his hands clasped together as if carrying a weapon, forcing the officer to shoot. However, an autopsy revealed that Mr. Johnson had been shot in the back of the neck. Officer Michnick had also shot a suspect to death when working as a police officer in California in 1987. A shooting panel found the shooting unjustified, and Officer Michnick was fired on Dec. 29, 1989. An inquest jury later determined that the shooting was justified, and criminal charges were never filed against the officer. In documents related to the officer's firing (which he contested), several officers complained about Michnick, including Officer C. Gonter, who wrote, "Personally I do not want to work around Officer Michnick. I do not want Officer Michnick backing me up on call and I will cancel him if he is responding. Officer Michnick escalates situations and is abusive to suspects in custody. I feel that Officer Michnick draws his weapon inappropriately and is dangerous to other officers and the public." Mr. Johnson's family was awarded $150,000 in a settlement. Mr. Johnson was from Tacoma. He is survived by his sister Brenda Cook. **Source:** Tacoma News-Tribune, 12/27/93; Seattle Times, 5/19/90 & 1/29/90

Unidentified Man   —   —

September 10, 1989. Tacoma (?):

The newspaper reported, "Computerized Fingerprint Check Will Be Necessary To Confirm ID Of Man Killed In Drug Raid." **Source:** Tacoma News-Tribune, 9/11/89

Dennis Tiles   38   *white*

September 8, 1989. Seattle:

Mr. Tiles, an unemployed man, was shot to death by Seattle police during a narcotics raid at 298 E. Estelle Street. **Source:** Seattle Times, 10/24/96

Allen Kinder   —   —

June 26, 1989 (?). Summit (?):

Mr. Kinder was shot to death by four Pierce County deputies in a standoff with a SWAT team. He allegedly pointed a gun at officers. **Source:** Tacoma News-Tribune, 6/27/89

Danny R. Spencer   28   —

June 17, 1989. Olympia:

Mr. Spencer died in a police car after being beaten and arrested by an Olympia police officer during a traffic stop. Police accused him of resisting arrest for an outstanding traffic ticket warrant. An autopsy found drugs in his bloodstream. A police review found no policies were violated. Mr. Spencer's family sued the police. Their attorney said that police hit him 15 to 20 times with batons and with a metal flashlight, pepper-sprayed and hog-tied him, then threw him in the back of a squad car where he slipped between the seats and suffocated on his own vomit. The family lost the lawsuit. Mr. Spencer was a logger from Olympia. He is survived by a brother and a nine-year-old son. **Source:** Tacoma News-Tribune, 6/20/89 & 2/19/92

Erdman Bascomb   41   *Black*

February 17, 1988. Seattle:

Seattle Police officers knocked down Mr. Bascomb's door in a drug raid at midnight. Surprised, Mr. Bascomb jumped up from the couch, and Seattle Police Officer Robert Lisoski shot him to death. The police claimed that they thought a TV remote control he was holding was a gun and that they had given a clear warning before breaking down the door. Neighbors testified at an inquest that no warning was given. No drugs were found in the apartment, which belonged to Mr. Bascomb's nephew. The inquest ruled that the shooting was justified. Mr. Bascomb's brother, Paul Bascomb, filed an unsuccessful lawsuit against the city, the police chief, and Officer Lisoski. Mr. Bascomb is survived by a large family in Seattle. **Source:** Seattle Times, 10/24/96 & 1/11/91; victim's family

| **Lynn C. Brooks** | 34 | *white* |

November 21, 1988. Seattle:
Mr. Brooks, an unemployed man, allegedly threatened a Seattle police officer with a gun during a traffic stop. The officer shot him to death. **Source:** Tacoma News-Tribune, 11/23/88

| **Paul Bickler** | 44 | *white* |

October 5, 1988. Seattle:
Mr. Bickler, a construction laborer, was shot to death by Seattle police after allegedly shooting at officers at the scene of a robbery call. **Source:** Seattle Times, 10/24/96

| **Michael T. Jacob** | 19 | *white* |

September 16, 1988. Seattle:
Mr. Jacob was shot to death by police after allegedly threatening an officer and struggling with him. **Source:** Seattle Times, 10/24/96

| **Charles Medina** | 6 months | — |

Aug. 18, 1988 (?). Tacoma (?):
Charles was killed when a car being chased by police crashed into his home. **Source:** Tacoma News-Tribune, 8/19/88

| **Shawn Robert McDowell** | 29 | *white* |

July 10, 1988. Seattle:
Mr. McDowell, a laborer, was shot to death during an alleged attempted robbery. Police surprised him while on a stakeout. **Source:** Seattle Times, 10/24/96

| **Mr. Isaac (?)** | — | — |

May 6, 1988. Tacoma:
Mr. Isaac was shot to death by a Tacoma police officer. **Source:** Tacoma News-Tribune, 5/7/88

| **Gary Pate** | 19 | — |

April 28, 1988. Orting (?):
Mr. Pate was shot to death by Pierce County sheriff's deputies. He was allegedly drunk and cops claim he fired two shots at them before he was killed. **Source:** Tacoma News-Tribune, 6/27/89

| **William Gravel** | — | — |

Apr. 18, 1988 (?). Tacoma:
Mr. Gravel died in a police chase. **Source:** Tacoma News-Tribune, 4/19/88

| **Johnny Lee McElroy** | 41 | *white* |

February 16, 1988. Seattle:
Mr. McElroy was shot to death by off-duty Seattle police officer Andrew Depola during an alleged bank robbery in Seattle. **Source:** Seattle Times, 10/24/96

| **Robert Knott** | — | — |

Feb. 16, 1988 (?). Lewis County:
Mr. Knott was "accidentally killed" by police. He was supposedly a suspect in a kidnapping and murder. **Source:** Tacoma News-Tribune, 2/17/88

Guadalupe Rios   32   *Chicano*

February 4, 1988. Renton:

Mr. Rios was shot to death at a Renton gas station by King County police officer Mathias Bachmeier. In 1997, Officer Bachmeier was convicted of the Aug. 10, 1996, first-degree murder of another James Bradley Wren. Similar to the 1996 killing for which he was tried and convicted, Officer Bachmeier was alone when he killed Mr. Rios. According to his own inquest testimony, he shot Mr. Rios twice, then walked over to him on the ground, and shot him a third time when Mr. Rios allegedly pointed his gun at him. Although Officer Bachmeier claimed that Mr. Rios shot at him twice with a rifle, three independent witnesses reported that the victim was unarmed. King County Prosecutor Norm Maleng refused to prosecute, claiming that he "couldn't find" these witnesses. Guadalupe Rios' family believes the rifle was planted. Officer Bachmeier was never prosecuted for this killing. In addition, although there was extensive coverage of the arrest and murder conviction of Bachmeier in 1996 and 1997, the Seattle media has barely mentioned this earlier case. Guadalupe Rios is survived by his sister, Mercedes Rios, and his wife, Lillian Angulo. **Source:** Seattle Times, 11/22/96

William M. Tucker   44   *Black*

February 2, 1988. Seattle:

Seattle police claim that during a drug raid on Mr. Tucker's house, an officer's gun "accidentally discharged", killing Mr. Tucker. **Source:** Seattle Times, 10/24/96

Leola Washington   24   —

December 1985. Seattle:

Ms. Washington's estate was awarded $325,000 in a lawsuit against the Seattle police on Dec. 12, 1989. The lawsuit charged that her death was caused by police negligence. **Source:** Tacoma News-Tribune, 12/13/89

WEST VIRGINIA

Name	Age	Nationality	Photo

Amanda Smailes   21   *white*

November 24, 1996. Marinsburg:

Ms. Smailes was killed in the early morning hours when an allegedly drunk driver being pursued by police in a high speed car chase crashed into her car. State Trooper Kevin Plumer, who was pursuing the other car at speeds of up to 100 mph, shouted "Die" at the driver of the car he was chasing shortly before the crash. After the crash, he shouted, "I killed that girl, man...I killed her...damn it." State Trooper Plumer was being taped by "Real Stories of the Highway Patrol" during the chase. Amanda's mother, Cynthia Smailes, said the presence of the cameras and a camera crew member saying "Go get him," had encouraged the Trooper to engage in the reckless chase. Ms. Smailes was returning from a late-night shift at Wal-mart and was living with her parents in Inwood, WV while studying nursing at Shepherd's College. Ms. Smailes' parents filed a wrongful death suit against the police. **Source:** The Washington Post, 12/14/97; The Dallas Morning News, 12/19/97; The Straits Times (Singapore), 12/18/97

WISCONSIN

Name	Age	Nationality	Photo

Deborah J. Meyer   31   —

January 28, 1999. Kenosha:

Ms. Meyer was shot nine times and killed by police outside a convenience store after she allegedly pointed a pistol at them. She reportedly left behind a job resignation note at the sandwich shop where she worked, saying, "What is going to happen must happen." Ms. Meyer had a history of mental illness and was reportedly not taking her medication. She leaves behind two sons, ages eight and nine, and her husband. **Source:** The San Francisco Examiner, 1/29/99

Unidentified Man	19	—

August 26, 1998. Milwaukee:

A young man was hit by a truck while being chased on foot by cops. He later died at the hospital. Cops claim the man pulled a gun after bolting from a car parked at an "unusual angle" when police stopped to question him and the driver of the car. Police allegedly seized a large wad of money and a white substance from the car. **Source:** The Milwaukee Journal Sentinel, 8/27/98

Brian J. Ackley	13	—
Scott A. Lunda	13	—

August 12, 1998. Marshall (east side):

The two 13-year-old boys were killed after the car they were driving went off the road and crashed into several trees during a police chase. Police allege that the car drove at speeds of up to 79 mph, though it was going less than 40 mph when it crashed. Authorities also claim that the officer pursuing the boys never exceeded 40 mph and did not follow the boys long enough to constitute a chase. The boys had reportedly hot-wired a neighbor's car. **Source:** The Milwaukee Journal Sentinel, 8/14/97

David L. Cross	39	—

August 11, 1998. Milwaukee:

Police received a domestic violence call from Mr. Cross' ex-girlfriend. When they arrived at her house, they found him lying on a bed. After telling Mr. Cross he was under arrest, a struggle reportedly ensued. Mr. Cross was pepper sprayed, which "apparently was not effective," according to police. He was then shot and killed by a Milwaukee police officer after he allegedly grabbed the holstered gun of the officer's partner. Police did not release the name of the officer who killed Mr. Cross. Four children, ranging in age from eight to 17, were in the house at the time of the shooting. Police claimed Mr. Cross had a "lengthy police record," including domestic violence and child abuse charges, and that he was wanted for theft at the time of his death. **Source:** The Milwaukee Journal Sentinel, 8/12/98

Antonio Davis, Jr.	24	—

July 3, 1998. Milwaukee (North Side):

Mr. Davis was shot in the neck and killed at a Mobil Mart gas station at 3510 N. 7th Street by a Milwaukee cop. The officer was presumably responding to a complaint by a woman that she was having trouble with Mr. Davis. The official story is that Mr. Davis came in contact with the cop's gun while driving his car past the officer and that this caused the officer's gun to discharge. People questioned this account. One of Mr. Davis's neighbors described him as "a well-liked individual...That's a young man that didn't bother nobody." Other neighbors said Mr. Davis used to break up neighborhood fights, that he had just gotten a decent paying job, that he took care of his three young children, and that he planned to get married. Mr. Davis' fiancee said the cop who killed him should be charged with a crime. The cop, whose name was not given, was placed on administrative duty pending an investigation. **Source:** Milwaukee Journal Sentinel, 7/5/98

Andy Gill	16	—
Eddie Gill	19	—

March 17, 1998. Milwaukee (northwest side):

The Gill brothers were killed just blocks from their home in an on-duty crash with Police Rookie David G. Pagan. The brothers allegedly turned their car in front of the cop's car. About ten days later, Officer Pagan was fired, though police maintain he did nothing wrong in the crash and that the firing was unrelated to the accident. **Source:** The Milwaukee Journal Sentinel, 3/28/98

David Fowler   23   *African American*

February 12, 1998. Milwaukee:

Police claim that patrol officers responded to a call by Mr. Fowler's girlfriend reporting a domestic dispute. They claim that when two patrol officers arrived, Mr. Fowler tried to flee and then struggled with the officers outside. Police also claim that Mr. Fowler grabbed a cop's gun and fired it, but a witness to the killing says Mr. Fowler never fired the gun - it went off during the struggle. This was the seventh time in 19 months that Milwaukee police have shot and killed someone. **Source:** Workers World, 3/12/98

James Ray Guerrero   22   —

November 1, 1997. Milwaukee:

Police claim that Mr. Guerrero struggled with Officer Jutiki Jackson and the cop's gun went off accidentally. A total of four witnesses, however, contradict the police version of events. A neighborhood pastor who witnessed the shooting said in a videotaped statement that at no time did he see Mr. Guerrero struggle with the officer or reach for his gun. The pastor described seeing Mr. Guerrero stumble, fall onto his side, and roll onto his back with his hands by his side. While in this position, the officer brought his gun up to Mr. Guerrero's head and fired it, killing him. An inquest by the District Attorney's office ruled it an accidental shooting, and the DA did not press charges against the officer. This was the sixth fatal shooting by Milwaukee police in the past 15 months. **Source:** Workers World, 3/12/98; Milwaukee Journal Sentinel, 11/5/97; Chicago Tribune, 12/11/97

Laura Sue Ackland   39   —

August 4, 1997. Milwaukee:

Mrs. Ackland was killed, and her son brain damaged, from a collision with a car driven by Josiphus Wilder, 19, whose car was being chased by police. Cops claim they suspected the occupants in Mr. Wilder's car of involvement in a shooting. Mr. Wilder was sentenced to seven years in prison. **Source:** The Milwaukee Journal Sentinel, 5/27/98 & 10/7/97

Calvin D. Harrington, Jr.   26   —

April 21, 1997. Milwaukee County:

Mr. Harrington was shot once in the chest and killed by an undercover detective who was allegedly making a drug buy in the 700 block of S. 23rd Street. Cops claim the detective went to the home and identified himself as a cop, at which point, "numerous" people in the house attacked him and began "grabbing at (the officer's) right hand.... (The) detective had to struggle to maintain possession of his firearm," causing the cop's weapon to discharge, which police maintain may have been accidental. Cops claim they recovered drugs and a weapon from the scene. **Source:** Milwaukee Journal Sentinel, 5/20/97

Thomas Jackson   —   —

April 16, 1997. Milwaukee:

Mr. Jackson was killed by positional asphyxiation.

Timothy D. Wing   38   —

March 21, 1997. Madison:

Mr. Wing was shot and killed in the basement of his parents' house by Madison Police Officer Timothy G. Hahn. Cops claim the victim had fired five shots, hitting Officer Hahn's partner three times, mostly in his bulletproof vest. Officer Hahn fired nine shots, hitting Mr. Wing four times, with the fatal bullet hitting his aorta. Within a week, the Dane County District Attorney's office said the cop had "used reasonable and minimum force" and cleared him of any wrongdoing. Cops claim they had come to the house to serve Mr. Wing with an arrest warrant. **Source:** Milwaukee Journal Sentinel, 3/27/97

Clarence Michael Thurman III   25   *African American*

August 3, 1996. Milwaukee (Northwest Side):
Mr. Thurman was shot to death by an off-duty cop. Police claim that Mr. Thurman had tried to steal a lawn mower from the officer's garage and that he was killed during a struggle over the officer's gun. Mr. Thurman's mother and uncle read a statement on a Black radio talk show saying, "This much we know: Michael was killed by a Milwaukee police officer over a lawn mower. This is totally unacceptable and consistent with a long history of actions by the Milwaukee Police Department. These actions have been consistently condoned by the so-called criminal justice system.... We cannot trust the office of the District Attorney to deliver justice in these actions. We the Black community must take it upon ourselves to see that justice is done." **Source:** Workers World, 3/12/98; information from family

---

Demetrik Moore   —   —

July 25, 1996. Milwaukee:
Mr. Moore was killed by police.

Mario Cenin   43   —

December 4, 1995. Melvina:
Mr. Cenin, a Vietnam vet with post traumatic stress syndrome, waved down an officer and allegedly threatened him with a rifle. After a six minute standoff, the officer rolled out of the car and a backup officer shot and killed Mr. Cenin. **Source:** Associated Press, 4/25/98

Kimberly Carr   18   —
Unidentified Man   —   —
Clifton Bernard Wallace   20   —

April 1995. Milwaukee (Northwest Side):
Three people were killed when an allegedly stolen car being chased by Milwaukee police crashed into the bus shelter where they were standing. Mr. Wallace and Ms. Carr were boyfriend and girlfriend. Another person standing in the bus shelter was killed, and a passenger in the car being chased was also killed. **Source:** Milwaukee Journal Sentinel, 5/27/98

Unidentified   —   —

April 1995. Milwaukee (Northwest Side):
A passenger in an allegedly stolen car was killed when the car crashed into a bus shelter while being chased by Milwaukee police. The accident also killed three people waiting in the bus shelter. **Source:** Milwaukee Journal Sentinel, 5/27/98

Reinhold Deering   69   —

March 1995. Shawano County (Gillett):
Mr. Deering was shot and killed by Shawano County Sheriff's Deputy James M. Reich. Deputy Reich was trying to serve a misdemeanor warrant on Mr. Deering, who friends described as having mental problems, when Mr. Deering allegedly fired at another deputy and then pointed his gun at Deputy Reich. Deputy Reich fired 11 shots, two of which hit Mr. Deering in the back near his side. Mr. Deering lived in a remote, isolated farmhouse on a 300-acre farm, and kept a gun on his back porch because he feared strangers who hunted on his farm. Reinhold Deering's brother, Walter Deering, filed a $2 million wrongful death suit against Deputy Reich and two other deputies. The judge dismissed the lawsuit against the other two deputies and, in June 1998, a jury found no wrongdoing on Deputy Reich's part after less than an hour of deliberations. **Source:** Milwaukee Journal Sentinel, 6/10/98

Rene Campos   23   *Chicano*

Date Unknown. Madison (in jail):
Mr. Campos was arrested. Authorities claim that, while in custody, he committed suicide by shoving more that half of his t-shirt down his own throat. The coroner said that the t-shirt was about 3/4 of the way down his throat, and that it would be impossible for anyone to do this and remain conscious. In other words, he could not have done this to himself. It appears that he was murdered by jail authorities.

WYOMING

Name	Age	Nationality	Photo

Zeb Richenberg — 18 — —

May 10, 1998. Basin:
Mr. Richenberg was shot and killed by Big Horn County deputies after he allegedly barricaded himself in his home and began firing a rifle randomly in all directions. Mr. Richenberg was a student at Riverside High School in Basin. **Source:** Wyoming Tribune-Eagle, 5/12/98

Hector Leon Aoah — teens — —

4 other teenagers — —

May 9, 1998. Wind River Indian Reservation:
Hector Aoah and four other teenagers died in a high speed police chase. Their allegedly stolen truck was pursued by a Lander police officer north of city limits. The cop claims he stopped the chase when the road became curvy. The truck "failed to negotiate a curve, became airborne and ejected all six passengers" (one evidently survived). Mr. Aoha's cousin reported that the cops were chasing the van because he and his friends allegedly had alcohol. After an investigation, the Wyoming Highway Patrol cleared the cop of responsibility for the crash. **Source:** The Rocky Mountain News (Denver, CO), 5/13/98

Thomas Cruz — 32 — —

June 10, 1996. Laramie:
Mr. Cruz, allegedly high on cocaine, suffocated to death as a result of being hog-tied by the police. His family sued the City of Laramie. City officials denied responsibility for Mr. Cruz's death. **Source:** Wyoming Tribune-Eagle, 7/9/98

Stolen Lives Pledge

I, _____, pledge that the life and humanity of these Stolen Lives will not be forgotten. I pledge that their highest hopes and aspirations will live on in us, and that I will seek justice for these and all the Stolen Lives. In this way I pledge that their memory will stay alive in us and will inspire us to fight for justice and a better world.